P9-CMF-910

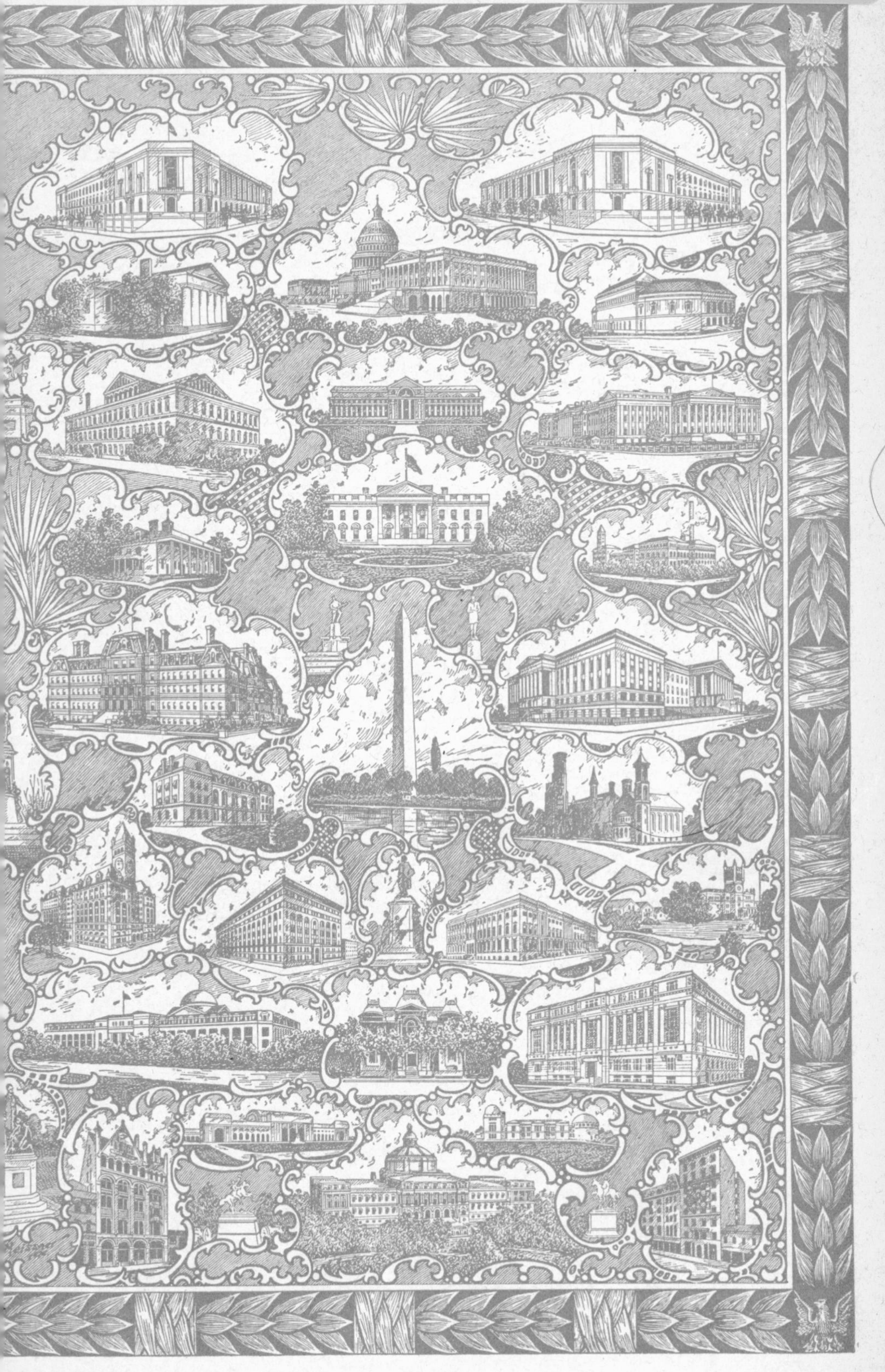

Patent Office

A COMPILATION

OF THE

MESSAGES AND PAPERS

OF THE

PRESIDENTS

Prepared Under the Direction of the Joint Committee on Printing, of the House and Senate, Pursuant to an Act of the Fifty-Second Congress of the United States

(With Additions and Encyclopedic Index by Private Enterprise)

VOLUME VI

PUBLISHED BY

BUREAU OF NATIONAL LITERATURE, Inc.
NEW YORK

ILLUSTRATIONS IN VOLUME SIX

the Mississippi. It is desirable that they should be removed, and in the event of a division of the country in the West, or of a new home being provided for a portion of the tribe, that they be permitted to join either party, as they may prefer, and be incorporated with them.

I submit the whole subject to Congress, that such legislative measures may be adopted as will be just to all the parties or bands of the tribe. Such measures, I am satisfied, are the only means of arresting the horrid and inhuman massacres which have marked the history of the Cherokees for the last few years, and especially for the last few months.

The Cherokees have been regarded as among the most enlightened of the Indian tribes, but experience has proved that they have not yet advanced to such a state of civilization as to dispense with the guardian care and control of the Government of the United States.

JAMES K. POLK.

To the Senate and House of Representatives:

In compliance with the act of the 3d of March, 1845, I communicate herewith to Congress a report of the Secretaries of War and the Navy on the subject of a permanent building for the War and Navy Departments, together with the plans and estimates. [illegible]

[illegible] while it is proper and [illegible] [illegible] and [illegible] that more [illegible] furnished [illegible] selection was made of such as would furnish the requisite room for the accommodation of the War and Navy Departments at the least expense.

All the plans and estimates which have been received are herewith communicated, for the information of Congress.

JAMES K. POLK.

WASHINGTON, *April* [illegible], *1846*.

To the House of Representatives:

I have considered the resolution of the House of Representatives of the 9th instant, by which I am requested "to cause to be furnished to that House an account of all payments made on President's certificates from the fund appropriated by law, through the agency of the State Department, for the contingent expenses of foreign intercourse from the 4th of March, 1841, until the retirement of Daniel Webster from the Department of State, with copies of all entries, receipts, letters, vouchers, memorandums, or other evidence of such payments, to whom paid, for what, and particularly all concerning the northeastern-boundary dispute with Great Britain."

the Mississippi. It is desirable that they should be removed, and in the event of a division of the country in the West, or of a new home being provided for a portion of the tribe, that they be permitted to join either party, as they may prefer, and be incorporated with them.

I submit the whole subject to Congress, that such legislative measures may be adopted as will be just to all the parties or bands of the tribe. Such measures, I am satisfied, are the only means of arresting the horrid and inhuman massacres which have marked the history of the Cherokees for the last few years, and especially for the last few months.

The Cherokees have been regarded as among the most enlightened of the Indian tribes, but experience has proved that they have not yet advanced to such a state of civilization as to dispense with the guardian care and control of the Government of the United States.

JAMES K. POLK.

WASHINGTON, *April 14, 1846.*

To the Senate and House of Representatives:

In compliance with the act of the 3d of March, 1845, I communicate herewith to Congress a report of the Secretaries of War and the Navy on the subject of a fireproof building for the War and Navy Departments, together with documents explaining the plans to which it refers and containing an estimate of the cost of erecting the buildings proposed.

Congress having made no appropriation for the employment of an architect to prepare and submit the necessary plans, none was appointed. Several skillful architects were invited to submit plans and estimates, and from those that were voluntarily furnished a selection has been made of such as would furnish the requisite building for the accommodation of the War and Navy Departments at the least expense.

All the plans and estimates which have been received are herewith communicated, for the information of Congress.

JAMES K. POLK.

WASHINGTON, *April 20, 1846.*

To the House of Representatives:

I have considered the resolution of the House of Representatives of the 9th instant, by which I am requested "to cause to be furnished to that House an account of all payments made on President's certificates from the fund appropriated by law, through the agency of the State Department, for the contingent expenses of foreign intercourse from the 4th of March, 1841, until the retirement of Daniel Webster from the Department of State, with copies of all entries, receipts, letters, vouchers, memorandums, or other evidence of such payments, to whom paid, for what, and particularly all concerning the northeastern-boundary dispute with Great Britain."

With an anxious desire to furnish to the House any information requested by that body which may be in the Executive Departments, I have felt bound by a sense of public duty to inquire how far I could with propriety, or consistently with the existing laws, respond to their call.

The usual annual appropriation "for the contingent expenses of intercourse between the United States and foreign nations" has been disbursed since the date of the act of May 1, 1810, in pursuance of its provisions. By the third section of that act it is provided—

That when any sum or sums of money shall be drawn from the Treasury under any law making appropriation for the contingent expenses of intercourse between the United States and foreign nations the President shall be, and he is hereby, authorized to cause the same to be duly settled annually with the accounting officers of the Treasury in the manner following; that is to say, by causing the same to be accounted for specially in all instances wherein the expenditure thereof may in his judgment be made public, and by making a certificate of the amount of such expenditures as he may think it advisable not to specify; and every such certificate shall be deemed a sufficient voucher for the sum or sums therein expressed to have been expended.

Two distinct classes of expenditure are authorized by this law—the one of a public and the other of a private and confidential character. The President in office at the time of the expenditure is made by the law the sole judge whether it shall be public or private. Such sums are to be "accounted for specially in all instances wherein the expenditure thereof may in his judgment be made public." All expenditures "accounted for specially" are settled at the Treasury upon vouchers, and not on "President's certificates," and, like all other public accounts, are subject to be called for by Congress, and are open to public examination. Had information as respects this class of expenditures been called for by the resolution of the House, it would have been promptly communicated.

Congress, foreseeing that it might become necessary and proper to apply portions of this fund for objects the original accounts and vouchers for which could not be "made public" without injury to the public interests, authorized the President, instead of such accounts and vouchers, to make a certificate of the amount "of such expenditures as he may think it advisable not to specify," and have provided that "every such certificate shall be deemed a sufficient voucher for the sum or sums therein expressed to have been expended."

The law making these provisions is in full force. It is binding upon all the departments of the Government, and especially upon the Executive, whose duty it is "to take care that the laws be faithfully executed." In the exercise of the discretion lodged by it in the Executive several of my predecessors have made "certificates" of the amount "of such expenditures as they have thought it advisable not to specify," and upon these certificates as the only vouchers settlements have been made at the Treasury.

It appears that within the period specified in the resolution of the

House certificates were given by my immediate predecessor, upon which settlements have been made at the Treasury, amounting to $5,460. He has solemnly determined that the objects and items of these expenditures should not be made public, and has given his certificates to that effect, which are placed upon the records of the country. Under the direct authority of an existing law, he has exercised the power of placing these expenditures under the seal of confidence, and the whole matter was terminated before I came into office. An important question arises, whether a subsequent President, either voluntarily or at the request of one branch of Congress, can without a violation of the spirit of the law revise the acts of his predecessor and expose to public view that which he had determined should not be "made public." If not a matter of strict duty, it would certainly be a safe general rule that this should not be done. Indeed, it may well happen, and probably would happen, that the President for the time being would not be in possession of the information upon which his predecessor acted, and could not, therefore, have the means of judging whether he had exercised his discretion wisely or not. The law requires no other voucher but the President's certificate, and there is nothing in its provisions which requires any "entries, receipts, letters, vouchers, memorandums, or other evidence of such payments" to be preserved in the executive department. The President who makes the "certificate" may, if he chooses, keep all the information and evidence upon which he acts in his own possession. If, for the information of his successors, he shall leave the evidence on which he acts and the items of the expenditures which make up the sum for which he has given his "certificate" on the confidential files of one of the Executive Departments, they do not in any proper sense become thereby public records. They are never seen or examined by the accounting officers of the Treasury when they settle an account on the "President's certificate." The First Congress of the United States on the 1st of July, 1790, passed an act "providing the means of intercourse between the United States and foreign nations," by which a similar provision to that which now exists was made for the settlement of such expenditures as in the judgment of the President ought not to be made public. This act was limited in its duration. It was continued for a limited term in 1793, and between that time and the date of the act of May 1, 1810, which is now in force, the same provision was revived and continued. Expenditures were made and settled under Presidential certificates in pursuance of these laws.

If the President may answer the present call, he must answer similar calls for every such expenditure of a confidential character, made under every Administration, in war and in peace, from the organization of the Government to the present period. To break the seal of confidence imposed by the law, and heretofore uniformly preserved, would be subversive of the very purpose for which the law was enacted, and might be productive of the most disastrous consequences. The expenditures of this confidential character, it is believed, were never before sought to be made public, and I should greatly apprehend the consequences of establishing a precedent which would render such disclosures hereafter inevitable.

I am fully aware of the strong and correct public feeling which exists throughout the country against secrecy of any kind in the administration of the Government, and especially in reference to public expenditures; yet our foreign negotiations are wisely and properly confined to the knowledge of the Executive during their pendency. Our laws require the accounts of every particular expenditure to be rendered and publicly settled at the Treasury Department. The single exception which exists is not that the amounts embraced under President's certificates shall be withheld from the public, but merely that the items of which these are composed shall not be divulged. To this extent, and no further, is secrecy observed.

The laudable vigilance of the people in regard to all the expenditures of the Government, as well as a sense of duty on the part of the President and a desire to retain the good opinion of his fellow-citizens, will prevent any sum expended from being accounted for by the President's certificate unless in cases of urgent necessity. Such certificates have therefore been resorted to but seldom throughout our past history.

For my own part, I have not caused any account whatever to be settled on a Presidential certificate. I have had no occasion rendering it necessary in my judgment to make such a certificate, and it would be an extreme case which would ever induce me to exercise this authority; yet if such a case should arise it would be my duty to assume the responsibility devolved on me by the law.

During my Administration all expenditures for contingent expenses of foreign intercourse in which the accounts have been closed have been settled upon regular vouchers, as all other public accounts are settled at the Treasury.

It may be alleged that the power of impeachment belongs to the House of Representatives, and that, with a view to the exercise of this power, that House has the right to investigate the conduct of all public officers under the Government. This is cheerfully admitted. In such a case the safety of the Republic would be the supreme law, and the power of the House in the pursuit of this object would penetrate into the most secret recesses of the Executive Departments. It could command the attendance of any and every agent of the Government, and compel them to produce all papers, public or private, official or unofficial, and to testify on oath to all facts within their knowledge. But even in a case of that kind they would adopt all wise precautions to prevent the exposure of all such matters the publication of which might injuriously affect the public interest, except so far as this might be necessary to accomplish the great ends of public justice. If the House of Representatives, as the grand inquest of the nation, should at any time have reason to believe that there has been malversation in office by an improper use or application of the public money by a public officer, and should think proper to institute an inquiry into the matter, all the archives and papers of the Executive Departments, public or private, would be subject to the inspection and control of a committee of their body and every facility in the power of the Executive be afforded to enable them to prosecute the investigation.

The experience of every nation on earth has demonstrated that emergencies may arise in which it becomes absolutely necessary for the public safety or the public good to make expenditures the very object of which would be defeated by publicity. Some governments have very large amounts at their disposal, and have made vastly greater expenditures than the small amounts which have from time to time been accounted for on President's certificates. In no nation is the application of such sums ever made public. In time of war or impending danger the situation of the country may make it necessary to employ individuals for the purpose of obtaining information or rendering other important services who could never be prevailed upon to act if they entertained the least apprehension that their names or their agency would in any contingency be divulged. So it may often become necessary to incur an expenditure for an object highly useful to the country; for example, the conclusion of a treaty with a barbarian power whose customs require on such occasions the use of presents. But this object might be altogether defeated by the intrigues of other powers if our purposes were to be made known by the exhibition of the original papers and vouchers to the accounting officers of the Treasury. It would be easy to specify other cases which may occur in the history of a great nation, in its intercourse with other nations, wherein it might become absolutely necessary to incur expenditures for objects which could never be accomplished if it were suspected in advance that the items of expenditure and the agencies employed would be made public.

Actuated undoubtedly by considerations of this kind, Congress provided such a fund, coeval with the organization of the Government, and subsequently enacted the law of 1810 as the permanent law of the land. While this law exists in full force I feel bound by a high sense of public policy and duty to observe its provisions and the uniform practice of my predecessors under it.

With great respect for the House of Representatives and an anxious desire to conform to their wishes, I am constrained to come to this conclusion.

If Congress disapprove the policy of the law, they may repeal its provisions.

In reply to that portion of the resolution of the House which calls for "copies of whatever communications were made from the Secretary of State during the last session of the Twenty-seventh Congress, particularly February, 1843, to Mr. Cushing and Mr. Adams, members of the Committee of this House on Foreign Affairs, of the wish of the President of the United States to institute a special mission to Great Britain," I have to state that no such communications or copies of them are found in the Department of State.

"Copies of all letters on the books of the Department of State to any officer of the United States or any person in New York concerning Alexander McLeod," which are also called for by the resolution, are herewith communicated.

JAMES K. POLK.

WASHINGTON, *April 20, 1846*.

To the Senate of the United States:

I herewith transmit to the Senate, in answer to their resolution of the 8th instant, a report from the Secretary of State, with accompanying papers, containing the information and correspondence referred to in that resolution, relative to the search of American vessels by British cruisers subsequent to the date of the treaty of Washington.

JAMES K. POLK.

WASHINGTON, *April 27, 1846*.

To the Senate of the United States:

I transmit herewith the information called for by a resolution of the Senate of the 3d December last, relating to "claims arising under the fourteenth article of the treaty of Dancing Rabbit Creek" with the Choctaw tribe of Indians, concluded in September, 1830.

JAMES K. POLK.

WASHINGTON, *April 27, 1846*.

To the House of Representatives:

I transmit herewith a report of the Secretary of War and accompanying papers, containing the information called for by the resolution of the House of Representatives of December 19, 1845, relating to certain claims of the Chickasaw tribe of Indians.

JAMES K. POLK.

WASHINGTON, *April 27, 1846*.

To the House of Representatives:

I transmit herewith a report and accompanying papers from the Secretary of War, in reply to the resolution of the House of Representatives of the 31st of December last, in relation to claims arising under the

Choctaw treaty of 1830 which have been presented to and allowed or rejected by commissioners appointed in pursuance of the acts of 3d of March, 1837, and 23d of August, 1842.

JAMES K. POLK.

WASHINGTON, *May 6, 1846.*

To the House of Representatives:

I transmit herewith reports from the Secretary of War and the Secretary of the Treasury, with additional papers, relative to the claims of certain Chickasaw Indians, which, with those heretofore communicated to Congress, contain all the information called for by the resolution of the House of Representatives of the 19th of December last.

JAMES K. POLK.

WASHINGTON, *May 6, 1846.*

To the House of Representatives:

I transmit herewith a report from the Secretary of State, with accompanying papers, in answer to a resolution of the House of Representatives of the 8th ultimo, requesting the President to communicate to that body, "if not incompatible with the public interest, copies of the correspondence of George William Gordon, late consul of the United States at Rio de Janeiro, with the Department of State, relating to the slave trade in vessels and by citizens of the United States between the coast of Africa and Brazil."

JAMES K. POLK.

WASHINGTON, *May 6, 1846.*

To the House of Representatives:

I transmit herewith a report of the Secretary of War, in answer to the resolution of the House of Representatives of the 4th instant, calling for information "whether any soldier or soldiers of the Army of the United States have been shot for desertion, or in the act of deserting, and, if so, by whose order and under what authority."

JAMES K. POLK.

WASHINGTON, *May 11, 1846.*

To the Senate and House of Representatives:

The existing state of the relations between the United States and Mexico renders it proper that I should bring the subject to the consideration of Congress. In my message at the commencement of your present session the state of these relations, the causes which led to the suspension of diplomatic intercourse between the two countries in March, 1845, and the long-continued and unredressed wrongs and injuries committed by the Mexican Government on citizens of the United States in their persons and property were briefly set forth.

As the facts and opinions which were then laid before you were carefully considered, I can not better express my present convictions of the condition of affairs up to that time than by referring you to that communication.

The strong desire to establish peace with Mexico on liberal and honorable terms, and the readiness of this Government to regulate and adjust our boundary and other causes of difference with that power on such fair and equitable principles as would lead to permanent relations of the most friendly nature, induced me in September last to seek the reopening of diplomatic relations between the two countries. Every measure adopted on our part had for its object the furtherance of these desired results. In communicating to Congress a succinct statement of the injuries which we had suffered from Mexico, and which have been accumulating during a period of more than twenty years, every expression that could tend to inflame the people of Mexico or defeat or delay a pacific result was carefully avoided. An envoy of the United States repaired to Mexico with full powers to adjust every existing difference. But though present on the Mexican soil by agreement between the two Governments, invested with full powers, and bearing evidence of the most friendly dispositions, his mission has been unavailing. The Mexican Government not only refused to receive him or listen to his propositions, but after a long-continued series of menaces have at last invaded our territory and shed the blood of our fellow-citizens on our own soil.

It now becomes my duty to state more in detail the origin, progress, and failure of that mission. In pursuance of the instructions given in September last, an inquiry was made on the 13th of October, 1845, in the most friendly terms, through our consul in Mexico, of the minister for foreign affairs, whether the Mexican Government "would receive an envoy from the United States intrusted with full powers to adjust all the questions in dispute between the two Governments," with the assurance that "should the answer be in the affirmative such an envoy would be immediately dispatched to Mexico." The Mexican minister on the 15th of October gave an affirmative answer to this inquiry, requesting at the same time that our naval force at Vera Cruz might be withdrawn, lest its continued presence might assume the appearance of menace and coercion pending the negotiations. This force was immediately withdrawn. On the 10th of November, 1845, Mr. John Slidell, of Louisiana, was commissioned by me as envoy extraordinary and minister plenipotentiary of the United States to Mexico, and was intrusted with full powers to adjust both the questions of the Texas boundary and of indemnification to our citizens. The redress of the wrongs of our citizens naturally and inseparably blended itself with the question of boundary. The settlement of the one question in any correct view of the subject involves that of the other. I could not for a moment entertain the idea that the claims of our much-injured and long-suffering citizens, many of which had existed for more than twenty years, should be postponed or separated from the settlement of the boundary question.

Mr. Slidell arrived at Vera Cruz on the 30th of November, and was courteously received by the authorities of that city. But the Government of General Herrera was then tottering to its fall. The revolutionary party had seized upon the Texas question to effect or hasten its overthrow. Its determination to restore friendly relations with the United States, and to receive our minister to negotiate for the settlement of this question, was violently assailed, and was made the great theme of denunciation against it. The Government of General Herrera, there is good reason to believe, was sincerely desirous to receive our minister; but it yielded to the storm raised by its enemies, and on the 21st of December refused to accredit Mr. Slidell upon the most frivolous pretexts. These are so fully and ably exposed in the note of Mr. Slidell of the 24th of December last to the Mexican minister of foreign relations, herewith transmitted, that I deem it unnecessary to enter into further detail on this portion of the subject.

Five days after the date of Mr. Slidell's note General Herrera yielded the Government to General Paredes without a struggle, and on the 30th of December resigned the Presidency. This revolution was accomplished solely by the army, the people having taken little part in the contest; and thus the supreme power in Mexico passed into the hands of a military leader.

Determined to leave no effort untried to effect an amicable adjustment with Mexico, I directed Mr. Slidell to present his credentials to the Government of General Paredes and ask to be officially received by him. There would have been less ground for taking this step had General Paredes come into power by a regular constitutional succession. In that event his administration would have been considered but a mere constitutional continuance of the Government of General Herrera, and the refusal of the latter to receive our minister would have been deemed conclusive unless an intimation had been given by General Paredes of his desire to reverse the decision of his predecessor. But the Government of General Paredes owes its existence to a military revolution, by which the subsisting constitutional authorities had been subverted. The form of government was entirely changed, as well as all the high functionaries by whom it was administered.

Under these circumstances, Mr. Slidell, in obedience to my direction, addressed a note to the Mexican minister of foreign relations, under date of the 1st of March last, asking to be received by that Government in the diplomatic character to which he had been appointed. This minister in his reply, under date of the 12th of March, reiterated the arguments of his predecessor, and in terms that may be considered as giving just grounds of offense to the Government and people of the United States denied the application of Mr. Slidell. Nothing therefore remained for our envoy but to demand his passports and return to his own country.

Thus the Government of Mexico, though solemnly pledged by official acts in October last to receive and accredit an American envoy, violated their plighted faith and refused the offer of a peaceful adjustment of our difficulties. Not only was the offer rejected, but the indignity of its rejection was enhanced by the manifest breach of faith in refusing to admit the envoy who came because they had bound themselves to receive him. Nor can it be said that the offer was fruitless from the want of opportunity of discussing it; our envoy was present on their own soil. Nor can it be ascribed to a want of sufficient powers; our envoy had full powers to adjust every question of difference. Nor was there room for complaint that our propositions for settlement were unreasonable; permission was not even given our envoy to make any proposition whatever. Nor can it be objected that we, on our part, would not listen to any reasonable terms of their suggestion; the Mexican Government refused all negotiation, and have made no proposition of any kind.

In my message at the commencement of the present session I informed you that upon the earnest appeal both of the Congress and convention of Texas I had ordered an efficient military force to take a position "between the Nueces and the Del Norte." This had become necessary to meet a threatened invasion of Texas by the Mexican forces, for which extensive military preparations had been made. The invasion was threatened solely because Texas had determined, in accordance with a solemn resolution of the Congress of the United States, to annex herself to our Union, and under these circumstances it was plainly our duty to extend our protection over her citizens and soil.

This force was concentrated at Corpus Christi, and remained there until after I had received such information from Mexico as rendered it probable, if not certain, that the Mexican Government would refuse to receive our envoy.

Meantime Texas, by the final action of our Congress, had become an integral part of our Union. The Congress of Texas, by its act of December 19, 1836, had declared the Rio del Norte to be the boundary of that Republic. Its jurisdiction had been extended and exercised beyond the Nueces. The country between that river and the Del Norte had been represented in the Congress and in the convention of Texas, had thus taken part in the act of annexation itself, and is now included within one of our Congressional districts. Our own Congress had, moreover, with great unanimity, by the act approved December 31, 1845, recognized the country beyond the Nueces as a part of our territory by including it within our own revenue system, and a revenue officer to reside within that district has been appointed by and with the advice and consent of the Senate. It became, therefore, of urgent necessity to provide for the defense of that portion of our country. Accordingly, on the 13th of January last instructions were issued to the general in command of these troops to occupy the left bank of the Del Norte. This river, which is the southwestern boundary of the State of Texas, is an exposed frontier.

From this quarter invasion was threatened; upon it and in its immediate vicinity, in the judgment of high military experience, are the proper stations for the protecting forces of the Government. In addition to this important consideration, several others occurred to induce this movement. Among these are the facilities afforded by the ports at Brazos Santiago and the mouth of the Del Norte for the reception of supplies by sea, the stronger and more healthful military positions, the convenience for obtaining a ready and a more abundant supply of provisions, water, fuel, and forage, and the advantages which are afforded by the Del Norte in forwarding supplies to such posts as may be established in the interior and upon the Indian frontier.

The movement of the troops to the Del Norte was made by the commanding general under positive instructions to abstain from all aggressive acts toward Mexico or Mexican citizens and to regard the relations between that Republic and the United States as peaceful unless she should declare war or commit acts of hostility indicative of a state of war. He was specially directed to protect private property and respect personal rights.

The Army moved from Corpus Christi on the 11th of March, and on the 28th of that month arrived on the left bank of the Del Norte opposite to Matamoras, where it encamped on a commanding position, which has since been strengthened by the erection of fieldworks. A depot has also been established at Point Isabel, near the Brazos Santiago, 30 miles in rear of the encampment. The selection of his position was necessarily confided to the judgment of the general in command.

The Mexican forces at Matamoras assumed a belligerent attitude, and on the 12th of April General Ampudia, then in command, notified General Taylor to break up his camp within twenty-four hours and to retire beyond the Nueces River, and in the event of his failure to comply with these demands announced that arms, and arms alone, must decide the question. But no open act of hostility was committed until the 24th of April. On that day General Arista, who had succeeded to the command of the Mexican forces, communicated to General Taylor that "he considered hostilities commenced and should prosecute them." A party of dragoons of 63 men and officers were on the same day dispatched from the American camp up the Rio del Norte, on its left bank, to ascertain whether the Mexican troops had crossed or were preparing to cross the river, "became engaged with a large body of these troops, and after a short affair, in which some 16 were killed and wounded, appear to have been surrounded and compelled to surrender."

The grievous wrongs perpetrated by Mexico upon our citizens throughout a long period of years remain unredressed, and solemn treaties pledging her public faith for this redress have been disregarded. A government either unable or unwilling to enforce the execution of such treaties fails to perform one of its plainest duties.

Our commerce with Mexico has been almost annihilated. It was formerly highly beneficial to both nations, but our merchants have been deterred from prosecuting it by the system of outrage and extortion which the Mexican authorities have pursued against them, whilst their appeals through their own Government for indemnity have been made in vain. Our forbearance has gone to such an extreme as to be mistaken in its character. Had we acted with vigor in repelling the insults and redressing the injuries inflicted by Mexico at the commencement, we should doubtless have escaped all the difficulties in which we are now involved.

Instead of this, however, we have been exerting our best efforts to propitiate her good will. Upon the pretext that Texas, a nation as independent as herself, thought proper to unite its destinies with our own, she has affected to believe that we have severed her rightful territory, and in official proclamations and manifestoes has repeatedly threatened to make war upon us for the purpose of reconquering Texas. In the meantime we have tried every effort at reconciliation. The cup of forbearance had been exhausted even before the recent information from the frontier of the Del Norte. But now, after reiterated menaces, Mexico has passed the boundary of the United States, has invaded our territory and shed American blood upon the American soil. She has proclaimed that hostilities have commenced, and that the two nations are now at war.

As war exists, and, notwithstanding all our efforts to avoid it, exists by the act of Mexico herself, we are called upon by every consideration of duty and patriotism to vindicate with decision the honor, the rights, and the interests of our country.

Anticipating the possibility of a crisis like that which has arrived, instructions were given in August last, "as a precautionary measure" against invasion or threatened invasion, authorizing General Taylor, if the emergency required, to accept volunteers, not from Texas only, but from the States of Louisiana, Alabama, Mississippi, Tennessee, and Kentucky, and corresponding letters were addressed to the respective governors of those States. These instructions were repeated, and in January last, soon after the incorporation of "Texas into our Union of States," General Taylor was further "authorized by the President to make a requisition upon the executive of that State for such of its militia force as may be needed to repel invasion or to secure the country against apprehended invasion." On the 2d day of March he was again reminded, "in the event of the approach of any considerable Mexican force, promptly and efficiently to use the authority with which he was clothed to call to him such auxiliary force as he might need." War actually existing and our territory having been invaded, General Taylor, pursuant to authority vested in him by my direction, has called on the governor of Texas for four regiments of State troops, two to be mounted and two to serve on foot, and on the governor of Louisiana for four regiments of infantry to be sent to him as soon as practicable.

In further vindication of our rights and defense of our territory, I invoke the prompt action of Congress to recognize the existence of the war, and to place at the disposition of the Executive the means of prosecuting the war with vigor, and thus hastening the restoration of peace. To this end I recommend that authority should be given to call into the public service a large body of volunteers to serve for not less than six or twelve months unless sooner discharged. A volunteer force is beyond question more efficient than any other description of citizen soldiers, and it is not to be doubted that a number far beyond that required would readily rush to the field upon the call of their country. I further recommend that a liberal provision be made for sustaining our entire military force and furnishing it with supplies and munitions of war.

The most energetic and prompt measures and the immediate appearance in arms of a large and overpowering force are recommended to Congress as the most certain and efficient means of bringing the existing collision with Mexico to a speedy and successful termination.

In making these recommendations I deem it proper to declare that it is my anxious desire not only to terminate hostilities speedily, but to bring all matters in dispute between this Government and Mexico to an early and amicable adjustment; and in this view I shall be prepared to renew negotiations whenever Mexico shall be ready to receive propositions or to make propositions of her own.

I transmit herewith a copy of the correspondence between our envoy to Mexico and the Mexican minister for foreign affairs, and so much of the correspondence between that envoy and the Secretary of State and between the Secretary of War and the general in command on the Del Norte as is necessary to a full understanding of the subject.

JAMES K. POLK.

WASHINGTON, *May 12, 1846*.

To the Senate and House of Representatives:

I herewith transmit to Congress a copy of a communication* from the officer commanding the Army in Texas, with the papers which accompanied it. They were received by the Southern mail of yesterday, some hours after my message of that date had been transmitted, and are of a prior date to one of the communications from the same officer which accompanied that message.

JAMES K. POLK.

WASHINGTON, *May 19, 1846*.

To the Senate of the United States:

I transmit herewith a report from the Secretary of War, in answer to a resolution of the Senate of the 4th of December last, which contains

*Relating to the operations of the Army near Matamoras, Mexico.

the information called for "with respect to the practicability and utility of a fort or forts on Ship Island, on the coast of Mississippi, with a view to the protection of said coast."

JAMES K. POLK.

WASHINGTON, *May 26, 1846.*

To the Senate of the United States:

A convention was concluded at Lima on 17th March, 1841, between the United States and the Republic of Peru, for the adjustment of claims of our citizens upon that Republic. It was stipulated by the seventh article of this convention that "it shall be ratified by the contracting parties, and the ratifications shall be exchanged within two years from its date, or sooner if possible, after having been approved by the President and Senate of the United States and by the Congress of Peru."

This convention was transmitted by the President to the Senate for their consideration during the extra session of 1841, but it did not receive their approbation until the 5th January, 1843. This delay rendered it impracticable that the convention should reach Lima before the 17th March, 1843, the last day when the ratifications could be exchanged under the terms of its seventh article. The Senate therefore extended the time for this purpose until the 20th December, 1843.

In the meantime, previous to the 17th March, 1843, General Menendez, the constitutional President of Peru, had ratified the convention, declaring, however, in the act of ratification itself (which is without date), that "the present convention and ratification are to be submitted within the time stipulated in the seventh article for the final approbation of the National Congress." This was, however, rendered impossible from the fact that no Peruvian Congress assembled from the date of the convention until the year 1845.

When the convention arrived at Lima General Menendez had been deposed by a revolution, and General Vivanco had placed himself at the head of the Government. On the 16th July, 1843, the convention was ratified by him in absolute terms without the reference to Congress which the constitution of Peru requires, because, as the ratification states, "under existing circumstances the Government exercises the legislative powers demanded by the necessities of the State." The ratifications were accordingly exchanged at Lima on the 22d July, 1843, and the convention itself was proclaimed at Washington by the President on the 21st day of February, 1844.

In the meantime General Vivanco was deposed, and on the 12th October, 1843, the Government then in existence published a decree declaring all his administrative acts to be null and void, and notwithstanding the earnest and able remonstrances of Mr. Pickett, our chargé d'affaires at Lima, the Peruvian Government have still persisted in declaring that the ratification of the convention by Vivanco was invalid.

After the meeting of the Peruvian Congress in 1845 the convention was submitted to that body, by which it was approved on the 21st of

October last, "with the condition, however, that the first installment of $30,000 on account of the principal of the debt thereby recognized, and to which the second article relates, should begin from the 1st day of January, 1846, and the interest on this annual sum, according to article 3, should be calculated and paid from the 1st day of January, 1842, following in all other respects besides this modification the terms of the convention."

I am not in possession of the act of the Congress of Peru containing this provision, but the information is communicated through a note under date of the 15th of November, 1845, from the minister of foreign affairs of Peru to the chargé d'affaires of the United States at Lima. A copy of this note has been transmitted to the Department of State both by our chargé d'affaires at Lima and by the Peruvian minister of foreign affairs, and a copy of the same is herewith transmitted.

Under these circumstances I submit to the Senate, for their consideration, the amendment to the convention thus proposed by the Congress of Peru, with a view to its ratification. It would have been more satisfactory to have submitted the act itself of the Peruvian Congress, but, on account of the great distance, if I should wait until its arrival another year might be consumed, whilst the American claimants have already been too long delayed in receiving the money justly due to them. Several of the largest of these claimants would, I am informed, be satisfied with the modification of the convention adopted by the Peruvian Congress.

A difficulty may arise in regard to the form of any proceeding which the Senate might think proper to adopt, from the fact that the original convention approved by them was sent to Peru and was exchanged for the other original, ratified by General Vivanco, which is now in the Department of State. In order to obviate this difficulty as far as may be in my power, I transmit a copy of the convention, under the seal of the United States, on which the Senate might found any action they may deem advisable.

I would suggest that should the Senate advise the adoption of the amendment proposed by the Peruvian Congress the time for exchanging the ratifications of the amended convention ought to be extended for a considerable period, so as to provide against all accidents in its transmission to Lima.

JAMES K. POLK.

WASHINGTON, *May 27, 1846.*

To the House of Representatives:

In compliance with the request contained in the resolution of the House of Representatives of this date, I transmit copies of all the official dispatches which have been received from General Taylor, commanding the army of occupation on the Rio Grande, relating to the battles* of the 8th and 9th instant.

JAMES K. POLK.

*Palo Alto and Resaca de la Palma.

WASHINGTON, *May 28, 1846*.

To the Senate and House of Representatives:

I transmit a copy of a note, under date the 26th instant, from the envoy extraordinary and minister plenipotentiary of Her Britannic Majesty to the Secretary of State, communicating a dispatch, under date of the 4th instant, received by him from Her Majesty's principal secretary of state for foreign affairs.

From these it will be seen that the claims of the two Governments upon each other for a return of duties which had been levied in violation of the commercial convention of 1815 have been finally and satisfactorily adjusted. In making this communication I deem it proper to express my satisfaction at the prompt manner in which the British Government has acceded to the suggestion of the Secretary of State for the speedy termination of this affair.

JAMES K. POLK.

WASHINGTON, *June 1, 1846*.

To the Senate of the United States:

I propose, for the reason stated in the accompanying communication of the Secretary of War, that the confirmation of Brevet Second Lieutenant L. B. Wood by the Senate on the 5th of February, as a second lieutenant in the Fifth Regiment of Infantry, be canceled; and I nominate the officers named in the same communication for regular promotion in the Army.

JAMES K. POLK.

WAR DEPARTMENT, *May 15, 1846*.

The PRESIDENT OF THE UNITED STATES.

SIR: On the 12th of December last a list of promotions and appointments of officers of the Army was submitted to the Senate for confirmation, in which list Brevet Second Lieutenant L. B. Wood, of the Eighth Infantry, was nominated to the grade of second lieutenant in the Fifth Regiment of Infantry, *vice* Second Lieutenant Deas, promoted. He was entitled to this vacancy by *seniority*, but in a letter dated November 30, 1845, and received at the Adjutant-General's Office December 30, 1845 (eighteen days *after* the list referred to above had been sent to the Senate), he says: "I respectfully beg leave to be permitted to decline promotion in any other regiment, and to fill the first vacancy which may happen in the Eighth." This request was acceded to, and accordingly, on the first subsequent list submitted to the Senate, dated January 8, 1846, Brevet Second Lieutenant Charles S. Hamilton, of the Second Infantry (the next below Lieutenant Wood), was nominated to fill the vacancy in the *Fifth* Regiment and Lieutenant Wood to a vacancy which has occurred meanwhile (December 31) in the *Eighth*.

The foregoing circumstances were explained in a note to the nomination list of January 8, but it is probable the explanation escaped observation in the Senate, as on the 5th of February Lieutenant Wood was confirmed in the Fifth Infantry, agreeably to the first nomination, while no action appears to have been taken on his nomination or that of Lieutenant Hamilton on the subsequent list of January 8, 1846.

As no commissions have yet been issued to these officers, and as Lieutenant Wood has renewed his application to be continued in the Eighth Infantry, I respectfully suggest that the Senate be requested to cancel their confirmation, on the 5th of February, of his promotion as a second lieutenant in the Fifth Regiment of Infantry; and I have the honor to propose the renomination of the lieutenants whose names are annexed for regular promotion, to wit:

Fifth Regiment of Infantry.

Brevet Second Lieutenant Charles S. Hamilton, of the Second Regiment of Infantry, to be second lieutenant, November 17, 1846, *vice* Deas, promoted.

Eighth Regiment of Infantry.

Brevet Second Lieutenant Lafayette B. Wood to be second lieutenant, December 31, 1846, *vice* Maclay, promoted.

I am, sir, with great respect, your obedient servant,

W. L. MARCY.

WASHINGTON, *June 5, 1846.*

To the Senate of the United States:

In answer to the resolution of the Senate of the 22d ultimo, calling for information upon the subject of the treaties which were concluded between the late Republic of Texas and England and France, respectively, I transmit a report from the Secretary of State and the documents by which it was accompanied.

JAMES K. POLK.

WASHINGTON, *June 6, 1846.*

To the Senate of the United States:

In answer to the resolutions of the Senate of the 10th, 11th, and 22d of April last, I communicate herewith a report from the Secretary of State, accompanied with the correspondence between the Government of the United States and that of Great Britain in the years 1840, 1841, 1842, and 1843 respecting the right or practice of visiting or searching merchant vessels in time of peace, and also the protest addressed by the minister of the United States at Paris in the year 1842 against the concurrence of France in the quintuple treaty, together with all correspondence relating thereto.

JAMES K. POLK.

WASHINGTON, *June 6, 1846.*

To the Senate of the United States:

I herewith communicate to the Senate, for its consideration, a convention signed on the 2d day of May, 1846, by the minister of the United States at Berlin with the plenipotentiary of Hesse-Cassel, for the mutual abolition of the *droit d'aubaine* and duties on emigration between that German State and the United States; and I communicate with the convention an explanatory dispatch of the minister of the United States dated on the same day of the present year and numbered 284.

JAMES K. POLK.

WASHINGTON, *June 8, 1846.*

To the Senate of the United States:

I communicate herewith a report from the Secretary of War, transmitting the correspondence called for by the resolution of the Senate of the 5th instant with General Edmund P. Gaines and General Winfield Scott, of the Army of the United States.

The report of the Secretary of War and the accompanying correspondence with General Gaines contain all the information in my possession in relation to calls for "volunteers or militia into the service of the United States" "by any officer of the Army" without legal "authority therefor," and of the "measures which have been adopted" "in relation to such officer or troops so called into service."

In addition to the information contained in the report of the Secretary of War and the accompanying correspondence with "Major-General Scott, of the United States Army, upon the subject of his taking the command of the army of occupation on the frontier of Texas," I state that on the same day on which I approved and signed the act of the 13th of May, 1846, entitled "An act providing for the prosecution of the existing war between the United States and the Republic of Mexico," I communicated to General Scott, through the Secretary of War, and also in a personal interview with that officer, my desire that he should take command of the Army on the Rio Grande and of the volunteer forces which I informed him it was my intention forthwith to call out to march to that frontier to be employed in the prosecution of the war against Mexico. The tender of the command to General Scott was voluntary on my part, and was made without any request or intimation on the subject from him. It was made in consideration of his rank as Commander in Chief of the Army. My communications with General Scott assigning him the command were verbal, first through the Secretary of War and afterwards in person. No written order was deemed to be necessary. General Scott assented to assume the command, and on the following day I had another interview with him and the Secretary of War, in relation to the number and apportionment among the several States of the volunteer forces to be called out for immediate service, the forces which were to be organized and held in readiness subject to a future call should it become necessary, and other military preparations and movements to be made with a view to the vigorous prosecution of the war. It was distinctly settled, and was well understood by General Scott, that he was to command the Army in the war against Mexico, and so continued to be settled and understood without any other intention on my part until the Secretary of War submitted to me the letter of General Scott addressed to him under date of the 21st of May, 1846, a copy of which is herewith communicated. The character of that letter made it proper, in my judgment, to change my determination in regard to the command of the Army, and the Secretary of War, by my direction, in his letter of the 25th of May, 1846, a copy of which is also herewith communicated, for the reasons therein assigned, informed General Scott that he was relieved from the command of the Army destined to prosecute the war against Mexico, and that he would remain in the discharge of his duties at Washington. The command of the Army on the frontier of Mexico has since been assigned to General Taylor, with his brevet rank of major-general recently conferred upon him.

JAMES K. POLK.

WASHINGTON, *June 10, 1846.*

To the Senate of the United States:

I lay before the Senate a proposal, in the form of a convention, presented to the Secretary of State on the 6th instant by the envoy extraordinary and minister plenipotentiary of Her Britannic Majesty, for the adjustment of the Oregon question, together with a protocol of this proceeding. I submit this proposal to the consideration of the Senate, and request their advice as to the action which in their judgment it may be proper to take in reference to it.

In the early periods of the Government the opinion and advice of the Senate were often taken in advance upon important questions of our foreign policy. General Washington repeatedly consulted the Senate and asked their previous advice upon pending negotiations with foreign powers, and the Senate in every instance responded to his call by giving their advice, to which he always conformed his action. This practice, though rarely resorted to in later times, was, in my judgment, eminently wise, and may on occasions of great importance be properly revived. The Senate are a branch of the treaty-making power, and by consulting them in advance of his own action upon important measures of foreign policy which may ultimately come before them for their consideration the President secures harmony of action between that body and himself. The Senate are, moreover, a branch of the war-making power, and it may be eminently proper for the Executive to take the opinion and advice of that body in advance upon any great question which may involve in its decision the issue of peace or war. On the present occasion the magnitude of the subject would induce me under any circumstances to desire the previous advice of the Senate, and that desire is increased by the recent debates and proceedings in Congress, which render it, in my judgment, not only respectful to the Senate, but necessary and proper, if not indispensable to insure harmonious action between that body and the Executive. In conferring on the Executive the authority to give the notice for the abrogation of the convention of 1827 the Senate acted publicly so large a part that a decision on the proposal now made by the British Government, without a definite knowledge of the views of that body in reference to it, might render the question still more complicated and difficult of adjustment. For these reasons I invite the consideration of the Senate to the proposal of the British Government for the settlement of the Oregon question, and ask their advice on the subject.

My opinions and my action on the Oregon question were fully made known to Congress in my annual message of the 2d of December last, and the opinions therein expressed remain unchanged.

Should the Senate, by the constitutional majority required for the ratification of treaties, advise the acceptance of this proposition, or advise it with such modifications as they may upon full deliberation deem proper, I shall conform my action to their advice. Should the Senate, however, decline by such constitutional majority to give such advice or to express an opinion on the subject, I shall consider it my duty to reject the offer.

I also communicate herewith an extract from a dispatch of the Secretary of State to the minister of the United States at London under date of the 28th of April last, directing him, in accordance with the joint resolution of Congress "concerning the Oregon Territory," to deliver the notice to the British Government for the abrogation of the convention of the 6th of August, 1827, and also a copy of the notice transmitted to him for that purpose, together with extracts from a dispatch of that minister to the Secretary of State bearing date on the 18th day of May last.

JAMES K. POLK.

WASHINGTON, *June 11, 1846.*

To the Senate of the United States:

I transmit herewith a communication from the Secretary of War, which is accompanied by documents relating to General Gaines's calls for volunteers, received since the answer was made to the resolution of the Senate of the 5th instant on that subject, and which I deem it proper to submit for the further information of the Senate.

JAMES K. POLK.

WASHINGTON, *June 12, 1846.*

To the Senate and House of Representatives:

I transmit herewith for the information of Congress, official reports received at the War Department from the officer commanding the Army on the Mexican frontier, giving a detailed report of the operations of the Army in that quarter, and particularly of the recent engagements* between the American and Mexican forces.

JAMES K. POLK.

WASHINGTON, *June 15, 1846.*

To the Senate of the United States:

I transmit herewith a communication from the Secretary of War, accompanied by a report of an expedition led by Lieutenant Abert on the

* Palo Alto and Resaca de la Palma.

Upper Arkansas and through the country of the Camanche Indians in the fall of the year 1845, as requested by the resolution of the Senate of the 9th instant.

JAMES K. POLK.

WASHINGTON, *June 16, 1846.*

To the Senate of the United States:

In answer to the resolution of the Senate of the 3d instant, I communicate herewith estimates prepared by the War and Navy Departments of the probable expenses of conducting the existing war with Mexico during the remainder of the present and the whole of the next fiscal year. I communicate also a report of the Secretary of the Treasury, based upon these estimates, containing recommendations of measures for raising the additional means required. It is probable that the actual expenses incurred during the period specified may fall considerably below the estimates submitted, which are for a larger number of troops than have yet been called to the field. As a precautionary measure, however, against any possible deficiency, the estimates have been made at the largest amount which any state of the service may require.

It will be perceived from the report of the Secretary of the Treasury that a considerable portion of the additional amount required may be raised by a modification of the rates of duty imposed by the existing tariff laws. The high duties at present levied on many articles totally exclude them from importation, whilst the quantity and amount of others which are imported are greatly diminished. By reducing these duties to a revenue standard, it is not doubted that a large amount of the articles on which they are imposed would be imported, and a corresponding amount of revenue be received at the Treasury from this source. By imposing revenue duties on many articles now permitted to be imported free of duty, and by regulating the rates within the revenue standard upon others, a large additional revenue will be collected. Independently of the high considerations which induced me in my annual message to recommend a modification and reduction of the rates of duty imposed by the act of 1842 as being not only proper in reference to a state of peace, but just to all the great interests of the country, the necessity of such modification and reduction as a war measure must now be manifest. The country requires additional revenue for the prosecution of the war. It may be obtained to a great extent by reducing the prohibitory and highly protective duties imposed by the existing laws to revenue rates, by imposing revenue duties on the free list, and by modifying the rates of duty on other articles.

The modifications recommended by the Secretary of the Treasury in his annual report in December last were adapted to a state of peace, and the additional duties now suggested by him are with a view strictly to raise revenue as a war measure. At the conclusion of the war these duties may and should be abolished and reduced to lower rates.

It is not apprehended that the existing war with Mexico will materially affect our trade and commerce with the rest of the world. On the contrary, the reductions proposed would increase that trade and augment the revenue derived from it.

When the country is in a state of war no contingency should be permitted to occur in which there would be a deficiency in the Treasury for the vigorous prosecution of the war, and to guard against such an event it is recommended that contingent authority be given to issue Treasury notes or to contract a loan for a limited amount, reimbursable at an early day. Should no occasion arise to exercise the power, still it may be important that the authority should exist should there be a necessity for it.

It is not deemed necessary to resort to direct taxes or excises, the measures recommended being deemed preferable as a means of increasing the revenue. It is hoped that the war with Mexico, if vigorously prosecuted, as is contemplated, may be of short duration. I shall be at all times ready to conclude an honorable peace whenever the Mexican Government shall manifest a like disposition. The existing war has been rendered necessary by the acts of Mexico, and whenever that power shall be ready to do us justice we shall be prepared to sheath the sword and tender to her the olive branch of peace.

JAMES K. POLK.

WASHINGTON, *June 16, 1846.*

To the Senate of the United States:

In accordance with the resolution of the Senate of the 12th instant, that "the President of the United States be, and he is hereby, advised to accept the proposal of the British Government accompanying his message to the Senate dated 10th June, 1846, for a convention to settle boundaries, etc., between the United States and Great Britain west of the Rocky or Stony Mountains," a convention was concluded and signed on the 15th instant by the Secretary of State, on the part of the United States, and the envoy extraordinary and minister plenipotentiary of Her Britannic Majesty, on the part of Great Britain.

This convention I now lay before the Senate, for their consideration with a view to its ratification.

JAMES K. POLK.

WASHINGTON, *June 17, 1846.*

To the House of Representatives of the United States:

I communicate herewith a report from the Secretary of the Navy, accompanied with the correspondence called for by the resolution of the House of Representatives of the 4th of May last, between Commander G. J. Pendergrast and the Governments on the Rio de la Plata, and the foreign naval commanders and the United States minister at Buenos

Ayres and the Navy Department, whilst or since said Pendergrast was in command of the United States ship *Boston* in the Rio de la Plata, touching said service.

JAMES K. POLK.

WASHINGTON, *June 23, 1846.*

To the Senate of the United States:

I herewith communicate to the Senate, for its consideration, a convention concluded by the minister of the United States at Berlin with the Duchy of Nassau, dated on the 27th May, 1846, for the mutual abolition of the *droit d'aubaine* and taxes on emigration between that State of the Germanic Confederation and the United States of America, and also a dispatch from the minister explanatory of the convention.

JAMES K. POLK.

WASHINGTON, *June 24, 1846.*

To the Senate:

I transmit herewith a communication from the Secretary of War, accompanied by a report from the Commissioner of Indian Affairs, in reply to the resolution of the Senate of the 9th instant, requiring information on the subject of the removal of the Chippewa Indians from the mineral lands on Lake Superior.

JAMES K. POLK.

WASHINGTON, *July 2, 1846.*

To the House of Representatives:

I transmit herewith a report from the Secretary of State, together with copies of the correspondence in the year 1841 between the President of the United States and the governor of New York relative to the appearance of Joshua A. Spencer, esq., district attorney of the United States for the western district of New York in the courts of the State of New York as counsel for Alexander McLeod, called for by the resolution of the House of Representatives of the 10th of April, 1846.

JAMES K. POLK.

WASHINGTON, *July 7, 1846.*

To the Senate of the United States:

I herewith communicate to the Senate, for its consideration, a treaty of commerce and navigation between the United States and the Kingdom of Hanover, concluded and signed at Hanover on the 10th ultimo by the respective plenipotentiaries.

And I communicate at the same time extracts of a dispatch from the agent of the United States explanatory of the treaty.

JAMES K. POLK.

WASHINGTON, *July 9, 1846.*

To the Senate of the United States:

I transmit herewith, for the consideration and advice of the Senate with regard to its ratification, a treaty concluded on the 5th and 17th days of June last by T. P. Andrews, Thomas A. Harvey, and Gideon C. Matlock, commissioners on the part of the United States, and the various bands of the Pottawatomies, Chippewa, and Ottawa Indians, together with a report of the Commissioner of Indian Affairs and other papers explanatory of the same.

JAMES K. POLK.

WASHINGTON, *July 9, 1846.*

To the Senate of the United States:

I communicate herewith a report from the Secretary of the Treasury, transmitting a report from the Commissioner of Public Lands in reply to the resolution of the Senate of the 22d of June, 1846, calling for information of the "progress which has been made in the surveys of the mineral region upon Lake Superior, and within what time such surveys may probably be prepared for the sales of the lands in that country." In answer to that portion of the resolution which calls for the "views" of the Executive "respecting the proper mode of disposing of said lands, keeping in view the interest of the United States and the equitable claims of individuals who, under the authority of the War Department, have made improvements thereon or acquired rights of possession," I recommend that these lands be brought into market and sold at such price and under such regulations as Congress may prescribe, and that the right of preemption be secured to such persons as have, under the authority of the War Department, made improvements or acquired rights of possession thereon. Should Congress deem it proper to authorize the sale of these lands, it will be necessary to attach them to suitable land districts, and that they be placed under the management and control of the General Land Office, as other public lands.

JAMES K. POLK.

WASHINGTON, *July 11, 1846.*

To the Senate of the United States.

I communicate herewith a report from the Secretary of War, together with copies of the reports of the board of engineers heretofore employed in an examination of the coast of Texas with a view to its defense and improvement, called for by the resolution of the 29th June, 1846.

JAMES K. POLK.

WASHINGTON, *July 15, 1846.*

To the Senate of the United States:

I transmit herewith, for the consideration of the Senate, a treaty concluded on the 15th day of May last with the Comanche and other tribes or bands of Indians of Texas and the Southwestern prairies. I also inclose a communication from the Secretary of War and a report from the Commissioner of Indian Affairs, with accompanying documents, which contain full explanations of the considerations which led to the negotiation of the treaty and the general objects sought to be accomplished by it.

JAMES K. POLK.

WASHINGTON, *July 21, 1846.*

To the Senate of the United States:

I herewith transmit, in compliance with the request of the Senate in their resolution of the 17th of June, 1846, a report of the Secretary of State, together with a copy of all "the dispatches and instructions" "relative to the Oregon treaty" "forwarded to our minister, Mr. McLane," "not heretofore communicated to the Senate," including a statement of the propositions for the adjustment of the Oregon question previously made and rejected by the respective Governments. This statement was furnished to Mr. McLane before his departure from the country, and is dated on the 12th July, 1845, the day on which the note was addressed by the Secretary of State to Mr. Pakenham offering to settle the controversy by the forty-ninth parallel of latitude, which was rejected by that minister on the 29th July following.

The Senate will perceive that extracts from but two of Mr. McLane's "dispatches and communications to this Government" are transmitted, and these only because they were necessary to explain the answers given to them by the Secretary of State.

These dispatches are both numerous and voluminous, and, from their confidential character, their publication, it is believed, would be highly prejudicial to the public interests.

Public considerations alone have induced me to withhold the dispatches of Mr. McLane addressed to the Secretary of State. I concur with the Secretary of State in the views presented in his report herewith transmitted, against the publication of these dispatches.

Mr. McLane has performed his whole duty to his country, and I am not only willing, but anxious, that every Senator who may desire it shall have an opportunity of perusing these dispatches at the Department of State. The Secretary of State has been instructed to afford every facility for this purpose.

JAMES K. POLK.

WASHINGTON, *July 21, 1846.*

To the Senate of the United States:

I communicate herewith a report from the Secretary of State, in answer to the resolution of the Senate of the 18th of June, 1846, calling for certain information in relation to the Oregon Territory.

JAMES K. POLK.

WASHINGTON, *August 4, 1846.*

To the Senate of the United States:

I herewith communicate to the Senate the copy of a letter, under date of the 27th ultimo, from the Secretary of State of the United States to the minister of foreign relations of the Mexican Republic, again proposing to open negotiations and conclude a treaty of peace which shall adjust all the questions in dispute between the two Republics. Considering the relative power of the two countries, the glorious events which have already signalized our arms, and the distracted condition of Mexico, I did not conceive that any point of national honor could exist which ought to prevent me from making this overture. Equally anxious to terminate by a peace honorable for both parties as I was originally to avoid the existing war, I have deemed it my duty again to extend the olive branch to Mexico. Should the Government of that Republic accept the offer in the same friendly spirit by which it was dictated, negotiations will speedily commence for the conclusion of a treaty.

The chief difficulty to be anticipated in the negotiation is the adjustment of the boundary between the parties by a line which shall at once be satisfactory to both, and such as neither will hereafter be inclined to disturb. This is the best mode of securing perpetual peace and good neighborhood between the two Republics. Should the Mexican Government, in order to accomplish these objects, be willing to cede any portion of their territory to the United States, we ought to pay them a fair equivalent—a just and honorable peace, and not conquest, being our purpose in the prosecution of the war.

Under these circumstances, and considering the exhausted and distracted condition of the Mexican Republic, it might become necessary in order to restore peace that I should have it in my power to advance a portion of the consideration money for any cession of territory which may be made. The Mexican Government might not be willing to wait for the payment of the whole until the treaty could be ratified by the Senate and an appropriation to carry it into effect be made by Congress, and the necessity for such a delay might defeat the object altogether. I would therefore suggest whether it might not be wise for Congress to appropriate a sum such as they might consider adequate for this purpose, to be paid, if necessary, immediately upon the ratification of the treaty by Mexico. This disbursement would of course be accounted for at the Treasury, not as secret-service money, but like other expenditures.

Two precedents for such a proceeding exist in our past history, during the Administration of Mr. Jefferson, to which I would call your attention. On the 26th February, 1803, Congress passed an act appropriating $2,000,000 "for the purpose of defraying any extraordinary expenses which may be incurred in the intercourse between the United States and foreign nations," "to be applied under the direction of the President of the United States, who shall cause an account of the expenditure thereof to be laid before Congress as soon as may be;" and on the 13th February, 1806, an appropriation was made of the same amount and in the same terms. The object in the first case was to enable the President to obtain the cession of Louisiana, and in the second that of the Florida. In neither case was the money actually drawn from the Treasury, and I should hope that the result might be similar in this respect on the present occasion, though the appropriation is deemed expedient as a precautionary measure.

I refer the whole subject to the Senate in executive session. If they should concur in opinion with me, then I recommend the passage of a law appropriating such a sum as Congress may deem adequate, to be used by the Executive, if necessary, for the purpose which I have indicated.

In the two cases to which I have referred the special purpose of the appropriation did not appear on the face of the law, as this might have defeated the object; neither, for the same reason, in my opinion, ought it now to be stated.

I also communicate to the Senate the copy of a letter from the Secretary of State to Commodore Conner of the 29th ultimo, which was transmitted to him on the day it bears date.

JAMES K. POLK.

WASHINGTON, *August 5, 1846.*

To the Senate and House of Representatives of the United States:

I communicate herewith a copy of a convention for the settlement and adjustment of the Oregon question, which was concluded in this city on the 15th day of June last between the United States and Her Britannic Majesty. This convention has since been duly ratified by the respective parties, and the ratifications were exchanged at London on the 17th day of July, 1846.

It now becomes important that provision should be made by law at the earliest practicable period for the organization of a Territorial government in Oregon.

It is also deemed proper that our laws regulating trade and intercourse with the Indian tribes east of the Rocky Mountains should be extended to such tribes within our territory as dwell beyond them, and that a suitable number of Indian agents should be appointed for the purpose of carrying these laws into execution.

It is likewise important that mail facilities, so indispensable for the diffusion of information and for binding together the different portions of our extended Confederacy, should be afforded to our citizens west of the Rocky Mountains.

There is another subject to which I desire to call your special attention. It is of great importance to our country generally, and especially to our navigating and whaling interests, that the Pacific Coast, and, indeed, the whole of our territory west of the Rocky Mountains, should speedily be filled up by a hardy and patriotic population. Emigrants to that territory have many difficulties to encounter and privations to endure in their long and perilous journey, and by the time they reach their place of destination their pecuniary means are generally much reduced, if not altogether exhausted. Under these circumstances it is deemed but an act of justice that these emigrants, whilst most effectually advancing the interests and policy of the Government, should be aided by liberal grants of land. I would therefore recommend that such grants be made to actual settlers upon the terms and under the restrictions and limitations which Congress may think advisable.

JAMES K. POLK.

WASHINGTON, *August 7, 1846.*

To the Senate of the United States:

I communicate herewith a report from the Secretary of the Navy, with the accompanying documents, in answer to the resolution of the Senate of August 6, 1846, calling for the report of the board of naval officers, recently in session in this city, including the orders under which it was convened and the evidence which may have been laid before it.

JAMES K. POLK.

WASHINGTON, *August 7, 1846.*

To the Senate of the United States:

I transmit herewith, for the consideration and constitutional action of the Senate, articles of a treaty which has been concluded by the commissioners appointed for the purpose with the different parties into which the Cherokee tribe of Indians has been divided, through their delegates now in Washington. The same commissioners had previously been appointed to investigate the subject of the difficulties which have for years existed among the Cherokees, and which have kept them in a state of constant excitement and almost entirely interrupted all progress on their part in civilization and improvement in agriculture and the mechanic arts, and have led to many unfortunate acts of domestic strife, against which the Government is bound by the treaty of 1835 to protect them. Their unfortunate internal dissensions had attracted the notice and excited the sympathies of the whole country, and it became evident that if something was not done to heal them they would terminate in a sanguinary war, in which other tribes of Indians might become involved and the lives and property of our own citizens on the frontier endangered. I recommended in my message to Congress on the 13th of April last such measures as I then thought it expedient should be adopted to restore peace and good order among the Cherokees, one of which was a division of the country which they occupy and separation of the tribe. This recommendation was made under the belief that the different factions could not be reconciled and live together in harmony—a belief based in a great degree upon the representations of the delegates of the two divisions of the tribe. Since then, however, there appears to have been a change of opinion on this subject on the part of these divisions of the tribe, and on representations being made to me that by the appointment of commissioners to hear and investigate the causes of grievance of the parties against each other and to examine into their claims against the Government it would probably be found that an arrangement could be made which would once more harmonize the tribe and adjust in a satisfactory manner their claims upon and relations with the United States, I did not hesitate to appoint three persons for the purpose. The commissioners entered into an able and laborious investigation, and on their making known to me the probability of their being able to conclude a new treaty with the delegates of all the divisions of the tribe, who were fully empowered to make any new arrangement which would heal all dissensions among the Cherokees and restore them to their ancient condition of peace and good brotherhood, I authorized and appointed them to enter into negotiations with these delegates for the accomplishment of that object. The treaty now transmitted is the result of their labors, and it is hoped that it will meet the approbation of Congress, and, if carried out in good faith by all parties to it, it is believed it will effect the great and desirable ends had in view.

Accompanying the treaty is the report of the commissioners, and also a communication to them from John Ross and others, who represent what is termed the government party of the Cherokees, and which is transmitted at their request for the consideration of the Senate.

JAMES K. POLK.

WASHINGTON, *August 8, 1846*.

To the Senate and House of Representatives of the United States:

I invite your attention to the propriety of making an appropriation to provide for any expenditure which it may be necessary to make in advance for the purpose of settling all our difficulties with the Mexican Republic. It is my sincere desire to terminate, as it was originally to avoid, the existing war with Mexico by a peace just and honorable to both parties. It is probable that the chief obstacle to be surmounted in accomplishing this desirable object will be the adjustment of a boundary between the two Republics which shall prove satisfactory and convenient to both, and such as neither will hereafter be inclined to disturb. In the adjustment of this boundary we ought to pay a fair equivalent for any concessions which may be made by Mexico.

Under these circumstances, and considering the other complicated questions to be settled by negotiation with the Mexican Republic, I deem it important that a sum of money should be placed under the control of the Executive to be advanced, if need be, to the Government of that Republic immediately after their ratification of a treaty. It might be inconvenient for the Mexican Government to wait for the whole sum the payment of which may be stipulated by this treaty until it could be ratified by our Senate and an appropriation to carry it into effect made by Congress. Indeed, the necessity for this delay might defeat the object altogether. The disbursement of this money would of course be accounted for, not as secret-service money, but like other expenditures.

Two precedents for such a proceeding exist in our past history, during the Administration of Mr. Jefferson, to which I would call your attention: On the 26th February, 1803, an act was passed appropriating $2,000,000 "for the purpose of defraying any extraordinary expenses which may be incurred in the intercourse between the United States and foreign nations," "to be applied under the direction of the President of the United States, who shall cause an account of the expenditure thereof to be laid before Congress as soon as may be;" and on the 13th of February, 1806, an appropriation was made of the same amount and in the same terms. In neither case was the money actually drawn from the Treasury, and I should hope that the result in this respect might be similar on the present occasion, although the appropriation may prove to be indispensable in accomplishing the object. I would therefore recommend the passage of a law appropriating $2,000,000 to be placed at the disposal of the Executive for the purpose which I have indicated.

In order to prevent all misapprehension, it is my duty to state that, anxious as I am to terminate the existing war with the least possible delay, it will continue to be prosecuted with the utmost vigor until a treaty of peace shall be signed by the parties and ratified by the Mexican Republic.

JAMES K. POLK.

VETO MESSAGES.

WASHINGTON, *August 3, 1846*.

To the House of Representatives:

I have considered the bill entitled "An act making appropriations for the improvement of certain harbors and rivers" with the care which its importance demands, and now return the same to the House of Representatives, in which it originated, with my objections to its becoming a law. The bill proposes to appropriate $1,378,450 to be applied to more than forty distinct and separate objects of improvement. On examining its provisions and the variety of objects of improvement which it embraces, many of them of a local character, it is difficult to conceive, if it shall be sanctioned and become a law, what practical constitutional restraint can hereafter be imposed upon the most extended system of internal improvements by the Federal Government in all parts of the Union. The Constitution has not, in my judgment, conferred upon the Federal Government the power to construct works of internal improvement within the States, or to appropriate money from the Treasury for that purpose. That this bill assumes for the Federal Government the right to exercise this power can not, I think, be doubted. The approved course of the Government and the deliberately expressed judgment of the people have denied the existence of such a power under the Constitution. Several of my predecessors have denied its existence in the most solemn forms.

The general proposition that the Federal Government does not possess this power is so well settled and has for a considerable period been so generally acquiesced in that it is not deemed necessary to reiterate the arguments by which it is sustained. Nor do I deem it necessary, after the full and elaborate discussions which have taken place before the country on this subject, to do more than to state the general considerations which have satisfied me of the unconstitutionality and inexpediency of the exercise of such a power.

It is not questioned that the Federal Government is one of limited powers. Its powers are such, and such only, as are expressly granted in the Constitution or are properly incident to the expressly granted powers and necessary to their execution. In determining whether a given power has been granted a sound rule of construction has been laid down by Mr. Madison. That rule is that—

> Whenever a question arises concerning a particular power, the first question is whether the power be expressed in the Constitution. If it be, the question is decided. If it be not expressed, the next inquiry must be whether it is properly an incident to an expressed power and necessary to its execution. If it be, it may be exercised by Congress. If it be not, Congress can not exercise it.

It is not pretended that there is any express grant in the Constitution conferring on Congress the power in question. Is it, then, an incidental power necessary and proper for the execution of any of the granted powers? All the granted powers, it is confidently affirmed, may be effectually executed without the aid of such an incident. "A power, to be incidental, must not be exercised for ends which make it a principal or substantive power, independent of the principal power to which it is an incident." It is not enough that it may be regarded by Congress as *convenient* or that its exercise would advance the public weal. It must be *necessary and proper* to the execution of the principal expressed power to which it is an incident, and without which such principal power can not be carried into effect. The whole frame of the Federal Constitution proves that the Government which it creates was intended to be one of limited and specified powers. A construction of the Constitution so broad as that by which the power in question is defended tends imperceptibly to a consolidation of power in a Government intended by its framers to be thus limited in its authority. "The obvious tendency and inevitable result of a consolidation of the States into one sovereignty would be to transform the republican system of the United States into a monarchy." To guard against the assumption of all powers which encroach upon the reserved sovereignty of the States, and which consequently tend to consolidation, is the duty of all the true friends of our political system. That the power in question is not properly an incident to any of the granted powers I am fully satisfied; but if there were doubts on this subject, experience has demonstrated the wisdom of the rule that all the functionaries of the Federal Government should abstain from the exercise of all questionable or doubtful powers. If an enlargement of the powers of the Federal Government should be deemed proper, it is safer and wiser to appeal to the States and the people in the mode prescribed by the Constitution for the grant desired than to assume its exercise without an amendment of the Constitution. If Congress does not possess the general power to construct works of internal improvement within the States, or to appropriate money from the Treasury for that purpose, what is there to exempt some, at least, of the objects of appropriation included in this bill from the operation of the general rule? This bill assumes the existence of the power, and in some of its provisions asserts the principle that Congress may exercise it as fully as though the appropriations which it proposes were applicable to the construction of roads and canals. If there be a distinction in principle, it is not perceived, and should be clearly defined. Some of the objects of appropriation contained in this bill are local in their character, and lie within the limits of a single State; and though in the language of the bill they are called *harbors*, they are not connected with foreign commerce, nor are they places of refuge or shelter for our Navy or commercial marine on the ocean or lake shores. To call the mouth of a creek or a shallow inlet on our coast a harbor can not confer the authority to expend the public money in its improvement. Congress have exercised the power coeval with the Constitution of establishing light-houses, beacons, buoys, and piers on our ocean and lake shores for the purpose of rendering navigation safe and easy and of affording protection and shelter for our Navy and other shipping. These are safeguards placed in existing channels of navigation. After the long acquiescence of the Government through all preceding Administrations, I am not disposed to question or disturb the authority to make appropriations for such purposes.

When we advance a step beyond this point, and, in addition to the establishment and support, by appropriations from the Treasury, of light-houses, beacons, buoys, piers, and other improvements within the bays, inlets, and harbors on our ocean and lake coasts immediately connected with our foreign commerce, attempt to make improvements in the inte-

By the President of the United States of America

A Proclamation.

Whereas, the Congress of the United States, by virtue of the constitutional authority vested in them, have declared by their act, bearing date this day, that "by the act of the Republic of Mexico, a state of war exists between that Government and the United States."

Now, therefore, I, James K. Polk, President of the United States of America, do hereby proclaim the same to all whom it may concern: and I do specially enjoin on all persons holding offices, civil or military, under the authority of the United States, that they be vigilant and zealous, in discharging the duties respectively incident thereto: And I do moreover exhort all the good people of the United States, as they love their country; as they feel the wrongs which have forced on them the last resort of injured Nations; and as they consult the best means, under the blessing of Divine Providence, of abridging its calamities; that they exert themselves in preserving order, in promoting concord, in maintaining the authority and the efficacy of the laws, and in supporting and invigorating all the measures which may be adopted by the constituted authorities for obtaining a speedy, a just, and an honorable peace.

In testimony whereof, I have hereunto set my hand, and caused the seal of the United States to be affixed to these presents.

Done at the City of Washington, the thirteenth day of May, one thousand eight hundred and forty-six, and of the Independence of the United States the seventieth.

James K. Polk

By the President:
James Buchanan
Secretary of State.

XLIV a

47

DECLARATION OF WAR AGAINST MEXICO.

rior at points unconnected with foreign commerce, and where they are not needed for the protection and security of our Navy and commercial marine, the difficulty arises in drawing a line beyond which appropriations may not be made by the Federal Government.

One of my predecessors, who saw the evil consequences of the system proposed to be revived by this bill, attempted to define this line by declaring that "expenditures of this character" should be "confined *below* the ports of entry or delivery established by law." Acting on this restriction, he withheld his sanction from a bill which had passed Congress "to improve the navigation of the Wabash River." He was at the same time "sensible that this restriction was not as satisfactory as could be desired, and that much embarrassment may be caused to the executive department in its execution, by appropriations for remote and not well-understood objects." This restriction, it was soon found, was subject to be evaded and rendered comparatively useless in checking the system of improvements which it was designed to arrest, in consequence of the facility with which ports of entry and delivery may be established by law upon the upper waters, and in some instances almost at the head springs of some of the most unimportant of our rivers, and at points on our coast possessing no commercial importance and not used as places of refuge and safety by our Navy and other shipping. Many of the ports of entry and delivery now authorized by law, so far as foreign commerce is concerned, exist only in the statute books. No entry of foreign goods is ever made and no duties are ever collected at them. No exports of American products bound for foreign countries ever clear from them. To assume that their existence in the statute book as ports of entry or delivery warrants expenditures on the waters leading to them, which would be otherwise unauthorized, would be to assert the proposition that the lawmaking power may ingraft new provisions on the Constitution. If the restriction is a sound one, it can only apply to the bays, inlets, and rivers connected with or leading to such ports as actually have foreign commerce—ports at which foreign importations arrive in bulk, paying the duties charged by law, and from which exports are made to foreign countries. It will be found by applying the restriction thus understood to the bill under consideration that it contains appropriations for more than twenty objects of internal improvement, called in the bill *harbors*, at places which have never been declared by law either ports of entry or delivery, and at which, as appears from the records of the Treasury, there has never been an arrival of foreign merchandise, and from which there has never been a vessel cleared for a foreign country. It will be found that many of these works are new, and at places for the improvement of which appropriations are now for the first time proposed. It will be found also that the bill contains appropriations for rivers upon which there not only exists no foreign commerce, but upon which there has not been established even a paper port of entry, and for the mouths of creeks, denominated harbors, which if improved can benefit only the particular neighborhood in which they are situated. It will be found, too, to contain appropriations the expenditure of which will only have the effect of improving one place at the expense of the local natural advantages of another in its vicinity. Should this bill become a law, the same *principle* which authorizes the appropriations which it proposes to make would also authorize similar appropriations for the improvement of all the other bays, inlets, and creeks, which may with equal propriety be called harbors, and of all the rivers, important or unimportant, in every part of the Union. To sanction the bill with such provisions would be to concede the *principle* that the Federal Government possesses the power to expend the public money in a general system of internal improvements, limited in its extent only by the ever-varying discretion of successive Congresses and successive Executives. It would be to efface and remove the limitations and restrictions of power which the Constitution has wisely provided to limit the authority and action of the Federal Government to a few well-defined and specified objects. Besides these objections, the practical evils which must flow from the exercise on the part of the Federal Government of the powers asserted in this bill impress my mind with a grave sense of my duty to avert them from the country as far as my constitutional action may enable me to do so.

It not only leads to a consolidation of power in the Federal Government at the expense of the rightful authority of the States, but its inevitable tendency is to embrace objects for the expenditure of the public money which are local in their character, benefiting but few at the expense of the common Treasury of the whole. It will engender sectional feelings and prejudices calculated to disturb the harmony of the Union. It will destroy the harmony which should prevail in our legislative councils.

It will produce combinations of local and sectional interests, strong enough when united to carry propositions for appropriations of public money which could not of themselves, and standing alone, succeed, and can not fail to lead to wasteful and extravagant expenditures.

It must produce a disreputable scramble for the public money, by the conflict which is inseparable from such a system between local and individual interests and the general interest of the whole. It is unjust to those States which have with their own means constructed their own internal improvements to make from the common Treasury appropriations for similar improvements in other States.

In its operation it will be oppressive and unjust toward those States whose representatives and people either deny or doubt the existence of the power or think its exercise inexpedient, and who, while they equally contribute to the Treasury, can not consistently with their opinions engage in a general competition for a share of the public money. Thus a large portion of the Union, in numbers and in geographical extent, contributing its equal proportion of taxes to the support of the Government, would under the operation of such a system be compelled to see the national treasure—the common stock of all—unequally disbursed, and often improvidently wasted for the advantage of small sections, instead of being applied to the great national purposes in which all have a common interest, and for which alone the power to collect the revenue was given. Should the system of internal improvements proposed prevail, all these evils will multiply and increase with the increase of the number of the States and the extension of the geographical limits of the settled portions of our country. With the increase of our numbers and the extension of our settlements the local objects demanding appropriations of the public money for their improvement will be proportionately increased. In each case the expenditure of the public money would confer benefits, direct or indirect, only on a section, while these sections would become daily less in comparison with the whole.

The wisdom of the framers of the Constitution in withholding power over such objects from the Federal Government and leaving them to the local governments of the States becomes more and more manifest with every year's experience of the operations of our system.

In a country of limited extent, with but few such objects of expenditure (if the form of government permitted it), a common treasury might be used for their improvement with much less inequality and injustice than in one of the vast extent which ours now presents in population and territory. The treasure of the world would hardly be equal to the improvement of every bay, inlet, creek, and river in our country which might be supposed to promote the agricultural, manufacturing, or commercial interests of a neighborhood.

The Federal Constitution was wisely adapted in its provisions to any expansion of our limits and population, and with the advance of the confederacy of the States in the career of national greatness it becomes the more apparent that the harmony of the Union and the equal justice to which all its parts are entitled require that the Federal Government should confine its action within the limits prescribed by the Constitution to its power and authority. Some of the provisions of this bill are not subject to the objections stated, and did they stand alone I should not feel it to be my duty to withhold my approval.

If no constitutional objections existed to the bill, there are others of a serious nature which deserve some consideration. It appropriates between $1,000,000 and $2,000,000 for objects which are of no pressing necessity, and this is proposed at a time when the country is engaged in a foreign war, and when Congress at its present session has authorized a loan or the issue of Treasury notes to defray the expenses of the war, to be resorted to if the "exigencies of the Government shall require it." It would seem to be the dictate of wisdom under such circumstances to husband our means, and not to waste them on comparatively unimportant objects, so that we may reduce the loan or issue of Treasury notes which may become necessary to the smallest practicable sum. It would seem to be wise, too, to abstain from such expenditures with a view to avoid the accumulation of a large public debt, the existence of which would be opposed to the interests of our people as well as to the genius of our free institutions.

Should this bill become a law, the principle which it establishes will inevitably lead to large and annually increasing appropriations and drains upon the Treasury, for it is not to be doubted that numerous other localities not embraced in its provisions, but quite as much entitled to the favor of the Government as those which are embraced, will demand, through their representatives in Congress, to be placed on an equal footing with them. With such an increase of expenditure must necessarily follow either an increased public debt or increased burdens upon the people by taxation to supply the Treasury with the means of meeting the accumulated demands upon it.

With profound respect for the opinions of Congress, and ever anxious, as far as I can consistently with my responsibility to our common constituents, to cooperate with them in the discharge of our respective duties, it is with unfeigned regret that I find myself constrained, for the reasons which I have assigned, to withhold my approval from this bill.

JAMES K. POLK.

WASHINGTON, *August 8, 1846*.

To the Senate of the United States:

I return to the Senate, in which it originated, the bill entitled "An act to provide for the ascertainment and satisfaction of claims of American citizens for spoliations committed by the French prior to the 31st day of July, 1801," which was presented to me on the 6th instant, with my objections to its becoming a law.

In attempting to give to the bill the careful examination it requires, difficulties presented themselves in the outset from the remoteness of the period to which the claims belong, the complicated nature of the transactions in which they originated, and the protracted negotiations to which they led between France and the United States.

The short time intervening between the passage of the bill by Congress and the approaching close of their session, as well as the pressure of other official duties, have not permitted me to extend my examination of the subject into its minute details; but in the consideration which I have been able to give to it I find objections of a grave character to its provisions.

For the satisfaction of the claims provided for by the bill it is proposed to appropriate $5,000,000. I can perceive no legal or equitable ground upon which this large appropriation can rest. A portion of the claims have been more than half a century before the Government in its executive or legislative departments, and all of them had their origin in events which occurred prior to the year 1800. Since 1802 they have been from time to time before Congress. No greater necessity or propriety exists for providing for these claims at this time than has existed for near half a century, during all which period this questionable measure has never until now received the favorable consideration of Congress. It is scarcely probable, if the claim had been regarded as obligatory upon the Government or constituting an equitable demand upon the Treasury, that those who were contemporaneous with the events which gave rise to it should not long since have done justice to the claimants. The Treasury has often been in a condition to enable the Government to do so without inconvenience if these claims had been considered just. Mr. Jefferson, who was fully cognizant of the early dissensions between the Governments of the United States and France, out of which the claims arose, in his annual message in 1808 adverted to the large surplus then in the Treasury and its "probable accumulation," and inquired whether it should "lie unproductive in the public vaults;" and yet these claims, though then before Congress, were not recognized or paid. Since that time the public debt of the Revolution and of the War of 1812 has been extinguished, and at several periods since the Treasury has been in possession of large surpluses over the demands upon it. In 1836 the surplus amounted to many millions of dollars, and, for want of proper objects to which to apply it, it was directed by Congress to be deposited with the States.

During this extended course of time, embracing periods eminently favorable for satisfying all just demands upon the Government, the claims embraced in this bill met with no favor in Congress beyond reports of committees in one or the other branch. These circumstances alone are calculated to raise strong doubts in respect to these claims, more especially as all the information necessary to a correct judgment concerning them has been long before the public. These doubts are strengthened in my mind by the examination I have been enabled to give to the transactions in which they originated.

The bill assumes that the United States have become liable in these ancient transactions to make reparation to the claimants for injuries committed by France. Nothing was obtained for the claimants by negotiation; and the bill assumes that the Government has become responsible to them for the aggressions of France. I have not been able to satisfy myself of the correctness of this assumption, or that the Government has become in any way responsible for these claims. The limited time allotted me before your adjournment precludes the possibility of reiterating the facts and arguments by which in preceding Congresses these claims have been successfully resisted.

The present is a period peculiarly unfavorable for the satisfaction of claims of so large an amount and, to say the least of them, of so doubtful a character. There is no surplus in the Treasury. A public debt of several millions of dollars has been created within the last few years.

We are engaged in a foreign war, uncertain in its duration and involving heavy expenditures, to prosecute which Congress has at its present session authorized a further loan; so that in effect the Government, should this bill become a law, borrows money and increases the public debt to pay these claims.

It is true that by the provisions of the bill payment is directed to be made in land scrip instead of money, but the effect upon the Treasury will be the same. The public lands constitute one of the sources of public revenue, and if these claims be paid in land scrip it will from the date of its issue to a great extent cut off from the Treasury the annual income from the sales of the public lands, because payments for lands sold by the Government may be expected to be made in scrip until it is all redeemed. If these claims be just, they ought to be paid in money, and not in anything less valuable. The bill provides that they shall be paid in land scrip, whereby they are made in effect to be a mortgage upon the public lands in the new States; a mortgage, too, held in great part, if not wholly, by nonresidents of the States in which the lands lie, who may secure these lands to the amount of several millions of acres, and then demand for them exorbitant prices from the citizens of the States who may desire to purchase them for settlement, or they may keep them out of the market, and thus retard the prosperity and growth of the States in which they are situated. Why this unusual mode of satisfying demands on the Treasury has been resorted to does not appear. It is not consistent with a sound public policy. If it be done in this case, it may be done in all others. It would form a precedent for the satisfaction of all other stale and questionable claims in the same manner, and would undoubtedly be resorted to by all claimants who after successive trials shall fail to have their claims recognized and paid in money by Congress.

This bill proposes to appropriate $5,000,000, to be paid in land scrip, and provides that "no claim or memorial shall be received by the commissioners" authorized by the act "unless accompanied by a release or discharge of the United States from all other and further compensation" than the claimant "may be entitled to receive under the provisions of this act." These claims are estimated to amount to a much larger sum than $5,000,000, and yet the claimant is required to release to the Government all other compensation, and to accept his share of a fund which is known to be inadequate. If the claims be well founded, it would be unjust to the claimants to repudiate any portion of them, and the payment of the remaining sum could not be hereafter resisted. This bill proposes to pay these claims not in the currency known to the Constitution, and not to their full amount.

Passed, as this bill has been, near the close of the session, and when many measures of importance necessarily claim the attention of Congress, and possibly without that full and deliberate consideration which the large sum it appropriates and the existing condition of the Treasury and of the country demand, I deem it to be my duty to withhold my approval, that it may hereafter undergo the revision of Congress. I have come to this conclusion with regret. In interposing my objections to its becoming a law I am fully sensible that it should be an extreme case which would make it the duty of the Executive to withhold his approval of any bill passed by Congress upon the ground of its inexpediency alone. Such a case I consider this to be.

JAMES K. POLK.

PROCLAMATIONS.

[From Statutes at Large (Little & Brown), Vol. IX, p. 999.]

BY THE PRESIDENT OF THE UNITED STATES OF AMERICA.

A PROCLAMATION.

Whereas by an act of the Congress of the United States of the 3d of March, 1845, entitled "An act allowing drawback upon foreign merchandise exported in the original packages to Chihuahua and Santa Fe, in Mexico, and to the British North American Provinces adjoining the United States," certain privileges are extended in reference to drawback to ports therein specially enumerated in the seventh section of said act, which also provides "that such other ports situated on the frontiers of the United States adjoining the British North American Provinces as may hereafter be found expedient may have extended to them the like privileges on the recommendation of the Secretary of the Treasury and proclamation duly made by the President of the United States specially designating the ports to which the aforesaid privileges are to be extended;" and

Whereas the Secretary of the Treasury has duly recommended to me the extension of the privileges of the law aforesaid to the port of Lewiston, in the collection district of Niagara, in the State of New York:

Now, therefore, I, James K. Polk, President of the United States of America, do hereby declare and proclaim that the port of Lewiston, in the collection district of Niagara, in the State of New York, is and shall be entitled to all the privileges extended to the other ports enumerated in the seventh section of the act aforesaid from and after the date of this proclamation.

In witness whereof I have hereunto set my hand and caused the seal of the United States to be affixed.

[SEAL.] Done at the city of Washington, this 17th day of January, A. D. 1846, and of the Independence of the United States of America the seventieth.

JAMES K. POLK.

By the President:

JAMES BUCHANAN,

Secretary of State.

BY THE PRESIDENT OF THE UNITED STATES OF AMERICA.

A PROCLAMATION.

Whereas the Congress of the United States, by virtue of the constitutional authority vested in them, have declared by their act bearing date this day that "by the act of the Republic of Mexico a state of war exists between that Government and the United States:"

Now, therefore, I, James K. Polk, President of the United States of America, do hereby proclaim the same to all whom it may concern; and I do specially enjoin on all persons holding offices, civil or military, under the authority of the United States that they be vigilant and zealous in discharging the duties respectively incident thereto; and I do, moreover, exhort all the good people of the United States, as they love their country, as they feel the wrongs which have forced on them the last resort of injured nations, and as they consult the best means, under the blessing of Divine Providence, of abridging its calamities, that they exert themselves in preserving order, in promoting concord, in maintaining the authority and the efficacy of the laws, and in supporting and invigorating all the measures which may be adopted by the constituted authorities for obtaining a speedy, a just, and an honorable peace.

In testimony whereof I have hereunto set my hand and caused the seal of the United States to be affixed to these presents.

[SEAL.] Done at the city of Washington, the 13th day of May, A. D. 1846, and of the Independence of the United States the seventieth.

JAMES K. POLK.

By the President:

JAMES BUCHANAN,
Secretary of State.

BY THE PRESIDENT OF THE UNITED STATES OF AMERICA.

A PROCLAMATION.

Whereas by the act of Congress approved July 9, 1846, entitled "An act to retrocede the county of Alexandria, in the District of Columbia, to the State of Virginia," it is enacted that, with the assent of the people of the county and town of Alexandria, to be ascertained in the manner therein prescribed, all that portion of the District of Columbia ceded to the United States by the State of Virginia and all the rights and jurisdiction therewith ceded over the same shall be ceded and forever relinquished to the State of Virginia in full and absolute right and jurisdiction, as well of soil as of persons residing or to reside thereon; and

Whereas it is further provided that the said act "shall not be in force until after the assent of the people of the county and town of Alexandria shall be given to it in the mode therein provided," and, if a majority of the votes should be in favor of accepting the provisions of the said act, it shall be the duty of the President to make proclamation of the fact; and

Whereas on the 17th day of August, 1846, after the close of the late session of the Congress of the United States, I duly appointed five citizens of the county or town of Alexandria, being freeholders within the same, as commissioners, who, being duly sworn to perform the duties imposed on them as prescribed in the said act, did proceed within ten days after they were notified to fix upon the 1st and 2d days of September, 1846, as the time, the court-house of the county of Alexandria as the place, and *viva voce* as the manner of voting, and gave due notice of the same; and at the time and at the place, in conformity with the said notice, the said commissioners presiding and deciding all questions arising in relation to the right of voting under the said act, the votes of the citizens qualified to vote were taken *viva voce* and recorded in poll books duly kept, and on the 3d day of September instant, after the said polls were closed, the said commissioners did make out and on the next day did transmit to me a statement of the polls so held, upon oath and under their seals; and of the votes so cast and polled there were in favor of accepting the provisions of the said act 763 votes, and against accepting the same 222, showing a majority of 541 votes for the acceptance of the same:

Now, therefore, be it known that I, James K. Polk, President of the United States of America, in fulfillment of the duty imposed upon me by the said act of Congress, do hereby make proclamation of the "result" of said "poll" as above stated, and do call upon all and singular the persons whom it doth or may concern to take notice that the act aforesaid "is in full force and effect."

In witness whereof I have hereunto set my hand and caused the seal of the United States to be affixed.

[SEAL.] Done at the city of Washington, this 7th day of September, A. D. 1846, and of the Independence of the United States the seventy-first.

JAMES K. POLK.

By the President:

N. P. TRIST,

Acting Secretary of State.

SECOND ANNUAL MESSAGE.

WASHINGTON, *December 8, 1846.*

Fellow-Citizens of the Senate and of the House of Representatives:

In resuming your labors in the service of the people it is a subject of congratulation that there has been no period in our past history when all the elements of national prosperity have been so fully developed. Since your last session no afflicting dispensation has visited our country. General good health has prevailed, abundance has crowned the toil of the husbandman, and labor in all its branches is receiving an ample reward, while education, science, and the arts are rapidly enlarging the means of social happiness. The progress of our country in her career of greatness, not only in the vast extension of our territorial limits and the rapid increase of our population, but in resources and wealth and in the happy condition of our people, is without an example in the history of nations.

As the wisdom, strength, and beneficence of our free institutions are unfolded, every day adds fresh motives to contentment and fresh incentives to patriotism.

Our devout and sincere acknowledgments are due to the gracious Giver of All Good for the numberless blessings which our beloved country enjoys.

It is a source of high satisfaction to know that the relations of the United States with all other nations, with a single exception, are of the most amicable character. Sincerely attached to the policy of peace early adopted and steadily pursued by this Government, I have anxiously desired to cultivate and cherish friendship and commerce with every foreign power. The spirit and habits of the American people are favorable to the maintenance of such international harmony. In adhering to this wise policy, a preliminary and paramount duty obviously consists in the protection of our national interests from encroachment or sacrifice and our national honor from reproach. These must be maintained at any hazard. They admit of no compromise or neglect, and must be scrupulously and constantly guarded. In their vigilant vindication collision and conflict with foreign powers may sometimes become unavoidable. Such has been our scrupulous adherence to the dictates of justice in all our foreign intercourse that, though steadily and rapidly advancing in prosperity and power, we have given no just cause of complaint to any nation and have enjoyed the blessings of peace for more than thirty years. From a policy so sacred to humanity and so salutary in its effects upon our political system we should never be induced voluntarily to depart.

The existing war with Mexico was neither desired nor provoked by the United States. On the contrary, all honorable means were resorted to to avert it. After years of endurance of aggravated and unredressed wrongs on our part, Mexico, in violation of solemn treaty stipulations and of every principle of justice recognized by civilized nations, commenced hostilities, and thus by her own act forced the war upon us. Long before the advance of our Army to the left bank of the Rio Grande we had ample cause of war against Mexico, and had the United States resorted to this extremity we might have appealed to the whole civilized world for the justice of our cause. I deem it to be my duty to present to you on the present occasion a condensed review of the injuries we had sustained, of the causes which led to the war, and of its progress since its commencement. This is rendered the more necessary because of the misapprehensions which have to some extent prevailed as to its origin and true character. The war has been represented as unjust and unnecessary and as one of aggression on our part upon a weak and injured enemy. Such erroneous views, though entertained by but few, have been widely and extensively circulated, not only at home, but have been spread throughout Mexico and the whole world. A more effectual means could not have been devised to encourage the enemy and protract the war than to advocate and adhere to their cause, and thus give them "aid and comfort." It is a source of national pride and exultation that the great body of our people have thrown no such obstacles in the way of the Government in prosecuting the war successfully, but have shown themselves to be eminently patriotic and ready to vindicate their country's honor and interests at any sacrifice. The alacrity and promptness with which our volunteer forces rushed to the field on their country's call prove not only their patriotism, but their deep conviction that our cause is just.

The wrongs which we have suffered from Mexico almost ever since she became an independent power and the patient endurance with which we have borne them are without a parallel in the history of modern civilized nations. There is reason to believe that if these wrongs had been resented and resisted in the first instance the present war might have been avoided. One outrage, however, permitted to pass with impunity almost necessarily encouraged the perpetration of another, until at last Mexico seemed to attribute to weakness and indecision on our part a forbearance which was the offspring of magnanimity and of a sincere desire to preserve friendly relations with a sister republic.

Scarcely had Mexico achieved her independence, which the United States were the first among the nations to acknowledge, when she commenced the system of insult and spoliation which she has ever since pursued. Our citizens engaged in lawful commerce were imprisoned, their vessels seized, and our flag insulted in her ports. If money was wanted, the lawless seizure and confiscation of our merchant vessels and their cargoes was a ready resource, and if to accomplish their purposes it became necessary to imprison the owners, captains, and crews, it was done. Rulers superseded rulers in Mexico in rapid succession, but still there was no change in this system of depredation. The Government of the United States made repeated reclamations on behalf of its citizens, but these were answered by the perpetration of new outrages. Promises of redress made by Mexico in the most solemn forms were postponed or evaded. The files and records of the Department of State contain conclusive proofs of numerous lawless acts perpetrated upon the property and persons of our citizens by Mexico, and of wanton insults to our national flag. The interposition of our Government to obtain redress was again and again invoked under circumstances which no nation ought to disregard. It was hoped that these outrages would cease and that

Mexico would be restrained by the laws which regulate the conduct of civilized nations in their intercourse with each other after the treaty of amity, commerce, and navigation of the 5th of April, 1831, was concluded between the two Republics; but this hope soon proved to be vain. The course of seizure and confiscation of the property of our citizens, the violation of their persons, and the insults to our flag pursued by Mexico previous to that time were scarcely suspended for even a brief period, although the treaty so clearly defines the rights and duties of the respective parties that it is impossible to misunderstand or mistake them. In less than seven years after the conclusion of that treaty our grievances had become so intolerable that in the opinion of President Jackson they should no longer be endured. In his message to Congress in February, 1837, he presented them to the consideration of that body, and declared that—

The length of time since some of the injuries have been committed, the repeated and unavailing applications for redress, the wanton character of some of the outrages upon the property and persons of our citizens, upon the officers and flag of the United States, independent of recent insults to this Government and people by the late extraordinary Mexican minister, would justify in the eyes of all nations immediate war.

In a spirit of kindness and forbearance, however, he recommended reprisals as a milder mode of redress. He declared that war should not be used as a remedy "by just and generous nations, confiding in their strength for injuries committed, if it can be honorably avoided," and added:

It has occurred to me that, considering the present embarrassed condition of that country, we should act with both wisdom and moderation by giving to Mexico one more opportunity to atone for the past before we take redress into our own hands. To avoid all misconception on the part of Mexico, as well as to protect our own national character from reproach, this opportunity should be given with the avowed design and full preparation to take immediate satisfaction if it should not be obtained on a repetition of the demand for it. To this end I recommend that an act be passed authorizing reprisals, and the use of the naval force of the United States by the Executive against Mexico to enforce them, in the event of a refusal by the Mexican Government to come to an amicable adjustment of the matters in controversy between us upon another demand thereof made from on board one of our vessels of war on the coast of Mexico.

Committees of both Houses of Congress, to which this message of the President was referred, fully sustained his views of the character of the wrongs which we had suffered from Mexico, and recommended that another demand for redress should be made before authorizing war or reprisals. The Committee on Foreign Relations of the Senate, in their report, say:

After such a demand, should prompt justice be refused by the Mexican Government, we may appeal to all nations, not only for the equity and moderation with which we shall have acted toward a sister republic, but for the necessity which will then compel us to seek redress for our wrongs, either by actual war or by reprisals. The subject will then be presented before Congress, at the commencement of the next session, in a clear and distinct form, and the committee can not doubt but that such measures will be immediately adopted as may be necessary to vindicate the honor of the country and insure ample reparation to our injured fellow-citizens.

The Committee on Foreign Affairs of the House of Representatives made a similar recommendation. In their report they say that—

They fully concur with the President that ample cause exists for taking redress into our own hands, and believe that we should be justified in the opinion of other nations for taking such a step. But they are willing to try the experiment of another demand, made in the most solemn form, upon the justice of the Mexican Government before any further proceedings are adopted.

No difference of opinion upon the subject is believed to have existed in Congress at that time; the executive and legislative departments concurred; and yet such has been our forbearance and desire to preserve peace with Mexico that the wrongs of which we then complained, and which gave rise to these solemn proceedings, not only remain unredressed to this day, but additional causes of complaint of an aggravated character have ever since been accumulating. Shortly after these proceedings a special messenger was dispatched to Mexico to make a final demand for redress, and on the 20th of July, 1837, the demand was made. The reply of the Mexican Government bears date on the 29th of the same month, and contains assurances of the "anxious wish" of the Mexican Government "not to delay the moment of that final and equitable adjustment which is to terminate the existing difficulties between the two Governments;" that "nothing should be left undone which may contribute to the most speedy and equitable determination of the subjects which have so seriously engaged the attention of the American Government;" that the "Mexican Government would adopt as the only guides for its conduct the plainest principles of public right, the sacred obligations imposed by international law, and the religious faith of treaties," and that "whatever reason and justice may dictate respecting each case will be done." The assurance was further given that the decision of the Mexican Government upon each cause of complaint for which redress had been demanded should be communicated to the Government of the United States by the Mexican minister at Washington.

These solemn assurances in answer to our demand for redress were disregarded. By making them, however, Mexico obtained further delay. President Van Buren, in his annual message to Congress of the 5th of December, 1837, states that "although the larger number" of our demands for redress, "and many of them aggravated cases of personal wrongs, have been now for years before the Mexican Government, and some of the causes of national complaint, and those of the most offensive character, admitted of immediate, simple, and satisfactory replies, it is only within a few days past that any specific communication in answer to our last demand, made five months ago, has been received from the Mexican minister;" and that "for not one of our public complaints has satisfaction been given or offered, that but one of the cases of personal wrong has been favorably considered, and that but four cases of both descriptions out of all those formally presented and earnestly pressed have as yet been decided upon by the Mexican Government." President Van Buren, believing that it would be vain to make any further attempt to obtain redress by the ordinary means within the power of the Executive, communicated this opinion to Congress in the message referred to, in which he said:

> On a careful and deliberate examination of their contents [of the correspondence with the Mexican Government], and considering the spirit manifested by the Mexican Government, it has become my painful duty to return the subject as it now stands to Congress, to whom it belongs to decide upon the time, the mode, and the measure of redress.

Had the United States at that time adopted compulsory measures and taken redress into their own hands, all our difficulties with Mexico would probably have been long since adjusted and the existing war have been averted. Magnanimity and moderation on our part only had the effect to complicate these difficulties and render an amicable settlement of them the more embarrassing. That such measures of redress under similar provocations committed by any of the powerful nations of Europe would have been promptly resorted to by the United States can not be doubted. The national honor and the preservation of the national character throughout the world, as well as our own self-respect and the protection due to our own citizens, would have rendered such a resort indispensable. The history of no civilized nation in modern times has presented within so brief a period so many wanton attacks upon the honor of its flag and upon the property and persons of its citizens as had at that time been borne by the United States from the Mexican authorities and people. But Mexico was a sister republic on the North American continent, occupying a territory contiguous to our own, and was in a feeble and distracted condition, and these considerations, it is presumed, induced Congress to forbear still longer.

Instead of taking redress into our own hands, a new negotiation was entered upon with fair promises on the part of Mexico, but with the real purpose, as the event has proved, of indefinitely postponing the reparation which we demanded, and which was so justly due. This negotiation, after more than a year's delay, resulted in the convention of the 11th of April, 1839, "for the adjustment of claims of citizens of the United States of America upon the Government of the Mexican Republic." The joint board of commissioners created by this convention to examine and decide upon these claims was not organized until the month of August, 1840, and under the terms of the convention they were to terminate their duties within eighteen months from that time. Four of the eighteen months were consumed in preliminary discussions on frivolous and dilatory points raised by the Mexican commissioners, and it was not until the month of December, 1840, that they commenced the examination of the claims of our citizens upon Mexico. Fourteen months only remained to examine and decide upon these numerous and complicated cases. In the month of February, 1842, the term of the commission expired, leaving many claims undisposed of for want of time. The claims which were allowed by the board and by the umpire authorized by the convention to decide in case of disagreement between the Mexican and American commissioners amounted to $2,026,139.68. There were pending before the umpire when the commission expired additional claims, which had been examined and awarded by the American commissioners and had not been allowed by the Mexican commissioners, amounting to $928,627.88, upon which he did not decide, alleging that his authority had ceased with the termination of the joint commission. Besides these claims, there were others of American citizens amounting to $3,336,837.05, which had been submitted to the board, and upon which they had not time to decide before their final adjournment.

The sum of $2,026,139.68, which had been awarded to the claimants, was a liquidated and ascertained debt due by Mexico, about which there could be no dispute, and which she was bound to pay according to the terms of the convention. Soon after the final awards for this amount had been made the Mexican Government asked for a postponement of the time of making payment, alleging that it would be inconvenient to make the payment at the time stipulated. In the spirit of forbearing kindness toward a sister republic, which Mexico has so long abused, the United States promptly complied with her request. A second convention was accordingly concluded between the two Governments on the 30th of January, 1843, which upon its face declares that "this new arrangement is entered into for the accommodation of Mexico." By the terms of this convention all the interest due on the awards which had been made in favor of the claimants under the convention of the 11th of April, 1839, was to be paid to them on the 30th of April, 1843, and "the principal of the said awards and the interest accruing thereon" was stipulated to "be paid in five years, in equal installments every three months." Notwithstanding this new convention was entered into at the request of Mexico and for the purpose of relieving her from embarrassment, the claimants have only received the interest due on the 30th of April, 1843, and three of the twenty installments. Although the payment of the sum thus liquidated and confessedly due by Mexico to our citizens as indemnity for acknowledged acts of outrage and wrong was secured by treaty, the obligations of which are ever held sacred by all just nations, yet Mexico has violated this solemn engagement by failing and refusing to make the payment. The two installments due in April and July, 1844, under the peculiar circumstances connected with them, have been assumed by the United States and discharged to the claimants, but they are still due by Mexico. But this is not all of which we have just cause of complaint. To provide a remedy for the claimants whose cases were not decided by the joint commission under the convention of April 11, 1839, it was expressly stipulated by the sixth article of the convention of the 30th of January, 1843, that—

A new convention shall be entered into for the settlement of all claims of the Government and citizens of the United States against the Republic of Mexico which were not finally decided by the late commission which met in the city of Washington, and of all claims of the Government and citizens of Mexico against the United States.

In conformity with this stipulation, a third convention was concluded and signed at the city of Mexico on the 20th of November, 1843, by the plenipotentiaries of the two Governments, by which provision was made for ascertaining and paying these claims. In January, 1844, this convention was ratified by the Senate of the United States with two amendments, which were manifestly reasonable in their character. Upon a reference of the amendments proposed to the Government of Mexico, the same evasions, difficulties, and delays were interposed which have so long marked the policy of that Government toward the United States. It has not even yet decided whether it would or would not accede to them, although the subject has been repeatedly pressed upon its consideration. Mexico has thus violated a second time the faith of treaties by failing or refusing to carry into effect the sixth article of the convention of January, 1843.

Such is the history of the wrongs which we have suffered and patiently endured from Mexico through a long series of years. So far from affording reasonable satisfaction for the injuries and insults we had borne, a great aggravation of them consists in the fact that while the United States, anxious to preserve a good understanding with Mexico, have been constantly but vainly employed in seeking redress for past wrongs, new outrages were constantly occurring, which have continued to increase our causes of complaint and to swell the amount of our demands. While the citizens of the United States were conducting a lawful commerce with Mexico under the guaranty of a treaty of "amity, commerce, and navigation," many of them have suffered all the injuries which would have resulted from open war. This treaty, instead of affording protection to our citizens, has been the means of inviting them into the ports of Mexico that they might be, as they have been in numerous instances, plundered of their property and deprived of their personal liberty if they dared insist on their rights. Had the unlawful seizures of American property and the violation of the personal liberty of our citizens, to say nothing of the insults to our flag, which have occurred in the ports of Mexico taken place on the high seas, they would themselves long since have constituted a state of actual war between the two countries. In so long suffering Mexico to violate her most solemn treaty obligations, plunder our citizens of their property, and imprison their persons without affording them any redress we have failed to perform one of the first and highest duties which every government owes to its citizens, and the consequence has been that many of them have been reduced from a state of affluence to bankruptcy. The proud name of American citizen, which ought to protect all who bear it from insult and injury throughout the world, has afforded no such protection to our citizens in Mexico. We had ample cause of war against Mexico long before the breaking out of hostilities; but even then we forbore to take redress into our own hands until Mexico herself became the aggressor by invading our soil in hostile array and shedding the blood of our citizens.

Such are the grave causes of complaint on the part of the United States against Mexico—causes which existed long before the annexation of Texas to the American Union; and yet, animated by the love of peace and a magnanimous moderation, we did not adopt those measures of redress which under such circumstances are the justified resort of injured nations.

The annexation of Texas to the United States constituted no just cause of offense to Mexico. The pretext that it did so is wholly inconsistent and irreconcilable with well-authenticated facts connected with the revolution by which Texas became independent of Mexico. That this may be the more manifest, it may be proper to advert to the causes and to the history of the principal events of that revolution.

Texas constituted a portion of the ancient Province of Louisiana, ceded to the United States by France in the year 1803. In the year 1819 the United States, by the Florida treaty, ceded to Spain all that part of Louisiana within the present limits of Texas, and Mexico, by the revolution which separated her from Spain and rendered her an independent nation, succeeded to the rights of the mother country over this territory. In the year 1824 Mexico established a federal constitution, under which the Mexican Republic was composed of a number of sovereign States confederated together in a federal union similar to our own. Each of these States had its own executive, legislature, and judiciary, and for all except federal purposes was as independent of the General Government and that of the other States as is Pennsylvania or Virginia under our Constitution. Texas and Coahuila united and formed one of these Mexican States. The State constitution which they adopted, and which was approved by the Mexican Confederacy, asserted that they were "free and independent of the other Mexican United States and of every other power and dominion whatsoever," and proclaimed the great principle of human liberty that "the sovereignty of the state resides originally and essentially in the general mass of the individuals who compose it." To the Government under this constitution, as well as to that under the federal constitution, the people of Texas owed allegiance.

Emigrants from foreign countries, including the United States, were invited by the colonization laws of the State and of the Federal Government to settle in Texas. Advantageous terms were offered to induce them to leave their own country and become Mexican citizens. This invitation was accepted by many of our citizens in the full faith that in their new home they would be governed by laws enacted by representatives elected by themselves, and that their lives, liberty, and property would be protected by constitutional guaranties similar to those which existed in the Republic they had left. Under a Government thus organized they continued until the year 1835, when a military revolution broke out in the City of Mexico which entirely subverted the federal and State constitutions and placed a military dictator at the head of the Government. By a sweeping decree of a Congress subservient to the will of the Dictator the several State constitutions were abolished and the States themselves converted into mere departments of the central Government. The people of Texas were unwilling to submit to this usurpation. Resistance to such tyranny became a high duty. Texas was fully absolved from all allegiance to the central Government of Mexico from the moment that Government had abolished her State constitution and in its place substituted an arbitrary and despotic central government. Such were the principal causes of the Texan revolution. The people of Texas at once determined upon resistance and flew to arms. In the midst of these important and exciting events, however, they did not omit to place their liberties upon a secure and permanent foundation. They elected members to a convention, who in the month of March, 1836, issued a formal declaration that their "political connection with the Mexican nation has forever ended, and that the people of Texas do now constitute a *free, sovereign, and independent Republic*, and are fully invested with all the rights and attributes which properly belong to independent nations." They also adopted for their government a liberal republican constitution. About the same time Santa Anna, then the Dictator of Mexico, invaded Texas with a numerous army for the purpose of subduing her people and enforcing obedience to his arbitrary and despotic Government. On the 21st of April, 1836, he was met by the Texan citizen soldiers, and on that day was achieved by them the memorable victory of San Jacinto, by which they conquered their independence. Considering the numbers engaged on the respective sides, history does not record a more brilliant achievement. Santa Anna himself was among the captives.

In the month of May, 1836, Santa Anna acknowledged by a treaty with the Texan authorities in the most solumn form "the full, entire, and perfect independence of the Republic of Texas." It is true he was then a prisoner of war, but it is equally true that he had failed to reconquer Texas, and had met with signal defeat; that his authority had not been revoked, and that by virtue of this treaty he obtained his personal release. By it hostilities were suspended, and the army which had invaded Texas under his command returned in pursuance of this arrangement unmolested to Mexico.

From the day that the battle of San Jacinto was fought until the present hour Mexico has never possessed the power to reconquer Texas. In the language of the Secretary of State of the United States in a dispatch to our minister in Mexico under date of the 8th of July, 1842—

Mexico may have chosen to consider, and may still choose to consider, Texas as having been at all times since 1835, and as still continuing, a rebellious province; but the world has been obliged to take a very different view of the matter. From the time of the battle of San Jacinto, in April, 1836, to the present moment, Texas has exhibited the same external signs of national independence as Mexico herself, and with quite as much stability of government. Practically free and independent, acknowledged as a political sovereignty by the principal powers of the world, no hostile foot finding rest within her territory for six or seven years, and Mexico herself refraining for all that period from any further attempt to reestablish her own authority over that territory, it can not but be surprising to find Mr. De Bocanegra [the secretary of foreign affairs of Mexico] complaining that for that whole period citizens of the United States or its Government have been favoring the rebels of Texas and supplying them with vessels, ammunition, and money, as if the war for the reduction of the Province of Texas had been constantly prosecuted by Mexico, and her success prevented by these influences from abroad.

In the same dispatch the Secretary of State affirms that—

Since 1837 the United States have regarded Texas as an independent sovereignty as much as Mexico, and that trade and commerce with citizens of a government at war with Mexico can not on that account be regarded as an intercourse by which assistance and succor are given to Mexican rebels. The whole current of Mr. De Bocanegra's remarks runs in the same direction, as if the independence of Texas had not been acknowledged. It has been acknowledged; it was acknowledged in 1837 against the remonstrance and protest of Mexico, and most of the acts of any importance of which Mr. De Bocanegra complains flow necessarily from that recognition. He speaks of Texas as still being "an integral part of the territory of the Mexican Republic," but he can not but understand that the United States do not so regard it. The real complaint of Mexico, therefore, is in substance neither more nor less than a complaint against the recognition of Texan independence. It may be thought rather late to repeat that complaint, and not quite just to confine it to the United States to the exemption of England, France, and Belgium, unless the United States, having been the first to acknowledge the independence of Mexico herself, are to be blamed for setting an example for the recognition of that of Texas.

And he added that—

The Constitution, public treaties, and the laws oblige the President to regard Texas as an independent state, and its territory as no part of the territory of Mexico.

Texas had been an independent state, with an organized government, defying the power of Mexico to overthrow or reconquer her, for more than ten years before Mexico commenced the present war against the United States. Texas had given such evidence to the world of her ability to maintain her separate existence as an independent nation that she had been formally recognized as such not only by the United States, but by several of the principal powers of Europe. These powers had entered into treaties of amity, commerce, and navigation with her. They had received and accredited her ministers and other diplomatic agents at their respective courts, and they had commissioned ministers and diplomatic agents on their part to the Government of Texas. If Mexico, notwithstanding all this and her utter inability to subdue or reconquer Texas, still stubbornly refused to recognize her as an independent nation, she was none the less so on that account. Mexico herself had been recognized as an independent nation by the United States and by other powers many years before Spain, of which before her revolution she had been a colony, would agree to recognize her as such; and yet Mexico was at that time in the estimation of the civilized world, and in fact, none the less an independent power because Spain still claimed her as a colony. If Spain had continued until the present period to assert that Mexico was one of her colonies in rebellion against her, this would not have made her so or changed the fact of her independent existence. Texas at the period of her annexation to the United States bore the same relation to Mexico that Mexico had borne to Spain for many years before Spain acknowledged her independence, with this important difference, that before the annexation of Texas to the United States was consummated Mexico herself, by a formal act of her Government, had acknowledged the independence of Texas as a nation. It is true that in the act of recognition she prescribed a condition which she had no power or authority to impose—that Texas should not annex herself to any other power—but this could not detract in any degree from the recognition which Mexico then made of her actual independence. Upon this plain statement of facts, it is absurd for Mexico to allege as a pretext for commencing hostilities against the United States that Texas is still a part of her territory.

But there are those who, conceding all this to be true, assume the ground that the true western boundary of Texas is the Nueces instead of the Rio Grande, and that therefore in marching our Army to the east bank of the latter river we passed the Texan line and invaded the territory of Mexico. A simple statement of facts known to exist will conclusively refute such an assumption. Texas, as ceded to the United States by France in 1803, has been always claimed as extending west to the Rio Grande or Rio Bravo. This fact is established by the authority of our most eminent statesmen at a period when the question was as well, if not better, understood than it is at present. During Mr. Jefferson's Administration Messrs. Monroe and Pinckney, who had been sent on a special mission to Madrid, charged among other things with the adjustment of boundary between the two countries, in a note addressed to the Spanish minister of foreign affairs under date of the 28th of January, 1805, assert that the boundaries of Louisiana, as ceded to the United States by France, "are the river Perdido on the east and the river Bravo on the west," and they add that "the facts and principles which justify this conclusion are so satisfactory to our Government as to convince it that the United States have not a better right to the island of New Orleans under the cession referred to than they have to the whole district of territory which is above described." Down to the conclusion of the

Florida treaty, in February, 1819, by which this territory was ceded to Spain, the United States asserted and maintained their territorial rights to this extent. In the month of June, 1818, during Mr. Monroe's Administration, information having been received that a number of foreign adventurers had landed at Galveston with the avowed purpose of forming a settlement in that vicinity, a special messenger was dispatched by the Government of the United States with instructions from the Secretary of State to warn them to desist, should they be found there, "or any other place north of the Rio Bravo, and within the territory claimed by the United States." He was instructed, should they be found in the country north of that river, to make known to them "the surprise with which the President has seen possession thus taken, without authority from the United States, of a place within their territorial limits, and upon which no lawful settlement can be made without their sanction." He was instructed to call upon them to "avow under what national authority they profess to act," and to give them due warning "that the place is within the United States, who will suffer no permanent settlement to be made there under any authority other than their own." As late as the 8th of July, 1842, the Secretary of State of the United States, in a note addressed to our minister in Mexico, maintains that by the Florida treaty of 1819 the territory as far west as the Rio Grande was confirmed to Spain. In that note he states that—

By the treaty of the 22d of February, 1819, between the United States and Spain, the Sabine was adopted as the line of boundary between the two powers. Up to that period no considerable colonization had been effected in Texas; but the territory between the Sabine and the Rio Grande being confirmed to Spain by the treaty, applications were made to that power for grants of land, and such grants or permissions of settlement were in fact made by the Spanish authorities in favor of citizens of the United States proposing to emigrate to *Texas* in numerous families before the declaration of independence by Mexico.

The Texas which was ceded to Spain by the Florida treaty of 1819 embraced all the country now claimed by the State of Texas between the Nueces and the Rio Grande. The Republic of Texas always claimed this river as her western boundary, and in her treaty made with Santa Anna in May, 1836, he recognized it as such. By the constitution which Texas adopted in March, 1836, senatorial and representative districts were organized extending west of the Nueces. The Congress of Texas on the 19th of December, 1836, passed "An act to define the boundaries of the Republic of Texas," in which they declared the Rio Grande from its mouth to its source to be their boundary, and by the said act they extended their "civil and political jurisdiction" over the country up to that boundary. During a period of more than nine years which intervened between the adoption of her constitution and her annexation as one of the States of our Union Texas asserted and exercised many acts of sovereignty and jurisdiction over the territory and inhabitants west of the Nueces. She organized and defined the limits of counties extending to the Rio Grande; she established courts of justice and extended her judicial system over the territory; she established a custom-house and collected duties, and also post-offices and post-roads, in it; she established a land office and issued numerous grants for land within its limits; a senator and a representative residing in it were elected to the Congress of the Republic and served as such before the act of annexation took place. In both the Congress and convention of Texas which gave their assent to the terms of annexation to the United States proposed by our Congress were representatives residing west of the Nueces, who took part in the act of annexation itself. This was the Texas which by the act of our Congress of the 29th of December, 1845, was admitted as one of the States of our Union. That the Congress of the United States understood the State of Texas which they admitted into the Union to extend beyond the Nueces is apparent from the fact that on the 31st of December, 1845, only two days after the act of admission, they passed a law "to establish a collection district in the State of Texas," by which they created a port of delivery at Corpus Christi, situated west of the Nueces, and being the same point at which the Texas custom-house under the laws of that Republic had been located, and directed that a surveyor to collect the revenue should be appointed for that port by the President, by and with the advice and consent of the Senate. A surveyor was accordingly nominated, and confirmed by the Senate, and has been ever since in the performance of his duties. All these acts of the Republic of Texas and of our Congress preceded the orders for the advance of our Army to the east bank of the Rio Grande. Subsequently Congress passed an act "establishing certain post routes" extending west of the Nueces. The country west of that river now constitutes a part of one of the Congressional districts of Texas and is represented in the House of Representatives. The Senators from that State were chosen by a legislature in which the country west of that river was represented. In view of all these facts it is difficult to conceive upon what ground it can be maintained that in occupying the country west of the Nueces with our Army, with a view solely to its security and defense, we invaded the territory of Mexico. But it would have been still more difficult to justify the Executive, whose duty it is to see that the laws be faithfully executed, if in the face of all these proceedings, both of the Congress of Texas and of the United States, he had assumed the responsibility of yielding up the territory west of the Nueces to Mexico or of refusing to protect and defend this territory and its inhabitants, including Corpus Christi as well as the remainder of Texas, against the threatened Mexican invasion.

But Mexico herself has never placed the war which she has waged upon the ground that our Army occupied the intermediate territory between the Nueces and the Rio Grande. Her refuted pretension that Texas was not in fact an independent state, but a rebellious province, was obstinately persevered in, and her avowed purpose in commencing a war with the United States was to reconquer Texas and to restore Mexican authority over the whole territory—not to the Nueces only, but to the Sabine. In view of the proclaimed menaces of Mexico to this effect, I deemed it my duty, as a measure of precaution and defense, to order our Army to occupy a position on our frontier as a military post, from which our troops could best resist and repel any attempted invasion which Mexico might make. Our Army had occupied a position at Corpus Christi, west of the Nueces, as early as August, 1845, without complaint from any quarter. Had the Nueces been regarded as the true western boundary of Texas, that boundary had been passed by our Army many months before it advanced to the eastern bank of the Rio Grande. In my annual message of December last I informed Congress that upon the invitation of both the Congress and convention of Texas I had deemed it proper to order a strong squadron to the coasts of Mexico and to concentrate an efficient military force on the western frontier of Texas to protect and defend the inhabitants against the menaced invasion of Mexico. In that message I informed Congress that the moment the terms of annexation offered by the United States were accepted by Texas the latter became so far a part of our own country as to make it our duty to afford such protection and defense, and that for that purpose our squadron had been ordered to the Gulf and our Army to take a "position between the Nueces and the Del Norte" or Rio Grande and to "repel any invasion of the Texan territory which might be attempted by the Mexican forces."

It was deemed proper to issue this order, because soon after the President of Texas, in April, 1845, had issued his proclamation convening the Congress of that Republic for the purpose of submitting to that body the terms of annexation proposed by the United States the Government of Mexico made serious threats of invading the Texan territory. These threats became more imposing as it became more apparent in the progress of the question that the people of Texas would decide in favor of accepting the terms of annexation, and finally they had assumed such a formidable character as induced both the Congress and convention of Texas to request that a military force should be sent by the United States into her territory for the purpose of protecting and defending her against the threatened invasion. It would have been a violation of good faith toward the people of Texas to have refused to afford the aid which they desired against a threatened invasion to which they had been exposed by their free determination to annex themselves to our Union in compliance with the overture made to them by the joint resolution of our Congress. Accordingly, a portion of the Army was ordered to advance into Texas. Corpus Christi was the position selected by General Taylor. He encamped at that place in August, 1845, and the Army remained in that position until the 11th of March, 1846, when it moved westward, and on the 28th of that month reached the east bank of the Rio Grande opposite to Matamoras. This movement was made in pursuance of orders from the War Department, issued on the 13th of January, 1846. Before these orders were issued the dispatch of our minister in Mexico transmitting the decision of the council of government of Mexico advising that he should not be received, and also the dispatch of our consul residing in the City of Mexico, the former bearing date on the 17th and the latter on the 18th of December, 1845, copies of both of which accompanied my message to Congress of the 11th of May last, were received at the Department of State. These communications rendered it highly probable, if not absolutely certain, that our minister would not be received by the Government of General Herrera. It was also well known that but little hope could be entertained of a different result from General Paredes in case the revolutionary movement which he was prosecuting should prove successful, as was highly probable. The partisans of Paredes, as our minister in the dispatch referred to states, breathed the fiercest hostility against the United States, denounced the proposed negotiation as treason, and openly called upon the troops and the people to put down the Government of Herrera by force. The reconquest of Texas and war with the United States were openly threatened. These were the circumstances existing when it was deemed proper to order the Army under the command of General Taylor to advance to the western frontier of Texas and occupy a position on or near the Rio Grande.

The apprehensions of a contemplated Mexican invasion have been since fully justified by the event. The determination of Mexico to rush into hostilities with the United States was afterwards manifested from the whole tenor of the note of the Mexican minister of foreign affairs to our minister bearing date on the 12th of March, 1846. Paredes had then revolutionized the Government, and his minister, after referring to the resolution for the annexation of Texas which had been adopted by our Congress in March, 1845, proceeds to declare that—

> A fact such as this, or, to speak with greater exactness, so notable an act of usurpation, created an imperious necessity that Mexico, for her own honor, should repel it with proper firmness and dignity. The supreme Government had beforehand declared that it would look upon such an act as a *casus belli*, and as a consequence of this declaration negotiation was by its very nature at an end, and war was the only recourse of the Mexican Government.

It appears also that on the 4th of April following General Paredes, through his minister of war, issued orders to the Mexican general in command on the Texan frontier to "attack" our Army "by every means which war permits." To this General Paredes had been pledged to the army and people of Mexico during the military revolution which had brought him into power. On the 18th of April, 1846, General Paredes addressed a letter to the commander on that frontier in which he stated to him: "At the present date I suppose you, at the head of that valiant army, either fighting already or preparing for the operations of a campaign;" and, "Supposing you already on the theater of operations and with all the forces assembled, it is indispensable that hostilities be commenced, yourself taking the initiative against the enemy."

The movement of our Army to the Rio Grande was made by the commanding general under positive orders to abstain from all aggressive acts toward Mexico or Mexican citizens, and to regard the relations between the two countries as peaceful unless Mexico should declare war or commit acts of hostility indicative of a state of war, and these orders he faithfully executed. Whilst occupying his position on the east bank of the Rio Grande, within the limits of Texas, then recently admitted as one of the States of our Union, the commanding general of the Mexican forces, who, in pursuance of the orders of his Government, had collected a large army on the opposite shore of the Rio Grande, crossed the river, invaded our territory, and commenced hostilities by attacking our forces. Thus, after all the injuries which we had received and borne from Mexico, and after she had insultingly rejected a minister sent to her on a mission of peace, and whom she had solemnly agreed to receive, she consummated her long course of outrage against our country by commencing an offensive war and shedding the blood of our citizens on our own soil.

The United States never attempted to acquire Texas by conquest. On the contrary, at an early period after the people of Texas had achieved their independence they sought to be annexed to the United States. At a general election in September, 1836, they decided with great unanimity in favor of "annexation," and in November following the Congress of the Republic authorized the appointment of a minister to bear their request to this Government. This Government, however, having remained neutral between Texas and Mexico during the war between them, and considering it due to the honor of our country and our fair fame among the nations of the earth that we should not at this early period consent to annexation, nor until it should be manifest to the whole world that the reconquest of Texas by Mexico was impossible, refused to accede to the overtures made by Texas. On the 12th of April, 1844, after more than seven years had elapsed since Texas had established her independence, a treaty was concluded for the annexation of that Republic to the United States, which was rejected by the Senate. Finally, on the 1st of March, 1845, Congress passed a joint resolution for annexing her to the United States upon certain preliminary conditions to which her assent was required. The solemnities which characterized the deliberations and conduct of the Government and people of Texas on the deeply interesting questions presented by these resolutions are known to the world. The Congress, the Executive, and the people of Texas, in a convention elected for that purpose, accepted with great unanimity the proposed terms of annexation, and thus consummated on her part the great act of restoring to our Federal Union a vast territory which had been ceded to Spain by the Florida treaty more than a quarter of a century before.

After the joint resolution for the annexation of Texas to the United States had been passed by our Congress the Mexican minister at Washington addressed a note to the Secretary of State, bearing date on the 6th of March, 1845, protesting against it as "an act of aggression the most unjust which can be found recorded in the annals of modern history, namely, that of despoiling a friendly nation like Mexico of a considerable portion of her territory," and protesting against the resolution of annexation as being an act "whereby the Province of Texas, an integral portion of the Mexican territory, is agreed and admitted into the American Union;" and he announced that as a consequence his mission to the United States had terminated, and demanded his passports, which were granted. It was upon the absurd pretext, made by Mexico (herself indebted for her independence to a successful revolution), that the Republic of Texas still continued to be, notwithstanding all that had passed, a Province of Mexico that this step was taken by the Mexican minister.

Every honorable effort has been used by me to avoid the war which followed, but all have proved vain. All our attempts to preserve peace have been met by insult and resistance on the part of Mexico. My efforts to this end commenced in the note of the Secretary of State of the 10th of March, 1845, in answer to that of the Mexican minister. Whilst declining to reopen a discussion which had already been exhausted, and proving again what was known to the whole world, that Texas had long since achieved her independence, the Secretary of State expressed the regret of this Government that Mexico should have taken offense at the resolution of annexation passed by Congress, and gave assurance that our "most strenuous efforts shall be devoted to the amicable adjustment of every cause of complaint between the two Governments and to the cultivation of the kindest and most friendly relations between the sister Republics." That I have acted in the spirit of this assurance will appear from the events which have since occurred. Notwithstanding Mexico had abruptly terminated all diplomatic intercourse with the United States, and ought, therefore, to have been the first to ask for its resumption, yet, waiving all ceremony, I embraced the earliest favorable opportunity "to ascertain from the Mexican Government whether they would receive an envoy from the United States intrusted with full power to adjust all the questions in dispute between the two Governments." In September, 1845, I believed the propitious moment for such an overture had arrived. Texas, by the enthusiastic and almost unanimous will of her people, had pronounced in favor of annexation. Mexico herself had agreed to acknowledge the independence of Texas, subject to a condition, it is true, which she had no right to impose and no power to enforce. The last lingering hope of Mexico, if she still could have retained any, that Texas would ever again become one of her Provinces, must have been abandoned.

The consul of the United States at the City of Mexico was therefore instructed by the Secretary of State on the 15th of September, 1845, to make the inquiry of the Mexican Government. The inquiry was made, and on the 15th of October, 1845, the minister of foreign affairs of the Mexican Government, in a note addressed to our consul, gave a favorable response, requesting at the same time that our naval force might be withdrawn from Vera Cruz while negotiations should be pending. Upon the receipt of this note our naval force was promptly withdrawn from Vera Cruz. A minister was immediately appointed, and departed to Mexico. Everything bore a promising aspect for a speedy and peaceful adjustment of all our difficulties. At the date of my annual message to Congress in December last no doubt was entertained but that he would be received by the Mexican Government, and the hope was cherished that all cause of misunderstanding between the two countries would be speedily removed. In the confident hope that such would be the result of his mission, I informed Congress that I forbore at that time to "recommend such ulterior measures of redress for the wrongs and injuries we had so long borne as it would have been proper to make had no such negotiation been instituted." To my surprise and regret the Mexican Government, though solemnly pledged to do so, upon the arrival of our minister in Mexico refused to receive and accredit him. When he reached Vera Cruz, on the 30th of November, 1845, he found that the aspect of affairs had undergone an unhappy change. The Government of General Herrera, who was at that time President of the Republic, was tottering to its fall. General Paredes, a military leader, had manifested his determination to overthrow the Government of Herrera by a military revolution, and one of the principal means which he employed to effect his purpose and render the Government of Herrera odious to the army and people of Mexico was by loudly condemning its determination to receive a minister of peace from the United States, alleging that it was the intention of Herrera, by a treaty with the United States, to dismember the territory of Mexico by ceding away the department of Texas. The Government of Herrera is believed to have been well disposed to a pacific adjustment of existing difficulties, but probably alarmed for its own security, and in order to ward off the danger of the revolution led by Paredes, violated its solemn agreement and refused to receive or accredit our minister; and this although informed that he had been invested with full power to adjust all questions in dispute between the two Governments. Among the frivolous pretexts for this refusal, the principal one was that our minister had not gone upon a special mission confined to the question of Texas alone, leaving all the outrages upon our flag and our citizens unredressed. The Mexican Government well knew that both our national honor and the protection due to our citizens imperatively required that the two questions of boundary and indemnity should be treated of together, as naturally and inseparably blended, and they ought to have seen that this course was best calculated to enable the United States to extend to them the most liberal justice. On the 30th of December, 1845, General Herrera resigned the Presidency and yielded up the Government to General Paredes without a struggle. Thus a revolution was accomplished solely by the army commanded by Paredes, and the supreme power in Mexico passed into the hands of a military usurper who was known to be bitterly hostile to the United States.

Although the prospect of a pacific adjustment with the new Government was unpromising from the known hostility of its head to the United States, yet, determined that nothing should be left undone on our part to restore friendly relations between the two countries, our minister was instructed to present his credentials to the new Government and ask to be accredited by it in the diplomatic character in which he had been commissioned. These instructions he executed by his note of the 1st of March, 1846, addressed to the Mexican minister of foreign affairs, but his request was insultingly refused by that minister in his answer of the 12th of the same month. No alternative remained for our minister but to demand his passports and return to the United States.

Thus was the extraordinary spectacle presented to the civilized world of a Government, in violation of its own express agreement, having twice rejected a minister of peace invested with full powers to adjust all the existing differences between the two countries in a manner just and honorable to both. I am not aware that modern history presents a parallel case in which in time of peace one nation has refused even to hear propositions from another for terminating existing difficulties between them. Scarcely a hope of adjusting our difficulties, even at a remote day, or of preserving peace with Mexico, could be cherished while Paredes remained at the head of the Government. He had acquired the supreme power by a military revolution and upon the most solemn pledges to wage war against the United States and to reconquer Texas, which he claimed as a revolted province of Mexico. He had denounced as guilty of treason all those Mexicans who considered Texas as no longer constituting a part of the territory of Mexico and who were friendly to the cause of peace. The duration of the war which he waged against the United States was indefinite, because the end which he proposed of the reconquest of Texas was hopeless. Besides, there was good reason to believe from all his conduct that it was his intention to convert the Republic of Mexico into a monarchy and to call a foreign European prince to the throne. Preparatory to this end, he had during his short rule destroyed the liberty of the press, tolerating that portion of it only which openly advocated the establishment of a monarchy. The better to secure the success of his ultimate designs, he had by an arbitrary decree convoked a Congress, not to be elected by the free voice of the people, but to be chosen in a manner to make them subservient to his will and to give him absolute control over their deliberations.

Under all these circumstances it was believed that any revolution in Mexico founded upon opposition to the ambitious projects of Paredes would tend to promote the cause of peace as well as prevent any attempted European interference in the affairs of the North American continent, both objects of deep interest to the United States. Any such foreign interference, if attempted, must have been resisted by the United States. My views upon that subject were fully communicated to Congress in my last annual message. In any event, it was certain that no change whatever in the Government of Mexico which would deprive Paredes of power could be for the worse so far as the United States were concerned, while it was highly probable that any change must be for the better. This was the state of affairs existing when Congress, on the 13th of May last, recognized the existence of the war which had been commenced by the Government of Paredes; and it became an object of much importance, with a view to a speedy settlement of our difficulties and the restoration of an honorable peace, that Paredes should not retain power in Mexico.

Before that time there were symptoms of a revolution in Mexico, favored, as it was understood to be, by the more liberal party, and especially by those who were opposed to foreign interference and to the monarchical form of government. Santa Anna was then in exile in Havana, having been expelled from power and banished from his country by a revolution which occurred in December, 1844; but it was known that he had still a considerable party in his favor in Mexico. It was also equally well known that no vigilance which could be exerted by our squadron would in all probability have prevented him from effecting a landing somewhere on the extensive Gulf coast of Mexico if he desired to return to his country. He had openly professed an entire change of policy, had expressed his regret that he had subverted the federal constitution of 1824, and avowed that he was now in favor of its restoration. He had publicly declared his hostility, in strongest terms, to the establishment of a monarchy and to European interference in the affairs of his country. Information to this effect had been received, from sources believed to be reliable, at the date of the recognition of the existence of the war by Congress, and was afterwards fully confirmed by the receipt of the dispatch of our consul in the City of Mexico, with the accompanying documents, which are herewith transmitted. Besides, it was reasonable to suppose that he must see the ruinous consequences to Mexico of a war with the United States, and that it would be his interest to favor peace.

It was under these circumstances and upon these considerations that it was deemed expedient not to obstruct his return to Mexico should he attempt to do so. Our object was the restoration of peace, and, with that view, no reason was perceived why we should take part with Paredes and aid him by means of our blockade in preventing the return of his rival to Mexico. On the contrary, it was believed that the intestine divisions which ordinary sagacity could not but anticipate as the fruit of Santa Anna's return to Mexico, and his contest with Paredes, might strongly tend to produce a disposition with both parties to restore and preserve peace with the United States. Paredes was a soldier by profession and a monarchist in principle. He had but recently before been successful in a military revolution, by which he had obtained power. He was the sworn enemy of the United States, with which he had involved his country in the existing war. Santa Anna had been expelled from power by the army, was known to be in open hostility to Paredes, and publicly pledged against foreign intervention and the restoration of monarchy in Mexico. In view of these facts and circumstances it was that when orders were issued to the commander of our naval forces in the Gulf, on the 13th day of May last, the same day on which the existence of the war was recognized by Congress, to place the coasts of Mexico under blockade, he was directed not to obstruct the passage of Santa Anna to Mexico should he attempt to return.

A revolution took place in Mexico in the early part of August following, by which the power of Paredes was overthrown, and he has since been banished from the country, and is now in exile. Shortly afterwards Santa Anna returned. It remains to be seen whether his return may not yet prove to be favorable to a pacific adjustment of the existing difficulties, it being manifestly his interest not to persevere in the prosecution of a war commenced by Paredes to accomplish a purpose so absurd as the reconquest of Texas to the Sabine. Had Paredes remained in power, it is morally certain that any pacific adjustment would have been hopeless.

Upon the commencement of hostilities by Mexico against the United States the indignant spirit of the nation was at once aroused. Congress promptly responded to the expectations of the country, and by the act of the 13th of May last recognized the fact that war existed, by the act of Mexico, between the United States and that Republic, and granted the means necessary for its vigorous prosecution. Being involved in a war thus commenced by Mexico, and for the justice of which on our part we may confidently appeal to the whole world, I resolved to prosecute it with the utmost vigor. Accordingly the ports of Mexico on the Gulf and on the Pacific have been placed under blockade and her territory invaded at several important points. The reports from the Departments of War and of the Navy will inform you more in detail of the measures adopted in the emergency in which our country was placed and of the gratifying results which have been accomplished.

The various columns of the Army have performed their duty under great disadvantages with the most distinguished skill and courage. The victories of Palo Alto and Resaca de la Palma and of Monterey, won against greatly superior numbers and against most decided advantages in other respects on the part of the enemy, were brilliant in their execution, and entitle our brave officers and soldiers to the grateful thanks of their country. The nation deplores the loss of the brave officers and men who have gallantly fallen while vindicating and defending their country's rights and honor.

It is a subject of pride and satisfaction that our volunteer citizen soldiers, who so promptly responded to their country's call, with an experience of the discipline of a camp of only a few weeks, have borne their part in the hard-fought battle of Monterey with a constancy and courage equal to that of veteran troops and worthy of the highest admiration. The privations of long marches through the enemy's country and through a wilderness have been borne without a murmur. By rapid movements the Province of New Mexico, with Santa Fe, its capital, has been captured without bloodshed. The Navy has cooperated with the Army and rendered important services; if not so brilliant, it is because the enemy had no force to meet them on their own element and because of the defenses which nature has interposed in the difficulties of the navigation on the Mexican coast. Our squadron in the Pacific, with the cooperation of a gallant officer of the Army and a small force hastily collected in that distant country, has acquired bloodless possession of the Californias, and the American flag has been raised at every important point in that Province.

I congratulate you on the success which has thus attended our military and naval operations. In less than seven months after Mexico commenced hostilities, at a time selected by herself, we have taken possession of many of her principal ports, driven back and pursued her invading army, and acquired military possession of the Mexican Provinces of New Mexico, New Leon, Coahuila, Tamaulipas, and the Californias, a territory larger in extent than that embraced in the original thirteen States of the Union, inhabited by a considerable population, and much of it more than 1,000 miles from the points at which we had to collect our forces and commence our movements. By the blockade the import and export trade of the enemy has been cut off. Well may the American people be proud of the energy and gallantry of our regular and volunteer officers and soldiers. The events of these few months afford a gratifying proof that our country can under any emergency confidently rely for the maintenance of her honor and the defense of her rights on an effective force, ready at all times voluntarily to relinquish the comforts of home for the perils and privations of the camp. And though such a force may be for the time expensive, it is in the end economical, as the ability to command it removes the necessity of employing a large standing army in time of peace, and proves that our people love their institutions and are ever ready to defend and protect them.

While the war was in a course of vigorous and successful prosecution, being still anxious to arrest its evils, and considering that after the brilliant victories of our arms on the 8th and 9th of May last the national honor could not be compromitted by it, another overture was made to Mexico, by my direction, on the 27th of July last to terminate hostilities by a peace just and honorable to both countries. On the 31st of August following the Mexican Government declined to accept this friendly overture, but referred it to the decision of a Mexican Congress to be assembled in the early part of the present month. I communicate to you herewith a copy of the letter of the Secretary of State proposing to reopen negotiations, of the answer of the Mexican Government, and of the reply thereto of the Secretary of State.

The war will continue to be prosecuted with vigor as the best means of securing peace. It is hoped that the decision of the Mexican Congress, to which our last overture has been referred, may result in a speedy and honorable peace. With our experience, however, of the unreasonable course of the Mexican authorities, it is the part of wisdom not to relax in the energy of our military operations until the result is made known. In this view it is deemed important to hold military possession of all the Provinces which have been taken until a definitive treaty of peace shall have been concluded and ratified by the two countries.

The war has not been waged with a view to conquest, but, having been commenced by Mexico, it has been carried into the enemy's country and will be vigorously prosecuted there with a view to obtain an honorable peace, and thereby secure ample indemnity for the expenses of the war, as well as to our much-injured citizens, who hold large pecuniary demands against Mexico.

By the laws of nations a conquered country is subject to be governed by the conqueror during his military possession and until there is either a treaty of peace or he shall voluntarily withdraw from it. The old civil government being necessarily superseded, it is the right and duty of the conqueror to secure his conquest and to provide for the maintenance of civil order and the rights of the inhabitants. This right has been exercised and this duty performed by our military and naval commanders by the establishment of temporary governments in some of the conquered Provinces of Mexico, assimilating them as far as practicable to the free institutions of our own country. In the Provinces of New Mexico and of the Californias little, if any, further resistance is apprehended from the inhabitants to the temporary governments which have thus, from the necessity of the case and according to the laws of war, been established. It may be proper to provide for the security of these important conquests by making an adequate appropriation for the purpose of erecting fortifications and defraying the expenses necessarily incident to the maintenance of our possession and authority over them.

Near the close of your last session, for reasons communicated to Congress, I deemed it important as a measure for securing a speedy peace with Mexico, that a sum of money should be appropriated and placed in the power of the Executive, similar to that which had been made upon two former occasions during the Administration of President Jefferson.

On the 26th of February, 1803, an appropriation of $2,000,000 was made and placed at the disposal of the President. Its object is well known. It was at that time in contemplation to acquire Louisiana from France, and it was intended to be applied as a part of the consideration which might be paid for that territory. On the 13th of February, 1806, the same sum was in like manner appropriated, with a view to the purchase of the Floridas from Spain. These appropriations were made to facilitate negotiations and as a means to enable the President to accomplish the important objects in view. Though it did not become necessary for the President to use these appropriations, yet a state of things might have arisen in which it would have been highly important for him to do so, and the wisdom of making them can not be doubted. It is believed that the measure recommended at your last session met with the approbation of decided majorities in both Houses of Congress. Indeed, in different forms, a bill making an appropriation of $2,000,000 passed each House, and it is much to be regretted that it did not become a law. The reasons which induced me to recommend the measure at that time still exist, and I again submit the subject for your consideration and suggest the importance of early action upon it. Should the appropriation be made and be not needed, it will remain in the Treasury; should it be deemed proper to apply it in whole or in part, it will be accounted for as other public expenditures.

Immediately after Congress had recognized the existence of the war with Mexico my attention was directed to the danger that privateers might be fitted out in the ports of Cuba and Porto Rico to prey upon the commerce of the United States, and I invited the special attention of the Spanish Government to the fourteenth article of our treaty with that power of the 27th of October, 1795, under which the citizens and subjects of either nation who shall take commissions or letters of marque to act as privateers against the other "shall be punished as pirates."

It affords me pleasure to inform you that I have received assurances from the Spanish Government that this article of the treaty shall be faithfully observed on its part. Orders for this purpose were immediately transmitted from that Government to the authorities of Cuba and Porto Rico to exert their utmost vigilance in preventing any attempts to fit out privateers in those islands against the United States. From the good faith of Spain I am fully satisfied that this treaty will be executed in its spirit as well as its letter, whilst the United States will on their part faithfully perform all the obligations which it imposes on them.

Information has been recently received at the Department of State that the Mexican Government has sent to Havana blank commissions to privateers and blank certificates of naturalization signed by General Salas, the present head of the Mexican Government. There is also reason to apprehend that similar documents have been transmitted to other parts of the world. Copies of these papers, in translation, are herewith transmitted.

As the preliminaries required by the practice of civilized nations for commissioning privateers and regulating their conduct appear not to have been observed, and as these commissions are in blank, to be filled up with the names of citizens and subjects of all nations who may be willing to purchase them, the whole proceeding can only be construed as an invitation to all the freebooters upon earth who are willing to pay for the privilege to cruise against American commerce. It will be for our courts of justice to decide whether under such circumstances these Mexican letters of marque and reprisal shall protect those who accept them, and commit robberies upon the high seas under their authority, from the pains and penalties of piracy.

If the certificates of naturalization thus granted be intended by Mexico to shield Spanish subjects from the guilt and punishment of pirates under our treaty with Spain, they will certainly prove unavailing. Such a subterfuge would be but a weak device to defeat the provisions of a solemn treaty.

I recommend that Congress should immediately provide by law for the trial and punishment as pirates of Spanish subjects who, escaping the vigilance of their Government, shall be found guilty of privateering against the United States. I do not apprehend serious danger from these privateers. Our Navy will be constantly on the alert to protect our commerce. Besides, in case prizes should be made of American vessels, the utmost vigilance will be exerted by our blockading squadron to prevent the captors from taking them into Mexican ports, and it is not apprehended that any nation will violate its neutrality by suffering such prizes to be condemned and sold within its jurisdiction.

I recommend that Congress should immediately provide by law for granting letters of marque and reprisal against vessels under the Mexican flag. It is true that there are but few, if any, commercial vessels of Mexico upon the high seas, and it is therefore not probable that many American privateers would be fitted out in case a law should pass authorizing this mode of warfare. It is, notwithstanding, certain that such privateers may render good service to the commercial interests of the country by recapturing our merchant ships should any be taken by armed vessels under the Mexican flag, as well as by capturing these vessels themselves. Every means within our power should be rendered available for the protection of our commerce.

The annual report of the Secretary of the Treasury will exhibit a detailed statement of the condition of the finances. The imports for the fiscal year ending on the 30th of June last were of the value of $121,691,797, of which the amount exported was $11,346,623, leaving the amount retained in the country for domestic consumption $110,345,174. The value of the exports for the same period was $113,488,516, of which $102,141,893 consisted of domestic productions and $11,346,623 of foreign articles.

The receipts into the Treasury for the same year were $29,499,247.06, of which there was derived from customs $26,712,667.87, from the sales of public lands $2,694,452.48, and from incidental and miscellaneous sources $92,126.71. The expenditures for the same period were $28,-031,114.20, and the balance in the Treasury on the 1st day of July last was $9,126,439.08.

The amount of the public debt, including Treasury notes, on the 1st of the present month was $24,256,494.60, of which the sum of $17,788,-799.62 was outstanding on the 4th of March, 1845, leaving the amount incurred since that time $6,467,694.98.

In order to prosecute the war with Mexico with vigor and energy, as the best means of bringing it to a speedy and honorable termination, a further loan will be necessary to meet the expenditures for the present and the next fiscal year. If the war should be continued until the 30th of June, 1848, being the end of the next fiscal year, it is estimated that an additional loan of $23,000,000 will be required. This estimate is made upon the assumption that it will be necessary to retain constantly in the Treasury $4,000,000 to guard against contingencies. If such surplus were not required to be retained, then a loan of $19,000,000 would be sufficient. If, however, Congress should at the present session impose a revenue duty on the principal articles now embraced in the free list, it is estimated that an additional annual revenue of about two millions and a half, amounting, it is estimated, on the 30th of June, 1848, to $4,000,000, would be derived from that source, and the loan required would be reduced by that amount. It is estimated also that should Congress graduate and reduce the price of such of the public lands as have been long in the market the additional revenue derived from that source would be annually, for several years to come, between half a million and a million dollars; and the loan required may be reduced by that amount also. Should these measures be adopted, the loan required would not probably exceed $18,000,000 or $19,000,000, leaving in the Treasury a constant surplus of $4,000,000. The loan proposed, it is estimated, will be sufficient to cover the necessary expenditures both for the war and for all other purposes up to the 30th of June, 1848, and an amount of this loan not exceeding one-half may be required during the present fiscal year, and the greater part of the remainder during the first half of the fiscal year succeeding.

In order that timely notice may be given and proper measures taken to effect the loan, or such portion of it as may be required, it is important that the authority of Congress to make it be given at an early period of your present session. It is suggested that the loan should be contracted for a period of twenty years, with authority to purchase the stock and pay it off at an earlier period at its market value out of any surplus which may at any time be in the Treasury applicable to that purpose. After the establishment of peace with Mexico, it is supposed that a considerable surplus will exist, and that the debt may be extinguished in a much shorter period than that for which it may be contracted. The period of twenty years, as that for which the proposed loan may be contracted, in preference to a shorter period, is suggested, because all experience, both at home and abroad, has shown that loans are effected upon much better terms upon long time than when they are reimbursable at short dates.

Necessary as this measure is to sustain the honor and the interests of the country engaged in a foreign war, it is not doubted but that Congress will promptly authorize it.

The balance in the Treasury on the 1st July last exceeded $9,000,000, notwithstanding considerable expenditures had been made for the war during the months of May and June preceding. But for the war the whole public debt could and would have been extinguished within a short period; and it was a part of my settled policy to do so, and thus relieve the people from its burden and place the Government in a position which would enable it to reduce the public expenditures to that economical standard which is most consistent with the general welfare and the pure and wholesome progress of our institutions.

Among our just causes of complaint against Mexico arising out of her refusal to treat for peace, as well before as since the war so unjustly commenced on her part, are the extraordinary expenditures in which we have been involved. Justice to our own people will make it proper that Mexico should be held responsible for these expenditures.

Economy in the public expenditures is at all times a high duty which all public functionaries of the Government owe to the people. This duty becomes the more imperative in a period of war, when large and extraordinary expenditures become unavoidable. During the existence of the war with Mexico all our resources should be husbanded, and no appropriations made except such as are absolutely necessary for its vigorous prosecution and the due administration of the Government. Objects of appropriation which in peace may be deemed useful or proper, but which are not indispensable for the public service, may when the country is engaged in a foreign war be well postponed to a future period. By the observance of this policy at your present session large amounts may be saved to the Treasury and be applied to objects of pressing and urgent necessity, and thus the creation of a corresponding amount of public debt may be avoided.

It is not meant to recommend that the ordinary and necessary appropriations for the support of Government should be withheld; but it is well known that at every session of Congress appropriations are proposed for numerous objects which may or may not be made without materially affecting the public interests, and these it is recommended should not be granted.

The act passed at your last session "reducing the duties on imports" not having gone into operation until the 1st of the present month, there has not been time for its practical effect upon the revenue and the business of the country to be developed. It is not doubted, however, that the just policy which it adopts will add largely to our foreign trade and promote the general prosperity. Although it can not be certainly foreseen what amount of revenue it will yield, it is estimated that it will exceed that produced by the act of 1842, which it superseded. The leading principles established by it are to levy the taxes with a view to raise revenue and to impose them upon the articles imported according to their actual value.

The act of 1842, by the excessive rates of duty which it imposed on many articles, either totally excluded them from importation or greatly reduced the amount imported, and thus diminished instead of producing revenue. By it the taxes were imposed not for the legitimate purpose of raising revenue, but to afford advantages to favored classes at the expense of a large majority of their fellow-citizens. Those employed in agriculture, mechanical pursuits, commerce, and navigation were compelled to contribute from their substance to swell the profits and overgrown wealth of the comparatively few who had invested their capital in manufactures. The taxes were not levied in proportion to the value of the articles upon which they were imposed, but, widely departing from this just rule, the lighter taxes were in many cases levied upon articles of luxury and high price and the heavier taxes on those of necessity and low price, consumed by the great mass of the people. It was a system the inevitable effect of which was to relieve favored classes and the wealthy few from contributing their just proportion for the support of Government, and to lay the burden on the labor of the many engaged in other pursuits than manufactures.

A system so unequal and unjust has been superseded by the existing law, which imposes duties not for the benefit or injury of classes or pursuits, but distributes and, as far as practicable, equalizes the public burdens among all classes and occupations. The favored classes who under the unequal and unjust system which has been repealed have heretofore realized large profits, and many of them amassed large fortunes at the expense of the many who have been made tributary to them, will have no reason to complain if they shall be required to bear their just proportion of the taxes necessary for the support of Government. So far from it, it will be perceived by an examination of the existing law that discriminations in the rates of duty imposed within the revenue principle have been retained in their favor. The incidental aid against foreign competition which they still enjoy gives them an advantage which no other pursuits possess, but of this none others will complain, because the duties levied are necessary for revenue. These revenue duties, including freights and charges, which the importer must pay before he can come in competition with the home manufacturer in our markets, amount on nearly all our leading branches of manufacture to more than one-third of the value of the imported article, and in some cases to almost one-half its value. With such advantages it is not doubted that our domestic manufacturers will continue to prosper, realizing in well-conducted establishments even greater profits than can be derived from any other regular business. Indeed, so far from requiring the protection of even incidental revenue duties, our manufacturers in several leading branches are extending their business, giving evidence of great ingenuity and skill and of their ability to compete, with increased prospect of success, for the open market of the world. Domestic manufactures to the value of several millions of dollars, which can not find a market at home, are annually exported to foreign countries. With such rates of duty as those established by the existing law the system will probably be permanent, and capitalists who are made or shall hereafter make their investments in manufactures will know upon what to rely. The country will be satisfied with these rates, because the advantages which the manufacturers still enjoy result necessarily from the collection of revenue for the support of Government. High protective duties, from their unjust operation upon the masses of the people, can not fail to give rise to extensive dissatisfaction and complaint and to constant efforts to change or repeal them, rendering all investments in manufactures uncertain and precarious. Lower and more permanent rates of duty, at the same time that they will yield to the manufacturer fair and remunerating profits, will secure him against the danger of frequent changes in the system, which can not fail to ruinously affect his interests.

Simultaneously with the relaxation of the restrictive policy by the United States, Great Britain, from whose example we derived the system, has relaxed hers. She has modified her corn laws and reduced many other duties to moderate revenue rates. After ages of experience the statesmen of that country have been constrained by a stern necessity and by a public opinion having its deep foundation in the sufferings and wants of impoverished millions to abandon a system the effect of which was to build up immense fortunes in the hands of the few and to reduce the laboring millions to pauperism and misery. Nearly in the same ratio that labor was depressed capital was increased and concentrated by the British protective policy.

The evils of the system in Great Britain were at length rendered intolerable, and it has been abandoned, but not without a severe struggle on the part of the protected and favored classes to retain the unjust advantages which they have so long enjoyed. It was to be expected that a similar struggle would be made by the same classes in the United States whenever an attempt was made to modify or abolish the same unjust system here. The protective policy had been in operation in the United States for a much shorter period, and its pernicious effects were not, therefore, so clearly perceived and felt. Enough, however, was known of these effects to induce its repeal.

It would be strange if in the face of the example of *Great Britain*, our principal foreign customer, and of the evils of a system rendered manifest in that country by long and painful experience, and in the face of the immense advantages which under a more liberal commercial policy we are already deriving, and must continue to derive, by supplying her starving population with food, the United States should restore a policy which she has been compelled to abandon, and thus diminish her ability to purchase from us the food and other articles which she so much needs and we so much desire to sell. By the simultaneous abandonment of the protective policy by Great Britain and the United States new and important markets have already been opened for our agricultural and other products, commerce and navigation have received a new impulse, labor and trade have been released from the artificial trammels which have so long fettered them, and to a great extent reciprocity in the exchange of commodities has been introduced at the same time by both countries, and greatly for the benefit of both. Great Britain has been forced by the pressure of circumstances at home to abandon a policy which has been upheld for ages, and to open her markets for our immense surplus of breadstuffs, and it is confidently believed that other powers of Europe will ultimately see the wisdom, if they be not compelled by the pauperism and sufferings of their crowded population, to pursue a similar policy.

Our farmers are more deeply interested in maintaining the just and liberal policy of the existing law than any other class of our citizens. They constitute a large majority of our population, and it is well known that when they prosper all other pursuits prosper also. They have heretofore not only received none of the bounties or favors of Government, but by the unequal operations of the protective policy have been made by the burdens of taxation which it imposed to contribute to the bounties which have enriched others.

When a foreign as well as a home market is opened to them, they must receive, as they are now receiving, increased prices for their products. They will find a readier sale, and at better prices, for their wheat, flour, rice, Indian corn, beef, pork, lard, butter, cheese, and other articles which they produce. The home market alone is inadequate to enable them to dispose of the immense surplus of food and other articles which they are capable of producing, even at the most reduced prices, for the manifest reason that they can not be consumed in the country. The United States can from their immense surplus supply not only the home demand, but the deficiencies of food required by the whole world.

That the reduced production of some of the chief articles of food in Great Britain and other parts of Europe may have contributed to increase the demand for our breadstuffs and provisions is not doubted, but that the great and efficient cause of this increased demand and of increased prices consists in the removal of artificial restrictions heretofore imposed is deemed to be equally certain. That our exports of food, already increased and increasing beyond former example under the more liberal policy which has been adopted, will be still vastly enlarged unless they be checked or prevented by a restoration of the protective policy can not be doubted. That our commercial and navigating interests will be enlarged in a corresponding ratio with the increase of our trade is equally certain, while our manufacturing interests will still be the favored interests of the country and receive the incidental protection afforded them by revenue duties; and more than this they can not justly demand.

In my annual message of December last a tariff of revenue duties based upon the principles of the existing law was recommended, and I have seen no reason to change the opinions then expressed. In view of the probable beneficial effects of that law, I recommend that the policy established by it be maintained. It has but just commenced to operate, and to abandon or modify it without giving it a fair trial would be inexpedient and unwise. Should defects in any of its details be ascertained by actual experience to exist, these may be hereafter corrected; but until such defects shall become manifest the act should be fairly tested.

It is submitted for your consideration whether it may not be proper, as a war measure, to impose revenue duties on some of the articles now embraced in the free list. Should it be deemed proper to impose such duties with a view to raise revenue to meet the expenses of the war with Mexico or to avoid to that extent the creation of a public debt, they may be repealed when the emergency which gave rise to them shall cease to exist, and constitute no part of the permanent policy of the country.

The act of the 6th of August last, "to provide for the better organization of the Treasury and for the collection, safe-keeping, transfer, and disbursement of the public revenue," has been carried into execution as rapidly as the delay necessarily arising out of the appointment of new officers, taking and approving their bonds, and preparing and securing proper places for the safe-keeping of the public money would permit. It is not proposed to depart in any respect from the principles or policy on which this great measure is founded. There are, however, defects in the details of the measure, developed by its practical operation, which are fully set forth in the report of the Secretary of the Treasury, to which the attention of Congress is invited. These defects would impair to some extent the successful operation of the law at all times, but are especially embarrassing when the country is engaged in a war, when the expenditures are greatly increased, when loans are to be effected and the disbursements are to be made at points many hundred miles distant, in some cases, from any depository, and a large portion of them in a foreign country. The modifications suggested in the report of the Secretary of the Treasury are recommended to your favorable consideration.

In connection with this subject I invite your attention to the importance of establishing a branch of the Mint of the United States at New York. Two-thirds of the revenue derived from customs being collected at that point, the demand for specie to pay the duties will be large, and a branch mint where foreign coin and bullion could be immediately converted into American coin would greatly facilitate the transaction of the public business, enlarge the circulation of gold and silver, and be at the same time a safe depository of the public money.

The importance of graduating and reducing the price of such of the public lands as have been long offered in the market at the minimum rate authorized by existing laws, and remain unsold, induces me again to recommend the subject to your favorable consideration. Many millions of acres of these lands have been offered in the market for more than thirty years and larger quantities for more than ten or twenty years, and, being of an inferior quality, they must remain unsalable for an indefinite period unless the price at which they may be purchased shall be reduced. To place a price upon them above their real value is not only to prevent their sale, and thereby deprive the Treasury of any income from that source, but is unjust to the States in which they lie, because it retards their growth and increase of population, and because they have no power to levy a tax upon them as upon other lands within their limits, held by other proprietors than the United States, for the support of their local governments.

The beneficial effects of the graduation principle have been realized by some of the States owning the lands within their limits in which it has been adopted. They have been demonstrated also by the United States acting as the trustee of the Chickasaw tribe of Indians in the sale of their lands lying within the States of Mississippi and Alabama. The Chickasaw lands, which would not command in the market the minimum price established by the laws of the United States for the sale of their lands, were, in pursuance of the treaty of 1834 with that tribe, subsequently offered for sale at graduated and reduced rates for limited periods. The result was that large quantities of these lands were purchased which would otherwise have remained unsold. The lands were disposed of at their real value, and many persons of limited means were enabled to purchase small tracts, upon which they have settled with their families. That similar results would be produced by the adoption of the graduation policy by the United States in all the States in which they are the owners of large bodies of lands which have been long in the market can not be doubted. It can not be a sound policy to withhold large quantities of the public lands from the use and occupation of our citizens by fixing upon them prices which experience has shown they will not command. On the contrary, it is a wise policy to afford facilities to our citizens to become the owners at low and moderate rates of freeholds of their own instead of being the tenants and dependents of others. If it be apprehended that these lands if reduced in price would be secured in large quantities by speculators or capitalists, the sales may be restricted in limited quantities to actual settlers or persons purchasing for purposes of cultivation.

In my last annual message I submitted for the consideration of Congress the present system of managing the mineral lands of the United States, and recommended that they should be brought into market and sold upon such terms and under such restrictions as Congress might prescribe. By the act of the 11th of July last "the reserved lead mines and contiguous lands in the States of Illinois and Arkansas and Territories of Wisconsin and Iowa" were authorized to be sold. The act is confined in its operation to "lead mines and contiguous lands." A large portion of the public lands, containing copper and other ores, is represented to be very valuable, and I recommend that provision be made authorizing the sale of these lands upon such terms and conditions as from their supposed value may in the judgment of Congress be deemed advisable, having due regard to the interests of such of our citizens as may be located upon them.

It will be important during your present session to establish a Territorial government and to extend the jurisdiction and laws of the United States over the Territory of Oregon. Our laws regulating trade and intercourse with the Indian tribes east of the Rocky Mountains should be extended to the Pacific Ocean; and for the purpose of executing them and preserving friendly relations with the Indian tribes within our limits, an additional number of Indian agencies will be required, and should be authorized by law. The establishment of custom-houses and of post-offices and post-roads and provision for the transportation of the mail on such routes as the public convenience will suggest require legislative authority. It will be proper also to establish a surveyor-general's office in that Territory and to make the necessary provision for surveying the public lands and bringing them into market. As our citizens who now reside in that distant region have been subjected to many hardships, privations, and sacrifices in their emigration, and by their improvements have enhanced the value of the public lands in the neighborhood of their settlements, it is recommended that liberal grants be made to them of such portions of these lands as they may occupy, and that similar grants or rights of preemption be made to all who may emigrate thither within a limited period, prescribed by law.

The report of the Secretary of War contains detailed information relative to the several branches of the public service connected with that Department. The operations of the Army have been of a satisfactory and highly gratifying character. I recommend to your early and favorable consideration the measures proposed by the Secretary of War for speedily filling up the rank and file of the Regular Army, for its greater efficiency in the field, and for raising an additional force to serve during the war with Mexico.

Embarrassment is likely to arise for want of legal provision authorizing compensation to be made to the agents employed in the several States and Territories to pay the Revolutionary and other pensioners the amounts allowed them by law. Your attention is invited to the recommendations of the Secretary of War on this subject. These agents incur heavy responsibilities and perform important duties, and no reason exists why they should not be placed on the same footing as to compensation with other disbursing officers.

Our relations with the various Indian tribes continue to be of a pacific character. The unhappy dissensions which have existed among the Cherokees for many years past have been healed. Since my last annual message important treaties have been negotiated with some of the tribes, by which the Indian title to large tracts of valuable land within the limits of the States and Territories has been extinguished and arrangements made for removing them to the country west of the Mississippi. Between 3,000 and 4,000 of different tribes have been removed to the country provided for them by treaty stipulations, and arrangements have been made for others to follow.

In our intercourse with the several tribes particular attention has been given to the important subject of education. The number of schools established among them has been increased, and additional means provided not only for teaching them the rudiments of education, but of instructing them in agriculture and the mechanic arts.

I refer you to the report of the Secretary of the Navy for a satisfactory view of the operations of the Department under his charge during the past year. It is gratifying to perceive that while the war with Mexico has rendered it necessary to employ an unusual number of our armed vessels on her coasts, the protection due to our commerce in other quarters of the world has not proved insufficient. No means will be spared to give efficiency to the naval service in the prosecution of the war; and I am happy to know that the officers and men anxiously desire to devote themselves to the service of their country in any enterprise, however difficult of execution.

I recommend to your favorable consideration the proposition to add to each of our foreign squadrons an efficient sea steamer, and, as especially demanding attention, the establishment at Pensacola of the necessary means of repairing and refitting the vessels of the Navy employed in the Gulf of Mexico.

There are other suggestions in the report which deserve and I doubt not will receive your consideration.

The progress and condition of the mail service for the past year are fully presented in the report of the Postmaster-General. The revenue for the year ending on the 30th of June last amounted to $3,487,199, which is $802,642.45 less than that of the preceding year. The payments for that Department during the same time amounted to $4,084,297.22. Of this sum $597,097.80 have been drawn from the Treasury. The disbursements for the year were $236,434.77 less than those of the preceding year. While the disbursements have been thus diminished, the mail facilities have been enlarged by new mail routes of 5,739 miles, an increase of transportation of 1,764,145 miles, and the establishment of 418 new post-offices. Contractors, postmasters, and others engaged in this branch of the service have performed their duties with energy and faithfulness deserving commendation. For many interesting details connected with the operations of this establishment you are referred to the report of the Postmaster-General, and his suggestions for improving its revenues are recommended to your favorable consideration. I repeat the opinion expressed in my last annual message that the business of this Department should be so regulated that the revenues derived from it should be made to equal the expenditures, and it is believed that this may be done by proper modifications of the present laws, as suggested in the report of the Postmaster-General, without changing the present rates of postage.

With full reliance upon the wisdom and patriotism of your deliberations, it will be my duty, as it will be my anxious desire, to cooperate with you in every constitutional effort to promote the welfare and maintain the honor of our common country.

JAMES K. POLK.

SPECIAL MESSAGES.

WASHINGTON, *December 14, 1846.*

To the Senate of the United States:

I transmit to the Senate, for their consideration and advice with regard to its ratification, a convention for the mutual surrender of criminals between the United States and the Swiss Confederation, signed by their respective plenipotentiaries on the 15th of September last at Paris.

I transmit also a copy of a dispatch from the plenipotentiary of the United States, with the accompanying documents.

JAMES K. POLK.

WASHINGTON, *December 22, 1846.*

To the House of Representatives of the United States:

In compliance with the request contained in the resolution of the House of Representatives of the 15th instant, I communicate herewith reports from the Secretary of War and the Secretary of the Navy, with the documents which accompany them.

These documents contain all the "orders or instructions" to any military, naval, or other officer of the Government "in relation to the establishment or organization of civil government in any portion of the territory of Mexico which has or might be taken possession of by the Army or Navy of the United States."

These orders and instructions were given to regulate the exercise of the rights of a belligerent engaged in actual war over such portions of the territory of our enemy as by military conquest might be "taken possession of" and be occupied by our armed forces—rights necessarily resulting from a state of war and clearly recognized by the laws of nations. This was all the authority which could be delegated to our military and naval commanders, and its exercise was indispensable to the secure occupation and possession of territory of the enemy which might be conquered. The regulations authorized were temporary, and dependent on the rights acquired by conquest. They were authorized as belligerent rights, and were to be carried into effect by military or naval officers. They were but the amelioration of martial law, which modern civilization requires, and were due as well to the security of the conquest as to the inhabitants of the conquered territory.

The documents communicated also contain the reports of several highly meritorious officers of our Army and Navy who have conquered and taken possession of portions of the enemy's territory.

Among the documents accompanying the report of the Secretary of War will be found a "form of government" "established and organized" by the military commander who conquered and occupied with his forces the Territory of New Mexico. This document was received at the War Department in the latter part of the last month, and, as will be perceived by the report of the Secretary of War, was not, for the reasons stated by that officer, brought to my notice until after my annual message of the 8th instant was communicated to Congress.

It is declared on its face to be a "temporary government of the said Territory," but there are portions of it which purport to "establish and organize" a permanent Territorial government of the United States over the Territory and to impart to its inhabitants political rights which under the Constitution of the United States can be enjoyed permanently only by citizens of the United States. These have not been "approved and recognized" by me. Such organized regulations as have been established in any of the conquered territories for the security of our conquest, for the preservation of order, for the protection of the rights of the inhabitants, and for depriving the enemy of the advantages of these territories while the military possession of them by the forces of the United States continues will be recognized and approved.

It will be apparent from the reports of the officers who have been required by the success which has crowned their arms to exercise the powers of temporary government over the conquered territories that if any excess of power has been exercised the departure has been the offspring of a patriotic desire to give to the inhabitants the privileges and immunities so cherished by the people of our own country, and which they believed calculated to improve their condition and promote their prosperity. Any such excess has resulted in no practical injury, but can and will be early corrected in a manner to alienate as little as possible the good feelings of the inhabitants of the conquered territory.

JAMES K. POLK.

WASHINGTON, *December 29, 1846.*

To the Senate and House of Representatives of the United States:

In order to prosecute the war against Mexico with vigor and success, it is necessary that authority should be promptly given by Congress to increase the Regular Army and to remedy existing defects in its organization. With this view your favorable attention is invited to the annual report of the Secretary of War, which accompanied my message of the 8th instant, in which he recommends that ten additional regiments of regular troops shall be raised, to serve during the war.

Of the additional regiments of volunteers which have been called for from several of the States, some have been promptly raised; but this has not been the case in regard to all. The existing law, requiring that they should be organized by the independent action of the State governments, has in some instances occasioned considerable delay, and it is yet uncertain when the troops required can be ready for service in the field.

It is our settled policy to maintain in time of peace as small a Regular Army as the exigencies of the public service will permit. In a state of war, notwithstanding the great advantage with which our volunteer citizen soldiers can be brought into the field, this small Regular Army must be increased in its numbers in order to render the whole force more efficient.

Additional officers as well as men then become indispensable. Under the circumstances of our service a peculiar propriety exists for increasing the officers, especially in the higher grades. The number of such officers who from age and other causes are rendered incapable of active service in the field has seriously impaired the efficiency of the Army.

From the report of the Secretary of War it appears that about two-thirds of the whole number of regimental field officers are either permanently disabled or are necessarily detached from their commands on other duties. The long enjoyment of peace has prevented us from experiencing much embarrassment from this cause, but now, in a state of war, conducted in a foreign country, it has produced serious injury to the public service.

An efficient organization of the Army, composed of regulars and volunteers, whilst prosecuting the war in Mexico, it is believed would require the appointment of a general officer to take the command of all our military forces in the field. Upon the conclusion of the war the services of such an officer would no longer be necessary, and should be dispensed with upon the reduction of the Army to a peace establishment.

I recommend that provision be made by law for the appointment of such a general officer to serve during the war.

It is respectfully recommended that early action should be had by Congress upon the suggestions submitted for their consideration, as necessary to insure active and efficient service in prosecuting the war, before the present favorable season for military operations in the enemy's country shall have passed away.

JAMES K. POLK.

WASHINGTON, *January 4, 1847.*

To the Senate of the United States:

I communicate herewith a report of the Postmaster-General, which contains the information called for by the resolution of the Senate of the 16th instant, in relation to the means which have been taken for the transmission of letters and papers to and from the officers and soldiers now in the service of the United States in Mexico. In answer to the inquiry whether any legislation is necessary to secure the speedy transmission and delivery of such letters and papers, I refer you to the suggestions of the Postmaster-General, which are recommended to your favorable consideration.

JAMES K. POLK.

WASHINGTON, *January 11, 1847.*

To the Senate of the United States:

In answer to the resolution of the Senate of the 22d ultimo, calling for information relative to the negotiation of the treaty of commerce with the Republic of New Granada signed on the 20th of December, 1844, I transmit a report from the Secretary of State and the documents by which it was accompanied.

JAMES K. POLK.

WASHINGTON, *January 19, 1847.*

To the House of Representatives of the United States:

I transmit herewith a report of the Secretary of War, with the accompanying report from the Adjutant-General of the Army, made in compliance with the resolution of the House of Representatives of the 5th instant, requesting the President to communicate to the House "the whole number of volunteers which have been mustered into the service of the United States since the 1st day of May last, designating the number mustered for three months, six months, and twelve months; the number of those who have been discharged before they served two months, number discharged after two months' service, and the number of volunteer officers who have resigned, and the dates of their resignations."

JAMES K. POLK.

WASHINGTON, *January 20, 1847.*

To the House of Representatives of the United States:

I communicate herewith a letter received from the president of the convention of delegates of the people of Wisconsin, transmitting a certified copy of the constitution adopted by the delegates of the people of Wisconsin in convention assembled, also a copy of the act of the legislature of the Territory of Wisconsin providing for the calling of said convention, and also a copy of the last census, showing the number of inhabitants in said Territory, requesting the President to "lay the same before the Congress of the United States with the request that Congress act upon the same at its present session."

JAMES K. POLK.

WASHINGTON, *January 25, 1847*.

To the House of Representatives of the United States:

I communicate herewith a report of the Secretary of the Treasury, accompanied by a statement of the Register of the Treasury prepared in compliance with a resolution of the House of Representatives of the 7th instant, requesting the President "to furnish the House with a statement showing the whole amount allowed and paid at the Treasury during the year ending 30th June, 1846, for postages of the Executive Departments of the Government and for the several officers and persons authorized by the act approved 3d March, 1846, to send or receive matter through the mails free, including the amount allowed or allowable, if charged in the postages of any officers or agents, military, naval, or civil, employed in or by any of said Departments." It will be perceived that said statement is as full and accurate as can be made during the present session of Congress.

JAMES K. POLK.

WASHINGTON, *January 29, 1847*.

To the House of Representatives of the United States:

I communicate herewith a report of the Secretary of War, together with reports of the Adjutant-General and Paymaster-General of the Army, in answer to a resolution of the House of Representatives of the 20th instant, requesting the President to communicate to the House "whether any, and, if any, which, of the Representatives named in the list annexed have held any office or offices under the United States since the commencement of the Twenty-ninth Congress, designating the office or offices held by each, and whether the same are now so held, and including in said information the names of all who are now serving in the Army of the United States as officers and receiving pay as such, and when and by whom they were commissioned."

JAMES K. POLK.

WASHINGTON, *February 3, 1847*.

To the Senate of the United States:

I communicate herewith reports of the Secretary of War and the Secretary of the Treasury, with accompanying documents, in answer to a resolution of the Senate "requesting the President to inform the Senate whether any funds of the Government, and, if any, what amount, have been remitted from the Atlantic States to New Orleans or to the disbursing officers of the American Army in Mexico since the 1st of September last, and, if any remitted, in what funds remitted, whether in gold or silver coin, Treasury notes, bank notes, or bank checks, and, if in whole or in part remitted in gold and silver, what has been the expense to the Government of each of said remittances."

JAMES K. POLK.

WASHINGTON, *February 10, 1847*.

To the Senate of the United States:

I transmit to the Senate, for their advice with regard to its ratification, "a general treaty of peace, amity, navigation, and commerce between the United States of America and the Republic of New Granada," concluded at Bogota on the 12th December last by Benjamin A. Bidlack, chargé d'affaires of the United States, on their part, and by Manuel Maria Mallarino, secretary of state and foreign relations, on the part of that Republic.

It will be perceived by the thirty-fifth article of this treaty that New Granada proposes to guarantee to the Government and citizens of the United States the right of passage across the Isthmus of Panama over the natural roads and over any canal or railroad which may be constructed to unite the two seas, on condition that the United States shall make a similar guaranty to New Granada of the neutrality of this portion of her territory and her sovereignty over the same.

The reasons which caused the insertion of this important stipulation in the treaty will be fully made known to the Senate by the accompanying documents. From these it will appear that our chargé d'affaires acted in this particular upon his own responsibility and without instructions. Under such circumstances it became my duty to decide whether I would submit the treaty to the Senate, and after mature consideration I have determined to adopt this course.

The importance of this concession to the commercial and political interests of the United States can not easily be overrated. The route by the Isthmus of Panama is the shortest between the two oceans, and from the information herewith communicated it would seem to be the most practicable for a railroad or canal.

The vast advantages to our commerce which would result from such a communication, not only with the west coast of America, but with Asia and the islands of the Pacific, are too obvious to require any detail. Such a passage would relieve us from a long and dangerous navigation of more than 9,000 miles around Cape Horn and render our communication with our possessions on the northwest coast of America comparatively easy and speedy.

The communication across the Isthmus has attracted the attention of the Government of the United States ever since the independence of the South American Republics. On the 3d of March, 1835, a resolution passed the Senate in the following words:

> *Resolved*, That the President of the United States be respectfully requested to consider the expediency of opening negotiations with the governments of other nations, and particularly with the Governments of Central America and New Granada, for the purpose of effectually protecting, by suitable treaty stipulations with them, such individuals or companies as may undertake to open a communication between the Atlantic and Pacific oceans by the construction of a ship canal across the isthmus which connects North and South America, and of securing forever by such stipulations the free and equal right of navigating such canal to all nations on the payment of such reasonable tolls as may be established to compensate the capitalists who may engage in such undertaking and complete the work.

No person can be more deeply sensible than myself of the danger of entangling alliances with any foreign nation. That we should avoid such alliances has become a maxim of our policy consecrated by the most venerated names which adorn our history and sanctioned by the unanimous voice of the American people. Our own experience has taught us the wisdom of this maxim in the only instance, that of the guaranty to France of her American possessions, in which we have ever entered into such an alliance. If, therefore, the very peculiar circumstances of the present case do not greatly impair, if not altogether destroy, the force of this objection, then we ought not to enter into the stipulation, whatever may be its advantages. The general considerations which have induced me to transmit the treaty to the Senate for their advice may be summed up in the following particulars:

1. The treaty does not propose to guarantee a territory to a foreign nation in which the United States will have no common interest with that nation. On the contrary, we are more deeply and directly interested in the subject of this guaranty than New Granada herself or any other country.

2. The guaranty does not extend to the territories of New Granada generally, but is confined to the single Province of the Isthmus of Panama, where we shall acquire by the treaty a common and coextensive right of passage with herself.

3. It will constitute no alliance for any political object, but for a purely commercial purpose, in which all the navigating nations of the world have a common interest.

4. In entering into the mutual guaranties proposed by the thirty-fifth article of the treaty neither the Government of New Granada nor that of the United States has any narrow or exclusive views. The ultimate object, as presented by the Senate of the United States in their resolution to which I have already referred, is to secure to all nations the free and equal right of passage over the Isthmus. If the United States, as the chief of the American nations, should first become a party to this guaranty, it can not be doubted—indeed, it is confidently expected by the Government of New Granada—that similar guaranties will be given to that Republic

by Great Britain and France. Should the proposition thus tendered be rejected we may deprive the United States of the just influence which its acceptance might secure to them and confer the glory and benefits of being the first among the nations in concluding such an arrangement upon the Government either of Great Britain or France. That either of these Governments would embrace the offer can not be doubted, because there does not appear to be any other effectual means of securing to all nations the advantages of this important passage but the guaranty of great commercial powers that the Isthmus shall be neutral territory. The interests of the world at stake are so important that the security of this passage between the two oceans can not be suffered to depend upon the wars and revolutions which may arise among different nations.

Besides, such a guaranty is almost indispensable to the construction of a railroad or canal across the territory. Neither sovereign states nor individuals would expend their capital in the construction of these expensive works without some such security for their investments.

The guaranty of the sovereignty of New Granada over the Isthmus is a natural consequence of the guaranty of its neutrality, and there does not seem to be any other practicable mode of securing the neutrality of this territory. New Granada would not consent to yield up this Province in order that it might become a neutral state, and if she should it is not sufficiently populous or wealthy to establish and maintain an independent sovereignty. But a civil government must exist there in order to protect the works which shall be constructed. New Granada is a power which will not excite the jealousy of any nation. If Great Britain, France, or the United States held the sovereignty over the Isthmus, other nations might apprehend that in case of war the Government would close up the passage against the enemy, but no such fears can ever be entertained in regard to New Granada.

This treaty removes the heavy discriminating duties against us in the ports of New Granada, which have nearly destroyed our commerce and navigation with that Republic, and which we have been in vain endeavoring to abolish for the last twenty years.

It may be proper also to call the attention of the Senate to the twenty-fifth article of the treaty, which prohibits privateering in case of war between the two Republics, and also to the additional article, which nationalizes all vessels of the parties which "shall be provided by the respective Governments with a patent issued according to its laws," and in this particular goes further than any of our former treaties.

JAMES K. POLK.

WASHINGTON, *February 13, 1847.*

To the Senate and House of Representatives of the United States:

Congress, by the act of the 13th of May last, declared that "by the act of the Republic of Mexico a state of war exists between that Government and the United States." and "for the purpose of enabling the

Government of the United States to prosecute said war to a speedy and successful termination" authority was vested in the President to employ the "naval and military forces of the United States."

It has been my unalterable purpose since the commencement of hostilities by Mexico and the declaration of the existence of war by Congress to prosecute the war in which the country was unavoidably involved with the utmost energy, with a view to its "speedy and successful termination" by an honorable peace.

Accordingly all the operations of our naval and military forces have been directed with this view. While the sword has been held in one hand and our military movements pressed forward into the enemy's country and its coasts invested by our Navy, the tender of an honorable peace has been constantly presented to Mexico in the other.

Hitherto the overtures of peace which have been made by this Government have not been accepted by Mexico. With a view to avoid a protracted war, which hesitancy and delay on our part would be so well calculated to produce, I informed you in my annual message of the 8th December last that the war would "continue to be prosecuted with vigor, as the best means of securing peace," and recommended to your early and favorable consideration the measures proposed by the Secretary of War in his report accompanying that message.

In my message of the 4th January last these and other measures deemed to be essential to the "speedy and successful termination" of the war and the attainment of a just and honorable peace were recommended to your early and favorable consideration.

The worst state of things which could exist in a war with such a power as Mexico would be a course of indecision and inactivity on our part. Being charged by the Constitution and the laws with the conduct of the war, I have availed myself of all the means at my command to prosecute it with energy and vigor.

The act "to raise for a limited time an additional military force, and for other purposes," and which authorizes the raising of ten additional regiments to the Regular Army, to serve during the war and to be disbanded at its termination, which was presented to me on the 11th instant and approved on that day, will constitute an important part of our military force. These regiments will be raised and moved to the seat of war with the least practicable delay.

It will be perceived that this act makes no provision for the organization into brigades and divisions of the increased force which it authorizes, nor for the appointment of general officers to command it. It will be proper that authority be given by law to make such organization, and to appoint, by and with the advice and consent of the Senate, such number of major-generals and brigadier-generals as the efficiency of the service may demand. The number of officers of these grades now in service are not more than are required for their respective commands; but further legislative action during your present session will, in my judgment, be required, and to which it is my duty respectfully to invite your attention.

Should the war, contrary to my earnest desire, be protracted to the close of the term of service of the volunteers now in Mexico, who engaged for twelve months, an additional volunteer force will probably become necessary to supply their place. Many of the volunteers now serving in Mexico, it is not doubted, will cheerfully engage at the conclusion of their present term to serve during the war. They would constitute a more efficient force than could be speedily obtained by accepting the services of any new corps who might offer their services. They would have the advantage of the experience and discipline of a year's service, and will have become accustomed to the climate and be in less danger than new levies of suffering from the diseases of the country. I recommend, therefore, that authority be given to accept the services of such of the volunteers now in Mexico as the state of the public service may require, and who may at the termination of their present term voluntarily engage to serve during the war with Mexico, and that provision be made for commissioning the officers. Should this measure receive the favorable consideration of Congress, it is recommended that a bounty be granted to them upon their voluntarily extending their term of service. This would not only be due to these gallant men, but it would be economy to the Government, because if discharged at the end of the twelve months the Government would be bound to incur a heavy expense in bringing them back to their homes and in sending to the seat of war new corps of fresh troops to supply their place.

By the act of the 13th of May last the President was authorized to accept the services of volunteers "in companies, battalions, squadrons, and regiments," but no provision was made for filling up vacancies which might occur by death or discharges from the service on account of sickness or other casualties. In consequence of this omission many of the corps now in service have been much reduced in numbers. Nor was any provision made for filling vacancies of regimental or company officers who might die or resign. Information has been received at the War Department of the resignation of more than 100 of these officers. They were appointed by the State authorities, and no information has been received except in a few instances that their places have been filled; and the efficiency of the service has been impaired from this cause. To remedy these defects, I recommend that authority be given to accept the services of individual volunteers to fill up the places of such as may die or become unfit for the service and be discharged, and that provision be also made for filling the places of regimental and company officers who may die or resign. By such provisions the volunteer corps may be constantly kept full or may approximate the maximum number authorized and called into service in the first instance.

While it is deemed to be our true policy to prosecute the war in the manner indicated, and thus make the enemy feel its pressure and its evils, I shall be at all times ready, with the authority conferred on me by the Constitution and with all the means which may be placed at my command by Congress, to conclude a just and honorable peace.

Of equal importance with an energetic and vigorous prosecution of the war are the means required to defray its expenses and to uphold and maintain the public credit.

In my annual message of the 8th December last I submitted for the consideration of Congress the propriety of imposing, as a war measure, revenue duties on some of the articles now embraced in the free list. The principal articles now exempt from duty from which any considerable revenue could be derived are tea and coffee. A moderate revenue duty on these articles it is estimated would produce annually an amount exceeding $2,500,000. Though in a period of peace, when ample means could be derived from duties on other articles for the support of the Government, it may have been deemed proper not to resort to a duty on these articles, yet when the country is engaged in a foreign war and all our resources are demanded to meet the unavoidable increased expenditure in maintaining our armies in the field no sound reason is perceived why we should not avail ourselves of the revenues which may be derived from this source. The objections which have heretofore existed to the imposition of these duties were applicable to a state of peace, when they were not needed. We are now, however, engaged in a foreign war. We need money to prosecute it and to maintain the public honor and credit. It can not be doubted that the patriotic people of the United States would cheerfully and without complaint submit to the payment of this additional duty or any other that may be necessary to maintain the honor of the country, provide for the unavoidable expenses of the Government, and to uphold the public credit. It is recommended that any duties which may be imposed on these articles be limited in their duration to the period of the war.

An additional annual revenue, it is estimated, of between half a million and a million of dollars would be derived from the graduation and reduction of the price of such of the public lands as have been long offered in the market at the minimum price established by the existing laws and have remained unsold. And in addition to other reasons commending the measure to favorable consideration, it is recommended as a financial measure. The duty suggested on tea and coffee and the graduation and reduction of the price of the public lands would secure an additional annual revenue to the Treasury of not less than $3,000,000, and would thereby prevent the necessity of incurring a public debt annually to that amount, the interest on which must be paid semiannually, and ultimately the debt itself by a tax on the people.

It is a sound policy and one which has long been approved by the Government and people of the United States never to resort to loans unless in cases of great public emergency, and then only for the smallest amount which the public necessities will permit.

The increased revenues which the measures now recommended would produce would, moreover, enable the Government to negotiate a loan for any additional sum which may be found to be needed with more facility and at cheaper rates than can be done without them.

Under the injunction of the Constitution which makes it my duty "from time to time to give to Congress information of the state of the Union and to recommend to their consideration such measures" as shall be judged "necessary and expedient," I respectfully and earnestly invite the action of Congress on the measures herein presented for their consideration. The public good, as well as a sense of my responsibility to our common constituents, in my judgment imperiously demands that I should present them for your enlightened consideration and invoke favorable action upon them before the close of your present session.

JAMES K. POLK.

WASHINGTON, *February 13, 1847.*

To the Senate of the United States:

I nominate the officers named in the accompanying communication for regular promotion in the Army of the United States, as proposed by the Secretary of War.

JAMES K. POLK.

WAR DEPARTMENT,
Washington, February 13, 1847.

The PRESIDENT OF THE UNITED STATES.

SIR: I have the honor respectfully to propose for your approbation the following-named captains* for promotion to the rank of major in the existing regiments of the Army, in conformity with the third section of the act approved February 11, 1847, which authorizes one additional major to each of the regiments of dragoons, artillery, infantry, and riflemen.

The promotions are all regular with one exception, that of Captain Washington Seawell, of the Seventh Infantry, instead of Captain Edgar Hawkins, of the same regiment, who stands at the head of the list of his grade in the infantry arm. Captain Hawkins, who distinguished himself in the defense of Fort Brown, is passed over on the ground of mental alienation, it being officially reported that he is "insane," on which account he was recently sent from the Army in Mexico. He is now in New York, and is reported to be "unable to perform any duty." An officer just returned from the Army in Mexico, and who had recently served with Captain Hawkins, informed the Adjutant-General that he was quite deranged, but that he had hopes of his recovery, as the malady was probably caused by sickness. Should these hopes be realized at some future day, Captain Hawkins will then of course be promoted without loss of rank; meanwhile I respectfully recommend that he be passed over, as the declared object of these additional majors (as set forth in the Adjutant-General's report to this Department of the 30th of July last) was to insure the presence of an adequate number of *efficient* field officers for duty with the marching regiments, which object would be neutralized in part should Captain Hawkins now receive the appointment.

I am, sir, with great respect, your obedient servant,

W. L. MARCY.

*List omitted.

WASHINGTON, *February 20, 1847.*

To the Senate of the United States:

I communicate herewith a report of the Secretary of State, with the accompanying documents, in answer to a resolution of the Senate of the 2d instant, requesting the President to communicate such information in possession of the Executive Departments in relation to the importation of foreign criminals and paupers as he may deem consistent with the public interests to communicate.

JAMES K. POLK.

WASHINGTON, *February 26, 1847.*

To the Senate of the United States:

I nominate the persons named in the accompanying list* of promotions and appointments in the Army of the United States to the several grades annexed to their names, as proposed by the Secretary of War.

JAMES K. POLK.

WAR DEPARTMENT, *February 26, 1847.*

The PRESIDENT OF THE UNITED STATES.

SIR: I have the honor respectfully to propose for your approbation the annexed list* of officers for regular promotion and persons for appointment in the Army of the United States.

It having been decided to be just and proper to restore Grafton D. Hanson, late a lieutenant in the Eighth Infantry, to his former regiment and rank, whose resignation was accepted in June, 1845, contrary to his wish, he having in due time recalled the same, it will be seen that he is reappointed accordingly. I deem it proper to state that the vacancy of first lieutenant in the Eighth Infantry, now proposed to be filled by Mr. Hanson's restoration and reappointment, has been occasioned by the appointment of the senior captain of the regiment to be major under the recent act authorizing an additional major to each regiment, being an original vacancy, and therefore the less reason for any objection in respect to the general principles and usages of the service, which guarantee regular promotions to fill vacancies which occur by accident, etc.

I am, sir, with great respect, your obedient servant,

W. L. MARCY.

WASHINGTON, *February 26, 1847.*

To the Senate of the United States:

I nominate the officers named in the accompanying list* for brevet promotion in the Army of the United States, for gallant conduct in the actions at Monterey.

JAMES K. POLK.

WAR DEPARTMENT, *February 19, 1847.*

The PRESIDENT.

SIR: I present to you the following list* of officers engaged in the actions at Monterey, whose distinguished conduct therein entitles them, in my judgment, to the promotion by brevet. This list has been prepared after a particular and careful examination of all the documents in this Department in relation to the military operations at that place.

*Omitted.

Lieutenant-Colonel Garland and Brevet Lieutenant-Colonel Childs (then a captain of the line) also behaved in the actions of Monterey in a manner deserving of particular notice, but as their names are now before the Senate for colonelcies by brevet, I have not presented them for further promotion. I am not aware that any officer below the lineal rank of colonel has ever been made a brigadier-general by brevet.

I have the honor to be, very respectfully, your obedient servant,

W. L. MARCY.

WASHINGTON, *February 27, 1847.*

To the House of Representatives of the United States:

I communicate herewith a report of the Secretary of War, with the accompanying documents, in answer to the resolution of the House of Representatives of the 1st instant, requesting the President "to communicate to the House of Representatives all the correspondence with General Taylor since the commencement of hostilities with Mexico which has not yet been published, and the publication of which may not be deemed detrimental to the public service; also the correspondence of the Quartermaster-General in relation to transportation for General Taylor's Army; also the reports of Brigadier-Generals Hamer and Quitman of the operations of their respective brigades on the 21st of September last."

As some of these documents relate to military operations of our forces which may not have been fully executed, I might have deemed it proper to withhold parts of them under the apprehension that their publication at this time would be detrimental to the public service; but I am satisfied that these operations are now so far advanced and that the enemy has already received so much information from other sources in relation to the intended movements of our Army as to render this precaution unnecessary.

JAMES K. POLK.

WASHINGTON, *March 2, 1847.*

To the Senate of the United States:

I communicate herewith a report of the Secretary of War, with the accompanying documents, in answer to the resolution of the Senate of the 27th ultimo, requesting to be informed "why the name of Captain Theophilus H. Holmes was not sent in for brevet promotion amongst the other officers who distinguished themselves at the military operations at Monterey."

The report of the Secretary of War discloses the reasons for the omission of the name of Captain Holmes in the list of brevet promotions in my message of the —— ultimo. Upon the additional testimony in Captain Holmes's case which has been received at the War Department, and to which the Secretary of War refers in his report, I deem it proper to nominate him for brevet promotion.

I therefore nominate Captain Theophilus H. Holmes, of the Seventh Regiment of Infantry, to be major by brevet from the 23d September, 1846, in the Army of the United States.

JAMES K. POLK.

WAR DEPARTMENT, *March 1, 1847.*

The PRESIDENT OF THE UNITED STATES.

SIR: With a special reference to the resolution of the Senate of the 27th ultimo, requesting to be informed "why the name of Captain Theophilus H. Holmes was not sent in for brevet promotion amongst the other officers who distinguished themselves at the military operations at Monterey," I have again examined the official reports of those operations. I do not find that Captain Holmes is mentioned in General Taylor's report, nor in that of any other officer except the report of Brigadier-General Worth. The following extract from the latter contains all that is said having relation to the conduct of Captain Holmes:

"My thanks are also especially due to Lieutenant-Colonel Stanford, Eighth, commanding First Brigade; Major Munroe, chief of artillery, general staff; Brevet Major Brown and Captain J. R. Vinton, artillery battalion; Captain J. B. Scott, artillery battalion, light troops; Major Scott (commanding) and Captain Merrill, Fifth; Captain Miles (commanding), Holmes, and Ross, Seventh Infantry, and Captain Screven, commanding Eighth Infantry; to Lieutenant-Colonel Walker, captain of rifles; Major Chevalier and Captain McCulloch, of the Texan, and Captain Blanchard, of the Louisiana, Volunteers; to Lieutenant Mackall, commanding battery; Roland, Martin, Hays, Irons, Clark, and Curd, horse artillery; Lieutenant Longstreet, commanding light company, Eighth; Lieutenant Ayers, artillery battalion, who was among the first in the assault upon the place and who secured the colors. Each of the officers named either headed special detachments, columns of attack, storming parties, or detached guns, and all were conspicuous for conduct and courage."

It will be perceived that in this list there are twenty-one officers (besides the medical staff and officers of volunteers) who are highly commended by General Worth for gallant conduct. That they were justly entitled to the praise bestowed on them is not doubted; but if I had recommended all of them to be brevetted, together with all those in the reports of other generals also in like manner highly commended, the number of officers in my list submitted for your consideration would have been probably trebled. Indeed, the whole Army behaved most gallantly on that occasion. It was deemed proper to discriminate and select from among the well deserving those who had peculiar claims to distinction. In making this selection I exercised my best judgment, regarding the official reports as the authentic source of information. Six or seven only of the officers named in the foregoing extract from General Worth's report were placed on the list. A close examination of the reports will, I think, disclose the ground for the discrimination, and I hope justify the distinction which I felt it my duty to make. Without disparagement to Captain Holmes, whose conduct was highly creditable, it appears to me that a rule of selection which would have brought him upon the list for promotion by brevet would also have placed on the same list nearly everyone named with him in General Worth's report, and many on the reports of other generals not presented in my report to you of the 19th ultimo. There is not time before the adjournment of the Senate to make the thorough examination which a due regard to the relative claims of the gallant officers engaged in the actions of Monterey would require if the list of brevet promotions is to be enlarged to this extent. Such enlargement would not accord with my own views on the subject of bestowing brevet rewards.

There are on file other papers relative to Captain Holmes. They were not written with reference to his brevet promotion, but for an appointment in the new regiments. Copies of those are herewith transmitted. The letter of the Hon. W. P.

Mangum inclosing the statement from Generals Twiggs and Smith is dated the 26th, and my report the 19th ultimo, and was not, consequently, received at this Department until some days after the list for brevets was made out and presented to you.

From the facts and recommendations of the official reports of the actions at Monterey I should not feel warranted in presenting Captain Holmes for brevet promotion without at the same time including on the same list many others not recommended in my report of the 19th ultimo; but as his conduct fell under the immediate observation of General Smith (General Twiggs commanded in a different part of the town), it may be proper to regard their statement, received since my former report was prepared and handed to you, as additional evidence of his gallantry and of claims to your particular notice. I therefore recommend him to be promoted major by brevet.

I have the honor to be, very respectfully, your obedient servant,

W. L. MARCY,
Secretary of War.

PROCLAMATIONS.

[From Statutes at Large (Little & Brown), Vol. IX, p. 1001.]

BY THE PRESIDENT OF THE UNITED STATES OF AMERICA.

A PROCLAMATION.

Whereas by an act of the Congress of the United States approved the 3d day of March, 1845, entitled "An act regulating commercial intercourse within the islands of Miquelon and St. Pierre," it is provided that all French vessels coming directly from those islands, either in ballast or laden with articles the growth or manufacture of either of said islands, and which are permitted to be exported therefrom in American vessels, may be admitted into the ports of the United States on payment of no higher duties of tonnage or on their cargoes aforesaid than are imposed on American vessels and on like cargoes imported in American vessels, provided that this act shall not take effect until the President of the United States shall have received satisfactory information that similar privileges have been allowed to American vessels and their cargoes at said islands by the Government of France and shall have made proclamation accordingly; and

Whereas satisfactory information has been received by me that similar privileges have been allowed to American vessels and their cargoes at said islands by the Government of France:

Now, therefore, I, James K. Polk, President of the United States of America, do hereby declare and proclaim that all French vessels coming directly from the islands of Miquelon and St. Pierre, either in ballast or laden with articles the growth or manufacture of either of said islands, and which are permitted to be exported therefrom in American vessels, shall from this date be admitted into the ports of the United States on payment of no higher duties on tonnage or on their cargoes aforesaid than are imposed on American vessels and on like cargoes imported in American vessels.

Given under my hand, at the city of Washington, the 20th day of April, A. D. 1847, and of the Independence of the United States the seventy-first.

JAMES K. POLK.

By the President:

JAMES BUCHANAN,
Secretary of State.

BY THE PRESIDENT OF THE UNITED STATES OF AMERICA.

A PROCLAMATION.

Whereas by an act of the Congress of the United States of the 24th of May, 1828, entitled "An act in addition to an act entitled 'An act concerning discriminating duties of tonnage and impost' and to equalize the duties on Prussian vessels and their cargoes," it is provided that upon satisfactory evidence being given to the President of the United States by the government of any foreign nation that no discriminating duties of tonnage or impost are imposed or levied in the ports of the said nation upon vessels wholly belonging to citizens of the United States, or upon the produce, manufactures, or merchandise imported in the same from the United States or from any foreign country, the President is thereby authorized to issue his proclamation declaring that the foreign discriminating duties of tonnage and impost within the United States are and shall be suspended and discontinued so far as respects the vessels of the said foreign nation and the produce, manufactures, or merchandise imported into the United States in the same from the said foreign nation or from any other foreign country, the said suspension to take effect from the time of such notification being given to the President of the United States and to continue so long as the reciprocal exemption of vessels belonging to citizens of the United States and their cargoes as aforesaid shall be continued, and no longer; and

Whereas satisfactory evidence has lately been received by me from His Majesty the Emperor of Brazil, through an official communication of Mr. Felippe José Pereira Leal, his chargé d'affaires in the United States, under date of the 25th of October, 1847, that no other or higher duties of tonnage and impost are imposed or levied in the ports of Brazil upon vessels wholly belonging to citizens of the United States and upon the produce, manufactures, or merchandise imported in the same from the United States and from any foreign country whatever than are levied on Brazilian ships and their cargoes in the same ports under like circumstances:

Now, therefore, I, James K. Polk, President of the United States of America, do hereby declare and proclaim that so much of the several acts imposing discriminating duties of tonnage and impost within the United States are and shall be suspended and discontinued so far as respects the vessels of Brazil and the produce, manufactures, and merchandise imported into the United States in the same from Brazil and from any other foreign country whatever, the said suspension to take effect from the day above mentioned and to continue thenceforward so long as the reciprocal exemption of the vessels of the United States and the produce, manufactures, and merchandise imported into Brazil in the same as aforesaid shall be continued on the part of the Government of Brazil.

Given under my hand, at the city of Washington, this 4th day of November, A. D. 1847, and the seventy-second of the Independence of the United States.

JAMES K. POLK.

By the President:

JAMES BUCHANAN,
Secretary of State.

EXECUTIVE ORDERS.

WASHINGTON, *March 23, 1847.*

The SECRETARY OF THE TREASURY.

SIR: The Government of Mexico having repeatedly rejected the friendly overtures of the United States to open negotiations with a view to the restoration of peace, sound policy and a just regard to the interests of our own country require that the enemy should be made, as far as practicable, to bear the expenses of a war of which they are the authors, and which they obstinately persist in protracting.

It is the right of the conqueror to levy contribution upon the enemy in their seaports, towns, or provinces which may be in his military possession by conquest and to apply the same to defray the expenses of the war. The conqueror possesses the right also to establish a temporary military government over such seaports, towns, or provinces and to prescribe the conditions and restrictions upon which commerce with such places may be permitted. He may, in his discretion, exclude all trade, or admit it with limitation or restriction, or impose terms the observance of which will be the condition of carrying it on. One of these conditions may be the payment of a prescribed rate of duties on tonnage and imports.

In the exercise of these unquestioned rights of war, I have, on full consideration, determined to order that all the ports or places in Mexico which now are or hereafter may be in the actual possession of our land and naval forces by conquest shall be opened while our military occupation may continue to the commerce of all neutral nations, as well as our own, in articles not contraband of war, upon the payment of prescribed rates of duties, which will be made known and enforced by our military and naval commanders.

While the adoption of this policy will be to impose a burden on the enemy, and at the same time to deprive them of the revenue to be derived from trade at such ports or places, as well as to secure it to ourselves, whereby the expenses of the war may be diminished, a just regard to the general interests of commerce and the obvious advantages of uniformity in the exercise of these belligerent rights require that well-considered regulations and restrictions should be prepared for the guidance of those who may be charged with carrying it into effect.

You are therefore instructed to examine the existing Mexican tariff of duties and report to me a schedule of articles of trade to be admitted at such ports or places as may be at any time in our military possession, with such rates of duty on them and also on tonnage as will be likely to produce the greatest amount of revenue. You will also communicate the considerations which may recommend the scale of duties which you may propose, and will submit such regulations as you may deem advisable in order to enforce their collection.

As the levy of the contribution proposed is a military right, derived from the laws of nations, the collection and disbursement of the duties will be made, under the orders of the Secretary of War and the Secretary of the Navy, by the military and naval commanders at the ports or places in Mexico which may be in possession of our arms. The report requested is therefore necessary in order to enable me to give the proper directions to the War and Navy Departments.

JAMES K. POLK.

TREASURY DEPARTMENT, *March 30, 1847*.

The PRESIDENT.

SIR: Your instructions of the 23d instant have been received by this Department, and in conformity thereto I present you herewith, for your consideration, a scale of duties proposed to be collected as a military contribution during the war in the ports of Mexico in possession of our Army or Navy by conquest, with regulations for the ascertainment and collection of such duties, together with the reasons which appear to me to recommend their adoption.

It is clear that we must either adopt our own tariff or that of Mexico, or establish a new system of duties. Our own tariff could not be adopted, because the Mexican exports and imports are so different from our own that different rates of duties are indispensable in order to collect the largest revenue. Thus upon many articles produced in great abundance here duties must be imposed at the lowest rate in order to collect any revenue, whereas many of the same articles are not produced in Mexico, or to a very inconsiderable extent, and would therefore bear there a much higher duty for revenue. A great change is also rendered necessary by the proposed exaction of duties on all imports to any Mexican port in our possession from any other Mexican port occupied by us in the same manner. This measure would largely increase the revenue which we might collect. It is recommended, however, for reasons of obvious safety, that this Mexican coastwise trade should be confined to our own vessels, as well as the interior trade above any port of entry in our possession, but that in all other respects the ports of Mexico held by us should be freely opened at the rate of duties herein recommended to the vessels and commerce of all the world. The *ad valorem* system of duties adopted by us, although by far the most just and equitable, yet requires an appraisement to ascertain the actual value of every article. This demands great mercantile skill, knowledge, and experience, and therefore, for the want of skillful appraisers (a class of officers wholly unknown in Mexico), could not at once be put into successful operation there. If also, as proposed, these duties are to be ascertained and collected as a military contribution through the officers of our Army and Navy, those brave men would more easily perform almost any other duty than that of estimating the value of every description of goods, wares, and merchandise.

The system of specific duties already prevails in Mexico, and may be put by us into immediate operation; and if, as conceded, specific duties should be more burdensome upon the people of Mexico, the more onerous the operation of these duties upon them the sooner it is likely that they will force their military rulers to agree to a peace. It is certain that a mild and forbearing system of warfare, collecting no duties in their ports in our possession on the Gulf and levying no contributions, whilst our armies purchase supplies from them at high prices, by rendering the war a benefit to the people of Mexico rather than an injury has not hastened the conclusion of a peace. It may be, however, that specific duties, onerous as they are, and heavy contributions, accompanied by a vigorous prosecution of the war, may more speedily insure that peace which we have failed to obtain from magnanimous forbearance, from brilliant victories, or from proffered negotiation. The duties, however, whilst they may be specific, and therefore more onerous than *ad valorem* duties, should not be so high as to defeat revenue.

It is impossible to adopt as a basis the tariff of Mexico, because the duties are extravagantly high, defeating importation, commerce, and revenue and producing innumerable frauds and smuggling. There are also sixty articles the importation of which into Mexico is strictly prohibited by their tariff, embracing most of the necessaries of life and far the greater portion of our products and fabrics.

Among the sixty prohibited articles are sugar, rice, cotton, boots and half-boots, coffee, nails of all kinds, leather of most kinds, flour, cotton yarn and thread, soap of all kinds, common earthenware, lard, molasses, timber of all kinds, saddles of all kinds, coarse woolen cloth, cloths for cloaks, ready-made clothing of all kinds, salt, tobacco of all kinds, cotton goods or textures, chiefly such as are made by ourselves; pork, fresh or salted, smoked or corned; woolen or cotton blankets or counterpanes, shoes and slippers, wheat and grain of all kinds. Such is a list of but part of the articles whose importation is prohibited by the Mexican tariff. These prohibitions should not be permitted to continue, because they exclude most of our products and fabrics and prevent the collection of revenue. We turn from the prohibitions to the actual duties imposed by Mexico. The duties are specific throughout, and almost universally by weight, irrespective of value; are generally protective or exorbitant, and without any discrimination for revenue. The duties proposed to be substituted are moderate when compared with those imposed by Mexico, being generally reduced to a standard more than one-half below the Mexican duties. The duties are also based upon a discrimination throughout for revenue, and, keeping in view the customs and habits of the people of Mexico, so different from our own, are fixed in each case at that rate which it is believed will produce in the Mexican ports the largest amount of revenue.

In order to realize from this system the largest amount of revenue, it would be necessary that our Army and Navy should seize every important port or place upon the Gulf of Mexico or California, or on the Pacific, and open the way through the interior for the free transit of exports and imports, and especially that the interior passage through the Mexican isthmus should be secured from ocean to ocean, for the benefit of our commerce and that of all the world. This measure, whilst it would greatly increase our revenue from these duties and facilitate communication between our forces upon the eastern and western coasts of Mexico, would probably lead at the conclusion of a peace to results of incalculable importance to our own commerce and to that of all the world.

In the meantime the Mexican Government monopoly in tobacco, from which a considerable revenue is realized by Mexico, together with the culture there which yields that revenue, should be abolished, so as to diminish the resources of that Government and augment our own by collecting the duty upon all the imported tobacco. The Mexican interior transit duties should also be abolished, and also their internal Government duty on coin and bullion. The prohibition of exports and the duties upon exports should be annulled, and especially the heavy export duty on coin and bullion, so as to cheapen and facilitate the purchase of imports and permit the precious metals, untaxed, to flow out freely from Mexico into general circulation. Quicksilver and machinery for working the mines of precious metals in Mexico, for the same reasons, should also be admitted duty free, which, with the measures above indicated, would largely increase the production and circulation of the precious metals, improve our own commerce and industry and that of all neutral powers.

In thus opening the ports of Mexico to the commerce of the world you will present to all nations with whom we are at peace the best evidence of your desire to maintain with them our friendly relations, to render the war to them productive of as little injury as possible, and even to advance their interests, so far as it safely can be done, by affording to them in common with ourselves the advantages of a liberal commerce with Mexico. To extend this commerce, you will have unsealed the ports of Mexico, repealed their interior transit duties, which obstruct the passage of merchandise to and from the coast; you will have annulled the Government duty on coin and bullion and abolished the heavy export duties on the precious metals, so as to permit them to flow out freely for the benefit of mankind; you will have expunged the long list of their prohibited articles and reduced more than one-half their duties on imports, whilst the freest scope would be left for the mining of the precious metals. These are great advantages which would be secured to friendly nations, especially when compared with the exclusion of their commerce by rigorous blockades. It is true, the duties collected from these imports would be for the benefit of our own Government, but it is equally true that the expenses of the war, which Mexico insists upon prosecuting, are borne exclusively by ourselves, and not by foreign nations. It can not be doubted but that all neutral nations will see in the adoption of such a course by you a manifestation of your good will toward them and a strong desire to advance those just and humane principles which make it the duty of belligerents, as we have always contended, to render the war in which they are engaged as little injurious as practicable to neutral powers.

These duties would not be imposed upon any imports into our own country, but only upon imports into Mexico, and the tax would fall upon the people of Mexico in the enhancement to them of the prices of these imports. Nearly all our own products are excluded by the Mexican tariff even in time of peace; they are excluded also during the war so far as we continue the system of blockading any of the ports of Mexico; and they are also excluded even from the ports not blockaded in possession of Mexico; whereas the new system would soon open to our commerce all the ports of Mexico as they shall fall into our military possession. Neither our own nor foreign merchants are required to send any goods to Mexico, and if they do so voluntarily it will be because they can make a profit upon the importation there, and therefore they will have no right to complain of the duties levied in the ports of Mexico upon the consumers of those goods—the people of Mexico. The whole money collected would inure to the benefit of our own Government and people, to sustain the war and to prevent to that extent new loans and increased taxation. Indeed, in view of the fact that the Government is thrown upon the ordinary revenues for peace, with no other additional resources but loans to carry on the war, the income to be derived from the new system, which it is believed will be large if these suggestions are adopted, would be highly important to sustain the credit of the Government, to prevent the embarrassment of the Treasury, and to save the country from such ruinous sacrifices as occurred during the last war, including the inevitable legacy to posterity of a large public debt and onerous taxation. The new system would not only arrest the expensive transfer and ruinous drain of specie to Mexico, but would cause it, in duties and in return for our exports, to reflow into our country to an amount, perhaps, soon exceeding the $9,000,000 which it had reached in 1835 even under the restrictive laws of Mexico, thus relieving our own people from a grievous tax and imposing it where it should fall, upon our enemies, the people of Mexico, as a contribution levied upon them to conquer a peace as well as to defray the expenses of the war; whereas by admitting our exports freely, without duty, into the Mexican ports which we may occupy from time to time, and affording those goods, including the necessaries of life, at less than one-half the prices which they had heretofore paid for them, the war might in time become a benefit instead of a burden to the people of Mexico, and they would therefore be unwilling to terminate the contest. It is hoped also that Mexico, after a peace, will never renew her present prohibitory and protective system, so nearly resembling that of ancient China or Japan, but that, liberalized, enlightened, and regenerated by the contact and intercourse with our people and those of other civilized nations, she will continue the far more moderate system of duties resembling that prescribed by these regulations.

In the meantime it is not just that Mexico, by her obstinate persistence in this contest, should compel us to overthrow our own financial policy and arrest this great nation in her high and prosperous career. To reimpose high duties would be alike injurious to ourselves and to all neutral powers, and, unless demanded by a stern necessity, ungenerous to those enlightened nations which have adopted cotemporaneously with us a more liberal commercial policy. The system you now propose of imposing the burden as far as practicable upon our enemies, the people of Mexico, and not upon ourselves or upon friendly nations, appears to be most just in itself, and is further recommended as the only policy which is likely to hasten the conclusion of a just and honorable peace.

A tonnage duty on all vessels, whether our own or of neutral powers, of $1 per ton, which is greatly less than that imposed by Mexico, is recommended in lieu of all port duties and charges. Appended to these regulations are tables of the rates at which foreign money is fixed by law, as also a separate table of currencies by usage, in which a certificate of value is required to be attached to the invoice. There is also annexed a table of foreign weights and measures reduced to the standard of the United States, together with blank forms to facilitate the transaction of business.

It is recommended that the duties herein suggested shall be collected exclusively in gold or silver coin. These duties can only be collected as a military contribution through the agency of our brave officers of the Army and Navy, who will no doubt cheerfully and faithfully collect and keep these moneys and account for them, not to the Treasury, but to the Secretaries of War or of the Navy, respectively.

It is recommended that these duties be performed by the commandant of the port, whether naval or military, aided by the paymaster or purser or other officer, the accounts of each being countersigned by the other, as a check upon mistakes or error, in the same manner as is now the case with the collector and naval officer of our several principal ports, which has introduced so much order and accuracy in our system. It is suggested that as in some cases the attention of the commandant of the port might be necessary for the performance of other duties that he be permitted to substitute some other officer, making known the fact to the Secretaries of War or of the Navy, and subject to their direction.

I have the honor to be, with great respect, your obedient servant,

R. J. WALKER,
Secretary of the Treasury.

WASHINGTON, *March 31, 1847.*

SIR:* Being charged by the Constitution with the prosecution of the existing war with Mexico, I deem it proper, in the exercise of an undoubted belligerent right, to order that military contributions be levied upon the enemy in such of their ports or other places as now are or may be hereafter in the possession of our land and naval forces by conquest, and that the same be collected and applied toward defraying the expenses of the war. As one means of effecting this object, the blockade at such conquered ports will be raised, and they will be opened to our own commerce and that of all neutral nations in articles not contraband of war during our military occupation of them, and duties on tonnage and imports will be levied and collected through the agency of our military and naval officers in command at such ports, acting under orders from the War and Navy Departments.

I transmit to you herewith, for your information and guidance, a copy of a communication addressed by me to the Secretary of the Treasury on the 23d instant, instructing him to examine the existing Mexican tariff and to report to me, for my consideration, a scale of duties which he would recommend to be levied on tonnage and imports in such conquered ports, together with such regulations as he would propose as necessary and proper in order to carry this policy into effect; and also a copy of the report of the Secretary of the Treasury made on the 30th instant in answer to my communication to him. The scale of duties and the regulations for their collection as military contributions exacted from the enemy, recommended by the Secretary of the Treasury in this report, have been approved by me.

*Addressed to the Secretaries of War and of the Navy.

You will, after consulting with the Secretary of the Navy, so as to secure concert of action between the War and Navy Departments, issue the necessary orders to carry the measure proposed into immediate effect.

JAMES K. POLK.

TREASURY DEPARTMENT, *June 10, 1847*.

The PRESIDENT.

SIR: In compliance with your directions, I have examined the questions presented by the Secretary of War in regard to the military contributions proposed to be levied in Mexico under the tariff and regulations sanctioned by you on the 31st of March last, and respectfully recommend the following modifications, namely:

First. On all manufactures of cotton, or of cotton mixed with any other material except wool, worsted, and silk, in the piece or in any other form, a duty, as a military contribution, of 30 per cent *ad valorem*.

Second. When goods on which the duties are levied by weight are imported into said ports in the package, the duties shall be collected on the net weight only; and in all cases an allowance shall be made for all deficiencies, leakage, breakage, or damage proved to have actually occurred during the voyage of importation, and made known before the goods are warehoused.

Third. The period named in the eighth of said regulations during which the goods may remain in warehouse before the payment of duties is extended from thirty to ninety days, and within said period of ninety days any portion of the said goods on which the duties, as a military contribution, have been paid may be taken, after such payment, from the warehouse and entered free of any further duty at any other port or ports of Mexico in our military possession, the facts of the case, with a particular description of said goods and a statement that the duties thereon have been paid, being certified by the proper officer of the port or ports of reshipment.

Fourth. It is intended to provide by the treaty of peace that all goods imported during the war into any of the Mexican ports in our military possession shall be exempt from any new import duty or confiscation by Mexico in the same manner as if said goods had been imported and paid the import duties prescribed by the Government of Mexico.

Most respectfully, your obedient servant,

R. J. WALKER,
Secretary of the Treasury.

JUNE 11, 1847.

The modifications as above recommended by the Secretary of the Treasury are approved by me, and the Secretary of War and the Secretary of the Navy will give the proper orders to carry them into effect.

JAMES K. POLK.

TREASURY DEPARTMENT, *November 5, 1847*.

The PRESIDENT.

SIR: The military contributions in the form of duties upon imports into Mexican ports have been levied by the Departments of War and of the Navy during the last six months under your order of the 31st of March last, and in view of the experience of the practical operation of the system I respectfully recommend the following modifications in some of its details, which will largely augment the revenue:

That the duty on silk, flax, hemp or grass, cotton, wool, worsted or any manufactures of the same, or of either or mixtures thereof; coffee, teas, sugar, molasses, tobacco and all manufactures thereof, including cigars and cigarritos; glass, china, and stoneware, iron and steel and all manufactures of either not prohibited, be 30 per cent *ad valorem;* on copper and all manufactures thereof, tallow, tallow candles, soap, fish, beef, pork, hams, bacon, tongues, butter, lard, cheese, rice, Indian corn and meal, potatoes, wheat, rye, oats, and all other grain, rye meal and oat meal, flour, whale and sperm oil, clocks, boots and shoes, pumps, bootees and slippers, bonnets, hats, caps, beer, ale, porter, cider, timber, boards, planks, scantling, shingles, laths, pitch, tar, rosin, turpentine, spirits of turpentine, vinegar, apples, ship bread, hides, leather and manufactures thereof, and paper of all kinds, 20 per cent *ad valorem;* and these reduced rates shall also apply to all goods on which the duties are not paid remaining not exceeding ninety days in deposit in the Mexican ports, introduced under previous regulations enforcing military contributions.

Yours, most respectfully,

R. J. WALKER,
Secretary of the Treasury.

NOVEMBER 6, 1847.

The modifications as above recommended by the Secretary of the Treasury are approved by me, and the Secretary of War and the Secretary of the Navy will give the proper orders to carry them into effect.

JAMES K. POLK.

TREASURY DEPARTMENT, *November 16, 1847*.

The PRESIDENT.

SIR: With a view to augment the military contributions now collected by the Departments of War and of the Navy under your order of the 31st of March last, I recommend that the export duty exacted before the war by the Government of Mexico be now collected at the port of exportation by the same officers of the Army or Navy of the United States in the Mexican ports in our possession who are authorized to collect the import duties, abolishing, however, the prohibition of export established in certain cases by the Mexican Government, as also all interior transit duties; dispensing also with the necessity of any certificate of having paid any duty to the Mexican Government.

The export duty would then be as follows:

	Per cent.
Gold, coined or wrought	3
Silver, coined	6
Silver, wrought, with or without certificate of having paid any duty to the Mexican Government	7
Silver, refined or pure, wrought in ingots, with or without certificate of having paid the Mexican Government duty	7
Gold, unwrought or in a state of ore or dust	3
Silver, unwrought or in a state of ore	7

Where gold or silver in any form is taken from any interior Mexican city in our military possession, the export duty must be paid there to the officer of the United States commanding, and his certificate of such prepayment must be produced at the Mexican port of exportation; otherwise a double duty will be collected upon the arrival of such gold or silver at the Mexican port of exportation. Whenever it is practicable, all internal taxes of every description, whether upon persons or property, exacted by the Government of Mexico, or by any department, town, or city thereof, should be collected by our military officers in possession and appropriated as a military contribution toward defraying the expenses of the war, excluding however, all duties on the transit of goods from one department to another, which duties, being prejudicial to revenue and restrictive of the exchange of imports for exports, were abolished by your order of the 31st of March last.

Yours, most respectfully,

R. J. WALKER,
Secretary of the Treasury.

NOVEMBER 16, 1847.

The modifications and military contributions as above recommended by the Secretary of the Treasury are approved by me, and the Secretary of War and the Secretary of the Navy will give the proper orders to carry them into effect.

JAMES K. POLK.

THIRD ANNUAL MESSAGE.

WASHINGTON, *December 7, 1847.*

Fellow-Citizens of the Senate and of the House of Representatives:

The annual meeting of Congress is always an interesting event. The representatives of the States and of the people come fresh from their constituents to take counsel together for the common good.

After an existence of near three-fourths of a century as a free and independent Republic, the problem no longer remains to be solved whether man is capable of self-government. The success of our admirable system is a conclusive refutation of the theories of those in other countries who maintain that a "favored few" are born to rule and that the mass of mankind must be governed by force. Subject to no arbitrary or hereditary authority, the people are the only sovereigns recognized by our Constitution.

Numerous emigrants, of every lineage and language, attracted by the civil and religious freedom we enjoy and by our happy condition, annually crowd to our shores, and transfer their heart, not less than their allegiance, to the country whose dominion belongs alone to the people.

No country has been so much favored, or should acknowledge with deeper reverence the manifestations of the divine protection. An all-wise Creator directed and guarded us in our infant struggle for freedom and has constantly watched over our surprising progress until we have become one of the great nations of the earth.

It is in a country thus favored, and under a Government in which the executive and legislative branches hold their authority for limited periods alike from the people, and where all are responsible to their respective constituencies, that it is again my duty to communicate with Congress upon the state of the Union and the present condition of public affairs.

During the past year the most gratifying proofs are presented that our country has been blessed with a widespread and universal prosperity. There has been no period since the Government was founded when all the industrial pursuits of our people have been more successful or when labor in all branches of business has received a fairer or better reward. From our abundance we have been enabled to perform the pleasing duty of furnishing food for the starving millions of less favored countries.

In the enjoyment of the bounties of Providence at home such as have rarely fallen to the lot of any people, it is cause of congratulation that our intercourse with all the powers of the earth except Mexico continues to be of an amicable character.

It has ever been our cherished policy to cultivate peace and good will with all nations, and this policy has been steadily pursued by me.

No change has taken place in our relations with Mexico since the adjournment of the last Congress. The war in which the United States were forced to engage with the Government of that country still continues.

I deem it unnecessary, after the full exposition of them contained in my message of the 11th of May, 1846, and in my annual message at the commencement of the session of Congress in December last, to reiterate the serious causes of complaint which we had against Mexico before she commenced hostilities.

It is sufficient on the present occasion to say that the wanton violation of the rights of person and property of our citizens committed by Mexico, her repeated acts of bad faith through a long series of years, and her disregard of solemn treaties stipulating for indemnity to our injured citizens not only constituted ample cause of war on our part, but were of such an aggravated character as would have justified us before the whole world in resorting to this extreme remedy. With an anxious desire to avoid a rupture between the two countries, we forbore for years to assert our clear rights by force, and continued to seek redress for the wrongs we had suffered by amicable negotiation in the hope that Mexico might yield to pacific counsels and the demands of justice. In this hope we were disappointed. Our minister of peace sent to Mexico was insultingly rejected. The Mexican Government refused even to hear the terms of adjustment which he was authorized to propose, and finally, under wholly unjustifiable pretexts, involved the two countries in war by invading the territory of the State of Texas, striking the first blow, and shedding the blood of our citizens on our own soil.

Though the United States were the aggrieved nation, Mexico commenced the war, and we were compelled in self-defense to repel the invader and to vindicate the national honor and interests by prosecuting it with vigor until we could obtain a just and honorable peace.

On learning that hostilities had been commenced by Mexico I promptly communicated that fact, accompanied with a succinct statement of our other causes of complaint against Mexico, to Congress, and that body, by the act of the 13th of May, 1846, declared that "by the act of the Republic of Mexico a state of war exists between that Government and the United States." This act declaring "the war to exist by the act of the Republic of Mexico," and making provision for its prosecution "to a speedy and successful termination," was passed with great unanimity by Congress, there being but two negative votes in the Senate and but fourteen in the House of Representatives.

The existence of the war having thus been declared by Congress, it became my duty under the Constitution and the laws to conduct and prosecute it. This duty has been performed, and though at every stage of its progress I have manifested a willingness to terminate it by a just peace, Mexico has refused to accede to any terms which could be accepted by the United States consistently with the national honor and interest.

The rapid and brilliant successes of our arms and the vast extent of the enemy's territory which had been overrun and conquered before the close of the last session of Congress were fully known to that body. Since that time the war has been prosecuted with increased energy, and, I am gratified to state, with a success which commands universal admiration. History presents no parallel of so many glorious victories achieved by any nation within so short a period. Our Army, regulars and volunteers, have covered themselves with imperishable honors. Whenever and wherever our forces have encountered the enemy, though he was in vastly superior numbers and often intrenched in fortified positions of his own selection and of great strength, he has been defeated. Too much praise can not be bestowed upon our officers and men, regulars and volunteers, for their gallantry, discipline, indomitable courage, and perseverance, all seeking the post of danger and vying with each other in deeds of noble daring.

While every patriot's heart must exult and a just national pride animate every bosom in beholding the high proofs of courage, consummate military skill, steady discipline, and humanity to the vanquished enemy exhibited by our gallant Army, the nation is called to mourn over the loss of many brave officers and soldiers, who have fallen in defense of their country's honor and interests. The brave dead met their melancholy fate in a foreign land, nobly discharging their duty, and with their country's flag waving triumphantly in the face of the foe. Their patriotic deeds are justly appreciated, and will long be remembered by their grateful countrymen. The parental care of the Government they loved and served should be extended to their surviving families.

Shortly after the adjournment of the last session of Congress the gratifying intelligence was received of the signal victory of Buena Vista, and of the fall of the city of Vera Cruz, and with it the strong castle of San Juan de Ulloa, by which it was defended. Believing that after these and other successes so honorable to our arms and so disastrous to Mexico the period was propitious to afford her another opportunity, if she thought proper to embrace it, to enter into negotiations for peace, a commissioner was appointed to proceed to the headquarters of our Army with full powers to enter upon negotiations and to conclude a just and honorable treaty of peace. He was not directed to make any new overtures of peace, but was the bearer of a dispatch from the Secretary of State of the United States to the minister of foreign affairs of Mexico, in reply to one received from the latter of the 22d of February, 1847, in which the Mexican Government was informed of his appointment and of his presence at the headquarters of our Army, and that he was invested with full powers to conclude a definitive treaty of peace whenever the Mexican Government might signify a desire to do so. While I was unwilling to subject the United States to another indignant refusal, I was yet resolved that the evils of the war should not be protracted a day longer than might be rendered absolutely necessary by the Mexican Government.

Care was taken to give no instructions to the commissioner which could in any way interfere with our military operations or relax our energies in the prosecution of the war. He possessed no authority in any manner to control these operations. He was authorized to exhibit his instructions to the general in command of the Army, and in the event of a treaty being concluded and ratified on the part of Mexico he was directed to give him notice of that fact. On the happening of such contingency, and on receiving notice thereof, the general in command was instructed by the Secretary of War to suspend further active military operations until further orders. These instructions were given with a view to intermit hostilities until the treaty thus ratified by Mexico could be transmitted to Washington and receive the action of the Government of the United States. The commissioner was also directed on reaching the Army to deliver to the general in command the dispatch which he bore from the Secretary of State to the minister of foreign affairs of Mexico, and on receiving it the general was instructed by the Secretary of War to cause it to be transmitted to the commander of the Mexican forces, with a request that it might be communicated to his Government.

The commissioner did not reach the headquarters of the Army until after another brilliant victory had crowned our arms at Cerro Gordo.

The dispatch which he bore from the Secretary of War to the general in command of the Army was received by that officer, then at Jalapa, on the 7th of May, 1847, together with the dispatch from the Secretary of State to the minister of foreign affairs of Mexico, having been transmitted to him from Vera Cruz. The commissioner arrived at the headquarters of the Army a few days afterwards. His presence with the Army and his diplomatic character were made known to the Mexican Government from Puebla on the 12th of June, 1847, by the transmission of the dispatch from the Secretary of State to the minister of foreign affairs of Mexico.

Many weeks elapsed after its receipt, and no overtures were made nor was any desire expressed by the Mexican Government to enter into negotiations for peace.

Our Army pursued its march upon the capital, and as it approached it was met by formidable resistance. Our forces first encountered the enemy, and achieved signal victories in the severely contested battles of Contreras and Churubusco. It was not until after these actions had resulted in decisive victories and the capital of the enemy was within our power that the Mexican Government manifested any disposition to enter into negotiations for peace, and even then, as events have proved, there is too much reason to believe they were insincere, and that in agreeing to go through the forms of negotiation the object was to gain time to strengthen the defenses of their capital and to prepare for fresh resistance.

The general in command of the Army deemed it expedient to suspend hostilities temporarily by entering into an armistice with a view to the opening of negotiations. Commissioners were appointed on the part of Mexico to meet the commissioner on the part of the United States. The result of the conferences which took place between these functionaries of the two Governments was a failure to conclude a treaty of peace.

The commissioner of the United States took with him the project of a treaty already prepared, by the terms of which the indemnity required by the United States was a cession of territory.

It is well known that the only indemnity which it is in the power of Mexico to make in satisfaction of the just and long-deferred claims of our citizens against her and the only means by which she can reimburse the United States for the expenses of the war is a cession to the United States of a portion of her territory. Mexico has no money to pay, and no other means of making the required indemnity. If we refuse this, we can obtain nothing else. To reject indemnity by refusing to accept a cession of territory would be to abandon all our just demands, and to wage the war, bearing all its expenses, without a purpose or definite object.

A state of war abrogates treaties previously existing between the belligerents and a treaty of peace puts an end to all claims for indemnity for tortious acts committed under the authority of one government against the citizens or subjects of another unless they are provided for in its stipulations. A treaty of peace which would terminate the existing war without providing for indemnity would enable Mexico, the acknowledged debtor and herself the aggressor in the war, to relieve herself from her just liabilities. By such a treaty our citizens who hold just demands against her would have no remedy either against Mexico or their own Government. Our duty to these citizens must forever prevent such a peace, and no treaty which does not provide ample means of discharging these demands can receive my sanction.

A treaty of peace should settle all existing differences between the two countries. If an adequate cession of territory should be made by such a treaty, the United States should release Mexico from all her liabilities and assume their payment to our own citizens. If instead of this the United States were to consent to a treaty by which Mexico should again engage to pay the heavy amount of indebtedness which a just indemnity to our Government and our citizens would impose on her, it is notorious that she does not possess the means to meet such an undertaking. From such a treaty no result could be anticipated but the same irritating disappointments which have heretofore attended the violations of similar treaty stipulations on the part of Mexico. Such a treaty would be but a temporary cessation of hostilities, without the restoration of the friendship and good understanding which should characterize the future intercourse between the two countries.

That Congress contemplated the acquisition of territorial indemnity when that body made provision for the prosecution of the war is obvious. Congress could not have meant when, in May, 1846, they appropriated $10,000,000 and authorized the President to employ the militia and naval and military forces of the United States and to accept the services of 50,000 volunteers to enable him to prosecute the war, and when, at their last session, and after our Army had invaded Mexico, they made additional appropriations and authorized the raising of additional troops for the same purpose, that no indemnity was to be obtained from Mexico at the conclusion of the war; and yet it was certain that if no Mexican territory was acquired no indemnity could be obtained. It is further manifest that Congress contemplated territorial indemnity from the fact that at their last session an act was passed, upon the Executive recommendation, appropriating $3,000,000 with that express object. This appropriation was made "to enable the President to conclude a treaty of peace, limits, and boundaries with the Republic of Mexico, to be used by him in the event that said treaty, when signed by the authorized agents of the two Governments and duly ratified by Mexico, shall call for the expenditure of the same or any part thereof." The object of asking this appropriation was distinctly stated in the several messages on the subject which I communicated to Congress. Similar appropriations made in 1803 and 1806, which were referred to, were intended to be applied in part consideration for the cession of Louisiana and the Floridas. In like manner it was anticipated that in settling the terms of a treaty of "limits and boundaries" with Mexico a cession of territory estimated to be of greater value than the amount of our demands against her might be obtained, and that the prompt payment of this sum in part consideration for the territory ceded, on the conclusion of a treaty and its ratification on her part, might be an inducement with her to make such a cession of territory as would be satisfactory to the United States; and although the failure to conclude such a treaty has rendered it unnecessary to use any part of the $3,000,000 appropriated by that act, and the entire sum remains in the Treasury, it is still applicable to that object should the contingency occur making such application proper.

The doctrine of no territory is the doctrine of no indemnity, and if sanctioned would be a public acknowledgment that our country was wrong and that the war declared by Congress with extraordinary unanimity was unjust and should be abandoned—an admission unfounded in fact and degrading to the national character.

The terms of the treaty proposed by the United States were not only just to Mexico, but, considering the character and amount of our claims, the unjustifiable and unprovoked commencement of hostilities by her, the expenses of the war to which we have been subjected, and the success which had attended our arms, were deemed to be of a most liberal character.

The commissioner of the United States was authorized to agree to the establishment of the Rio Grande as the boundary from its entrance into the Gulf to its intersection with the southern boundary of New Mexico, in north latitude about 32°, and to obtain a cession to the United States of the Provinces of New Mexico and the Californias and the privilege of the right of way across the Isthmus of Tehuantepec. The boundary of the Rio Grande and the cession to the United States of New Mexico and Upper California constituted an ultimatum which our commissioner was under no circumstances to yield.

That it might be manifest, not only to Mexico, but to all other nations, that the United States were not disposed to take advantage of a feeble power by insisting upon wresting from her all the other Provinces, including many of her principal towns and cities, which we had conquered and held in our military occupation, but were willing to conclude a treaty in a spirit of liberality, our commissioner was authorized to stipulate for the restoration to Mexico of all our other conquests.

As the territory to be acquired by the boundary proposed might be estimated to be of greater value than a fair equivalent for our just demands, our commissioner was authorized to stipulate for the payment of such additional pecuniary consideration as was deemed reasonable.

The terms of a treaty proposed by the Mexican commissioners were wholly inadmissible. They negotiated as if Mexico were the victorious, and not the vanquished, party. They must have known that their ultimatum could never be accepted. It required the United States to dismember Texas by surrendering to Mexico that part of the territory of that State lying between the Nueces and the Rio Grande, included within her limits by her laws when she was an independent republic, and when she was annexed to the United States and admitted by Congress as one of the States of our Union. It contained no provision for the payment by Mexico of the just claims of our citizens. It required indemnity to Mexican citizens for injuries they may have sustained by our troops in the prosecution of the war. It demanded the right for Mexico to levy and collect the Mexican tariff of duties on goods imported into her ports while in our military occupation during the war, and the owners of which had paid to officers of the United States the military contributions which had been levied upon them; and it offered to cede to the United States, for a pecuniary consideration, that part of Upper California lying north of latitude 37°. Such were the unreasonable terms proposed by the Mexican commissioners.

The cession to the United States by Mexico of the Provinces of New Mexico and the Californias, as proposed by the commissioner of the United States, it was believed would be more in accordance with the convenience and interests of both nations than any other cession of territory which it was probable Mexico could be induced to make.

It is manifest to all who have observed the actual condition of the Mexican Government for some years past and at present that if these Provinces should be retained by her she could not long continue to hold and govern them. Mexico is too feeble a power to govern these Provinces, lying as they do at a distance of more than 1,000 miles from her capital, and if attempted to be retained by her they would constitute but for a short time even nominally a part of her dominions. This would be especially the case with Upper California.

The sagacity of powerful European nations has long since directed their attention to the commercial importance of that Province, and there can be little doubt that the moment the United States shall relinquish their present occupation of it and their claim to it as indemnity an effort would be made by some foreign power to possess it, either by conquest or by purchase. If no foreign government should acquire it in either of these modes, an independent revolutionary government would probably be established by the inhabitants and such foreigners as may remain in or remove to the country as soon as it shall be known that the United States have abandoned it. Such a government would be too feeble long to maintain its separate independent existence, and would finally become annexed to or be a dependent colony of some more powerful state.

Should any foreign government attempt to possess it as a colony, or otherwise to incorporate it with itself, the principle avowed by President Monroe in 1824, and reaffirmed in my first annual message, that no foreign power shall with our consent be permitted to plant or establish any new colony or dominion on any part of the North American continent must be maintained. In maintaining this principle and in resisting its invasion by any foreign power we might be involved in other wars more expensive and more difficult than that in which we are now engaged.

The Provinces of New Mexico and the Californias are contiguous to the territories of the United States, and if brought under the government of our laws their resources—mineral, agricultural, manufacturing, and commercial—would soon be developed.

Upper California is bounded on the north by our Oregon possessions, and if held by the United States would soon be settled by a hardy, enterprising, and intelligent portion of our population. The Bay of San Francisco and other harbors along the Californian coast would afford shelter for our Navy, for our numerous whale ships, and other merchant vessels employed in the Pacific Ocean, and would in a short period become the marts of an extensive and profitable commerce with China and other countries of the East.

These advantages, in which the whole commercial world would participate, would at once be secured to the United States by the cession of this territory; while it is certain that as long as it remains a part of the Mexican dominions they can be enjoyed neither by Mexico herself nor by any other nation.

New Mexico is a frontier Province, and has never been of any considerable value to Mexico. From its locality it is naturally connected with our Western settlements. The territorial limits of the State of Texas, too, as defined by her laws before her admission into our Union, embrace all that portion of New Mexico lying east of the Rio Grande, while Mexico still claims to hold this territory as a part of her dominions. The adjustment of this question of boundary is important.

There is another consideration which induced the belief that the Mexican Government might even desire to place this Province under the protection of the Government of the United States. Numerous bands of fierce and warlike savages wander over it and upon its borders. Mexico has been and must continue to be too feeble to restrain them from committing depredations, robberies, and murders, not only upon the inhabitants of New Mexico itself, but upon those of the other northern States of Mexico. It would be a blessing to all these northern States to have their citizens protected against them by the power of the United States. At this moment many Mexicans, principally females and children, are in captivity among them. If New Mexico were held and governed by the United States, we could effectually prevent these tribes from committing such outrages, and compel them to release these captives and restore them to their families and friends.

In proposing to acquire New Mexico and the Californias, it was known that but an inconsiderable portion of the Mexican people would be transferred with them, the country embraced within these Provinces being chiefly an uninhabited region.

These were the leading considerations which induced me to authorize the terms of peace which were proposed to Mexico. They were rejected, and, negotiations being at an end, hostilities were renewed. An assault was made by our gallant Army upon the strongly fortified places near the gates of the City of Mexico and upon the city itself, and after several days of severe conflict the Mexican forces, vastly superior in number to our own, were driven from the city, and it was occupied by our troops.

Immediately after information was received of the unfavorable result of the negotiations, believing that his continued presence with the Army could be productive of no good, I determined to recall our commissioner. A dispatch to this effect was transmitted to him on the 6th of October last. The Mexican Government will be informed of his recall, and that in the existing state of things I shall not deem it proper to make any further overtures of peace, but shall be at all times ready to receive and consider any proposals which may be made by Mexico.

Since the liberal proposition of the United States was authorized to be made, in April last, large expenditures have been incurred and the precious blood of many of our patriotic fellow-citizens has been shed in the prosecution of the war. This consideration and the obstinate perseverance of Mexico in protracting the war must influence the terms of peace which it may be deemed proper hereafter to accept.

Our arms having been everywhere victorious, having subjected to our military occupation a large portion of the enemy's country, including his capital, and negotiations for peace having failed, the important questions arise, in what manner the war ought to be prosecuted and what should be our future policy. I can not doubt that we should secure and render available the conquests which we have already made, and that with this view we should hold and occupy by our naval and military forces all the ports, towns, cities, and Provinces now in our occupation or which may hereafter fall into our possession; that we should press forward our military operations and levy such military contributions on the enemy as may, as far as practicable, defray the future expenses of the war.

Had the Government of Mexico acceded to the equitable and liberal terms proposed, that mode of adjustment would have been preferred. Mexico having declined to do this and failed to offer any other terms which could be accepted by the United States, the national honor, no less than the public interests, requires that the war should be prosecuted with increased energy and power until a just and satisfactory peace can be obtained. In the meantime, as Mexico refuses all indemnity, we should adopt measures to indemnify ourselves by appropriating permanently a portion of her territory. Early after the commencement of the war New Mexico and the Californias were taken possession of by our forces. Our military and naval commanders were ordered to conquer and hold them, subject to be disposed of by a treaty of peace.

These Provinces are now in our undisputed occupation, and have been so for many months, all resistance on the part of Mexico having ceased within their limits. I am satisfied that they should never be surrendered to Mexico. Should Congress concur with me in this opinion, and that they should be retained by the United States as indemnity, I can perceive no good reason why the civil jurisdiction and laws of the United States should not at once be extended over them. To wait for a treaty of peace such as we are willing to make, by which our relations toward them would not be changed, can not be good policy; whilst our own interest and that of the people inhabiting them require that a stable, responsible, and free government under our authority should as soon as possible be established over them. Should Congress, therefore, determine to hold these Provinces permanently, and that they shall hereafter be considered as constituent parts of our country, the early establishment of Territorial governments over them will be important for the more perfect protection of persons and property; and I recommend that such Territorial governments be established. It will promote peace and tranquillity among the inhabitants, by allaying all apprehension that they may still entertain of being again subjected to the jurisdiction of Mexico. I invite the early and favorable consideration of Congress to this important subject.

Besides New Mexico and the Californias, there are other Mexican Provinces which have been reduced to our possession by conquest. These other Mexican Provinces are now governed by our military and naval commanders under the general authority which is conferred upon a conqueror by the laws of war. They should continue to be held, as a means of coercing Mexico to accede to just terms of peace. Civil as well as military officers are required to conduct such a government. Adequate compensation, to be drawn from contributions levied on the enemy, should be fixed by law for such officers as may be thus employed. What further provision may become necessary and what final disposition it may be proper to make of them must depend on the future progress of the war and the course which Mexico may think proper hereafter to pursue.

With the views I entertain I can not favor the policy which has been suggested, either to withdraw our Army altogether or to retire to a designated line and simply hold and defend it. To withdraw our Army

THE SIEGE OF VERA CRUZ

SIEGE AND CAPTURE OF VERA CRUZ

Gen. Winfield Scott reached the mouth of the Rio Grande in January, 1847. On March 9th 12,000 troops were landed near Vera Cruz. By March 13th the city and its island fortress, called the Castle of San Juan de Ulloa, which the Mexicans considered invulnerable, were thoroughly invested. On March 22d Scott was ready to commence the bombardment, and demanded the surrender of the city, called "the key to the country." The demand being refused, the artillerymen commenced to throw iron into the city, firing during the brief bombardment 6700 rounds of shot and shell. On March 26th overtures were made by the besieged, and on the 29th the place was handed over. Five thousand Mexicans marched out and laid down their arms, munitions and flags. One thousand Mexicans were killed and an indefinite number were wounded. The American forces lost only 80 men in killed and wounded.

See the article "Vera Cruz, Mexico, Siege and Capture of," in the index in volume eleven.

altogether from the conquests they have made by deeds of unparalleled bravery, and at the expense of so much blood and treasure, in a just war on our part, and one which, by the act of the enemy, we could not honorably have avoided, would be to degrade the nation in its own estimation and in that of the world. To retire to a line and simply hold and defend it would not terminate the war. On the contrary, it would encourage Mexico to persevere and tend to protract it indefinitely. It is not to be expected that Mexico, after refusing to establish such a line as a permanent boundary when our victorious Army are in possession of her capital and in the heart of her country, would permit us to hold it without resistance. That she would continue the war, and in the most harassing and annoying forms, there can be no doubt. A border warfare of the most savage character, extending over a long line, would be unceasingly waged. It would require a large army to be kept constantly in the field, stationed at posts and garrisons along such a line, to protect and defend it. The enemy, relieved from the pressure of our arms on his coasts and in the populous parts of the interior, would direct his attention to this line, and, selecting an isolated post for attack, would concentrate his forces upon it. This would be a condition of affairs which the Mexicans, pursuing their favorite system of guerrilla warfare, would probably prefer to any other. Were we to assume a defensive attitude on such a line, all the advantages of such a state of war would be on the side of the enemy. We could levy no contributions upon him, or in any other way make him feel the pressure of the war, but must remain inactive and await his approach, being in constant uncertainty at what point on the line or at what time he might make an assault. He may assemble and organize an overwhelming force in the interior on his own side of the line, and, concealing his purpose, make a sudden assault upon some one of our posts so distant from any other as to prevent the possibility of timely succor or reenforcements, and in this way our gallant Army would be exposed to the danger of being cut off in detail; or if by their unequaled bravery and prowess everywhere exhibited during this war they should repulse the enemy, their numbers stationed at any one post may be too small to pursue him. If the enemy be repulsed in one attack, he would have nothing to do but to retreat to his own side of the line, and, being in no fear of a pursuing army, may reenforce himself at leisure for another attack on the same or some other post. He may, too, cross the line between our posts, make rapid incursions into the country which we hold, murder the inhabitants, commit depredations on them, and then retreat to the interior before a sufficient force can be concentrated to pursue him. Such would probably be the harassing character of a mere defensive war on our part. If our forces when attacked, or threatened with attack, be permitted to cross the line, drive back the enemy, and conquer him, this would be again to invade the enemy's country after having lost all the advantages of the conquests we have already made by having voluntarily abandoned them.

To hold such a line successfully and in security it is far from being certain that it would not require as large an army as would be necessary to hold all the conquests we have already made and to continue the prosecution of the war in the heart of the enemy's country. It is also far from being certain that the expenses of the war would be diminished by such a policy.

I am persuaded that the best means of vindicating the national honor and interest and of bringing the war to an honorable close will be to prosecute it with increased energy and power in the vital parts of the enemy's country.

In my annual message to Congress of December last I declared that—

> The war has not been waged with a view to conquest, but, having been commenced by Mexico, it has been carried into the enemy's country and will be vigorously prosecuted there with a view to obtain an honorable peace, and thereby secure ample indemnity for the expenses of the war, as well as to our much-injured citizens, who hold large pecuniary demands against Mexico.

Such, in my judgment, continues to be our true policy; indeed, the only policy which will probably secure a permanent peace.

It has never been contemplated by me, as an object of the war, to make a permanent conquest of the Republic of Mexico or to annihilate her separate existence as an independent nation. On the contrary, it has ever been my desire that she should maintain her nationality, and under a good government adapted to her condition be a free, independent, and prosperous Republic. The United States were the first among the nations to recognize her independence, and have always desired to be on terms of amity and good neighborhood with her. This she would not suffer. By her own conduct we have been compelled to engage in the present war. In its prosecution we seek not her overthrow as a nation, but in vindicating our national honor we seek to obtain redress for the wrongs she has done us and indemnity for our just demands against her. We demand an honorable peace, and that peace must bring with it indemnity for the past and security for the future. Hitherto Mexico has refused all accommodation by which such a peace could be obtained.

Whilst our armies have advanced from victory to victory from the commencement of the war, it has always been with the olive branch of peace in their hands, and it has been in the power of Mexico at every step to arrest hostilities by accepting it.

One great obstacle to the attainment of peace has undoubtedly arisen from the fact that Mexico has been so long held in subjection by one faction or military usurper after another, and such has been the condition of insecurity in which their successive governments have been placed that each has been deterred from making peace lest for this very cause a rival faction might expel it from power. Such was the fate of President Herrera's administration in 1845 for being disposed even to listen to the overtures of the United States to prevent the war, as is fully confirmed by an official correspondence which took place in the month of August last between him and his Government, a copy of which is herewith communicated. "For this cause alone the revolution which displaced him from power was set on foot" by General Paredes. Such may be the condition of insecurity of the present Government.

There can be no doubt that the peaceable and well-disposed inhabitants of Mexico are convinced that it is the true interest of their country to conclude an honorable peace with the United States, but the apprehension of becoming the victims of some military faction or usurper may have prevented them from manifesting their feelings by any public act. The removal of any such apprehension would probably cause them to speak their sentiments freely and to adopt the measures necessary for the restoration of peace. With a people distracted and divided by contending factions and a Government subject to constant changes by successive revolutions, the continued successes of our arms may fail to secure a satisfactory peace. In such event it may become proper for our commanding generals in the field to give encouragement and assurances of protection to the friends of peace in Mexico in the establishment and maintenance of a free republican government of their own choice, able and willing to conclude a peace which would be just to them and secure to us the indemnity we demand. This may become the only mode of obtaining such a peace. Should such be the result, the war which Mexico has forced upon us would thus be converted into an enduring blessing to herself. After finding her torn and distracted by factions, and ruled by military usurpers, we should then leave her with a republican government in the enjoyment of real independence and domestic peace and prosperity, performing all her relative duties in the great family of nations and promoting her own happiness by wise laws and their faithful execution.

If, after affording this encouragement and protection, and after all the persevering and sincere efforts we have made from the moment Mexico commenced the war, and prior to that time, to adjust our differences with her, we shall ultimately fail, then we shall have exhausted all honorable means in pursuit of peace, and must continue to occupy her country with our troops, taking the full measure of indemnity into our own hands, and must enforce the terms which our honor demands.

To act otherwise in the existing state of things in Mexico, and to withdraw our Army without a peace, would not only leave all the wrongs of which we complain unredressed, but would be the signal for new and fierce civil dissensions and new revolutions—all alike hostile to peaceful relations with the United States. Besides, there is danger, if our troops were withdrawn before a peace was concluded, that the Mexican people, wearied with successive revolutions and deprived of protection for their persons and property, might at length be inclined to yield to foreign influences and to cast themselves into the arms of some European monarch for protection from the anarchy and suffering which would ensue. This, for our own safety and in pursuance of our established policy, we should be compelled to resist. We could never consent that Mexico should be thus converted into a monarchy governed by a foreign prince.

Mexico is our near neighbor, and her boundaries are coterminous with our own through the whole extent across the North American continent, from ocean to ocean. Both politically and commercially we have the deepest interest in her regeneration and prosperity. Indeed, it is impossible that, with any just regard to our own safety, we can ever become indifferent to her fate.

It may be that the Mexican Government and people have misconstrued or misunderstood our forbearance and our objects in desiring to conclude an amicable adjustment of the existing differences between the two countries. They may have supposed that we would submit to terms degrading to the nation, or they may have drawn false inferences from the supposed division of opinion in the United States on the subject of the war, and may have calculated to gain much by protracting it, and, indeed, that we might ultimately abandon it altogether without insisting on any indemnity, territorial or otherwise. Whatever may be the false impressions under which they have acted, the adoption and prosecution of the energetic policy proposed must soon undeceive them.

In the future prosecution of the war the enemy must be made to feel its pressure more than they have heretofore done. At its commencement it was deemed proper to conduct it in a spirit of forbearance and liberality. With this end in view, early measures were adopted to conciliate, as far as a state of war would permit, the mass of the Mexican population; to convince them that the war was waged, not against the peaceful inhabitants of Mexico, but against their faithless Government, which had commenced hostilities; to remove from their minds the false impressions which their designing and interested rulers had artfully attempted to make, that the war on our part was one of conquest, that it was a war against their religion and their churches, which were to be desecrated and overthrown, and that their rights of person and private property would be violated. To remove these false impressions, our commanders in the field were directed scrupulously to respect their religion, their churches, and their church property, which were in no manner to be violated; they were directed also to respect the rights of persons and property of all who should not take up arms against us.

Assurances to this effect were given to the Mexican people by Major-General Taylor in a proclamation issued in pursuance of instructions from the Secretary of War in the month of June, 1846, and again by Major-General Scott, who acted upon his own convictions of the propriety of issuing it, in a proclamation of the 11th of May, 1847. In this spirit of liberality and conciliation, and with a view to prevent the body of the Mexican population from taking up arms against us, was the war conducted on our part. Provisions and other supplies furnished to our

Army by Mexican citizens were paid for at fair and liberal prices, agreed upon by the parties. After the lapse of a few months it became apparent that these assurances and this mild treatment had failed to produce the desired effect upon the Mexican population. While the war had been conducted on our part according to the most humane and liberal principles observed by civilized nations, it was waged in a far different spirit on the part of Mexico. Not appreciating our forbearance, the Mexican people generally became hostile to the United States, and availed themselves of every opportunity to commit the most savage excesses upon our troops. Large numbers of the population took up arms, and, engaging in guerrilla warfare, robbed and murdered in the most cruel manner individual soldiers or small parties whom accident or other causes had separated from the main body of our Army; bands of guerrilleros and robbers infested the roads, harassed our trains, and whenever it was in their power cut off our supplies.

The Mexicans having thus shown themselves to be wholly incapable of appreciating our forbearance and liberality, it was deemed proper to change the manner of conducting the war, by making them feel its pressure according to the usages observed under similar circumstances by all other civilized nations.

Accordingly, as early as the 22d of September, 1846, instructions were given by the Secretary of War to Major-General Taylor to "draw supplies" for our Army "from the enemy without paying for them, and to require contributions for its support, if in that way he was satisfied he could get abundant supplies for his forces." In directing the execution of these instructions much was necessarily left to the discretion of the commanding officer, who was best acquainted with the circumstances by which he was surrounded, the wants of the Army, and the practicability of enforcing the measure. General Taylor, on the 26th of October, 1846, replied from Monterey that "it would have been impossible hitherto, and is so now, to sustain the Army to any extent by forced contributions of money or supplies." For the reasons assigned by him, he did not adopt the policy of his instructions, but declared his readiness to do so "should the Army in its future operations reach a portion of the country which may be made to supply the troops with advantage." He continued to pay for the articles of supply which were drawn from the enemy's country.

Similar instructions were issued to Major-General Scott on the 3d of April, 1847, who replied from Jalapa on the 20th of May, 1847, that if it be expected "that the Army is to support itself by forced contributions levied upon the country we may ruin and exasperate the inhabitants and starve ourselves." The same discretion was given to him that had been to General Taylor in this respect. General Scott, for the reasons assigned by him, also continued to pay for the articles of supply for the Army which were drawn from the enemy.

After the Army had reached the heart of the most wealthy portion of Mexico it was supposed that the obstacles which had before that time prevented it would not be such as to render impracticable the levy of forced contributions for its support, and on the 1st of September and again on the 6th of October, 1847, the order was repeated in dispatches addressed by the Secretary of War to General Scott, and his attention was again called to the importance of making the enemy bear the burdens of the war by requiring them to furnish the means of supporting our Army, and he was directed to adopt this policy unless by doing so there was danger of depriving the Army of the necessary supplies. Copies of these dispatches were forwarded to General Taylor for his government.

On the 31st of March last I caused an order to be issued to our military and naval commanders to levy and collect a military contribution upon all vessels and merchandise which might enter any of the ports of Mexico in our military occupation, and to apply such contributions toward defraying the expenses of the war. By virtue of the right of conquest and the laws of war, the conqueror, consulting his own safety or convenience, may either exclude foreign commerce altogether from all such ports or permit it upon such terms and conditions as he may prescribe. Before the principal ports of Mexico were blockaded by our Navy the revenue derived from import duties under the laws of Mexico was paid into the Mexican treasury. After these ports had fallen into our military possession the blockade was raised and commerce with them permitted upon prescribed terms and conditions. They were opened to the trade of all nations upon the payment of duties more moderate in their amount than those which had been previously levied by Mexico, and the revenue, which was formerly paid into the Mexican treasury, was directed to be collected by our military and naval officers and applied to the use of our Army and Navy. Care was taken that the officers, soldiers, and sailors of our Army and Navy should be exempted from the operations of the order, and, as the merchandise imported upon which the order operated must be consumed by Mexican citizens, the contributions exacted were in effect the seizure of the public revenues of Mexico and the application of them to our own use. In directing this measure the object was to compel the enemy to contribute as far as practicable toward the expenses of the war.

For the amount of contributions which have been levied in this form I refer you to the accompanying reports of the Secretary of War and of the Secretary of the Navy, by which it appears that a sum exceeding half a million of dollars has been collected. This amount would undoubtedly have been much larger but for the difficulty of keeping open communications between the coast and the interior, so as to enable the owners of the merchandise imported to transport and vend it to the inhabitants of the country. It is confidently expected that this difficulty will to a great extent be soon removed by our increased forces which have been sent to the field.

Measures have recently been adopted by which the internal as well as the external revenues of Mexico in all places in our military occupation will be seized and appropriated to the use of our Army and Navy.

The policy of levying upon the enemy contributions in every form consistently with the laws of nations, which it may be practicable for our military commanders to adopt, should, in my judgment, be rigidly enforced, and orders to this effect have accordingly been given. By such a policy, at the same time that our own Treasury will be relieved from a heavy drain, the Mexican people will be made to feel the burdens of the war, and, consulting their own interests, may be induced the more readily to require their rulers to accede to a just peace.

After the adjournment of the last session of Congress events transpired in the prosecution of the war which in my judgment required a greater number of troops in the field than had been anticipated. The strength of the Army was accordingly increased by "accepting" the services of all the volunteer forces authorized by the act of the 13th of May, 1846, without putting a construction on that act the correctness of which was seriously questioned. The volunteer forces now in the field, with those which had been "accepted" to "serve for twelve months" and were discharged at the end of their term of service, exhaust the 50,000 men authorized by that act. Had it been clear that a proper construction of the act warranted it, the services of an additional number would have been called for and accepted; but doubts existing upon this point, the power was not exercised. It is deemed important that Congress should at an early period of their session confer the authority to raise an additional regular force to serve during the war with Mexico and to be discharged upon the conclusion and ratification of a treaty of peace. I invite the attention of Congress to the views presented by the Secretary of War in his report upon this subject.

I recommend also that authority be given by law to call for and accept the services of an additional number of volunteers, to be exercised at such time and to such extent as the emergencies of the service may require.

In prosecuting the war with Mexico, whilst the utmost care has been taken to avoid every just cause of complaint on the part of neutral nations, and none has been given, liberal privileges have been granted to their commerce in the ports of the enemy in our military occupation.

The difficulty with the Brazilian Government, which at one time threatened to interrupt the friendly relations between the two countries, will, I trust, be speedily adjusted. I have received information that an envoy extraordinary and minister plenipotentiary to the United States will shortly be appointed by His Imperial Majesty, and it is hoped that he will come instructed and prepared to adjust all remaining differences between the two Governments in a manner acceptable and honorable to both. In the meantime, I have every reason to believe that nothing will occur to interrupt our amicable relations with Brazil.

.....

It has been my constant effort to maintain and cultivate the most intimate relations of friendship with all the independent powers of South America, and this policy has been attended with the happiest results. It is true that the settlement and payment of many just claims of American citizens against these nations have been long delayed. The peculiar position in which they have been placed and the desire on the part of my predecessors as well as myself to grant them the utmost indulgence have hitherto prevented these claims from being urged in a manner demanded by strict justice. The time has arrived when they ought to be finally adjusted and liquidated, and efforts are now making for that purpose.

It is proper to inform you that the Government of Peru has in good faith paid the first two installments of the indemnity of $30,000 each, and the greater portion of the interest due thereon, in execution of the convention between that Government and the United States the ratifications of which were exchanged at Lima on the 31st of October, 1846. The Attorney-General of the United States early in August last completed the adjudication of the claims under this convention, and made his report thereon in pursuance of the act of the 8th of August, 1846. The sums to which the claimants are respectively entitled will be paid on demand at the Treasury.

I invite the early attention of Congress to the present condition of our citizens in China. Under our treaty with that power American citizens are withdrawn from the jurisdiction, whether civil or criminal, of the Chinese Government and placed under that of our public functionaries in that country. By these alone can our citizens be tried and punished for the commission of any crime; by these alone can questions be decided between them involving the rights of persons and property, and by these alone can contracts be enforced into which they may have entered with the citizens or subjects of foreign powers. The merchant vessels of the United States lying in the waters of the five ports of China open to foreign commerce are under the exclusive jurisdiction of officers of their own Government. Until Congress shall establish competent tribunals to try and punish crimes and to exercise jurisdiction in civil cases in China, American citizens there are subject to no law whatever. Crimes may be committed with impunity and debts may be contracted without any means to enforce their payment. Inconveniences have already resulted from the omission of Congress to legislate upon the subject, and still greater are apprehended. The British authorities in China have already complained that this Government has not provided for the punishment of crimes or the enforcement of contracts against American citizens in that country, whilst their Government has established tribunals by which an American citizen can recover debts due from British subjects.

Accustomed, as the Chinese are, to summary justice, they could not be made to comprehend why criminals who are citizens of the United States should escape with impunity, in violation of treaty obligations, whilst the punishment of a Chinese who had committed any crime against an American citizen would be rigorously exacted. Indeed, the consequences might be fatal to American citizens in China should a flagrant crime be committed by any one of them upon a Chinese, and should trial and punishment not follow according to the requisitions of the treaty. This might disturb, if not destroy, our friendly relations with that Empire, and cause an interruption of our valuable commerce.

Our treaties with the Sublime Porte, Tripoli, Tunis, Morocco, and Muscat also require the legislation of Congress to carry them into execution, though the necessity for immediate action may not be so urgent as in regard to China.

The Secretary of State has submitted an estimate to defray the expense of opening diplomatic relations with the Papal States. The interesting political events now in progress in these States, as well as a just regard to our commercial interests, have, in my opinion, rendered such a measure highly expedient.

Estimates have also been submitted for the outfits and salaries of chargés d'affaires to the Republics of Bolivia, Guatemala, and Ecuador. The manifest importance of cultivating the most friendly relations with all the independent States upon this continent has induced me to recommend appropriations necessary for the maintenance of these missions.

I recommend to Congress that an appropriation be made to be paid to the Spanish Government for the purpose of distribution among the claimants in the *Amistad* case. I entertain the conviction that this is due to Spain under the treaty of the 20th of October, 1795, and, moreover, that from the earnest manner in which the claim continues to be urged so long as it shall remain unsettled it will be a source of irritation and discord between the two countries, which may prove highly prejudicial to the interests of the United States. Good policy, no less than a faithful compliance with our treaty obligations, requires that the inconsiderable appropriation demanded should be made.

A detailed statement of the condition of the finances will be presented in the annual report of the Secretary of the Treasury. The imports for the last fiscal year, ending on the 30th of June, 1847, were of the value of $146,545,638, of which the amount exported was $8,011,158, leaving $138,534,480 in the country for domestic use. The value of the exports for the same period was $158,648,622, of which $150,637,464 consisted of domestic productions and $8,011,158 of foreign articles.

The receipts into the Treasury for the same period amounted to $26,-346,790.37, of which there was derived from customs $23,747,864.66, from sales of public lands $2,498,335.20, and from incidental and miscellaneous sources $100,570.51. The last fiscal year, during which this amount was received, embraced five months under the operation of the tariff act of 1842 and seven months during which the tariff act of 1846 was in force. During the five months under the act of 1842 the amount received from customs was $7,842,306.90, and during the seven months under the act of 1846 the amount received was $15,905,557.76.

The net revenue from customs during the year ending on the 1st of December, 1846, being the last year under the operation of the tariff act of 1842, was $22,971,403.10, and the net revenue from customs during the year ending on the 1st of December, 1847, being the first year under the operations of the tariff act of 1846, was about $31,500,000, being an increase of revenue for the first year under the tariff of 1846 of more than $8,500,000 over that of the last year under the tariff of 1842.

The expenditures during the fiscal year ending on the 30th of June last were $59,451,177.65, of which $3,522,082.37 was on account of payment of principal and interest of the public debt, including Treasury notes redeemed and not funded. The expenditures exclusive of payment of public debt were $55,929,095.28.

It is estimated that the receipts into the Treasury for the fiscal year ending on the 30th of June, 1848, including the balance in the Treasury on the 1st of July last, will amount to $42,886,545.80, of which $31,000,000, it is estimated, will be derived from customs, $3,500,000 from the sale of the public lands, $400,000 from incidental sources, including sales made by the Solicitor of the Treasury, and $6,285,294.55 from loans already authorized by law, which, together with the balance in the Treasury on the 1st of July last, make the sum estimated.

The expenditures for the same period, if peace with Mexico shall not be concluded and the Army shall be increased as is proposed, will amount, including the necessary payments on account of principal and interest of the public debt and Treasury notes, to $58,615,660.07.

On the 1st of the present month the amount of the public debt actually incurred, including Treasury notes, was $45,659,659.40. The public debt due on the 4th of March, 1845, including Treasury notes, was $17,788,799.62, and consequently the addition made to the public debt since that time is $27,870,859.78.

Of the loan of twenty-three millions authorized by the act of the 28th of January, 1847, the sum of five millions was paid out to the public creditors or exchanged at par for specie; the remaining eighteen millions was offered for specie to the highest bidder not below par, by an advertisement issued by the Secretary of the Treasury and published from the 9th of February until the 10th of April, 1847, when it was awarded to the several highest bidders at premiums varying from one-eighth of 1 per cent to 2 per cent above par. The premium has been paid into the Treasury and the sums awarded deposited in specie in the Treasury as fast as it was required by the wants of the Government.

To meet the expenditures for the remainder of the present and for the next fiscal year, ending on the 30th of June, 1849, a further loan in aid of the ordinary revenues of the Government will be necessary. Retaining a sufficient surplus in the Treasury, the loan required for the remainder of the present fiscal year will be about $18,500,000. If the duty on tea and coffee be imposed and the graduation of the price of the public lands shall be made at an early period of your session, as recommended, the loan for the present fiscal year may be reduced to $17,000,000. The loan may be further reduced by whatever amount of expenditures can be saved by military contributions collected in Mexico. The most vigorous measures for the augmentation of these contributions have been directed and a very considerable sum is expected from that source. Its amount can not, however, be calculated with any certainty. It is recommended that the loan to be made be authorized upon the same terms and for the same time as that which was authorized under the provisions of the act of the 28th of January, 1847.

Should the war with Mexico be continued until the 30th of June, 1849, it is estimated that a further loan of $20,500,000 will be required for the fiscal year ending on that day, in case no duty be imposed on tea and coffee, and the public lands be not reduced and graduated in price, and no military contributions shall be collected in Mexico. If the duty on tea and coffee be imposed and the lands be reduced and graduated in price as proposed, the loan may be reduced to $17,000,000, and will be subject to be still further reduced by the amount of the military contributions which may be collected in Mexico. It is not proposed, however, at present to ask Congress for authority to negotiate this loan for the next fiscal year, as it is hoped that the loan asked for the remainder of the present fiscal year, aided by military contributions which may be collected in Mexico, may be sufficient. If, contrary to my expectation, there should be a necessity for it, the fact will be communicated to Congress in time for their action during the present session. In no event will a sum exceeding $6,000,000 of this amount be needed before the meeting of the session of Congress in December, 1848.

The act of the 30th of July, 1846, "reducing the duties on imports," has been in force since the 1st of December last, and I am gratified to state that all the beneficial effects which were anticipated from its operation have been fully realized. The public revenue derived from customs during the year ending on the 1st of December, 1847, exceeds by more than $8,000,000 the amount received in the preceding year under the operation of the act of 1842, which was superseded and repealed by it. Its effects are visible in the great and almost unexampled prosperity which prevails in every branch of business.

While the repeal of the prohibitory and restrictive duties of the act of 1842 and the substitution in their place of reasonable revenue rates levied on articles imported according to their actual value has increased the revenue and augmented our foreign trade, all the great interests of the country have been advanced and promoted.

The great and important interests of agriculture, which had been not only too much neglected, but actually taxed under the protective policy for the benefit of other interests, have been relieved of the burdens which that policy imposed on them; and our farmers and planters, under a more just and liberal commercial policy, are finding new and profitable markets abroad for their augmented products. Our commerce is rapidly increasing, and is extending more widely the circle of international exchanges. Great as has been the increase of our imports during the past year, our exports of domestic products sold in foreign markets have been still greater.

Our navigating interest is eminently prosperous. The number of vessels built in the United States has been greater than during any preceding period of equal length. Large profits have been derived by those who have constructed as well as by those who have navigated them. Should the ratio of increase in the number of our merchant vessels be progressive, and be as great for the future as during the past year, the time is not distant when our tonnage and commercial marine will be larger than that of any other nation in the world.

Whilst the interests of agriculture, of commerce, and of navigation have been enlarged and invigorated, it is highly gratifying to observe that our manufactures are also in a prosperous condition. None of the ruinous effects upon this interest which were apprehended by some as the result of the operation of the revenue system established by the act of 1846 have been experienced. On the contrary, the number of manufactories and the amount of capital invested in them is steadily and rapidly increasing, affording gratifying proofs that American enterprise and skill employed in this branch of domestic industry, with no other advantages than those fairly and incidentally accruing from a just system of revenue duties, are abundantly able to meet successfully all competition from abroad and still derive fair and remunerating profits. While capital invested in manufactures is yielding adequate and fair profits under the new system, the wages of labor, whether employed in manufactures, agriculture, commerce, or navigation, have been augmented. The toiling millions whose daily labor furnishes the supply of food and raiment and all the necessaries and comforts of life are receiving higher wages and more steady and permanent employment than in any other country or at any previous period of our own history.

So successful have been all branches of our industry that a foreign war, which generally diminishes the resources of a nation, has in no essential degree retarded our onward progress or checked our general prosperity.

With such gratifying evidences of prosperity and of the successful operation of the revenue act of 1846, every consideration of public policy recommends that it shall remain unchanged. It is hoped that the system of impost duties which it established may be regarded as the permanent policy of the country, and that the great interests affected by it may not again be subject to be injuriously disturbed, as they have heretofore been, by frequent and sometimes sudden changes.

For the purpose of increasing the revenue, and without changing or modifying the rates imposed by the act of 1846 on the dutiable articles embraced by its provisions, I again recommend to your favorable consideration the expediency of levying a revenue duty on tea and coffee. The policy which exempted these articles from duty during peace, and when the revenue to be derived from them was not needed, ceases to exist when the country is engaged in war and requires the use of all of its available resources. It is a tax which would be so generally diffused among the people that it would be felt oppressively by none and be complained of by none. It is believed that there are not in the list of imported articles any which are more properly the subject of war duties than tea and coffee.

It is estimated that $3,000,000 would be derived annually by a moderate duty imposed on these articles.

Should Congress avail itself of this additional source of revenue, not only would the amount of the public loan rendered necessary by the war with Mexico be diminished to that extent, but the public credit and the public confidence in the ability and determination of the Government to meet all its engagements promptly would be more firmly established, and the reduced amount of the loan which it may be necessary to negotiate could probably be obtained at cheaper rates.

Congress is therefore called upon to determine whether it is wiser to impose the war duties recommended or by omitting to do so increase the public debt annually $3,000,000 so long as loans shall be required to prosecute the war, and afterwards provide in some other form to pay the semiannual interest upon it, and ultimately to extinguish the principal. If in addition to these duties Congress should graduate and reduce the price of such of the public lands as experience has proved will not command the price placed upon them by the Government, an additional annual income to the Treasury of between half a million and a million of dollars, it is estimated, would be derived from this source. Should both measures receive the sanction of Congress, the annual amount of public debt necessary to be contracted during the continuance of the war would be reduced near $4,000,000. The duties recommended to be levied on tea and coffee it is proposed shall be limited in their duration to the end of the war, and until the public debt rendered necessary to be contracted by it shall be discharged. The amount of the public debt to be contracted should be limited to the lowest practicable sum, and should be extinguished as early after the conclusion of the war as the means of the Treasury will permit.

With this view, it is recommended that as soon as the war shall be over all the surplus in the Treasury not needed for other indispensable objects shall constitute a sinking fund and be applied to the purchase of the funded debt, and that authority be conferred by laws for that purpose.

The act of the 6th of August, 1846, "to establish a warehousing system," has been in operation more than a year, and has proved to be an important auxiliary to the tariff act of 1846 in augmenting the revenue and extending the commerce of the country. Whilst it has tended to enlarge commerce, it has been beneficial to our manufactures by diminishing forced sales at auction of foreign goods at low prices to raise the duties to be advanced on them, and by checking fluctuations in the market. The system, although sanctioned by the experience of other countries, was entirely new in the United States, and is susceptible of improvement in some of its provisions. The Secretary of the Treasury, upon whom was devolved large discretionary powers in carrying this measure into effect, has collected and is now collating the practical results of the system in other countries where it has long been established, and will report at an early period of your session such further regulations suggested by the investigation as may render it still more effective and beneficial.

By the act to "provide for the better organization of the Treasury and for the collection, safe-keeping, and disbursement of the public revenue" all banks were discontinued as fiscal agents of the Government, and the paper currency issued by them was no longer permitted to be received in payment of public dues. The constitutional treasury created by this act went into operation on the 1st of January last. Under the system established by it the public moneys have been collected, safely kept, and disbursed by the direct agency of officers of the Government in gold and silver, and transfers of large amounts have been made from points of collection to points of disbursement without loss to the Treasury or injury or inconvenience to the trade of the country.

While the fiscal operations of the Government have been conducted with regularity and ease under this system, it has had a salutary effect in checking and preventing an undue inflation of the paper currency issued by the banks which exist under State charters. Requiring, as it does, all dues to the Government to be paid in gold and silver, its effect is to restrain excessive issues of bank paper by the banks disproportioned to the specie in their vaults, for the reason that they are at all times liable to be called on by the holders of their notes for their redemption in order to obtain specie for the payment of duties and other public dues. The banks, therefore, must keep their business within prudent limits, and be always in a condition to meet such calls, or run the hazard of being compelled to suspend specie payments and be thereby discredited. The amount of specie imported into the United States during the last fiscal year was $24,121,289, of which there was retained in the country $22,276,170. Had the former financial system prevailed and the public moneys been placed on deposit in the banks, nearly the whole of this amount would have gone into their vaults, not to be thrown into circulation by them, but to be withheld from the hands of the people as a currency and made the basis of new and enormous issues of bank paper. A large proportion of the specie imported has been paid into the Treasury for public dues, and after having been to a great extent recoined at the

Mint has been paid out to the public creditors and gone into circulation as a currency among the people. The amount of gold and silver coin now in circulation in the country is larger than at any former period.

The financial system established by the constitutional treasury has been thus far eminently successful in its operations, and I recommend an adherence to all its essential provisions, and especially to that vital provision which wholly separates the Government from all connection with banks and excludes bank paper from all revenue receipts.

In some of its details, not involving its general principles, the system is defective and will require modification. These defects and such amendments as are deemed important were set forth in the last annual report of the Secretary of the Treasury. These amendments are again recommended to the early and favorable consideration of Congress.

During the past year the coinage at the Mint and its branches has exceeded $20,000,000. This has consisted chiefly in converting the coins of foreign countries into American coin.

The largest amount of foreign coin imported has been received at New York, and if a branch mint were established at that city all the foreign coin received at that port could at once be converted into our own coin without the expense, risk, and delay of transporting it to the Mint for that purpose, and the amount recoined would be much larger.

Experience has proved that foreign coin, and especially foreign gold coin, will not circulate extensively as a currency among the people. The important measure of extending our specie circulation, both of gold and silver, and of diffusing it among the people can only be effected by converting such foreign coin into American coin. I repeat the recommendation contained in my last annual message for the establishment of a branch of the Mint of the United States at the city of New York.

All the public lands which had been surveyed and were ready for market have been proclaimed for sale during the past year. The quantity offered and to be offered for sale under proclamations issued since the 1st of January last amounts to 9,138,531 acres. The prosperity of the Western States and Territories in which these lands lie will be advanced by their speedy sale. By withholding them from market their growth and increase of population would be retarded, while thousands of our enterprising and meritorious frontier population would be deprived of the opportunity of securing freeholds for themselves and their families. But in addition to the general considerations which rendered the early sale of these lands proper, it was a leading object at this time to derive as large a sum as possible from this source, and thus diminish by that amount the public loan rendered necessary by the existence of a foreign war.

It is estimated that not less than 10,000,000 acres of the public lands will be surveyed and be in a condition to be proclaimed for sale during the year 1848.

In my last annual message I presented the reasons which in my judgment rendered it proper to graduate and reduce the price of such of the public lands as have remained unsold for long periods after they had been offered for sale at public auction.

Many millions of acres of public lands lying within the limits of several of the Western States have been offered in the market and been subject to sale at private entry for more than twenty years and large quantities for more than thirty years at the lowest price prescribed by the existing laws, and it has been found that they will not command that price. They must remain unsold and uncultivated for an indefinite period unless the price demanded for them by the Government shall be reduced. No satisfactory reason is perceived why they should be longer held at rates above their real value. At the present period an additional reason exists for adopting the measure recommended. When the country is engaged in a foreign war, and we must necessarily resort to loans, it would seem to be the dictate of wisdom that we should avail ourselves of all our resources and thus limit the amount of the public indebtedness to the lowest possible sum.

I recommend that the existing laws on the subject of preemption rights be amended and modified so as to operate prospectively and to embrace all who may settle upon the public lands and make improvements upon them, before they are surveyed as well as afterwards, in all cases where such settlements may be made after the Indian title shall have been extinguished.

If the right of preemption be thus extended, it will embrace a large and meritorious class of our citizens. It will increase the number of small freeholders upon our borders, who will be enabled thereby to educate their children and otherwise improve their condition, while they will be found at all times, as they have ever proved themselves to be in the hour of danger to their country, among our hardiest and best volunteer soldiers, ever ready to attend to their services in cases of emergencies and among the last to leave the field as long as an enemy remains to be encountered. Such a policy will also impress these patriotic pioneer emigrants with deeper feelings of gratitude for the parental care of their Government, when they find their dearest interests secured to them by the permanent laws of the land and that they are no longer in danger of losing their homes and hard-earned improvements by being brought into competition with a more wealthy class of purchasers at the land sales.

The attention of Congress was invited at their last and the preceding session to the importance of establishing a Territorial government over our possessions in Oregon, and it is to be regretted that there was no legislation on the subject. Our citizens who inhabit that distant region of country are still left without the protection of our laws, or any regularly organized government. Before the question of limits and boundaries of the Territory of Oregon was definitely settled, from the necessity

THE CHARGE AT CERRO GORDO

THE BATTLE OF CERRO GORDO

After the Battle of Buena Vista, Santa Ana, by extraordinary efforts, collected at Cerro Gordo an army of 12,000 men. Cerro Gordo is a difficult mountain pass on the great national road from Vera Cruz to the City of Mexico, and was directly in the path of Scott's army. On April 13, 1847, Scott came upon this obstacle to his progress, reconnoitered the fortifications and then issued his orders. These directions were minutely detailed. They were followed to the letter and victory was the result. On the 18th the battle began. On one side was a deep, dark river; on the other was a frowning slope of rock, 1,000 feet in height, bristling with batteries; and above that rose the fortress of Cerro Gordo. The place was stormed and taken from 12,000 Mexicans by less than 8,000 Americans, the furious character of the fighting being well depicted in the illustration.

The article entitled "Cerro Gordo (Mexico), Battle of," in the index tells the full story, and underneath is a citation of a presidential reference to the affair.

of their condition the inhabitants had established a temporary government of their own. Besides the want of legal authority for continuing such a government, it is wholly inadequate to protect them in their rights of person and property, or to secure to them the enjoyment of the privileges of other citizens, to which they are entitled under the Constitution of the United States. They should have the right of suffrage, be represented in a Territorial legislature and by a Delegate in Congress, and possess all the rights and privileges which citizens of other portions of the territories of the United States have heretofore enjoyed or may now enjoy.

Our judicial system, revenue laws, laws regulating trade and intercourse with the Indian tribes, and the protection of our laws generally should be extended over them.

In addition to the inhabitants in that Territory who had previously emigrated to it, large numbers of our citizens have followed them during the present year, and it is not doubted that during the next and subsequent years their numbers will be greatly increased.

Congress at its last session established post routes leading to Oregon, and between different points within that Territory, and authorized the establishment of post-offices at "Astoria and such other places on the coasts of the Pacific within the territory of the United States as the public interests may require." Post-offices have accordingly been established, deputy postmasters appointed, and provision made for the transportation of the mails.

The preservation of peace with the Indian tribes residing west of the Rocky Mountains will render it proper that authority should be given by law for the appointment of an adequate number of Indian agents to reside among them.

I recommend that a surveyor-general's office be established in that Territory, and that the public lands be surveyed and brought into market at an early period.

I recommend also that grants, upon liberal terms, of limited quantities of the public lands be made to all citizens of the United States who have emigrated, or may hereafter within a prescribed period emigrate, to Oregon and settle upon them. These hardy and adventurous citizens, who have encountered the dangers and privations of a long and toilsome journey, and have at length found an abiding place for themselves and their families upon the utmost verge of our western limits, should be secured in the homes which they have improved by their labor.

I refer you to the accompanying report of the Secretary of War for a detailed account of the operations of the various branches of the public service connected with the Department under his charge. The duties devolving on this Department have been unusually onerous and responsible during the past year, and have been discharged with ability and success.

Pacific relations continue to exist with the various Indian tribes, and most of them manifest a strong friendship for the United States. Some depredations were committed during the past year upon our trains transporting supplies for the Army, on the road between the western border of Missouri and Santa Fe. These depredations, which are supposed to have been committed by bands from the region of New Mexico, have been arrested by the presence of a military force ordered out for that purpose. Some outrages have been perpetrated by a portion of the northwestern bands upon the weaker and comparatively defenseless neighboring tribes. Prompt measures were taken to prevent such occurrences in future.

Between 1,000 and 2,000 Indians, belonging to several tribes, have been removed during the year from the east of the Mississippi to the country allotted to them west of that river as their permanent home, and arrangements have been made for others to follow.

Since the treaty of 1846 with the Cherokees the feuds among them appear to have subsided, and they have become more united and contented than they have been for many years past. The commissioners appointed in pursuance of the act of June 27, 1846, to settle claims arising under the treaty of 1835–36 with that tribe have executed their duties, and after a patient investigation and a full and fair examination of all the cases brought before them closed their labors in the month of July last. This is the fourth board of commissioners which has been organized under this treaty. Ample opportunity has been afforded to all those interested to bring forward their claims. No doubt is entertained that impartial justice has been done by the late board, and that all valid claims embraced by the treaty have been considered and allowed. This result and the final settlement to be made with this tribe under the treaty of 1846, which will be completed and laid before you during your session, will adjust all questions of controversy between them and the United States and produce a state of relations with them simple, well defined, and satisfactory.

Under the discretionary authority conferred by the act of the 3d of March last the annuities due to the various tribes have been paid during the present year to the heads of families instead of to their chiefs or such persons as they might designate, as required by the law previously existing. This mode of payment has given general satisfaction to the great body of the Indians. Justice has been done to them, and they are grateful to the Government for it. A few chiefs and interested persons may object to this mode of payment, but it is believed to be the only mode of preventing fraud and imposition from being practiced upon the great body of common Indians, constituting a majority of all the tribes.

It is gratifying to perceive that a number of the tribes have recently manifested an increased interest in the establishment of schools among them, and are making rapid advances in agriculture, some of them producing a sufficient quantity of food for their support and in some cases a surplus to dispose of to their neighbors. The comforts by which those who have received even a very limited education and have engaged in agriculture are surrounded tend gradually to draw off their less civilized brethren from the precarious means of subsistence by the chase to habits of labor and civilization.

The accompanying report of the Secretary of the Navy presents a satisfactory and gratifying account of the condition and operations of the naval service during the past year. Our commerce has been pursued with increased activity and with safety and success in every quarter of the globe under the protection of our flag, which the Navy has caused to be respected in the most distant seas.

In the Gulf of Mexico and in the Pacific the officers and men of our squadrons have displayed distinguished gallantry and performed valuable services. In the early stages of the war with Mexico her ports on both coasts were blockaded, and more recently many of them have been captured and held by the Navy. When acting in cooperation with the land forces, the naval officers and men have performed gallant and distinguished services on land as well as on water, and deserve the high commendation of the country.

While other maritime powers are adding to their navies large numbers of war steamers, it was a wise policy on our part to make similar additions to our Navy. The four war steamers authorized by the act of the 3d of March, 1847, are in course of construction.

In addition to the four war steamers authorized by this act, the Secretary of the Navy has, in pursuance of its provisions, entered into contracts for the construction of five steamers to be employed in the transportation of the United States mail "from New York to New Orleans, touching at Charleston, Savannah, and Havana, and from Havana to Chagres;" for three steamers to be employed in like manner from Panama to Oregon, "so as to connect with the mail from Havana to Chagres across the Isthmus;" and for five steamers to be employed in like manner from New York to Liverpool. These steamers will be the property of the contractors, but are to be built "under the superintendence and direction of a naval constructor in the employ of the Navy Department, and to be so constructed as to render them convertible at the least possible expense into war steamers of the first class." A prescribed number of naval officers, as well as a post-office agent, are to be on board of them, and authority is reserved to the Navy Department at all times to "exercise control over said steamships" and "to have the right to take them for the exclusive use and service of the United States upon making proper compensation to the contractors therefor."

Whilst these steamships will be employed in transporting the mails of the United States coastwise and to foreign countries upon an annual compensation to be paid to the owners, they will be always ready, upon an emergency requiring it, to be converted into war steamers; and the right reserved to take them for public use will add greatly to the efficiency and strength of this description of our naval force. To the steamers thus authorized under contracts made by the Secretary of the Navy should be added five other steamers authorized under contracts made in pursuance of laws by the Postmaster-General, making an addition, in the whole, of eighteen war steamers subject to be taken for public use. As further contracts for the transportation of the mail to foreign countries may be authorized by Congress, this number may be enlarged indefinitely.

The enlightened policy by which a rapid communication with the various distant parts of the globe is established, by means of American-built sea steamers, would find an ample reward in the increase of our commerce and in making our country and its resources more favorably known abroad; but the national advantage is still greater—of having our naval officers made familiar with steam navigation and of having the privilege of taking the ships already equipped for immediate service at a moment's notice, and will be cheaply purchased by the compensation to be paid for the transportation of the mail in them over and above the postages received.

A just national pride, no less than our commercial interests, would seem to favor the policy of augmenting the number of this description of vessels. They can be built in our country cheaper and in greater numbers than in any other in the world.

I refer you to the accompanying report of the Postmaster-General for a detailed and satisfactory account of the condition and operations of that Department during the past year. It is gratifying to find that within so short a period after the reduction in the rates of postage, and notwithstanding the great increase of mail service, the revenue received for the year will be sufficient to defray all the expenses, and that no further aid will be required from the Treasury for that purpose.

The first of the American mail steamers authorized by the act of the 3d of March, 1845, was completed and entered upon the service on the 1st of June last, and is now on her third voyage to Bremen and other intermediate ports. The other vessels authorized under the provisions of that act are in course of construction, and will be put upon the line as soon as completed. Contracts have also been made for the transportation of the mail in a steamer from Charleston to Havana.

A reciprocal and satisfactory postal arrangement has been made by the Postmaster-General with the authorities of Bremen, and no difficulty is apprehended in making similar arrangements with all other powers with which we may have communications by mail steamers, except with Great Britain.

On the arrival of the first of the American steamers bound to Bremen at Southampton, in the month of June last, the British post-office directed the collection of discriminating postages on all letters and other mailable matter which she took out to Great Britain or which went into the British post-office on their way to France and other parts of Europe. The effect of the order of the British post-office is to subject all letters and other matter transported by American steamers to double postage, one postage having been previously paid on them to the United States, while letters transported in British steamers are subject to pay but a single postage. This measure was adopted with the avowed object of protecting the British line of mail steamers now running between Boston and Liverpool, and if permitted to continue must speedily put an end to the transportation of all letters and other matter by American steamers and give to British steamers a monopoly of the business. A just and fair reciprocity is all that we desire, and on this we must insist. By our laws no such discrimination is made against British steamers bringing letters into our ports, but all letters arriving in the United States are subject to the same rate of postage, whether brought in British or American vessels. I refer you to the report of the Postmaster-General for a full statement of the facts of the case and of the steps taken by him to correct this inequality. He has exerted all the power conferred upon him by the existing laws.

The minister of the United States at London has brought the subject to the attention of the British Government, and is now engaged in negotiations for the purpose of adjusting reciprocal postal arrangements which shall be equally just to both countries. Should he fail in concluding such arrangements, and should Great Britain insist on enforcing the unequal and unjust measure she has adopted, it will become necessary to confer additional powers on the Postmaster-General in order to enable him to meet the emergency and to put our own steamers on an equal footing with British steamers engaged in transporting the mails between the two countries, and I recommend that such powers be conferred.

In view of the existing state of our country, I trust it may not be inappropriate, in closing this communication, to call to mind the words of wisdom and admonition of the first and most illustrious of my predecessors in his Farewell Address to his countrymen.

That greatest and best of men, who served his country so long and loved it so much, foresaw with "serious concern" the danger to our Union of "characterizing parties by *geographical* discriminations—*Northern* and *Southern*, *Atlantic* and *Western*—whence designing men may endeavor to excite a belief that there is a real difference of local interests and views," and warned his countrymen against it.

So deep and solemn was his conviction of the importance of the Union and of preserving harmony between its different parts, that he declared to his countrymen in that address:

> It is of infinite moment that you should properly estimate the immense value of your national union to your collective and individual happiness; that you should cherish a cordial, habitual, and immovable attachment to it; accustoming yourselves to think and speak of it as of the palladium of your political safety and prosperity; watching for its preservation with jealous anxiety; discountenancing whatever may suggest even a suspicion that it can in any event be abandoned, and indignantly frowning upon the first dawning of every attempt to alienate any portion of our country from the rest or to enfeeble the sacred ties which now link together the various parts.

After the lapse of half a century these admonitions of Washington fall upon us with all the force of truth. It *is* difficult to estimate the "immense value" of our glorious Union of confederated States, to which we are so much indebted for our growth in population and wealth and for all that constitutes us a great and a happy nation. How unimportant are all our differences of opinion upon minor questions of public policy compared with its preservation, and how scrupulously should we avoid all agitating topics which may tend to distract and divide us into contending parties, separated by geographical lines, whereby it may be weakened or endangered.

Invoking the blessing of the Almighty Ruler of the Universe upon your deliberations, it will be my highest duty, no less than my sincere pleasure, to cooperate with you in all measures which may tend to promote the honor and enduring welfare of our common country.

JAMES K. POLK.

SPECIAL MESSAGES.

WASHINGTON, *December 20, 1847.*

To the Senate of the United States:

I herewith communicate to the Senate, for their consideration and advice with regard to its ratification, a convention between the United States and the Swiss Confederation, signed in this city by their respective plenipotentiaries on the 18th day of May last, for the mutual abolition of the *droit d'aubaine* and of taxes on emigration.

JAMES K. POLK.

WASHINGTON, *December 21, 1847.*

To the Senate of the United States:

I submit herewith, for the consideration and constitutional action of the Senate, two treaties with the Chippewa Indians of Lake Superior and the Upper Mississippi, for a portion of the lands possessed by those Indians west of the Mississippi River. The treaties are accompanied by communications from the Secretary of War and Commissioner of Indian Affairs, which fully explain their nature and objects.

JAMES K. POLK.

WASHINGTON, *December 22, 1847.*

To the Senate and House of Representatives:

I communicate herewith a report of the Secretary of the Navy, containing a statement of the measures which have been taken in execution of the act of 3d March last, relating to the construction of floating dry docks at Pensacola, Philadelphia, and Kittery.

JAMES K. POLK.

WASHINGTON, *January 4, 1848.*

To the House of Representatives of the United States:

I communicate herewith a report of the Secretary of War, with accompanying documents, being in addition to a report made on the 27th of February, 1847, in answer to a resolution of the House of Representatives of the 1st of that month, requesting the President "to communicate to the House of Representatives all the correspondence with General Taylor since the commencement of hostilities with Mexico which has not yet been published, and the publication of which may not be deemed detrimental to the public service; also the correspondence of the Quartermaster-General in relation to transportation for General Taylor's Army; also the reports of Brigadier-Generals Hamer and Quitman of the operations of their respective brigades on the 21st of September last" (1846).

JAMES K. POLK.

WASHINGTON, *January 12, 1848.*

To the House of Representatives of the United States:

I have carefully considered the resolution of the House of Representatives of the 4th instant, requesting the President to communicate to that House "any instructions which may have been given to any of the officers of the Army or Navy of the United States, or other persons, in regard to the return of President General Lopez de Santa Anna, or any other Mexican, to the Republic of Mexico prior or subsequent to the order of the President or Secretary of War issued in January, 1846, for the march of the Army from the Nueces River, across the 'stupendous deserts' which intervene, to the Rio Grande; that the date of all such instructions, orders, and correspondence be set forth, together with the instructions and orders issued to Mr. Slidell at any time prior or subsequent to his departure for Mexico as minister plenipotentiary of the United States to that Republic;" and requesting the President also to "communicate all the orders and correspondence of the Government in relation to the return of General Paredes to Mexico."

I transmit herewith reports from the Secretary of State, the Secretary of War, and the Secretary of the Navy, with the documents accompanying the same, which contain all the information in the possession of the Executive which it is deemed compatible with the public interests to communicate.

For further information relating to the return of Santa Anna to Mexico I refer you to my annual message of December 8, 1846. The facts and considerations stated in that message induced the order of the Secretary of the Navy to the commander of our squadron in the Gulf of Mexico a copy of which is herewith communicated. This order was issued simultaneously with the order to blockade the coasts of Mexico, both bearing date the 13th of May, 1846, the day on which the existence of the war with Mexico was recognized by Congress. It was issued solely upon the views of policy presented in that message, and without any understanding on the subject, direct or indirect, with Santa Anna or any other person.

General Paredes evaded the vigilance of our combined forces by land and sea, and made his way back to Mexico from the exile into which he had been driven, landing at Vera Cruz after that city and the castle of San Juan de Ulloa were in our military occupation, as will appear from the accompanying reports and documents.

The resolution calls for the "instructions and orders issued to Mr. Slidell at any time prior or subsequent to his departure for Mexico as minister plenipotentiary of the United States to that Republic." The customary and usual reservation contained in calls of either House of Congress upon the Executive for information relating to our intercourse with foreign nations has been omitted in the resolution before me. The call of the House is unconditional. It is that the information requested be communicated, and thereby be made public, whether in the opinion of the Executive (who is charged by the Constitution with the duty of conducting negotiations with foreign powers) such information, when disclosed, would be prejudicial to the public interest or not. It has been a subject of serious deliberation with me whether I could, consistently with my constitutional duty and my sense of the public interests involved and to be affected by it, violate an important principle, always heretofore held sacred by my predecessors, as I should do by a compliance with the request of the House. President Washington, in a message to the House of Representatives of the 30th of March, 1796, declined to comply with a request contained in a resolution of that body, to lay before them "a copy of the instructions to the minister of the United States who negotiated the treaty with the King of Great Britain, together with the correspondence and other documents relative to that treaty, excepting such of the said papers as any existing negotiation may render improper to be disclosed." In assigning his reasons for declining to comply with the call he declared that—

> The nature of foreign negotiations requires caution, and their success must often depend on secrecy; and even when brought to a conclusion a full disclosure of all the measures, demands, or eventual concessions which may have been proposed or contemplated would be extremely impolitic; for this might have a pernicious influence on future negotiations, or produce immediate inconveniences, perhaps danger and mischief, in relation to other powers. The necessity of such caution and secrecy was one cogent reason for vesting the power of making treaties in the President, with the advice and consent of the Senate, the principle on which that body was formed confining it to a small number of members. To admit, then, a right in the House of Representatives to demand and to have as a matter of course all the papers respecting a negotiation with a foreign power would be to establish a dangerous precedent.

In that case the instructions and documents called for related to a treaty which had been concluded and ratified by the President and Senate, and the negotiations in relation to it had been terminated. There was an express reservation, too, "excepting" from the call all such papers as related to "any existing negotiations" which it might be improper to disclose. In that case President Washington deemed it to be a violation of an important principle, the establishment of a "dangerous precedent," and prejudicial to the public interests to comply with the call of the House. Without deeming it to be necessary on the present occasion to examine or decide upon the other reasons assigned by him for his refusal to communicate the information requested by the House, the one which is herein recited is in my judgment conclusive in the case under consideration.

Indeed, the objections to complying with the request of the House contained in the resolution before me are much stronger than those which existed in the case of the resolution in 1796. This resolution calls for the "instructions and orders" to the minister of the United States to Mexico which relate to negotiations which have not been terminated, and which may be resumed. The information called for respects negotiations which the United States offered to open with Mexico immediately preceding the commencement of the existing war. The instructions given to the minister of the United States relate to the differences between the two countries out of which the war grew and the terms of adjustment which we were prepared to offer to Mexico in our anxiety to prevent the war. These differences still remain unsettled, and to comply with the call of the House would be to make public through that channel, and to communicate to Mexico, now a public enemy engaged in war, information which could not fail to produce serious embarrassment in any future negotiation between the two countries. I have heretofore communicated to Congress all the correspondence of the minister of the United States to Mexico which in the existing state of our relations with that Republic can, in my judgment, be at this time communicated without serious injury to the public interest.

Entertaining this conviction, and with a sincere desire to furnish any information which may be in possession of the executive department, and which either House of Congress may at any time request, I regard it to be my constitutional right and my solemn duty under the circumstances of this case to decline a compliance with the request of the House contained in their resolution.

JAMES K. POLK.

WASHINGTON, *January 21, 1848.*

To the Senate of the United States:

I herewith communicate to the Senate, for its consideration, a declaration of the Government of the Grand Duchy of Mecklenburg-Schwerin, bearing date at the city of Schwerin on the 9th December, 1847, acceding substantially to the stipulations of our treaty of commerce and navigation with Hanover of the 10th June, 1846.

Under the twelfth article of this treaty—

The United States agree to extend all the advantages and privileges contained in the stipulations of the present treaty to one or more of the other States of the Germanic Confederation which may wish to accede to them, by means of an official exchange of declarations, provided that such State or States shall confer similar favors upon the said United States to those conferred by the Kingdom of Hanover, and observe and be subject to the same conditions, stipulations, and obligations.

This declaration of the Grand Duchy of Mecklenburg-Schwerin is submitted to the Senate, because in its eighth and eleventh articles it is not the same in terms with the corresponding articles of our treaty with Hanover. The variations, however, are deemed unimportant, while the admission of our "paddy," or rice in the husk, into Mecklenburg-Schwerin free of import duty is an important concession not contained in the Hanoverian treaty. Others might be mentioned, which will appear upon inspection. Still, as the stipulations in the two articles just mentioned in the declaration are not the same as those contained in the corresponding articles of our treaty with Hanover, I deem it proper to submit this declaration to the Senate for their consideration before issuing a proclamation to give it effect.

I also communicate a dispatch from the special agent on the part of the United States, which accompanied the declaration.

JAMES K. POLK.

WASHINGTON, *January 24, 1848.*

To the Senate of the United States:

In compliance with the request of the Senate in their resolution of the 13th instant, I herewith communicate a report from the Secretary of War, with the accompanying correspondence, containing the information called for, in relation to forced contributions in Mexico.

JAMES K. POLK.

WASHINGTON, *January 31, 1848.*

To the Senate of the United States:

I transmit herewith a report from the Secretary of War, containing the information called for in the resolution of the Senate of the 20th instant, in relation to General Orders, No. 376,* issued by General Scott at headquarters, Mexico, bearing date the 15th December last.

JAMES K. POLK.

WASHINGTON, *January 31, 1848.*

To the Senate of the United States:

I communicate herewith a report of the Secretary of War, with the accompanying documents, in answer to the resolution of the Senate of

*Relating to the levying of taxes and duties upon Mexican products, etc., for the support of the United States Army in Mexico.

the 24th instant, requesting to be furnished with "copies of the letters, reports, or other communications which are referred to in the letter of General Zachary Taylor dated at New Orleans, 20th July, 1845, and addressed to the Secretary of War, and which are so referred to as containing the views of General Taylor, previously communicated, in regard to the line proper to be occupied at that time by the troops of the United States; and any similar communication from any officer of the Army on the same subject."

JAMES K. POLK.

WASHINGTON, *February 2, 1848.*

To the Senate of the United States:

In answer to a resolution of the Senate of the 13th January, 1848, calling for information on the subject of the negotiation between the commissioner of the United States and the commissioners of Mexico during the suspension of hostilities after the battles of Contreras and Churubusco, I transmit a report from the Secretary of State and the documents which accompany it.

I deem it proper to add that the invitation from the commissioner of the United States to submit the proposition of boundary referred to in his dispatch (No. 15) of the 4th of September, 1847, herewith communicated, was unauthorized by me, and was promptly disapproved; and this disapproval was communicated to the commissioner of the United States with the least possible delay.

JAMES K. POLK.

WASHINGTON, *February 3, 1848.*

To the House of Representatives of the United States:

In compliance with the request of the House of Representatives contained in their resolution of the 31st of January, 1848, I communicate herewith a report of the Secretary of War, transmitting "a copy of General Taylor's answer* to the letter dated January 27, 1847," addressed to him by the Secretary of War.

JAMES K. POLK.

WASHINGTON, *February 8, 1848.*

To the House of Representatives of the United States:

In compliance with the resolution of the House of Representatives of the 31st January last, I communicate herewith the report of the Secretary of State, accompanied by "the documents and correspondence not already published relating to the final adjustment of the difficulties between Great Britain and the United States concerning rough rice and paddy."

JAMES K. POLK.

*Relating to the publication of a letter from General Taylor to General Gaines concerning the operations of the United States forces in Mexico.

WASHINGTON, *February 10, 1848*.

To the Senate of the United States:

In answer to the resolution of the Senate of the 1st instant, requesting to be informed whether "any taxes, duties, or imposts" have been "laid and collected upon goods and merchandise belonging to citizens of the United States exported by such citizens from the United States to Mexico, and, if so, what is the rate of such duties, and what amount has been collected, and also by what authority of law the same have been laid and collected," I refer the Senate to my annual message of the 7th of December last, in which I informed Congress that orders had been given to our military and naval commanders in Mexico to adopt the policy, as far as practicable, of levying military contributions upon the enemy for the support of our Army.

As one of the modes adopted for levying such contributions, it was stated in that message that—

> On the 31st of March last I caused an order to be issued to our military and naval commanders to levy and collect a military contribution upon all vessels and merchandise which might enter any of the ports of Mexico in our military occupation, and to apply such contributions toward defraying the expenses of the war. By virtue of the right of conquest and the laws of war, the conqueror, consulting his own safety or convenience, may either exclude foreign commerce altogether from all such ports or permit it upon such terms and conditions as he may prescribe. Before the principal ports of Mexico were blockaded by our Navy the revenue derived from import duties under the laws of Mexico was paid into the Mexican treasury. After these ports had fallen into our military possession the blockade was raised and commerce with them permitted upon prescribed terms and conditions. They were opened to the trade of all nations upon the payment of duties more moderate in their amount than those which had been previously levied by Mexico, and the revenue, which was formerly paid into the Mexican treasury, was directed to be collected by our military and naval officers and applied to the use of our Army and Navy. Care was taken that the officers, soldiers, and sailors of our Army and Navy should be exempted from the operations of the order, and, as the merchandise imported upon which the order operated must be consumed by Mexican citizens, the contributions exacted were in effect the seizure of the public revenues of Mexico and the application of them to our own use. In directing this measure the object was to compel the enemy to contribute as far as practicable toward the expenses of the war.

A copy of the order referred to, with the documents accompanying it, has been communicated to Congress.

The order operated upon the vessels and merchandise of all nations, whether belonging to citizens of the United States or to foreigners, arriving in any of the ports in Mexico in our military occupation. The contributions levied were a tax upon Mexican citizens, who were the consumers of the merchandise imported. But for the permit or license granted by the order all vessels and merchandise belonging to citizens of the United States were necessarily excluded from all commerce with Mexico from the commencement of the war. The coasts and ports of Mexico were ordered to be placed under blockade on the day Congress declared the war to exist, and by the laws of nations the blockade applied to the vessels of the United States as well as to the vessels of all other nations. Had no blockade been declared, or had any of our merchant vessels entered any of the ports of Mexico not blockaded, they would have been liable to be seized and condemned as lawful prize by the Mexican authorities. When the order was issued, it operated as a privilege to the vessels of the United States as well as to those of foreign countries to enter the ports held by our arms upon prescribed terms and conditions. It was altogether optional with citizens of the United States and foreigners to avail themselves of the privileges granted upon the terms prescribed.

Citizens of the United States and foreigners have availed themselves of these privileges.

No principle is better established than that a nation at war has the right of shifting the burden off itself and imposing it on the enemy by exacting military contributions. The mode of making such exactions must be left to the discretion of the conqueror, but it should be exercised in a manner conformable to the rules of civilized warfare.

The right to levy these contributions is essential to the successful prosecution of war in an enemy's country, and the practice of nations has been in accordance with this principle. It is as clearly necessary as the right to fight battles, and its exercise is often essential to the subsistence of the army.

Entertaining no doubt that the military right to exclude commerce altogether from the ports of the enemy in our military occupation included the minor right of admitting it under prescribed conditions, it became an important question at the date of the order whether there should be a discrimination between vessels and cargoes belonging to citizens of the United States and vessels and cargoes belonging to neutral nations.

Had the vessels and cargoes belonging to citizens of the United States been admitted without the payment of any duty, while a duty was levied on foreign vessels and cargoes, the object of the order would have been defeated. The whole commerce would have been conducted in American vessels, no contributions could have been collected, and the enemy would have been furnished with goods without the exaction from him of any contribution whatever, and would have been thus benefited by our military occupation, instead of being made to feel the evils of the war. In order to levy these contributions and to make them available for the support of the Army, it became, therefore, absolutely necessary that they should be collected upon imports into Mexican ports, whether in vessels belonging to citizens of the United States or to foreigners.

It was deemed proper to extend the privilege to vessels and their cargoes belonging to neutral nations. It has been my policy since the commencement of the war with Mexico to act justly and liberally toward all neutral nations, and to afford to them no just cause of complaint; and we have seen the good consequences of this policy by the general satisfaction which it has given.

In answer to the inquiry contained in the resolution as to the rates of duties imposed, I refer you to the documents which accompanied my annual message of the 7th of December last, which contain the information.

From the accompanying reports of the Secretary of War and the Secretary of the Navy it will be seen that the contributions have been collected on all vessels and cargoes, whether American or foreign; but the returns to the Departments do not show with exactness the amounts collected on American as distinguishable from foreign vessels and merchandise.

JAMES K. POLK.

WASHINGTON, *February 10, 1848.*

To the House of Representatives of the United States:

In answer to the resolution of the House of Representatives of the 7th instant, I transmit herewith a report from the Secretary of State.

No communication has been received from Mexico "containing propositions from the Mexican authorities or commissioners for a treaty of peace," except the "counter projet" presented by the Mexican commissioners to the commissioners of the United States on the 6th of September last, a copy of which, with the documents accompanying it, I communicated to the Senate of the United States on the 2d instant. A copy of my communication to the Senate embracing this "projet" is herewith communicated.

JAMES K. POLK.

WASHINGTON, *February 14, 1848.*

To the Senate of the United States:

I transmit, for the consideration of the Senate with a view to ratification, a treaty of peace, friendship, commerce, and navigation between the United States and the Republic of Peru, concluded and signed in this city on the 9th instant by the Secretary of State and the minister plenipotentiary of Peru, in behalf of their respective Governments. I also transmit a copy of the correspondence between them which led to the treaty.

JAMES K. POLK.

WASHINGTON, *February 15, 1848.*

To the Senate of the United States:

I communicate herewith a report of the Secretary of War, together with the accompanying report of the Adjutant-General, in answer to the resolution of the Senate of the 7th instant, calling for information in regard to the order or law by virtue of which certain words "in relation to the promotion of cadets have been inserted in the Army Register of the United States, page 45, in the year 1847."

JAMES K. POLK.

WASHINGTON, *February 22, 1848.*

To the Senate of the United States:

I lay before the Senate, for their consideration and advice as to its ratification, a treaty of peace, friendship, limits, and settlement, signed at the city of Guadalupe Hidalgo on the 2d day of February, 1848, by N. P. Trist on the part of the United States, and by plenipotentiaries appointed for that purpose on the part of the Mexican Government.

I deem it to be my duty to state that the recall of Mr. Trist as commissioner of the United States, of which Congress was informed in my annual message, was dictated by a belief that his continued presence with the Army could be productive of no good, but might do much harm by encouraging the delusive hopes and false impressions of the Mexicans, and that his recall would satisfy Mexico that the United States had no terms of peace more favorable to offer. Directions were given that any propositions for peace which Mexico might make should be received and transmitted by the commanding general of our forces to the United States.

It was not expected that Mr. Trist would remain in Mexico or continue in the exercise of the functions of the office of commissioner after he received his letter of recall. He has, however, done so, and the plenipotentiaries of the Government of Mexico, with a knowledge of the fact, have concluded with him this treaty. I have examined it with a full sense of the extraneous circumstances attending its conclusion and signature, which might be objected to, but conforming as it does substantially on the main questions of boundary and indemnity to the terms which our commissioner, when he left the United States in April last, was authorized to offer, and animated as I am by the spirit which has governed all my official conduct toward Mexico, I have felt it to be my duty to submit it to the Senate for their consideration with a view to its ratification.

To the tenth article of the treaty there are serious objections, and no instructions given to Mr. Trist contemplated or authorized its insertion. The public lands within the limits of Texas belong to that State, and this Government has no power to dispose of them or to change the conditions of grants already made. All valid titles to lands within the other territories ceded to the United States will remain unaffected by the change of sovereignty; and I therefore submit that this article should not be ratified as a part of the treaty.

There may be reason to apprehend that the ratification of the "additional and secret article" might unreasonably delay and embarrass the final action on the treaty by Mexico. I therefore submit whether that article should not be rejected by the Senate.

If the treaty shall be ratified as proposed to be amended, the cessions of territory made by it to the United States as indemnity, the provision for the satisfaction of the claims of our injured citizens, and the permanent establishment of the boundary of one of the States of the Union are objects gained of great national importance, while the magnanimous forbearance exhibited toward Mexico, it is hoped, may insure a lasting peace and good neighborhood between the two countries.

I communicate herewith a copy of the instructions given to Mr. Slidell in November, 1845, as envoy extraordinary and minister plenipotentiary to Mexico; a copy of the instructions given to Mr. Trist in April last, and such of the correspondence of the latter with the Department of State, not heretofore communicated to Congress, as will enable the Senate to understand the action which has been had with a view to the adjustment of our difficulties with Mexico.

JAMES K. POLK.

WASHINGTON, *February 28, 1848.*

To the Senate of the United States:

In answer to the resolution of the Senate of the 24th instant, requesting to be informed whether the active operations of the Army of the United States in Mexico have been, and now are, suspended, and, if so, by whose agency and in virtue of what authority such armistice has been effected, I have to state that I have received no information relating to the subject other than that communicated to the Senate with my executive message of the 22d instant.

JAMES K. POLK.

WASHINGTON, *February 29, 1848.*

To the Senate of the United States:

In compliance with the resolution of the Senate passed in "executive session" on yesterday, requesting the President "to communicate to the Senate, *in confidence*, the entire correspondence between Mr. Trist and the Mexican commissioners from the time of his arrival in Mexico until the time of the negotiation of the treaty submitted to the Senate; and also the entire correspondence between Mr. Trist and the Secretary of State in relation to his negotiations with the Mexican commissioners; also all the correspondence between General Scott and the Government and between General Scott and Mr. Trist since the arrival of Mr. Trist in Mexico which may be in the possession of the Government," I transmit herewith the correspondence called for. These documents are very voluminous, and presuming that the Senate desired them in reference to early action on the treaty with Mexico submitted to the consideration of that body by my message of the 22d instant, the originals of several of the letters of Mr. Trist are herewith communicated, in order to save the time which would necessarily be required to make copies of them. These original letters, it is requested, may be returned when the Senate shall have no further use for them.

The letters of Mr. Trist to the Secretary of State, and especially such of them as bear date subsequent to the receipt by him of his letter of recall as commissioner, it will be perceived, contain much matter that is impertinent, irrelevant, and highly exceptionable. Four of these letters, bearing date, respectively, the 29th December, 1847, January 12, January 22, and January 25, 1848, have been received since the treaty was submitted to the Senate. In the latter it is stated that the Mexican commissioners who signed the treaty derived "their full powers, bearing date on the 30th December, 1847, from the President *ad interim* of the Republic (General Anaya), constitutionally elected to that office in November by the Sovereign Constituent Congress" of Mexico. It is impossible that I can approve the conduct of Mr. Trist in disobeying the positive orders of his Government contained in the letter recalling him, or do otherwise than condemn much of the matter with which he has chosen to encumber his voluminous correspondence. Though all of his acts since his recall might have been disavowed by his Government, yet Mexico can take no such exception. The treaty which the Mexican commissioners have negotiated with him, with a full knowledge on their part that he had been recalled from his mission, *is* binding on Mexico.

Looking at the actual condition of Mexico, and believing that if the present treaty be rejected the war will probably be continued at great expense of life and treasure for an indefinite period, and considering that the terms, with the exceptions mentioned in my message of the 22d instant, conform substantially, so far as relates to the main question of boundary, to those authorized by me in April last, I considered it to be my solemn duty to the country, uninfluenced by the exceptionable conduct of Mr. Trist, to submit the treaty to the Senate with a recommendation that it be ratified, with the modifications suggested.

Nothing contained in the letters received from Mr. Trist since it was submitted to the Senate has changed my opinion on the subject.

The resolution also calls for "all the correspondence between General Scott and the Government since the arrival of Mr. Trist in Mexico." A portion of that correspondence, relating to Mr. Trist and his mission, accompanies this communication. The remainder of the "correspondence between General Scott and the Government" relates mainly, if not exclusively, to military operations. A part of it was communicated to Congress with my annual message, and the whole of it will be sent to the Senate if it shall be desired by that body. As coming within the purview of the resolution, I also communicate copies of the letters of the Secretary of War to Major-General Butler in reference to Mr. Trist's remaining at the headquarters of the Army in the assumed exercise of his powers of commissioner.

JAMES K. POLK.

WASHINGTON, *March 2, 1848.*

To the Senate of the United States:

In answer to a resolution of the Senate of the 3d of January, 1848, I communicate herewith a report from the Secretary of State, with the accompanying documents, containing the correspondence of Mr. Wise, late minister of the United States at the Court of Brazil, relating to the subject of the slave trade.

JAMES K. POLK.

WASHINGTON, *March 2, 1848.*

To the Senate of the United States:

I communicate herewith a report of the Secretary of War, with the accompanying documents, in answer to the resolution of the Senate of the 28th February, 1848, requesting the President to communicate "any information he may at any time have received of the desire of any considerable portion of the people of any of the States of Mexico to be incorporated within the limits of any territory to be acquired from the Republic of Mexico, and particularly that he communicate any late proposition which has been made to that effect through General Wool or any other military officer in Mexico."

JAMES K. POLK.

WASHINGTON, *March 7, 1848.*

To the Senate of the United States:

I lay before the Senate a letter of the 12th February, 1848, from N. P. Trist, together with the authenticated map of the United Mexican States and of the plan of the port of San Diego, referred to in the fifth article of the treaty "of peace, friendship, limits, and settlement between the United States of America and the Mexican Republic," which treaty was transmitted to the Senate with my message of the 22d ultimo.

JAMES K. POLK.

WASHINGTON, *March 8, 1848.*

To the Senate of the United States:

In answer to the resolution of the Senate of this date, requesting the President "to inform the Senate of the terms of the authority given to Mr. Trist to draw for the $3,000,000 authorized by the act of the 2d of March, 1847," I communicate herewith a report from the Secretary of State, with the accompanying documents, which contain the information called for.

JAMES K. POLK.

WASHINGTON, *March 8, 1848.*

To the Senate of the United States:

In answer to the resolution of the Senate of this date, requesting the President to communicate to that body, "confidentially, any additional dispatches which may have been received from Mr. Trist, and especially those which are promised by him in his letter to Mr. Buchanan of the 2d of February last, if the same have been received," I have to state that all the dispatches which have been received from Mr. Trist have been heretofore communicated to the Senate.

JAMES K. POLK.

WASHINGTON, *March 10, 1848.*

To the House of Representatives:

I transmit herewith reports from the Secretary of State and the Secretary of War, with the accompanying documents, in compliance with the resolution of the House of Representatives of the 7th February, 1848, requesting the President to communicate to that House "copies of all correspondence between the Secretary of War and Major-General Scott, and between the Secretary of War and Major-General Taylor, and between Major-General Scott and N. P. Trist, late commissioner of the United States to Mexico, and between the latter and Secretary of State, which has not heretofore been published, and the publication of which may not be incompatible with the public interest."

JAMES K. POLK.

To the House of Representatives:

I communicate herewith a copy of the constitution of State government formed by a convention of the people of the Territory of Wisconsin in pursuance of the act of Congress of August 6, 1846, entitled "An act to enable the people of Wisconsin Territory to form a constitution and State government, and for the admission of such State into the Union."

I communicate also the documents accompanying the constitution, which have been transmitted to me by the president of the convention.

JAMES K. POLK.

MARCH 16, 1848.

WASHINGTON, *March 18, 1848.*

To the Senate of the United States:

Sudden and severe indisposition has prevented, and may for an indefinite period continue to prevent, Ambrose H. Sevier, recently appointed commissioner to Mexico, from departing on his mission. The public interest requires that a diplomatic functionary should proceed without delay to Mexico, bearing with him the treaty between the United States and the Mexican Republic, lately ratified, with amendments, by and with the advice and consent of the Senate of the United States. It is deemed proper, with this view, to appoint an associate commissioner, with full powers to act separately or jointly with Mr. Sevier.

I therefore nominate Nathan Clifford, of the State of Maine, to be a commissioner, with the rank of envoy extraordinary and minister plenipotentiary, of the United States to the Mexican Republic.

JAMES K. POLK.

WASHINGTON, *March 22, 1848.*

To the Senate of the United States:

I transmit herewith a report from the Secretary of State, with the accompanying documents, in compliance with the resolution of the Senate of the 24th January, 1848, requesting the President to communicate to the Senate, if not inconsistent with the public interest, the correspondence of Mr. Wise, late minister of the United States at the Court of Brazil, with the Department of State of the United States.

JAMES K. POLK.

WASHINGTON, *March 24, 1848.*

To the Senate of the United States:

In answer to the resolution of the Senate of the 17th instant, requesting the President to transmit to that body "a copy of a dispatch to the United States consul at Monterey, T. O. Larkin, esq., forwarded in November, 1845, by Captain Gillespie, of the Marine Corps, and which was by him destroyed before entering the port of Vera Cruz, if a communication of the same be not, in his opinion, incompatible with the public interests," I communicate herewith a report of the Secretary of State, with a copy of the dispatch referred to. The resolution of the Senate appears to have been passed in legislative session. Entertaining the opinion that the publication of this dispatch at this time will not be "compatible with the public interests," but unwilling to withhold from the Senate information deemed important by that body, I communicate a copy of it to the Senate in executive session.

JAMES K. POLK.

To the House of Representatives of the United States:

I transmit herewith a report from the Secretary of State, with the accompanying documents, in compliance with the resolution of the House of Representatives of the 8th instant, calling for "any correspondence which may have recently taken place with the British Government relative to the adoption of principles of reciprocity in the trade and shipping of the two countries."

JAMES K. POLK.

MARCH 24, 1848.

To the Senate of the United States:

I transmit herewith a report of the Secretary of State, with accompanying documents, in compliance with the resolution of the Senate of the 17th instant, requesting the President to communicate to that body "copies of the correspondence between the minister of the United States at London and any authorities of the British Government in relation to a postal arrangement between the two countries."

JAMES K. POLK.

MARCH 27, 1848.

WASHINGTON, *April 3, 1848.*

To the Senate and House of Representatives of the United States:

I communicate to Congress, for their information, a copy of a dispatch, with the accompanying documents, received at the Department of State from the envoy extraordinary and minister plenipotentiary of the United States at Paris, giving official information of the overthrow of the French Monarchy, and the establishment in its stead of a "provisional government based on republican principles."

This great event occurred suddenly, and was accomplished almost without bloodshed. The world has seldom witnessed a more interesting or sublime spectacle than the peaceful rising of the French people, resolved to secure for themselves enlarged liberty, and to assert, in the majesty of their strength, the great truth that in this enlightened age man is capable of governing himself.

The prompt recognition of the new Government by the representative of the United States at the French Court meets my full and unqualified approbation, and he has been authorized in a suitable manner to make known this fact to the constituted authorities of the French Republic.

Called upon to act upon a sudden emergency, which could not have been anticipated by his instructions, he judged rightly of the feelings and sentiments of his Government and of his countrymen, when, in advance of the diplomatic representatives of other countries, he was the first to recognize, so far as it was in his power, the free Government established by the French people.

The policy of the United States has ever been that of nonintervention in the domestic affairs of other countries, leaving to each to establish the form of government of its own choice. While this wise policy will be maintained toward France, now suddenly transformed from a monarchy into a republic, all our sympathies are naturally enlisted on the side of a great people who, imitating our example, have resolved to be free. That such sympathy should exist on the part of the people of the United States with the friends of free government in every part of the world, and especially in France, is not remarkable. We can never forget that France was our early friend in our eventful Revolution, and generously aided us in shaking off a foreign yoke and becoming a free and independent people.

We have enjoyed the blessings of our system of well-regulated self-government for near three-fourths of a century, and can properly appreciate its value. Our ardent and sincere congratulations are extended to the patriotic people of France upon their noble and thus far successful efforts to found for their future government liberal institutions similar to our own.

It is not doubted that under the benign influence of free institutions the enlightened statesmen of republican France will find it to be for her true interests and permanent glory to cultivate with the United States the most liberal principles of international intercourse and commercial reciprocity, whereby the happiness and prosperity of both nations will be promoted.

JAMES K. POLK.

WASHINGTON, *April 7, 1848.*

To the Senate of the United States:

In answer to a resolution of the Senate of the 29th of March, 1848, I transmit herewith a report of the Secretary of War, with the accompanying documents, containing the information called for, relative to the services of Captain McClellan's company of Florida volunteers in the year 1840.

JAMES K. POLK.

WASHINGTON, *April 7, 1848.*

To the Senate of the United States:

I communicate herewith a report of the Secretary of War, transmitting a copy of the proceedings of the general court-martial in the case of Lieutenant-Colonel Frémont, called for by a resolution of the Senate of the 29th February, 1848.

JAMES K. POLK.

WASHINGTON, *April 10, 1848.*

To the Senate of the United States:

I communicate herewith a report of the Secretary of State, together with a copy of the correspondence between the Secretary of State and "the Brazilian chargé d'affaires at Washington," called for by the resolution of the Senate of the 28th of March, 1848.

JAMES K. POLK.

WASHINGTON, *April 13, 1848.*

To the Senate of the United States:

In answer to the resolution of the Senate of the 28th of March, 1848, I communicate herewith a report of the Secretary of War, transmitting a report of the head of the Ordnance Bureau, with the accompanying papers, relative to "the repeating firearms invented by Samuel Colt."

Such is the favorable opinion entertained of the value of this arm, particularly for a mounted corps, that the Secretary of War, as will be seen by his report, has contracted with Mr. Colt for 2,000 of his pistols. He has offered to contract for an additional number at liberal prices, but the inventor is unwilling to furnish them at the prices offered.

The invention for the construction of these arms being patented, the United States can not manufacture them at the Government armories without a previous purchase of the right so to do. The right to use his patent by the United States the inventor is unwilling to dispose of at a price deemed reasonable.

JAMES K. POLK.

WASHINGTON, *April 25, 1848.*

To the House of Representatives of the United States:

I communicate herewith a report of the Secretary of War, with accompanying documents, submitted by him as embracing the papers and the correspondence* between the Secretary of War and Major-General Scott, called for by the resolution of the House of Representatives of the 17th instant.

JAMES K. POLK.

WASHINGTON, *April 29, 1848.*

To the Senate and House of Representatives of the United States:

I submit for the consideration of Congress several communications received at the Department of State from Mr. Justo Sierra, commissioner of Yucatan, and also a communication from the Governor of that State, representing the condition of extreme suffering to which their country has been reduced by an insurrection of the Indians within its limits, and asking the aid of the United States.

These communications present a case of human suffering and misery which can not fail to excite the sympathies of all civilized nations. From these and other sources of information it appears that the Indians of Yucatan are waging a war of extermination against the white race. In this civil war they spare neither age nor sex, but put to death, indiscriminately, all who fall within their power. The inhabitants, panic stricken and destitute of arms, are flying before their savage pursuers toward the coast, and their expulsion from their country or their extermination would seem to be inevitable unless they can obtain assistance from abroad.

In this condition they have, through their constituted authorities, implored the aid of this Government to save them from destruction, offering in case this should be granted to transfer the "dominion and sovereignty of the peninsula" to the United States. Similar appeals for aid and protection have been made to the Spanish and the English Governments.

Whilst it is not my purpose to recommend the adoption of any measure with a view to the acquisition of the "dominion and sovereignty"

* Relating to the conduct of the war in Mexico and the recall of General Scott from the command of the Army.

over Yucatan, yet, according to our established policy, we could not consent to a transfer of this "dominion and sovereignty" either to Spain, Great Britain, or any other European power. In the language of President Monroe in his message of December, 1823—

> We should consider any attempt on their part to extend their system to any portion of this hemisphere as dangerous to our peace and safety.

In my annual message of December, 1845, I declared that—

> Near a quarter of a century ago the principle was distinctly announced to the world, in the annual message of one of my predecessors, that "the American continents, by the free and independent condition which they have assumed and maintain, are henceforth not to be considered as subjects for future colonization by any European powers." This principle will apply with greatly increased force should any European power attempt to establish any new colony in North America. In the existing circumstances of the world, the present is deemed a proper occasion to reiterate and reaffirm the principle avowed by Mr. Monroe, and to state my cordial concurrence in its wisdom and sound policy. The reassertion of this principle, especially in reference to North America, is at this day but the promulgation of a policy which no European power should cherish the disposition to resist. Existing rights of every European nation should be respected, but it is due alike to our safety and our interests that the efficient protection of our laws should be extended over our whole territorial limits, and that it should be distinctly announced to the world as our settled policy that no future European colony or dominion shall with our consent be planted or established on any part of the North American continent.

Our own security requires that the established policy thus announced should guide our conduct, and this applies with great force to the peninsula of Yucatan. It is situate in the Gulf of Mexico, on the North American continent, and, from its vicinity to Cuba, to the capes of Florida, to New Orleans, and, indeed, to our whole southwestern coast, it would be dangerous to our peace and security if it should become a colony of any European nation.

We have now authentic information that if the aid asked from the United States be not granted such aid will probably be obtained from some European power, which may hereafter assert a claim to "dominion and sovereignty" over Yucatan.

Our existing relations with Yucatan are of a peculiar character, as will be perceived from the note of the Secretary of State to their commissioner dated on the 24th of December last, a copy of which is herewith transmitted. Yucatan has never declared her independence, and we treated her as a State of the Mexican Republic. For this reason we have never officially received her commissioner; but whilst this is the case, we have to a considerable extent recognized her as a neutral in our war with Mexico. Whilst still considering Yucatan as a portion of Mexico, if we had troops to spare for this purpose I would deem it proper, during the continuance of the war with Mexico, to occupy and hold military possession of her territory and to defend the white inhabitants against the incursions of the Indians, in the same way that we have employed our troops in other States of the Mexican Republic in our possession in repelling the attacks of savages upon the inhabitants who have maintained their neutrality in the war. But, unfortunately, we can not at the present time, without serious danger, withdraw our forces from other portions of the Mexican territory now in our occupation and send them to Yucatan. All that can be done under existing circumstances is to employ our naval forces in the Gulf not required at other points to afford them relief; but it is not to be expected that any adequate protection can thus be afforded, as the operations of such naval forces must of necessity be confined to the coast.

I have considered it proper to communicate the information contained in the accompanying correspondence, and I submit to the wisdom of Congress to adopt such measures as in their judgment may be expedient to prevent Yucatan from becoming a colony of any European power, which in no event could be permitted by the United States, and at the same time to rescue the white race from extermination or expulsion from their country.

JAMES K. POLK.

WASHINGTON, *May 5, 1848.*

To the Senate of the United States:

I communicate herewith a report from the Secretary of State, together with the correspondence "between the Secretary of State and Don Justo Sierra, the representative of Yucatan," called for by the resolution of the Senate of the 4th instant.

I communicate also additional documents relating to the same subject.

JAMES K. POLK.

WASHINGTON, *May 8, 1848.*

To the Senate of the United States:

I communicate herewith a report of the Secretary of War, together with the accompanying documents, in compliance with the resolution of the Senate of the 25th April, requesting the President to cause to be sent to the Senate a copy of the opinion of the Attorney-General, with copies of the accompanying papers, on the claim made by the Choctaw Indians for $5,000, with interest thereon from the date of the transfer, being the difference between the cost of the stock and the par value thereof transferred to them by the Chickasaws under the convention of the 17th of January, 1837.

JAMES K. POLK.

WASHINGTON, *May 9, 1848.*

To the Senate of the United States:

In answer to the resolution of the Senate of the 8th instant, requesting further information in relation to the condition of Yucatan, I transmit herewith a report of the Secretary of the Navy, with the accompanying copies of communications from officers of the Navy on the subject.

JAMES K. POLK.

WASHINGTON, *May 9, 1848*.

To the Senate of the United States:

I herewith communicate to the Senate, for their consideration with a view to its ratification, a convention for the extension of certain stipulations* contained in the treaty of commerce and navigation of August 27, 1829, between the United States and Austria, concluded and signed in this city on the 8th instant by the respective plenipotentiaries.

JAMES K. POLK.

WASHINGTON, *May 15, 1848*.

To the Senate of the United States:

I communicate herewith a report from the Secretary of the Navy, together with the accompanying documents, in compliance with the resolution of the Senate of the 13th instant, requesting information as to the measures taken for the protection of the white population of Yucatan by the naval forces of the United States.

JAMES K. POLK.

WASHINGTON, *May 19, 1848*.

To the Senate and House of Representatives of the United States:

I transmit for the information of Congress a communication from the Secretary of War and a report from the Commissioner of Indian Affairs, showing the result of the settlement required by the treaty of August, 1846, with the Cherokees, and the appropriations requisite to carry the provisions of that treaty into effect.

JAMES K. POLK.

WASHINGTON, *May 29, 1848*.

To the Senate and House of Representatives of the United States:

I lay before Congress the accompanying memorial and papers, which have been transmitted to me, by a special messenger employed for that purpose, by the governor and legislative assembly of Oregon Territory, who constitute the temporary government which the inhabitants of that distant region of our country have, from the necessity of their condition, organized for themselves. The memorialists are citizens of the United States. They express ardent attachment to their native land, and in their present perilous and distressed situation they earnestly invoke the aid and protection of their Government.

They represent that "the proud and powerful tribes of Indians" residing in their vicinity have recently raised "the war whoop and crimsoned their tomahawks in the blood of their citizens;" that they apprehend that "many of the powerful tribes inhabiting the upper valley of the

*Relating to disposal of property, etc.

Columbia have formed an alliance for the purpose of carrying on hostilities against their settlements;" that the number of the white population is far inferior to that of the savages; that they are deficient in arms and money, and fear that they do not possess strength to repel the "attack of so formidable a foe and protect their families and property from violence and rapine." They conclude their appeal to the Government of the United States for relief by declaring:

If it be at all the intention of our honored parent to spread her guardian wing over her sons and daughters in Oregon, she surely will not refuse to do it now, when they are struggling with all the ills of a weak and temporary government, and when perils are daily thickening around them and preparing to burst upon their heads. When the ensuing summer's sun shall have dispelled the snow from the mountains, we shall look with glowing hope and restless anxiety for the coming of your laws and your arms.

In my message of the 5th of August, 1846, communicating "a copy of the convention for the settlement and adjustment of the Oregon boundary," I recommended to Congress that "provision should be made by law, at the earliest practicable period, for the organization of a Territorial government in Oregon." In my annual message of December, 1846, and again in December, 1847, this recommendation was repeated.

The population of Oregon is believed to exceed 12,000 souls, and it is known that it will be increased by a large number of emigrants during the present season. The facts set forth in the accompanying memorial and papers show that the dangers to which our fellow-citizens are exposed are so imminent that I deem it to be my duty again to impress on Congress the strong claim which the inhabitants of that distant country have to the benefit of our laws and to the protection of our Government.

I therefore again invite the attention of Congress to the subject, and recommend that laws be promptly passed establishing a Territorial government and granting authority to raise an adequate volunteer force for the defense and protection of its inhabitants. It is believed that a regiment of mounted men, with such additional force as may be raised in Oregon, will be sufficient to afford the required protection. It is recommended that the forces raised for this purpose should engage to serve for twelve months, unless sooner discharged. No doubt is entertained that, with proper inducements in land bounties, such a force can be raised in a short time. Upon the expiration of their service many of them will doubtless desire to remain in the country and settle upon the land which they may receive as bounty. It is deemed important that provision be made for the appointment of a suitable number of Indian agents to reside among the various tribes in Oregon, and that appropriations be made to enable them to treat with these tribes with a view to restore and preserve peace between them and the white inhabitants.

Should the laws recommended be promptly passed, the measures for their execution may be completed during the present season, and before the severity of winter will interpose obstacles in crossing the Rocky

Mountains. If not promptly passed, a delay of another year will be the consequence, and may prove destructive to the white settlements in Oregon.

JAMES K. POLK.

WASHINGTON, *May 31, 1848.*

To the Senate of the United States:

I transmit herewith reports from the Secretary of State and the Secretary of the Navy, with the accompanying correspondence, which contains the information called for by the Senate in their resolution of the 30th instant, relating to the existing condition of affairs in Yucatan.

JAMES K. POLK.

WASHINGTON, *June 12, 1848.*

To the Senate of the United States:

I communicate herewith a report of the Secretary of State, together with the accompanying documents, in compliance with the resolution of the Senate of the 31st ultimo, "requesting the President to communicate the correspondence not heretofore communicated between the Secretary of State and the minister of the United States at Paris since the recent change in the Government of France."

JAMES K. POLK.

WASHINGTON, *June 23, 1848.*

To the Senate of the United States:

I communicate herewith a report of the Secretary of War, with the accompanying documents, in answer to a resolution of the Senate of the 21st instant, requesting the President to communicate to the Senate, in executive session, as early as practicable, the papers heretofore in the possession of the Senate and returned to the War Department, together with a statement from the Adjutant-General of the Army as to the merits or demerits of the claim of James W. Schaumburg to be restored to rank in the Army.

JAMES K. POLK.

WASHINGTON, *July 5, 1848.*

To the Senate of the United States:

I submit herewith, for such action as the Senate shall deem proper, a report of the Secretary of War, suggesting a discrepancy between the resolutions of the Senate of the 15th and the 27th ultimo, advising and consenting to certain appointments and promotions in the Army of the United States.

JAMES K. POLK.

WAR DEPARTMENT,
Washington, July 1, 1848.

The PRESIDENT OF THE UNITED STATES.

SIR: I have the honor to submit herewith a report from the Adjutant-General of the Army, inviting attention to a difficulty arising from the terms of certain confirmations made by the resolutions of the Senate of the 15th and 27th ultimo, the former advising and consenting to the reappointment of Captain Edward Deas, Fourth Artillery, who had been dismissed the service, and the latter advising and consenting to the promotion of First Lieutenant Joseph Roberts to be captain, *vice* Deas, dismissed, and Second Lieutenant John A. Brown to be first lieutenant, *vice* Roberts, promoted.

Very respectfully, your obedient servant,

W. L. MARCY,
Secretary of War.

ADJUTANT-GENERAL'S OFFICE,
Washington, June 29, 1848.

Hon. W. L. MARCY,
Secretary of War.

SIR: In a list of confirmations of regular promotions just received from the Senate, dated the 27th instant, it is observed, under the heading "Fourth Regiment of Artillery," that First Lieutenant Joseph Roberts is confirmed as a captain, *vice* Deas, dismissed, and Second Lieutenant John A. Brown as first lieutenant, *vice* Roberts, promoted.

The President, having decided to reinstate Captain Deas, nominated him for restoration to the Senate the 12th instant, withdrawing, as the records show, at the same time the names of Lieutenants Roberts and Brown. This nomination of Captain Deas was confirmed the 15th of June, and he has been commissioned accordingly. I respectfully bring this matter to your notice under the impression that as the resolutions of June 15 and June 27 conflict with each other it may be the wish of the Senate to reconcile them by rescinding that portion of the latter which advises and consents to the promotions of Lieutenants Roberts and Brown.

Respectfully submitted.

R. JONES, *Adjutant-General.*

WASHINGTON, *July 6, 1848.*

To the Senate and House of Representatives of the United States:

I lay before Congress copies of a treaty of peace, friendship, limits, and settlement between the United States and the Mexican Republic, the ratifications of which were duly exchanged at the city of Queretaro, in Mexico, on the 30th day of May, 1848.

The war in which our country was reluctantly involved, in the necessary vindication of the national rights and honor, has been thus terminated, and I congratulate Congress and our common constituents upon the restoration of an honorable peace.

The extensive and valuable territories ceded by Mexico to the United States constitute indemnity for the past, and the brilliant achievements and signal successes of our arms will be a guaranty of security for the future, by convincing all nations that our rights must be respected. The results of the war with Mexico have given to the United States a national character abroad which our country never before enjoyed. Our power and our resources have become known and are respected throughout the world, and we shall probably be saved from the necessity of engaging in another foreign war for a long series of years. It is a subject of congratulation that we have passed through a war of more than two years' duration with the business of the country uninterrupted, with our resources unexhausted, and the public credit unimpaired.

I communicate for the information of Congress the accompanying documents and correspondence, relating to the negotiation and ratification of the treaty.

Before the treaty can be fully executed on the part of the United States legislation will be required.

It will be proper to make the necessary appropriations for the payment of the $12,000,000 stipulated by the twelfth article to be paid to Mexico in four equal annual installments. Three million dollars were appropriated by the act of March 3, 1847, and that sum was paid to the Mexican Government after the exchange of the ratifications of the treaty.

The fifth article of the treaty provides that—

> In order to designate the boundary line with due precision upon authoritative maps, and to establish upon the ground landmarks which shall show the limits of both Republics as described in the present article, the two Governments shall each appoint a commissioner and a surveyor, who, before the expiration of one year from the date of the exchange of ratifications of this treaty, shall meet at the port of San Diego and proceed to run and mark the said boundary in its whole course to the mouth of the Rio Bravo del Norte.

It will be necessary that provision should be made by law for the appointment of a commissioner and surveyor on the part of the United States to act in conjunction with a commissioner and surveyor appointed by Mexico in executing the stipulations of this article.

It will be proper also to provide by law for the appointment of a "board of commissioners" to adjudicate and decide upon all claims of our citizens against the Mexican Government, which by the treaty have been assumed by the United States.

New Mexico and Upper California have been ceded by Mexico to the United States, and now constitute a part of our country. Embracing nearly ten degrees of latitude, lying adjacent to the Oregon Territory, and extending from the Pacific Ocean to the Rio Grande, a mean distance of nearly 1,000 miles, it would be difficult to estimate the value of these possessions to the United States. They constitute of themselves a country large enough for a great empire, and their acquisition is second only in importance to that of Louisiana in 1803. Rich in mineral and agricultural resources, with a climate of great salubrity, they embrace the most important ports on the whole Pacific coast of the continent of North America. The possession of the ports of San Diego and Monterey and the Bay of San Francisco will enable the United States to command the already valuable and rapidly increasing commerce of the Pacific. The number of our whale ships alone now employed in that sea exceeds 700, requiring more than 20,000 seamen to navigate them, while the capital invested in this particular branch of commerce is estimated at not less than $40,000,000. The excellent harbors of Upper California will under our flag afford security and repose to our commercial marine, and American mechanics will soon furnish ready means of shipbuilding and repair, which are now so much wanted in that distant sea.

By the acquisition of these possessions we are brought into immediate proximity with the west coast of America, from Cape Horn to the Russian possessions north of Oregon, with the islands of the Pacific Ocean, and by a direct voyage in steamers we will be in less than thirty days of Canton and other ports of China.

In this vast region, whose rich resources are soon to be developed by American energy and enterprise, great must be the augmentation of our commerce, and with it new and profitable demands for mechanic labor in all its branches and new and valuable markets for our manufactures and agricultural products.

While the war has been conducted with great humanity and forbearance and with complete success on our part, the peace has been concluded on terms the most liberal and magnanimous to Mexico. In her hands the territories now ceded had remained, and, it is believed, would have continued to remain, almost unoccupied, and of little value to her or to any other nation, whilst as a part of our Union they will be productive of vast benefits to the United States, to the commercial world, and the general interests of mankind.

The immediate establishment of Territorial governments and the extension of our laws over these valuable possessions are deemed to be not only important, but indispensable to preserve order and the due administration of justice within their limits, to afford protection to the inhabitants, and to facilitate the development of the vast resources and wealth which their acquisition has added to our country.

The war with Mexico having terminated, the power of the Executive to establish or to continue temporary civil governments over these territories, which existed under the laws of nations whilst they were regarded as conquered provinces in our military occupation, has ceased. By their cession to the United States Mexico has no longer any power over them, and until Congress shall act the inhabitants will be without any organized government. Should they be left in this condition, confusion and anarchy will be likely to prevail.

Foreign commerce to a considerable amount is now carried on in the ports of Upper California, which will require to be regulated by our laws. As soon as our system shall be extended over this commerce, a revenue of considerable amount will be at once collected, and it is not doubted that it will be annually increased. For these and other obvious reasons I deem it to be my duty earnestly to recommend the action of Congress on the subject at the present session.

In organizing governments over these territories, fraught with such vast advantages to every portion of our Union, I invoke that spirit of concession, conciliation, and compromise in your deliberations in which the Constitution was framed, in which it should be administered, and which is so indispensable to preserve and perpetuate the harmony and union of the States. We should never forget that this Union of confederated States was established and cemented by kindred blood and by the common toils, sufferings, dangers, and triumphs of all its parts, and has been the ever-augmenting source of our national greatness and of all our blessings.

There has, perhaps, been no period since the warning so impressively given to his countrymen by Washington to guard against geographical divisions and sectional parties which appeals with greater force than the present to the patriotic, sober-minded, and reflecting of all parties and of all sections of our country. Who can calculate the value of our glorious Union? It is a model and example of free government to all the world, and is the star of hope and haven of rest to the oppressed of every clime. By its preservation we have been rapidly advanced as a nation to a height of strength, power, and happiness without a parallel in the history of the world. As we extend its blessings over new regions, shall we be so unwise as to endanger its existence by geographical divisions and dissensions?

With a view to encourage the early settlement of these distant possessions, I recommend that liberal grants of the public lands be secured to all our citizens who have settled or may in a limited period settle within their limits.

In execution of the provisions of the treaty, orders have been issued to our military and naval forces to evacuate without delay the Mexican Provinces, cities, towns, and fortified places in our military occupation, and which are not embraced in the territories ceded to the United States. The Army is already on its way to the United States. That portion of it, as well regulars as volunteers, who engaged to serve during the war with Mexico will be discharged as soon as they can be transported or marched to convenient points in the vicinity of their homes. A part of the Regular Army will be employed in New Mexico and Upper California to afford protection to the inhabitants and to guard our interests in these territories.

The old Army, as it existed before the commencement of the war with Mexico, especially if authority be given to fill up the rank and file of the several corps to the maximum number authorized during the war, it is believed, will be a sufficient force to be retained in service during a period of peace. A few additional officers in the line and staff of the Army have been authorized, and these, it is believed, will be necessary in the peace establishment, and should be retained in the service.

The number of the general officers may be reduced, as vacancies occur by the casualties of the service, to what it was before the war.

While the people of other countries who live under forms of government less free than our own have been for ages oppressed by taxation to support large standing armies in periods of peace, our experience has

STORMING OF CHAPULTEPEC

THE BATTLE OF CHAPULTEPEC

September 12th and 13th, 1847

By means of ladders Scott's gallant storming-party, under severe fire all the time, swarmed over the walls of the castle of Chapultepec. It stood 150 feet above the plain on the summit of a hill, and in addition to the walls of the fortress proper, the Americans had to make their way through two other walls, which surrounded the entire building and were from twelve to fifteen feet high, with a ten-foot interval between them. Over their heads screamed the projectiles from the American artillery, while the Mexican gunners, under the direction of French experts, replied in kind. But after penetrating the outer walls, the troops rushed up their ladders into the fort itself, and after the kind of fighting shown in the picture, the Mexican flag came down and in its place fluttered Old Glory.

The full account is given in the article entitled "Chapultepec (Mexico), Battle of," in the Encyclopedic Index, and a presidential reference to the event is noted just below.

shown that such establishments are unnecessary in a republic. Our standing army is to be found in the bosom of society. It is composed of free citizens, who are ever ready to take up arms in the service of their country when an emergency requires it. Our experience in the war just closed fully confirms the opinion that such an army may be raised upon a few weeks' notice, and that our citizen soldiers are equal to any troops in the world. No reason, therefore, is perceived why we should enlarge our land forces and thereby subject the Treasury to an annual increased charge. Sound policy requires that we should avoid the creation of a large standing army in a period of peace. No public exigency requires it. Such armies are not only expensive and unnecessary, but may become dangerous to liberty.

Besides making the necessary legislative provisions for the execution of the treaty and the establishment of Territorial governments in the ceded country, we have, upon the restoration of peace, other important duties to perform. Among these I regard none as more important than the adoption of proper measures for the speedy extinguishment of the national debt. It is against sound policy and the genius of our institutions that a public debt should be permitted to exist a day longer than the means of the Treasury will enable the Government to pay it off. We should adhere to the wise policy laid down by President Washington, of "avoiding likewise the accumulation of debt, not only by shunning occasions of expense, but by vigorous exertions in time of peace to discharge the debts which unavoidable wars have occasioned, not ungenerously throwing upon posterity the burthen which we ourselves ought to bear."

At the commencement of the present Administration the public debt amounted to $17,788,799.62. In consequence of the war with Mexico, it has been necessarily increased, and now amounts to $65,778,450.41, including the stock and Treasury notes which may yet be issued under the act of January 28, 1847, and the $16,000,000 loan recently negotiated under the act of March 31, 1848.

In addition to the amount of the debt, the treaty stipulates that $12,000,000 shall be paid to Mexico, in four equal annual installments of $3,000,000 each, the first of which will fall due on the 30th day of May, 1849. The treaty also stipulates that the United States shall "assume and pay" to our own citizens "the claims already liquidated and decided against the Mexican Republic," and "all claims not heretofore decided against the Mexican Government," "to an amount not exceeding three and a quarter millions of dollars." The "liquidated" claims of citizens of the United States against Mexico, as decided by the joint board of commissioners under the convention between the United States and Mexico of the 11th of April, 1839, amounted to $2,026,139.68. This sum was payable in twenty equal annual installments. Three of them have been paid to the claimants by the Mexican Government and two by the

United States, leaving to be paid of the principal of the liquidated amount assumed by the United States the sum of $1,519,604.76, together with the interest thereon. These several amounts of "liquidated" and unliquidated claims assumed by the United States, it is believed, may be paid as they fall due out of the accruing revenue, without the issue of stock or the creation of any additional public debt.

I can not too strongly recommend to Congress the importance of husbanding all our national resources, of limiting the public expenditures to necessary objects, and of applying all the surplus at any time in the Treasury to the redemption of the debt. I recommend that authority be vested in the Executive by law to anticipate the period of reimbursement of such portion of the debt as may not be now redeemable, and to purchase it at par, or at the premium which it may command in the market, in all cases in which that authority has not already been granted. A premium has been obtained by the Government on much the larger portion of the loans, and if when the Government becomes a purchaser of its own stock it shall command a premium in the market, it will be sound policy to pay it rather than to pay the semiannual interest upon it. The interest upon the debt, if the outstanding Treasury notes shall be funded, from the end of the last fiscal year until it shall fall due and be redeemable will be very nearly equal to the principal, which must itself be ultimately paid.

Without changing or modifying the present tariff of duties, so great has been the increase of our commerce under its benign operation that the revenue derived from that source and from the sales of the public lands will, it is confidently believed, enable the Government to discharge annually several millions of the debt and at the same time possess the means of meeting necessary appropriations for all other proper objects. Unless Congress shall authorize largely increased expenditures for objects not of absolute necessity, the whole public debt existing before the Mexican war and that created during its continuance may be paid off without any increase of taxation on the people long before it falls due.

Upon the restoration of peace we should adopt the policy suited to a state of peace. In doing this the earliest practicable payment of the public debt should be a cardinal principle of action. Profiting by the experience of the past, we should avoid the errors into which the country was betrayed shortly after the close of the war with Great Britain in 1815. In a few years after that period a broad and latitudinous construction of the powers of the Federal Government unfortunately received but too much countenance. Though the country was burdened with a heavy public debt, large, and in some instances unnecessary and extravagant, expenditures were authorized by Congress. The consequence was that the payment of the debt was postponed for more than twenty years, and even then it was only accomplished by the stern will and unbending policy of President Jackson, who made its payment a leading measure of his Administration. He resisted the attempts which were made to divert the public money from that great object and apply it in wasteful and extravagant expenditures for other objects, some of them of more than doubtful constitutional authority and expediency.

If the Government of the United States shall observe a proper economy in its expenditures, and be confined in its action to the conduct of our foreign relations and to the few general objects of its care enumerated in the Constitution, leaving all municipal and local legislation to the States, our greatness as a nation, in moral and physical power and in wealth and resources, can not be calculated.

By pursuing this policy oppressive measures, operating unequally and unjustly upon sections and classes, will be avoided, and the people, having no cause of complaint, will pursue their own interests under the blessings of equal laws and the protection of a just and paternal Government. By abstaining from the exercise of all powers not clearly conferred, the current of our glorious Union, now numbering thirty States, will be strengthened as we grow in age and increase in population, and our future destiny will be without a parallel or example in the history of nations.

JAMES K. POLK.

WASHINGTON, *July 7, 1848.*

To the Senate of the United States:

For the reasons mentioned in the accompanying letter of the Secretary of War, I ask that the date in the promotion of Captain W. J. Hardee, Second Dragoons, to be major by brevet for gallant and meritorious conduct in the affair at Madellin, Mexico, be changed to the 25th of March, 1847, the day on which the action occurred.

JAMES K. POLK.

WAR DEPARTMENT,
Washington, July 7, 1848.

The PRESIDENT OF THE UNITED STATES.

SIR: Captain W. J. Hardee, Second Dragoons, has been promoted to be major by brevet for gallant and meritorious conduct in the affair at Madellin, Mexico, to date from the 26th of March, 1847. As this affair took place on the 25th of that month, I respectfully recommend that the Senate be asked to change the date of Captain Hardee's brevet rank so as to correspond with the date of the action, to wit, the 25th of March, 1847. Brevets which have been conferred upon other officers in the same affair take the latter date.

Very respectfully, your obedient servant,

W. L. MARCY,
Secretary of War.

WASHINGTON, *July 12, 1848.*

To the Senate of the United States:

In compliance with a resolution of the Senate, of the 21st June, 1848, I herewith communicate to the Senate a report of the Secretary of War, with the accompanying documents, containing the proceedings of a court of inquiry which convened at Saltillo, Mexico, January 12, 1848, and which was instituted for the purpose of obtaining full information relative to an alleged mutiny in the camp of Buena Vista, Mexico, on or about the 15th of August, 1847.

JAMES K. POLK.

WASHINGTON, *July 14, 1848.*

To the Senate of the United States:

In compliance with the resolution of the Senate of July 13, 1848, I transmit herewith a report of the Secretary of War and accompanying documents, containing all the proceedings of the two courts of inquiry in the case of Major-General Pillow, the one commenced and terminated in Mexico, the other commenced in Mexico and terminated in the United States.

JAMES K. POLK.

WASHINGTON, *July 24, 1848.*

To the House of Representatives of the United States:

In answer to the resolutions of the House of Representatives of the 10th instant, requesting information in relation to New Mexico and California, I communicate herewith reports from the Secretary of State, the Secretary of the Treasury, the Secretary of War, and the Secretary of the Navy, with the documents which accompany the same. These reports and documents contain information upon the several points of inquiry embraced by the resolutions. "The proper limits and boundaries of New Mexico and California" are delineated on the map referred to in the late treaty with Mexico, an authentic copy of which is herewith transmitted; and all the additional information upon that subject, and also the most reliable information in respect to the population of these respective Provinces, which is in the possession of the Executive will be found in the accompanying report of the Secretary of State.

The resolutions request information in regard to the existence of civil governments in New Mexico and California, their "form and character," by "whom instituted," by "what authority," and how they are "maintained and supported."

In my message of December 22, 1846, in answer to a resolution of the House of Representatives calling for information "in relation to the establishment or organization of civil government in any portion of the territory of Mexico which has or might be taken possession of by the Army or Navy of the United States," I communicated the orders which had been given to the officers of our Army and Navy, and stated the general authority upon which temporary military governments had been established over the conquered portion of Mexico then in our military occupation.

The temporary governments authorized were instituted by virtue of the rights of war. The power to declare war against a foreign country, and to prosecute it according to the general laws of war, as sanctioned by civilized nations, it will not be questioned, exists under our Constitution. When Congress has declared that war exists with a foreign nation, "the general laws of war apply to our situation," and it becomes the duty of the President, as the constitutional "Commander in Chief of the Army and Navy of the United States," to prosecute it.

In prosecuting a foreign war thus duly declared by Congress, we have the right, by "conquest and military occupation," to acquire possession of the territories of the enemy, and, during the war, to "exercise the fullest rights of sovereignty over it." The sovereignty of the enemy is in such case "suspended," and his laws can "no longer be rightfully enforced" over the conquered territory "or be obligatory upon the inhabitants who remain and submit to the conqueror. By the surrender the inhabitants pass under a temporary allegiance" to the conqueror, and are "bound by such laws, and such only, as" he may choose to recognize and impose. "From the nature of the case, no other laws could be obligatory upon them, for where there is no protection or allegiance or sovereignty there can be no claim to obedience." These are well-established principles of the laws of war, as recognized and practiced by civilized nations, and they have been sanctioned by the highest judicial tribunal of our own country.

The orders and instructions issued to the officers of our Army and Navy, applicable to such portions of the Mexican territory as had been or might be conquered by our arms, were in strict conformity to these principles. They were, indeed, ameliorations of the rigors of war upon which we might have insisted. They substituted for the harshness of military rule something of the mildness of civil government, and were not only the exercise of no excess of power, but were a relaxation in favor of the peaceable inhabitants of the conquered territory who had submitted to our authority, and were alike politic and humane.

It is from the same source of authority that we derive the unquestioned right, after the war has been declared by Congress, to blockade the ports and coasts of the enemy, to capture his towns, cities, and provinces, and to levy contributions upon him for the support of our Army. Of the same character with these is the right to subject to our temporary military government the conquered territories of our enemy. They are all belligerent rights, and their exercise is as essential to the successful prosecution of a foreign war as the right to fight battles.

New Mexico and Upper California were among the territories conquered and occupied by our forces, and such temporary governments were established over them. They were established by the officers of our Army and Navy in command, in pursuance of the orders and instructions accompanying my message to the House of Representatives of

December 22, 1846. In their form and detail, as at first established, they exceeded in some respects, as was stated in that message, the authority which had been given, and instructions for the correction of the error were issued in dispatches from the War and Navy Departments of the 11th of January, 1847, copies of which are herewith transmitted. They have been maintained and supported out of the military exactions and contributions levied upon the enemy, and no part of the expense has been paid out of the Treasury of the United States.

In the routine of duty some of the officers of the Army and Navy who first established temporary governments in California and New Mexico have been succeeded in command by other officers, upon whom light duties devolved; and the agents employed or designated by them to conduct the temporary governments have also, in some instances, been superseded by others. Such appointments for temporary civil duty during our military occupation were made by the officers in command in the conquered territories, respectively.

On the conclusion and exchange of ratifications of a treaty of peace with Mexico, which was proclaimed on the 4th instant, these temporary governments necessarily ceased to exist. In the instructions to establish a temporary government over New Mexico, no distinction was made between that and the other Provinces of Mexico which might be conquered and held in our military occupation.

The Province of New Mexico, according to its ancient boundaries, as claimed by Mexico, lies on both sides of the Rio Grande. That part of it on the east of that river was in dispute when the war between the United States and Mexico commenced. Texas, by a successful revolution in April, 1836, achieved, and subsequently maintained, her independence. By an act of the Congress of Texas passed in December, 1836, her western boundary was declared to be the Rio Grande from its mouth to its source, and thence due north to the forty-second degree of north latitude. Though the Republic of Texas, by many acts of sovereignty which she asserted and exercised, some of which were stated in my annual message of December, 1846, had established her clear title to the country west of the Nueces, and bordering upon that part of the Rio Grande which lies below the Province of New Mexico, she had never conquered or reduced to actual possession and brought under her Government and laws that part of New Mexico lying east of the Rio Grande, which she claimed to be within her limits. On the breaking out of the war we found Mexico in possession of this disputed territory. As our Army approached Sante Fe (the capital of New Mexico) it was found to be held by a governor under Mexican authority, with an armed force collected to resist our advance. The inhabitants were Mexicans, acknowledging allegiance to Mexico. The boundary in dispute was the line between the two countries engaged in actual war, and the settlement of it of necessity depended on a treaty of peace. Finding the Mexican authorities and people in possession, our forces conquered them, and extended military rule over them and the territory which they actually occupied, in lieu of the sovereignty which was displaced. It was not possible to disturb or change the practical boundary line in the midst of the war, when no negotiation for its adjustment could be opened, and when Texas was not present, by her constituted authorities, to establish and maintain government over a hostile Mexican population who acknowledged no allegiance to her. There was, therefore, no alternative left but to establish and maintain military rule during the war over the conquered people in the disputed territory who had submitted to our arms, or to forbear the exercise of our belligerent rights and leave them in a state of anarchy and without control.

Whether the country in dispute rightfully belonged to Mexico or to Texas, it was our right in the first case, and our duty as well as our right in the latter, to conquer and hold it. Whilst this territory was in our possession as conquerors, with a population hostile to the United States, which more than once broke out in open insurrection, it was our unquestionable duty to continue our military occupation of it until the conclusion of the war, and to establish over it a military government, necessary for our own security as well as for the protection of the conquered people.

By the joint resolution of Congress of March 1, 1845, "for annexing Texas to the United States," the "adjustment of all questions of boundary which may arise with other governments" was reserved to this Government. When the conquest of New Mexico was consummated by our arms, the question of boundary remained still unadjusted. Until the exchange of the ratifications of the late treaty, New Mexico never became an undisputed portion of the United States, and it would therefore have been premature to deliver over to Texas that portion of it on the east side of the Rio Grande, to which she asserted a claim. However just the right of Texas may have been to it, that right had never been reduced into her possession, and it was contested by Mexico.

By the cession of the whole of New Mexico, on both sides of the Rio Grande, to the United States, the question of disputed boundary, so far as Mexico is concerned, has been settled, leaving the question as to the true limits of Texas in New Mexico to be adjusted between that State and the United States.

Under the circumstances existing during the pendency of the war, and while the whole of New Mexico, as claimed by our enemy, was in our military occupation, I was not unmindful of the rights of Texas to that portion of it which she claimed to be within her limits. In answer to a letter from the governor of Texas dated on the 4th of January, 1847, the Secretary of State, by my direction, informed him in a letter of the 12th of February, 1847, that in the President's annual message of December, 1846—

You have already perceived that New Mexico is at present in the temporary occupation of the troops of the United States, and the government over it is military in its character. It is merely such a government as must exist under the laws of nations and of war to preserve order and protect the rights of the inhabitants, and will cease on the conclusion of a treaty of peace with Mexico. Nothing, therefore, can be more certain than that this temporary government, resulting from necessity, can never injuriously affect the right which the President believes to be justly asserted by Texas to the whole territory on this side of the Rio Grande whenever the Mexican claim to it shall have been extinguished by treaty. But this is a subject which more properly belongs to the legislative than the executive branch of the Government.

The result of the whole is that Texas had asserted a right to that part of New Mexico east of the Rio Grande, which is believed, under the acts of Congress for the annexation and admission of Texas into the Union as a State, and under the constitution and laws of Texas, to be well founded; but this right had never been reduced to her actual possession and occupancy. The General Government, possessing exclusively the war-making power, had the right to take military possession of this disputed territory, and until the title to it was perfected by a treaty of peace it was their duty to hold it and to establish a temporary military government over it for the preservation of the conquest itself, the safety of our Army, and the security of the conquered inhabitants.

The resolutions further request information whether any persons have been tried and condemned for "treason against the United States in that part of New Mexico lying east of the Rio Grande since the same has been in the occupancy of our Army," and, if so, before "what tribunal" and "by what authority of law such tribunal was established." It appears that after the territory in question was "in the occupancy of our Army" some of the conquered Mexican inhabitants, who had at first submitted to our authority, broke out in open insurrection, murdering our soldiers and citizens and committing other atrocious crimes. Some of the principal offenders who were apprehended were tried and condemned by a tribunal invested with civil and criminal jurisdiction, which had been established in the conquered country by the military officer in command. That the offenders deserved the punishment inflicted upon them there is no reason to doubt, and the error in the proceedings against them consisted in designating and describing their crimes as "treason against the United States." This error was pointed out, and its recurrence thereby prevented, by the Secretary of War in a dispatch to the officer in command in New Mexico dated on the 26th of June, 1847, a copy of which, together with copies of all communications relating to the subject which have been received at the War Department, is herewith transmitted.

The resolutions call for information in relation to the quantity of the public lands acquired within the ceded territory, and "how much of the same is within the boundaries of Texas as defined by the act of the Congress of the Republic of Texas of the 19th day of December, 1836." No means of making an accurate estimate on the subject is in the possession of the executive department. The information which is possessed will be found in the accompanying report of the Secretary of the Treasury.

The country ceded to the United States lying west of the Rio Grande, and to which Texas has no title, is estimated by the commissioner of the General Land Office to contain 526,078 square miles, or 336,689,920 acres.

The period since the exchange of ratifications of the treaty has been too short to enable the Government to have access to or to procure abstracts or copies of the land titles issued by Spain or by the Republic of Mexico. Steps will be taken to procure this information at the earliest practicable period. It is estimated, as appears from the accompanying report of the Secretary of the Treasury, that much the larger portion of the land within the territories ceded remains vacant and unappropriated, and will be subject to be disposed of by the United States. Indeed, a very inconsiderable portion of the land embraced in the cession, it is believed, has been disposed of or granted either by Spain or Mexico.

What amount of money the United States may be able to realize from the sales of these vacant lands must be uncertain, but it is confidently believed that with prudent management, after making liberal grants to emigrants and settlers, it will exceed the cost of the war and all the expenses to which we have been subjected in acquiring it.

The resolutions also call for "the evidence, or any part thereof, that the 'extensive and valuable territories ceded by Mexico to the United States constitute indemnity for the past.'"

The immense value of the ceded country does not consist alone in the amount of money for which the public lands may be sold. If not a dollar could be realized from the sale of these lands, the cession of the jurisdiction over the country and the fact that it has become a part of our Union and can not be made subject to any European power constitute ample "indemnity for the past" in the immense value and advantages which its acquisition must give to the commercial, navigating, manufacturing, and agricultural interests of our country.

The value of the public lands embraced within the limits of the ceded territory, great as that value may be, is far less important to the people of the United States than the sovereignty over the country. Most of our States contain no public lands owned by the United States, and yet the sovereignty and jurisdiction over them is of incalculable importance to the nation. In the State of New York the United States is the owner of no public lands, and yet two-thirds of our whole revenue is collected at the great port of that State, and within her limits is found about one-seventh of our entire population. Although none of the future cities on our coast of California may ever rival the city of New York in wealth, population, and business, yet that important cities will grow up on the magnificent harbors of that coast, with a rapidly increasing commerce and population, and yielding a large revenue, would seem to be certain. By the possession of the safe and capacious harbors on the Californian coast we shall have great advantages in securing the rich commerce of the East, and shall thus obtain for our products new and increased markets and greatly enlarge our coasting and foreign trade, as well as augment our tonnage and revenue.

These great advantages, far more than the simple value of the public lands in the ceded territory, "constitute our indemnity for the past."

JAMES K. POLK.

WASHINGTON, *July 28, 1848.*

To the Senate of the United States:

I have received from the Senate the "convention for the mutual delivery of criminals, fugitives from justice, in certain cases, concluded on the 29th of January, 1845, between the United States on the one part and Prussia and other States of the German Confederation on the other part," with a copy of their resolution of the 21st of June last, advising and consenting to its ratification, with an amendment extending the period for the exchange of ratifications until the 28th of September, 1848.

I have taken this subject into serious and deliberate consideration, and regret that I can not ratify this convention, in conformity with the advice of the Senate, without violating my convictions of duty. Having arrived at this conclusion, I deem it proper and respectful, considering the peculiar circumstances of the present case and the intimate relations which the Constitution has established between the President and Senate, to make known to you the reasons which influence me to come to this determination.

On the 16th of December, 1845, I communicated this convention to the Senate for its consideration, at the same time stating my objections to the third article. I deemed this to be a more proper and respectful course toward the Senate, as well as toward Prussia and the other parties to it, than if I had withheld it and disapproved it altogether. Had the Senate concurred with me in opinion and rejected the third article, then the convention thus amended would have conformed to our treaties of extradition with Great Britain and France.

But the Senate did not act upon it within the period limited for the exchange of ratifications. From this I concluded that they had concurred with me in opinion in regard to the third article, and had for this and other reasons deemed it proper to take no proceedings upon the convention. After this date, therefore, I considered the affair as terminated.

Upon the presumption that this was the fact, new negotiations upon the subject were commenced, and several conferences were held between the Secretary of State and the Prussian minister. These resulted in a protocol signed at the Department of State on the 27th of April, 1847, in which the Secretary proposed either that the two Governments might agree to extend the time for the exchange of ratifications, and thus revive the convention, provided the Prussian Government would previously intimate its consent to the omission of the third article, or he "expressed his willingness immediately to conclude with Mr. Gerolt a new convention, if he possessed the requisite powers from his Government, embracing all the provisions contained in that of the 29th January, 1845, with the exception of the third article. To this Mr. Gerolt observed that he had no powers to conclude such a convention, but would submit the propositions of Mr. Buchanan to the Prussian Government for further instructions."

Mr. Gerolt has never yet communicated in writing to the Department of State the answer of his Government to these propositions, but the Secretary of State, a few months after the date of the protocol, learned from him in conversation that they insisted upon the third article of the convention as a *sine qua non*. Thus the second negotiation had finally terminated by a disagreement between the parties, when, more than a year afterwards, on the 21st June, 1848, the Senate took the original convention into consideration and ratified it, retaining the third article.

After the second negotiation with the Prussian Government, in which the objections to the third article were stated, as they had been previously in my message of the 16th December, 1845, a strong additional difficulty was interposed to the ratification of the convention; but I might overcome this difficulty if my objections to the third article had not grown stronger by further reflection. For a statement of them in detail I refer you to the accompanying memorandum, prepared by the Secretary of State by my direction.

I can not believe that the sovereign States of this Union, whose administration of justice would be almost exclusively affected by such a convention, will ever be satisfied with a treaty of extradition under which if a German subject should commit murder or any other high crime in New York or New Orleans, and could succeed in escaping to his own country, he would thereby be protected from trial and punishment under the jurisdiction of our State laws which he had violated. It is true, as has been stated, that the German States, acting upon a principle springing from the doctrine of perpetual allegiance, still assert the jurisdiction of trying and punishing their subjects for crimes committed in the United States or any other portion of the world. It must, however, be manifest that individuals throughout our extended country would rarely, if ever, follow criminals to Germany with the necessary testimony for the purpose of prosecuting them to conviction before German courts for crimes committed in the United States.

On the other hand, the Constitution and laws of the United States, as well as of the several States, would render it impossible that crimes committed by our citizens in Germany could be tried and punished in any portion of this Union.

But if no other reason existed for withholding my ratification from this treaty, the great change which has recently occurred in the organization of the Government of the German States would be sufficient. By the last advices we learn that the German Parliament, at Frankfort, have already established a federal provisional Executive for all the States of Germany, and have elected the Archduke John of Austria to be "Administrator of the Empire." One of the attributes of this Executive is "to represent the Confederation in its relations with foreign nations and to appoint diplomatic agents, ministers, and consuls." Indeed, our minister at Berlin has already suggested the propriety of his transfer to Frankfort. In case this convention with nineteen of the thirty-nine German States should be ratified, this could amount to nothing more than a proposition on the part of the Senate and President to these nineteen States who were originally parties to the convention to negotiate anew on the subject of extradition. In the meantime a central German Government has been provisionally established, which extinguishes the right of these separate parties to enter into negotiations with foreign Governments on subjects of several interest to the whole.

Admitting such a treaty as that which has been ratified by the Senate to be desirable, the obvious course would now be to negotiate with the General Government of Germany. A treaty concluded with it would embrace all the thirty-nine States of Germany, and its authority, being coextensive with the Empire, fugitives from justice found in any of these States would be surrendered up on the requisition of our minister at Frankfort. This would be more convenient and effectual than to address such separate requisitions to each of the nineteen German States with which the convention was concluded.

I communicate herewith, for the information of the Senate, copies of a dispatch from our minister at Berlin and a communication from our consul at Darmstadt.

JAMES K. POLK.

WASHINGTON, *July 29, 1848.*

To the House of Representatives of the United States:

In answer to the resolution of the House of Representatives of the 17th instant, requesting the President "to communicate, if not inconsistent with the public interests, copies of all instructions given to the Hon. Ambrose H. Sevier and Nathan Clifford, commissioners appointed to conduct negotiations for the ratification of the treaty lately concluded between the United States and the Republic of Mexico," I have to state that in my opinion it would be "inconsistent with the public interests" to give publicity to these instructions at the present time.

I avail myself of this occasion to observe that, as a general rule applicable to all our important negotiations with foreign powers, it could not fail to be prejudicial to the public interest to publish the instructions to our ministers until some time had elapsed after the conclusion of such negotiations.

In the present case the object of the mission of our commissioners to

Mexico has been accomplished. The treaty, as amended by the Senate of the United States, has been ratified. The ratifications have been exchanged and the treaty has been proclaimed as the supreme law of the land. No contingency occurred which made it either necessary or proper for our commissioners to enter upon any negotiations with the Mexican Government further than to urge upon that Government the ratification of the treaty in its amended form.

JAMES K. POLK.

WASHINGTON, *July 31, 1848.*

To the Senate of the United States:

I communicate herewith a report from the Secretary of State, containing the information called for by the resolution of the Senate of the 24th of April, 1848, in relation "to the claim of the owners of the ship *Miles*, of Warren, in the State of Rhode Island, upon the Government of Portugal for the payment of a cargo of oil taken by the officers and applied to the uses of that Government."

JAMES K. POLK.

WASHINGTON, *July 31, 1848.*

To the Senate of the United States:

In compliance with the resolution of the Senate of the 28th instant, requesting the President to communicate to that body, "in confidence, if not inconsistent with the public interest, what steps, if any, have been taken by the Executive to extinguish the rights of the Hudsons Bay and Puget Sound Land Company within the Territory of Oregon, and such communications, if any, which may have been received from the British Government in relation to this subject," I communicate herewith a report from the Secretary of State, with the accompanying documents.

JAMES K. POLK.

WASHINGTON, *August 1, 1848.*

To the House of Representatives of the United States:

I communicate herewith a report from the Secretary of War, containing the information called for by the resolution of the House of Representatives of the 17th July, 1848, in relation to the number of Indians in Oregon, California, and New Mexico, the number of military posts, the number of troops which will be required in each, and "the whole military force which should constitute the peace establishment."

I have seen no reason to change the opinion expressed in my message to Congress of the 6th July, 1848, transmitting the treaty of peace with Mexico, that "the old Army, as it existed before the commencement of the war with Mexico, especially if authority be given to fill up the rank and file of the several corps to the maximum number authorized during the war, will be a sufficient force to be retained in service during a period of peace."

The old Army consists of fifteen regiments. By the act of the 13th of May, 1846, the President was authorized, by "voluntary enlistments, to increase the number of privates in each or any of the companies of the existing regiments of dragoons, artillery, and infantry to any number not exceeding 100," and to "reduce the same to 64 when the exigencies requiring the present increase shall cease." Should this act remain in force, the maximum number of the rank and file of the Army authorized by it would be over 16,000 men, exclusive of officers. Should the authority conferred by this act be continued, it would depend on the exigencies of the service whether the number of the rank and file should be increased, and, if so, to what amount beyond the minimum number of 64 privates to a company.

Allowing 64 privates to a company, the Army would be over 10,000 men, exclusive of commissioned and noncommissioned officers, a number which, it is believed, will be sufficient; but, as a precautionary measure, it is deemed expedient that the Executive should possess the power of increasing the strength of the respective corps should the exigencies of the service be such as to require it. Should these exigencies not call for such increase, the discretionary power given by the act to the President will not be exercised.

It will be seen from the report of the Secretary of War that a portion of the forces will be employed in Oregon, New Mexico, and Upper California; a portion for the protection of the Texas frontier adjoining the Mexican possessions, and bordering on the territory occupied by the Indian tribes within her limits. After detailing the force necessary for these objects, it is believed a sufficient number of troops will remain to afford security and protection to our Indian frontiers in the West and Northwest and to occupy with sufficient garrisons the posts on our northern and Atlantic borders.

I have no reason at present to believe that any increase of the number of regiments or corps will be required during a period of peace.

JAMES K. POLK.

WASHINGTON, *August 3, 1848.*

To the Senate of the United States:

I communicate herewith a report from the Secretary of War, together with the accompanying documents, in compliance with the resolution of the Senate of the 24th July, 1848, requesting the President "to transmit to the Senate the proceedings of the two courts of inquiry in the case of Major-General Pillow, the one commenced and terminated in Mexico, and the other commenced in Mexico and terminated in the United States."

JAMES K. POLK.

WASHINGTON, *August 5, 1848.*

To the Senate of the United States:

I nominate Andrew J. Donelson, of Tennessee, to be envoy extraordinary and minister plenipotentiary of the United States to the Federal Government of Germany.

In submitting this nomination I transmit, for the information of the Senate, an official dispatch received from the consul of the United States at Darmstadt, dated July 10, 1848. I deem it proper also to state that no such diplomatic agent as that referred to by the consul has been appointed by me. Mr. Deverre, the person alluded to, is unknown to me and has no authority to represent this Government in any capacity whatever.

JAMES K. POLK.

WASHINGTON, *August 5, 1848.*

To the House of Representatives of the United States:

I communicate herewith a report from the Secretary of War, together with the accompanying documents, in compliance with a resolution of the House of Representatives of the 17th of July, 1848, requesting the President to communicate to the House of Representatives "a copy of the proceedings of the court of inquiry in Mexico touching the matter which led to the dismissal from the public service of Lieutenants Joseph S. Pendée and George E. B. Singletary, of the North Carolina regiment of volunteers, and all the correspondence between the War Department and Generals Taylor and Wool in relation to the same."

JAMES K. POLK.

WASHINGTON, *August 8, 1848.*

To the Senate of the United States:

In reply to the resolution of the Senate of the 7th instant, requesting the President to inform that body "whether he has any information that any citizen or citizens of the United States is or are now preparing or intending to prepare within the United States an expedition to revolutionize by force any part of the Republic of Mexico, or to assist in so doing, and, if he has, what is the extent of such preparation, and whether he has or is about to take any steps to arrest the same," I have to state that the Executive is not in possession of any information of the character called for by the resolution.

The late treaty of peace with Mexico has been and will be faithfully observed on our part.

JAMES K. POLK.

WASHINGTON, *August 8, 1848.*

To the Senate and House of Representatives of the United States:

It affords me satisfaction to communicate herewith, for the information of Congress, copies of a decree adopted by the National Assembly of France in response to the resolution of the Congress of the United States passed on the 13th of April last, "tendering the congratulations of the American to the French people upon the success of their recent efforts to consolidate the principles of liberty in a republican form of government."

JAMES K. POLK.

WASHINGTON, *August 10, 1848.*

To the Senate of the United States:

I communicate herewith a report of the Secretary of the Navy, together with the accompanying documents, in answer to a resolution of the Senate of the 18th July, 1848, requesting the President to communicate to that body "any information which may be in the possession of the Executive relating to the seizure or capture of the American ship *Admittance* on the coast of California by a vessel of war of the United States, and whether any, and what, proceedings have occurred in regard to said vessel or her cargo, and to furnish the Senate with copies of all documents, papers, and communications in the possession of the Executive relating to the same."

JAMES K. POLK.

WASHINGTON, *August 11, 1848.*

To the House of Representatives of the United States:

I communicate herewith reports from the Secretary of the Treasury and the Secretary of War, together with the accompanying documents, in answer to a resolution of the House of Representatives of the 17th of July, 1848, requesting the President to inform that body what amount of public moneys had been respectively paid to Lewis Cass and Zachary Taylor from the time of their first entrance into the public service up to this time, distinguishing between regular and extra compensation; that he also state what amount of extra compensation has been claimed by either; the items composing the same; when filed; when and by whom allowed; if disallowed, when and by whom; the reasons for such disallowance; and whether or not any items so disallowed were subsequently presented for payment, and, if allowed, when and by whom.

JAMES K. POLK.

WASHINGTON, *August 14, 1848.*

To the House of Representatives of the United States:

When the President has given his official sanction to a bill which has passed Congress, usage requires that he shall notify the House in which it originated of that fact. The mode of giving this notification has been by an oral message delivered by his private secretary.

Having this day approved and signed an act entitled "An act to establish the Territorial government of Oregon," I deem it proper, under

STORMING OF TETE DE PONT, CHURUBUSCO

THE BATTLE OF CHURUBUSCO

On August 20, 1847, after the victory at Contreras, the Americans pursued the fleeing Mexicans to a small village called Churubusco. Here, at the head of the causeway running to Mexico City, and in front of a bridge over the Churubusco River, stood a strong redoubt. Inside the hamlet stood the convent church of San Pablo, its walls pierced for cannon and filled with munitions of war saved from the wreck at Contreras. Twelve thousand Mexicans under Santa Ana held the place. The redoubt at the bridge was carried, as shown in the illustration, at the point of the bayonet. For three hours the troops in the church held out, the stubbornest resistance being made by deserters from the American Army, who hauled down the white flag each time it was raised, knowing that escape was impossible and that capture meant court-martial and the gallows.

In the Encyclopedic Index, there is an article describing the action under the heading "Churubusco (Mexico), Battle of." Beneath is an entry directing the reader to a presidential reference to the victory.

the existing circumstances, to communicate the fact in a more solemn form. The deeply interesting and protracted discussions which have taken place in both Houses of Congress and the absorbing interest which the subject has excited throughout the country justify, in my judgment, this departure from the form of notice observed in other cases. In this communication with a coordinate branch of the Government, made proper by the considerations referred to, I shall frankly and without reserve express the reasons which have constrained me not to withhold my signature from the bill to establish a government over Oregon, even though the two territories of New Mexico and California are to be left for the present without governments. None doubt that it is proper to establish a government in Oregon. Indeed, it has been too long delayed. I have made repeated recommendations to Congress to this effect. The petitions of the people of that distant region have been presented to the Government, and ought not to be disregarded. To give to them a regularly organized government and the protection of our laws, which, as citizens of the United States, they claim, is a high duty on our part, and one which we are bound to perform, unless there be controlling reasons to prevent it.

In the progress of all governments questions of such transcendent importance occasionally arise as to cast in the shade all those of a mere party character. But one such question can now be agitated in this country, and this may endanger our glorious Union, the source of our greatness and all our political blessings. This question is slavery. With the slaveholding States this does not embrace merely the rights of property, however valuable, but it ascends far higher, and involves the domestic peace and security of every family.

The fathers of the Constitution, the wise and patriotic men who laid the foundation of our institutions, foreseeing the danger from this quarter, acted in a spirit of compromise and mutual concession on this dangerous and delicate subject, and their wisdom ought to be the guide of their successors. Whilst they left to the States exclusively the question of domestic slavery within their respective limits, they provided that slaves who might escape into other States not recognizing the institution of slavery shall be "delivered up on the claim of the party to whom such service or labor may be due."

Upon this foundation the matter rested until the Missouri question arose.

In December, 1819, application was made to Congress by the people of the Missouri Territory for admission into the Union as a State. The discussion upon the subject in Congress involved the question of slavery, and was prosecuted with such violence as to produce excitements alarming to every patriot in the Union. But the good genius of conciliation, which presided at the birth of our institutions, finally prevailed, and the Missouri compromise was adopted. The eighth section of the act of Congress of the 6th of March, 1820, "to authorize the people of the

Missouri Territory to form a constitution and State government," etc., provides:

That in all that territory ceded by France to the United States under the name of Louisiana which lies north of 36° 30′ north latitude, not included within the limits of the State contemplated by this act, slavery and involuntary servitude, otherwise than in the punishment of crimes, whereof the parties shall have been duly convicted, shall be, and is hereby, forever prohibited: *Provided always*, That any person escaping into the same from whom labor or service is lawfully claimed in any State or Territory of the United States, such fugitive may be lawfully reclaimed and conveyed to the person claiming his or her labor or service as aforesaid.

This compromise had the effect of calming the troubled waves and restoring peace and good will throughout the States of the Union.

The Missouri question had excited intense agitation of the public mind, and threatened to divide the country into geographical parties, alienating the feelings of attachment which each portion of our Union should bear to every other. The compromise allayed the excitement, tranquilized the popular mind, and restored confidence and fraternal feelings. Its authors were hailed as public benefactors.

I do not doubt that a similar adjustment of the questions which now agitate the public mind would produce the same happy results. If the legislation of Congress on the subject of the other Territories shall not be adopted in a spirit of conciliation and compromise, it is impossible that the country can be satisfied or that the most disastrous consequences shall fail to ensue.

When Texas was admitted into the Union, the same spirit of compromise which guided our predecessors in the admission of Missouri a quarter of a century before prevailed without any serious opposition. The joint resolution for annexing Texas to the United States, approved March 1, 1845, provides that—

Such States as may be formed out of that portion of said territory lying south of 36° 30′ north latitude, commonly known as the Missouri compromise line, shall be admitted into the Union with or without slavery, as the people of each State asking admission may desire; and in such State or States as shall be formed out of said territory north of the Missouri compromise line slavery or involuntary servitude (except for crime) shall be prohibited.

The Territory of Oregon lies far north of 36° 30′, the Missouri and Texas compromise line. Its southern boundary is the parallel of 42°, leaving the intermediate distance to be 330 geographical miles. And it is because the provisions of this bill are not inconsistent with the laws of the Missouri compromise, if extended from the Rio Grande to the Pacific Ocean, that I have not felt at liberty to withhold my sanction. Had it embraced territories south of that compromise, the question presented for my consideration would have been of a far different character, and my action upon it must have corresponded with my convictions.

Ought we now to disturb the Missouri and Texas compromises? Ought we at this late day, in attempting to annul what has been so long established and acquiesced in, to excite sectional divisions and jealousies, to alienate the people of different portions of the Union from each other, and to endanger the existence of the Union itself?

From the adoption of the Federal Constitution, during a period of sixty years, our progress as a nation has been without example in the annals of history. Under the protection of a bountiful Providence, we have advanced with giant strides in the career of wealth and prosperity. We have enjoyed the blessings of freedom to a greater extent than any other people, ancient or modern, under a Government which has preserved order and secured to every citizen life, liberty, and property. We have now become an example for imitation to the whole world. The friends of freedom in every clime point with admiration to our institutions. Shall we, then, at the moment when the people of Europe are devoting all their energies in the attempt to assimilate their institutions to our own, peril all our blessings by despising the lessons of experience and refusing to tread in the footsteps which our fathers have trodden? And for what cause would we endanger our glorious Union? The Missouri compromise contains a prohibition of slavery throughout all that vast region extending twelve and a half degrees along the Pacific, from the parallel of 36° 30′ to that of 49°, and east from that ocean to and beyond the summit of the Rocky Mountains. Why, then, should our institutions be endangered because it is proposed to submit to the people of the remainder of our newly acquired territory lying south of 36° 30′, embracing less than four degrees of latitude, the question whether, in the language of the Texas compromise, they "shall be admitted [as a State] into the Union with or without slavery." Is this a question to be pushed to such extremities by excited partisans on the one side or the other, in regard to our newly acquired distant possessions on the Pacific, as to endanger the Union of thirty glorious States, which constitute our Confederacy? I have an abiding confidence that the sober reflection and sound patriotism of the people of all the States will bring them to the conclusion that the dictate of wisdom is to follow the example of those who have gone before us, and settle this dangerous question on the Missouri compromise, or some other equitable compromise which would respect the rights of all and prove satisfactory to the different portions of the Union.

Holding as a sacred trust the Executive authority for the whole Union, and bound to guard the rights of all, I should be constrained by a sense of duty to withhold my official sanction from any measure which would conflict with these important objects.

I can not more appropriately close this message than by quoting from the Farewell Address of the Father of his Country. His warning voice can never be heard in vain by the American people. If the spirit of prophecy had distinctly presented to his view more than a half century ago the present distracted condition of his country, the language which he then employed could not have been more appropriate than it is to the present occasion. He declared:

The unity of government which constitutes you one people is also now dear to you. It is justly so, for it is a main pillar in the edifice of your real independence, the support of your tranquillity at home, your peace abroad, of your safety, of your prosperity, of that very liberty which you so highly prize. But as it is easy to foresee that from different causes and from different quarters much pains will be taken, many artifices employed, to weaken in your minds the conviction of this truth, as this is the point in your political fortress against which the batteries of internal and external enemies will be most constantly and actively (though often covertly and insidiously) directed, it is of infinite moment that you should properly estimate the immense value of your national union to your collective and individual happiness; that you should cherish a cordial, habitual, and immovable attachment to it; accustoming yourselves to think and speak of it as of the palladium of your political safety and prosperity; watching for its preservation with jealous anxiety; discountenancing whatever may suggest even a suspicion that it can in any event be abandoned, and indignantly frowning upon the first dawning of every attempt to alienate any portion of our country from the rest or to enfeeble the sacred ties which now link together the various parts.

For this you have every inducement of sympathy and interest. Citizens by birth or choice of a common country, that country has a right to concentrate your affections. The name of American, which belongs to you in your national capacity, must always exalt the just pride of patriotism more than any appellation derived from local discriminations. With slight shades of difference, you have the same religion, manners, habits, and political principles. You have in a common cause fought and triumphed together. The independence and liberty you possess are the work of joint councils and joint efforts, of common dangers, sufferings, and successes.

* * * * * * *

With such powerful and obvious motives to union affecting all parts of our country, while experience shall not have demonstrated its impracticability, there will always be reason to distrust the patriotism of those who in any quarter may endeavor to weaken its bands.

In contemplating the causes which may disturb our union it occurs as matter of serious concern that any ground should have been furnished for characterizing parties by *geographical* discriminations—*Northern* and *Southern*, *Atlantic* and *Western*—whence designing men may endeavor to excite a belief that there is a real difference of local interests and views. One of the expedients of party to acquire influence within particular districts is to misrepresent the opinions and aims of other districts. You can not shield yourselves too much against the jealousies and heartburnings which spring from these misrepresentations; they tend to render alien to each other those who ought to be bound together by fraternal affection.

JAMES K. POLK.

VETO MESSAGE.*

WASHINGTON, *December 15, 1847*.

To the House of Representatives:

On the last day of the last session of Congress a bill entitled "An act to provide for continuing certain works in the Territory of Wisconsin, and for other purposes," which had passed both Houses, was presented to me for my approval. I entertained insuperable objections to its becom-

*Pocket veto.

ing a law, but the short period of the session which remained afforded me no sufficient opportunity to prepare my objections and communicate them with the bill to the House of Representatives, in which it originated. For this reason the bill was retained, and I deem it proper now to state my objections to it.

Although from the title of the bill it would seem that its main object was to make provision for continuing certain works already commenced in the Territory of Wisconsin, it appears on examination of its provisions that it contains only a single appropriation of $6,000 to be applied within that Territory, while it appropriates more than half a million of dollars for the improvement of numerous harbors and rivers lying within the limits and jurisdiction of several of the States of the Union.

At the preceding session of Congress it became my duty to return with my objections to the House in which it originated a bill making similar appropriations and involving like principles, and the views then expressed remain unchanged.

The circumstances under which this heavy expenditure of public money was proposed were of imposing weight in determining upon its expediency. Congress had recognized the existence of war with Mexico, and to prosecute it to "a speedy and successful termination" had made appropriations exceeding our ordinary revenues. To meet the emergency and provide for the expenses of the Government, a loan of $23,000,000 was authorized at the same session, which has since been negotiated. The practical effect of this bill, had it become a law, would have been to add the whole amount appropriated by it to the national debt. It would, in fact, have made necessary an additional loan to that amount as effectually as if in terms it had required the Secretary of the Treasury to borrow the money therein appropriated. The main question in that aspect is whether it is wise, while all the means and credit of the Government are needed to bring the existing war to an honorable close, to impair the one and endanger the other by borrowing money to be expended in a system of internal improvements capable of an expansion sufficient to swallow up the revenues not only of our own country, but of the civilized world? It is to be apprehended that by entering upon such a career at this moment confidence at home and abroad in the wisdom and prudence of the Government would be so far impaired as to make it difficult, without an immediate resort to heavy taxation, to maintain the public credit and to preserve the honor of the nation and the glory of our arms in prosecuting the existing war to a successful conclusion. Had this bill become a law, it is easy to foresee that largely increased demands upon the Treasury would have been made at each succeeding session of Congress for the improvements of numerous other harbors, bays, inlets, and rivers of equal importance with those embraced by its provisions. Many millions would probably have been added to the necessary amount of the war debt, the annual interest on which must also have been borrowed, and finally a permanent national debt been fastened on the country and entailed on posterity.

The policy of embarking the Federal Government in a general system of internal improvements had its origin but little more than twenty years ago. In a very few years the applications to Congress for appropriations in furtherance of such objects exceeded $200,000,000. In this alarming crisis President Jackson refused to approve and sign the Maysville road bill, the Wabash River bill, and other bills of similar character. His interposition put a check upon the new policy of throwing the cost of local improvements upon the National Treasury, preserved the revenues of the nation for their legitimate objects, by which he was enabled to extinguish the then existing public debt and to present to an admiring world the unprecedented spectacle in modern times of a nation free from debt and advancing to greatness with unequaled strides under a Government which was content to act within its appropriate sphere in protecting the States and individuals in their own chosen career of improvement and of enterprise. Although the bill under consideration proposes no appropriation for a road or canal, it is not easy to perceive the difference in principle or mischievous tendency between appropriations for making roads and digging canals and appropriations to deepen rivers and improve harbors. All are alike within the limits and jurisdiction of the States, and rivers and harbors alone open an abyss of expenditure sufficient to swallow up the wealth of the nation and load it with a debt which may fetter its energies and tax its industry for ages to come.

The experience of several of the States, as well as that of the United States, during the period that Congress exercised the power of appropriating the public money for internal improvements is full of eloquent warnings. It seems impossible, in the nature of the subject, as connected with local representation, that the several objects presented for improvement shall be weighed according to their respective merits and appropriations confined to those whose importance would justify a tax on the whole community to effect their accomplishment.

In some of the States systems of internal improvements have been projected, consisting of roads and canals, many of which, taken separately, were not of sufficient public importance to justify a tax on the entire population of the State to effect their construction, and yet by a combination of local interests, operating on a majority of the legislature, the whole have been authorized and the States plunged into heavy debts. To an extent so ruinous has this system of legislation been carried in some portions of the Union that the people have found it necessary to their own safety and prosperity to forbid their legislatures, by constitutional restrictions, to contract public debts for such purposes without their immediate consent.

If the abuse of power has been so fatal in the States, where the systems of taxation are direct and the representatives responsible at short periods to small masses of constituents, how much greater danger of abuse is to be apprehended in the General Government, whose revenues are raised by indirect taxation and whose functionaries are responsible to the people in larger masses and for longer terms.

Regarding only objects of improvement of the nature of those embraced in this bill, how inexhaustible we shall find them. Let the imagination run along our coast from the river St. Croix to the Rio Grande and trace every river emptying into the Atlantic and Gulf of Mexico to its source; let it coast along our lakes and ascend all their tributaries; let it pass to Oregon and explore all its bays, inlets, and streams; and then let it raise the curtain of the future and contemplate the extent of this Republic and the objects of improvement it will embrace as it advances to its high destiny, and the mind will be startled at the immensity and danger of the power which the principle of this bill involves.

Already our Confederacy consists of twenty-nine States. Other States may at no distant period be expected to be formed on the west of our present settlements. We own an extensive country in Oregon, stretching many hundreds of miles from east to west and seven degrees of latitude from south to north. By the admission of Texas into the Union we have recently added many hundreds of miles to our seacoast. In all this vast country, bordering on the Atlantic and Pacific, there are many thousands of bays, inlets, and rivers equally entitled to appropriations for their improvement with the objects embraced in this bill.

We have seen in our States that the interests of individuals or neighborhoods, combining against the general interest, have involved their governments in debts and bankruptcy; and when the system prevailed in the General Government, and was checked by President Jackson, it had begun to be considered the highest merit in a member of Congress to be able to procure appropriations of public money to be expended within his district or State, whatever might be the object. We should be blind to the experience of the past if we did not see abundant evidences that if this system of expenditure is to be indulged in combinations of individual and local interests will be found strong enough to control legislation, absorb the revenues of the country, and plunge the Government into a hopeless indebtedness.

What is denominated a harbor by this system does not necessarily mean a bay, inlet, or arm of the sea on the ocean or on our lake shores, on the margin of which may exist a commercial city or town engaged in foreign or domestic trade, but is made to embrace waters where there is not only no such city or town, but no commerce of any kind. By it a bay or sheet of shoal water is called a *harbor*, and appropriations demanded from Congress to deepen it with a view to draw commerce to it or to enable individuals to build up a town or city on its margin upon speculation and for their own private advantage.

What is denominated a river which may be improved in the system is equally undefined in its meaning. It may be the Mississippi or it may be the smallest and most obscure and unimportant stream bearing the name of river which is to be found in any State in the Union.

Such a system is subject, moreover, to be perverted to the accomplishment of the worst of political purposes. During the few years it was in full operation, and which immediately preceded the veto of President Jackson of the Maysville road bill, instances were numerous of public men seeking to gain popular favor by holding out to the people interested in particular localities the promise of large disbursements of public money. Numerous reconnoissances and surveys were made during that period for roads and canals through many parts of the Union, and the people in the vicinity of each were led to believe that their property would be enhanced in value and they themselves be enriched by the large expenditures which they were promised by the advocates of the system should be made from the Federal Treasury in their neighborhood. Whole sections of the country were thus sought to be influenced, and the system was fast becoming one not only of profuse and wasteful expenditure, but a potent political engine.

If the power to improve a harbor be admitted, it is not easy to perceive how the power to deepen every inlet on the ocean or the lakes and make harbors where there are none can be denied. If the power to clear out or deepen the channel of rivers near their mouths be admitted, it is not easy to perceive how the power to improve them to their fountain head and make them navigable to their sources can be denied. Where shall the exercise of the power, if it be assumed, stop? Has Congress the power when an inlet is deep enough to admit a schooner to deepen it still more, so that it will admit ships of heavy burden, and has it not the power when an inlet will admit a boat to make it deep enough to admit a schooner? May it improve rivers deep enough already to float ships and steamboats, and has it no power to improve those which are navigable only for flatboats and barges? May the General Government exercise power and jurisdiction over the soil of a State consisting of rocks and sand bars in the beds of its rivers, and may it not excavate a canal around its waterfalls or across its lands for precisely the same object?

Giving to the subject the most serious and candid consideration of which my mind is capable, I can not perceive any intermediate grounds. The power to improve harbors and rivers for purposes of navigation, by deepening or clearing out, by dams and sluices, by locking or canalling, must be admitted without any other limitation than the discretion of Congress, or it must be denied altogether. If it be admitted, how broad and how susceptible of enormous abuses is the power thus vested in the General Government! There is not an inlet of the ocean or the Lakes, not a river, creek, or streamlet within the States, which is not brought for this purpose within the power and jurisdiction of the General Government.

Speculation, disguised under the cloak of public good, will call on Congress to deepen shallow inlets, that it may build up new cities on their shores, or to make streams navigable which nature has closed by bars and rapids, that it may sell at a profit its lands upon their banks. To enrich neighborhoods by spending within them the moneys of the nation will be the aim and boast of those who prize their local interests above the good of the nation, and millions upon millions will be abstracted by tariffs and taxes from the earnings of the whole people to foster speculation and subserve the objects of private ambition.

Such a system could not be administered with any approach to equality among the several States and sections of the Union. There is no equality among them in the objects of expenditure, and if the funds were distributed according to the merits of those objects some would be enriched at the expense of their neighbors. But a greater practical evil would be found in the art and industry by which appropriations would be sought and obtained. The most artful and industrious would be the most successful. The true interests of the country would be lost sight of in an annual scramble for the contents of the Treasury, and the Member of Congress who could procure the largest appropriations to be expended in his district would claim the reward of victory from his enriched constituents. The necessary consequence would be sectional discontents and heartburnings, increased taxation, and a national debt never to be extinguished.

In view of these portentous consequences, I can not but think that this course of legislation should be arrested, even were there nothing to forbid it in the fundamental laws of our Union. This conclusion is fortified by the fact that the Constitution itself indicates a process by which harbors and rivers within the States may be improved—a process not susceptible of the abuses necessarily to flow from the assumption of the power to improve them by the General Government, just in its operation, and actually practiced upon, without complaint or interruption, during more than thirty years from the organization of the present Government.

The Constitution provides that "no State shall, without the consent of Congress, lay any duty of tonnage." With the "consent" of Congress, such duties may be levied, collected, and expended by the States. We are not left in the dark as to the objects of this reservation of power to the States. The subject was fully considered by the Convention that framed the Constitution. It appears in Mr. Madison's report of the proceedings of that body that one object of the reservation was that the States should not be restrained from laying duties of tonnage for the purpose of clearing harbors. Other objects were named in the debates, and among them the support of seamen. Mr. Madison, treating on this subject in the Federalist, declares that—

The restraint on the power of the States over imports and exports is enforced by all the arguments which prove the necessity of submitting the regulation of trade to the Federal councils. It is needless, therefore, to remark further on this head than that the manner in which the restraint is qualified seems well calculated at once to secure to the States a reasonable discretion in providing for the conveniency of their imports and exports, and to the United States a reasonable check against the abuse of this discretion.

The States may lay tonnage duties for clearing harbors, improving rivers, or for other purposes, but are restrained from abusing the power, because before such duties can take effect the "consent" of Congress must be obtained. Here is a safe provision for the improvement of harbors and rivers in the reserved powers of the States and in the aid they may derive from duties of tonnage levied with the consent of Congress. Its safeguards are, that both the State legislatures and Congress have to concur in the act of raising the funds; that they are in every instance to be levied upon the commerce of those ports which are to profit by the proposed improvement; that no question of conflicting power or jurisdiction is involved; that the expenditure, being in the hands of those who are to pay the money and be immediately benefited, will be more carefully managed and more productive of good than if the funds were drawn from the National Treasury and disbursed by the officers of the General Government; that such a system will carry with it no enlargement of Federal power and patronage, and leave the States to be the sole judges of their own wants and interests, with only a conservative negative in Congress upon any abuse of the power which the States may attempt.

Under this wise system the improvement of harbors and rivers was commenced, or rather continued, from the organization of the Government under the present Constitution. Many acts were passed by the several States levying duties of tonnage, and many were passed by Congress giving their consent to those acts. Such acts have been passed by Massachusetts, Rhode Island, Pennsylvania, Maryland, Virginia, North Carolina, South Carolina, and Georgia, and have been sanctioned by the consent of Congress. Without enumerating them all, it may be instructive to refer to some of them, as illustrative of the mode of improving harbors and rivers in the early periods of our Government, as to the constitutionality of which there can be no doubt.

In January, 1790, the State of Rhode Island passed a law levying a tonnage duty on vessels arriving in the port of Providence, "for the purpose of clearing and deepening the channel of Providence River and making the same more navigable."

On the 2d of February, 1798, the State of Massachusetts passed a law levying a tonnage duty on all vessels, whether employed in the foreign or coasting trade, which might enter into the Kennebunk River, for the improvement of the same by "rendering the passage in and out of said river less difficult and dangerous."

On the 1st of April, 1805, the State of Pennsylvania passed a law levying a tonnage duty on vessels, "to remove the obstructions to the navigation of the river Delaware below the city of Philadelphia."

On the 23d of January, 1804, the State of Virginia passed a law levying a tonnage duty on vessels, "for improving the navigation of James River."

On the 22d of February, 1826, the State of Virginia passed a law levying a tonnage duty on vessels, "for improving the navigation of James River from Warwick to Rocketts Landing."

On the 8th of December, 1824, the State of Virginia passed a law levying a tonnage duty on vessels, "for improving the navigation of Appomattox River from Pocahontas Bridge to Broadway."

In November, 1821, the State of North Carolina passed a law levying a tonnage duty on vessels, "for the purpose of opening an inlet at the lower end of Albemarle Sound, near a place called Nags Head, and improving the navigation of said sound, with its branches;" and in November, 1828, an amendatory law was passed.

On the 21st of December, 1804, the State of South Carolina passed a law levying a tonnage duty, for the purpose of "building a marine hospital in the vicinity of Charleston," and on the 17th of December, 1816, another law was passed by the legislature of that State for the "maintenance of a marine hospital."

On the 10th of February, 1787, the State of Georgia passed a law levying a tonnage duty on all vessels entering into the port of Savannah, for the purpose of "clearing" the Savannah River of "wrecks and other obstructions" to the navigation.

On the 12th of December, 1804, the State of Georgia passed a law levying a tonnage duty on vessels, "to be applied to the payment of the fees of the harbor master and health officer of the ports of Savannah and St. Marys."

In April, 1783, the State of Maryland passed a law laying a tonnage duty on vessels, for the improvement of the "basin" and "harbor" of Baltimore and the "river Patapsco."

On the 26th of December, 1791, the State of Maryland passed a law levying a tonnage duty on vessels, for the improvement of the "harbor and port of Baltimore."

On the 28th of December, 1793, the State of Maryland passed a law authorizing the appointment of a health officer for the port of Baltimore, and laying a tonnage duty on vessels to defray the expenses.

Congress has passed many acts giving its "consent" to these and other State laws, the first of which is dated in 1790 and the last in 1843. By the latter act the "consent" of Congress was given to the law of the legislature of the State of Maryland laying a tonnage duty on vessels for the improvement of the harbor of Baltimore, and continuing it in force until the 1st day of June, 1850. I transmit herewith copies of such of the acts of the legislatures of the States on the subject, and also the acts of Congress giving its "consent" thereto, as have been collated.

That the power was constitutionally and rightfully exercised in these cases does not admit of a doubt.

The injustice and inequality resulting from conceding the power to both Governments is illustrated by several of the acts enumerated. Take that for the improvement of the harbor of Baltimore. That improvement is paid for exclusively by a tax on the commerce of that city, but if an appropriation be made from the National Treasury for the improvement of the harbor of Boston it must be paid in part out of taxes levied on the commerce of Baltimore. The result is that the commerce of Baltimore pays the full cost of the harbor improvement designed for its own benefit, and in addition contributes to the cost of all other harbor and river improvements in the Union. The facts need but be stated to prove the inequality and injustice which can not but flow from the practice embodied in this bill. Either the subject should be left as it was during the first third of a century, or the practice of levying tonnage duties by the States should be abandoned altogether and all harbor and river improvements made under the authority of the United States, and by means of direct appropriations. In view not only of the constitutional difficulty, but as a question of policy, I am clearly of opinion that the whole subject should be left to the States, aided by such tonnage duties on vessels navigating their waters as their respective legislatures may think proper to propose and Congress see fit to sanction. This "consent" of Congress would never be refused in any case where the duty proposed to be levied by the State was reasonable and where the object of improvement was one of importance. The funds required for the improvement of harbors and rivers may be raised in this mode, as was done in the earlier periods of the Government, and thus avoid a resort to a strained construction of the Constitution not warranted by its letter. If direct appropriations be made of the money in the Federal Treasury for such purposes, the expenditures will be unequal and unjust. The money in the Federal Treasury is paid by a tax on the whole people of the United States, and if applied to the purposes of improving harbors and rivers it will be partially distributed and be expended for the advantage of particular States, sections, or localities at the expense of others.

By returning to the early and approved construction of the Constitution and to the practice under it this inequality and injustice will be avoided and at the same time all the really important improvements be made, and, as our experience has proved, be better made and at less cost than they would be by the agency of officers of the United States. The interests benefited by these improvements, too, would bear the cost of making them, upon the same principle that the expenses of the Post-Office establishment have always been defrayed by those who derive benefits from it. The power of appropriating money from the Treasury for such improvements was not claimed or exercised for more than thirty years after the organization of the Government in 1789, when a more latitudinous construction was indicated, though it was not broadly asserted and exercised until 1825. Small appropriations were first made in 1820 and 1821 for surveys. An act was passed on the 3d of March, 1823, authorizing the President to "cause an examination and survey to be made of the obstructions between the harbor of Gloucester and the harbor of Squam, in the State of Massachusetts," and of "the entrance of the harbor of the port of Presque Isle, in Pennsylvania," with a view to their removal, and a small appropriation was made to pay the necessary expenses. This appears to have been the commencement of harbor improvements by Congress, thirty-four years after the Government went into operation under the present Constitution. On the 30th of April, 1824, an act was passed making an appropriation of $30,000, and directing "surveys and estimates to be made of the routes of such roads and canals" as the President "may deem of national importance in a commercial or military point of view or necessary for the transportation of the mails." This act evidently looked to the adoption of a general system of internal improvements, to embrace roads and canals as well as harbors and rivers. On the 26th May, 1824, an act was passed making appropriations for "deepening the channel leading into the harbor of Presque Isle, in the State of Pennsylvania," and to "repair Plymouth Beach, in the State of Massachusetts, and thereby prevent the harbor at that place from being destroyed."

President Monroe yielded his approval to these measures, though he entertained, and had, in a message to the House of Representatives on the 4th of May, 1822, expressed, the opinion that the Constitution had not conferred upon Congress the power to "adopt and execute a system of internal improvements." He placed his approval upon the ground, not that Congress possessed the power to "adopt and execute" such a system by virtue of any or all of the enumerated grants of power in the Constitution, but upon the assumption that the power to make appropriations of the public money was limited and restrained only by the discretion of Congress. In coming to this conclusion he avowed that "in the more early stage of the Government" he had entertained a different opinion. He avowed that his first opinion had been that "as the National Government is a Government of limited powers, it has no right to expend money except in the performance of acts authorized by the other specific grants, according to a strict construction of their powers," and that the power to make appropriations gave to Congress no discretionary authority to apply the public money to any other purposes or objects except to "carry into effect the powers contained in the other grants." These sound views, which Mr. Monroe entertained "in the early stage of the Government," he gave up in 1822, and declared that—

> The right of appropriation is nothing more than a right to apply the public money to this or that purpose. It has no incidental power, nor does it draw after it any consequences of that kind. All that Congress could do under it in the case of internal improvements would be to appropriate the money necessary to make them. For every act requiring legislative sanction or support the State authority must be relied on. The condemnation of the land, if the proprietors should refuse to sell it, the

establishment of turnpikes and tolls, and the protection of the work when finished must be done by the State. To these purposes the powers of the General Government are believed to be utterly incompetent.

But it is impossible to conceive on what principle the power of appropriating public money when in the Treasury can be construed to extend to objects for which the Constitution does not authorize Congress to levy taxes or imposts to raise money. The power of appropriation is but the consequence of the power to raise money; and the true inquiry is whether Congress has the right to levy taxes for the object over which power is claimed.

During the four succeeding years embraced by the Administration of President Adams the power not only to appropriate money, but to apply it, under the direction and authority of the General Government, as well to the construction of roads as to the improvement of harbors and rivers, was fully asserted and exercised.

Among other acts assuming the power was one passed on the 20th of May, 1826, entitled "An act for improving certain harbors and the navigation of certain rivers and creeks, and for authorizing surveys to be made of certain bays, sounds, and rivers therein mentioned." By that act large appropriations were made, which were to be "applied, under the direction of the President of the United States," to numerous improvements in ten of the States. This act, passed thirty-seven years after the organization of the present Government, contained the first appropriation ever made for the improvement of a navigable river, unless it be small appropriations for examinations and surveys in 1820. During the residue of that Administration many other appropriations of a similar character were made, embracing roads, rivers, harbors, and canals, and objects claiming the aid of Congress multiplied without number.

This was the first breach effected in the barrier which the universal opinion of the framers of the Constitution had for more than thirty years thrown in the way of the assumption of this power by Congress. The general mind of Congress and the country did not appreciate the distinction taken by President Monroe between the right to appropriate money for an object and the right to apply and expend it without the embarrassment and delay of applications to the State governments. Probably no instance occurred in which such an application was made, and the flood gates being thus hoisted the principle laid down by him was disregarded, and applications for aid from the Treasury, virtually to make harbors as well as improve them, clear out rivers, cut canals, and construct roads, poured into Congress in torrents until arrested by the veto of President Jackson. His veto of the Maysville road bill was followed up by his refusal to sign the "Act making appropriations for building light-houses, light-boats, beacons, and monuments, placing buoys, improving harbors, and directing surveys;" "An act authorizing subscriptions for stock in the Louisville and Portland Canal Company;" "An act for the improvement of certain harbors and the navigation of certain rivers;" and, finally, "An act to improve the navigation of the Wabash River." In his objections to the act last named he says:

> The desire to embark the Federal Government in works of internal improvement prevailed in the highest degree during the first session of the first Congress that I had the honor to meet in my present situation. When the bill authorizing a subscription on the part of the United States for stock in the Maysville and Lexington Turnpike Company passed the two Houses, there had been reported by the Committees of Internal Improvements bills containing appropriations for such objects, inclusive of those for the Cumberland road and for harbors and light-houses, to the amount of $106,000,000. In this amount was included authority to the Secretary of the Treasury to subscribe for the stock of different companies to a great extent, and the residue was principally for the direct construction of roads by this Government. In addition to these projects, which had been presented to the two Houses under the sanction and recommendation of their respective Committees on Internal Improvements, there were then still pending before the committees and in memorials to Congress presented but not referred different projects for works of a similar character, the expense of which can not be estimated with certainty, but must have exceeded $100,000,000.

Thus, within the brief period of less than ten years after the commencement of internal improvements by the General Government the sum asked for from the Treasury for various projects amounted to more than $200,000,000. President Jackson's powerful and disinterested appeals to his country appear to have put down forever the assumption of power to make roads and cut canals, and to have checked the prevalent disposition to bring all rivers in any degree navigable within the control of the General Government. But an immense field for expending the public money and increasing the power and patronage of this Government was left open in the concession of even a limited power of Congress to improve harbors and rivers—a field which millions will not fertilize to the satisfaction of those local and speculating interests by which these projects are in general gotten up. There can not be a just and equal distribution of public burdens and benefits under such a system, nor can the States be relieved from the danger of fatal encroachment, nor the United States from the equal danger of consolidation, otherwise than by an arrest of the system and a return to the doctrines and practices which prevailed during the first thirty years of the Government.

How forcibly does the history of this subject illustrate the tendency of power to concentration in the hands of the General Government. The power to improve their own harbors and rivers was clearly reserved to the States, who were to be aided by tonnage duties levied and collected by themselves, with the consent of Congress. For thirty-four years improvements were carried on under that system, and so careful was Congress not to interfere, under any implied power, with the soil or jurisdiction of the States that they did not even assume the power to erect light-houses or build piers without first purchasing the ground, with the consent of the States, and obtaining jurisdiction over it. At length, after the lapse of thirty-three years, an act is passed providing for the examination of certain obstructions at the mouth of one or two harbors almost unknown. It is followed by acts making small appropriations for the removal of those obstructions. The obstacles interposed by President Monroe, after conceding the power to appropriate, were soon swept away. Congress virtually assumed jurisdiction of the soil and waters of the States, without their consent, for the purposes of internal improvement, and the eyes of eager millions were turned from the State governments to Congress as the fountain whose golden streams were to deepen their harbors and rivers, level their mountains, and fill their valleys with canals. To what consequences this assumption of power was rapidly leading is shown by the veto messages of President Jackson, and to what end it is again tending is witnessed by the provisions of this bill and bills of similar character.

In the proceedings and debates of the General Convention which formed the Constitution and of the State conventions which adopted it nothing is found to countenance the idea that the one intended to propose or the others to concede such a grant of power to the General Government as the building up and maintaining of a system of internal improvements within the States necessarily implies. Whatever the General Government may constitutionally create, it may lawfully protect. If it may make a road upon the soil of the States, it may protect it from destruction or injury by penal laws. So of canals, rivers, and harbors. If it may put a dam in a river, it may protect that dam from removal or injury, in direct opposition to the laws, authorities, and people of the State in which it is situated. If it may deepen a harbor, it may by its own laws protect its agents and contractors from being driven from their work even by the laws and authorities of the State. The power to make a road or canal or to dig up the bottom of a harbor or river implies a right in the soil of the State and a jurisdiction over it, for which it would be impossible to find any warrant.

The States were particularly jealous of conceding to the General Government any right of jurisdiction over their soil, and in the Constitution restricted the exclusive legislation of Congress to such places as might be "purchased with the consent of the States in which the same shall be, for the erection of forts, magazines, dockyards, and other needful buildings." That the United States should be prohibited from purchasing lands within the States without their consent, even for the most essential purposes of national defense, while left at liberty to purchase or seize them for roads, canals, and other improvements of immeasurably less importance, is not to be conceived.

A proposition was made in the Convention to provide for the appointment of a "Secretary of Domestic Affairs," and make it his duty, among other things, "to attend to the opening of roads and navigation and the facilitating communications through the United States." It was referred to a committee, and that appears to have been the last of it. On a subsequent occasion a proposition was made to confer on Congress the power to "provide for the cutting of canals when deemed necessary," which was rejected by the strong majority of eight States to three. Among the reasons given for the rejection of this proposition, it was urged that "the expense in such cases will fall on the United States and the benefits accrue to the places where the canals may be cut."

During the consideration of this proposition a motion was made to enlarge the proposed power for "cutting canals" into a power "to grant charters of incorporation when the interest of the United States might require and the legislative provisions of the individual States may be incompetent;" and the reason assigned by Mr. Madison for the proposed enlargement of the power was that it would "secure an easy communication between the States, which the free intercourse now to be opened seemed to call for. The political obstacles being removed, a removal of the natural ones, as far as possible, ought to follow."

The original proposition and all the amendments were rejected, after deliberate discussion, not on the ground, as so much of that discussion as has been preserved indicates, that no direct grant was necessary, but because it was deemed inexpedient to grant it at all. When it is considered that some of the members of the Convention, who afterwards participated in the organization and administration of the Government, advocated and practiced upon a very liberal construction of the Constitution, grasping at many high powers as implied in its various provisions, not one of them, it is believed, at that day claimed the power to make roads and canals, or improve rivers and harbors, or appropriate money for that purpose. Among our early statesmen of the strict-construction class the opinion was universal, when the subject was first broached, that Congress did not possess the power, although some of them thought it desirable.

President Jefferson, in his message to Congress in 1806, recommended an amendment of the Constitution, with a view to apply an anticipated surplus in the Treasury "to the great purposes of the public education, roads, rivers, canals, and such other objects of public improvement as it may be thought proper to add to the constitutional enumeration of Federal powers." And he adds:

I suppose an amendment to the Constitution, by consent of the States, necessary, because the objects now recommended are not among those enumerated in the Constitution, and to which it permits the public moneys to be applied.

In 1825 he repeated, in his published letters, the opinion that no such power has been conferred upon Congress.

President Madison, in a message to the House of Representatives of the 3d of March, 1817, assigning his objections to a bill entitled "An act to set apart and pledge certain funds for internal improvements," declares that—

"The power to regulate commerce among the several States" can not include a power to construct roads and canals and to *improve the navigation of water courses* in order to facilitate, promote, and secure such a commerce without a latitude of construction departing from the ordinary import of the terms, strengthened by the known inconveniences which doubtless led to the grant of this remedial power to Congress.

President Monroe, in a message to the House of Representatives of the 4th of May, 1822, containing his objections to a bill entitled "An act for the preservation and repair of the Cumberland road," declares:

Commerce between independent powers or communities is universally regulated by duties and imposts. It was so regulated by the States before the adoption of this Constitution, equally in respect to each other and to foreign powers. The goods and vessels employed in the trade are the only subjects of regulation. It can act on none other. A power, then, to impose such duties and imposts in regard to foreign nations and to prevent any on the trade between the States was the only power granted.

If we recur to the causes which produced the adoption of this Constitution, we shall find that injuries resulting from the regulation of trade by the States respectively and the advantages anticipated from the transfer of the power to Congress were among those which had the most weight. Instead of acting as a nation in regard to foreign powers, the States individually had commenced a system of restraint on each other whereby the interests of foreign powers were promoted at their expense. If one State imposed high duties on the goods or vessels of a foreign power to countervail the regulations of such power, the next adjoining States imposed lighter duties to invite those articles into their ports, that they might be transferred thence into the other States, securing the duties to themselves. This contracted policy in some of the States was soon counteracted by others. Restraints were immediately laid on such commerce by the suffering States; and thus had grown up a state of affairs disorderly and unnatural, the tendency of which was to destroy the Union itself and with it all hope of realizing those blessings which we had anticipated from the glorious Revolution which had been so recently achieved. From this deplorable dilemma, or, rather, certain ruin, we were happily rescued by the adoption of the Constitution.

Among the first and most important effects ot this great Revolution was the complete abolition of this pernicious policy. The States were brought together by the Constitution, as to commerce, into one community, equally in regard to foreign nations and each other. The regulations that were adopted regarded us in both respects as one people. The duties and imposts that were laid on the vessels and merchandise of foreign nations were all uniform throughout the United States, and in the intercourse between the States themselves no duties of any kind were imposed other than between different ports and counties within the same State.

This view is supported by a series of measures, all of a marked character, preceding the adoption of the Constitution. As early as the year 1781 Congress recommended it to the States to vest in the United States a power to levy a duty of 5 per cent on all goods imported from foreign countries into the United States for the term of fifteen years. In 1783 this recommendation, with alterations as to the kind of duties and an extension of this term to twenty-five years, was repeated and more earnestly urged. In 1784 it was recommended to the States to authorize Congress to prohibit, under certain modifications, the importation of goods from foreign powers into the United States for fifteen years. In 1785 the consideration of the subject was resumed, and a proposition presented in a new form, with an address to the States explaining fully the principles on which a grant of the power to regulate trade was deemed indispensable. In 1786 a meeting took place at Annapolis of delegates from several of the States on this subject, and on their report a convention was formed at Philadelphia the ensuing year from all the States, to whose deliberations we are indebted for the present Constitution.

In none of these measures was the subject of internal improvement mentioned or even glanced at. Those of 1784, 1785, 1786, and 1787, leading step by step to the adoption of the Constitution, had in view only the obtaining of a power to enable Congress to regulate trade with foreign powers. It is manifest that the regulation of trade with the several States was altogether a secondary object, suggested by and adopted in connection with the other. If the power necessary to this system of improvement is included under either branch of this grant, I should suppose that it was the first rather than the second. The pretension to it, however, under that branch has never been set up. In support of the claim under the second no reason has been assigned which appears to have the least weight.

Such is a brief history of the origin, progress, and consequences of a system which for more than thirty years after the adoption of the Constitution was unknown. The greatest embarrassment upon the subject consists in the departure which has taken place from the early construction of the Constitution and the precedents which are found in the legislation of Congress in later years. President Jackson, in his veto of the Wabash River bill, declares that "to inherent embarrassments have been added others resulting from the course of our legislation concerning it." In his vetoes on the Maysville road bill, the Rockville road bill, the Wabash River bill, and other bills of like character he reversed the precedents which existed prior to that time on the subject of internal improvements. When our experience, observation, and reflection have convinced us that a legislative precedent is either unwise or unconstitutional, it should not be followed.

No express grant of this power is found in the Constitution. Its advocates have differed among themselves as to the source from which it is derived as an incident. In the progress of the discussions upon this subject the power to regulate commerce seems now to be chiefly relied upon, especially in reference to the improvement of harbors and rivers.

In relation to the regulation of commerce, the language of the grant in the Constitution is:

> Congress shall have power to regulate commerce with foreign nations, and among the several States, and with the Indian tribes.

That to "regulate commerce" does not mean to make a road, or dig a canal, or clear out a river, or deepen a harbor would seem to be obvious to the common understanding. To "regulate" admits or affirms the preexistence of the thing to be regulated. In this case it presupposes the existence of commerce, and, of course, the means by which and the channels through which commerce is carried on. It confers no creative power; it only assumes control over that which may have been brought into existence through other agencies, such as State legislation and the industry and enterprise of individuals. If the definition of the word "regulate" is to include the provision of means to carry on commerce, then have Congress not only power to deepen harbors, clear out rivers, dig canals, and make roads, but also to build ships, railroad cars, and other vehicles, all of which are necessary to commerce. There is no middle ground. If the power to regulate can be legitimately construed into a power to create or facilitate, then not only the bays and harbors, but the roads and canals and all the means of transporting merchandise among the several States, are put at the disposition of Congress. This power to regulate commerce was construed and exercised immediately after the adoption of the Constitution, and has been exercised to the present day, by prescribing general rules by which commerce should be conducted. With foreign nations it has been regulated by treaties defining the rights of citizens and subjects, as well as by acts of Congress imposing duties and restrictions embracing vessels, seamen, cargoes, and passengers. It has been regulated among the States by acts of Congress relating to the coasting trade and the vessels employed therein, and for the better security of passengers in vessels propelled by steam, and by the removal of all restrictions upon internal trade. It has been regulated with the Indian tribes by our intercourse laws, prescribing the manner in which it shall be carried on. Thus each branch of this grant of power was exercised soon after the adoption of the Constitution, and has continued to be exercised to the present day. If a more extended construction be adopted, it is impossible for the human mind to fix on a limit to the exercise of the power other than the will and discretion of Congress. It sweeps into the vortex of national power and jurisdiction not only harbors and inlets, rivers and little streams, but canals, turnpikes, and railroads—every species of improvement which can facilitate or create trade and intercourse "with foreign nations, and among the several States, and with the Indian tribes."

Should any great object of improvement exist in our widely extended country which can not be effected by means of tonnage duties levied by the States with the concurrence of Congress, it is safer and wiser to apply to the States in the mode prescribed by the Constitution for an amendment of that instrument whereby the powers of the General Government may be enlarged, with such limitations and restrictions as experience has shown to be proper, than to assume and exercise a power which has not been granted, or which may be regarded as doubtful in the opinion of a large portion of our constituents. This course has been recommended successively by Presidents Jefferson, Madison, Monroe, and Jackson, and I fully concur with them in opinion. If an enlargement of power should be deemed proper, it will unquestionably be granted by the States; if otherwise, it will be withheld; and in either case their decision should be final. In the meantime I deem it proper to add that the investigation of this subject has impressed me more strongly than ever with the solemn conviction that the usefulness and permanency of this Government and the happiness of the millions over whom it spreads its protection will be best promoted by carefully abstaining from the exercise of all powers not clearly granted by the Constitution.

JAMES K. POLK

PROCLAMATION.

BY THE PRESIDENT OF THE UNITED STATES OF AMERICA.

A PROCLAMATION.

Whereas a treaty of peace, friendship, limits, and settlement between the United States of America and the Mexican Republic was concluded and signed at the city of Guadalupe Hidalgo on the 2d day of February, 1848, which treaty, as amended by the Senate of the United States, and being in the English and Spanish languages, is word for word as follows:

[Here follows the treaty.]

And whereas the said treaty, as amended, has been duly ratified on both parts, and the respective ratifications of the same were exchanged at Queretaro on the 30th day of May last by Ambrose H. Sevier and Nathan Clifford, commissioners on the part of the Government of the United States, and by Señor Don Luis de la Rosa, minister of relations of the Mexican Republic, on the part of that Government:

Now, therefore, be it known that I, James K. Polk, President of the United States of America, have caused the said treaty to be made public, to the end that the same and every clause and article thereof may be observed and fulfilled with good faith by the United States and the citizens thereof.

In witness whereof I have hereunto set my hand and caused the seal of the United States to be affixed.

[SEAL.] Done at the city of Washington, this 4th day of July, 1848, and of the Independence of the United States the seventy-third.

JAMES K. POLK.

By the President:

JAMES BUCHANAN, *Secretary of State.*

EXECUTIVE ORDER.

GENERAL ORDERS, NO. 9.

WAR DEPARTMENT, ADJUTANT-GENERAL'S OFFICE,
Washington, February 24, 1848.

I. The following orders of the President of the United States and Secretary of War announce to the Army the death of the illustrious ex-President John Quincy Adams:

BY THE PRESIDENT OF THE UNITED STATES.

WASHINGTON, *February 24, 1848.*

It has pleased Divine Providence to call hence a great and patriotic citizen. John Quincy Adams is no more. At the advanced age of more than fourscore years, he was suddenly stricken from his seat in the House of Representatives by the hand of disease on the 21st, and expired in the Capitol a few minutes after 7 o'clock on the evening of the 23d of February, 1848.

He had for more than half a century filled the most important public stations, and among them that of President of the United States. The two Houses of Congress, of one of which he was a venerable and most distinguished member, will doubtless prescribe appropriate ceremonies to be observed as a mark of respect for the memory of this eminent citizen.

The nation mourns his loss; and as a further testimony of respect for his memory I direct that all the executive offices at Washington be placed in mourning and that all business be suspended during this day and to-morrow.

JAMES K. POLK.

WAR DEPARTMENT, *February 24, 1848.*

The President of the United States with deep regret announces to the Army the death of John Quincy Adams, our eminent and venerated fellow-citizen.

While occupying his seat as a member of the House of Representatives, on the 21st instant he was suddenly prostrated by disease, and on the 23d expired, without having been removed from the Capitol. He had filled many honorable and responsible stations in the service of his country, and among them that of President of the United States; and he closed his long and eventful life in the actual discharge of his duties as one of the Representatives of the people.

From sympathy with his relatives and the American people for his loss and from respect for his distinguished public services, the President orders that funeral honors shall be paid to his memory at each of the military stations.

The Adjutant-General will give the necessary instructions for carrying into effect the foregoing orders.

W. L. MARCY,
Secretary of War.

II. On the day succeeding the arrival of this general order at each military post the troops will be paraded at 10 o'clock a. m. and the order read to them, after which all labors for the day will cease.

The national flag will be displayed at half-staff.

At dawn of day thirteen guns will be fired, and afterwards, at intervals of thirty minutes between the rising and setting sun, a single gun, and at the close of the day a national salute of twenty-nine guns.

The officers of the Army will wear crape on the left arm and on their swords and the colors of the several regiments will be put in mourning for the period of six months.

By order:

R. JONES,
Adjutant-General.

FOURTH ANNUAL MESSAGE.

WASHINGTON, *December 5, 1848.*

Fellow-Citizens of the Senate and of the House of Representatives:

Under the benignant providence of Almighty God the representatives of the States and of the people are again brought together to deliberate for the public good. The gratitude of the nation to the Sovereign Arbiter of All Human Events should be commensurate with the boundless blessings which we enjoy.

Peace, plenty, and contentment reign throughout our borders, and our beloved country presents a sublime moral spectacle to the world.

The troubled and unsettled condition of some of the principal European powers has had a necessary tendency to check and embarrass trade and to depress prices throughout all commercial nations, but notwithstanding these causes, the United States, with their abundant products, have felt their effects less severely than any other country, and all our great interests are still prosperous and successful.

In reviewing the great events of the past year and contrasting the agitated and disturbed state of other countries with our own tranquil and happy condition, we may congratulate ourselves that we are the most favored people on the face of the earth. While the people of other countries are struggling to establish free institutions, under which man may govern himself, we are in the actual enjoyment of them—a rich inheritance from our fathers. While enlightened nations of Europe are convulsed and distracted by civil war or intestine strife, we settle all our political controversies by the peaceful exercise of the rights of freemen at the ballot box.

The great republican maxim, so deeply engraven on the hearts of our people, that the will of the majority, constitutionally expressed, shall prevail, is our sure safeguard against force and violence. It is a subject of just pride that our fame and character as a nation continue rapidly to advance in the estimation of the civilized world.

To our wise and free institutions it is to be attributed that while other nations have achieved glory at the price of the suffering, distress, and impoverishment of their people, we have won our honorable position in the midst of an uninterrupted prosperity and of an increasing individual comfort and happiness.

I am happy to inform you that our relations with all nations are friendly and pacific. Advantageous treaties of commerce have been concluded within the last four years with New Granada, Peru, the Two Sicilies, Belgium, Hanover, Oldenburg, and Mecklenburg-Schwerin. Pursuing our example, the restrictive system of Great Britain, our principal foreign customer, has been relaxed, a more liberal commercial policy has been adopted by other enlightened nations, and our trade has been greatly enlarged and extended. Our country stands higher in the respect of the world than at any former period. To continue to occupy this proud position, it is only necessary to preserve peace and faithfully adhere to the great and fundamental principle of our foreign policy of noninterference in the domestic concerns of other nations. We recognize in all nations the right which we enjoy ourselves, to change and reform their political institutions according to their own will and pleasure. Hence we do not look behind existing governments capable of maintaining their own authority. We recognize all such actual governments, not only from the dictates of true policy, but from a sacred regard for the independence of nations. While this is our settled policy, it does not follow that we can ever be indifferent spectators of the progress of liberal principles. The Government and people of the United States hailed with enthusiasm and delight the establishment of the French Republic, as we now hail the efforts in progress to unite the States of Germany in a confederation similar in many respects to our own Federal Union. If the great and enlightened German States, occupying, as they do, a central and commanding position in Europe, shall succeed in establishing such a confederated government, securing at the same time to the citizens of each State local governments adapted to the peculiar condition of each, with unrestricted trade and intercourse with each other, it will be an important era in the history of human events. Whilst it will consolidate and strengthen the power of Germany, it must essentially promote the cause of peace, commerce, civilization, and constitutional liberty throughout the world.

With all the Governments on this continent our relations, it is believed, are now on a more friendly and satisfactory footing than they have ever been at any former period.

Since the exchange of ratifications of the treaty of peace with Mexico our intercourse with the Government of that Republic has been of the most friendly character. The envoy extraordinary and minister plenipotentiary of the United States to Mexico has been received and accredited, and a diplomatic representative from Mexico of similar rank has been received and accredited by this Government The amicable relations between the two countries, which had been suspended, have been happily restored, and are destined, I trust, to be long preserved. The two Republics, both situated on this continent, and with coterminous territories, have every motive of sympathy and of interest to bind them together in perpetual amity.

This gratifying condition of our foreign relations renders it unnecessary for me to call your attention more specifically to them.

It has been my constant aim and desire to cultivate peace and commerce with all nations. Tranquillity at home and peaceful relations abroad constitute the true permanent policy of our country. War, the scourge of nations, sometimes becomes inevitable, but is always to be avoided when it can be done consistently with the rights and honor of a nation.

One of the most important results of the war into which we were recently forced with a neighboring nation is the demonstration it has afforded of the military strength of our country. Before the late war with Mexico European and other foreign powers entertained imperfect and erroneous views of our physical strength as a nation and of our ability to prosecute war, and especially a war waged out of our own country. They saw that our standing Army on the peace establishment did not exceed 10,000 men. Accustomed themselves to maintain in peace large standing armies for the protection of thrones against their own subjects, as well as against foreign enemies, they had not conceived that it was possible for a nation without such an army, well disciplined and of long service, to wage war successfully. They held in low repute our militia, and were far from regarding them as an effective force, unless it might be for temporary defensive operations when invaded on our own soil. The events of the late war with Mexico have not only undeceived them, but have removed erroneous impressions which prevailed to some extent even among a portion of our own countrymen. That war has demonstrated that upon the breaking out of hostilities not anticipated, and for which no previous preparation had been made, a volunteer army of citizen soldiers equal to veteran troops, and in numbers equal to any emergency, can in a short period be brought into the field. Unlike what would have occurred in any other country, we were under no necessity of resorting to drafts or conscriptions. On the contrary, such was the number of volunteers who patriotically tendered their services that the chief difficulty was in making selections and determining who should be disappointed and compelled to remain at home. Our citizen soldiers are unlike those drawn from the population of any other country. They are composed indiscriminately of all professions and pursuits—of farmers, lawyers, physicians, merchants, manufacturers, mechanics, and laborers—and this not only among the officers, but the private soldiers in the ranks. Our citizen soldiers are unlike those of any other country in other respects. They are armed, and have been accustomed from their youth up to handle and use firearms, and a large proportion of them, especially in the Western and more newly settled States, are expert marksmen. They are men who have a reputation to maintain at home by their good conduct in the field. They are intelligent, and there is an individuality of character which is found in the ranks of no other army. In battle each private man, as well as every officer, fights not only for his country, but for glory and distinction among his fellow-citizens when he shall return to civil life.

The war with Mexico has demonstrated not only the ability of the Government to organize a numerous army upon a sudden call, but also to provide it with all the munitions and necessary supplies with dispatch, convenience, and ease, and to direct its operations with efficiency. The strength of our institutions has not only been displayed in the valor and skill of our troops engaged in active service in the field, but in the organization of those executive branches which were charged with the general direction and conduct of the war. While too great praise can not be bestowed upon the officers and men who fought our battles, it would be unjust to withhold from those officers necessarily stationed at home, who were charged with the duty of furnishing the Army in proper time and at proper places with all the munitions of war and other supplies so necessary to make it efficient, the commendation to which they are entitled. The credit due to this class of our officers is the greater when it is considered that no army in ancient or modern times was ever better appointed or provided than our Army in Mexico. Operating in an enemy's country, removed 2,000 miles from the seat of the Federal Government, its different corps spread over a vast extent of territory, hundreds and even thousands of miles apart from each other, nothing short of the untiring vigilance and extraordinary energy of these officers could have enabled them to provide the Army at all points and in proper season with all that was required for the most efficient service.

It is but an act of justice to declare that the officers in charge of the several executive bureaus, all under the immediate eye and supervision of the Secretary of War, performed their respective duties with ability, energy, and efficiency. They have reaped less of the glory of the war, not having been personally exposed to its perils in battle, than their companions in arms; but without their forecast, efficient aid, and cooperation those in the field would not have been provided with the ample means they possessed of achieving for themselves and their country the unfading honors which they have won for both.

When all these facts are considered, it may cease to be a matter of so much amazement abroad how it happened that our noble Army in Mexico, regulars and volunteers, were victorious upon every battlefield, however fearful the odds against them.

The war with Mexico has thus fully developed the capacity of republican governments to prosecute successfully a just and necessary foreign war with all the vigor usually attributed to more arbitrary forms of government. It has been usual for writers on public law to impute to republics a want of that unity, concentration of purpose, and vigor of execution which are generally admitted to belong to the monarchical and aristocratic forms; and this feature of popular government has been supposed to display itself more particularly in the conduct of a war carried on in an enemy's territory. The war with Great Britain in 1812 was to a great extent confined within our own limits, and shed but little light on this subject; but the war which we have just closed by an honorable peace evinces beyond all doubt that a popular representative government is equal to any emergency which is likely to arise in the affairs of a nation.

The war with Mexico has developed most strikingly and conspicuously another feature in our institutions. It is that without cost to the Government or danger to our liberties we have in the bosom of our society of freemen, available in a just and necessary war, virtually a standing army of 2,000,000 armed citizen soldiers, such as fought the battles of Mexico. But our military strength does not consist alone in our capacity for extended and successful operations on land. The Navy is an important arm of the national defense. If the services of the Navy were not so brilliant as those of the Army in the late war with Mexico, it was because they had no enemy to meet on their own element. While the Army had opportunity of performing more conspicuous service, the Navy largely participated in the conduct of the war. Both branches of the service performed their whole duty to the country. For the able and gallant services of the officers and men of the Navy, acting independently as well as in cooperation with our troops, in the conquest of the Californias, the capture of Vera Cruz, and the seizure and occupation of other important positions on the Gulf and Pacific coasts, the highest praise is due. Their vigilance, energy, and skill rendered the most effective service in excluding munitions of war and other supplies from the enemy, while they secured a safe entrance for abundant supplies for our own Army. Our extended commerce was nowhere interrupted, and for this immunity from the evils of war the country is indebted to the Navy.

High praise is due to the officers of the several executive bureaus, navy-yards, and stations connected with the service, all under the immediate direction of the Secretary of the Navy, for the industry, foresight, and energy with which everything was directed and furnished to give efficiency to that branch of the service. The same vigilance existed in directing the operations of the Navy as of the Army. There was concert of action and of purpose between the heads of the two arms of the service. By the orders which were from time to time issued, our vessels of war on the Pacific and the Gulf of Mexico were stationed in proper time and in proper positions to cooperate efficiently with the Army. By this means their combined power was brought to bear successfully on the enemy.

The great results which have been developed and brought to light by this war will be of immeasurable importance in the future progress of our country. They will tend powerfully to preserve us from foreign collisions, and to enable us to pursue uninterruptedly our cherished policy of "peace with all nations, entangling alliances with none."

Occupying, as we do, a more commanding position among nations than at any former period, our duties and our responsibilities to ourselves and to posterity are correspondingly increased. This will be the more obvious when we consider the vast additions which have been recently made to our territorial possessions and their great importance and value.

Within less than four years the annexation of Texas to the Union has been consummated; all conflicting title to the Oregon Territory south of the forty-ninth degree of north latitude, being all that was insisted on by any of my predecessors, has been adjusted, and New Mexico and Upper California have been acquired by treaty. The area of these several Territories, according to a report carefully prepared by the Commissioner of the General Land Office from the most authentic information in his possession, and which is herewith transmitted, contains 1,193,061 square miles, or 763,559,040 acres; while the area of the remaining twenty-nine States and the territory not yet organized into States east of the Rocky Mountains contains 2,059,513 square miles, or 1,318,126,058 acres. These estimates show that the territories recently acquired, and over which our exclusive jurisdiction and dominion have been extended, constitute a country more than half as large as all that which was held by the United States before their acquisition. If Oregon be excluded from the estimate, there will still remain within the limits of Texas, New Mexico, and California 851,598 square miles, or 545,012,720 acres, being an addition equal to more than one-third of all the territory owned by the United States before their acquisition, and, including Oregon, nearly as great an extent of territory as the whole of Europe, Russia only excepted. The Mississippi, so lately the frontier of our country, is now only its center. With the addition of the late acquisitions, the United States are now estimated to be nearly as large as the whole of Europe. It is estimated by the Superintendent of the Coast Survey in the accompanying report that the extent of the seacoast of Texas on the Gulf of Mexico is upward of 400 miles; of the coast of Upper California on the Pacific, of 970 miles, and of Oregon, including the Straits of Fuca, of 650 miles, making the whole extent of seacoast on the Pacific 1,620 miles and the whole extent on both the Pacific and the Gulf of Mexico 2,020 miles. The length of the coast on the Atlantic from the northern limits of the United States around the capes of Florida to the Sabine, on the eastern boundary of Texas, is estimated to be 3,100 miles; so that the addition of seacoast, including Oregon, is very nearly two-thirds as great as all we possessed before, and, excluding Oregon, is an addition of 1,370 miles, being nearly equal to one-half of the extent of coast which we possessed before these acquisitions. We have now three great maritime fronts—on the Atlantic, the Gulf of Mexico, and the Pacific—making in the whole an extent of seacoast exceeding 5,000 miles. This is the extent of the seacoast of the United States, not including bays, sounds, and small irregularities of the main shore and of the sea islands. If these be included, the length of the shore line of coast, as estimated by the Superintendent of the Coast Survey in his report, would be 33,063 miles.

It would be difficult to calculate the value of these immense additions to our territorial possessions. Texas, lying contiguous to the western boundary of Louisiana, embracing within its limits a part of the navigable tributary waters of the Mississippi and an extensive seacoast, could not long have remained in the hands of a foreign power without endangering the peace of our southwestern frontier. Her products in the vicinity of the tributaries of the Mississippi must have sought a market through these streams, running into and through our territory, and the danger of irritation and collision of interests between Texas as a foreign state and ourselves would have been imminent, while the embarrassments in the commercial intercourse between them must have been constant and unavoidable. Had Texas fallen into the hands or under the influence and control of a strong maritime or military foreign power, as she might have done, these dangers would have been still greater. They have been avoided by her voluntary and peaceful annexation to the United States. Texas, from her position, was a natural and almost indispensable part of our territories. Fortunately, she has been restored to our country, and now constitutes one of the States of our Confederacy, "upon an equal footing with the original States." The salubrity of climate, the fertility of soil, peculiarly adapted to the production of some of our most valuable staple commodities, and her commercial advantages must soon make her one of our most populous States.

New Mexico, though situated in the interior and without a seacoast, is known to contain much fertile land, to abound in rich mines of the precious metals, and to be capable of sustaining a large population. From its position it is the intermediate and connecting territory between our settlements and our possessions in Texas and those on the Pacific Coast.

Upper California, irrespective of the vast mineral wealth recently developed there, holds at this day, in point of value and importance, to the rest of the Union the same relation that Louisiana did when that fine territory was acquired from France forty-five years ago. Extending nearly ten degrees of latitude along the Pacific, and embracing the only safe and commodious harbors on that coast for many hundred miles, with a temperate climate and an extensive interior of fertile lands, it is scarcely possible to estimate its wealth until it shall be brought under the government of our laws and its resources fully developed. From its position it must command the rich commerce of China, of Asia, of the islands of the Pacific, of western Mexico, of Central America, the South American States, and of the Russian possessions bordering on that ocean. A great emporium will doubtless speedily arise on the Californian coast which may be destined to rival in importance New Orleans itself. The depot of the vast commerce which must exist on the Pacific will probably be at some point on the Bay of San Francisco, and will occupy the same relation to the whole western coast of that ocean as New Orleans does to the valley of the Mississippi and the Gulf of Mexico. To this depot our numerous whale ships will resort with their cargoes to trade, refit, and obtain supplies. This of itself will largely contribute to build up a city, which would soon become the center of a great and rapidly increasing commerce. Situated on a safe harbor, sufficiently capacious for all the navies as well as the marine of the world, and convenient to excellent timber for shipbuilding, owned by the United States, it must become our great Western naval depot.

It was known that mines of the precious metals existed to a considerable extent in California at the time of its acquisition. Recent discoveries render it probable that these mines are more extensive and valuable than was anticipated. The accounts of the abundance of gold in that territory are of such an extraordinary character as would scarcely command belief were they not corroborated by the authentic reports of officers in the public service who have visited the mineral district and derived the facts which they detail from personal observation. Reluctant to credit the reports in general circulation as to the quantity of gold, the officer commanding our forces in California visited the mineral district in July last for the purpose of obtaining accurate information on the subject. His report to the War Department of the result of his examination and the facts obtained on the spot is herewith laid before Congress. When he visited the country there were about 4,000 persons engaged in collecting gold. There is every reason to believe that the number of persons so employed has since been augmented. The explorations already made warrant the belief that the supply is very large and that gold is found at various places in an extensive district of country.

Information received from officers of the Navy and other sources, though not so full and minute, confirms the accounts of the commander of our military force in California. It appears also from these reports that mines of quicksilver are found in the vicinity of the gold region. One of them is now being worked, and is believed to be among the most productive in the world.

The effects produced by the discovery of these rich mineral deposits and the success which has attended the labors of those who have resorted to them have produced a surprising change in the state of affairs in California. Labor commands a most exorbitant price, and all other pursuits but that of searching for the precious metals are abandoned. Nearly the whole of the male population of the country have gone to the gold districts. Ships arriving on the coast are deserted by their crews and their voyages suspended for want of sailors. Our commanding officer there entertains apprehensions that soldiers can not be kept in the public service without a large increase of pay. Desertions in his command have become frequent, and he recommends that those who shall withstand the strong temptation and remain faithful should be rewarded.

This abundance of gold and the all-engrossing pursuit of it have already caused in California an unprecedented rise in the price of all the necessaries of life.

That we may the more speedily and fully avail ourselves of the undeveloped wealth of these mines, it is deemed of vast importance that a branch of the Mint of the United States be authorized to be established

THE DAYS OF FORTY-NINE IN CALIFORNIA

THE DAYS OF FORTY-NINE IN CALIFORNIA

Sutter's discovery of gold in 1848 could not be kept secret; by May of that year San Francisco was deserted by its male population. By March, 1849, more than seventeen thousand gold hunters had embarked at Atlantic and Gulf ports for California, either intending to make the seven-month's journey around Cape Horn, or, after landing in Panama, Nicaragua or Mexico, cross overland to the Pacific and there re-embark. By May an equal number had begun the overland journey. San Francisco was their objective point. It was composed of a few old Mexican residences and a host of shacks, tents and shanties for the temporary accommodation of the hordes who made the town a stopping-place on their route to the El Dorado. Four or five hundred ships, whose crews and captains had caught the gold fever and deserted, lay rotting in the harbor; cargoes of goods, unsuitable to the population but worth fortunes, were strewn on the beach; gold was the only currency in use, an ounce of it being worth $16; unskilled labor received $10 per diem, while carpenters and blacksmiths received $16; a candle cost $3; a shirt, $40; a barrel of pork, $210; a tin basin, $9. El Dorado, the chief gambling tent, paid $40,000 a year rent; the Parker House, a two-story hotel, paid $120,000 a year rent. The law was meted out by an alcalde, who heard complaints, settled disputes and summoned juries. Punishments in the shape of fines, flogging, expulsion from the camps and death were awarded. Each man's right to his claim was carefully guarded.

The pictures, being contemporary, are unquestionably truthful representations of (1) a faro outfit, (2) a dance hall, and (3) Chinese employees of the miners.

See the article "California" in the Encyclopedic Index.

at your present session in California. Among other signal advantages which would result from such an establishment would be that of raising the gold to its par value in that territory. A branch mint of the United States at the great commercial depot on the west coast would convert into our own coin not only the gold derived from our own rich mines, but also the bullion and specie which our commerce may bring from the whole west coast of Central and South America. The west coast of America and the adjacent interior embrace the richest and best mines of Mexico, New Granada, Central America, Chili, and Peru. The bullion and specie drawn from these countries, and especially from those of western Mexico and Peru, to an amount in value of many millions of dollars, are now annually diverted and carried by the ships of Great Britain to her own ports, to be recoined or used to sustain her national bank, and thus contribute to increase her ability to command so much of the commerce of the world. If a branch mint be established at the great commercial point upon that coast, a vast amount of bullion and specie would flow thither to be recoined, and pass thence to New Orleans, New York, and other Atlantic cities. The amount of our constitutional currency at home would be greatly increased, while its circulation abroad would be promoted. It is well known to our merchants trading to China and the west coast of America that great inconvenience and loss are experienced from the fact that our coins are not current at their par value in those countries.

The powers of Europe, far removed from the west coast of America by the Atlantic Ocean, which intervenes, and by a tedious and dangerous navigation around the southern cape of the continent of America, can never successfully compete with the United States in the rich and extensive commerce which is opened to us at so much less cost by the acquisition of California.

The vast importance and commercial advantages of California have heretofore remained undeveloped by the Government of the country of which it constituted a part. Now that this fine province is a part of our country, all the States of the Union, some more immediately and directly than others, are deeply interested in the speedy development of its wealth and resources. No section of our country is more interested or will be more benefited than the commercial, navigating, and manufacturing interests of the Eastern States. Our planting and farming interests in every part of the Union will be greatly benefited by it. As our commerce and navigation are enlarged and extended, our exports of agricultural products and of manufactures will be increased, and in the new markets thus opened they can not fail to command remunerating and profitable prices.

The acquisition of California and New Mexico, the settlement of the Oregon boundary, and the annexation of Texas, extending to the Rio Grande, are results which, combined, are of greater consequence and will add more to the strength and wealth of the nation than any which have preceded them since the adoption of the Constitution.

But to effect these great results not only California, but New Mexico, must be brought under the control of regularly organized governments. The existing condition of California and of that part of New Mexico lying west of the Rio Grande and without the limits of Texas imperiously demands that Congress should at its present session organize Territorial governments over them.

Upon the exchange of ratifications of the treaty of peace with Mexico, on the 30th of May last, the temporary governments which had been established over New Mexico and California by our military and naval commanders by virtue of the rights of war ceased to derive any obligatory force from that source of authority, and having been ceded to the United States, all government and control over them under the authority of Mexico had ceased to exist. Impressed with the necessity of establishing Territorial governments over them, I recommended the subject to the favorable consideration of Congress in my message communicating the ratified treaty of peace, on the 6th of July last, and invoked their action at that session. Congress adjourned without making any provision for their government. The inhabitants by the transfer of their country had become entitled to the benefit of our laws and Constitution, and yet were left without any regularly organized government. Since that time the very limited power possessed by the Executive has been exercised to preserve and protect them from the inevitable consequences of a state of anarchy. The only government which remained was that established by the military authority during the war. Regarding this to be a *de facto* government, and that by the presumed consent of the inhabitants it might be continued temporarily, they were advised to conform and submit to it for the short intervening period before Congress would again assemble and could legislate on the subject. The views entertained by the Executive on this point are contained in a communication of the Secretary of State dated the 7th of October last, which was forwarded for publication to California and New Mexico, a copy of which is herewith transmitted. The small military force of the Regular Army which was serving within the limits of the acquired territories at the close of the war was retained in them, and additional forces have been ordered there for the protection of the inhabitants and to preserve and secure the rights and interests of the United States.

No revenue has been or could be collected at the ports in California, because Congress failed to authorize the establishment of custom-houses or the appointment of officers for that purpose.

The Secretary of the Treasury, by a circular letter addressed to collectors of the customs on the 7th day of October last, a copy of which is herewith transmitted, exercised all the power with which he was invested by law.

In pursuance of the act of the 14th of August last, extending the benefit of our post-office laws to the people of California, the Postmaster-General has appointed two agents, who have proceeded, the one to California and the other to Oregon, with authority to make the necessary arrangements for carrying its provisions into effect.

The monthly line of mail steamers from Panama to Astoria has been required to "stop and deliver and take mails at San Diego, Monterey, and San Francisco." These mail steamers, connected by the Isthmus of Panama with the line of mail steamers on the Atlantic between New York and Chagres, will establish a regular mail communication with California.

It is our solemn duty to provide with the least practicable delay for New Mexico and California regularly organized Territorial governments. The causes of the failure to do this at the last session of Congress are well known and deeply to be regretted. With the opening prospects of increased prosperity and national greatness which the acquisition of these rich and extensive territorial possessions affords, how irrational it would be to forego or to reject these advantages by the agitation of a domestic question which is coeval with the existence of our Government itself, and to endanger by internal strifes, geographical divisions, and heated contests for political power, or for any other cause, the harmony of the glorious Union of our confederated States—that Union which binds us together as one people, and which for sixty years has been our shield and protection against every danger. In the eyes of the world and of posterity how trivial and insignificant will be all our internal divisions and struggles compared with the preservation of this Union of the States in all its vigor and with all its countless blessings! No patriot would foment and excite geographical and sectional divisions. No lover of his country would deliberately calculate the value of the Union. Future generations would look in amazement upon the folly of such a course. Other nations at the present day would look upon it with astonishment, and such of them as desire to maintain and perpetuate thrones and monarchical or aristocratical principles will view it with exultation and delight, because in it they will see the elements of faction, which they hope must ultimately overturn our system. Ours is the great example of a prosperous and free self-governed republic, commanding the admiration and the imitation of all the lovers of freedom throughout the world. How solemn, therefore, is the duty, how impressive the call upon us and upon all parts of our country, to cultivate a patriotic spirit of harmony, of good-fellowship, of compromise and mutual concession, in the administration of the incomparable system of government formed by our fathers in the midst of almost insuperable difficulties, and transmitted to us with the injunction that we should enjoy its blessings and hand it down unimpaired to those who may come after us.

In view of the high and responsible duties which we owe to ourselves and to mankind, I trust you may be able at your present session to approach the adjustment of the only domestic question which seriously threatens, or probably ever can threaten, to disturb the harmony and successful operations of our system.

The immensely valuable possessions of New Mexico and California are already inhabited by a considerable population. Attracted by their great fertility, their mineral wealth, their commercial advantages, and the salubrity of the climate, emigrants from the older States in great numbers are already preparing to seek new homes in these inviting regions. Shall the dissimilarity of the domestic institutions in the different States prevent us from providing for them suitable governments? These institutions existed at the adoption of the Constitution, but the obstacles which they interposed were overcome by that spirit of compromise which is now invoked. In a conflict of opinions or of interests, real or imaginary, between different sections of our country, neither can justly demand all which it might desire to obtain. Each, in the true spirit of our institutions, should concede something to the other.

Our gallant forces in the Mexican war, by whose patriotism and unparalleled deeds of arms we obtained these possessions as an indemnity for our just demands against Mexico, were composed of citizens who belonged to no one State or section of our Union. They were men from slaveholding and nonslaveholding States, from the North and the South, from the East and the West. They were all companions in arms and fellow-citizens of the same common country, engaged in the same common cause. When prosecuting that war they were brethren and friends, and shared alike with each other common toils, dangers, and sufferings. Now, when their work is ended, when peace is restored, and they return again to their homes, put off the habiliments of war, take their places in society, and resume their pursuits in civil life, surely a spirit of harmony and concession and of equal regard for the rights of all and of all sections of the Union ought to prevail in providing governments for the acquired territories—the fruits of their common service. The whole people of the United States, and of every State, contributed to defray the expenses of that war, and it would not be just for any one section to exclude another from all participation in the acquired territory. This would not be in consonance with the just system of government which the framers of the Constitution adopted.

The question is believed to be rather abstract than practical, whether slavery ever can or would exist in any portion of the acquired territory even if it were left to the option of the slaveholding States themselves. From the nature of the climate and productions in much the larger portion of it it is certain it could never exist, and in the remainder the probabilities are it would not. But however this may be, the question, involving, as it does, a principle of equality of rights of the separate and several States as equal copartners in the Confederacy, should not be disregarded.

In organizing governments over these territories no duty imposed on Congress by the Constitution requires that they should legislate on the subject of slavery, while their power to do so is not only seriously questioned, but denied by many of the soundest expounders of that instrument. Whether Congress shall legislate or not, the people of the acquired territories, when assembled in convention to form State constitutions, will possess the sole and exclusive power to determine for themselves whether slavery shall or shall not exist within their limits. If Congress shall abstain from interfering with the question, the people of these territories will be left free to adjust it as they may think proper when they apply for admission as States into the Union. No enactment of Congress could restrain the people of any of the sovereign States of the Union, old or new, North or South, slaveholding or nonslaveholding, from determining the character of their own domestic institutions as they may deem wise and proper. Any and all the States possess this right, and Congress can not deprive them of it. The people of Georgia might if they chose so alter their constitution as to abolish slavery within its limits, and the people of Vermont might so alter their constitution as to admit slavery within its limits. Both States would possess the right, though, as all know, it is not probable that either would exert it.

It is fortunate for the peace and harmony of the Union that this question is in its nature temporary and can only continue for the brief period which will intervene before California and New Mexico may be admitted as States into the Union. From the tide of population now flowing into them it is highly probable that this will soon occur.

Considering the several States and the citizens of the several States as equals and entitled to equal rights under the Constitution, if this were an original question it might well be insisted on that the principle of noninterference is the true doctrine and that Congress could not, in the absence of any express grant of power, interfere with their relative rights. Upon a great emergency, however, and under menacing dangers to the Union, the Missouri compromise line in respect to slavery was adopted. The same line was extended farther west in the acquisition of Texas. After an acquiescence of nearly thirty years in the principle of compromise recognized and established by these acts, and to avoid the danger to the Union which might follow if it were now disregarded, I have heretofore expressed the opinion that that line of compromise should be extended on the parallel of 36° 30′ from the western boundary of Texas, where it now terminates, to the Pacific Ocean. This is the middle ground of compromise, upon which the different sections of the Union may meet, as they have heretofore met. If this be done, it is confidently believed a large majority of the people of every section of the country, however widely their abstract opinions on the subject of slavery may differ, would cheerfully and patriotically acquiesce in it, and peace and harmony would again fill our borders.

The restriction north of the line was only yielded to in the case of Missouri and Texas upon a principle of compromise, made necessary for the sake of preserving the harmony and possibly the existence of the Union.

It was upon these considerations that at the close of your last session I gave my sanction to the principle of the Missouri compromise line by approving and signing the bill to establish "the Territorial government of Oregon." From a sincere desire to preserve the harmony of the Union, and in deference for the acts of my predecessors, I felt constrained to yield my acquiescence to the extent to which they had gone in compromising this delicate and dangerous question. But if Congress shall now reverse the decision by which the Missouri compromise was effected, and shall propose to extend the restriction over the whole territory, south as well as north of the parallel of 36° 30′, it will cease to be a compromise, and must be regarded as an original question.

If Congress, instead of observing the course of noninterference, leaving the adoption of their own domestic institutions to the people who may inhabit these territories, or if, instead of extending the Missouri compromise line to the Pacific, shall prefer to submit the legal and constitutional questions which may arise to the decision of the judicial tribunals, as was proposed in a bill which passed the Senate at your last session, an adjustment may be effected in this mode. If the whole subject be referred to the judiciary, all parts of the Union should cheerfully acquiesce in the final decision of the tribunal created by the Constitution for the settlement of all questions which may arise under the Constitution, treaties, and laws of the United States.

Congress is earnestly invoked, for the sake of the Union, its harmony, and our continued prosperity as a nation, to adjust at its present session this, the only dangerous question which lies in our path, if not in some one of the modes suggested, in some other which may be satisfactory.

In anticipation of the establishment of regular governments over the acquired territories, a joint commission of officers of the Army and Navy has been ordered to proceed to the coast of California and Oregon for the purpose of making reconnoissances and a report as to the proper sites for the erection of fortifications or other defensive works on land and of suitable situations for naval stations. The information which may be expected from a scientific and skillful examination of the whole face of the coast will be eminently useful to Congress when they come to consider the propriety of making appropriations for these great national objects. Proper defenses on land will be necessary for the security and protection of our possessions, and the establishment of navy-yards and a dock for the repair and construction of vessels will be important alike to our Navy and commercial marine. Without such establishments every vessel, whether of the Navy or of the merchant service, requiring repair must at great expense come round Cape Horn to one of our Atlantic yards for that purpose. With such establishments vessels, it is believed, may be built or repaired as cheaply in California as upon the Atlantic coast. They would give employment to many of our enterprising ship-builders and mechanics and greatly facilitate and enlarge our commerce in the Pacific.

As it is ascertained that mines of gold, silver, copper, and quicksilver exist in New Mexico and California, and that nearly all the lands where they are found belong to the United States, it is deemed important to the public interest that provision be made for a geological and mineralogical examination of these regions. Measures should be adopted to preserve the mineral lands, especially such as contain the precious metals, for the use of the United States, or, if brought into market, to separate them from the farming lands and dispose of them in such manner as to secure a large return of money to the Treasury and at the same time to lead to the development of their wealth by individual proprietors and purchasers. To do this it will be necessary to provide for an immediate survey and location of the lots. If Congress should deem it proper to dispose of the mineral lands, they should be sold in small quantities and at a fixed minimum price.

I recommend that surveyors-general's offices be authorized to be established in New Mexico and California and provision made for surveying and bringing the public lands into market at the earliest practicable period. In disposing of these lands, I recommend that the right of preemption be secured and liberal grants made to the early emigrants who have settled or may settle upon them.

It will be important to extend our revenue laws over these territories, and especially over California, at an early period. There is already a considerable commerce with California, and until ports of entry shall be established and collectors appointed no revenue can be received.

If these and other necessary and proper measures be adopted for the development of the wealth and resources of New Mexico and California and regular Territorial governments be established over them, such will probably be the rapid enlargement of our commerce and navigation and such the addition to the national wealth that the present generation may live to witness the controlling commercial and monetary power of the world transferred from London and other European emporiums to the city of New York.

The apprehensions which were entertained by some of our statesmen in the earlier periods of the Government that our system was incapable of operating with sufficient energy and success over largely extended territorial limits, and that if this were attempted it would fall to pieces by its own weakness, have been dissipated by our experience. By the division of power between the States and Federal Government the latter is found to operate with as much energy in the extremes as in the center. It is as efficient in the remotest of the thirty States which now compose the Union as it was in the thirteen States which formed our Constitution. Indeed, it may well be doubted whether if our present population had been confined within the limits of the original thirteen States the tendencies to centralization and consolidation would not have been such as to have encroached upon the essential reserved rights of the States, and thus to have made the Federal Government a widely different one, practically, from what it is in theory and was intended to be by its framers. So far from entertaining apprehensions of the safety of our system by the extension of our territory, the belief is confidently entertained that each new State gives strength and an additional guaranty for the preservation of the Union itself.

In pursuance of the provisions of the thirteenth article of the treaty of peace, friendship, limits, and settlement with the Republic of Mexico, and of the act of July 29, 1848, claims of our citizens, which had been "already liquidated and decided, against the Mexican Republic" amounting, with the interest thereon, to $2,023,832.51 have been liquidated and paid. There remain to be paid of these claims $74,192.26.

Congress at its last session having made no provision for executing the fifteenth article of the treaty, by which the United States assume to make satisfaction for the "unliquidated claims" of our citizens against Mexico to "an amount not exceeding three and a quarter millions of dollars," the subject is again recommended to your favorable consideration.

The exchange of ratifications of the treaty with Mexico took place on the 30th of May, 1848. Within one year after that time the commissioner and surveyor which each Government stipulates to appoint are required to meet "at the port of San Diego and proceed to run and mark the said boundary in its whole course to the mouth of the Rio Bravo del Norte." It will be seen from this provision that the period within which a commissioner and surveyor of the respective Governments are to meet at San Diego will expire on the 30th of May, 1849. Congress at the close of its last session made an appropriation for "the expenses of running and marking the boundary line" between the two countries, but did not fix the amount of salary which should be paid to the commissioner and surveyor to be appointed on the part of the United States. It is desirable that the amount of compensation which they shall receive should be prescribed by law, and not left, as at present, to Executive discretion.

Measures were adopted at the earliest practicable period to organize the "Territorial government of Oregon," as authorized by the act of the 14th of August last. The governor and marshal of the Territory, accompanied by a small military escort, left the frontier of Missouri in September last, and took the southern route, by the way of Santa Fe and the river Gila, to California, with the intention of proceeding thence in one of our vessels of war to their destination. The governor was fully advised of the great importance of his early arrival in the country, and it is confidently believed he may reach Oregon in the latter part of the present month or early in the next. The other officers for the Territory have proceeded by sea.

In the month of May last I communicated information to Congress that an Indian war had broken out in Oregon, and recommended that authority be given to raise an adequate number of volunteers to proceed without delay to the assistance of our fellow-citizens in that Territory. The authority to raise such a force not having been granted by Congress, as soon as their services could be dispensed with in Mexico orders were issued to the regiment of mounted riflemen to proceed to Jefferson Barracks, in Missouri, and to prepare to march to Oregon as soon as the necessary provision could be made. Shortly before it was ready to march it was arrested by the provision of the act passed by Congress on the last day of the last session, which directed that all the noncommissioned officers, musicians, and privates of that regiment who had been in service in Mexico should, upon their application, be entitled to be discharged. The effect of this provision was to disband the rank and file of the regiment, and before their places could be filled by recruits the season had so far advanced that it was impracticable for it to proceed until the opening of the next spring.

In the month of October last the accompanying communication was received from the governor of the temporary government of Oregon, giving information of the continuance of the Indian disturbances and of the destitution and defenseless condition of the inhabitants. Orders were immediately transmitted to the commander of our squadron in the Pacific to dispatch to their assistance a part of the naval forces on that station, to furnish them with arms and ammunition, and to continue to give them such aid and protection as the Navy could afford until the Army could reach the country.

It is the policy of humanity, and one which has always been pursued by the United States, to cultivate the good will of the aboriginal tribes of this continent and to restrain them from making war and indulging in excesses by mild means rather than by force. That this could have been done with the tribes in Oregon had that Territory been brought under the government of our laws at an earlier period, and had other suitable measures been adopted by Congress, such as now exist in our intercourse with the other Indian tribes within our limits, can not be doubted. Indeed, the immediate and only cause of the existing hostility of the Indians of Oregon is represented to have been the long delay of the United States in making to them some trifling compensation, in such articles as they wanted, for the country now occupied by our emigrants, which the Indians claimed and over which they formerly roamed. This compensation had been promised to them by the temporary government established in Oregon, but its fulfillment had been postponed from time to time for nearly two years, whilst those who made it had been anxiously waiting for Congress to establish a Territorial government over the country. The Indians became at length distrustful of their good faith and sought redress by plunder and massacre, which finally led to the present difficulties. A few thousand dollars in suitable presents, as a compensation for the country which had been taken possession of by our citizens, would have satisfied the Indians and have prevented the war. A small amount properly distributed, it is confidently believed, would soon restore quiet. In this Indian war our fellow-citizens of Oregon have been compelled to take the field in their own defense, have performed valuable military services, and been subjected to expenses which have fallen heavily upon them. Justice demands that provision should be made by Congress to compensate them for their services and to refund to them the necessary expenses which they have incurred.

I repeat the recommendation heretofore made to Congress, that provision be made for the appointment of a suitable number of Indian agents to reside among the tribes of Oregon, and that a small sum be appropriated to enable these agents to cultivate friendly relations with them. If this be done, the presence of a small military force will be all that is necessary to keep them in check and preserve peace. I recommend that similar provisions be made as regards the tribes inhabiting northern Texas, New Mexico, California, and the extensive region lying between our settlements in Missouri and these possessions, as the most effective means of preserving peace upon our borders and within the recently acquired territories.

The Secretary of the Treasury will present in his annual report a highly satisfactory statement of the condition of the finances.

The imports for the fiscal year ending on the 30th of June last were of the value of $154,977,876, of which the amount exported was $21,128,010, leaving $133,849,866 in the country for domestic use. The value of the exports for the same period was $154,032,131, consisting of domestic productions amounting to $132,904,121 and $21,128,010 of foreign articles. The receipts into the Treasury for the same period, exclusive of loans, amounted to $35,436,750.59, of which there was derived from customs $31,757,070.96, from sales of public lands $3,328,642.56, and from miscellaneous and incidental sources $351,037.07.

It will be perceived that the revenue from customs for the last fiscal year exceeded by $757,070.96 the estimate of the Secretary of the Treasury in his last annual report, and that the aggregate receipts during the same period from customs, lands, and miscellaneous sources also exceeded the estimate by the sum of $536,750.59, indicating, however, a very near approach in the estimate to the actual result.

The expenditures during the fiscal year ending on the 30th of June last, including those for the war and exclusive of payments of principal and interest for the public debt, were $42,811,970.03.

It is estimated that the receipts into the Treasury for the fiscal year ending on the 30th of June, 1849, including the balance in the Treasury on the 1st of July last, will amount to the sum of $57,048,969.90, of which $32,000,000, it is estimated, will be derived from customs, $3,000,000 from the sales of the public lands, and $1,200,000 from miscellaneous and incidental sources, including the premium upon the loan, and the amount paid and to be paid into the Treasury on account of military contributions in Mexico, and the sales of arms and vessels and other public property rendered unnecessary for the use of the Government by the termination of the war, and $20,695,435.30 from loans already negotiated, including Treasury notes funded, which, together with the balance in the Treasury on the 1st of July last, make the sum estimated.

The expenditures for the same period, including the necessary payment on account of the principal and interest of the public debt, and the principal and interest of the first installment due to Mexico on the 30th of May next, and other expenditures growing out of the war to be paid during the present year, will amount, including the reimbursement of Treasury notes, to the sum of $54,195,275.06, leaving an estimated balance in the Treasury on the 1st of July, 1849, of $2,853,694.84.

The Secretary of the Treasury will present, as required by law, the estimate of the receipts and expenditures for the next fiscal year. The expenditures as estimated for that year are $33,213,152.73, including $3,799,102.18 for the interest on the public debt and $3,540,000 for the principal and interest due to Mexico on the 30th of May, 1850, leaving the sum of $25,874,050.35, which, it is believed, will be ample for the ordinary peace expenditures.

The operations of the tariff act of 1846 have been such during the past year as fully to meet the public expectation and to confirm the opinion heretofore expressed of the wisdom of the change in our revenue system which was effected by it. The receipts under it into the Treasury for the first fiscal year after its enactment exceeded by the sum of $5,044,403.09 the amount collected during the last fiscal year under the tariff act of 1842, ending the 30th of June, 1846. The total revenue realized from the commencement of its operation, on the 1st of December, 1846, until the close of the last quarter, on the 30th of September last, being twenty-two months, was $56,654,563.79, being a much larger sum than was ever before received from duties during any equal period under the tariff acts of 1824, 1828, 1832, and 1842. Whilst by the repeal of highly protective and prohibitory duties the revenue has been increased, the taxes on the people have been diminished. They have been relieved from the heavy amounts with which they were burthened under former laws in the form of increased prices or bounties paid to favored classes and pursuits.

The predictions which were made that the tariff act of 1846 would reduce the amount of revenue below that collected under the act of 1842, and would prostrate the business and destroy the prosperity of the country, have not been verified. With an increased and increasing revenue, the finances are in a highly flourishing condition. Agriculture, commerce, and navigation are prosperous; the prices of manufactured fabrics and of other products are much less injuriously affected than was to have been anticipated from the unprecedented revulsions which during the last and the present year have overwhelmed the industry and paralyzed the credit and commerce of so many great and enlightened nations of Europe.

Severe commercial revulsions abroad have always heretofore operated to depress and often to affect disastrously almost every branch of American industry. The temporary depression of a portion of our manufacturing interests is the effect of foreign causes, and is far less severe than has prevailed on all former similar occasions.

It is believed that, looking to the great aggregate of all our interests, the whole country was never more prosperous than at the present period, and never more rapidly advancing in wealth and population. Neither the foreign war in which we have been involved, nor the loans which have absorbed so large a portion of our capital, nor the commercial revulsion in Great Britain in 1847, nor the paralysis of credit and commerce throughout Europe in 1848, have affected injuriously to any considerable extent any of the great interests of the country or arrested our onward march to greatness, wealth, and power.

Had the disturbances in Europe not occurred, our commerce would undoubtedly have been still more extended, and would have added still more to the national wealth and public prosperity. But notwithstanding these disturbances, the operations of the revenue system established by the tariff act of 1846 have been so generally beneficial to the Government and the business of the country that no change in its provisions is demanded by a wise public policy, and none is recommended.

The operations of the constitutional treasury established by the act of the 6th of August, 1846, in the receipt, custody, and disbursement of the public money have continued to be successful. Under this system the public finances have been carried through a foreign war, involving the necessity of loans and extraordinary expenditures and requiring distant transfers and disbursements, without embarrassment, and no loss has occurred of any of the public money deposited under its provisions. Whilst it has proved to be safe and useful to the Government, its effects have been most beneficial upon the business of the country. It has tended powerfully to secure an exemption from that inflation and fluctuation of the paper currency so injurious to domestic industry and rendering so uncertain the rewards of labor, and, it is believed, has largely contributed to preserve the whole country from a serious commercial revulsion, such as often occurred under the bank deposit system. In the year 1847 there was a revulsion in the business of Great Britain of great extent and intensity, which was followed by failures in that Kingdom unprecedented in number and amount of losses. This is believed to be the first instance when such disastrous bankruptcies, occurring in a country with which we have such extensive commerce, produced little or no injurious effect upon our trade or currency. We remained but little affected in our money market, and our business and industry were still prosperous and progressive.

During the present year nearly the whole continent of Europe has been convulsed by civil war and revolutions, attended by numerous bankruptcies, by an unprecedented fall in their public securities, and an almost universal paralysis of commerce and industry; and yet, although our trade and the prices of our products must have been somewhat unfavorably affected by these causes, we have escaped a revulsion, our money market is comparatively easy, and public and private credit have advanced and improved.

It is confidently believed that we have been saved from their effect by the salutary operation of the constitutional treasury. It is certain that if the twenty-four millions of specie imported into the country during the fiscal year ending on the 30th of June, 1847, had gone into the banks, as to a great extent it must have done, it would in the absence of this system have been made the basis of augmented bank paper issues, probably to an amount not less than $60,000,000 or $70,000,000, producing, as an inevitable consequence of an inflated currency, extravagant prices for a time and wild speculation, which must have been followed, on the reflux to Europe the succeeding year of so much of that specie, by the prostration of the business of the country, the suspension of the banks, and most extensive bankruptcies. Occurring, as this would have done, at a period when the country was engaged in a foreign war, when considerable loans of specie were required for distant disbursements, and when the banks, the fiscal agents of the Government and the depositories of its money, were suspended, the public credit must have sunk, and many millions of dollars, as was the case during the War of 1812, must have been sacrificed in discounts upon loans and upon the depreciated paper currency which the Government would have been compelled to use.

Under the operations of the constitutional treasury not a dollar has been lost by the depreciation of the currency. The loans required to prosecute the war with Mexico were negotiated by the Secretary of the Treasury above par, realizing a large premium to the Government. The restraining effect of the system upon the tendencies to excessive paper issues by banks has saved the Government from heavy losses and thousands of our business men from bankruptcy and ruin. The wisdom of the system has been tested by the experience of the last two years, and it is the dictate of sound policy that it should remain undisturbed. The modifications in some of the details of this measure, involving none of its essential principles, heretofore recommended, are again presented for your favorable consideration.

In my message of the 6th of July last, transmitting to Congress the ratified treaty of peace with Mexico, I recommended the adoption of measures for the speedy payment of the public debt. In reiterating that recommendation I refer you to the considerations presented in that message in its support. The public debt, including that authorized to be negotiated in pursuance of existing laws, and including Treasury notes, amounted at that time to $65,778,450.41.

Funded stock of the United States amounting to about half a million of dollars has been purchased, as authorized by law, since that period, and the public debt has thus been reduced, the details of which will be presented in the annual report of the Secretary of the Treasury.

The estimates of expenditures for the next fiscal year, submitted by the Secretary of the Treasury, it is believed will be ample for all necessary purposes. If the appropriations made by Congress shall not exceed the amount estimated, the means in the Treasury will be sufficient to defray all the expenses of the Government, to pay off the next installment of $3,000,000 to Mexico, which will fall due on the 30th of May next, and still a considerable surplus will remain, which should be applied to the further purchase of the public stock and reduction of the debt. Should enlarged appropriations be made, the necessary consequence will be to postpone the payment of the debt. Though our debt, as compared with that of most other nations, is small, it is our true policy, and in harmony with the genius of our institutions, that we should present to the world the rare spectacle of a great Republic, possessing vast resources and wealth, wholly exempt from public indebtedness. This would add still more to our strength, and give to us a still more commanding position among the nations of the earth.

The public expenditures should be economical, and be confined to such necessary objects as are clearly within the powers of Congress. All such as are not absolutely demanded should be postponed, and the payment of the public debt at the earliest practicable period should be a cardinal principle of our public policy.

For the reason assigned in my last annual message, I repeat the recommendation that a branch of the Mint of the United States be established at the city of New York. The importance of this measure is greatly increased by the acquisition of the rich mines of the precious metals in New Mexico and California, and especially in the latter.

I repeat the recommendation heretofore made in favor of the graduation and reduction of the price of such of the public lands as have been long offered in the market and have remained unsold, and in favor of extending the rights of preemption to actual settlers on the unsurveyed as well as the surveyed lands.

The condition and operations of the Army and the state of other branches of the public service under the supervision of the War Department are satisfactorily presented in the accompanying report of the Secretary of War.

On the return of peace our forces were withdrawn from Mexico, and the volunteers and that portion of the Regular Army engaged for the war were disbanded. Orders have been issued for stationing the forces of our permanent establishment at various positions in our extended country where troops may be required. Owing to the remoteness of some of these positions, the detachments have not yet reached their destination. Notwithstanding the extension of the limits of our country and the forces required in the new territories, it is confidently believed that our present military establishment is sufficient for all exigencies so long as our peaceful relations remain undisturbed.

Of the amount of military contributions collected in Mexico, the sum of $769,650 was applied toward the payment of the first installment due under the treaty with Mexico. The further sum of $346,369.30 has been paid into the Treasury, and unexpended balances still remain in the hands of disbursing officers and those who were engaged in the collection of these moneys. After the proclamation of peace no further disbursements were made of any unexpended moneys arising from this source. The balances on hand were directed to be paid into the Treasury, and individual claims on the fund will remain unadjusted until Congress shall authorize their settlement and payment. These claims are not considerable in number or amount.

I recommend to your favorable consideration the suggestions of the Secretary of War and the Secretary of the Navy in regard to legislation on this subject.

Our Indian relations are presented in a most favorable view in the report from the War Department. The wisdom of our policy in regard to the tribes within our limits is clearly manifested by their improved and rapidly improving condition.

A most important treaty with the Menomonies has been recently negotiated by the Commissioner of Indian Affairs in person, by which all their land in the State of Wisconsin—being about 4,000,000 acres—has been ceded to the United States. This treaty will be submitted to the Senate for ratification at an early period of your present session.

Within the last four years eight important treaties have been negotiated with different Indian tribes, and at a cost of $1,842,000; Indian lands to the amount of more than 18,500,000 acres have been ceded to the United States, and provision has been made for settling in the country west of the Mississippi the tribes which occupied this large extent of the public domain. The title to all the Indian lands within the several States of our Union, with the exception of a few small reservations, is now extinguished, and a vast region opened for settlement and cultivation.

The accompanying report of the Secretary of the Navy gives a satisfactory exhibit of the operations and condition of that branch of the public service.

A number of small vessels, suitable for entering the mouths of rivers, were judiciously purchased during the war, and gave great efficiency to the squadron in the Gulf of Mexico. On the return of peace, when no longer valuable for naval purposes, and liable to constant deterioration, they were sold and the money placed in the Treasury.

The number of men in the naval service authorized by law during the war has been reduced by discharges below the maximum fixed for the peace establishment. Adequate squadrons are maintained in the several quarters of the globe where experience has shown their services may be most usefully employed, and the naval service was never in a condition of higher discipline or greater efficiency.

I invite attention to the recommendation of the Secretary of the Navy on the subject of the Marine Corps. The reduction of the Corps at the end of the war required that four officers of each of the three lower grades should be dropped from the rolls. A board of officers made the selection, and those uesignated were necessarily dismissed, but without any alleged fault. I concur in opinion with the Secretary that the service would be improved by reducing the number of landsmen and increasing the marines. Such a measure would justify an increase of the number of officers to the extent of the reduction by dismissal, and still the Corps would have fewer officers than a corresponding number of men in the Army.

The contracts for the transportation of the mail in steamships, convertible into war steamers, promise to realize all the benefits to our commerce and to the Navy which were anticipated. The first steamer thus secured to the Government was launched in January, 1847. There are now seven, and in another year there will probably be not less than seventeen afloat. While this great national advantage is secured, our social and commercial intercourse is increased and promoted with Germany, Great Britain, and other parts of Europe, with all the countries on the west coast of our continent, especially with Oregon and California, and between the northern and southern sections of the United States. Considerable revenue may be expected from postages, but the connected line from New York to Chagres, and thence across the Isthmus to Oregon, can not fail to exert a beneficial influence, not now to be estimated, on the interests of the manufactures, commerce, navigation, and currency of the United States. As an important part of the system, I recommend to your favorable consideration the establishment of the proposed line of steamers between New Orleans and Vera Cruz. It promises the most happy results in cementing friendship between the two Republics and extending reciprocal benefits to the trade and manufactures of both.

The report of the Postmaster-General will make known to you the operations of that Department for the past year.

It is gratifying to find the revenues of the Department, under the rates of postage now established by law, so rapidly increasing. The gross amount of postages during the last fiscal year amounted to $4,371,077, exceeding the annual average received for the nine years immediately preceding the passage of the act of the 3d of March, 1845, by the sum of $6,453, and exceeding the amount received for the year ending the 30th of June, 1847, by the sum of $425,184.

The expenditures for the year, excluding the sum of $94,672, allowed by Congress at its last session to individual claimants, and including the sum of $100,500, paid for the services of the line of steamers between Bremen and New York, amounted to $4,198,845, which is less than the annual average for the nine years previous to the act of 1845 by $300,748.

The mail routes on the 30th day of June last were 163,208 miles in extent, being an increase during the last year of 9,390 miles. The mails were transported over them during the same time 41,012,579 miles, making an increase of transportation for the year of 2,124,680 miles, whilst the expense was less than that of the previous year by $4,235.

The increase in the mail transportation within the last three years has been 5,378,310 miles, whilst the expenses were reduced $456,738, making an increase of service at the rate of 15 per cent and a reduction in the expenses of more than 15 per cent.

During the past year there have been employed, under contracts with the Post-Office Department, two ocean steamers in conveying the mails monthly between New York and Bremen, and one, since October last, performing semimonthly service between Charleston and Havana; and a contract has been made for the transportation of the Pacific mails across the Isthmus from Chagres to Panama.

Under the authority given to the Secretary of the Navy, three ocean steamers have been constructed and sent to the Pacific, and are expected to enter upon the mail service between Panama and Oregon and the intermediate ports on the 1st of January next; and a fourth has been engaged by him for the service between Havana and Chagres, so that a regular monthly mail line will be kept up after that time between the United States and our territories on the Pacific.

Notwithstanding this great increase in the mail service, should the revenue continue to increase the present year as it did in the last, there will be received near $450,000 more than the expenditures.

These considerations have satisfied the Postmaster-General that, with certain modifications of the act of 1845, the revenue may be still further increased and a reduction of postages made to a uniform rate of 5 cents, without an interference with the principle, which has been constantly and properly enforced, of making that Department sustain itself.

A well-digested cheap-postage system is the best means of diffusing intelligence among the people, and is of so much importance in a country so extensive as that of the United States that I recommend to your favorable consideration the suggestions of the Postmaster-General for its improvement.

Nothing can retard the onward progress of our country and prevent us from assuming and maintaining the first rank among nations but a disregard of the experience of the past and a recurrence to an unwise public policy. We have just closed a foreign war by an honorable peace—a war rendered necessary and unavoidable in vindication of the national rights and honor. The present condition of the country is similar in some respects to that which existed immediately after the close of the war with Great Britain in 1815, and the occasion is deemed to be a proper one to take a retrospect of the measures of public policy which followed that war. There was at that period of our history a departure from our earlier policy. The enlargement of the powers of the Federal Government by *construction*, which obtained, was not warranted by any just interpretation of the Constitution. A few years after the close of that war a series of measures was adopted which, united and combined, constituted what was termed by their authors and advocates the "American system."

The introduction of the new policy was for a time favored by the condition of the country, by the heavy debt which had been contracted during the war, by the depression of the public credit, by the deranged state of the finances and the currency, and by the commercial and pecuniary embarrassment which extensively prevailed. These were not the only causes which led to its establishment. The events of the war with Great Britain and the embarrassments which had attended its prosecution had left on the minds of many of our statesmen the impression that our Government was not strong enough, and that to wield its resources successfully in great emergencies, and especially in war, more power should be concentrated in its hands. This increased power they did not seek to obtain by the legitimate and prescribed mode—an amendment of the Constitution—but by *construction*. They saw Governments in the Old World based upon different orders of society, and so constituted as to throw the whole power of nations into the hands of a few, who taxed and controlled the many without responsibility or restraint. In that arrangement they conceived the strength of nations in war consisted. There was also something fascinating in the ease, luxury, and display of the higher orders, who drew their wealth from the toil of the laboring millions. The authors of the system drew their ideas of political economy from what they had witnessed in Europe, and particularly in Great Britain. They had viewed the enormous wealth concentrated in few hands and had seen the splendor of the overgrown establishments of an aristocracy which was upheld by the restrictive policy. They forgot to look down upon the poorer classes of the English population, upon whose daily and yearly labor the great establishments they so much admired were sustained and supported. They failed to perceive that the scantily fed and half-clad operatives were not only in abject poverty, but were bound in chains of oppressive servitude for the benefit of favored classes, who were the exclusive objects of the care of the Government.

It was not possible to reconstruct society in the United States upon the European plan. Here there was a written Constitution, by which orders and titles were not recognized or tolerated. A system of measures was therefore devised, calculated, if not intended, to withdraw power gradually and silently from the States and the mass of the people, and by *construction* to approximate our Government to the European models, substituting an aristocracy of wealth for that of orders and titles.

Without reflecting upon the dissimilarity of our institutions and of the condition of our people and those of Europe, they conceived the vain idea of building up in the United States a system similar to that which they admired abroad. Great Britain had a national bank of large capital, in whose hands was concentrated the controlling monetary and financial power of the nation—an institution wielding almost kingly power, and exerting vast influence upon all the operations of trade and upon the policy of the Government itself. Great Britain had an enormous public debt, and it had become a part of her public policy to regard this as a "public blessing." Great Britain had also a restrictive policy, which placed fetters and burdens on trade and trammeled the productive industry of the mass of the nation. By her combined system of policy the landlords and other property holders were protected and enriched by the enormous taxes which were levied upon the labor of the country for their advantage. Imitating this foreign policy, the first step in establishing the new system in the United States was the creation of a national bank. Not foreseeing the dangerous power and countless evils which such an institution might entail on the country, nor perceiving the connection which it was designed to form between the bank and the other branches of the miscalled "American system," but feeling the embarrassments of the Treasury and of the business of the country consequent upon the war, some of our statesmen who had held different and sounder views were induced to yield their scruples and, indeed, settled convictions of its unconstitutionality, and to give it their sanction as an expedient which they vainly hoped might produce relief. It was a most unfortunate error, as the subsequent history and final catastrophe of that dangerous and corrupt institution have abundantly proved. The bank, with its numerous branches ramified into the States, soon brought many of the active political and commercial men in different sections of the country into the relation of debtors to it and dependents upon it for pecuniary favors, thus diffusing throughout the mass of society a great number of individuals of power and influence to give tone to public opinion and to act in concert in cases of emergency. The corrupt power of such a political engine is no longer a matter of speculation, having been displayed in numerous instances, but most signally in the political struggles of 1832, 1833, and 1834 in opposition to the public will represented by a fearless and patriotic President.

But the bank was but one branch of the new system. A public debt of more than $120,000,000 existed, and it is not to be disguised that many of the authors of the new system did not regard its speedy payment as essential to the public prosperity, but looked upon its continuance as no national evil. Whilst the debt existed it furnished aliment to the national bank and rendered increased taxation necessary to the amount of the interest, exceeding $7,000,000 annually.

This operated in harmony with the next branch of the new system, which was a high protective tariff. This was to afford bounties to favored classes and particular pursuits at the expense of all others. A proposition to tax the whole people for the purpose of enriching a few was too monstrous to be openly made. The scheme was therefore veiled under the plausible but delusive pretext of a measure to protect "home industry," and many of our people were for a time led to believe that a tax which in the main fell upon labor was for the benefit of the laborer who paid it. This branch of the system involved a partnership between the Government and the favored classes, the former receiving the proceeds of the tax imposed on articles imported and the latter the increased price of similar articles produced at home, caused by such tax. It is obvious that the portion to be received by the favored classes would, as a general rule, be increased in proportion to the increase of the rates of tax imposed and diminished as those rates were reduced to the revenue standard required by the wants of the Government. The rates required to produce a sufficient revenue for the ordinary expenditures of Government for necessary purposes were not likely to give to the private partners in this scheme profits sufficient to satisfy their cupidity, and hence a variety of expedients and pretexts were resorted to for the purpose of enlarging the expenditures and thereby creating a necessity for keeping up a high protective tariff. The effect of this policy was to interpose artificial restrictions upon the natural course of the business and trade of the country, and to advance the interests of large capitalists and monopolists at the expense of the great mass of the people, who were taxed to increase their wealth.

Another branch of this system was a comprehensive scheme of internal improvements, capable of indefinite enlargement and sufficient to swallow up as many millions annually as could be exacted from the foreign commerce of the country. This was a convenient and necessary adjunct of the protective tariff. It was to be the great absorbent of any surplus which might at any time accumulate in the Treasury and of the taxes levied on the people, not for necessary revenue purposes, but for the avowed object of affording protection to the favored classes.

Auxiliary to the same end, if it was not an essential part of the system itself, was the scheme, which at a later period obtained, for distributing the proceeds of the sales of the public lands among the States. Other expedients were devised to take money out of the Treasury and prevent its coming in from any other source than the protective tariff. The authors and supporters of the system were the advocates of the largest expenditures, whether for necessary or useful purposes or not, because the larger the expenditures the greater was the pretext for high taxes in the form of protective duties.

These several measures were sustained by popular names and plausible arguments, by which thousands were deluded. The bank was represented to be an indispensable fiscal agent for the Government; was to equalize exchanges and to regulate and furnish a sound currency, always and everywhere of uniform value. The protective tariff was to give employment to "American labor" at advanced prices; was to protect "home industry" and furnish a steady market for the farmer. Internal improvements were to bring trade into every neighborhood and enhance the value of every man's property. The distribution of the land money was to enrich the States, finish their public works, plant schools throughout their borders, and relieve them from taxation. But the fact that for every dollar taken out of the Treasury for these objects a much larger sum was transferred from the pockets of the people to the favored classes was carefully concealed, as was also the tendency, if not the ultimate design, of the system to build up an aristocracy of wealth, to control the masses of society, and monopolize the political power of the country.

The several branches of this system were so intimately blended together that in their operation each sustained and strengthened the others. Their joint operation was to add new burthens of taxation and to encourage a largely increased and wasteful expenditure of public money. It was the interest of the bank that the revenue collected and the disbursements made by the Government should be large, because, being the depository of the public money, the larger the amount the greater would be the bank profits by its use. It was the interest of the favored classes, who were enriched by the protective tariff, to have the rates of that protection as high as possible, for the higher those rates the greater would be their advantage. It was the interest of the people of all those sections and localities who expected to be benefited by expenditures for internal improvements that the amount collected should be as large as possible, to the end that the sum disbursed might also be the larger. The States, being the beneficiaries in the distribution of the land money, had an interest in having the rates of tax imposed by the protective tariff large enough to yield a sufficient revenue from that source to meet the wants of the Government without disturbing or taking from them the land fund; so that each of the branches constituting the system had a common interest in swelling the public expenditures. They had a direct interest in maintaining the public debt unpaid and increasing its amount, because this would produce an annual increased drain upon the Treasury to the amount of the interest and render augmented taxes necessary. The operation and necessary effect of the whole system were to encourage large and extravagant expenditures, and thereby to increase the public patronage, and maintain a rich and splendid government at the expense of a taxed and impoverished people.

It is manifest that this scheme of enlarged taxation and expenditures, had it continued to prevail, must soon have converted the Government of the Union, intended by its framers to be a plain, cheap, and simple confederation of States, united together for common protection and charged with a few specific duties, relating chiefly to our foreign affairs, into a consolidated empire, depriving the States of their reserved rights and the people of their just power and control in the administration of their Government. In this manner the whole form and character of the Government would be changed, not by an amendment of the Constitution, but by resorting to an unwarrantable and unauthorized construction of that instrument.

The indirect mode of levying the taxes by a duty on imports prevents the mass of the people from readily perceiving the amount they pay, and has enabled the few who are thus enriched, and who seek to wield the political power of the country, to deceive and delude them. Were the taxes collected by a direct levy upon the people, as is the case in the States, this could not occur.

The whole system was resisted from its inception by many of our ablest statesmen, some of whom doubted its constitutionality and its expediency, while others believed it was in all its branches a flagrant and dangerous infraction of the Constitution.

That a national bank, a protective tariff—levied not to raise the revenue needed, but for protection merely—internal improvements, and the distribution of the proceeds of the sale of the public lands are measures without the warrant of the Constitution would, upon the maturest consideration, seem to be clear. It is remarkable that no one of these measures, involving such momentous consequences, is authorized by any express grant of power in the Constitution. No one of them is "incident to, as being necessary and proper for the execution of, the specific powers" granted by the Constitution. The authority under which it has been attempted to justify each of them is derived from inferences and constructions of the Constitution which its letter and its whole object and design do not warrant. Is it to be conceived that such immense powers would have been left by the framers of the Constitution to mere inferences and doubtful constructions? Had it been intended to confer them on the Federal Government, it is but reasonable to conclude that it would have been done by plain and unequivocal grants. This was not done; but the whole structure of which the "American system" consisted was reared on no other or better foundation than forced implications and inferences of power, which its authors assumed might be deduced by construction from the Constitution.

But it has been urged that the national bank, which constituted so essential a branch of this combined system of measures, was not a new measure, and that its constitutionality had been previously sanctioned, because a bank had been chartered in 1791 and had received the official signature of President Washington. A few facts will show the just weight to which this precedent should be entitled as bearing upon the question of constitutionality.

Great division of opinion upon the subject existed in Congress. It is well known that President Washington entertained serious doubts both as to the constitutionality and expediency of the measure, and while the bill was before him for his official approval or disapproval so great were these doubts that he required "the opinion in writing" of the members of his Cabinet to aid him in arriving at a decision. His Cabinet gave their opinions and were divided upon the subject, *General Hamilton* being in favor of and *Mr. Jefferson* and *Mr. Randolph* being opposed to the constitutionality and expediency of the bank. It is well known also that President Washington retained the bill from Monday, the 14th, when it was presented to him, until Friday, the 25th of February, being the last moment permitted him by the Constitution to deliberate, when he finally yielded to it his reluctant assent and gave it his signature. It is certain that as late as the 23d of February, being the ninth day after the bill was presented to him, he had arrived at no satisfactory conclusion, for on that day he addressed a note to General Hamilton in which he informs him that "this bill was presented to me by the joint committee of Congress at 12 o'clock on Monday, the 14th instant," and he requested his opinion "to what precise period, by legal interpretation of the Constitution, can the President retain it in his possession before it becomes a law by the lapse of ten days." If the proper construction was that the day on which the bill was presented to the President and the day on which his action was had upon it were both to be counted inclusive, then the time allowed him within which it would be competent for him to return it to the House in which it originated with his objections would expire on Thursday, the 24th of February. General Hamilton on the same day returned an answer, in which he states:

I give it as my opinion that you have ten days exclusive of that on which the bill was delivered to you and Sundays; hence, in the present case if it is returned on Friday it will be in time.

By this construction, which the President adopted, he gained another day for deliberation, and it was not until the 25th of February that he signed the bill, thus affording conclusive proof that he had at last obtained his own consent to sign it not without great and almost insuperable difficulty. Additional light has been recently shed upon the serious doubts which he had on the subject, amounting at one time to a conviction that it was his duty to withhold his approval from the bill. This is found among the manuscript papers of *Mr. Madison*, authorized to be purchased for the use of the Government by an act of the last session of Congress, and now for the first time accessible to the public. From these papers it appears that President Washington, while he yet held the bank bill in his hands, actually requested *Mr. Madison*, at that time a member of the House of Representatives, to prepare the draft of a veto message for him. *Mr. Madison*, at his request, did prepare the draft of such a message, and sent it to him on the 21st of February, 1791. A copy of this original draft, in Mr. Madison's own handwriting, was carefully preserved by him, and is among the papers lately purchased by Congress. It is preceded by a note, written on the same sheet, which is also in Mr. Madison's handwriting, and is as follows:

February 21, 1791.—Copy of a paper made out and sent to the President, *at his request*, to be ready in case his judgment should finally decide against the bill for incorporating a national bank, the bill being then before him.

Among the objections assigned in this paper to the bill, and which were submitted for the consideration of the President, are the following:

I object to the bill, because it is an essential principle of the Government that powers not delegated by the Constitution can not be rightfully exercised; because the power proposed by the bill to be exercised is not expressly delegated, and because I can not satisfy myself that it results from any express power by fair and safe rules of interpretation.

The weight of the precedent of the bank of 1791 and the sanction of the great name of Washington, which has been so often invoked in its support, are greatly weakened by the development of these facts.

The experiment of that bank satisfied the country that it ought not to be continued, and at the end of twenty years Congress refused to recharter it. It would have been fortunate for the country, and saved thousands from bankruptcy and ruin, had our public men of 1816 resisted the temporary pressure of the times upon our financial and pecuniary interests and refused to charter the second bank. Of this the country became abundantly satisfied, and at the close of its twenty years' duration, as in the case of the first bank, it also ceased to exist. Under the repeated blows of *President Jackson* it reeled and fell, and a subsequent attempt to charter a similar institution was arrested by the *veto* of President Tyler.

Mr. Madison, in yielding his signature to the charter of 1816, did so upon the ground of the respect due to precedents; and, as he subsequently declared—

The Bank of the United States, though on the original question held to be unconstitutional, received the Executive signature.

It is probable that neither the bank of 1791 nor that of 1816 would have been chartered but for the embarrassments of the Government in its finances, the derangement of the currency, and the pecuniary pressure which existed, the first the consequence of the War of the Revolution and the second the consequence of the War of 1812. Both were resorted to in the delusive hope that they would restore public credit and afford relief to the Government and to the business of the country.

Those of our public men who opposed the whole "American system" at its commencement and throughout its progress foresaw and predicted that it was fraught with incalculable mischiefs and must result in serious injury to the best interests of the country. For a series of years their wise counsels were unheeded, and the system was established. It was soon apparent that its practical operation was unequal and unjust upon different portions of the country and upon the people engaged in different pursuits. All were equally entitled to the favor and protection of the Government. It fostered and elevated the money power and enriched the favored few by taxing labor, and at the expense of the many. Its effect was to "make the rich richer and the poor poorer." Its tendency was to create distinctions in society based on wealth and to give to the favored classes undue control and sway in our Government. It was an organized money power, which resisted the popular will and sought to shape and control the public policy.

Under the pernicious workings of this combined system of measures the country witnessed alternate seasons of temporary apparent prosperity, of sudden and disastrous commercial revulsions, of unprecedented fluctuation of prices and depression of the great interests of agriculture, navigation, and commerce, of general pecuniary suffering, and of final bankruptcy of thousands. After a severe struggle of more than a quarter of a century, the system was overthrown.

The bank has been succeeded by a practical system of finance, conducted and controlled solely by the Government. The constitutional currency has been restored, the public credit maintained unimpaired even in a period of a foreign war, and the whole country has become satisfied that banks, national or State, are not necessary as fiscal agents of the Government. Revenue duties have taken the place of the protective tariff. The distribution of the money derived from the sale of the public lands has been abandoned and the corrupting system of internal improvements, it is hoped, has been effectually checked.

It is not doubted that if this whole train of measures, designed to take wealth from the many and bestow it upon the few, were to prevail the effect would be to change the entire character of the Government. One only danger remains. It is the seductions of that branch of the system which consists in internal improvements, holding out, as it does, inducements to the people of particular sections and localities to embark the Government in them without stopping to calculate the inevitable consequences. This branch of the system is so intimately combined and linked with the others that as surely as an effect is produced by an adequate cause, if it be resuscitated and revived and firmly established it requires no sagacity to foresee that it will necessarily and speedily draw after it the reestablishment of a national bank, the revival of a protective tariff, the distribution of the land money, and not only the postponement to the distant future of the payment of the present national debt, but its annual increase.

I entertain the solemn conviction that if the internal-improvement branch of the "American system" be not firmly resisted at this time the whole series of measures composing it will be speedily reestablished and the country be thrown back from its present high state of prosperity, which the existing policy has produced, and be destined again to witness all the evils, commercial revulsions, depression of prices, and pecuniary embarrassments through which we have passed during the last twenty-five years.

To guard against consequences so ruinous is an object of high national importance, involving, in my judgment, the continued prosperity of the country.

I have felt it to be an imperative obligation to withhold my constitutional sanction from two bills which had passed the two Houses of Congress, involving the principle of the internal-improvement branch of the "American system" and conflicting in their provisions with the views here expressed.

This power, conferred upon the President by the Constitution, I have on three occasions during my administration of the executive department of the Government deemed it my duty to exercise, and on this last occasion of making to Congress an annual communication "of the state of the Union" it is not deemed inappropriate to review the principles and considerations which have governed my action. I deem this the more necessary because, after the lapse of nearly sixty years since the adoption of the Constitution, the propriety of the exercise of this undoubted constitutional power by the President has for the first time been drawn seriously in question by a portion of my fellow-citizens.

The Constitution provides that—

> Every bill which shall have passed the House of Representatives and the Senate shall, before it become a law, be presented to the President of the United States. If he approve he *shall* sign it, but if not he *shall* return it with his objections to that House in which it shall have originated, who shall enter the objections at large on their Journal and proceed to reconsider it.

The preservation of the Constitution from infraction is the President's highest duty. He is bound to discharge that duty at whatever hazard of incurring the displeasure of those who may differ with him in opinion. He is bound to discharge it as well by his obligations to the people who have clothed him with his exalted trust as by his oath of office, which he may not disregard. Nor are the obligations of the President in any degree lessened by the prevalence of views different from his own in one or both Houses of Congress. It is not alone hasty and inconsiderate legislation that he is required to check; but if at any time Congress shall, after apparently full deliberation, resolve on measures which he deems subversive of the Constitution or of the vital interests of the country, it is his solemn duty to stand in the breach and resist them. The President is bound to approve or disapprove every bill which passes Congress and is presented to him for his signature. The Constitution makes this his duty, and he can not escape it if he would. He has no election. In deciding upon any bill presented to him he must exercise his own best judgment. If he can not approve, the Constitution commands him to return the bill to the House in which it originated with his objections, and if he fail to do this within ten days (Sundays excepted) it shall become a law without his signature. Right or wrong, he may be overruled by a vote of two-thirds of each House, and in that event the bill becomes a law without his sanction. If his objections be not thus overruled, the subject is only postponed, and is referred to the States and the people for their consideration and decision. The President's power is negative merely, and not affirmative. He can enact no law. The only effect, therefore, of his withholding his approval of a bill passed by Congress is to suffer the existing laws to remain unchanged, and the delay occasioned is only that required to enable the States and the people to consider and act upon the subject in the election of public agents who will carry out their wishes and instructions. Any attempt to coerce the President to yield his sanction to measures which he can not approve would be a violation of the spirit of the Constitution, palpable and flagrant, and if successful would break down the independence of the executive department and make the President, elected by the people and clothed by the Constitution with power to defend their rights, the mere instrument of a majority of Congress. A surrender on his part of the powers with which the Constitution has invested his office would effect a practical alteration of that instrument without resorting to the prescribed process of amendment.

With the motives or considerations which may induce Congress to pass any bill the President can have nothing to do. He must presume them to be as pure as his own, and look only to the practical effect of their measures when compared with the Constitution or the public good.

But it has been urged by those who object to the exercise of this undoubted constitutional power that it assails the representative principle and the capacity of the people to govern themselves; that there is greater safety in a numerous representative body than in the single Executive created by the Constitution, and that the Executive veto is a "one-man power," despotic in its character. To expose the fallacy of this objection it is only necessary to consider the frame and true character of our system. Ours is not a consolidated empire, but a confederated union. The States before the adoption of the Constitution were coordinate, coequal, and separate independent sovereignties, and by its adoption they did not lose that character. They clothed the Federal Government with certain powers and reserved all others, including their own sovereignty, to themselves. They guarded their own rights as States and the rights of the people by the very limitations which they incorporated into the Federal Constitution, whereby the different departments of the General Government were checks upon each other. That the majority should govern is a general principle controverted by none, but they must govern according to the Constitution, and not according to an undefined and unrestrained discretion, whereby they may oppress the minority.

The people of the United States are not blind to the fact that they may be temporarily misled, and that their representatives, legislative and executive, may be mistaken or influenced in their action by improper motives. They have therefore interposed between themselves and the laws which may be passed by their public agents various representations, such as assemblies, senates, and governors in their several States, a House of Representatives, a Senate, and a President of the United States. The people can by their own direct agency make no law, nor can the House of Representatives, immediately elected by them, nor can the Senate, nor can both together without the concurrence of the President or a vote of two-thirds of both Houses.

Happily for themselves, the people in framing our admirable system of government were conscious of the infirmities of their representatives, and in delegating to them the power of legislation they have fenced them around with checks to guard against the effects of hasty action, of error, of combination, and of possible corruption. Error, selfishness, and faction have often sought to rend asunder this web of checks and subject the Government to the control of fanatic and sinister influences, but these efforts have only satisfied the people of the wisdom of the checks which they have imposed and of the necessity of preserving them unimpaired.

The true theory of our system is not to govern by the acts or decrees of any one set of representatives. The Constitution interposes checks upon all branches of the Government, in order to give time for error to be corrected and delusion to pass away; but if the people settle down into a firm conviction different from that of their representatives they give effect to their opinions by changing their public servants. The checks which the people imposed on their public servants in the adoption of the Constitution are the best evidence of their capacity for self-government. They know that the men whom they elect to public stations are of like infirmities and passions with themselves, and not to be trusted without being restricted by coordinate authorities and constitutional limitations. Who that has witnessed the legislation of Congress for the last thirty years will say that he knows of no instance in which measures not demanded by the public good have been carried? Who will deny that in the State governments, by combinations of individuals and sections, in derogation of the general interest, banks have been chartered, systems of internal improvements adopted, and debts entailed upon the people repressing their growth and impairing their energies for years to come?

After so much experience it can not be said that absolute unchecked power is safe in the hands of any one set of representatives, or that the capacity of the people for self-government, which is admitted in its broadest extent, is a conclusive argument to prove the prudence, wisdom, and integrity of their representatives.

The people, by the Constitution, have commanded the President, as much as they have commanded the legislative branch of the Government, to execute their will. They have said to him in the Constitution, which they require he shall take a solemn oath to support, that if Congress pass any bill which he can not approve "he shall return it to the House in which it originated with his objections." In withholding from it his approval and signature he is executing the will of the people, constitutionally expressed, as much as the Congress that passed it. No bill is presumed to be in accordance with the popular will until it shall have passed through all the branches of the Government required by the Constitution to make it a law. A bill which passes the House of Representatives may be rejected by the Senate, and so a bill passed by the Senate may be rejected by the House. In each case the respective Houses exercise the veto power on the other.

Congress, and each House of Congress, hold under the Constitution a check upon the President, and he, by the power of the qualified veto, a check upon Congress. When the President recommends measures to Congress, he avows in the most solemn form his opinions, gives his voice in their favor, and pledges himself in advance to approve them if passed by Congress. If he acts without due consideration, or has been influenced by improper or corrupt motives, or if from any other cause Congress, or either House of Congress, shall differ with him in opinion, they exercise their *veto* upon his recommendations and reject them; and there is no appeal from their decision but to the people at the ballot box. These are proper checks upon the Executive, wisely interposed by the Constitution. None will be found to object to them or to wish them removed. It is equally important that the constitutional checks of the Executive upon the legislative branch should be preserved.

If it be said that the Representatives in the popular branch of Congress are chosen directly by the people, it is answered, the people elect the President. If both Houses represent the States and the people, so does the President. The President represents in the executive department the whole people of the United States, as each member of the legislative department represents portions of them.

The doctrine of restriction upon legislative and executive power, while a well-settled public opinion is enabled within a reasonable time to accomplish its ends, has made our country what it is, and has opened to us a career of glory and happiness to which all other nations have been strangers.

In the exercise of the power of the veto the President is responsible not only to an enlightened public opinion, but to the people of the whole Union, who elected him, as the representatives in the legislative branches who differ with him in opinion are responsible to the people of particular States or districts, who compose their respective constituencies. To deny to the President the exercise of this power would be to repeal that provision of the Constitution which confers it upon him. To charge that its exercise unduly controls the legislative will is to complain of the Constitution itself.

If the Presidential veto be objected to upon the ground that it checks and thwarts the popular will, upon the same principle the equality of representation of the States in the Senate should be stricken out of the Constitution. The vote of a Senator from Delaware has equal weight in deciding upon the most important measures with the vote of a Senator from New York, and yet the one represents a State containing, according to the existing apportionment of Representatives in the House of Representatives, but one thirty-fourth part of the population of the other. By the constitutional composition of the Senate a majority of that body from the smaller States represent less than one-fourth of the people of the Union. There are thirty States, and under the existing apportionment of Representatives there are 230 Members in the House of Representatives. Sixteen of the smaller States are represented in that House by but 50 Members, and yet the Senators from these States constitute a majority of the Senate. So that the President may recommend a measure to Congress, and it may receive the sanction and approval of more than three-fourths of the House of Representatives and of all the Senators from the large States, containing more than three-fourths of the whole population of the United States, and yet the measure may be defeated by the votes of the Senators from the smaller States. None, it is presumed, can be found ready to change the organization of the Senate on this account, or to strike that body practically out of existence by requiring that its action shall be conformed to the will of the more numerous branch.

Upon the same principle that the *veto* of the President should be practically abolished the power of the Vice-President to give the casting vote upon an equal division of the Senate should be abolished also. The Vice-President exercises the *veto* power as effectually by rejecting a bill by his casting vote as the President does by refusing to approve and sign it. This power has been exercised by the Vice-President in a few instances, the most important of which was the rejection of the bill to recharter the Bank of the United States in 1811. It may happen that a bill may be passed by a large majority of the House of Representatives, and may be supported by the Senators from the larger States, and the Vice-President may reject it by giving his vote with the Senators from the smaller States; and yet none, it is presumed, are prepared to deny to him the exercise of this power under the Constitution.

But it is, in point of fact, untrue that an act passed by Congress is conclusive evidence that it is an emanation of the popular will. A majority of the whole number elected to each House of Congress constitutes a quorum, and a majority of that quorum is competent to pass laws. It might happen that a quorum of the House of Representatives, consisting of a single member more than half of the whole number elected to that House, might pass a bill by a majority of a single vote, and in that case a fraction more than one-fourth of the people of the United States would be represented by those who voted for it. It might happen that the same bill might be passed by a majority of one of a quorum of the Senate, composed of Senators from the fifteen smaller States and a single Senator from a sixteenth State; and if the Senators voting for it happened to be from the eight of the smallest of these States, it would be passed by the votes of Senators from States having but fourteen Representatives in the House of Representatives, and containing less than one-sixteenth of the whole population of the United States. This extreme case is stated to illustrate the fact that the mere passage of a bill by Congress is no conclusive evidence that those who passed it represent the majority of the people of the United States or truly reflect their will. If such an extreme case is not likely to happen, cases that approximate it are of constant occurrence. It is believed that not a single law has been passed since the adoption of the Constitution upon which all the members elected to both Houses have been present and voted. Many of the most important acts which have passed Congress have been carried by a close vote in thin Houses. Many instances of this might be given. Indeed, our experience proves that many of the most important acts of Congress are postponed to the last days, and often the last hours, of a session, when they are disposed of in haste, and by Houses but little exceeding the number necessary to form a quorum.

Besides, in most of the States the members of the House of Representatives are chosen by pluralities, and not by majorities of all the voters in their respective districts, and it may happen that a majority of that House may be returned by a less aggregate vote of the people than that received by the minority.

If the principle insisted on be sound, then the Constitution should be so changed that no bill shall become a law unless it is voted for by members representing in each House a majority of the whole people of the United States. We must remodel our whole system, strike down and abolish not only the salutary checks lodged in the executive branch, but must strike out and abolish those lodged in the Senate also, and thus practically invest the whole power of the Government in a majority of a single assembly—a majority uncontrolled and absolute, and which may become despotic. To conform to this doctrine of the right of majorities to rule, independent of the checks and limitations of the Constitution, we must revolutionize our whole system; we must destroy the constitutional compact by which the several States agreed to form a Federal Union and rush into consolidation, which must end in monarchy or despotism. No one advocates such a proposition, and yet the doctrine maintained, if carried out, must lead to this result.

One great object of the Constitution in conferring upon the President a qualified negative upon the legislation of Congress was to protect minorities from injustice and oppression by majorities. The equality of their representation in the Senate and the veto power of the President are the constitutional guaranties which the smaller States have that their rights will be respected. Without these guaranties all their interests would be at the mercy of majorities in Congress representing the larger States. To the smaller and weaker States, therefore, the preservation of this power and its exercise upon proper occasions demanding it is of vital importance. They ratified the Constitution and entered into the Union, securing to themselves an equal representation with the larger States in the Senate; and they agreed to be bound by all laws passed by Congress upon the express condition, and none other, that they should be approved by the President or passed, his objections to the contrary notwithstanding, by a vote of two-thirds of both Houses. Upon this condition they have a right to insist as a part of the compact to which they gave their assent.

A bill might be passed by Congress against the will of the whole people of a particular State and against the votes of its Senators and all its Representatives. However prejudicial it might be to the interests of such State, it would be bound by it if the President shall approve it or it shall be passed by a vote of two-thirds of both Houses; but it has a right to demand that the President shall exercise his constitutional power and arrest it if his judgment is against it. If he surrender this power, or fail to exercise it in a case where he can not approve, it would make his formal approval a mere mockery, and would be itself a violation of the Constitution, and the dissenting State would become bound by a law which had not been passed according to the sanctions of the Constitution.

The objection to the exercise of the *veto* power is founded upon an idea respecting the popular will, which, if carried out, would annihilate State sovereignty and substitute for the present Federal Government a consolidation directed by a supposed numerical majority. A revolution of the Government would be silently effected and the States would be subjected to laws to which they had never given their constitutional consent.

The Supreme Court of the United States is invested with the power to declare, and has declared, acts of Congress passed with the concurrence of the Senate, the House of Representatives, and the approval of the President to be unconstitutional and void, and yet none, it is presumed, can be found who will be disposed to strip this highest judicial tribunal under the Constitution of this acknowledged power—a power necessary alike to its independence and the rights of individuals.

For the same reason that the Executive veto should, according to the doctrine maintained, be rendered nugatory, and be practically expunged from the Constitution, this power of the court should also be rendered nugatory and be expunged, because it restrains the legislative and Executive will, and because the exercise of such a power by the court may be regarded as being in conflict with the capacity of the people to govern themselves. Indeed, there is more reason for striking this power of the court from the Constitution than there is that of the qualified veto of the President, because the decision of the court is final, and can never be reversed even though both Houses of Congress and the President should be unanimous in opposition to it, whereas the veto of the President may be overruled by a vote of two-thirds of both Houses of Congress or by the people at the polls.

It is obvious that to preserve the system established by the Constitution each of the coordinate branches of the Government—the executive, legislative, and judicial—must be left in the exercise of its appropriate powers. If the executive or the judicial branch be deprived of powers conferred upon either as checks on the legislative, the preponderance of the latter will become disproportionate and absorbing and the others impotent for the accomplishment of the great objects for which they were established. Organized, as they are, by the Constitution, they work together harmoniously for the public good. If the Executive and the judiciary shall be deprived of the constitutional powers invested in them, and of their due proportions, the equilibrium of the system must be destroyed, and consolidation, with the most pernicious results, must ensue—a consolidation of unchecked, despotic power, exercised by majorities of the legislative branch.

The executive, legislative, and judicial each constitutes a separate coordinate department of the Government, and each is independent of the others. In the performance of their respective duties under the Constitution neither can in its legitimate action control the others. They each act upon their several responsibilities in their respective spheres. But if the doctrines now maintained be correct, the executive must become practically subordinate to the legislative, and the judiciary must become subordinate to both the legislative and the executive; and thus the whole power of the Government would be merged in a single department. Whenever, if ever, this shall occur, our glorious system of well-regulated self-government will crumble into ruins, to be succeeded, first by anarchy, and finally by monarchy or despotism. I am far from believing that this doctrine is the sentiment of the American people; and during the short period which remains in which it will be my duty to administer the executive department it will be my aim to maintain its independence and discharge its duties without infringing upon the powers or duties of either of the other departments of the Government.

The power of the Executive veto was exercised by the first and most illustrious of my predecessors and by four of his successors who preceded me in the administration of the Government, and it is believed in no instance prejudicially to the public interests. It has never been and there is but little danger that it ever can be abused. No President will ever desire unnecessarily to place his opinion in opposition to that of Congress. He must always exercise the power reluctantly, and only in cases where his convictions make it a matter of stern duty, which he can not escape. Indeed, there is more danger that the President, from the repugnance he must always feel to come in collision with Congress, may fail to exercise it in cases where the preservation of the Constitution from infraction, or the public good, may demand it than that he will ever exercise it unnecessarily or wantonly.

During the period I have administered the executive department of the Government great and important questions of public policy, foreign and domestic, have arisen, upon which it was my duty to act. It may, indeed, be truly said that my Administration has fallen upon eventful times. I have felt most sensibly the weight of the high responsibilities devolved upon me. With no other object than the public good, the enduring fame, and permanent prosperity of my country, I have pursued the convictions of my own best judgment. The impartial arbitrament of enlightened public opinion, present and future, will determine how far the public policy I have maintained and the measures I have from time to time recommended may have tended to advance or retard the public prosperity at home and to elevate or depress the estimate of our national character abroad.

Invoking the blessings of the Almighty upon your deliberations at your present important session, my ardent hope is that in a spirit of harmony and concord you may be guided to wise results, and such as may redound to the happiness, the honor, and the glory of our beloved country.

JAMES K. POLK.

SPECIAL MESSAGES.

WASHINGTON, *December 12, 1848*.

To the Senate of the United States:

I nominate Second Lieutenant Ulysses S. Grant (since promoted first lieutenant), of the Fourth Regiment of Infantry, to be first lieutenant by brevet for gallant and meritorious services in the battle of Chapultepec, September 13, 1847, as proposed in the accompanying communication from the Secretary of War.

JAMES K. POLK.

WAR DEPARTMENT, *December 11, 1848*.

The PRESIDENT OF THE UNITED STATES.

SIR: The brevet of captain conferred on Second Lieutenant Ulysses S. Grant (since promoted first lieutenant), of the Fourth Regiment of Infantry, and confirmed by the Senate on the 13th of July, 1848, "for gallant and meritorious conduct in the battle of Chapultepec, September 13, 1847," being the result of a misapprehension as to the grade held by that officer on the 13th of September, 1847 (he being then a second lieutenant), I have to propose that the brevet of captain be canceled and that the brevet of first lieutenant "for gallant and meritorious services in the battle of Chapultepec, September 13, 1847," be conferred in lieu thereof.

I am, sir, with great respect, your obedient servant,

W. L. MARCY.

WASHINGTON, *December 12, 1848.*

To the Senate of the United States:

I transmit herewith, for the consideration and advice of the Senate with regard to its ratification, a treaty concluded on the 6th of August, 1848, by L. E. Powell, on the part of the United States, and the chiefs and headmen of the confederated bands of the Pawnee Indians, together with a report of the Commissioner of Indian Affairs and other papers explanatory of the same.

JAMES K. POLK.

WASHINGTON, *December 12, 1848.*

To the Senate of the United States:

I transmit herewith, for the consideration and advice of the Senate with regard to its ratification, a treaty concluded on the 18th of October, 1848, by William Medill, Commissioner of Indian Affairs, on the part of the United States, and the chiefs and headmen of the Menomonee Indians, together with a report of the Commissioner of Indian Affairs and other papers explanatory of the same.

JAMES K. POLK.

WASHINGTON, *December 27, 1848.*

To the House of Representatives:

In compliance with the resolution of the House of the 11th instant, requesting the President to inform that body "whether he has received any information that American citizens have been imprisoned or arrested by British authorities in Ireland, and, if so, what have been the causes thereof and what steps have been taken for their release, and if not, in his opinion, inconsistent with public interest to furnish this House with copies of all correspondence in relation thereto," I communicate herewith a report of the Secretary of State, together with the accompanying correspondence upon the subject.

JAMES K. POLK.

WASHINGTON, *December 27, 1848.*

To the Senate of the United States:

I communicate herewith, in compliance with the request contained in the resolution of the Senate of the 19th instant, a report of the Secretary of the Treasury, with the accompanying statement, prepared by the Register of the Treasury, which exhibits the annual amount appropriated on account of the Coast Survey from the commencement of said Survey.

JAMES K. POLK.

WASHINGTON, *January 2, 1849.*

To the House of Representatives of the United States:

In answer to the resolution of the House of Representatives of the 18th of December, 1848, requesting information "under what law or provision of the Constitution, or by what other authority," the Secretary of the Treasury, with the "sanction and approval" of the President, established "a tariff of duties in the ports of the Mexican Republic during the war with Mexico," and "by what legal, constitutional, or other authority" the "revenue thus derived" was appropriated to "the support of the Army in Mexico," I refer the House to my annual message of the 7th of December, 1847, to my message to the Senate of the 10th of February, 1848, responding to a call of that body, a copy of which is herewith communicated, and to my message to the House of Representatives of the 24th of July, 1848, responding to a call of that House. The resolution assumes that the Secretary of the Treasury "established a tariff of duties in the ports of the Mexican Republic." The contributions collected in this mode were not established by the Secretary of the Treasury, but by a military order issued by the President through the War and Navy Departments. For his information the President directed the Secretary of the Treasury to prepare and report to him a scale of duties. That report was made, and the President's military order of the 31st of March, 1847, was based upon it. The documents communicated to Congress with my annual message of December, 1847, show the true character of that order.

The authority under which military contributions were exacted and collected from the enemy and applied to the support of our Army during the war with Mexico was stated in the several messages referred to. In the first of these messages I informed Congress that—

On the 31st of March last I caused an order to be issued to our military and naval commanders to levy and collect a military contribution upon all vessels and merchandise which might enter any of the ports of Mexico in our military occupation, and to apply such contributions toward defraying the expenses of the war. By virtue of the right of conquest and the laws of war, the conqueror, consulting his own safety or convenience, may either exclude foreign commerce altogether from all such ports or permit it upon such terms and conditions as he may prescribe. Before the principal ports of Mexico were blockaded by our Navy the revenue derived from import duties under the laws of Mexico was paid into the Mexican treasury. After these ports had fallen into our military possession the blockade was raised and commerce with them permitted upon prescribed terms and conditions. They were opened to the trade of all nations upon the payment of duties more moderate in their amount than those which had been previously levied by Mexico, and the revenue, which was formerly paid into the Mexican treasury, was directed to be collected by our military and naval officers and applied to the use of our Army and Navy. Care was taken that the officers, soldiers, and sailors of our Army and Navy should be exempted from the operations of the order, and, as the merchandise imported upon which the order operated must be consumed by Mexican citizens, the contributions exacted were in effect the seizure of the public revenues of Mexico and the application of them to our own use. In directing this measure the object was to compel the enemy to contribute as far as practicable toward the expenses of the war.

It was also stated in that message that—

Measures have recently been adopted by which the internal as well as the external revenues of Mexico in all places in our military occupation will be seized and appropriated to the use of our Army and Navy.

The policy of levying upon the enemy contributions in every form consistently with the laws of nations, which it may be practicable for our military commanders to adopt, should, in my judgment, be rigidly enforced, and orders to this effect have accordingly been given. By such a policy, at the same time that our own Treasury will be relieved from a heavy drain, the Mexican people will be made to feel the burdens of the war, and, consulting their own interests, may be induced the more readily to require their rulers to accede to a just peace.

In the same message I informed Congress that the amount of the "loan" which would be required for the further prosecution of the war might be "reduced by whatever amount of expenditures can be saved by military contributions collected in Mexico," and that "the most rigorous measures for the augmentation of these contributions have been directed, and a very considerable sum is expected from that source." The Secretary of the Treasury, in his annual report of that year, in making his estimate of the amount of loan which would probably be required, reduced the sum in consideration of the amount which would probably be derived from these contributions, and Congress authorized the loan upon this reduced estimate.

In the message of the 10th of February, 1848, to the Senate, it was stated that—

No principle is better established than that a nation at war has the right of shifting the burden off itself and imposing it on the enemy by exacting military contributions. The mode of making such exactions must be left to the discretion of the conqueror, but it should be exercised in a manner conformable to the rules of civilized warfare.

The right to levy these contributions is essential to the successful prosecution of war in an enemy's country, and the practice of nations has been in accordance with this principle. It is as clearly necessary as the right to fight battles, and its exercise is often essential to the subsistence of the army.

Entertaining no doubt that the military right to exclude commerce altogether from the ports of the enemy in our military occupation included the minor right of admitting it under prescribed conditions, it became an important question at the date of the order whether there should be a discrimination between vessels and cargoes belonging to citizens of the United States and vessels and cargoes belonging to neutral nations.

In the message to the House of Representatives of the 24th of July, 1848, it was stated that—

It is from the same source of authority that we derive the unquestioned right, after the war has been declared by Congress, to blockade the ports and coasts of the enemy, to capture his towns, cities, and provinces, and to levy contributions upon him for the support of our Army. Of the same character with these is the right to subject to our temporary military government the conquered territories of our enemy. They are all belligerent rights, and their exercise is as essential to the successful prosecution of a foreign war as the right to fight battles.

By the Constitution the power to "declare war" is vested in Congress, and by the same instrument it is provided that "the President shall be Commander in Chief of the Army and Navy of the United States" and that "he shall take care that the laws be faithfully executed."

When Congress have exerted their power by declaring war against a foreign nation, it is the duty of the President to prosecute it. The Constitution has prescribed no particular mode in which he shall perform this duty. The manner of conducting the war is not defined by the Constitution. The term *war* used in that instrument has a well-understood meaning among nations. That meaning is derived from the laws of nations, a code which is recognized by all civilized powers as being obligatory in a state of war. The power is derived from the Constitution and the manner of exercising it is regulated by the laws of nations. When Congress have declared war, they in effect make it the duty of the President in prosecuting it, by land and sea, to resort to all the modes and to exercise all the powers and rights which other nations at war possess. He is invested with the same power in this respect as if he were personally present commanding our fleets by sea or our armies by land. He may conduct the war by issuing orders for fighting battles, besieging and capturing cities, conquering and holding the provinces of the enemy, or by capturing his vessels and other property on the high seas. But these are not the only modes of prosecuting war which are recognized by the laws of nations and to which he is authorized to resort. The levy of contributions on the enemy is a right of war well established and universally acknowledged among nations, and one which every belligerent possessing the ability may properly exercise. The most approved writers on public law admit and vindicate this right as consonant with reason, justice, and humanity.

No principle is better established than that—

> We have a right to deprive our enemy of his possessions, of everything which may augment his strength and enable him to make war. This everyone endeavors to accomplish in the manner most suitable to him. Whenever we have an opportunity we seize on the enemy's property and convert it to our own use, and thus, besides diminishing the enemy's power, we augment our own and obtain at least a partial indemnification or equivalent, either for what constitutes the subject of the war or for the expenses and losses incurred in its prosecution. In a word, we do ourselves justice.

"Instead of the custom of pillaging the open country and defenseless places," the levy of contributions has been "substituted."

> Whoever carries on a just war has a right to make the enemy's country contribute to the support of his army and toward defraying all the charges of the war. Thus he obtains a part of what is due to him, and the enemy's subjects, by consenting to pay the sum demanded, have their property secured from pillage and the country is preserved.

These principles, it is believed, are uncontroverted by any civilized nation in modern times. The public law of nations, by which they are recognized, has been held by our highest judicial tribunal as a code which is applicable to our "situation" in a state of war and binding on the United States, while in admiralty and maritime cases it is often the governing rule. It is in a just war that a nation has the "right to make the enemy's country contribute to the support of his army." Not doubting that our late war with Mexico was just on the part of the United States, I did not hesitate when charged by the Constitution with its prosecution to exercise a power common to all other nations, and Congress was duly informed of the mode and extent to which that power had been and would be exercised at the commencement of their first session thereafter.

Upon the declaration of war against Mexico by Congress the United States were entitled to all the rights which any other nation at war would have possessed. These rights could only be demanded and enforced by the President, whose duty it was, as "Commander in Chief of the Army and Navy of the United States," to execute the law of Congress which declared the war. In the act declaring war Congress provided for raising men and money to enable the President "to prosecute it to a speedy and successful termination." Congress prescribed no mode of conducting it, but left the President to prosecute it according to the laws of nations as his guide. Indeed, it would have been impracticable for Congress to have provided for all the details of a campaign.

The mode of levying contributions must necessarily be left to the discretion of the conqueror, subject to be exercised, however, in conformity with the laws of nations. It may be exercised by requiring a given sum or a given amount of provisions to be furnished by the authorities of a captured city or province; it may be exercised by imposing an internal tax or a tax on the enemy's commerce, whereby he may be deprived of his revenues, and these may be appropriated to the use of the conqueror. The latter mode was adopted by the collection of duties in the ports of Mexico in our military occupation during the late war with that Republic.

So well established is the military right to do this under the laws of nations that our military and naval officers commanding our forces on the theater of war adopted the same mode of levying contributions from the enemy before the order of the President of the 31st of March, 1847, was issued. The general in command of the Army at Vera Cruz, upon his own view of his powers and duties, and without specific instructions to that effect, immediately after the capture of that city adopted this mode. By his order of the 28th of March, 1847, heretofore communicated to the House of Representatives, he directed a "temporary and moderate tariff of duties to be established." Such a tariff was established, and contributions were collected under it and applied to the uses of our Army. At a still earlier period the same power was exercised by the naval officers in command of our squadron on the Pacific coast. * * * Not doubting the authority to resort to this mode, the order of the 31st of March, 1847, was issued, and was in effect but a modification of the previous orders of these officers, by making the rates of contribution uniform and directing their collection in all the ports of the enemy in our military occupation and under our temporary military government.

The right to levy contributions upon the enemy in the form of import and export duties in his ports was sanctioned by the treaty of peace with Mexico. By that treaty both Governments recognized * * * and confirmed the exercise of that right. By its provisions "the custom-houses at all the ports occupied by the forces of the United States" were, upon the exchange of ratifications, to be delivered up to the Mexican authorities, "together with all bonds and evidences of debt for duties on importations and exportations *not yet fallen due;*" and "all duties on imports and on exports collected at such custom-houses or elsewhere in Mexico by authority of the United States" before the ratification of the treaty by the Mexican Government were to be retained by the United States, and only the net amount of the duties collected after this period was to be "delivered to the Mexican Government." By its provisions also all merchandise "imported previously to the restoration of the custom-houses to the Mexican authorities" or "exported from any Mexican port whilst in the occupation of the forces of the United States" was protected from confiscation and from the payment of any import or export duties to the Mexican Government, even although the importation of such merchandise "be prohibited by the Mexican tariff." The treaty also provides that should the custom-houses be surrendered to the Mexican authorities in less than sixty days from the date of its signature, the rates of duty on merchandise imposed by the United States were in that event to survive the war until the end of this period; and in the meantime Mexican custom-house officers were bound to levy no other duties thereon "than the duties established by the tariff found in force at such custom-houses at the time of the restoration of the same." The "tariff found in force at such custom-houses," which is recognized and sustained by this stipulation, was that established by the military order of the 31st of March, 1847, as a mode of levying and collecting military contributions from the enemy.

The right to blockade the ports and coasts of the enemy in war is no more provided for or prescribed by the Constitution than the right to levy and collect contributions from him in the form of duties or otherwise, and yet it has not been questioned that the President had the power after war had been declared by Congress to order our Navy to blockade the ports and coasts of Mexico. The right in both cases exists under the laws of nations. If the President can not order military contributions to be collected without an act of Congress, for the same reason he can not order a blockade; nor can he direct the enemy's vessels to be captured on the high seas; nor can he order our military and naval officers to invade the enemy's country, conquer, hold, and subject to our military government his cities and provinces; nor can he give to our military and naval commanders orders to perform many other acts essential to success in war.

If when the City of Mexico was captured the commander of our forces had found in the Mexican treasury public money which the enemy had provided to support his army, can it be doubted that he possessed the right to seize and appropriate it for the use of our own Army? If the money captured from the enemy could have been thus lawfully seized and appropriated, it would have been by virtue of the laws of war, recognized by all civilized nations; and by the same authority the sources of revenue and of supply of the enemy may be cut off from him, whereby he may be weakened and crippled in his means of continuing or waging the war. If the commanders of our forces, while acting under the orders of the President, in the heart of the enemy's country and surrounded by a hostile population, possess none of these essential and indispensable powers of war, but must halt the Army at every step of its progress and wait for an act of Congress to be passed to authorize them to do that which every other nation has the right to do by virtue of the laws of nations, then, indeed, is the Government of the United States in a condition of imbecility and weakness, which must in all future time render it impossible to prosecute a foreign war in an enemy's country successfully or to vindicate the national rights and the national honor by war.

The contributions levied were collected in the enemy's country, and were ordered to be "applied" in the enemy's country "toward defraying the expenses of the war," and the appropriations made by Congress for that purpose were thus relieved, and considerable balances remained undrawn from the Treasury. The amount of contributions remaining unexpended at the close of the war, as far as the accounts of collecting and disbursing officers have been settled, have been paid into the Treasury in pursuance of an order for that purpose, except the sum "applied toward the payment of the first installment due under the treaty with Mexico," as stated in my last annual message, for which an appropriation had been made by Congress. The accounts of some of these officers, as stated in the report of the Secretary of War accompanying that message, will require legislation before they can be finally settled.

In the late war with Mexico it is confidently believed that the levy of contributions and the seizure of the sources of public revenue upon which the enemy relied to enable him to continue the war essentially contributed to hasten peace. By those means the Government and people of Mexico were made to feel the pressure of the war and to realize that if it were protracted its burdens and inconveniences must be borne by themselves. Notwithstanding the great success of our arms, it may well be doubted whether an honorable peace would yet have been obtained but for the very contributions which were exacted.

JAMES K. POLK.

WASHINGTON, *January 4, 1849.*

To the Senate of the United States:

I transmit to the Senate, for their consideration and advice with regard to its ratification, a convention between the United States of America and the Government of Her Britannic Majesty, for the improvement of the communication by post between their respective territories, concluded and signed at London on the 15th December last, together with an explanatory dispatch from our minister at that Court.

JAMES K. POLK.

WASHINGTON, *January 29, 1849.*

To the Senate of the United States:

I communicate herewith a report of the Secretary of State, with the accompanying documents, in answer to a resolution of the Senate of the 21st December, 1848, requesting the President "to communicate to the Senate (if, in his opinion, not incompatible with the public service) a copy of the dispatches transmitted to the Secretary of State in August last by the resident minister at Rio de Janeiro in reference to the service and general conduct of Commodore G. W. Storer, commander in chief of the United States naval forces on the coast of Brazil."

JAMES K. POLK.

WASHINGTON, *January 29, 1849.*

To the House of Representatives of the United States:

I communicate herewith reports from the Secretary of War and the Secretary of the Navy, together with the accompanying documents, in answer to a resolution of the House of Representatives of December 20, 1848, requesting the President "to communicate to the House the amount of moneys and property received during the late war with the Republic of Mexico at the different ports of entry, or in any other way within her limits, and in what manner the same has been expended or appropriated."

JAMES K. POLK

WASHINGTON, *February 1, 1849*

To the Senate of the United States:

I communicate herewith reports from the Secretary of State, the Secretary of the Treasury, the Secretary of War, and the Secretary of the

Navy, together with the accompanying documents, in answer to a resolution of the Senate of the 15th January, 1849, "that the petition and papers of John B. Emerson be referred to the President of the United States, and that he be requested to cause a report thereon to be made to the Senate, wherein the public officer making such report shall state in what cases, if any, the United States have used or employed the invention of said Emerson contrary to law, and, further, whether any compensation therefor is justly due to said Emerson, and, if so, to what amount in each case."

JAMES K. POLK.

WASHINGTON, *February 5, 1849.*

To the Senate of the United States:

I transmit herewith, for the consideration and advice of the Senate with regard to its ratification, a treaty concluded on the 24th day of November, 1848, by Morgan L. Martin and Albert G. Ellis, commissioners on the part of the United States, and the sachem, councilors, and headmen of the Stockbridge tribe of Indians, together with a report of the Commissioner of Indian Affairs and other papers explanatory of the same.

JAMES K. POLK.

WASHINGTON, *February 8, 1849.*

To the House of Representatives of the United States:

In reply to the resolutions of the House of Representatives of the 5th instant, I communicate herewith a report from the Secretary of State, accompanied with all the documents and correspondence relating to the treaty of peace concluded between the United States and Mexico at Guadalupe Hidalgo on the 2d February, 1848, and to the amendments of the Senate thereto, as requested by the House in the said resolutions.

Amongst the documents transmitted will be found a copy of the instructions given to the commissioners of the United States who took to Mexico the treaty as amended by the Senate and ratified by the President of the United States. In my message to the House of Representatives of the 29th of July, 1848, I gave as my reason for declining to furnish these instructions in compliance with a resolution of the House that "in my opinion it would be inconsistent with the public interests to give publicity to them at the present time." Although it may still be doubted whether giving them publicity in our own country, and, as a necessary consequence, in Mexico, may not have a prejudicial influence on our public interests, yet, as they have been again called for by the House, and called for in connection with other documents, to the correct understanding of which they are indispensable, I have deemed it my duty to transmit them.

I still entertain the opinion expressed in the message referred to, that—

As a general rule applicable to all our important negotiations with foreign powers, it could not fail to be prejudicial to the public interests to publish the instructions to our ministers until some time had elapsed after the conclusion of such negotiations.

In these instructions of the 18th of March, 1848, it will be perceived that—

The task was assigned to the commissioners of the United States of consummating the treaty of peace, which was signed at Guadalupe Hidalgo on the 2d day of February last, between the United States and the Mexican Republic, and which on the 10th of March last was ratified by the Senate with amendments.

They were informed that—

This brief statement will indicate to you clearly the line of your duty. You are not sent to Mexico for the purpose of negotiating any new treaty, or of changing in any particular the ratified treaty which you will bear with you. None of the amendments adopted by the Senate can be rejected or modified except by the authority of that body. Your whole duty will, then, consist in using every honorable effort to obtain from the Mexican Government a ratification of the treaty in the form in which it has been ratified by the Senate, and this with the least practicable delay. * * * For this purpose it may, and most probably will, become necessary that you should explain to the Mexican minister for foreign affairs, or to the authorized agents of the Mexican Government, the reasons which have influenced the Senate in adopting these several amendments to the treaty. This duty you will perform as much as possible by personal conferences. Diplomatic notes are to be avoided unless in case of necessity. These might lead to endless discussions and indefinite delay. Besides, they could not have any practical result, as your mission is confined to procuring a ratification from the Mexican Government of the treaty as it came from the Senate, and does not extend to the slightest modification in any of its provisions.

The commissioners were sent to Mexico to procure the ratification of the treaty *as amended by the Senate*. Their instructions confined them to this point. It was proper that the amendments to the treaty adopted by the United States should be explained to the Mexican Government, and explanations were made by the Secretary of State in his letter of the 18th of March, 1848, to the Mexican minister for foreign affairs, under my direction. This dispatch was communicated to Congress with my message of the 6th of July last, communicating the treaty of peace, and published by their order. This dispatch was transmitted by our commissioners from the City of Mexico to the Mexican Government, then at Queretaro, on the 17th of April, 1848, and its receipt acknowledged on the 19th of the same month. During the whole time that the treaty, as amended, was before the Congress of Mexico these explanations of the Secretary of State, and these alone, were before them.

The President of Mexico, on these explanations, on the 8th day of May, 1848, submitted the amended treaty to the Mexican Congress, and on the 25th of May that Congress approved the treaty as amended, without modification or alteration. The final action of the Mexican Congress had taken place before the commissioners of the United States had been officially received by the Mexican authorities, or held any conference with them, or had any other communication on the subject of the treaty except to transmit the letter of the Secretary of State.

In their dispatch transmitted to Congress with my message of the 6th of July last, communicating the treaty of peace, dated "City of Queretaro, May 25, 1848, 9 o'clock p. m.," the commissioners say:

We have the satisfaction to inform you that we reached this city this afternoon at about 5 o'clock, and that the treaty, as amended by the Senate of the United States, passed the Mexican Senate about the hour of our arrival by a vote of 33 to 5. It having previously passed the House of Deputies, nothing now remains but to exchange the ratifications of the treaty.

On the next day (the 26th of May) the commissioners were for the first time presented to the President of the Republic and their credentials placed in his hands. On this occasion the commissioners delivered an address to the President of Mexico, and he replied. In their dispatch of the 30th of May the commissioners say:

We inclose a copy of our address to the President, and also a copy of his reply. Several conferences afterwards took place between Messrs. Rosa, Cuevas, Conto, and ourselves, which it is not thought necessary to recapitulate, as we inclose a copy of the protocol, which contains the substance of the conversations. We have now the satisfaction to announce that the exchange of ratifications was effected to-day.

This dispatch was communicated with my message of the 6th of July last, and published by order of Congress.

The treaty, as amended by the Senate of the United States, with the accompanying papers and the evidence that in that form it had been ratified by Mexico, was received at Washington on the 4th day of July, 1848, and immediately proclaimed as the supreme law of the land. On the 6th of July I communicated to Congress the ratified treaty, with such accompanying documents as were deemed material to a full understanding of the subject, to the end that Congress might adopt the legislation necessary and proper to carry the treaty into effect. Neither the address of the commissioners, nor the reply of the President of Mexico on the occasion of their presentation, nor the memorandum of conversations embraced in the paper called a protocol, nor the correspondence now sent, were communicated, because they were not regarded as in any way material; and in this I conformed to the practice of our Government. It rarely, if ever, happens that all the correspondence, and especially the instructions to our ministers, is communicated. Copies of these papers are now transmitted, as being within the resolutions of the House calling for all such "correspondence as appertains to said treaty."

When these papers were received at Washington, peace had been restored, the first installment of three millions paid to Mexico, the blockades were raised, the City of Mexico evacuated, and our troops on their return home. The war was at an end, and the treaty, as ratified by the United States, was binding on both parties, and already executed in a great degree. In this condition of things it was not competent for the

President alone, or for the President and Senate, or for the President, Senate, and House of Representatives combined, to abrogate the treaty, to annul the peace and restore a state of war, except by a solemn declaration of war.

Had the protocol varied the treaty as amended by the Senate of the United States, it would have had no binding effect.

It was obvious that the commissioners of the United States did not regard the protocol as in any degree a part of the treaty, nor as modifying or altering the treaty as amended by the Senate. They communicated it as the substance of conversations held after the Mexican Congress had ratified the treaty, and they knew that the approval of the Mexican Congress was as essential to the validity of a treaty in all its parts as the advice and consent of the Senate of the United States. They knew, too, that they had no authority to alter or modify the treaty in the form in which it had been ratified by the United States, but that, if failing to procure the ratification of the Mexican Government otherwise than with amendments, their duty, imposed by express instructions, was to ask of Mexico to send without delay a commissioner to Washington to exchange ratifications here if the amendments of the treaty proposed by Mexico, on being submitted, should be adopted by the Senate of the United States.

I was equally well satisfied that the Government of Mexico had agreed to the treaty as amended by the Senate of the United States, and did not regard the protocol as modifying, enlarging, or diminishing its terms or effect. The President of that Republic, in submitting the amended treaty to the Mexican Congress, in his message on the 8th day of May, 1848, said:

> If the treaty could have been submitted to your deliberation precisely as it came from the hands of the plenipotentiaries, my satisfaction at seeing the war at last brought to an end would not have been lessened as it this day is in consequence of the modifications introduced into it by the Senate of the United States, and which have received the sanction of the President. * * * At present it is sufficient for us to say to you that if in the opinion of the Government justice had not been evinced on the part of the Senate and Government of the United States in introducing such modifications, it is presumed, on the other hand, that they are not of such importance that they should set aside the treaty. I believe, on the contrary, that it ought to be ratified upon the same terms in which it has already received the sanction of the American Government. My opinion is also greatly strengthened by the fact that a new negotiation is neither expected nor considered possible. Much less could another be brought forward upon a basis more favorable for the Republic.

The deliberations of the Mexican Congress, with no explanation before that body from the United States except the letter of the Secretary of State, resulted in the ratification of the treaty, as recommended by the President of that Republic, in the form in which it had been amended and ratified by the United States. The conversations embodied in the paper called a protocol took place after the action of the Mexican Congress was complete, and there is no reason to suppose that the Government of Mexico ever submitted the protocol to the Congress, or ever treated or regarded it as in any sense a new negotiation, or as operating any modification or change of the amended treaty. If such had been its effect, it was a nullity until approved by the Mexican Congress; and such approval was never made or intimated to the United States. In the final consummation of the ratification of the treaty by the President of Mexico no reference is made to it. On the contrary, this ratification, which was delivered to the commissioners of the United States, and is now in the State Department, contains a full and explicit recognition of the amendments of the Senate just as they had been communicated to that Government by the Secretary of State and been afterwards approved by the Mexican Congress. It declares that—

Having seen and examined the said treaty and the modifications made by the Senate of the United States of America, and having given an account thereof to the General Congress, conformably to the requirement in the fourteenth paragraph of the one hundred and tenth article of the federal constitution of these United States, that body has thought proper to approve of the said treaty, with the modifications thereto, in all their parts; and in consequence thereof, exerting the power granted to me by the constitution, I accept, ratify, and confirm the said treaty with its modifications, and promise, in the name of the Mexican Republic, to fulfill and observe it, and to cause it to be fulfilled and observed.

Upon an examination of this protocol, when it was received with the ratified treaty, I did not regard it as material or as in any way attempting to modify or change the treaty as it had been amended by the Senate of the United States.

The first explanation which it contains is:

That the American Government, by suppressing the ninth article of the treaty of Guadalupe and substituting the third article of the treaty of Louisiana, did not intend to diminish in any way what was agreed upon by the aforesaid article (ninth) in favor of the inhabitants of the territories ceded by Mexico. Its understanding is that all of that agreement is contained in the third article of the treaty of Louisiana. In consequence, all the privileges and guaranties—civil, political, and religious—which would have been possessed by the inhabitants of the ceded territories if the ninth article of the treaty had been retained will be enjoyed by them without any difference under the article which has been substituted.

The ninth article of the original treaty stipulated for the incorporation of the Mexican inhabitants of the ceded territories and their admission into the Union "as soon as possible, according to the principles of the Federal Constitution, to the enjoyment of all the rights of citizens of the United States." It provided also that in the meantime they should be maintained in the enjoyment of their liberty, their property, and their civil rights now vested in them according to the Mexican laws. It secured to them similar political rights with the inhabitants of the other Territories of the United States, and at least equal to the inhabitants of Louisiana and Florida when they were in a Territorial condition. It then proceeded to guarantee that ecclesiastics and religious corporations should be protected in the discharge of the offices of their ministry and the enjoyment of their property of every kind, whether individual or corporate, and, finally, that there should be a free communication between the Catholics of the ceded territories and their ecclesiastical authorities "even although such authority should reside within the limits of the Mexican Republic as defined by this treaty."

The ninth article of the treaty, as adopted by the Senate, is much more comprehensive in its terms and explicit in its meaning, and it clearly embraces in comparatively few words all the guaranties inserted in the original article. It is as follows:

> Mexicans who, in the territories aforesaid, shall not preserve the character of citizens of the Mexican Republic, conformably with what is stipulated in the preceding article, shall be incorporated into the Union of the United States and be admitted at the proper time (to be judged of by the Congress of the United States) to the enjoyment of all the rights of citizens of the United States, according to the principles of the Constitution, and in the meantime shall be maintained and protected in the free enjoyment of their liberty and property and secured in the free exercise of their religion without restriction.

This article, which was substantially copied from the Louisiana treaty, provides equally with the original article for the admission of these inhabitants into the Union, and in the meantime, whilst they shall remain in a Territorial state, by one sweeping provision declares that they "shall be maintained and protected in the free enjoyment of their liberty and property and secured in the free exercise of their religion without restriction."

This guaranty embraces every kind of property, whether held by ecclesiastics or laymen, whether belonging to corporations or individuals. It secures to these inhabitants the free exercise of their religion without restriction, whether they choose to place themselves under the spiritual authority of pastors resident within the Mexican Republic or the ceded territories. It was, it is presumed, to place this construction beyond all question that the Senate superadded the words "without restriction" to the religious guaranty contained in the corresponding article of the Louisiana treaty. Congress itself does not possess the power under the Constitution to make any law prohibiting the free exercise of religion.

If the ninth article of the treaty, whether in its original or amended form, had been entirely omitted in the treaty, all the rights and privileges which either of them confers would have been secured to the inhabitants of the ceded territories by the Constitution and laws of the United States.

The protocol asserts that "the American Government, by suppressing the tenth article of the treaty of Guadalupe, did not in any way intend to annul the grants of lands made by Mexico in the ceded territories;" that "these grants, notwithstanding the suppression of the article of the treaty, preserve the legal value which they may possess; and the grantees may cause their legitimate titles to be acknowledged before the American tribunals;" and then proceeds to state that, "conformably to the law of the United States, legitimate titles to every description of property, personal and real, existing in the ceded territories are those which were legitimate titles under the Mexican law in California and New Mexico up to the 13th of May, 1846, and in Texas up to the 2d of March, 1836."

The former was the date of the declaration of war against Mexico and the latter that of the declaration of independence by Texas.

The objection to the tenth article of the original treaty was not that it protected legitimate titles, which our laws would have equally protected without it, but that it most unjustly attempted to resuscitate grants which had become a mere nullity by allowing the grantees the same period after the exchange of the ratifications of the treaty to which they had been originally entitled after the date of their grants for the purpose of performing the conditions on which they had been made. In submitting the treaty to the Senate I had recommended the rejection of this article. That portion of it in regard to lands in Texas did not receive a single vote in the Senate. This information was communicated by the letter of the Secretary of State to the minister for foreign affairs of Mexico, and was in possession of the Mexican Government during the whole period the treaty was before the Mexican Congress; and the article itself was reprobated in that letter in the strongest terms. Besides, our commissioners to Mexico had been instructed that—

> Neither the President nor the Senate of the United States can ever consent to ratify any treaty containing the tenth article of the treaty of Guadalupe Hidalgo, in favor of grantees of land in Texas or elsewhere.

And again:

> Should the Mexican Government persist in retaining this article, then all prospect of immediate peace is ended; and of this you may give them an absolute assurance.

On this point the language of the protocol is free from ambiguity, but if it were otherwise is there any individual American or Mexican who would place such a construction upon it as to convert it into a vain attempt to revive this article, which had been so often and so solemnly condemned? Surely no person could for one moment suppose that either the commissioners of the United States or the Mexican minister for foreign affairs ever entertained the purpose of thus setting at naught the deliberate decision of the President and Senate, which had been communicated to the Mexican Government with the assurance that their abandonment of this obnoxious article was essential to the restoration of peace.

But the meaning of the protocol is plain. It is simply that the nullification of this article was not intended to destroy valid, legitimate titles to land which existed and were in full force independently of the provisions and without the aid of this article. Notwithstanding it has been expunged from the treaty, these grants were to "preserve the legal value which they may possess." The refusal to revive grants which had become extinct was not to invalidate those which were in full force and vigor. That such was the clear understanding of the Senate of the United States, and this in perfect accordance with the protocol, is manifest from the fact that whilst they struck from the treaty this unjust article, they at the same time sanctioned and ratified the last paragraph of the eighth article of the treaty, which declares that—

In the said territories property of every kind now belonging to Mexicans not established there shall be inviolably respected. The present owners, the heirs of these, and all Mexicans who may hereafter acquire said property by contract shall enjoy with respect to it guaranties equally ample as if the same belonged to citizens of the United States.

Without any stipulation in the treaty to this effect, all such valid titles under the Mexican Government would have been protected under the Constitution and laws of the United States.

The third and last explanation contained in the protocol is that—

The Government of the United States, by suppressing the concluding paragraph of article 12 of the treaty, did not intend to deprive the Mexican Republic of the free and unrestrained faculty of ceding, conveying, or transferring at any time (as it may judge best) the sum of the $12,000,000 which the same Government of the United States is to deliver in the places designated by the amended article.

The concluding paragraph of the original twelfth article, thus suppressed by the Senate, is in the following language:

Certificates in proper form for the said installments, respectively, in such sums as shall be desired by the Mexican Government, and transferable by it, shall be delivered to the said Government by that of the United States.

From this bare statement of facts the meaning of the protocol is obvious. Although the Senate had declined to create a Government stock for the $12,000,000, and issue transferable certificates for the amount in such sums as the Mexican Government might desire, yet they could not have intended thereby to deprive that Government of the faculty which every creditor possesses of transferring for his own benefit the obligation of his debtor, whatever this may be worth, according to his will and pleasure.

It can not be doubted that the twelfth article of the treaty as it now stands contains a positive obligation, "in consideration of the extension acquired by the boundaries of the United States," to pay to the Mexican Republic $12,000,000 in four equal annual installments of three millions each. This obligation may be assigned by the Mexican Government to any person whatever, but the assignee in such case would stand in no better condition than the Government. The amendment of the Senate prohibiting the issue of a Government transferable stock for the amount produces this effect and no more.

The protocol contains nothing from which it can be inferred that the assignee could rightfully demand the payment of the money in case the consideration should fail which is stated on the face of the obligation.

With this view of the whole protocol, and considering that the explanations which it contained were in accordance with the treaty, I did not deem it necessary to take any action upon the subject. Had it varied from the terms of the treaty as amended by the Senate, although it would even then have been a nullity in itself, yet duty might have required that I should make this fact known to the Mexican Government. This not being the case, I treated it in the same manner I would have done had these explanations been made verbally by the commissioners to the Mexican minister for foreign affairs and communicated in a dispatch to the State Department.

JAMES K. POLK.

WASHINGTON, *February 9, 1849.*

To the Senate of the United States:

In compliance with the resolution of the Senate of the 6th instant, requesting the President to cause to be laid before that body, in "executive or open session, in his discretion, any instructions given to Ambrose H. Sevier and Nathan Clifford, commissioned as ministers plenipotentiary on the part of the United States to the Government of Mexico, or to either of said ministers, prior to the ratification by the Government of Mexico of the treaty of peace between the United States and that Republic," and certain correspondence and other papers specified in the said resolution, I communicate herewith a report from the Secretary of State, together with copies of the documents called for.

Having on the 8th instant, in compliance with a resolution of the House of Representatives in its terms more comprehensive than that of the Senate, communicated these and all other papers appertaining to the same subject, with a message to that House, this communication is made to the Senate in "open" and not in "executive" session.

JAMES K. POLK.

WASHINGTON, *February 12, 1849.*

To the Senate of the United States:

I communicate herewith a report from the Secretary of the Treasury, with the accompanying documents, in answer to the resolution of the Senate of December 28, 1848, requesting "to be informed of the number of vessels annually employed in the Coast Survey, and the annual cost thereof, and out of what fund they were paid; also the number of persons annually employed in said Survey who were not of the Army and Navy of the United States; also the amount of money received by the United States for maps and charts made under such Survey and sold under the act of 1844."

JAMES K. POLK.

WASHINGTON, *February 14, 1849.*

To the Senate of the United States:

I transmit herewith a report from the Secretary of War, together with the accompanying papers, in compliance with a resolution of the

Senate of the 12th instant, requesting the President to communicate to that body the proceedings under the act of Congress of the last session to compensate R. M. Johnson for the erection of certain buildings for the use of the Choctaw academy; also the evidence of the cost of said buildings.

JAMES K. POLK.

WASHINGTON, *February 23, 1849.*

To the Senate of the United States:

I communicate herewith a report of the Secretary of State, together with the accompanying documents, in compliance with a resolution of the Senate of the 23d ultimo, requesting the President "to transmit to the Senate, so far as is consistent with the public service, any correspondence between the Department of State and the Spanish authorities in the island of Cuba relating to the imprisonment in said island of William Henry Rush, a citizen of the United States."

JAMES K. POLK.

WASHINGTON, *February 27, 1849.*

To the Senate of the United States:

I communicate herewith a report from the Secretary of State, in compliance with a resolution of the Senate of the 3d ultimo, requesting the President to communicate to the Senate a list of all the treaties of commerce and navigation between the United States and foreign nations conferring upon the vessels of such nations the right of trading between the United States and the rest of the world in the productions of every country upon the same terms with American vessels, with the date of the proclamation of such treaties; also a list of the proclamations conferring similar rights upon the vessels of foreign nations issued by the President of the United States under the provisions of the first section of the act entitled "An act in addition to an act entitled 'An act concerning discriminating duties on tonnage and impost and to equalize the duties on Prussian vessels and their cargoes,'" approved May 24, 1828.

JAMES K. POLK.

WASHINGTON, *March 2, 1849.*

To the House of Representatives of the United States:

I communicate herewith a report of the Secretary of State, together with the accompanying papers, in compliance with the resolution of the House of Representatives of the 23d of December, 1848, requesting the President "to cause to be transmitted to the House, if compatible with the public interest, the correspondence of George W. Gordon, late, and Gorham Parks, the present, consul of the United States at Rio de Janeiro, with the Department of State on the subject of the African slave trade; also any unpublished correspondence on the same subject by the Hon. Henry A. Wise, our late minister to Brazil."

JAMES K. POLK.

WASHINGTON, *March 2, 1849.*

To the House of Representatives of the United States:

I communicate herewith a report of the Secretary of State, together with the accompanying papers, in compliance with the resolution of the House of Representatives of the 20th ultimo, requesting the President to communicate to that House a list of all consuls, vice-consuls, and commercial agents now in the service of the United States, their residence, distinguishing such as are citizens of the United States from such as are not, and to inform the said House whether regular returns of their fees and perquisites and the tonnage and commerce of the United States within their respective consulates or agencies have been regularly made by each, and to communicate the amount of such fees and perquisites for certain years therein specified, together with the number of vessels and amount of tonnage which entered and cleared within each of the consulates and agencies for the same period; also the number of seamen of the United States who have been provided for and sent home from each of the said consulates for the time aforesaid.

JAMES K. POLK.

WASHINGTON, *March 2, 1849.*

To the Senate of the United States:

I herewith transmit a communication from the Secretary of the Treasury, accompanying a report from the Solicitor of the Treasury presenting a view of the operations of that office since its organization.

JAMES K. POLK.

PROCLAMATIONS.

[From Senate Journal, Thirtieth Congress, second session, p. 349.]

WASHINGTON, *January 2, 1849.*

To the Senators of the United States, respectively.

SIR: Objects interesting to the United States requiring that the Senate should be in session on Monday, the 5th of March next, to receive and act upon such communications as may be made to it on the part of the Executive, your attention in the Senate Chamber, in this city, on that day at 10 o'clock in the forenoon is accordingly requested.

JAMES K. POLK.

BY THE PRESIDENT OF THE UNITED STATES.

A PROCLAMATION.

Whereas by an act of the Congress of the United States of the 10th January, 1849, entitled "An act to extend certain privileges to the town of Whitehall, in the State of New York," the President of the United States, on the recommendation of the Secretary of the Treasury, is authorized to extend to the town of Whitehall the same privileges as are conferred on certain ports named in the seventh section of an act entitled "An act allowing drawback upon foreign merchandise exported in the original packages to Chihuahua and Santa Fe, in Mexico, and to the British North American Provinces adjoining the United States," passed 3d March, 1845, in the manner prescribed by the proviso contained in said section; and

Whereas the Secretary of the Treasury has duly recommended to me the extension of the privileges of the law aforesaid to the port of Whitehall, in the collection district of Champlain, in the State of New York:

Now, therefore, I, James K. Polk, President of the United States of America, do hereby declare and proclaim that the port of Whitehall, in the collection district of Champlain, in the State of New York, is and shall be entitled to all the privileges extended to the other ports enumerated in the seventh section of the act aforesaid from and after the date of this proclamation.

In witness whereof I have hereunto set my hand and caused the seal of the United States to be affixed.

[SEAL.] Done at the city of Washington, this 2d day of March, A. D. 1849, and of the Independence of the United States of America the seventy-third.

JAMES K. POLK.

By the President:

JAMES BUCHANAN,

Secretary of State.

Zachary Taylor

March 5, 1849, to July 9, 1850

SEE ENCYCLOPEDIC INDEX.

The Encyclopedic Index is not only an index to the other volumes, not only a key that unlocks the treasures of the entire publication, but it is in itself an alphabetically arranged brief history or story of the great controlling events constituting the History of the United States.

Under its proper alphabetical classification the story is told of every great subject referred to by any of the Presidents in their official Messages, and at the end of each article the official utterances of the Presidents themselves are cited upon the subject, so that you may readily turn to the page in the body of the work itself for this original information.

Next to the possession of knowledge is the ability to turn at will to where knowledge is to be found.

HOME AT BATON ROUGE, LOUISIANA, OF

ZACHARY TAYLOR

With official portrait engraved from copy of original in steel

Zachary Taylor

Zachary Taylor

ZACHARY TAYLOR was born in Orange County, Va., November 24, 1784. He was the third son of Richard Taylor, a colonel in the War of the Revolution, who was conspicuous for his zeal and courage. In 1785 his father removed to Kentucky, then a sparsely occupied county of Virginia, and made his home near the present city of Louisville, where he died. Zachary had but little opportunity for attending school in this new settlement, but was surrounded during all the years of his childhood and early manhood by conditions and circumstances well adapted to form the character illustrated by his eventful career. In 1808 he was appointed a lieutenant in the Seventh Infantry, and in 1810 was promoted to the grade of captain in the same regiment. The same year was married to Miss Margaret Smith, of Maryland. For meritorious conduct in defending Fort Harrison, on the Wabash River, against the Indians received the brevet of major. In 1814 commanded in a campaign against hostile Indians and their British allies on Rock River. Was made lieutenant-colonel of the First Infantry in 1819, and in 1832 became full colonel of that regiment, with headquarters at Fort Crawford, Prairie du Chien. Was occupied with his regiment fighting the Indians in the Black Hawk and other campaigns until 1836, when he was transferred to Florida for service in the Seminole War. For gallant conduct there the next year received the brevet of brigadier-general, and in 1838 was appointed to the chief command in Florida. In 1840 was assigned to command the southern division of the western department of the Army. About this time he made his family home at Baton Rouge, La. In 1845 was ordered to the defense of Texas, which had been annexed to the United States. He went to Corpus Christi, and on March 8, 1846, advanced, and after some fighting, in which he routed and drove the enemy across the Rio Grande, on May 18 occupied Matamoras. He remained there for a short period, obtaining reenforcements. In September fought the enemy at Monterey and captured that town. The following February fought and won the battle of Buena Vista. In the meantime, besides engagements less important, he had won the victories of Palo Alto and Resaca de la Palma, which created great enthusiasm throughout the Union. The terms of capitulation granted by him to the enemy at Monterey were not approved by the Government at Washington. Soon after the battles of Palo Alto and Resaca de la Palma he received the rank of brevet major-general, and on June 27, 1846, was appointed major-general and was commander in chief of all the American forces in Mexico until Major-General Scott was ordered there in 1846. The latter part of November returned to his home in Louisiana. Upon his return to the United States he was received wherever he went with popular demonstrations. Was nominated for President by the national convention of the Whig party at Philadelphia on June 7, 1848, on the fourth ballot, defeating General Scott, Mr. Clay, and Mr. Webster. At the election on November 7 the Whig ticket (Taylor and Fillmore) was successful, receiving 163 electoral votes, while the Democratic candidates (Cass and Butler) each received 127 votes. He was inaugurated March 5, 1849, and died in Washington City July 9, 1850. Was buried in Cave Hill Cemetery, Louisville, Ky.

INAUGURAL ADDRESS.

Elected by the American people to the highest office known to our laws, I appear here to take the oath prescribed by the Constitution, and, in compliance with a time-honored custom, to address those who are now assembled.

The confidence and respect shown by my countrymen in calling me to be the Chief Magistrate of a Republic holding a high rank among the nations of the earth have inspired me with feelings of the most profound gratitude; but when I reflect that the acceptance of the office which their partiality has bestowed imposes the discharge of the most arduous duties and involves the weightiest obligations, I am conscious that the position which I have been called to fill, though sufficient to satisfy the loftiest ambition, is surrounded by fearful responsibilities. Happily, however, in the performance of my new duties I shall not be without able cooperation. The legislative and judicial branches of the Government present prominent examples of distinguished civil attainments and matured experience, and it shall be my endeavor to call to my assistance in the Executive Departments individuals whose talents, integrity, and purity of character will furnish ample guaranties for the faithful and honorable performance of the trusts to be committed to their charge. With such aids and an honest purpose to do whatever is right, I hope to execute diligently, impartially, and for the best interests of the country the manifold duties devolved upon me.

In the discharge of these duties my guide will be the Constitution, which I this day swear to "preserve, protect, and defend." For the interpretation of that instrument I shall look to the decisions of the judicial tribunals established by its authority and to the practice of the Government under the earlier Presidents, who had so large a share in its formation. To the example of those illustrious patriots I shall always defer with reverence, and especially to his example who was by so many titles "the Father of his Country."

To command the Army and Navy of the United States; with the advice and consent of the Senate, to make treaties and to appoint ambassadors and other officers; to give to Congress information of the state of the Union and recommend such measures as he shall judge to be necessary; and to take care that the laws shall be faithfully executed—these are the most important functions intrusted to the President by the Constitution, and it may be expected that I shall briefly indicate the principles which will control me in their execution.

Chosen by the body of the people under the assurance that my Administration would be devoted to the welfare of the whole country, and not to the support of any particular section or merely local interest, I this day renew the declarations I have heretofore made and proclaim my fixed determination to maintain to the extent of my ability the Government in its original purity and to adopt as the basis of my public policy those great republican doctrines which constitute the strength of our national existence.

In reference to the Army and Navy, lately employed with so much distinction on active service, care shall be taken to insure the highest condition of efficiency, and in furtherance of that object the military and naval schools, sustained by the liberality of Congress, shall receive the special attention of the Executive.

As American freemen we can not but sympathize in all efforts to extend the blessings of civil and political liberty, but at the same time we are warned by the admonitions of history and the voice of our own beloved Washington to abstain from entangling alliances with foreign nations. In all disputes between conflicting governments it is our interest not less than our duty to remain strictly neutral, while our geographical position, the genius of our institutions and our people, the advancing spirit of civilization, and, above all, the dictates of religion direct us to the cultivation of peaceful and friendly relations with all other powers. It is to be hoped that no international question can now arise which a government confident in its own strength and resolved to protect its own just rights may not settle by wise negotiation; and it eminently becomes a government like our own, founded on the morality and intelligence of its citizens and upheld by their affections, to exhaust every resort of honorable diplomacy before appealing to arms. In the conduct of our foreign relations I shall conform to these views, as I believe them essential to the best interests and the true honor of the country.

The appointing power vested in the President imposes delicate and onerous duties. So far as it is possible to be informed, I shall make honesty, capacity, and fidelity indispensable prerequisites to the bestowal of office, and the absence of either of these qualities shall be deemed sufficient cause for removal.

It shall be my study to recommend such constitutional measures to Congress as may be necessary and proper to secure encouragement and protection to the great interests of agriculture, commerce, and manufactures, to improve our rivers and harbors, to provide for the speedy extinguishment of the public debt, to enforce a strict accountability on the part of all officers of the Government and the utmost economy in all public expenditures; but it is for the wisdom of Congress itself, in which all legislative powers are vested by the Constitution, to regulate these and other matters of domestic policy. I shall look with confidence to the enlightened patriotism of that body to adopt such measures of conciliation as may harmonize conflicting interests and tend to perpetuate that Union which should be the paramount object of our hopes and affections. In any action calculated to promote an object so near the heart of everyone who truly loves his country I will zealously unite with the coordinate branches of the Government.

In conclusion I congratulate you, my fellow-citizens, upon the high state of prosperity to which the goodness of Divine Providence has conducted our common country. Let us invoke a continuance of the same protecting care which has led us from small beginnings to the eminence we this day occupy, and let us seek to deserve that continuance by prudence and moderation in our councils, by well-directed attempts to assuage the bitterness which too often marks unavoidable differences of opinion, by the promulgation and practice of just and liberal principles, and by an enlarged patriotism, which shall acknowledge no limits but those of our own widespread Republic.

MARCH 5, 1849.

SPECIAL MESSAGES.

WASHINGTON, *March 13, 1849.*

To the Senate of the United States:

I herewith communicate to the Senate, in confidence, a report and accompanying papers* from the Secretary of State, in answer to its resolution of the 12th instant.

Z. TAYLOR.

*Instructions to United States minister at London relative to further extension of reciprocity and equality in the laws of navigation, and contemplating the opening of the coasting trade of the United States to the vessels of other nations.

WASHINGTON, *March 20, 1849*.

To the Senate of the United States:

In answer to the resolution of the Senate of yesterday, passed in executive session, requesting a communication of certain papers relative to the amendments made by the Senate to the treaty of Guadalupe Hidalgo, I transmit a report from the Secretary of State and the documents by which it was accompanied. It is desirable that the latter should be returned to the Department of State.

Z. TAYLOR.

WASHINGTON, *March 22, 1849*.

To the Senate of the United States:

In compliance with the request contained in the resolution of the Senate yesterday, adopted in executive session, calling for certain papers in relation to the amendments made by the Senate in the treaty of Guadalupe Hidalgo, I transmit a report from the Secretary of State and the documents by which it was accompanied.

Z. TAYLOR.

PROCLAMATION.

BY THE PRESIDENT OF THE UNITED STATES.

A PROCLAMATION.

There is reason to believe that an armed expedition is about to be fitted out in the United States with an intention to invade the island of Cuba or some of the Provinces of Mexico. The best information which the Executive has been able to obtain points to the island of Cuba as the object of this expedition. It is the duty of this Government to observe the faith of treaties and to prevent any aggression by our citizens upon the territories of friendly nations. I have therefore thought it necessary and proper to issue this my proclamation to warn all citizens of the United States who shall connect themselves with an enterprise so grossly in violation of our laws and our treaty obligations that they will thereby subject themselves to the heavy penalties denounced against them by our acts of Congress and will forfeit their claim to the protection of their country. No such persons must expect the interference of this Government in any form on their behalf, no matter to what extremities they may be reduced in consequence of their conduct. An enterprise to invade the territories of a friendly nation, set on foot and prosecuted within the limits of the United States, is in the highest degree criminal, as tending to endanger the peace and compromit the honor of this nation; and therefore I exhort all good citizens, as they regard our national reputation, as they respect their own laws and the laws of nations, as they value the blessings of peace and the welfare of their country, to discountenance and prevent by all lawful means any such enterprise; and I call upon every officer of this Government, civil or military, to use all efforts in his power to arrest for trial and punishment every such offender against the laws providing for the performance of our sacred obligations to friendly powers.

Given under my hand the 11th day of August, A. D. 1849, and the seventy-fourth of the Independence of the United States.

Z. TAYLOR.

By the President:

J. M. CLAYTON,
Secretary of State.

EXECUTIVE ORDER.

GENERAL ORDERS, No. 34.

WAR DEPARTMENT,
ADJUTANT-GENERAL'S OFFICE,
Washington, June 19, 1849.

I. The following orders of the President of the United States and Secretary of War communicate to the Army the death of the late ex-President, James K. Polk:

WASHINGTON, *June 19, 1849.*

The President with deep regret announces to the American people the death of James K. Polk, late President of the United States, which occurred at Nashville on the 15th instant.

A nation is suddenly called upon to mourn the loss of one the recollection of whose long services in its councils will be forever preserved on the tablets of history.

As a mark of respect to the memory of a citizen who has been distinguished by the highest honors which his country could bestow, it is ordered that the Executive Mansion and the several Departments at Washington be immediately placed in mourning and all business be suspended during to-morrow.

It is further ordered that the War and Navy Departments cause suitable military and naval honors to be paid on this occasion to the memory of the illustrious dead.

Z. TAYLOR.

WAR DEPARTMENT, *June 19, 1849.*

The President of the United States with deep regret announces to the Army the death of James K. Polk, our distinguished and honored fellow-citizen.

He died at Nashville the 15th instant, having but recently left the theater of his high public duties at this capital and retired to his home amid the congratulations of his fellow-citizens. He died in the prime of life, after having received and enjoyed the highest honors of the Republic.

His Administration was eventful. No branch of the Government will be more intimately associated with it in history than the Army and its glorious achievements. Accordingly, the President orders that appropriate military honors shall be paid to his memory by the Army of the United States.

The Adjutant-General will give the necessary instructions for carrying into effect the foregoing orders.

G. W. CRAWFORD,
Secretary of War.

II. On the day succeeding the arrival of this general order at each military post the troops will be paraded at 10 o'clock a. m. and the order read to them, after which all labors for the day will cease.

The national flag will be displayed at half-staff.

At dawn of day thirteen guns will be fired, and afterwards at intervals of thirty minutes between the rising and setting sun a single gun, and at the close of the day a national salute of thirty guns.

The officers of the Army will wear crape on the left arm and on their swords and the colors of the several regiments will be put in mourning for the period of six months.

By order:

R. JONES, *Adjutant-General.*

FIRST ANNUAL MESSAGE.

WASHINGTON, *December 4, 1849.*

Fellow-Citizens of the Senate and House of Representatives:

Sixty years have elapsed since the establishment of this Government, and the Congress of the United States again assembles to legislate for an empire of freemen. The predictions of evil prophets, who formerly pretended to foretell the downfall of our institutions, are now remembered only to be derided, and the United States of America at this moment present to the world the most stable and permanent Government on earth.

Such is the result of the labors of those who have gone before us. Upon Congress will eminently depend the future maintenance of our system of free government and the transmission of it unimpaired to posterity.

We are at peace with all the other nations of the world, and seek to maintain our cherished relations of amity with them. During the past year we have been blessed by a kind Providence with an abundance of the fruits of the earth, and although the destroying angel for a time visited extensive portions of our territory with the ravages of a dreadful pestilence, yet the Almighty has at length deigned to stay his hand and to restore the inestimable blessing of general health to a people who have acknowledged His power, deprecated His wrath, and implored His merciful protection.

While enjoying the benefits of amicable intercourse with foreign nations, we have not been insensible to the distractions and wars which have prevailed in other quarters of the world. It is a proper theme of thanksgiving to Him who rules the destinies of nations that we have been able to maintain amidst all these contests an independent and neutral position toward all belligerent powers.

Our relations with Great Britain are of the most friendly character. In consequence of the recent alteration of the British navigation acts, British vessels, from British and other foreign ports, will under our existing laws, after the 1st day of January next, be admitted to entry in our ports with cargoes of the growth, manufacture, or production of any part of the world on the same terms as to duties, imposts, and charges as vessels of the United States with their cargoes, and our vessels will be admitted to the same advantages in British ports, entering therein on the same terms as British vessels. Should no order in council disturb this legislative arrangement, the late act of the British Parliament, by which Great Britain is brought within the terms proposed by the act of Congress of the 1st of March, 1817, it is hoped will be productive of benefit to both countries.

A slight interruption of diplomatic intercourse which occurred between this Government and France, I am happy to say, has been terminated, and our minister there has been received. It is therefore unnecessary to refer now to the circumstances which led to that interruption. I need not express to you the sincere satisfaction with which we shall welcome the arrival of another envoy extraordinary and minister plenipotentiary from a sister Republic to which we have so long been, and still remain, bound by the strongest ties of amity.

Shortly after I had entered upon the discharge of the Executive duties I was apprised that a war steamer belonging to the German Empire was being fitted out in the harbor of New York with the aid of some of our naval officers, rendered under the permission of the late Secretary of the Navy. This permission was granted during an armistice between that Empire and the Kingdom of Denmark, which had been engaged in the Schleswig-Holstein war. Apprehensive that this act of intervention on our part might be viewed as a violation of our neutral obligations incurred by the treaty with Denmark and of the provisions of the act of Congress of the 20th of April, 1818, I directed that no further aid should be rendered by any agent or officer of the Navy; and I instructed the Secretary of State to apprise the minister of the German Empire accredited to this

Government of my determination to execute the law of the United States and to maintain the faith of treaties with all nations. The correspondence which ensued between the Department of State and the minister of the German Empire is herewith laid before you. The execution of the law and the observance of the treaty were deemed by me to be due to the honor of the country, as well as to the sacred obligations of the Constitution. I shall not fail to pursue the same course should a similar case arise with any other nation. Having avowed the opinion on taking the oath of office that in disputes between conflicting foreign governments it is our interest not less than our duty to remain strictly neutral, I shall not abandon it. You will perceive from the correspondence submitted to you in connection with this subject that the course adopted in this case has been properly regarded by the belligerent powers interested in the matter.

Although a minister of the United States to the German Empire was appointed by my predecessor in August, 1848, and has for a long time been in attendance at Frankfort-on-the-Main, and although a minister appointed to represent that Empire was received and accredited here, yet no such government as that of the German Empire has been definitively constituted. Mr. Donelson, our representative at Frankfort, remained there several months in the expectation that a union of the German States under one constitution or form of government might at length be organized. It is believed by those well acquainted with the existing relations between Prussia and the States of Germany that no such union can be permanently established without her cooperation. In the event of the formation of such a union and the organization of a central power in Germany of which she should form a part, it would become necessary to withdraw our minister at Berlin; but while Prussia exists as an independent kingdom and diplomatic relations are maintained with her there can be no necessity for the continuance of the mission to Frankfort. I have therefore recalled Mr. Donelson and directed the archives of the legation at Frankfort to be transferred to the American legation at Berlin.

Having been apprised that a considerable number of adventurers were engaged in fitting out a military expedition within the United States against a foreign country, and believing from the best information I could obtain that it was destined to invade the island of Cuba, I deemed it due to the friendly relations existing between the United States and Spain, to the treaty between the two nations, to the laws of the United States, and, above all, to the American honor to exert the lawful authority of this Government in suppressing the expedition and preventing the invasion. To this end I issued a proclamation enjoining it upon the officers of the United States, civil and military, to use all lawful means within their power. A copy of that proclamation is herewith submitted. The expedition has been suppressed. So long as the act of Congress of the 20th of April, 1818, which owes its existence to the law of nations and to the policy of Washington himself, shall remain on our statute books, I hold it to be the duty of the Executive faithfully to obey its injunctions.

While this expedition was in progress I was informed that a foreigner who claimed our protection had been clandestinely and, as was supposed, forcibly carried off in a vessel from New Orleans to the island of Cuba. I immediately caused such steps to be taken as I thought necessary, in case the information I had received should prove correct, to vindicate the honor of the country and the right of every person seeking an asylum on our soil to the protection of our laws. The person alleged to have been abducted was promptly restored, and the circumstances of the case are now about to undergo investigation before a judicial tribunal. I would respectfully suggest that although the crime charged to have been committed in this case is held odious, as being in conflict with our opinions on the subject of national sovereignty and personal freedom, there is no prohibition of it or punishment for it provided in any act of Congress. The expediency of supplying this defect in our criminal code is therefore recommended to your consideration.

I have scrupulously avoided any interference in the wars and contentions which have recently distracted Europe. During the late conflict between Austria and Hungary there seemed to be a prospect that the latter might become an independent nation. However faint that prospect at the time appeared, I thought it my duty, in accordance with the general sentiment of the American people, who deeply sympathized with the Magyar patriots, to stand prepared, upon the contingency of the establishment by her of a permanent government, to be the first to welcome independent Hungary into the family of nations. For this purpose I invested an agent then in Europe with power to declare our willingness promptly to recognize her independence in the event of her ability to sustain it. The powerful intervention of Russia in the contest extinguished the hopes of the struggling Magyars. The United States did not at any time interfere in the contest, but the feelings of the nation were strongly enlisted in the cause, and by the sufferings of a brave people, who had made a gallant, though unsuccessful, effort to be free.

Our claims upon Portugal have been during the past year prosecuted with renewed vigor, and it has been my object to employ every effort of honorable diplomacy to procure their adjustment. Our late chargé d'affaires at Lisbon, the Hon. George W. Hopkins, made able and energetic, but unsuccessful, efforts to settle these unpleasant matters of controversy and to obtain indemnity for the wrongs which were the subjects of complaint. Our present chargé d'affaires at that Court will also bring to the prosecution of these claims ability and zeal. The revolutionary and distracted condition of Portugal in past times has been represented as one of the leading causes of her delay in indemnifying our suffering citizens.

But I must now say it is matter of profound regret that these claims have not yet been settled. The omission of Portugal to do justice to the American claimants has now assumed a character so grave and serious that I shall shortly make it the subject of a special message to Congress, with a view to such ultimate action as its wisdom and patriotism may suggest.

With Russia, Austria, Prussia, Sweden, Denmark, Belgium, the Netherlands, and the Italian States we still maintain our accustomed amicable relations.

During the recent revolutions in the Papal States our chargé d'affaires at Rome has been unable to present his letter of credence, which, indeed, he was directed by my predecessor to withhold until he should receive further orders. Such was the unsettled condition of things in those States that it was not deemed expedient to give him any instructions on the subject of presenting his credential letter different from those with which he had been furnished by the late Administration until the 25th of June last, when, in consequence of the want of accurate information of the exact state of things at that distance from us, he was instructed to exercise his own discretion in presenting himself to the then existing Government if in his judgment sufficiently stable, or, if not, to await further events. Since that period Rome has undergone another revolution, and he abides the establishment of a government sufficiently permanent to justify him in opening diplomatic intercourse with it.

With the Republic of Mexico it is our true policy to cultivate the most friendly relations. Since the ratification of the treaty of Guadalupe Hidalgo nothing has occurred of a serious character to disturb them. A faithful observance of the treaty and a sincere respect for her rights can not fail to secure the lasting confidence and friendship of that Republic. The message of my predecessor to the House of Representatives of the 8th of February last, communicating, in compliance with a resolution of that body, a copy of a paper called a protocol, signed at Queretaro on the 30th of May, 1848, by the commissioners of the United States and the minister of foreign affairs of the Mexican Government, having been a subject of correspondence between the Department of State and the envoy extraordinary and minister plenipotentiary of that Republic accredited to this Government, a transcript of that correspondence is herewith submitted.

The commissioner on the part of the United States for marking the boundary between the two Republics, though delayed in reaching San Diego by unforeseen obstacles, arrived at that place within a short period after the time required by the treaty, and was there joined by the commissioner on the part of Mexico. They entered upon their duties, and at the date of the latest intelligence from that quarter some progress had been made in the survey. The expenses incident to the organization of the commission and to its conveyance to the point where its operations were to begin have so much reduced the fund appropriated by Congress that a further sum, to cover the charges which must be incurred during the present fiscal year, will be necessary. The great length of frontier along which the boundary extends, the nature of the adjacent territory, and the difficulty of obtaining supplies except at or near the extremes of the line render it also indispensable that a liberal provision should be made to meet the necessary charges during the fiscal year ending on the 30th of June, 1851. I accordingly recommend this subject to your attention.

In the adjustment of the claims of American citizens on Mexico, provided for by the late treaty, the employment of counsel on the part of the Government may become important for the purpose of assisting the commissioners in protecting the interests of the United States. I recommend this subject to the early and favorable consideration of Congress.

Complaints have been made in regard to the inefficiency of the means provided by the Government of New Granada for transporting the United States mail across the Isthmus of Panama, pursuant to our postal convention with that Republic of the 6th of March, 1844. Our chargé d'affaires at Bogota has been directed to make such representations to the Government of New Granada as will, it is hoped, lead to a prompt removal of this cause of complaint.

The sanguinary civil war with which the Republic of Venezuela has for some time past been ravaged has been brought to a close. In its progress the rights of some of our citizens resident or trading there have been violated. The restoration of order will afford the Venezuelan Government an opportunity to examine and redress these grievances and others of longer standing which our representatives at Caracas have hitherto ineffectually urged upon the attention of that Government.

The extension of the coast of the United States on the Pacific and the unexampled rapidity with which the inhabitants of California especially are increasing in numbers have imparted new consequence to our relations with the other countries whose territories border upon that ocean. It is probable that the intercourse between those countries and our possessions in that quarter, particularly with the Republic of Chili, will become extensive and mutually advantageous in proportion as California and Oregon shall increase in population and wealth. It is desirable, therefore, that this Government should do everything in its power to foster and strengthen its relations with those States, and that the spirit of amity between us should be mutual and cordial.

I recommend the observance of the same course toward all other American States. The United States stand as the great American power, to which, as their natural ally and friend, they will always be disposed first to look for mediation and assistance in the event of any collision between them and any European nation. As such we may often kindly mediate in their behalf without entangling ourselves in foreign wars or unnecessary controversies. Whenever the faith of our treaties with any of them shall require our interference, we must necessarily interpose.

A convention has been negotiated with Brazil providing for the satisfaction of American claims on that Government, and it will be submitted to the Senate. Since the last session of Congress we have received an envoy extraordinary and minister plenipotentiary from that Empire, and our relations with it are founded upon the most amicable understanding.

Your attention is earnestly invited to an amendment of our existing laws relating to the African slave trade with a view to the effectual suppression of that barbarous traffic. It is not to be denied that this trade is still in part carried on by means of vessels built in the United States and owned or navigated by some of our citizens. The correspondence between the Department of State and the minister and consul of the United States at Rio de Janeiro, which has from time to time been laid before Congress, represents that it is a customary device to evade the penalties of our laws by means of sea letters. Vessels sold in Brazil, when provided with such papers by the consul, instead of returning to the United States for a new register proceed at once to the coast of Africa for the purpose of obtaining cargoes of slaves. Much additional information of the same character has recently been transmitted to the Department of State. It has not been considered the policy of our laws to subject an American citizen who in a foreign country purchases a vessel built in the United States to the inconvenience of sending her home for a new register before permitting her to proceed on a voyage. Any alteration of the laws which might have a tendency to impede the free transfer of property in vessels between our citizens, or the free navigation of those vessels between different parts of the world when employed in lawful commerce, should be well and cautiously considered; but I trust that your wisdom will devise a method by which our general policy in this respect may be preserved, and at the same time the abuse of our flag by means of sea letters, in the manner indicated, may be prevented.

Having ascertained that there is no prospect of the reunion of the five States of Central America which formerly composed the Republic of that name, we have separately negotiated with some of them treaties of amity and commerce, which will be laid before the Senate.

A contract having been concluded with the State of Nicaragua by a company composed of American citizens for the purpose of constructing a ship canal through the territory of that State to connect the Atlantic and Pacific oceans, I have directed the negotiation of a treaty with Nicaragua pledging both Governments to protect those who shall engage in and perfect the work. All other nations are invited by the State of Nicaragua to enter into the same treaty stipulations with her; and the benefit to be derived by each from such an arrangement will be the protection of this great interoceanic communication against any power which might seek to obstruct it or to monopolize its advantages. All States entering into such a treaty will enjoy the right of passage through the canal on payment of the same tolls. The work, if constructed under these guaranties, will become a bond of peace instead of a subject of contention and strife between the nations of the earth. Should the great maritime States of Europe consent to this arrangement (and we have no reason to suppose that a proposition so fair and honorable will be opposed by any), the energies of their people and ours will cooperate in promoting the success of the enterprise. I do not recommend any appropriation from the National Treasury for this purpose, nor do I believe that such an appropriation is necessary. Private enterprise, if properly protected, will complete the work should it prove to be feasible. The parties who have procured the charter from Nicaragua for its construction desire no assistance from this Government beyond its protection; and they profess that, having examined the proposed line of communication, they will be ready to commence the undertaking whenever that protection shall be extended to them. Should there appear to be reason, on examining the whole evidence, to entertain a serious doubt of the practicability of constructing such a canal, that doubt could be speedily solved by an actual exploration of the route.

Should such a work be constructed under the common protection of all nations, for equal benefits to all, it would be neither just nor expedient that any great maritime state should command the communication. The territory through which the canal may be opened ought to be freed from the claims of any foreign power. No such power should occupy a position that would enable it hereafter to exercise so controlling an influence over the commerce of the world or to obstruct a highway which ought to be dedicated to the common uses of mankind.

The routes across the Isthmus at Tehuantepec and Panama are also worthy of our serious consideration. They did not fail to engage the attention of my predecessor. The negotiator of the treaty of Guadalupe Hidalgo was instructed to offer a very large sum of money for the right of transit across the Isthmus of Tehuantepec. The Mexican Government did not accede to the proposition for the purchase of the right of way, probably because it had already contracted with private individuals for the construction of a passage from the Guasacualco River to Tehuantepec. I shall not renew any proposition to purchase for money a right which ought to be equally secured to all nations on payment of a reasonable toll to the owners of the improvement, who would doubtless be well contented with that compensation and the guaranties of the maritime states of the world in separate treaties negotiated with Mexico, binding her and them to protect those who should construct the work. Such guaranties would do more to secure the completion of the communication through the territory of Mexico than any other reasonable consideration that could be offered; and as Mexico herself would be the greatest gainer by the opening of this communication between the Gulf and the Pacific Ocean, it is presumed that she would not hesitate to yield her aid in the manner proposed to accomplish an improvement so important to her own best interests.

We have reason to hope that the proposed railroad across the Isthmus at Panama will be successfully constructed under the protection of the late treaty with New Granada, ratified and exchanged by my predecessor on the 10th day of June, 1848, which guarantees the perfect neutrality of the Isthmus and the rights of sovereignty and property of New Granada over that territory, "with a view that the free transit from ocean to ocean may not be interrupted or embarrassed" during the existence of the treaty. It is our policy to encourage every practicable route across the isthmus which connects North and South America, either by railroad or canal, which the energy and enterprise of our citizens may induce them to complete, and I consider it obligatory upon me to adopt that policy, especially in consequence of the absolute necessity of facilitating intercourse with our possessions on the Pacific.

The position of the Sandwich Islands with reference to the territory of the United States on the Pacific, the success of our persevering and benevolent citizens who have repaired to that remote quarter in Christianizing the natives and inducing them to adopt a system of government and laws suited to their capacity and wants, and the use made by our numerous whale ships of the harbors of the islands as places of resort for obtaining refreshments and repairs all combine to render their destiny peculiarly interesting to us. It is our duty to encourage the authorities of those islands in their efforts to improve and elevate the moral and political condition of the inhabitants, and we should make reasonable allowances for the difficulties inseparable from this task. We desire that the islands may maintain their independence and that other nations should concur with us in this sentiment. We could in no event be indifferent to their passing under the dominion of any other power. The principal commercial states have in this a common interest, and it is to be hoped that no one of them will attempt to interpose obstacles to the entire independence of the islands.

The receipts into the Treasury for the fiscal year ending on the 30th of June last were, in cash, $48,830,097.50, and in Treasury notes funded $10,833,000, making an aggregate of $59,663,097.50; and the expenditures for the same time were, in cash, $46,798,667.82, and in Treasury notes funded $10,833,000, making an aggregate of $57,631,667.82.

The accounts and estimates which will be submitted to Congress in the report of the Secretary of the Treasury show that there will probably be a deficit occasioned by the expenses of the Mexican War and treaty on the 1st day of July next of $5,828,121.66, and on the 1st day of July, 1851, of $10,547,092.73, making in the whole a probable deficit to be provided for of $16,375,214.39. The extraordinary expenses of the war with Mexico and the purchase of California and New Mexico exceed in amount this deficit, together with the loans heretofore made for those objects. I therefore recommend that authority be given to borrow whatever sum may be necessary to cover that deficit. I recommend the observance of strict economy in the appropriation and expenditure of public money.

I recommend a revision of the existing tariff and its adjustment on a basis which may augment the revenue. I do not doubt the right or duty of Congress to encourage domestic industry, which is the great source of national as well as individual wealth and prosperity. I look to the wisdom and patriotism of Congress for the adoption of a system which may place home labor at last on a sure and permanent footing and by due encouragement of manufactures give a new and increased stimulus to agriculture and promote the development of our vast resources and the extension of our commerce. Believing that to the attainment of these ends, as well as the necessary augmentation of the revenue and the prevention of frauds, a system of specific duties is best adapted, I strongly recommend to Congress the adoption of that system, fixing the duties at rates high enough to afford substantial and sufficient encouragement to our own industry and at the same time so adjusted as to insure stability.

The question of the continuance of the subtreasury system is respectfully submitted to the wisdom of Congress. If continued, important modifications of it appear to be indispensable.

For further details and views on the above and other matters connected with commerce, the finances, and revenue I refer to the report of the Secretary of the Treasury.

No direct aid has been given by the General Government to the improvement of agriculture except by the expenditure of small sums for the collection and publication of agricultural statistics and for some chemical analyses, which have been thus far paid for out of the patent fund. This aid is, in my opinion, wholly inadequate. To give to this leading branch of American industry the encouragement which it merits, I respectfully recommend the establishment of an agricultural bureau, to be connected with the Department of the Interior. To elevate the social condition of the agriculturist, to increase his prosperity, and to extend his means of usefulness to his country, by multiplying his sources of information, should be the study of every statesman and a primary object with every legislator.

No civil government having been provided by Congress for California, the people of that Territory, impelled by the necessities of their political condition, recently met in convention for the purpose of forming a constitution and State government, which the latest advices give me reason to suppose has been accomplished; and it is believed they will shortly apply for the admission of California into the Union as a sovereign State. Should such be the case, and should their constitution be conformable to the requisitions of the Constitution of the United States, I recommend their application to the favorable consideration of Congress.

The people of New Mexico will also, it is believed, at no very distant period present themselves for admission into the Union. Preparatory to the admission of California and New Mexico the people of each will have instituted for themselves a republican form of government, "laying its foundation in such principles and organizing its powers in such form as to them shall seem most likely to effect their safety and happiness." By awaiting their action all causes of uneasiness may be avoided and confidence and kind feeling preserved. With a view of maintaining the harmony and tranquillity so dear to all, we should abstain from the introduction of those exciting topics of a sectional character which have hitherto produced painful apprehensions in the public mind; and I repeat the solemn warning of the first and most illustrious of my predecessors against furnishing "any ground for characterizing parties by geographical discriminations."

A collector has been appointed at San Francisco under the act of Congress extending the revenue laws over California, and measures have been taken to organize the custom-houses at that and the other ports mentioned in that act at the earliest period practicable. The collector proceeded overland, and advices have not yet been received of his arrival at San Francisco. Meanwhile, it is understood that the customs have continued to be collected there by officers acting under the military authority, as they were during the Administration of my predecessor. It will, I think, be expedient to confirm the collections thus made, and direct the avails (after such allowances as Congress may think fit to authorize) to be expended within the Territory or to be paid into the Treasury for the purpose of meeting appropriations for the improvement of its rivers and harbors.

A party engaged on the coast survey was dispatched to Oregon in January last. According to the latest advices, they had not left California; and directions have been given to them, as soon as they shall have fixed on the sites of the two light-houses and the buoys authorized to be constructed and placed in Oregon, to proceed without delay to make reconnoissances of the most important points on the coast of California, and especially to examine and determine on sites for light-houses on that coast, the speedy erection of which is urgently demanded by our rapidly increasing commerce.

I have transferred the Indian agencies from upper Missouri and Council Bluffs to Santa Fe and Salt Lake, and have caused to be appointed subagents in the valleys of the Gila, the Sacramento, and the San Joaquin rivers. Still further legal provisions will be necessary for the effective and successful extension of our system of Indian intercourse over the new territories.

I recommend the establishment of a branch mint in California, as it will, in my opinion, afford important facilities to those engaged in mining, as well as to the Government in the disposition of the mineral lands.

I also recommend that commissions be organized by Congress to examine and decide upon the validity of the present subsisting land titles in California and New Mexico, and that provision be made for the establishment of offices of surveyor-general in New Mexico, California, and Oregon and for the surveying and bringing into market the public lands in those Territories. Those lands, remote in position and difficult of access, ought to be disposed of on terms liberal to all, but especially favorable to the early emigrants.

In order that the situation and character of the principal mineral deposits in California may be ascertained, I recommend that a geological and mineralogical exploration be connected with the linear surveys, and that the mineral lands be divided into small lots suitable for mining and be disposed of by sale or lease, so as to give our citizens an opportunity of procuring a permanent right of property in the soil. This would seem to be as important to the success of mining as of agricultural pursuits.

The great mineral wealth of California and the advantages which its ports and harbors and those of Oregon afford to commerce, especially with the islands of the Pacific and Indian oceans and the populous regions of eastern Asia, make it certain that there will arise in a few years large and prosperous communities on our western coast. It therefore becomes important that a line of communication, the best and most expeditious which the nature of the country will admit, should be opened within the territory of the United States from the navigable waters of the Atlantic or the Gulf of Mexico to the Pacific. Opinion, as elicited and expressed by two large and respectable conventions lately assembled at St. Louis and Memphis, points to a railroad as that which, if practicable, will best meet the wishes and wants of the country. But while this, if in successful operation, would be a work of great national importance and of a value to the country which it would be difficult to estimate, it ought also to be regarded as an undertaking of vast magnitude and expense, and one which must, if it be indeed practicable, encounter many difficulties in its construction and use. Therefore, to avoid failure and disappointment; to enable Congress to judge whether in the condition of the country through which it must pass the work be feasible, and, if it be found so, whether it should be undertaken as a national improvement or left to individual enterprise, and in the latter alternative what aid, if any, ought to be extended to it by the Government, I recommend as a preliminary measure a careful reconnoissance of the several proposed routes by a scientific corps and a report as to the practicability of making such a road, with an estimate of the cost of its construction and support.

For further views on these and other matters connected with the duties of the home department I refer you to the report of the Secretary of the Interior.

I recommend early appropriations for continuing the river and harbor improvements which have been already begun, and also for the construction of those for which estimates have been made, as well as for examinations and estimates preparatory to the commencement of such others as the wants of the country, and especially the advance of our population over new districts and the extension of commerce, may render necessary. An estimate of the amount which can be advantageously expended within the next fiscal year under the direction of the Bureau of Topographical Engineers accompanies the report of the Secretary of War, to which I respectfully invite the attention of Congress.

The cession of territory made by the late treaty with Mexico has greatly extended our exposed frontier and rendered its defense more difficult. That treaty has also brought us under obligations to Mexico, to comply with which a military force is requisite. But our military establishment is not materially changed as to its efficiency from the condition in which it stood before the commencement of the Mexican War. Some addition to it will therefore be necessary, and I recommend to the favorable consideration of Congress an increase of the several corps of the Army at our distant Western posts, as proposed in the accompanying report of the Secretary of War.

Great embarrassment has resulted from the effect upon rank in the Army heretofore given to brevet and staff commissions. The views of the Secretary of War on this subject are deemed important, and if carried into effect will, it is believed, promote the harmony of the service. The plan proposed for retiring disabled officers and providing an asylum for such of the rank and file as from age, wounds, and other infirmities occasioned by service have become unfit to perform their respective duties is recommended as a means of increasing the efficiency of the Army and as an act of justice due from a grateful country to the faithful soldier.

The accompanying report of the Secretary of the Navy presents a full and satisfactory account of the condition and operations of the naval service during the past year. Our citizens engaged in the legitimate pursuits of commerce have enjoyed its benefits. Wherever our national vessels have gone they have been received with respect, our officers have been treated with kindness and courtesy, and they have on all occasions pursued a course of strict neutrality, in accordance with the policy of our Government.

The naval force at present in commission is as large as is admissible with the number of men authorized by Congress to be employed.

I invite your attention to the recommendation of the Secretary of the Navy on the subject of a reorganization of the Navy in its various grades of officers, and the establishing of a retired list for such of the officers as are disqualified for active and effective service. Should Congress adopt some such measure as is recommended, it will greatly increase the efficiency of the Navy and reduce its expenditures.

I also ask your attention to the views expressed by him in reference to the employment of war steamers and in regard to the contracts for the transportation of the United States mails and the operation of the system upon the prosperity of the Navy.

By an act of Congress passed August 14, 1848, provision was made for extending post-office and mail accommodations to California and Oregon. Exertions have been made to execute that law, but the limited provisions of the act, the inadequacy of the means it authorizes, the ill adaptation of our post-office laws to the situation of that country, and the measure of compensation for services allowed by those laws, compared with the prices of labor and rents in California, render those exertions in a great degree ineffectual. More particular and efficient provision by law is required on this subject.

The act of 1845 reducing postage has now, by its operation during four years, produced results fully showing that the income from such reduced postage is sufficient to sustain the whole expense of the service of the Post-Office Department, not including the cost of transportation in mail steamers on the lines from New York to Chagres and from Panama to Astoria, which have not been considered by Congress as properly belonging to the mail service.

It is submitted to the wisdom of Congress whether a further reduction of postage should not now be made, more particularly on the letter correspondence. This should be relieved from the unjust burden of transporting and delivering the franked matter of Congress, for which public service provision should be made from the Treasury. I confidently believe that a change may safely be made reducing all single-letter postage to the uniform rate of 5 cents, regardless of distance, without thereby imposing any greater tax on the Treasury than would constitute a very moderate compensation for this public service; and I therefore respectfully recommend such a reduction. Should Congress prefer to abolish the franking privilege entirely, it seems probable that no demand on the Treasury would result from the proposed reduction of postage. Whether any further diminution should now be made, or the result of the reduction to 5 cents, which I have recommended, should be first tested, is submitted to your decision.

Since the commencement of the last session of Congress a postal treaty with Great Britain has been received and ratified, and such relations have been formed by the post-office departments of the two countries in pursuance of that treaty as to carry its provisions into full operation. The attempt to extend this same arrangement through England to France has not been equally successful, but the purpose has not been abandoned.

For a particular statement of the condition of the Post-Office Department and other matters connected with that branch of the public service I refer you to the report of the Postmaster-General.

By the act of the 3d of March, 1849, a board was constituted to make arrangements for taking the Seventh Census, composed of the Secretary of State, the Attorney-General, and the Postmaster-General; and it was made the duty of this board "to prepare and cause to be printed such forms and schedules as might be necessary for the full enumeration of the inhabitants of the United States, and also proper forms and schedules for collecting in statistical tables, under proper heads, such information as to mines, agriculture, commerce, manufactures, education, and other topics as would exhibit a full view of the pursuits, industry, education, and resources of the country." The duties enjoined upon the census board thus established having been performed, it now rests with Congress to enact a law for carrying into effect the provision of the Constitution which requires an actual enumeration of the people of the United States within the ensuing year.

Among the duties assigned by the Constitution to the General Government is one of local and limited application, but not on that account the less obligatory. I allude to the trust committed to Congress as the exclusive legislator and sole guardian of the interests of the District of Columbia. I beg to commend these interests to your kind attention. As the national metropolis the city of Washington must be an object of general interest; and founded, as it was, under the auspices of him whose immortal name it bears, its claims to the fostering care of Congress present themselves with additional strength. Whatever can contribute to its prosperity must enlist the feelings of its constitutional guardians and command their favorable consideration.

Our Government is one of limited powers, and its successful administration eminently depends on the confinement of each of its coordinate branches within its own appropriate sphere. The first section of the Constitution ordains that—

> All legislative powers herein granted shall be vested in a Congress of the United States, which shall consist of a Senate and House of Representatives.

The Executive has authority to recommend (not to dictate) measures to Congress. Having performed that duty, the executive department of the Government can not rightfully control the decision of Congress on any subject of legislation until that decision shall have been officially submitted to the President for approval. The check provided by the Constitution in the clause conferring the qualified veto will never be exercised by me except in the cases contemplated by the fathers of the Republic. I view it as an extreme measure, to be resorted to only in extraordinary cases, as where it may become necessary to defend the executive against the encroachments of the legislative power or to prevent hasty and inconsiderate or unconstitutional legislation. By cautiously confining this remedy within the sphere prescribed to it in the cotemporaneous expositions of the framers of the Constitution, the will of the people, legitimately expressed on all subjects of legislation through their constitutional organs, the Senators and Representatives of the United States, will have its full effect. As indispensable to the preservation of our system of self-government, the independence of the representatives of the States and the people is guaranteed by the Constitution, and they owe no responsibility to any human power but their constituents. By holding the representative responsible only to the people, and exempting him from all other influences, we elevate the character of the constituent and quicken his sense of responsibility to his country. It is under these circumstances only that the elector can feel that in the choice of the lawmaker he is himself truly a component part of the sovereign power of the nation. With equal care we should study to defend the rights of the executive and judicial departments. Our Government can only be preserved in its purity by the suppression and entire elimination of every claim or tendency of one coordinate branch to encroachment upon another. With the strict observance of this rule and the other injunctions of the Constitution, with a sedulous inculcation of that respect and love for the Union of the States which our fathers cherished and enjoined upon their children, and with the aid of that overruling Providence which has so long and so kindly guarded our liberties and institutions, we may reasonably expect to transmit them, with their innumerable blessings, to the remotest posterity.

But attachment to the Union of the States should be habitually fostered in every American heart. For more than half a century, during which kingdoms and empires have fallen, this Union has stood unshaken. The patriots who formed it have long since descended to the grave; yet still it remains, the proudest monument to their memory and the object of affection and admiration with everyone worthy to bear the American name. In my judgment its dissolution would be the greatest of calamities, and to avert that should be the study of every American. Upon its preservation must depend our own happiness and that of countless generations to come. Whatever dangers may threaten it, I shall stand by it and maintain it in its integrity to the full extent of the obligations imposed and the powers conferred upon me by the Constitution.

Z. TAYLOR.

SPECIAL MESSAGES.

WASHINGTON, *December 17, 1849.*

To the Senate of the United States:

I transmit to the Senate, for its consideration with a view to ratification, a convention between the United States and His Majesty the Emperor of Brazil, signed at Rio de Janeiro on the 27th of January last, providing for the adjustment of claims of citizens of the United States on the Brazilian Government. A copy of a dispatch from Mr. Tod, the United States minister at Rio de Janeiro, relative to the convention is also herewith communicated. As it is understood that the Emperor's ratification is ready to be exchanged for that of the United States, and as the period limited for the exchange will expire on the 27th of next month, it is desirable that the decision of the Senate in regard to the instrument should be known as soon as may be convenient.

Z. TAYLOR.

WASHINGTON, *December 21, 1849.*

To the Senate of the United States:

I transmit to the Senate, for its consideration with a view to ratification, a treaty between the United States and His Majesty the King of the Hawaiian Islands, yesterday concluded and signed in this city on the part of the respective Governments by the Secretary of State of the United States and by James Jackson Jarves, His Hawaiian Majesty's special commissioner.

Z. TAYLOR.

WASHINGTON, *December 27, 1849.*

To the Senate and House of Representatives:

In consequence of the unexpected delay in proceeding to business, I deem it necessary to invite the immediate attention of Congress to so much of the report of the Secretary of the Treasury as relates to the appropriations required for the expenses of collecting the revenue for the second half of the current fiscal year.

Z. TAYLOR.

WASHINGTON, *January 4, 1850.*

To the Senate and House of Representatives of the United States:

I herewith submit to you copies of a correspondence with the lady of Sir John Franklin, relative to the well-known expedition under his command to the arctic regions for the discovery of a northwest passage. On the receipt of her first letter imploring the aid of the American Government in a search for the missing ships engaged in an enterprise which interested all civilized nations, I anxiously sought the means of affording that assistance, but was prevented from accomplishing the object I had in view in consequence of the want of vessels suitable to encounter the perils of a proper exploration, the lateness of the season, and the want of an appropriation by Congress to enable me to furnish and equip an efficient squadron for that object. All that I could do in compliance with a request which I was deeply anxious to gratify was to cause the advertisements of reward promulged by the British Government and the best information I could obtain as to the means of finding the vessels under the command of Sir John Franklin to be widely circulated among our whalers and seafaring men whose spirit of enterprise might lead them to the inhospitable regions where that heroic officer and his brave followers, who periled their lives in the cause of science and for the benefit of the world, were supposed to be imprisoned among the icebergs or wrecked upon a desert shore.

Congress being now in session, the propriety and expediency of an appropriation for fitting out an expedition to proceed in search of the missing ships, with their officers and crews, is respectfully submitted to your consideration.

Z. TAYLOR.

EXECUTIVE OFFICE, *January 14, 1850.*

The PRESIDENT OF THE SENATE OF THE UNITED STATES.

SIR: I transmit herewith, to be laid before the Senate for its constitutional action thereon, a treaty concluded with the half-breeds of the Dacotah or Sioux Indians for lands reserved for them in the treaty of July 15, 1830, with the Sioux and other Indians, with accompanying papers.

Z. TAYLOR.

WASHINGTON, *January 14, 1850.*

To the Senate of the United States:

I herewith transmit reports from the Secretary of State and the Secretary of the Navy, containing the information called for by the resolution of the Senate of the 7th instant, in relation to the abduction* of Rey, *alias* Garcia, from New Orleans.

Z. TAYLOR.

WASHINGTON, *January 14, 1850.*

To the Senate of the United States:

I transmit to the Senate, for their consideration, a copy of a correspondence between the Department of State and the chargé d'affaires of Austria near this Government, on the subject of the convention for the extension of certain stipulations contained in the treaty of commerce and navigation of August 27, 1829, between the United States and Austria, concluded and signed on the 8th of May, 1848, and submitted to the Senate on the same day by my predecessor.

Z. TAYLOR.

WASHINGTON, *January 23, 1850.*

To the Senate of the United States:

I transmit to the Senate, in answer to a resolution of that body passed on the 17th instant, the accompanying reports of heads of Departments, which contain all the official information in the possession of the Executive asked for by the resolution.

*By the Spanish consul at New Orleans.

On coming into office I found the military commandant of the Department of California exercising the functions of civil governor in that Territory, and left, as I was, to act under the treaty of Guadalupe Hidalgo, without the aid of any legislative provision establishing a government in that Territory, I thought it best not to disturb that arrangement, made under my predecessor, until Congress should take some action on that subject. I therefore did not interfere with the powers of the military commandant, who continued to exercise the functions of civil governor as before; but I made no such appointment, conferred no such authority, and have allowed no increased compensation to the commandant for his services.

With a view to the faithful execution of the treaty so far as lay in the power of the Executive, and to enable Congress to act at the present session with as full knowledge and as little difficulty as possible on all matters of interest in these Territories, I sent the Hon. Thomas Butler King as bearer of dispatches to California, and certain officers to California and New Mexico, whose duties are particularly defined in the accompanying letters of instruction addressed to them severally by the proper Departments.

I did not hesitate to express to the people of those Territories my desire that each Territory should, if prepared to comply with the requisitions of the Constitution of the United States, form a plan of a State constitution and submit the same to Congress with a prayer for admission into the Union as a State, but I did not anticipate, suggest, or authorize the establishment of any such government without the assent of Congress, nor did I authorize any Government agent or officer to interfere with or exercise any influence or control over the election of delegates or over any convention in making or modifying their domestic institutions or any of the provisions of their proposed constitution. On the contrary, the instructions given by my orders were that all measures of domestic policy adopted by the people of California must originate solely with themselves; that while the Executive of the United States was desirous to protect them in the formation of any government republican in its character, to be at the proper time submitted to Congress, yet it was to be distinctly understood that the plan of such a government must at the same time be the result of their own deliberate choice and originate with themselves, without the interference of the Executive.

I am unable to give any information as to laws passed by any supposed government in California or of any census taken in either of the Territories mentioned in the resolution, as I have no information on those subjects.

As already stated, I have not disturbed the arrangements which I found had existed under my predecessor.

In advising an early application by the people of these Territories for admission as States I was actuated principally by an earnest desire to afford to the wisdom and patriotism of Congress the opportunity of avoiding occasions of bitter and angry dissensions among the people of the United States.

Under the Constitution every State has the right of establishing and from time to time altering its municipal laws and domestic institutions independently of every other State and of the General Government, subject only to the prohibitions and guaranties expressly set forth in the Constitution of the United States. The subjects thus left exclusively to the respective States were not designed or expected to become topics of national agitation. Still, as under the Constitution Congress has power to make all needful rules and regulations respecting the Territories of the United States, every new acquisition of territory has led to discussions on the question whether the system of involuntary servitude which prevails in many of the States should or should not be prohibited in that territory. The periods of excitement from this cause which have heretofore occurred have been safely passed, but during the interval, of whatever length, which may elapse before the admission of the Territories ceded by Mexico as States it appears probable that similar excitement will prevail to an undue extent.

Under these circumstances I thought, and still think, that it was my duty to endeavor to put it in the power of Congress, by the admission of California and New Mexico as States, to remove all occasion for the unnecessary agitation of the public mind.

It is understood that the people of the western part of California have formed a plan of a State constitution and will soon submit the same to the judgment of Congress and apply for admission as a State. This course on their part, though in accordance with, was not adopted exclusively in consequence of, any expression of my wishes, inasmuch as measures tending to this end had been promoted by the officers sent there by my predecessor, and were already in active progress of execution before any communication from me reached California. If the proposed constitution shall, when submitted to Congress, be found to be in compliance with the requisitions of the Constitution of the United States, I earnestly recommend that it may receive the sanction of Congress.

The part of California not included in the proposed State of that name is believed to be uninhabited, except in a settlement of our countrymen in the vicinity of Salt Lake.

A claim has been advanced by the State of Texas to a very large portion of the most populous district of the Territory commonly designated by the name of New Mexico. If the people of New Mexico had formed a plan of a State government for that Territory as ceded by the treaty of Guadalupe Hidalgo, and had been admitted by Congress as a State, our Constitution would have afforded the means of obtaining an adjustment of the question of boundary with Texas by a judicial decision. At present, however, no judicial tribunal has the power of deciding that

In witness whereof, I have hereunto set my hand, and caused the seal of the United States to be affixed. Done at the City of Washington, this fifth day of July, in the year of our Lord one thousand eight hundred and fifty, and of the Independence of the United States the seventy-fifth.

Z. Taylor

By the President:

J. M. Clayton – Secretary of State.

SIGNATURES OF TAYLOR AND SECRETARY JOHN M. CLAYTON TO A STATE DOCUMENT.

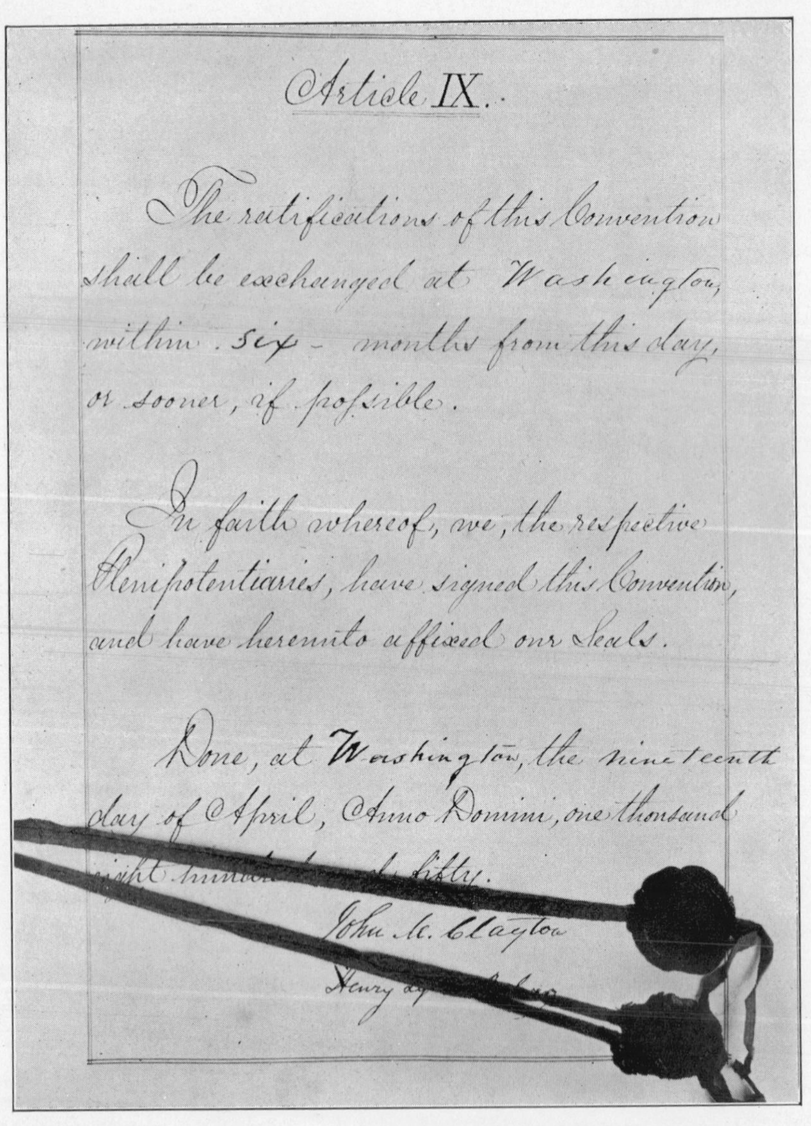

Article IX.

The ratifications of this Convention shall be exchanged at Washington, within six months from this day, or sooner, if possible.

In faith whereof, we, the respective Plenipotentiaries, have signed this Convention, and have hereunto affixed our Seals.

Done, at Washington, the nineteenth day of April, Anno Domini, one thousand eight hundred and fifty.

John M. Clayton

Henry [illegible]

LAST PAGE OF THE CLAYTON-BULWER TREATY, RATIFIED DURING TAYLOR'S ADMINISTRATION.

question, and it remains for Congress to devise some mode for its adjustment. Meanwhile I submit to Congress the question whether it would be expedient before such adjustment to establish a Territorial government, which by including the district so claimed would practically decide the question adversely to the State of Texas, or by excluding it would decide it in her favor. In my opinion such a course would not be expedient, especially as the people of this Territory still enjoy the benefit and protection of their municipal laws originally derived from Mexico and have a military force stationed there to protect them against the Indians. It is undoubtedly true that the property, lives, liberties, and religion of the people of New Mexico are better protected than they ever were before the treaty of cession.

Should Congress, when California shall present herself for incorporation into the Union, annex a condition to her admission as a State affecting her domestic institutions contrary to the wishes of her people, and even compel her temporarily to comply with it, yet the State could change her constitution at any time after admission when to her it should seem expedient. Any attempt to deny to the people of the State the right of self-government in a matter which peculiarly affects themselves will infallibly be regarded by them as an invasion of their rights, and, upon the principles laid down in our own Declaration of Independence, they will certainly be sustained by the great mass of the American people. To assert that they are a conquered people and must as a State submit to the will of their conquerors in this regard will meet with no cordial response among American freemen. Great numbers of them are native citizens of the United States, not inferior to the rest of our countrymen in intelligence and patriotism, and no language of menace to restrain them in the exercise of an undoubted right, substantially guaranteed to them by the treaty of cession itself, shall ever be uttered by me or encouraged and sustained by persons acting under my authority. It is to be expected that in the residue of the territory ceded to us by Mexico the people residing there will at the time of their incorporation into the Union as a State settle all questions of domestic policy to suit themselves.

No material inconvenience will result from the want for a short period of a government established by Congress over that part of the territory which lies eastward of the new State of California; and the reasons for my opinion that New Mexico will at no very distant period ask for admission into the Union are founded on unofficial information which, I suppose, is common to all who have cared to make inquiries on that subject.

Seeing, then, that the question which now excites such painful sensations in the country will in the end certainly be settled by the silent effect of causes independent of the action of Congress, I again submit to your wisdom the policy recommended in my annual message of awaiting the salutary operation of those causes, believing that we shall thus avoid the creation of geographical parties and secure the harmony of feeling so necessary to the beneficial action of our political system. Connected, as the Union is, with the remembrance of past happiness, the sense of present blessings, and the hope of future peace and prosperity, every dictate of wisdom, every feeling of duty, and every emotion of patriotism tend to inspire fidelity and devotion to it and admonish us cautiously to avoid any unnecessary controversy which can either endanger it or impair its strength, the chief element of which is to be found in the regard and affection of the people for each other.

Z. TAYLOR.

[A similar message, dated January 21, 1850, was sent to the House of Representatives, in answer to a resolution of that body.]

WASHINGTON, *January 23, 1850*.

To the Senate of the United States:

I transmit to the Senate a copy of the convention between the United States and His Majesty the Emperor of Brazil, providing for the satisfaction of claims of citizens of the United States against the Brazilian Government, signed at Rio de Janeiro on the 27th of January last, and the ratifications of which were exchanged in this city on the 18th instant. It is desirable that Congress should prescribe the mode in which the claims referred to are to be adjusted and the money stipulated to be paid by Brazil shall be distributed amongst the claimants. Extracts from dispatches of the minister of the United States at Rio de Janeiro and a copy of a letter from an agent of claimants there are also herewith communicated, to which your attention is invited. I have authorized our minister to demand, receive, and give acquittances for the amount payable by Brazil, and have caused him to be instructed to remit the same to the Treasury of the United States.

Z. TAYLOR.

[The same message was sent to the House of Representatives.]

WASHINGTON, *January 30, 1850*.

To the Senate of the United States:

In reply to the resolution of the Senate of the 7th instant, requesting of me all the official correspondence since the 4th of March last between this Government and its military authorities at Santa Fe or with the authorities of the State of Texas relating to the boundary or occupation of Texas, and the reasons why the judicial authority of Texas has not been recognized by the military authority at Santa Fe, I herewith submit the accompanying reports, which contain the information called for by the resolution.

I have not been informed of any acts of interference by the military forces stationed at Santa Fe with the judicial authority of Texas established or sought to be established there. I have received no communication from the governor of Texas on any of the matters referred to in the resolution. And I concur in the opinion expressed by my predecessor in the letter addressed by the late Secretary of State to the governor of Texas on the 12th day of February, 1847, that the boundary between the State of Texas and the Territory of New Mexico "is a subject which more properly belongs to the legislative than to the executive branch of the Government."

Z. TAYLOR.

WASHINGTON, *February 6, 1850.*

To the Senate of the United States:

In reply to the resolution of the Senate of the 28th ultimo, I have to state that the resolution of the Senate of the 2d of March, 1849, respecting James W. Schaumburg, was in April of that year submitted for the opinion of the Attorney-General upon questions arising in the case. No opinion had been given by him when it became necessary, prior to the meeting of the Senate, to prepare the nominations for promotions in the Army. The nomination of Lieutenant Ewell was then decided upon, after due consideration was given to the resolution of the Senate of the 2d of March, 1849.

I herewith submit a report from the Secretary of War, showing the grounds upon which the decision above referred to was made.

Z. TAYLOR.

WASHINGTON, *February 13, 1850.*

To the Senate of the United States:

I have received a resolution of the Senate of the 28th ultimo, requesting the President of the United States "to cause to be laid before the Senate, in open session if in his opinion consistent with the public interest, otherwise in executive session, copies of all instructions and communications of the late Secretary of State to our late chargé d'affaires to Guatemala and all dispatches and communications from said chargé d'affaires to the Department of State, including any conventions or treaties he may have concluded with either of the States composing the late Republic of Central America; and also all correspondence between our said chargé d'affaires and the Government or representatives of either of said States; and also all instructions and communications from the present Secretary of State to our late chargé d'affaires or our present chargé d'affaires to either of said States and all dispatches or communications from our chargé d'affaires to the Department of State, including any conventions or treaties he may have concluded with either of said States; and also all correspondence between the Department of State and either of said chargés d'affaires touching the so-called Kingdom of the Mosquitos and the right of way from the Atlantic to the Pacific through Lake Nicaragua."

The information called for by this resolution will be cheerfully communicated to the Senate as soon as it shall be found to be compatible with the public interest.

Z. TAYLOR.

WASHINGTON, *February 13, 1850.*

To the House of Representatives of the United States:

I have received a resolution of the House of Representatives of the 24th ultimo, requesting the President of the United States "to communicate to that body (provided the publication thereof be not prejudicial to the public interest) all such information as may be within the knowledge of the executive department relative to the alleged extraordinary proceedings of the English Government in the forcible seizure and occupation of the island of Tigre, in the State of Nicaragua, Central America; also all facts, circumstances, or communications within the knowledge of the Executive relative to any seizure, occupation, or attempted seizure or occupation, by the English Government of any port, river, town, territory, or island belonging to or claimed by any of the States of Central America; also that he be requested to communicate to this House, if not incompatible with the public interest, all treaties not heretofore published which may have been negotiated with any of the States of Central America by any person acting by authority from the late Administration or under the auspices of the present Executive." The information called for by this resolution will be cheerfully communicated to the House as soon as it shall be found compatible with the public interest.

Z. TAYLOR.

WASHINGTON, *February 13, 1850.*

To the House of Representatives of the United States:

I transmit herewith to the House of Representatives, for the information of that body, an authenticated copy of the constitution of the State of California, received by me from General Riley.

Z. TAYLOR.

WASHINGTON, *February 13, 1850.*

To the Senate of the United States:

I transmit herewith to the Senate, for the information of that body, an authenticated copy of the constitution of California, received by me from the Hon. William M. Gwyn.

Z. TAYLOR.

WASHINGTON, *March 1, 1850.*

To the Senate of the United States:

In reply to the resolution of the Senate of the 12th ultimo, requesting the President of the United States "to inform the Senate of the amount of prize money paid into the Treasury in conformity with the eighteenth section of the act of March 3, 1849," etc., I transmit herewith a report from the Secretary of the Navy, with accompanying documents.

Z. TAYLOR.

WASHINGTON, *March 4, 1850.*

To the Senate and House of Representatives of the United States:

I herewith transmit to Congress copies of a recent correspondence between the Department of State and the British minister at Washington, relating to subjects* which seem to require the consideration of the legislative rather than the executive branch of the Government.

Z. TAYLOR.

WASHINGTON, *March 6, 1850.*

To the Senate of the United States:

In answer to the inquiries contained in the resolution of the Senate of the 4th instant, in relation to the appointment of postmasters by the Postmaster-General, I send to the Senate herewith the letter of the Postmaster-General furnishing the desired information.

Z. TAYLOR.

MARCH 8, 1850.

To the Senate of the United States:

The Postmaster-General has this day communicated to me the letter herewith transmitted, in addition to his communication by me sent to the Senate on the 6th instant, in relation to the inquiries contained in the resolution of the Senate as to the appointment of postmasters.

Z. TAYLOR.

WASHINGTON, *March 19, 1850.*

To the Senate of the United States:

I transmit herewith, for the consideration and constitutional action of the Senate, a communication from the Secretary of the Interior, covering two treaties with Indians of New Mexico, one negotiated with the Navajo tribe on the 9th of September last by Colonel John Washington, of the Army, and J. S. Calhoun, United States Indian agent at Santa Fe, and the other with the Utah tribe, negotiated by J. S. Calhoun on the 13th of December last.

Z. TAYLOR.

WASHINGTON, *March 19, 1850.*

To the Senate of the United States:

I herewith transmit to the Senate, for their advice in regard to its ratification, "a general treaty of amity, navigation, and commerce" between

*Navigation laws and tariff on British productions.

the United States of America and the State of Nicaragua, concluded at Leon by E. George Squier, chargé d'affaires of the United States, on their part, and Señor Zepeda, on the part of the Republic of Nicaragua.

I also transmit, for the advice of the Senate in regard to its ratification, "a general treaty of amity, navigation, and commerce" negotiated by Mr. Squier with the Republic of San Salvador.

I also transmit to the Senate a copy of the instructions to and correspondence with the said chargé d'affaires relating to those treaties.

I also transmit, for the advice of the Senate in regard to its ratification, "a general treaty of peace, amity, commerce, and navigation" negotiated by Elijah Hise, our late chargé d'affaires, with the State of Guatemala.

I also transmit, for the information of the Senate, a copy of a treaty negotiated by Mr. Hise with the Government of Nicaragua on the 21st of June last, accompanied by copies of his instructions from and correspondence with the Department of State.

On the 12th day of November, 1847, Señor Buétrago, secretary of state and of the affairs of war and foreign relations and domestic administration of the Supreme Government of the State of Nicaragua, addressed a letter from the Government House at Leon to Mr. Buchanan, then Secretary of State of the United States, asking the friendly offices of this Government to prevent an attack upon the town of San Juan de Nicaragua, then contemplated by the British authorities as the allies of the Mosquito King. That letter, a translation of which is herewith sent, distinctly charges that—

> The object of the British in taking this key of the continent is not to protect the small tribe of the Mosquitos, but to establish their own empire over the Atlantic extremity of the line, by which a canal connecting the two oceans is most practicable, insuring to them the preponderance on the American continent, as well as their direct relations with Asia, the East Indies, and other important countries in the world.

No answer appears to have been returned to this letter.

A communication was received by my predecessor from Don José Guerrero, President and Supreme Director of the State of Nicaragua, dated the 15th day of December, 1847, expressing his desire to establish relations of amity and commerce with the United States, a translation of which is herewith inclosed. In this the President of Nicaragua says:

> My desire was carried to the utmost on seeing in your message at the opening of the Twenty-ninth Congress of your Republic a sincere profession of political faith in all respects conformable with the principles professed by these States, determined, as they are, to sustain with firmness the continental cause, the rights of Americans in general, and the noninterference of European powers in their concerns.

This letter announces the critical situation in which Nicaragua was placed and charges upon the Court of St. James a "well-known design to establish colonies on the coast of Nicaragua and to render itself master of the interoceanic canal, for which so many facilities are presented by the isthmus in that State." No reply was made to this letter.

The British ships of war *Alarm* and *Vixen* arrived at San Juan de Nicaragua on the 8th day of February, 1848, and on the 12th of that month the British forces, consisting of 260 officers and men, attacked and captured the post of Serapaqui, garrisoned, according to the British statements, by about 200 soldiers, after a sharp action of one hour and forty minutes.

On the 7th day of March, 1848, articles of agreement were concluded by Captain Locke, on the part of Great Britain, with the commissioners of the State of Nicaragua in the island of Cuba, in the Lake of Nicaragua, a copy of which will be found in the correspondence relating to the Mosquito Territory presented to and published by the House of Commons of Great Britain on the 3d day of July, 1848, herewith submitted. A copy of the same document will also be found accompanying the note of the minister for foreign affairs of Nicaragua to the Secretary of State of the United States under date the 17th March, 1848.

By the third article of the agreement it is provided that Nicaragua "shall not disturb the inhabitants of San Juan, understanding that any such act will be considered by Great Britain as a declaration of open hostilities." By the sixth article it is provided that these articles of agreement will not "hinder Nicaragua from soliciting by means of a commissioner to Her Britannic Majesty a final arrangement of these affairs."

The communication from Señor Sebastian Salinas, the secretary of foreign affairs of the State of Nicaragua, to Mr. Buchanan, the Secretary of State of the United States, dated 17th March, 1848, a translation of which is herewith submitted, recites the aggressions of Great Britain and the seizure of a part of the Nicaraguan territory in the name of the Mosquito King. No answer appears to have been given to this letter.

On the 28th day of October, 1847, Joseph W. Livingston was appointed by this Government consul of the United States for the port of San Juan de Nicaragua. On the 16th day of December, 1847, after having received his exequatur from the Nicaraguan Government, he addressed a letter to Mr. Buchanan, Secretary of State, a copy of which is herewith submitted, representing that he had been informed that the English Government would take possession of San Juan de Nicaragua in January, 1848.

In another letter, dated the 8th of April, 1848, Mr. Livingston states that "at the request of the minister for foreign affairs of Nicaragua he transmits a package of papers containing the correspondence relative to the occupation of the port of San Juan by British forces in the name of the Mosquito nation."

On the 3d day of June, 1848, Elijah Hise, being appointed chargé d'affaires of the United States to Guatemala, received his instructions, a copy of which is herewith submitted. In these instructions the following passages occur:

The independence as well as the interests of the nations on this continent require that they should maintain the American system of policy entirely distinct from that which prevails in Europe. To suffer any interference on the part of the European Governments with the domestic concerns of the American Republics and to permit them to establish new colonies upon this continent would be to jeopard their independence and to ruin their interests. These truths ought everywhere throughout this continent to be impressed on the public mind. But what can the United States do to resist such European interference whilst the Spanish American Republics continue to weaken themselves by division and civil war and deprive themselves of the ability of doing anything for their own protection?

This last significant inquiry seems plainly to intimate that the United States could do nothing to arrest British aggression while the Spanish American Republics continue to weaken themselves by division and civil war and deprive themselves of the ability of doing anything for their protection.

These instructions, which also state the dissolution of the Central American Republic, formerly composed of the five States of Nicaragua, Costa Rica, Honduras, San Salvador, and Guatemala, and their continued separation, authorize Mr. Hise to conclude treaties of commerce with the Republics of Guatemala and San Salvador, but conclude with saying that it was not deemed advisable to empower Mr. Hise to conclude a treaty with either Nicaragua, Honduras, or Costa Rica until more full and statistical information should have been communicated by him to the Department in regard to those States than that which it possesses.

The States of Nicaragua, Costa Rica, and Honduras are the only Central American States whose consent or cooperation would in any event be necessary for the construction of the ship canal contemplated between the Pacific and Atlantic oceans by the way of Lake Nicaragua.

In pursuance of the sixth article of the agreement of the 7th of March, 1848, between the forces of Great Britain and the authorities of Nicaragua, Señor Francisco Castillon was appointed commissioner from Nicaragua to Great Britain, and on the 5th day of November, 1848, while at Washington on his way to London, addressed a letter to the Secretary of State, a translation of which is herewith submitted, asking this Government to instruct its minister plenipotentiary residing in London to sustain the right of Nicaragua to her territory claimed by Mosquito, and especially to the port of San Juan, expressing the hope of Nicaragua "that the Government of the Union, firmly adhering to its principle of resisting all foreign intervention in America, would not hesitate to order such steps to be taken as might be effective before things reached a point in which the intervention of the United States would prove of no avail."

To this letter also no answer appears to have been returned, and no instructions were given to our minister in London in pursuance of the request contained in it.

On the 3d day of March, 1847, Christopher Hempstead was appointed consul at Belize, and an application was then made for his exequatur through our minister in London, Mr. Bancroft. Lord Palmerston referred Mr. Bancroft's application for an exequatur for Mr. Hempstead to the colonial office. The exequatur was granted, and Mr. Hempstead, in a letter to the Department of State bearing date the 12th day of February, 1848, a copy of which is herewith submitted, acknowledged the receipt of his exequatur from Her Britannic Majesty, by virtue of which he has discharged his consular functions. Thus far this Government has recognized the existence of a British colony at Belize, within the territory of Honduras. I have recalled the consul, and have appointed no one to supply his place.

On the 26th day of May, 1848, Mr. Hempstead represented in a letter to the Department of State that the Indians had "applied to Her Majesty's superintendent at Belize for protection, and had desired him to take possession of the territory which they occupied and take them under his protection as British subjects;" and he added that in the event of the success of their application "the British Government would then have possession of the entire coast from Cape Conte to San Juan de Nicaragua." In another letter, dated the 29th day of July, 1848, he wrote:

> I have not a doubt but the designs of Her Majesty's officers here and on the Mosquito shore are to obtain territory on this continent.

The receipt of this letter was regularly acknowledged on the 29th day of August, 1848.

When I came into office I found the British Government in possession of the port of San Juan, which it had taken by force of arms after we had taken possession of California and while we were engaged in the negotiation of a treaty for the cession of it, and that no official remonstrance had been made by this Government against the aggression, nor any attempt to resist it. Efforts were then being made by certain private citizens of the United States to procure from the State of Nicaragua by contract the right to cut the proposed ship canal by the way of the river San Juan and the lakes of Nicaragua and Managua to Realejo, on the Pacific Ocean. A company of American citizens entered into such a contract with the State of Nicaragua. Viewing the canal as a matter of great importance to the people of the United States, I resolved to adopt the policy of protecting the work and binding the Government of Nicaragua, through whose territory it would pass, also to protect it. The instructions to E. George Squier, appointed by me chargé d'affaires to Guatemala on the 2d day of April, 1849, are herewith submitted, as fully indicating the views which governed me in directing a treaty to be made with Nicaragua. I considered the interference of the British Government on this continent in seizing the port of San Juan, which commanded the route believed to be the most eligible for the canal across the Isthmus, and occupying it at the very moment when it was known, as I believe, to Great Britain that we were engaged in the negotiation for the purchase of California, as an unfortunate coincidence, and one calculated to lead to the inference that she entertained designs by no means in harmony with the interests of the United States.

Seeing that Mr. Hise had been positively instructed to make no treaty, not even a treaty of commerce, with Nicaragua, Costa Rica, or Honduras, I had no suspicion that he would attempt to act in opposition to his instructions, and in September last I was for the first time informed that he had actually negotiated two treaties with the State of Nicaragua, the one a treaty of commerce, the other a treaty for the construction of the proposed ship canal, which treaties he brought with him on his return home. He also negotiated a treaty of commerce with Honduras; and in each of these treaties it is recited that he had full powers for the purpose. He had no such powers, and the whole proceeding on his part with reference to those States was not only unauthorized by instructions, but in opposition to those he had received from my predecessor and after the date of his letter of recall and the appointment of his successor. But I have no evidence that Mr. Hise, whose letter of recall (a copy of which is herewith submitted) bears date the 2d day of May, 1849, had received that letter on the 21st day of June, when he negotiated the treaty with Nicaragua. The difficulty of communicating with him was so great that I have reason to believe he had not received it. He did not acknowledge it.

The twelfth article of the treaty negotiated by Mr. Hise in effect guarantees the perfect independence of the State of Nicaragua and her sovereignty over her alleged limits from the Caribbean Sea to the Pacific Ocean, pledging the naval and military power of the United States to support it. This treaty authorizes the chartering of a corporation by this Government to cut a canal outside of the limits of the United States, and gives to us the exclusive right to fortify and command it. I have not approved it, nor have I now submitted it for ratification; not merely because of the facts already mentioned, but because on the 31st day of December last Señor Edwardo Carcache, on being accredited to this Government as chargé d'affaires from the State of Nicaragua, in a note to the Secretary of State, a translation of which is herewith sent, declared that he was "only empowered to exchange ratifications of the treaty concluded with Mr. Squier, and that the special convention concluded at Guatemala by Mr. Hise, the chargé d'affaires of the United States, and Señor Selva, the commissioner of Nicaragua, had been, as was publicly and universally known, disapproved by his Government."

We have no precedent in our history to justify such a treaty as that negotiated by Mr. Hise since the guaranties we gave to France of her American possessions. The treaty negotiated with New Granada on the 12th day of December, 1846, did not guarantee the sovereignty of New Granada on the whole of her territory, but only over "the single Province of the Isthmus of Panama," immediately adjoining the line of the railroad, the neutrality of which was deemed necessary by the President and Senate to the construction and security of the work.

The thirty-fifth article of the treaty with Nicaragua, negotiated by Mr. Squier, which is submitted for your advice in regard to its ratification, distinctly recognizes the rights of sovereignty and property which the State of Nicaragua possesses in and over the line of the canal therein provided for. If the Senate doubt on that subject, it will be clearly wrong to involve us in a controversy with England by adopting the treaty; but after the best consideration which I have been able to give to the subject my own judgment is convinced that the claims of Nicaragua are just, and that as our commerce and intercourse with the Pacific require the opening of this communication from ocean to ocean it is our duty to ourselves to assert their justice.

This treaty is not intended to secure to the United States any monopoly or exclusive advantage in the use of the canal. Its object is to guarantee protection to American citizens and others who shall construct the canal, and to defend it when completed against unjust confiscations or obstructions, and to deny the advantages of navigation through it to those nations only which shall refuse to enter into the same guaranties. A copy of the contract of the canal company is herewith transmitted, from which, as well as from the treaty, it will be perceived that the same benefits are offered to all nations in the same terms.

The message of my predecessor to the Senate of the 10th February, 1847, transmitting for ratification the treaty with New Granada, contains in general the principles by which I have been actuated in directing the negotiation with Nicaragua. The only difference between the two cases consists in this: In that of Nicaragua the British Government has seized upon part of her territory and was in possession of it when we negotiated the treaty with her. But that possession was taken after our occupation of California, when the effect of it was to obstruct or control the most eligible route for a ship communication to the territories acquired by us on the Pacific. In the case of New Granada, her possession was undisturbed at the time of the treaty, though the British possession in the right of the Mosquito King was then extended into the territories claimed by New Granada as far as Boca del Toro. The professed objects of both the treaties are to open communications across the Isthmus to all nations and to invite their guaranties on the same terms. Neither of them proposes to guarantee territory to a foreign nation in which the United States will not have a common interest with that nation. Neither of them constitutes an alliance for any political object, but for a purely commercial purpose, in which all the navigating nations of the world have a common interest. Nicaragua, like New Granada, is a power which will not excite the jealousy of any nation.

As there is nothing narrow, selfish, illiberal, or exclusive in the views of the United States as set forth in this treaty, as it is indispensable to the successful completion of the contemplated canal to secure protection to it from the local authorities and this Government, and as I have no doubt that the British pretension to the port of San Juan in right of the Mosquito King is without just foundation in any public law ever before recognized in any other instance by Americans or Englishmen as applicable to Indian titles on this continent, I shall ratify this treaty in case the Senate shall advise that course. Its principal defect is taken from the treaty with New Granada, the negotiator having made it liable to be abrogated on notice after twenty years. Both treaties should have been perpetual or limited only by the duration of the improvements they were intended to protect. The instructions to our chargé d'affaires, it will be seen, prescribe no limitation for the continuance of the treaty with Nicaragua. Should the Senate approve of principle of the treaty, an amendment in this respect is deemed advisable; and it will be well to invite by another amendment the protection of other nations, by expressly offering them in the treaty what is now offered by implication only—the same advantages which we propose for ourselves on the same conditions upon which we shall have acquired them. The policy of this treaty is not novel, nor does it originate from any suggestion either of my immediate predecessor or myself. On the 3d day of March, 1835, the following resolution, referred to by the late President in his message to the Senate relative to the treaty with New Granada, was adopted in executive session by the Senate without division:

Resolved, That the President of the United States be respectfully requested to consider the expediency of opening negotiations with the Governments of Central America and New Granada for the purpose of effectually protecting, by suitable treaty stipulations with them, such individuals or companies as may undertake to open a communication between the Atlantic and Pacific oceans by the construction of a ship canal across the isthmus which connects North and South America, and of securing forever by such stipulations the free and equal rights of navigating such a canal to all such nations on the payment of such reasonable tolls as may be established to compensate the capitalists who may engage in such undertaking and complete the work.

President Jackson accorded with the policy suggested in this resolution, and in pursuance of it sent Charles Biddle as agent to negotiate with the Governments of Central America and New Granada. The result is fully set forth in the report of a select committee of the House of Representatives of the 20th of February, 1849, upon a joint resolution of Congress to authorize the survey of certain routes for a canal or railroad between the Atlantic and Pacific oceans. The policy indicated in the resolution of the 3d March, 1835, then adopted by the President and Senate, is that now proposed for the consideration and sanction of the Senate. So far as my knowledge extends, such has ever been the liberal policy of the leading statesmen of this country, and by no one has it been more earnestly recommended than by my lamented predecessor.

Z. TAYLOR.

WASHINGTON, *March 26, 1850.*

To the House of Representatives of the United States:

I herewith transmit, for the information of Congress, a copy of the report* of Thomas Butler King, esq., appointed bearer of dispatches and special agent to California, made in pursuance of instructions issued from the Department of State on the 3d day of April last.

Z. TAYLOR.

WASHINGTON, *March 28, 1850.*

To the Senate of the United States:

In compliance with a resolution of the Senate of the 22d instant, requesting the President of the United States to communicate to that body a copy of the instructions given to the agent of the United States who was employed to visit Hungary during the recent war between that country and Austria, and of the correspondence by and with such agent, so far as the publication of the same may be consistent with the public interest, I herewith transmit to the Senate a copy of the instructions to A. Dudley Mann, esq., relating to Hungary, he having been appointed by me special agent to that country on the 18th day of June last, together with a copy of the correspondence with our late chargé d'affaires to Austria referred to in those instructions and of other papers disclosing the policy of this Government in reference to Hungary and her people. I also transmit, in compliance with the resolution of the Senate, but in a separate packet, a copy of the correspondence of Mr. Mann with the Department of State. The latter I have caused to be marked "*executive*"—the information contained in it being such as will be found on examination most appropriately to belong to the Senate in the exercise of its executive functions. The publication of this correspondence of the agent sent by me to Hungary is a matter referred entirely to the judgment and discretion of the Senate.

It will be seen by the documents now transmitted that no minister or agent was accredited by the Government of Hungary to this Government at any period since I came into office, nor was any communication ever received by this Government from the minister of foreign affairs of Hungary or any other executive officer authorized to act in her behalf.

My purpose, as freely avowed in this correspondence, was to have acknowledged the independence of Hungary had she succeeded in establishing a government *de facto* on a basis sufficiently permanent in its character to have justified me in doing so according to the usages and settled principles of this Government; and although she is now fallen and many of her gallant patriots are in exile or in chains, I am free still to declare that had she been successful in the maintenance of such a government as we could have recognized we should have been the first to welcome her into the family of nations.

Z. TAYLOR.

*On California affairs.

WASHINGTON, *April 3, 1850.*

To the Senate and House of Representatives of the United States:

I transmit a translation of a note, under date the 20th of last month, addressed to the Secretary of State by the minister of the Mexican Republic accredited to this Government, expressing the views of that Government with reference to the control of the wild Indians of the United States on the frontier of Mexico, as stipulated for in the eleventh article of the treaty of Guadalupe Hidalgo.

Z. TAYLOR.

WASHINGTON, *April 22, 1850.*

To the Senate of the United States:

I herewith transmit to the Senate, for their advice with regard to its ratification, a convention between the United States and Great Britain, concluded at Washington on the 19th instant by John M. Clayton, Secretary of State, on the part of the United States, and by the Right Hon. Sir Henry Lytton Bulwer, on the part of Great Britain.

This treaty has been negotiated in accordance with the general views expressed in my message to Congress in December last. Its object is to establish a commercial alliance with all great maritime states for the protection of a contemplated ship canal through the territory of Nicaragua to connect the Atlantic and Pacific oceans, and at the same time to insure the same protection to the contemplated railways or canals by the Tehuantepec and Panama routes, as well as to every other interoceanic communication which may be adopted to shorten the transit to or from our territories on the Pacific.

It will be seen that this treaty does not propose to take money from the public Treasury to effect any object contemplated by it. It yields protection to the capitalists who may undertake to construct any canal or railway across the Isthmus, commencing in the southern part of Mexico and terminating in the territory of New Granada. It gives no preference to any one route over another, but proposes the same measure of protection for all which ingenuity and enterprise can construct. Should this treaty be ratified, it will secure in future the liberation of all Central America from any kind of foreign aggression.

At the time negotiations were opened with Nicaragua for the construction of a canal through her territory I found Great Britain in possession of nearly half of Central America, as the ally and protector of the Mosquito King. It has been my object in negotiating this treaty not only to secure the passage across the Isthmus to the Government and citizens of the United States by the construction of a great highway dedicated to the use of all nations on equal terms, but to maintain the independence and sovereignty of all the Central American Republics. The Senate will judge how far these objects have been effected.

If there be any who would desire to seize and annex any portion of the territories of these weak sister republics to the American Union, or to extend our dominion over them, I do not concur in their policy; and I wish it to be understood in reference to that subject that I adopt the views entertained, so far as I know, by all my predecessors.

The principles by which I have been regulated in the negotiation of this treaty are in accordance with the sentiments well expressed by my immediate predecessor on the 10th of February, 1847, when he communicated to the Senate the treaty with New Granada for the protection of the railroad at Panama. It is in accordance with the whole spirit of the resolution of the Senate of the 3d of March, 1835, referred to by President Polk, and with the policy adopted by President Jackson immediately after the passage of that resolution, who dispatched an agent to Central America and New Granada "to open negotiations with those Governments for the purpose of effectually protecting, by suitable treaty stipulations with them, such individuals or companies as might undertake to open a communication between the Atlantic and Pacific oceans by the construction of a ship canal across the isthmus which connects North and South America, and of securing forever by such stipulations the free and equal right of navigating such canal to all such nations on the payment of such reasonable tolls as might be established to compensate the capitalists who should engage in such undertaking and complete the work."

I also communicate herewith a copy of the correspondence between the American Secretary of State and the British plenipotentiary at the time of concluding the treaty. Whatever honor may be due to the party first proposing such a treaty justly belongs to the United States. My predecessor, in his message of the 10th of February, 1847, referring to the treaty with New Granada for the protection of the Panama Railroad, observes that—

> Should the proposition thus tendered be rejected we may deprive the United States of the just influence which its acceptance might secure to them, and confer the glory and benefits of being the first among the nations in concluding such an arrangement upon the Government either of Great Britain or France. That either of these Governments would embrace the offer can not be doubted, because there does not appear to be any other effectual means of securing to all nations the advantages of this important passage but the guaranty of great commercial powers that the Isthmus shall be neutral territory. The interests of the world at stake are so important that the security of this passage between the two oceans can not be suffered to depend upon the wars and revolutions which may arise among different nations.

Should the Senate in its wisdom see fit to confirm this treaty, and the treaty heretofore submitted by me for their advice in regard to its ratification, negotiated with the State of Nicaragua on the 3d day of September last, it will be necessary to amend one or both of them, so that both treaties may stand in conformity with each other in their spirit and intention. The Senate will discover by examining them both that this is a task of no great difficulty.

I have good reason to believe that France and Russia stand ready to accede to this treaty, and that no other great maritime state will refuse its accession to an arrangement so well calculated to diffuse the blessings of peace, commerce, and civilization, and so honorable to all nations which may enter into the engagement.

Z. TAYLOR.

WASHINGTON, *May 6, 1850.*

To the Senate of the United States:

I transmit to the Senate, for its consideration with a view to ratification, a consular convention between the United States and the Republic of New Granada, signed in this city on the 4th of this month by the Secretary of State on the part of the United States, and by Señor Don Rafael Rivas, chargé d'affaires of New Granada, on the part of that Republic.

Z. TAYLOR.

WASHINGTON, *May 7, 1850.*

To the House of Representatives of the United States:

I herewith transmit to the House of Representatives copies of a correspondence between the Department of State and the British legation in this city, relative to the reciprocal admission of the natural products of the United States and Canada free of duty into the territories of both countries. It will be seen by the accompanying documents that the late Secretary of the Treasury recommended, in his correspondence with the Committee on Commerce in the House of Representatives, reciprocal free trade in the natural products of the United States and Canada; that in March and June, 1849, a correspondence was opened between the British chargé d'affaires then residing in Washington and the Secretary of State upon the subject of a commercial convention or treaty to carry out the views of Her Majesty's Government in relation thereto, and that the proposition for such a convention or treaty was declined on the part of the American Government for reasons which are fully set forth in the note of the Secretary of State to Mr. Crampton of the 26th of June last. During the negotiations connected with this correspondence, not considering the markets of Canada as an equivalent for those of the United States, I directed the Secretary of State to inquire what other benefits of trade and commerce would be yielded by the British authorities in connection with such a measure, and particularly whether the free navigation of the St. Lawrence would be conceded to us. That subject has accordingly been presented to the British Government, and the result was communicated by Her Majesty's minister in Washington on the 27th of March last in reply to a note from the Secretary of State of the 26th of that month. From these papers it will be perceived that the navigation of the St. Lawrence and of the canals connecting it with the Western lakes will be opened to the citizens of the United States in the event that the bill referred to in the correspondence, providing for the admission of their natural products, should become a law. The whole subject is now submitted to the consideration of Congress, and especially whether the concession proposed by Great Britain is an equivalent for the reciprocity desired by her.

Z. TAYLOR.

WASHINGTON, *May 8, 1850.*

To the Senate of the United States:

With reference to the convention between the United States and Her Britannic Majesty relative to interoceanic communication by the way of Nicaragua, recently submitted to the Senate, I transmit a copy of a note, under date the 29th ultimo, addressed to the Secretary of State by Sir Henry L. Bulwer, Her Britannic Majesty's minister here, and of Mr. Clayton's reply, under date the 30th ultimo. Intelligence received from the chargé d'affaires of the United States in Central America and from other quarters having led to an apprehension that Mr. Chatfield, Her Britannic Majesty's minister in that country, had concluded a treaty with the Government of Costa Rica placing that State under the protection of the British Government, I deemed it my duty to cause inquiries upon the subject to be addressed to Her Majesty's Government through Sir Henry L. Bulwer. The note of that functionary communicates the answer to those inquiries, and may be deemed satisfactory, both from the denial of the fact that any such treaty has been concluded and from its positive disavowal on behalf of the British Government of the policy intended to be subserved by such treaties.

Z. TAYLOR.

WASHINGTON, *May 18, 1850.*

To the House of Representatives of the United States:

I herewith transmit to the House of Representatives a report of the Secretary of State, with accompanying papers,* in answer to its resolution of the 28th of March last.

Z. TAYLOR.

WASHINGTON, *May 20, 1850.*

To the Senate of the United States:

I transmit herewith reports from the Secretary of the Interior and Secretary of War, in reply to the resolution of the Senate of the 30th ultimo, calling for information in relation to the hostilities and outrages committed during the past year by the Seminole Indians in Florida, the steps taken for their removal west of the Mississippi, the area now occupied by them, etc.

Z. TAYLOR.

*Communications from the United States consul at Vienna.

WASHINGTON, *May 22, 1850.*

To the Senate of the United States:

I herewith transmit to the Senate reports of the several heads of Departments, to whom were referred the resolutions of the Senate of the 9th instant, "requesting the President of the United States to furnish to the Senate copies of all correspondence between any of the Executive Departments and General Persifor F. Smith and Brigadier-General B. Riley, or either of them, relative to affairs in California, which had not been communicated to the Senate; and also all information existing in any of the Executive Departments respecting the transactions of the convention in California by which the project of a State government was prepared, and particularly a copy of the journals of said convention and of such of the ordinances adopted by it as may in any way have been communicated to any of the said Departments; and likewise to inform the Senate if the surrender of General Riley to the jurisdiction and civil authority of the government made by the aforesaid convention was by order of the Executive of the United States, and, if not, whether the proclamation of General Riley recognizing the said State government and submitting to its jurisdiction has received the sanction of the Executive; and also that he furnish to the Senate whatever intelligence may have been received in the executive department respecting the condition of civil affairs in the Oregon Territory."

The reports, with the official correspondence accompanying them, it is believed, embrace all the information in the Departments called for by the resolutions.

Z. TAYLOR.

WASHINGTON, *May 24, 1850.*

To the Senate of the United States:

In the month of January last I nominated Thomas Sewall to be consul of the United States for the port of Santiago de Cuba, to which office he had been appointed by me during the recess of the Senate. The Spanish Government having refused to recognize Mr. Sewall as consul for that port, I now withdraw that nomination and nominate William N. Adams to fill the vacancy thus occasioned.

Z. TAYLOR.

WASHINGTON, *May 29, 1850.*

To the Senate of the United States:

I transmit to the Senate a copy of a dispatch from the minister of the United States at London, together with the memorial and other documents addressed to the Senate and House of Representatives of the United States by Count de Bronno Bronski which accompanied it, relative to an improved breed of silkworms which he desires to have introduced into this country.

Z. TAYLOR.

WASHINGTON, *June 3, 1850.*

To the Senate of the United States:

I transmit to the Senate herewith reports from the several heads of Departments, which contain all the information in possession of the Executive relative to the subject of the resolution of the 23d instant [ultimo].

No information has been received establishing the existence of any revolutionary movement in the island of Cuba among the inhabitants of that island. The correspondence submitted discloses, however, the fact that repeated attempts have been made under the direction of foreigners enjoying the hospitality of this country to get up armed expeditions in the United States for the purpose of invading Cuba. It will be seen by that correspondence that this Government has been faithful in the discharge of its treaty obligations with Spain and in the execution of the acts of Congress which have for their object the maintenance in this regard of the peace and honor of this country.

Z. TAYLOR

WASHINGTON, *June 10, 1850.*

To the Senate of the United States:

I submit herewith, in reply to a resolution of the Senate of the 3d instant, calling for "copies of the instructions given and orders issued in relation to the assemblage of persons on Round Island, coast of Mississippi, during the summer of 1849, and of the correspondence between the President or heads of Departments and the governor of Mississippi and the officers, naval or military, of the United States in reference to the observation, investment, and dispersion of said assemblage upon said island," a report from the Secretary of the Navy and accompanying documents, which contain all the information on the subject not heretofore communicated to the Senate.

Z. TAYLOR.

WASHINGTON, *June 13, 1850.*

To the House of Representatives of the United States:

I transmit to the House of Representatives a copy of a dispatch addressed by the minister of the United States at Paris to the Secretary of State, with a translation of the documents which accompanied it, relative to the memorial of Pierre Piron, a citizen of the French Republic, who, it will be perceived, presents a just claim to pecuniary remuneration from this Government on account of services rendered to citizens of the United States.

Z. TAYLOR.

WASHINGTON, *June 17, 1850.*

To the Senate of the United States:

I have received a copy of the resolution of the Senate of the 11th June instant, requesting me "to inform the Senate whether any orders have been issued to any military officer or officers at Santa Fe to hold possession against the authority of Texas, or in any way to embarrass or prevent the exercise of her jurisdiction over that country, and to furnish the Senate with copies of any correspondence which may have taken place between the War Department and the military stationed at Santa Fe since the date of my last communication to the Senate on that subject."

In reply to that resolution I state that no such orders have been given.

I herewith present to the Senate copies of all the correspondence referred to in the resolution. All the other orders relating to the subject-matter of the resolution have been heretofore communicated to the Senate.

I have already, in a former message, referred to the fact that the boundary between Texas and New Mexico is disputed. I have now to state that information has been recently received that a certain Robert S. Neighbors, styling himself commissioner of the State of Texas, has proceeded to Santa Fe with a view of organizing counties in that district under the authority of Texas. While I have no power to decide the question of boundary, and no desire to interfere with it, as a question of title, I have to observe that the possession of the territory into which it appears that Mr. Neighbors has thus gone was actually acquired by the United States from Mexico, and has since been held by the United States, and, in my opinion, ought so to remain until the question of boundary shall have been determined by some competent authority. Meanwhile, I think there is no reason for seriously apprehending that Texas will practically interfere with the possession of the United States.

Z. TAYLOR.

WASHINGTON, *June 26, 1850.*

To the House of Representatives of the United States:

I herewith transmit a report of the Secretary of War, communicating the information, as far as it can be furnished, required by the resolution of the House of Representatives of the 17th instant, respecting the amount of money collected from customs in California from the conclusion of the war until the collector appointed under the act of March 3, 1849, entered upon his duties, the objects for which said money has been expended, and the authority under which the collections and disbursements were made.

Z. TAYLOR.

WASHINGTON, *June 27, 1850.*

To the Senate of the United States:

In compliance with the resolution of the Senate of the 3d instant, requesting information in regard to the indemnity stipulated to be paid by the Government of Peru to the Government of the United States pursuant to the modified convention of the 17th of March, 1841, I transmit a report from the Secretary of State and the documents by which it was accompanied. The sums paid by that Government under the convention are mentioned in the letters of Messrs. E. McCall & Co., of Lima, who were appointed by my predecessor the agents to receive the installments as they might fall due.

Z. TAYLOR.

WASHINGTON, *July 1, 1850.*

To the House of Representatives of the United States:

In reply to the resolution of the House of Representatives of the 17th ultimo, in regard to the number of vessels, guns, and men constituting the African squadron, the annual expenses of that squadron, etc., I submit herewith a report from the Secretary of the Navy, with accompanying documents.

Z. TAYLOR.

WASHINGTON, *July 1, 1850.*

To the Senate of the United States:

I herewith transmit a report from the Secretary of War, prepared in answer to a resolution of the Senate of the 27th ultimo, requesting information of the proceedings of the Executive in regard to the appointment of the officer now commanding in New Mexico, the orders and instructions given to and correspondence with him, and upon other subjects mentioned in the resolution.

Z. TAYLOR.

WASHINGTON, *July 2, 1850.*

To the Senate of the United States:

In the month of March last I nominated William McNeir to be a justice of the peace in and for the county of Washington, in the District of Columbia, and on the 24th day of June the Senate advised and consented to the nomination. Since then I have learned from the late mayor of the city of Washington, upon whose recommendation the nomination was made, that the person whom he intended to recommend for that office was George McNeir, whom I now nominate to be a justice of the peace in and for the county of Washington, in the District of Columbia.

In the month of February last I nominated Benjamin Riddells as consul of the United States for Chihuahua, and on the 10th day of June last the Senate advised and consented to that nomination. I have since learned that the persons recommending the appointment of Mr. Riddells by the prænomen of Benjamin intended to recommend Bennet Riddells, whom I now nominate to be consul of the United States for Chihuahua in order to correct the mistake thus inadvertently made.

Z. TAYLOR.

PROCLAMATIONS.

ZACHARY TAYLOR, PRESIDENT OF THE UNITED STATES OF AMERICA.

To all whom it may concern:

An exequatur having been granted to Señor Carlos de España, bearing date the 29th October, 1846, recognizing him as the consul of Her Catholic Majesty at the port of New Orleans and declaring him free to exercise and enjoy such functions, powers, and privileges as are allowed to the consuls of the most favored nations in the United States:

These are now to declare that I do no longer recognize the said Carlos de España as consul of Her Catholic Majesty in any part of the United States, nor permit him to exercise and enjoy any of the functions, powers, or privileges allowed to the consuls of Spain; and I do hereby wholly revoke and annul the said exequatur heretofore given, and do declare the same to be absolutely null and void from this day forward.

In testimony whereof I have caused these letters to be made patent and the seal of the United States of America to be hereunto affixed.

[SEAL.] Given under my hand this 4th day of January, A. D. 1850, and of the Independence of the United States the seventy-fourth.

Z. TAYLOR.

By the President:

JOHN M. CLAYTON, *Secretary of State.*

BY THE PRESIDENT OF THE UNITED STATES.

A PROCLAMATION.

Whereas by an act of the Congress of the United States of the 14th of August, 1848, entitled "An act to establish the Territorial government of Oregon," the President of the United States is authorized to establish such ports of delivery in the collection district created by that act, not exceeding two in number (one of which shall be located on Pugets Sound), as he may deem proper:

Now, therefore, I, Zachary Taylor, President of the United States of America, do hereby declare and proclaim the ports of Nesqually (on Pugets Sound) and Portland, in the collection district of Oregon, in the Territory of Oregon, to be constituted ports of delivery, with all the privileges authorized by law to such ports.

In witness whereof I have hereunto set my hand and caused the seal of the United States to be affixed.

[SEAL.] Done at the city of Washington, this 10th day of January, A. D. 1850, and of the Independence of the United States the seventy-fourth.

Z. TAYLOR.

By the President:

J. M. CLAYTON, *Secretary of State.*

DEATH OF PRESIDENT TAYLOR.

ANNOUNCEMENT TO MR. FILLMORE.

[From official records in the State Department.]

DEPARTMENT OF STATE,
Washington, July 9, 1850.

MILLARD FILLMORE,
President of the United States.

SIR: The melancholy and most painful duty devolves on us to announce to you that Zachary Taylor, late President of the United States, is no more. He died at the President's mansion this evening at half-past 10 o'clock.

We have the honor to be, etc.,

JOHN M. CLAYTON,
Secretary of State.

W. M. MEREDITH,
Secretary of the Treasury.

T. EWING,
Secretary of the Interior.

GEO. W. CRAWFORD,
Secretary of War.

WM. BALLARD PRESTON,
Secretary of the Navy.

J. COLLAMER,
Postmaster-General.

[The announcement as published in the Daily National Intelligencer of July 11, 1850, contains also the signature of Reverdy Johnson, Attorney-General.]

REPLY OF MR. FILLMORE.

[From official records in the State Department.]

WASHINGTON, *July 9, 1850.*

To the Hons. JOHN M. CLAYTON, Secretary of State; W. M. MEREDITH, Secretary of the Treasury; T. EWING, Secretary of the Interior; GEO. W. CRAWFORD, Secretary of War; WM. BALLARD PRESTON, Secretary of the Navy; J. COLLAMER, Postmaster-General; REVERDY JOHNSON, Attorney-General.

GENTLEMEN: I have just received your note conveying the melancholy and painful intelligence of the decease of Zachary Taylor, late President of the United States. I have no language to express the emotions of my heart. The shock is so sudden and unexpected that I am overwhelmed with grief.

I shall avail myself of the earliest moment to communicate this sad intelligence to Congress, and shall appoint a time and place for taking the oath of office prescribed to the President of the United States. You are requested to be present and witness the ceremony.

I am, gentlemen, etc.,

MILLARD FILLMORE.

COMMUNICATION TO THE SENATE FROM MR. FILLMORE.

[From Senate Journal, Thirty-first Congress, first session, p. 443.]

WASHINGTON, *July 10, 1850.*

To the Senate of the United States:

In consequence of the lamented death of Zachary Taylor, late President of the United States, I shall no longer occupy the chair of the Senate, and I have thought that a formal communication to the Senate to that effect, through your Secretary, might enable you the more promptly to proceed to the choice of a presiding officer.

MILLARD FILLMORE.

ANNOUNCEMENT TO CONGRESS.

[From Senate Journal, Thirty-first Congress, first session, p. 443.]

WASHINGTON, *July 10, 1850.*

Fellow-Citizens of the Senate and House of Representatives:

I have to perform the melancholy duty of announcing to you that it has pleased Almighty God to remove from this life Zachary Taylor, late President of the United States. He deceased last evening at the hour of half-past 10 o'clock, in the midst of his family and surrounded by affectionate friends, calmly and in the full possession of all his faculties. Among his last words were these, which he uttered with emphatic distinctness:

I have always done my duty. I am ready to die. My only regret is for the friends I leave behind me.

Having announced to you, fellow-citizens, this most afflicting bereavement, and assuring you that it has penetrated no heart with deeper grief than mine, it remains for me to say that I propose this day at 12 o'clock, in the Hall of the House of Representatives, in the presence of both Houses of Congress, to take the oath prescribed by the Constitution, to enable me to enter on the execution of the office which this event has devolved on me.

MILLARD FILLMORE.

ANNOUNCEMENT TO REPRESENTATIVES OF THE UNITED STATES ABROAD.

[From official records in the State Department.]

CIRCULAR.

DEPARTMENT OF STATE, *Washington, July 10, 1850.*

SIR: It has become my most painful duty to announce to you the decease of Zachary Taylor, late President of the United States.

This afflicting event took place on the 9th instant at the Executive Mansion in this city, at thirty minutes after 10 o'clock in the evening.

I am, sir, respectfully, your obedient servant,

JOHN M. CLAYTON.

ANNOUNCEMENT TO REPRESENTATIVES OF FOREIGN GOVERNMENTS IN THE UNITED STATES.

[From official records in the State Department.]

CIRCULAR.

DEPARTMENT OF STATE, *Washington, July 10, 1850.*

SIR: It is my great misfortune to be obliged to inform you of an event not less afflicting to the people of the United States than distressing to my own feelings and the feelings of all those connected with the Government.

The President, Zachary Taylor, departed this life yesterday at half-past 10 o'clock in the evening.

You are respectfully invited to attend the funeral ceremonies, which will take place on Saturday next, and with the particular arrangements for which you will be made acquainted in due time.

Not doubting your sympathy and condolence with the Government and people of the country on this bereavement, I have the honor to be, sir, with high consideration, your obedient servant,

JOHN M. CLAYTON.

ANNOUNCEMENT TO THE ARMY.

[From official records in the War Department.]

GENERAL ORDERS, NO. 21.

WAR DEPARTMENT, ADJUTANT-GENERAL'S OFFICE,
Washington, July 11, 1850.

I. The following order of the President of the United States announces to the Army the lamented death of the illustrious General Zachary Taylor, late President of the United States:

WAR DEPARTMENT, *July 11, 1850.*

The President of the United States with profound sorrow announces to the Army, the Navy, and Marine Corps the death of Zachary Taylor, late President of the United States. He died at the Executive Mansion on the night of the 9th instant at half-past 10 o'clock.

His last public appearance was in participating in the ceremonies of our national anniversary at the base of the monument now rearing to the memory of Washington. His last official act was to affix his signature to the convention recently concluded between the United States and Great Britain.

The vigor of a constitution strong by nature and confirmed by active and temperate habits had in later years become impaired by the arduous toils and exposures of his military life.

Solely engrossed in maintaining the honor and advancing the glory of his country, in a career of forty years in the Army of the United States he rendered himself signal and illustrious. An unbroken current of success and victory, terminated by an achievement unsurpassed in our annals, left nothing to be accomplished for his military fame.

His conduct and courage gave him this career of unexampled fortune, and with the crowning virtues of moderation and humanity under all circumstances, and especially in the moment of victory, revealed to his countrymen those great and good qualities which induced them unsolicited to call him from his high military command to the highest civil office of honor and trust in the Republic; not that he desired to be first, but that he was felt to be worthiest.

The simplicity of his character, the singleness of his purpose, the elevation and patriotism of his principles, his moral courage, his justice, magnanimity and benevolence, his wisdom, moderation, and power of command, while they have endeared him to the heart of the nation, add to the deep sense of the national calamity in the loss of a Chief Magistrate whom death itself could not appall in the consciousness of "having always done his duty."

The officers of the Army, of the Navy, and Marine Corps will, as a manifestation of their respect for the exalted character and eminent public services of the illustrious dead, and of their sense of the calamity the country has sustained by this afflicting dispensation of Providence, wear crape on the left arm and upon the hilt of the sword for six months.

It is further directed that funeral honors be paid at each of the military posts according to general regulations, and at navy-yards and on board all public vessels in commission, by firing thirty minute guns, commencing at meridian, on the day after the receipt of this order, and by wearing their flags at half-mast.

By order of the President:

GEORGE W. CRAWFORD,
Secretary of War.

II. The day after the receipt of this general order at each military post the troops will be paraded at 10 o'clock a. m. and the order read to them, after which all labors for the day will cease.

The national flag will be displayed at half-staff.

At dawn of day thirteen guns will be fired, and afterwards at intervals of thirty minutes between the rising and setting sun a single gun, and at the close of the day a national salute of thirty guns.

The officers of the Army will wear the badge of mourning on the left arm and on their swords and the colors of the several regiments will be put in mourning for the period of six months.

By order:

R. JONES,
Adjutant-General.

[The Secretary of the Navy made the same announcement to the Navy as that portion of the above signed by the Secretary of War.]

ORDER OF THE PRESIDENT.

[From the Daily National Intelligencer, July 12, 1850.]

WASHINGTON, *July 10, 1850.*

In consequence of the death of the President of the United States, I direct that the several Executive Departments be closed until after the funeral of the illustrious deceased, and that they, as well as the Executive Mansion, be placed in mourning, and that the several officers of the Government wear the usual badge of mourning for the term of six months.

MILLARD FILLMORE.

ACTION OF CONGRESS.

[From Senate Journal, Thirty-first Congress, first session, p. 445.]

RESOLUTION OF THE SENATE.

Whereas it has pleased Divine Providence to remove from this life Zachary Taylor, late President of the United States, the Senate, sharing in the general sorrow which this melancholy event must produce, is desirous of manifesting its sensibility on this occasion: Therefore

Resolved, That a committee consisting of Messrs. Webster, Cass, and King be appointed on the part of the Senate to meet such committee as may be appointed on the part of the House of Representatives to consider and report what measures it may be deemed proper to adopt to show the respect and affection of Congress for the memory of the illustrious deceased and to make the necessary arrangements for his funeral.

[From House Journal, Thirty-first Congress, first session, p. 1121.]

RESOLUTION OF THE HOUSE OF REPRESENTATIVES.

Whereas it has pleased Divine Providence to remove from this life Zachary Taylor, late President of the United States, the House of Representatives, sharing in the general sorrow which this melancholy event must produce, is desirous of manifesting its sensibility on the occasion: Therefore

Resolved, That a committee consisting of thirteen members be appointed on the part of this House to meet such committee as may be appointed on the part of the Senate to consider and report what measures it may be deemed proper to adopt in order to show the respect and affection of Congress for the memory of the illustrious deceased and to make the necessary arrangements for his funeral.

[The committee consisted of Messrs. Conrad, of Louisiana; McDowell, of Virginia; Winthrop, of Massachusetts; Bissell, of Illinois; Duer, of New York; Orr, of South Carolina; Breck, of Kentucky; Strong, of Pennsylvania; Vinton, of Ohio; Cabell, of Florida; Kerr, of Maryland; Stanly, of North Carolina; Littlefield, of Maine.]

OFFICIAL ARRANGEMENTS FOR THE FUNERAL.

[From the Daily National Intelligencer, July 13, 1850.]

WASHINGTON, *July 11, 1850.*

The Committee of Arrangements of the two Houses of Congress, having consulted with the family of the deceased, have concluded that the funeral of the late President be solemnized on Saturday, the 13th of July, at 12 o'clock; the religious services to be performed by the Rev. Dr. Pyne at the Executive Mansion, according to the usage of the Episcopal Church, in which church the deceased most usually worshiped; the body to be afterwards taken from the President's house to the Congress Burying Ground, accompanied by a military escort and civic procession, and deposited in the receiving tomb.

The military arrangements to be under the direction of Major-General Scott, the General Commanding in Chief of the Army of the United States, and Major-General Walter Jones, of the militia of the District of Columbia.

Commodore Warrington, the senior naval officer now in the city, to have the direction of the naval arrangements.

The marshal of the District of Columbia to have the direction of the civic procession.

All the members of the diplomatic corps, all officers of Government, the clergy of the District and elsewhere, all associations and fraternities, and citizens generally are invited to attend.

And it is respectfully recommended to the officers of the Government that they wear the usual badge of mourning.

ORDER OF THE PROCESSION.

FUNERAL ESCORT.

(In column of march.)

Composed of such corps of the Army and the militia as may be ordered or as may report themselves for duty on the occasion.

CIVIC PROCESSION.

The United States marshal of the District of Columbia and his aids.
The mayors of Washington and Georgetown.
The Committee of Arrangements of the two Houses of Congress.
The chaplains of the two Houses of Congress and the officiating clergyman of the occasion.
Attending physicians to the late President.

Pallbearers.—Hon. Henry Clay, Hon. T. H. Benton, Hon. Lewis Cass, Hon. Daniel Webster, Hon. J. M. Berrien, Hon. Truman Smith, Hon. R. C. Winthrop, Hon. Linn Boyd, Hon. James McDowell, Hon. S. F. Vinton, Hon. Hugh White, Hon. Isaac E. Holmes, G. W. P. Custis, esq., Hon. R. J. Walker, Chief Justice Cranch, Joseph Gales, esq., Major-General Jesup, Major-General Gibson, Commodore Ballard, Brigadier-General Henderson.

The horse used by General Taylor in the late war.

Family and relatives of the late President.

The President of the United States and the heads of Departments.

The Sergeant-at-Arms of the Senate.

The Senate of the United States, preceded by the President *pro tempore* and Secretary.

The Sergeant-at-Arms of the House of Representatives.

The House of Repr sentatives, preceded by their Speaker and Clerk.

The Chief Justice and associate justices of the Supreme Court of the United States and its officers.

The diplomatic corps.

Governors of States and Territories.

Ex-members of Congress.

Members of State legislatures.

District judges of the United States.

Judges of the circuit and criminal courts of the District of Columbia, with the members of the bar and officers of the courts.

The judges of the several States.

The Comptroller of the Treasury, Auditors, Treasurer, Register, Solicitor, and Commissioners of Land Office, Pensions, Indian Affairs, Patents, and Public Buildings.

The clerks, etc., of the several Departments, preceded by their respective chief clerks, and all other civil officers of the Government.

Clergy of the District of Columbia and elsewhere.

Officers and soldiers of the Revolution.

Corporate authorities of Washington.

Corporate authorities of Georgetown.

Officers and soldiers who served in the War of 1812 and in the late war.

Presidents, professors, and students of the colleges of the District of Columbia.

Such societies and fraternities as may wish to join the procession, to report to the marshal of the District, who will assign them their respective positions.

Citizens and strangers.

The procession will move from the President's house at 1 o'clock precisely, or on the conclusion of the religious services.

DANIEL WEBSTER,
Chairman of the Committee on the part of the Senate.

CHAS. M. CONRAD,
Chairman of the Committee on the part of the House of Representatives.

[From official records in the War Department.]

GENERAL ORDERS, NO. 22.

WAR DEPARTMENT, ADJUTANT-GENERAL'S OFFICE,
Washington, July 11, 1850.

The joint committees of the Congress of the United States having designated the General in Chief, Major-General Scott, to take charge of the military arrangements for the funeral ceremonies of the late President of the United States, the Secretary of War directs that the Commanding General of the Army give the necessary orders and instructions accordingly. The military arrangements will conform to the directions found in the reports of the special committees of the Senate and House of Representatives.

By order of the Secretary of War:

R. JONES, *Adjutant-General.*

GENERAL ORDERS.

HEADQUARTERS OF THE ARMY,
ADJUTANT-GENERAL'S OFFICE,
Washington, July 12, 1850.

The Major-General Commanding the Army of the United States, having been charged by the joint committees of Congress with the military preparations for the funeral honors to be paid to the illustrious statesman, soldier, and citizen, Zachary Taylor, late President of the United States, directs the following order of arrangement:

ORDER OF THE MILITARY PROCESSION.

FUNERAL ESCORT.

(In column of march.)

Infantry.—Maryland volunteers; volunteer troops from other States; battalion of volunteers from the District of Columbia.

Firing party (to be commanded by an officer of the Army).—Two companies of volunteers from Washington; two companies of volunteers from Baltimore; battalion of United States marines; battalion of United States artillery, as infantry; troop of United States light artillery.

Dismounted officers of volunteers, Marine Corps, Navy, and Army, in the order named.

Mounted officers of volunteers, Marine Corps, Navy, and Army, in the order named.

Major-General Walter Jones, commanding the militia; aids-de-camp.

Major-General Winfield Scott, commanding the Army; aids-de-camp.

The troops will be formed in line in the Avenue, north of the President's mansion, precisely at 11 o'clock a. m., Saturday, the 13th instant, with the right (Brevet Major Sedgwick's troop of light artillery) resting opposite the War Department.

The procession will move at 1 o'clock p. m., when minute guns will be fired by detachments of artillery stationed near St. John's church, the City Hall, and the Capitol, respectively.

On arriving on the north front of the Congressional Burial Ground the escort will be formed in two lines, the first consisting of the firing party, facing the cemetery and 30 paces from it; the second composed of the rest of the infantry, 20 paces in rear; the battery of artillery to take position on the rising ground 100 paces in rear of the second line.

At sunrise to-morrow (the 13th instant) a Federal salute will be fired from the military stations in the vicinity of Washington, minute guns between the hours of 1 and 3, and a national salute at the setting of the sun.

The usual badge of mourning will be worn on the left arm and on the hilt of the sword.

The Adjutant-General of the Army is charged with the details of the military arrangements of the day, aided by the Assistant Adjutants-General on duty at Washington, by Brevet Lieutenant-Colonel Swords, of the staff, and Lieutenant W. T. Sherman, Third Artillery.

The United States marshal of the District of Columbia having been charged with the direction of the civic procession, the military will co-operate in the general order of arrangements.

By command of Major-General Scott:

R. JONES,
Adjutant-General.

[From the Daily National Intelligencer, July 12, 1850.]

GENERAL ORDER.

The major-general, zealous to execute the honorable commission in which the joint committees of Congress have associated him with the General in Chief of the Army, deems it proper and conducive to the end in view to make the best preparation in his power for carrying into effect the field arrangements of the military movements in the procession of the funeral of the late President, arrangements which must necessarily await the arrival of the General in Chief. For that purpose he thinks it expedient to appoint a general rendezvous where all the corps and companies of militia, including all who may march from any of the States with those of this District, may assemble at an early hour in the morning of Saturday, the 13th instant, and there receive final orders for being formed and posted. They are therefore requested to take notice that such rendezvous is in front of the City Hall. The corps and companies from the States are requested to repair to this general rendezvous immediately on arrival; those of the District not later than 9 o'clock a. m. The commandants of corps and companies are expected to report, immediately on arriving at the rendezvous, to the major-general or such staff officer as may be detailed for the purpose, the strength of their respective commands.

All officers not on duty in their respective corps or companies are requested to appear in full uniform and mounted. The post intended for them is in the personal suite of the General in Chief. The major-general knows of no more honorable or more interesting post that he could assign them in time of peace than that of following the lead of the renowned Scott in the procession of the funeral of the renowned Taylor.

WALTER JONES,
Major-General Militia District of Columbia.

RESOLUTION OF CONDOLENCE BY CONGRESS.

[From original in the State Department.]

A RESOLUTION expressing the condolence of Congress for Mrs. Margaret S. Taylor.

Resolved by the Senate and House of Representatives of the United States of America in Congress assembled, That the President of the United States be requested to transmit a copy of the proceedings of the two Houses on the 10th instant in relation to the death of the late President of the United States to Mrs. Margaret S. Taylor, and to assure her of the profound respect of the two Houses of Congress for her person and character and of their sincere condolence on the late afflicting dispensation of Providence.

Millard Fillmore

July 10, 1850, to March 4, 1853

SEE ENCYCLOPEDIC INDEX.

The Encyclopedic Index is not only an index to the other volumes, not only a key that unlocks the treasures of the entire publication, but it is in itself an alphabetically arranged brief history or story of the great controlling events constituting the History of the United States.

Under its proper alphabetical classification the story is told of every great subject referred to by any of the Presidents in their official Messages, and at the end of each article the official utterances of the Presidents themselves are cited upon the subject, so that you may readily turn to the page in the body of the work itself for this original information.

Next to the possession of knowledge is the ability to turn at will to where knowledge is to be found.

OLD HOME AT BUFFALO, NEW YORK, OF

MILLARD FILLMORE

With official portrait engraved from copy of original in steel

Millard Fillmore

Millard Fillmore

MILLARD FILLMORE was born February 7, 1800, in the township of Locke (now Summerhill), Cayuga County, N. Y. He was the second son of Nathaniel Fillmore and Phœbe Millard. His ancestors served with distinction in the French and Revolutionary wars. He attended the primitive schools in the neighborhood three months in the year, devoting the other nine to working on his father's farm. His father, having formed a distaste for farming, was desirous that his sons should follow other occupations. Accordingly, Millard, after serving an apprenticeship for a few months, began in 1815 the business of carding and dressing cloth. Was afterwards a school-teacher. In 1819 decided to become a lawyer, and in 1823, although he had not completed the usual course required, was admitted as an attorney by the court of common pleas of Erie County. February 5, 1826, was married to Miss Abigail Powers, daughter of a clergyman. In 1827 was admitted as an attorney and two years later as counselor before the supreme court. In 1830 removed to Buffalo and became a successful lawyer. His political career began and ended with the birth and extinction of the Whig party. Was elected to the legislature of his State in 1828, and served three terms; while there he was distinguished by his advocacy of the act to abolish imprisonment for debt, which passed in 1831. In 1832 was elected to Congress, and after serving one term retired till 1836, when he was reelected, and again returned in 1838 and 1840, declining a renomination in 1842. Was the author of the tariff of 1842. He retired from Congress in 1843. Was an unsuccessful candidate for Vice-President before the Whig convention at Baltimore in 1844. Was nominated by acclamation for governor of New York in the following September, but was defeated by Silas Wright. In 1847 was elected comptroller of the State. In 1848 was nominated by the Whigs for Vice-President on the ticket with General Taylor and was elected in the following November. He presided as Vice-President with strict impartiality during exciting debates in the Senate. By the death of President Taylor became President July 10, 1850. Was a candidate for President at the Whig convention in 1852, but General Scott received the nomination. Three weeks after the close of his Administration his wife died. Afterwards married Caroline C. McIntosh, who survived him. In 1856, while in Rome, he was nominated for the Presidency by the

American (Whig) party, but was defeated by Mr. Buchanan. After his retirement from office he resided in Buffalo the remainder of his life. He established the Buffalo Historical Society. Was called upon to welcome distinguished visitors to his city, and frequently presided over conventions and other public meetings, but held no office after retiring from the Presidency. He again visited Europe in 1866. Died at Buffalo, N. Y., March 8, 1874, and was buried in that city in Forest Lawn Cemetery.

SPECIAL MESSAGES.

WASHINGTON, *July 10, 1850.*

Fellow-Citizens of the Senate and House of Representatives:

A great man has fallen among us, and a whole country is called to an occasion of unexpected, deep, and general mourning.

I recommend to the two Houses of Congress to adopt such measures as in their discretion may seem proper to perform with due solemnities the funeral obsequies of Zachary Taylor, late President of the United States, and thereby to signify the great and affectionate regard of the American people for the memory of one whose life has been devoted to the public service, whose career in arms has not been surpassed in usefulness or brilliancy, who has been so recently raised by the unsolicited voice of the people to the highest civil authority in the Government, which he administered with so much honor and advantage to his country, and by whose sudden death so many hopes of future usefulness have been blighted forever.

To you, Senators and Representatives of a nation in tears, I can say nothing which can alleviate the sorrow with which you are oppressed. I appeal to you to aid me, under the trying circumstances which surround me, in the discharge of the duties from which, however much I may be oppressed by them, I dare not shrink; and I rely upon Him who holds in His hands the destinies of nations to endow me with the requisite strength for the task and to avert from our country the evils apprehended from the heavy calamity which has befallen us.

I shall most readily concur in whatever measures the wisdom of the two Houses may suggest as befitting this deeply melancholy occasion.

MILLARD FILLMORE.

WASHINGTON, *July 15, 1850.*

To the Senate of the United States:

I transmit to the Senate, for its consideration with a view to ratification, a treaty between the United States and the Republic of Peru, signed in this city on the 13th instant by the plenipotentiaries of the parties,

A report from the Secretary of State relative to the treaty, and the documents therein referred to, are also herewith transmitted.

MILLARD FILLMORE.

WASHINGTON, *July 17, 1850*.

To the Senate of the United States:

In further answer to a resolution of the Senate of the 27th ultimo, in reference to a proclamation issued by the military officer commanding in New Mexico and other matters, I herewith transmit a report from the Secretary of War, communicating information not received at the Department until after the date of his report of the 1st instant on this subject.

MILLARD FILLMORE.

WASHINGTON, *July 17, 1850*.

To the Senate of the United States:

In answer to a resolution of the Senate of the 1st instant, requesting the President to furnish the Senate with "the report and map of Lieutenant J. D. Webster, Corps of Topographical Engineers, of a survey of the Gulf coast at the mouth of the Rio Grande and its vicinity," and in compliance therewith, I transmit herewith a report from the Secretary of War, accompanied by the report and map above referred to.

MILLARD FILLMORE.

WASHINGTON, *July 18, 1850*.

To the House of Representatives of the United States:

I herewith transmit to the House of Representatives, in compliance with the request contained in their resolution of the 24th day of January last, the information asked for by that resolution, relating to certain proceedings of the British Government in the forcible seizure and occupation of the island of Tigre; also all the "facts, circumstances, and communications within the knowledge of the Executive relative to any seizure or occupation, or attempted seizure or occupation, by the British Government of any port, river, town, territory, or island belonging to or claimed by any of the States of Central America."

The resolution of the House speaks of the island of Tigre, in the State of Nicaragua. I am not aware of the existence of any such island in that State, and presume that the resolution refers to the island of the same name in the Gulf of Fonseca, in the State of Honduras.

The concluding part of the resolution, requesting the President to communicate to the House all treaties not heretofore published which may have been negotiated with any of the States of Central America "by any person acting by authority of the late Administration or under the auspices of the present Administration," so far as it has reference to treaties negotiated with any of those States by instructions from this Government, can not be complied with, inasmuch as those treaties have not been acted upon by the Senate of the United States, and are now in the possession of that body, to whom by the Constitution they are directed to be transmitted for advice in regard to their ratification.

But as its communication is not liable to the same objection, I transmit for the information of the House a copy of a treaty in regard to a ship canal across the Isthmus, negotiated by Elijah Hise, our late chargé d'affaires in Guatemala, with the Government of Nicaragua on the 21st day of June, 1849, accompanied by copies of his instructions from and correspondence with the Department of State.

I shall cheerfully comply with the request of the House of Representatives to lay before them the treaties negotiated with the States of Central America, now before the Senate, whenever it shall be compatible with the public interest to make the communication. For the present I communicate herewith a copy of the treaty with Great Britain and of the correspondence between the American Secretary of State and the British plenipotentiary at the time it was concluded. The ratifications of it were exchanged at Washington on the 4th day of July instant.

I also transmit the report of the Secretary of State, to whom the resolution of the House was referred, and who conducted the negotiations relative to Central America, under the direction of my lamented predecessor.

MILLARD FILLMORE.

WASHINGTON, *July 20, 1850.*

To the Senate of the United States:

I herewith transmit to the Senate, with a view to its ratification, a convention between the United States and the Mexican Republic for the extradition of fugitives from justice. This convention was negotiated under the directions of my predecessor, and was signed this day by John M. Clayton, Secretary of State, on the part of the United States, and by Señor Don Luis de la Rosa, envoy extraordinary and minister plenipotentiary of Mexico, on the part of that Republic. The length of the boundary line between the two countries, extending, as it does, from the Pacific to the Gulf, renders such a convention indispensable to the maintenance of good order and the amicable relations now so happily subsisting between the sister Republics.

MILLARD FILLMORE.

WASHINGTON, *July 23, 1850.*

To the Senate of the United States:

I lay before the Senate, for their consideration and advice as to its ratification, a treaty concluded in the city of Washington on the 1st day of

April, 1850, by and between Ardavan S. Loughery, commissioner on the part of the United States, and delegates of the Wyandott tribe of Indians.

I also lay before the Senate a letter from the Secretary of the Interior and the papers therein referred to.

MILLARD FILLMORE.

WASHINGTON, *July 30, 1850*.

To the Senate of the United States:

I herewith transmit to the Senate, in answer to its resolution of the 5th instant, requesting the President to communicate to that body "any information, if any has been received by the Government, showing that an American vessel has been recently stopped upon the high seas and searched by a British ship of war," the accompanying copies of papers. The Government has no knowledge of any alleged stopping or searching on the high seas of American vessels by British ships of war except in the cases therein mentioned. The circumstances of these cases will appear by the inclosed correspondence, taken from the files of the Navy Department. No remonstrance or complaint by the owners of these vessels has been presented to the Government of the United States.

MILLARD FILLMORE.

WASHINGTON, *August 2, 1850*.

To the Senate of the United States:

I have the honor to transmit herewith a report of the Secretary of War, in answer to a resolution of the Senate passed on the 8th of July last, calling for information in relation to the removal of Fort Polk, etc. The documents accompanying the report contain all the information required by the resolution.

MILLARD FILLMORE.

WASHINGTON, *August 6, 1850*.

To the Senate and House of Representatives:

I herewith transmit to the two Houses of Congress a letter from his excellency the governor of Texas, dated on the 14th day of June last, addressed to the late President of the United States, which, not having been answered by him, came to my hands on his death; and I also transmit a copy of the answer which I have felt it to be my duty to cause to be made to that communication.

Congress will perceive that the governor of Texas officially states that by authority of the legislature of that State he dispatched a special commissioner with full power and instructions to extend the civil jurisdiction of the State over the unorganized counties of El Paso, Worth, Presidio, and Santa Fe, situated on its northwestern limits.

He proceeds to say that the commissioner had reported to him in an official form that the military officers employed in the service of the United States stationed at Santa Fe interposed adversely with the inhabitants to the fulfillment of his object in favor of the establishment of a separate State government east of the Rio Grande, and within the rightful limits of the State of Texas. These four counties, which Texas thus proposes to establish and organize as being within her own jurisdiction, extend over the whole of the territory east of the Rio Grande, which has heretofore been regarded as an essential and integral part of the department of New Mexico, and actually governed and possessed by her people until conquered and severed from the Republic of Mexico by the American arms.

The legislature of Texas has been called together by her governor for the purpose, as is understood, of maintaining her claim to the territory east of the Rio Grande and of establishing over it her own jurisdiction and her own laws by force.

These proceedings of Texas may well arrest the attention of all branches of the Government of the United States, and I rejoice that they occur while the Congress is yet in session. It is, I fear, far from being impossible that, in consequence of these proceedings of Texas, a crisis may be brought on which shall summon the two Houses of Congress, and still more emphatically the executive government, to an immediate readiness for the performance of their respective duties.

By the Constitution of the United States the President is constituted Commander in Chief of the Army and Navy, and of the militia of the several States when called into the actual service of the United States. The Constitution declares also that he shall take care that the laws be faithfully executed and that he shall from time to time give to the Congress information of the state of the Union.

Congress has power by the Constitution to provide for calling forth the militia to execute the laws of the Union, and suitable and appropriate acts of Congress have been passed as well for providing for calling forth the militia as for placing other suitable and efficient means in the hands of the President to enable him to discharge the constitutional functions of his office.

The second section of the act of the 28th of February, 1795, declares that whenever the laws of the United States shall be opposed or their execution obstructed in any State by combinations too powerful to be suppressed by the ordinary course of judicial proceedings or the power vested in the marshals, the President may call forth the militia, as far as may be necessary, to suppress such combinations and to cause the laws to be duly executed.

By the act of March 3, 1807, it is provided that in all cases of obstruction to the laws either of the United States or any individual State or Territory, where it is lawful for the President to call forth the militia for the purpose of causing the laws to be duly executed, it shall be lawful for him to employ for the same purposes such part of the land or naval force of the United States as shall be judged necessary.

These several enactments are now in full force, so that if the laws of the United States are opposed or obstructed in any State or Territory by combinations too powerful to be suppressed by the judicial or civil authorities it becomes a case in which it is the duty of the President either to call out the militia or to employ the military and naval force of the United States, or to do both if in his judgment the exigency of the occasion shall so require, for the purpose of suppressing such combinations. The constitutional duty of the President is plain and peremptory and the authority vested in him by law for its performance clear and ample.

Texas is a State, authorized to maintain her own laws so far as they are not repugnant to the Constitution, laws, and treaties of the United States; to suppress insurrections against her authority, and to punish those who may commit treason against the State according to the forms provided by her own constitution and her own laws.

But all this power is local and confined entirely within the limits of Texas herself. She can possibly confer no authority which can be lawfully exercised beyond her own boundaries.

All this is plain, and hardly needs argument or elucidation. If Texas militia, therefore, march into any one of the other States or into any Territory of the United States, there to execute or enforce any law of Texas, they become at that moment trespassers; they are no longer under the protection of any lawful authority, and are to be regarded merely as intruders; and if within such State or Territory they obstruct any law of the United States, either by power of arms or mere power of numbers, constituting such a combination as is too powerful to be suppressed by the civil authority, the President of the United States has no option left to him, but is bound to obey the solemn injunction of the Constitution and exercise the high powers vested in him by that instrument and by the acts of Congress.

Or if any civil posse, armed or unarmed, enter into any Territory of the United States, under the protection of the laws thereof, with intent to seize individuals, to be carried elsewhere for trial for alleged offenses, and this posse be too powerful to be resisted by the local civil authorities, such seizure or attempt to seize is to be prevented or resisted by the authority of the United States.

The grave and important question now arises whether there be in the Territory of New Mexico any existing law of the United States opposition to which or the obstruction of which would constitute a case calling for the interposition of the authority vested in the President.

The Constitution of the United States declares that—

This Constitution, and the laws of the United States which shall be made in pursuance thereof, and all treaties made, or which shall be made, under the authority of the United States, shall be the supreme law of the land.

If, therefore, New Mexico be a Territory of the United States, and if any treaty stipulation be in force therein, such treaty stipulation is the supreme law of the land, and is to be maintained and upheld accordingly.

In the letter to the governor of Texas my reasons are given for believing that New Mexico is now a Territory of the United States, with the same extent and the same boundaries which belonged to it while in the actual possession of the Republic of Mexico, and before the late war. In the early part of that war both California and New Mexico were conquered by the arms of the United States, and were in the military possession of the United States at the date of the treaty of peace.

By that treaty the title by conquest was confirmed and these territories, provinces, or departments separated from Mexico forever, and by the same treaty certain important rights and securities were solemnly guaranteed to the inhabitants residing therein.

By the fifth article of the treaty it is declared that—

> The boundary line between the two Republics shall commence in the Gulf of Mexico 3 leagues from land, opposite the mouth of the Rio Grande, otherwise called Rio Bravo del Norte, or opposite the mouth of its deepest branch if it should have more than one branch emptying directly into the sea; from thence up the middle of that river, following the deepest channel where it has more than one, to the point where it strikes the southern boundary of New Mexico; thence westwardly, along the whole southern boundary of New Mexico (which runs north of the town called Paso) to its western termination; thence northward along the western line of New Mexico until it intersects the first branch of the river Gila (or, if it should not intersect any branch of that river, then to the point on the said line nearest to such branch, and thence in a direct line to the same); thence down the middle of the said branch and of the said river until it empties into the Rio Colorado; thence across the Rio Colorado, following the division line between Upper and Lower California, to the Pacific Ocean.

The eighth article of the treaty is in the following terms:

> Mexicans now established in territories previously belonging to Mexico, and which remain for the future within the limits of the United States as defined by the present treaty, shall be free to continue where they now reside or to remove at any time to the Mexican Republic, retaining the property which they possess in the said territories, or disposing thereof and removing the proceeds wherever they please without their being subjected on this account to any contribution, tax, or charge whatever.
>
> Those who shall prefer to remain in the said territories may either retain the title and rights of Mexican citizens or acquire those of citizens of the United States; but they shall be under the obligation to make their election within one year from the date of the exchange of ratifications of this treaty; and those who shall remain in the said territories after the expiration of that year without having declared their intention to retain the character of Mexicans shall be considered to have elected to become citizens of the United States.
>
> In the said territories property of every kind now belonging to Mexicans not established there shall be inviolably respected. The present owners, the heirs of these, and all Mexicans who may hereafter acquire said property by contract shall enjoy with respect to it guaranties equally ample as if the same belonged to citizens of the United States.

The ninth article of the treaty is in these words:

The Mexicans who, in the territories aforesaid, shall not preserve the character of citizens of the Mexican Republic, conformably with what is stipulated in the preceding article, shall be incorporated into the Union of the United States and be admitted at the proper time (to be judged of by the Congress of the United States) to the enjoyment of all the rights of citizens of the United States according to the principles of the Constitution, and in the meantime shall be maintained and protected in the free enjoyment of their liberty and property and secured in the free exercise of their religion without restriction.

It is plain, therefore, on the face of these treaty stipulations that all Mexicans established in territories north or east of the line of demarcation already mentioned come within the protection of the ninth article, and that the treaty, being a part of the supreme law of the land, does extend over all such Mexicans, and assures to them perfect security in the free enjoyment of their liberty and property, as well as in the free exercise of their religion; and this supreme law of the land, being thus in actual force over this territory, is to be maintained until it shall be displaced or superseded by other legal provisions; and if it be obstructed or resisted by combinations too powerful to be suppressed by the civil authority the case is one which comes within the provisions of law and which obliges the President to enforce those provisions. Neither the Constitution nor the laws nor my duty nor my oath of office leave me any alternative or any choice in my mode of action.

The executive government of the United States has no power or authority to determine what was the true line of boundary between Mexico and the United States before the treaty of Guadalupe Hidalgo, nor has it any such power now, since the question has become a question between the State of Texas and the United States. So far as this boundary is doubtful, that doubt can only be removed by some act of Congress, to which the assent of the State of Texas may be necessary, or by some appropriate mode of legal adjudication; but in the meantime, if disturbances or collisions arise or should be threatened, it is absolutely incumbent on the executive government, however painful the duty, to take care that the laws be faithfully maintained; and he can regard only the actual state of things as it existed at the date of the treaty, and is bound to protect all inhabitants who were then established and who now remain north and east of the line of demarcation in the full enjoyment of their liberty and property, according to the provisions of the ninth article of the treaty. In other words, all must be now regarded as New Mexico which was possessed and occupied as New Mexico by citizens of Mexico at the date of the treaty until a definite line of boundary shall be established by competent authority.

This assertion of duty to protect the people of New Mexico from threatened violence, or from seizure to be carried into Texas for trial for alleged offenses against Texan laws, does not at all include any claim of power on the part of the Executive to establish any civil or military government within that Territory. *That power* belongs exclusively to the legislative department, and Congress is the sole judge of the time and manner of creating or authorizing any such government.

The duty of the Executive extends only to the execution of laws and the maintenance of treaties already in force and the protection of all the people of the United States in the enjoyment of the rights which those treaties and laws guarantee.

It is exceedingly desirable that no occasion should arise for the exercise of the powers thus vested in the President by the Constitution and the laws. With whatever mildness those powers might be executed, or however clear the case of necessity, yet consequences might, nevertheless, follow of which no human sagacity can foresee either the evils or the end.

Having thus laid before Congress the communication of his excellency the governor of Texas and the answer thereto, and having made such observations as I have thought the occasion called for respecting constitutional obligations which may arise in the further progress of things and may devolve on me to be performed, I hope I shall not be regarded as stepping aside from the line of my duty, notwithstanding that I am aware that the subject is now before both Houses, if I express my deep and earnest conviction of the importance of an immediate decision or arrangement or settlement of the question of boundary between Texas and the Territory of New Mexico. All considerations of justice, general expediency, and domestic tranquillity call for this. It seems to be in its character and by position the first, or one of the first, of the questions growing out of the acquisition of California and New Mexico, and now requiring decision.

No government can be established for New Mexico, either State or Territorial, until it shall be first ascertained what New Mexico is, and what are her limits and boundaries. These can not be fixed or known till the line of division between her and Texas shall be ascertained and established; and numerous and weighty reasons conspire, in my judgment, to show that this divisional line should be established by Congress with the assent of the government of Texas. In the first place, this seems by far the most prompt mode of proceeding by which the end can be accomplished. If judicial proceedings were resorted to, such proceedings would necessarily be slow, and years would pass by, in all probability, before the controversy could be ended. So great a delay in this case is to be avoided if possible. Such delay would be every way inconvenient, and might be the occasion of disturbances and collisions. For the same reason I would, with the utmost deference to the wisdom of Congress, express a doubt of the expediency of the appointment of commissioners, and of an examination, estimate, and an award of indemnity to be made by them. This would be but a species of arbitration, which might last as long as a suit at law.

So far as I am able to comprehend the case, the general facts are now all known, and Congress is as capable of deciding on it justly and properly now as it probably would be after the report of the commissioners. If the claim of title on the part of Texas appears to Congress to be well founded in whole or in part, it is in the competency of Congress to offer her an indemnity for the surrender of that claim. In a case like this, surrounded, as it is, by many cogent considerations, all calling for amicable adjustment and immediate settlement, the Government of the United States would be justified, in my opinion, in allowing an indemnity to Texas, not unreasonable or extravagant, but fair, liberal, and awarded in a just spirit of accommodation.

I think no event would be hailed with more gratification by the people of the United States than the amicable adjustment of questions of difficulty which have now for a long time agitated the country and occupied, to the exclusion of other subjects, the time and attention of Congress.

Having thus freely communicated the results of my own reflections on the most advisable mode of adjusting the boundary question, I shall nevertheless cheerfully acquiesce in any other mode which the wisdom of Congress may devise. And in conclusion I repeat my conviction that every consideration of the public interest manifests the necessity of a provision by Congress for the settlement of this boundary question before the present session be brought to a close. The settlement of other questions connected with the same subject within the same period is greatly to be desired, but the adjustment of this appears to me to be in the highest degree important. In the train of such an adjustment we may well hope that there will follow a return of harmony and good will, an increased attachment to the Union, and the general satisfaction of the country.

MILLARD FILLMORE.

WASHINGTON, *August 8, 1850.*

To the Senate and House of Representatives:

It has been suggested that the language in the first paragraph of my message to the two Houses of Congress of the 6th instant may convey the idea that Governor Bell's letter to my predecessor was received by him before his death. It was addressed to him, but appears, in point of fact, to have been sent to me from the post-office after his death.

I make this communication to accompany the message and prevent misapprehension.

MILLARD FILLMORE.

WASHINGTON, *August 10, 1850.*

To the Senate of the United States:

I transmit herewith a communication from the Department of the Interior and the papers which accompanied it, being the first part of the results of investigations by Henry R. Schoolcraft, esq., under the provisions of an act of Congress approved March 3, 1847, requiring the Secretary of War "to collect and digest such statistics and materials as may illustrate the history, the present condition, and future prospects of the Indian tribes of the United States."

MILLARD FILLMORE.

WASHINGTON, *August 24, 1850.*

To the Senate of the United States:

I have the honor to transmit herewith a report submitted by the Secretary of the Treasury, to whom was referred the resolution of the Senate of the 31st July last, requesting to be furnished with certain information in relation to the commerce, etc., of the district of Brazos Santiago, in Texas.

MILLARD FILLMORE.

WASHINGTON, *August 26, 1850.*

To the Senate of the United States:

I have the honor to inclose herewith a letter just received from the Secretary of War, transmitting a communication from the Colonel of the Corps of Topographical Engineers, with accompanying papers, which he requests may be taken as a supplement to the "report and map of Lieutenant J. D. Webster, Corps of Topographical Engineers, of a survey of the Gulf coast at the mouth of the Rio Grande and its vicinity," called for by a resolution of the Senate of the 1st of July last.

MILLARD FILLMORE.

WASHINGTON, *September 2, 1850.*

To the Senate of the United States:

I have the honor herewith to transmit to your honorable body a report from the Secretary of the Navy, accompanied by copies of the correspondence relating to the resignation of Edward C. Anderson, a lieutenant in the Navy, in answer to a resolution of the Senate of August 28, 1850, adopted in executive session.

MILLARD FILLMORE.

WASHINGTON, *September 9, 1850.*

To the Senate of the United States:

In answer to a resolution of the Senate of the 5th instant, I have the honor herewith to transmit to the Senate a letter from the Secretary of State, accompanied by a copy of the report of the commissioner to China made in pursuance of the provisions of the act to carry into effect certain provisions of the treaties between the United States and China and the Ottoman Porte, giving certain judicial powers, etc.

MILLARD FILLMORE.

WASHINGTON, *September 9, 1850.*

To the Senate of the United States:

In compliance with the request of the Hon. Manuel Alvarez, acting governor, etc., I have the honor to transmit to the Senate herewith a copy of the constitution recently adopted by the inhabitants of New Mexico, together with a digest of the votes for and against it.

Congress having just passed a bill providing a Territorial government for New Mexico, I do not deem it advisable to submit any recommendation on the subject of a State government.

MILLARD FILLMORE.

WASHINGTON, *September 12, 1850.*

The SPEAKER OF THE HOUSE OF REPRESENTATIVES.

SIR: In answer to a resolution of the House of Representatives adopted September 2, 1850, calling upon me to communicate the full and exact cost of each of the lines of mail steamers now in service, etc., I have the honor to transmit herewith reports from the Secretary of the Navy and Postmaster-General, containing the desired information.

MILLARD FILLMORE.

WASHINGTON, *September 16, 1850.*

To the Senate of the United States:

In answer to a resolution of the Senate of the 9th instant, adopted in executive session, asking information in reference to the nomination of John Howard Payne as consul to Tunis, I have the honor to transmit a report from the Secretary of State, giving the desired information.

MILLARD FILLMORE.

WASHINGTON, *September 23, 1850.*

To the Senate and House of Representatives:

Having been informed that it is the wish of the family and relatives of the late lamented President of the United States that his remains should be removed to the State of Kentucky, and being desirous of manifesting the most sincere and profound respect for the character of the deceased, in which I doubt not Congress will fully concur, I have felt it to be my duty to make known to you the wishes of the family, that you might previous to your adjournment adopt such proceedings and take such order on the subject as in your wisdom may seem meet and proper on the occasion.

MILLARD FILLMORE.

[The remains of the late President of the United States were removed from Washington to Louisville, Ky., October 25, 1850.]

WASHINGTON, *September 27, 1850.*

To the Senate of the United States:

I herewith transmit to the Senate, in answer to their resolution of the 23d instant, a report from the Secretary of State, with the papers* therein referred to.

MILLARD FILLMORE.

WASHINGTON, *September 28, 1850.*

To the Senate of the United States:

In answer to your resolution of the 24th instant, expressing an opinion adverse to the alleged resignation of Lieutenant Anderson, of the Navy, I have the honor herewith to transmit a report from the Secretary of the Navy, accompanied by the correspondence in reference to such resignation.

Regarding the opinion of the Senate in this matter with the most profound respect, I have given to the subject the most anxious consideration, and submitted the question to the deliberation of my Cabinet, and after a careful examination of the whole correspondence they are unanimously of opinion that Lieutenant Anderson tendered his resignation, which was duly accepted, and that he was therefore rightfully dropped from the Register. I concur fully in this opinion. With these convictions I feel compelled to adhere to the decision of my lamented predecessor, and can only regret that I have the misfortune in this instance to differ from those for whom, individually and collectively, I entertain the highest respect.

MILLARD FILLMORE.

PROCLAMATION.

BY THE PRESIDENT OF THE UNITED STATES OF AMERICA.

A PROCLAMATION.

Whereas by an act of the Congress of the United States of the 24th of May, 1828, entitled "An act in addition to an act entitled 'An act concerning discriminating duties of tonnage and impost' and to equalize the duties on Prussian vessels and their cargoes," it is provided that upon satisfactory evidence being given to the President of the United States by the government of any foreign nation that no discriminating duties of tonnage or impost are imposed or levied in the ports of the said nation upon vessels wholly belonging to citizens of the United States, or upon the produce, manufactures, or merchandise imported in the same from the United States or from any foreign country, the President is thereby authorized to issue his proclamation declaring that the foreign discriminating duties of tonnage and impost within the United States

*Communications from the United States minister to Turkey relative to the Hungarian exiles.

are and shall be suspended and discontinued so far as respects the vessels of the said foreign nation and the produce, manufactures, or merchandise imported into the United States in the same from the said foreign nation or from any other foreign country, the said suspension to take effect from the time of such notification being given to the President of the United States and to continue so long as the reciprocal exemption of vessels belonging to citizens of the United States and their cargoes, as aforesaid, shall be continued, and no longer; and

Whereas satisfactory evidence has lately been received by me from the Government of the Republic of Chile, through an official communication of Señor Don Manuel Carvallo, accredited to this Government as envoy extraordinary and minister plenipotentiary of that Republic, under date of the 31st of October, 1850, that no other or higher duties of tonnage and impost are imposed or levied in the ports of Chile upon vessels wholly belonging to citizens of the United States and upon the produce, manufactures, or merchandise imported in the same from the United States and from any foreign country whatever than are levied on Chilean ships and their cargoes in the same ports and under like circumstances:

Now, therefore, I, Millard Fillmore, President of the United States of America, do hereby declare and proclaim that so much of the several acts imposing discriminating duties of tonnage and impost within the United States are and shall be suspended and discontinued so far as respects the vessels of Chile and the produce, manufactures, and merchandise imported into the United States in the same from Chile and from any other foreign country whatever, the said suspension to take effect from the day above mentioned and to continue thenceforward so long as the reciprocal exemption of the vessels of the United States and the produce, manufactures, and merchandise imported into Chile in the same, as aforesaid, shall be continued on the part of the Government of Chile.

Given under my hand, at the city of Washington, this 1st day of November, A. D. 1850, and the seventy-fifth of the Independence of the United States.

MILLARD FILLMORE.

By the President:

W. S. DERRICK, *Acting Secretary of State.*

FIRST ANNUAL MESSAGE.

WASHINGTON, *December 2, 1850.*

Fellow-Citizens of the Senate and of the House of Representatives:

Being suddenly called in the midst of the last session of Congress by a painful dispensation of Divine Providence to the responsible station which I now hold, I contented myself with such communications to the Legislature as the exigency of the moment seemed to require. The country was shrouded in mourning for the loss of its venerable Chief Magistrate and all hearts were penetrated with grief. Neither the time nor the occasion appeared to require or to justify on my part any general expression of political opinions or any announcement of the principles which would govern me in the discharge of the duties to the performance of which I had been so unexpectedly called. I trust, therefore, that it may not be deemed inappropriate if I avail myself of this opportunity of the reassembling of Congress to make known my sentiments in a general manner in regard to the policy which ought to be pursued by the Government both in its intercourse with foreign nations and its management and administration of internal affairs.

Nations, like individuals in a state of nature, are equal and independent, possessing certain rights and owing certain duties to each other, arising from their necessary and unavoidable relations; which rights and duties there is no common human authority to protect and enforce. Still, they are rights and duties, binding in morals, in conscience, and in honor, although there is no tribunal to which an injured party can appeal but the disinterested judgment of mankind, and ultimately the arbitrament of the sword.

Among the acknowledged rights of nations is that which each possesses of establishing that form of government which it may deem most conducive to the happiness and prosperity of its own citizens, of changing that form as circumstances may require, and of managing its internal affairs according to its own will. The people of the United States claim this right for themselves, and they readily concede it to others. Hence it becomes an imperative duty not to interfere in the government or internal policy of other nations; and although we may sympathize with the unfortunate or the oppressed everywhere in their struggles for freedom, our principles forbid us from taking any part in such foreign contests. We make no wars to promote or to prevent successions to thrones, to maintain any theory of a balance of power, or to suppress the actual government which any country chooses to establish for itself. We instigate no revolutions, nor suffer any hostile military expeditions to be fitted out in the United States to invade the territory or provinces of a friendly nation. The great law of morality ought to have a national as well as a personal and individual application. We should act toward other nations as we wish them to act toward us, and justice and conscience should form the rule of conduct between governments, instead of mere power, self-interest, or the desire of aggrandizement. To maintain a strict neutrality in foreign wars, to cultivate friendly relations, to reciprocate every noble and generous act, and to perform punctually and scrupulously every treaty obligation—these are the duties which we owe to other states, and by the performance of which we best entitle ourselves to like treatment from them; or, if that, in any case, be refused, we can enforce our own rights with justice and a clear conscience.

In our domestic policy the Constitution will be my guide, and in questions of doubt I shall look for its interpretation to the judicial decisions of that tribunal which was established to expound it and to the usage of the Government, sanctioned by the acquiescence of the country. I regard all its provisions as equally binding. In all its parts it is the will of the people expressed in the most solemn form, and the constituted authorities are but agents to carry that will into effect. Every power which it has granted is to be exercised for the public good; but no pretense of utility, no honest conviction, even, of what might be expedient, can justify the assumption of any power not granted. The powers conferred upon the Government and their distribution to the several departments are as clearly expressed in that sacred instrument as the imperfection of human language will allow, and I deem it my first duty not to question its wisdom, add to its provisions, evade its requirements, or nullify its commands.

Upon you, fellow-citizens, as the representatives of the States and the people, is wisely devolved the legislative power. I shall comply with my duty in laying before you from time to time any information calculated to enable you to discharge your high and responsible trust for the benefit of our common constituents.

My opinions will be frankly expressed upon the leading subjects of legislation; and if—which I do not anticipate—any act should pass the two Houses of Congress which should appear to me unconstitutional, or an encroachment on the just powers of other departments, or with provisions hastily adopted and likely to produce consequences injurious and unforeseen, I should not shrink from the duty of returning it to you, with my reasons, for your further consideration. Beyond the due performance of these constitutional obligations, both my respect for the Legislature and my sense of propriety will restrain me from any attempt to control or influence your proceedings. With you is the power, the honor, and the responsibility of the legislation of the country.

The Government of the United States is a limited Government. It is confined to the exercise of powers expressly granted and such others as may be necessary for carrying those powers into effect; and it is at all times an especial duty to guard against any infringement on the just rights of the States. Over the objects and subjects intrusted to Congress its legislative authority is supreme. But here that authority ceases, and every citizen who truly loves the Constitution and desires the continuance of its existence and its blessings will resolutely and firmly resist any interference in those domestic affairs which the Constitution has clearly and unequivocally left to the exclusive authority of the States. And every such citizen will also deprecate useless irritation among the several members of the Union and all reproach and crimination tending to alienate one portion of the country from another. The beauty of our system of government consists, and its safety and durability must consist, in avoiding mutual collisions and encroachments and in the regular separate action of all, while each is revolving in its own distinct orbit.

The Constitution has made it the duty of the President to take care that the laws be faithfully executed. In a government like ours, in which all laws are passed by a majority of the representatives of the people, and these representatives are chosen for such short periods that any injurious or obnoxious law can very soon be repealed, it would appear unlikely that any great numbers should be found ready to resist the execution of the laws. But it must be borne in mind that the country is extensive; that there may be local interests or prejudices rendering a law odious in one part which is not so in another, and that the thoughtless and inconsiderate, misled by their passions or their imaginations, may be induced madly to resist such laws as they disapprove. Such persons should recollect that without law there can be no real practical liberty; that when law is trampled under foot tyranny rules, whether it appears in the form of a military despotism or of popular violence. The law is the only sure protection of the weak and the only efficient restraint upon the strong. When impartially and faithfully administered, none is beneath its protection and none above its control. You, gentlemen, and the country may be assured that to the utmost of my ability and to the extent of the power vested in me I shall at all times and in all places take care that the laws be faithfully executed. In the discharge of this duty, solemnly imposed upon me by the Constitution and by my oath of office, I shall shrink from no responsibility, and shall endeavor to meet events as they may arise with firmness, as well as with prudence and discretion.

The appointing power is one of the most delicate with which the Executive is invested. I regard it as a sacred trust, to be exercised with the sole view of advancing the prosperity and happiness of the people. It shall be my effort to elevate the standard of official employment by selecting for places of importance individuals fitted for the posts to which they are assigned by their known integrity, talents, and virtues. In so extensive a country, with so great a population, and where few persons appointed to office can be known to the appointing power, mistakes will sometimes unavoidably happen and unfortunate appointments be made notwithstanding the greatest care. In such cases the power of removal may be properly exercised; and neglect of duty or malfeasance in office will be no more tolerated in individuals appointed by myself than in those appointed by others.

I am happy in being able to say that no unfavorable change in our foreign relations has taken place since the message at the opening of the last session of Congress. We are at peace with all nations and we enjoy in an eminent degree the blessings of that peace in a prosperous and growing commerce and in all the forms of amicable national intercourse. The unexampled growth of the country, the present amount of its population, and its ample means of self-protection assure for it the respect of all nations, while it is trusted that its character for justice and a regard to the rights of other States will cause that respect to be readily and cheerfully paid.

A convention was negotiated between the United States and Great Britain in April last for facilitating and protecting the construction of a ship canal between the Atlantic and Pacific oceans and for other purposes. The instrument has since been ratified by the contracting parties, the exchange of ratifications has been effected, and proclamation thereof has been duly made.

In addition to the stipulations contained in this convention, two other objects remain to be accomplished between the contracting powers:

First. The designation and establishment of a free port at each end of the canal.

Second. An agreement fixing the distance from the shore within which belligerent maritime operations shall not be carried on.

On these points there is little doubt that the two Governments will come to an understanding.

The company of citizens of the United States who have acquired from the State of Nicaragua the privilege of constructing a ship canal between the two oceans through the territory of that State have made progress in their preliminary arrangements. The treaty between the United States and Great Britain of the 19th of April last, above referred to, being now in operation, it is to be hoped that the guaranties which it offers will be sufficient to secure the completion of the work with all practicable expedition. It is obvious that this result would be indefinitely postponed if any other than peaceful measures for the purpose of harmonizing conflicting claims to territory in that quarter should be adopted. It will consequently be my endeavor to cause any further negotiations on the part of this Government which may be requisite for this purpose to be so conducted as to bring them to a speedy and successful close.

Some unavoidable delay has occurred, arising from distance and the difficulty of intercourse between this Government and that of Nicaragua, but as intelligence has just been received of the appointment of an envoy extraordinary and minister plenipotentiary of that Government to reside at Washington, whose arrival may soon be expected, it is hoped that no further impediments will be experienced in the prompt transaction of business between the two Governments.

Citizens of the United States have undertaken the connection of the two oceans by means of a railroad across the Isthmus of Tehuantepec, under grants of the Mexican Government to a citizen of that Republic. It is understood that a thorough survey of the course of the communication is in preparation, and there is every reason to expect that it will be prosecuted with characteristic energy, especially when that Government shall have consented to such stipulations with the Government of the United States as may be necessary to impart a feeling of security to those who may embark their property in the enterprise. Negotiations are pending for the accomplishment of that object, and a hope is confidently entertained that when the Government of Mexico shall become duly sensible of the advantages which that country can not fail to derive from the work, and learn that the Government of the United States desires that the right of sovereignty of Mexico in the Isthmus shall remain unimpaired, the stipulations referred to will be agreed to with alacrity.

By the last advices from Mexico it would appear, however, that that Government entertains strong objections to some of the stipulations which the parties concerned in the project of the railroad deem necessary for their protection and security. Further consideration, it is to be hoped, or some modification of terms, may yet reconcile the differences existing between the two Governments in this respect.

Fresh instructions have recently been given to the minister of the United States in Mexico, who is prosecuting the subject with promptitude and ability.

Although the negotiations with Portugal for the payment of claims of citizens of the United States against that Government have not yet resulted in a formal treaty, yet a proposition, made by the Government of Portugal for the final adjustment and payment of those claims, has recently been accepted on the part of the United States. It gives me pleasure to say that Mr. Clay, to whom the negotiation on the part of the United States had been intrusted, discharged the duties of his appointment with ability and discretion, acting always within the instructions of his Government.

It is expected that a regular convention will be immediately negotiated for carrying the agreement between the two Governments into effect.

The commissioner appointed under the act of Congress for carrying into effect the convention with Brazil of the 27th of January, 1849, has entered upon the performance of the duties imposed upon him by that act. It is hoped that those duties may be completed within the time which it prescribes. The documents, however, which the Imperial Government, by the third article of the convention, stipulates to furnish to the Government of the United States have not yet been received. As it is presumed that those documents will be essential for the correct disposition of the claims, it may become necessary for Congress to extend the period limited for the duration of the commission. The sum stipulated by the fourth article of the convention to be paid to this Government has been received.

The collection in the ports of the United States of discriminating duties upon the vessels of Chili and their cargoes has been suspended, pursuant to the provisions of the act of Congress of the 24th of May, 1828. It is to be hoped that this measure will impart a fresh impulse to the commerce between the two countries, which of late, and especially since our acquisition of California, has, to the mutual advantage of the parties, been much augmented.

Peruvian guano has become so desirable an article to the agricultural interest of the United States that it is the duty of the Government to employ all the means properly in its power for the purpose of causing that article to be imported into the country at a reasonable price. Nothing will be omitted on my part toward accomplishing this desirable end. I am persuaded that in removing any restraints on this traffic the Peruvian Government will promote its own best interests, while it will afford a proof of a friendly disposition toward this country, which will be duly appreciated.

The treaty between the United States and His Majesty the King of the Hawaiian Islands, which has recently been made public, will, it is believed, have a beneficial effect upon the relations between the two countries.

The relations between those parts of the island of St. Domingo which were formerly colonies of Spain and France, respectively, are still in an unsettled condition. The proximity of that island to the United States and the delicate questions involved in the existing controversy there render it desirable that it should be permanently and speedily adjusted. The interests of humanity and of general commerce also demand this; and as intimations of the same sentiment have been received from other governments, it is hoped that some plan may soon be devised to effect the object in a manner likely to give general satisfaction. The Government of the United States will not fail, by the exercise of all proper friendly offices, to do all in its power to put an end to the destructive war which has raged between the different parts of the island and to secure to them both the benefits of peace and commerce.

I refer you to the report of the Secretary of the Treasury for a detailed statement of the finances.

The total receipts into the Treasury for the year ending 30th of June last were $47,421,748.90.

The total expenditures during the same period were $43,002,168.90.

The public debt has been reduced since the last annual report from the Treasury Department $495,276.79.

By the nineteenth section of the act of 28th January, 1847, the proceeds of the sales of the public lands were pledged for the interest and principal of the public debt. The great amount of those lands subsequently granted by Congress for military bounties will, it is believed, very nearly supply the public demand for several years to come, and but little reliance can, therefore, be placed on that hitherto fruitful source of revenue. Aside from the permanent annual expenditures, which have necessarily largely increased, a portion of the public debt, amounting to $8,075,986.59, must be provided for within the next two fiscal years. It is most desirable that these accruing demands should be met without resorting to new loans.

All experience has demonstrated the wisdom and policy of raising a large portion of revenue for the support of Government from duties on goods imported. The power to lay these duties is unquestionable, and its chief object, of course, is to replenish the Treasury. But if in doing this an incidental advantage may be gained by encouraging the industry of our own citizens, it is our duty to avail ourselves of that advantage.

A duty laid upon an article which can not be produced in this country, such as tea or coffee, adds to the cost of the article, and is chiefly or wholly paid by the consumer. But a duty laid upon an article which may be produced here stimulates the skill and industry of our own country to produce the same article, which is brought into the market in competition with the foreign article, and the importer is thus compelled to reduce his price to that at which the domestic article can be sold, thereby throwing a part of the duty upon the producer of the foreign article. The continuance of this process creates the skill and invites the capital which finally enable us to produce the article much cheaper than it could have been procured from abroad, thereby benefiting both the producer and the consumer at home. The consequence of this is that the artisan and the agriculturist are brought together, each affords a ready market for the produce of the other, the whole country becomes prosperous, and the ability to produce every necessary of life renders us independent in war as well as in peace.

A high tariff can never be permanent. It will cause dissatisfaction, and will be changed. It excludes competition, and thereby invites the investment of capital in manufactures to such excess that when changed it brings distress, bankruptcy, and ruin upon all who have been misled by its faithless protection. What the manufacturer wants is uniformity and permanency, that he may feel a confidence that he is not to be ruined by sudden changes. But to make a tariff uniform and permanent it is not only necessary that the laws should not be altered, but that the duty should not fluctuate. To effect this all duties should be specific wherever the nature of the article is such as to admit of it. *Ad valorem* duties fluctuate with the price and offer strong temptations to fraud and perjury. Specific duties, on the contrary, are equal and uniform in all ports and at all times, and offer a strong inducement to the importer to bring the best article, as he pays no more duty upon that than upon one of inferior quality. I therefore strongly recommend a modification of the present tariff, which has prostrated some of our most important and necessary manufactures, and that specific duties be imposed sufficient to raise the requisite revenue, making such discriminations in favor of the industrial pursuits of our own country as to encourage home production without excluding foreign competition. It is also important that an unfortunate provision in the present tariff, which imposes a much higher duty upon the raw material that enters into our manufactures than upon the manufactured article, should be remedied.

The papers accompanying the report of the Secretary of the Treasury will disclose frauds attempted upon the revenue, in variety and amount so great as to justify the conclusion that it is impossible under any system of *ad valorem* duties levied upon the foreign cost or value of the article to secure an honest observance and an effectual administration of the laws. The fraudulent devices to evade the law which have been detected by the vigilance of the appraisers leave no room to doubt that similar impositions not discovered, to a large amount, have been successfully practiced since the enactment of the law now in force. This state of things has already had a prejudicial influence upon those engaged in foreign commerce. It has a tendency to drive the honest trader from the business of importing and to throw that important branch of employment into the hands of unscrupulous and dishonest men, who are alike regardless of law and the obligations of an oath. By these means the plain intentions of Congress, as expressed in the law, are daily defeated. Every motive of policy and duty, therefore, impels me to ask the earnest attention of Congress to this subject. If Congress should deem it unwise to attempt any important changes in the system of levying duties at this session, it will become indispensable to the protection of the revenue that such remedies as in the judgment of Congress may mitigate the evils complained of should be at once applied.

As before stated, specific duties would, in my opinion, afford the most perfect remedy for this evil; but if you should not concur in this view, then, as a partial remedy, I beg leave respectfully to recommend that instead of taking the invoice of the article abroad as a means of determining its value here, the correctness of which invoice it is in many cases impossible to verify, the law be so changed as to require a home valuation or appraisal, to be regulated in such manner as to give, as far as practicable, uniformity in the several ports.

There being no mint in California, I am informed that the laborers in the mines are compelled to dispose of their gold dust at a large discount. This appears to me to be a heavy and unjust tax upon the labor of those employed in extracting this precious metal, and I doubt not you will be disposed at the earliest period possible to relieve them from it by the establishment of a mint. In the meantime, as an assayer's office is established there, I would respectfully submit for your consideration the propriety of authorizing gold bullion which has been assayed and stamped to be received in payment of Government dues. I can not conceive that the Treasury would suffer any loss by such a provision, which will at once raise bullion to its par value, and thereby save (if I am rightly informed) many millions of dollars to the laborers which are now paid in brokerage to convert this precious metal into available funds. This discount upon their hard earnings is a heavy tax, and every effort should be made by the Government to relieve them from so great a burden.

More than three-fourths of our population are engaged in the cultivation of the soil. The commercial, manufacturing, and navigating interests are all to a great extent dependent on the agricultural. It is therefore the most important interest of the nation, and has a just claim to the fostering care and protection of the Government so far as they can be extended consistently with the provisions of the Constitution. As this can not be done by the ordinary modes of legislation, I respectfully recommend the establishment of an agricultural bureau, to be charged with the duty of giving to this leading branch of American industry the encouragement which it so well deserves. In view of the immense mineral resources of our country, provision should also be made for the employment of a competent mineralogist and chemist, who should be required, under the direction of the head of the bureau, to collect specimens of the various minerals of our country and to ascertain by careful analysis their respective elements and properties and their adaptation to useful purposes. He should also be required to examine and report upon the qualities of different soils and the manures best calculated to improve their productiveness. By publishing the results of such experiments, with suitable explanations, and by the collection and distribution of rare seeds and plants, with instructions as to the best system of cultivation, much may be done to promote this great national interest.

In compliance with the act of Congress passed on the 23d of May, 1850, providing, among other things, for taking the Seventh Census, a superintendent was appointed and all other measures adopted which were deemed necessary to insure the prompt and faithful performance of that duty. The appropriation already made will, it is believed, be sufficient to defray the whole expense of the work, but further legislation may be necessary in regard to the compensation of some of the marshals of the Territories. It will also be proper to make provision by law at an early day for the publication of such abstracts of the returns as the public interests may require.

The unprecedented growth of our territories on the Pacific in wealth and population and the consequent increase of their social and commercial relations with the Atlantic States seem to render it the duty of the Government to use all its constitutional power to improve the means of intercourse with them. The importance of opening "a line of communication, the best and most expeditious of which the nature of the country will admit," between the Valley of the Mississippi and the Pacific was brought to your notice by my predecessor in his annual message; and as the reasons which he presented in favor of the measure still exist in full force, I beg leave to call your attention to them and to repeat the recommendations then made by him.

The uncertainty which exists in regard to the validity of land titles in California is a subject which demands your early consideration. Large bodies of land in that State are claimed under grants said to have been made by authority of the Spanish and Mexican Governments. Many of these have not been perfected, others have been revoked, and some are believed to be fraudulent. But until they shall have been judicially investigated they will continue to retard the settlement and improvement of the country. I therefore respectfully recommend that provision be made by law for the appointment of commissioners to examine all such claims with a view to their final adjustment.

I also beg leave to call your attention to the propriety of extending at an early day our system of land laws, with such modifications as may be necessary, over the State of California and the Territories of Utah and New Mexico. The mineral lands of California will, of course, form an exception to any general system which may be adopted. Various methods of disposing of them have been suggested. I was at first inclined to favor the system of leasing, as it seemed to promise the largest revenue to the Government and to afford the best security against monopolies; but further reflection and our experience in leasing the lead mines and selling lands upon credit have brought my mind to the conclusion that there would be great difficulty in collecting the rents, and that the relation of debtor and creditor between the citizens and the Government would be attended with many mischievous consequences. I therefore recommend that instead of retaining the mineral lands under the permanent control of the Government they be divided into small parcels and sold, under such restrictions as to quantity and time as will insure the best price and guard most effectually against combinations of capitalists to obtain monopolies.

The annexation of Texas and the acquisition of California and New Mexico have given increased importance to our Indian relations. The various tribes brought under our jurisdiction by these enlargements of our boundaries are estimated to embrace a population of 124,000.

Texas and New Mexico are surrounded by powerful tribes of Indians, who are a source of constant terror and annoyance to the inhabitants. Separating into small predatory bands, and always mounted, they overrun the country, devastating farms, destroying crops, driving off whole herds of cattle, and occasionally murdering the inhabitants or carrying them into captivity. The great roads leading into the country are infested with them, whereby traveling is rendered extremely dangerous and immigration is almost entirely arrested. The Mexican frontier, which by the eleventh article of the treaty of Guadalupe Hidalgo we are bound to protect against the Indians within our border, is exposed to these incursions equally with our own. The military force stationed in that country, although forming a large proportion of the Army, is represented as entirely inadequate to our own protection and the fulfillment of our treaty stipulations with Mexico. The principal deficiency is in cavalry, and I recommend that Congress should, at as early a period as practicable, provide for the raising of one or more regiments of mounted men.

For further suggestions on this subject and others connected with our domestic interests and the defense of our frontier, I refer you to the reports of the Secretary of the Interior and of the Secretary of War.

I commend also to your favorable consideration the suggestion contained in the last-mentioned report and in the letter of the General in Chief relative to the establishment of an asylum for the relief of disabled and destitute soldiers. This subject appeals so strongly to your sympathies that it would be superfluous in me to say anything more than barely to express my cordial approbation of the proposed object.

The Navy continues to give protection to our commerce and other national interests in the different quarters of the globe, and, with the exception of a single steamer on the Northern lakes, the vessels in commission are distributed in six different squadrons.

The report of the head of that Department will exhibit the services of these squadrons and of the several vessels employed in each during the past year. It is a source of gratification that, while they have been constantly prepared for any hostile emergency, they have everywhere met with the respect and courtesy due as well to the dignity as to the peaceful dispositions and just purposes of the nation.

The two brigantines accepted by the Government from a generous citizen of New York and placed under the command of an officer of the Navy to proceed to the Arctic Seas in quest of the British commander Sir John Franklin and his companions, in compliance with the act of Congress approved in May last, had when last heard from penetrated into a high northern latitude; but the success of this noble and humane enterprise is yet uncertain.

I invite your attention to the view of our present naval establishment and resources presented in the report of the Secretary of the Navy, and the suggestions therein made for its improvement, together with the naval policy recommended for the security of our Pacific Coast and the protection and extension of our commerce with eastern Asia. Our facilities for a larger participation in the trade of the East, by means of our recent settlements on the shores of the Pacific, are too obvious to be overlooked or disregarded.

The questions in relation to rank in the Army and Navy and relative rank between officers of the two branches of the service, presented to the Executive by certain resolutions of the House of Representatives at the last session of Congress, have been submitted to a board of officers in each branch of the service, and their report may be expected at an early day.

I also earnestly recommend the enactment of a law authorizing officers of the Army and Navy to be retired from the service when incompetent for its vigorous and active duties, taking care to make suitable provision for those who have faithfully served their country and awarding distinctions by retaining in appropriate commands those who have been particularly conspicuous for gallantry and good conduct. While the obligation of the country to maintain and honor those who, to the exclusion of other pursuits, have devoted themselves to its arduous service is acknowledged, this obligation should not be permitted to interfere with the efficiency of the service itself.

I am gratified in being able to state that the estimates of expenditure for the Navy in the ensuing year are less by more than $1,000,000 than those of the present, excepting the appropriation which may become necessary for the construction of a dock on the coast of the Pacific, propositions for which are now being considered and on which a special report may be expected early in your present session.

There is an evident justness in the suggestion of the same report that appropriations for the naval service proper should be separated from those for fixed and permanent objects, such as building docks and navy-yards and the fixtures attached, and from the extraordinary objects under the care of the Department which, however important, are not essentially naval.

A revision of the code for the government of the Navy seems to require the immediate consideration of Congress. Its system of crimes and punishments had undergone no change for half a century until the last session, though its defects have been often and ably pointed out; and the abolition of a particular species of corporal punishment, which then took place, without providing any substitute, has left the service in a state of defectiveness which calls for prompt correction. I therefore recommend that the whole subject be revised without delay and such a system established for the enforcement of discipline as shall be at once humane and effectual.

The accompanying report of the Postmaster-General presents a satisfactory view of the operations and condition of that Department.

At the close of the last fiscal year the length of the inland mail routes in the United States (not embracing the service in Oregon and California) was 178,672 miles, the annual transportation thereon 46,541,423 miles, and the annual cost of such transportation $2,724,426.

The increase of the annual transportation over that of the preceding year was 3,997,354 miles and the increase in cost was $342,440.

The number of post-offices in the United States on the 1st day of July last was 18,417, being an increase of 1,670 during the preceding year.

The gross revenues of the Department for the fiscal year ending June 30, 1850, amounted to $5,552,971.48, including the annual appropriation of $200,000 for the franked matter of the Departments and excluding the foreign postages collected for and payable to the British Government.

The expenditures for the same period were $5,212,953.43, leaving a balance of revenue over expenditures of $340,018.05.

I am happy to find that the fiscal condition of the Department is such as to justify the Postmaster-General in recommending the reduction of our inland letter postage to 3 cents the single letter when prepaid and 5 cents when not prepaid. He also recommends that the prepaid rate shall be reduced to 2 cents whenever the revenues of the Department, after the reduction, shall exceed its expenditures by more than 5 per cent for two consecutive years; that the postage upon California and other letters sent by our ocean steamers shall be much reduced, and that the rates of postage on newspapers, pamphlets, periodicals, and other printed matter shall be modified and some reduction thereon made.

It can not be doubted that the proposed reductions will for the present diminish the revenues of the Department. It is believed that the deficiency, after the surplus already accumulated shall be exhausted, may be almost wholly met either by abolishing the existing privileges of sending free matter through the mails or by paying out of the Treasury to the Post-Office Department a sum equivalent to the postage of which it is deprived by such privileges. The last is supposed to be the preferable mode, and will, if not entirely, so nearly supply that deficiency as to make any further appropriation that may be found necessary so inconsiderable as to form no obstacle to the proposed reductions.

I entertain no doubt of the authority of Congress to make appropriations for leading objects in that class of public works comprising what are usually called works of internal improvement. This authority I suppose to be derived chiefly from the power of regulating commerce with foreign nations and among the States and the power of laying and collecting imposts. Where commerce is to be carried on and imposts collected there must be ports and harbors as well as wharves and custom-houses. If ships laden with valuable cargoes approach the shore or sail along the coast, light-houses are necessary at suitable points for the protection of life and property. Other facilities and securities for commerce and navigation are hardly less important; and those clauses of the Constitution, therefore, to which I have referred have received from the origin of the Government a liberal and beneficial construction. Not only have light-houses, buoys, and beacons been established and floating lights maintained, but harbors have been cleared and improved, piers constructed, and even breakwaters for the safety of shipping and sea walls to protect harbors from being filled up and rendered useless by the action of the ocean, have been erected at very great expense. And this construction of the Constitution appears the more reasonable from the consideration that if these works, of such evident importance and utility, are not to be accomplished by Congress they can not be accomplished at all. By the adoption of the Constitution the several States voluntarily parted with the power of collecting duties of imposts in their own ports, and it is not to be expected that they should raise money by internal taxation, direct or indirect, for the benefit of that commerce the revenues derived from which do not, either in whole or in part, go into their own treasuries. Nor do I perceive any difference between the power of Congress to make appropriations for objects of this kind on the ocean and the power to make appropriations for similar objects on lakes and rivers, wherever they are large enough to bear on their waters an extensive traffic. The magnificent Mississippi and its tributaries and the vast lakes of the North and Northwest appear to me to fall within the exercise of the power as justly and as clearly as the ocean and the Gulf of Mexico. It is a mistake to regard expenditures judiciously made for these objects as expenditures for local purposes. The position or sight of the work is necessarily local, but its utility is general. A ship canal around the Falls of St. Mary of less than a mile in length, though local in its construction, would yet be national in its purpose and its benefits, as it would remove the only obstruction to a navigation of more than 1,000 miles, affecting several States, as well as our commercial relations with Canada. So, too, the breakwater at the mouth of the Delaware is erected, not for the exclusive benefit of the States bordering on the bay and river of that name, but for that of the whole coastwise navigation of the United States and, to a considerable extent, also of foreign commerce. If a ship be lost on the bar at the entrance of a Southern port for want of sufficient depth of water, it is very likely to be a Northern ship; and if a steamboat be sunk in any part of the Mississippi on account of its channel not having been properly cleared of obstructions, it may be a boat belonging to either of eight or ten States. I may add, as somewhat remarkable, that among all the thirty-one States there is none that is not to a greater or less extent bounded on the ocean, or the Gulf of Mexico, or one of the Great Lakes, or some navigable river.

In fulfilling our constitutional duties, fellow-citizens, on this subject, as in carrying into effect all other powers conferred by the Constitution, we should consider ourselves as deliberating and acting for one and the same country, and bear constantly in mind that our regard and our duty are due not to a particular part only, but to the whole.

I therefore recommend that appropriations be made for completing such works as have been already begun and for commencing such others as may seem to the wisdom of Congress to be of public and general importance.

The difficulties and delays incident to the settlement of private claims by Congress amount in many cases to a denial of justice. There is reason to apprehend that many unfortunate creditors of the Government have thereby been unavoidably ruined. Congress has so much business of a public character that it is impossible it should give much attention to mere private claims, and their accumulation is now so great that many claimants must despair of ever being able to obtain a hearing. It may well be doubted whether Congress, from the nature of its organization, is properly constituted to decide upon such cases. It is impossible that each member should examine the merits of every claim on which he is compelled to vote, and it is preposterous to ask a judge to decide a case which he has never heard. Such decisions may, and frequently must, do injustice either to the claimant or the Government, and I perceive no better remedy for this growing evil than the establishment of some tribunal to adjudicate upon such claims. I beg leave, therefore, most respectfully to recommend that provision be made by law for the appointment of a commission to settle all private claims against the United States; and as an *ex parte* hearing must in all contested cases be very unsatisfactory, I also recommend the appointment of a solicitor, whose duty it shall be to represent the Government before such commission and protect it against all illegal, fraudulent, or unjust claims which may be presented for their adjudication.

This District, which has neither voice nor vote in your deliberations, looks to you for protection and aid, and I commend all its wants to your favorable consideration, with a full confidence that you will meet them not only with justice, but with liberality. It should be borne in mind that in this city, laid out by Washington and consecrated by his name, is located the Capitol of our nation, the emblem of our Union and the symbol of our greatness. Here also are situated all the public buildings necessary for the use of the Government, and all these are exempt from taxation. It should be the pride of Americans to render this place attractive to the people of the whole Republic and convenient and safe for the transaction of the public business and the preservation of the public records. The Government should therefore bear a liberal proportion of the burdens of all necessary and useful improvements. And as nothing could contribute more to the health, comfort, and safety of the city and the security of the public buildings and records than an abundant supply of pure water, I respectfully recommend that you make such provisions for obtaining the same as in your wisdom you may deem proper.

The act, passed at your last session, making certain propositions to Texas for settling the disputed boundary between that State and the Territory of New Mexico was, immediately on its passage, transmitted by express to the governor of Texas, to be laid by him before the general assembly for its agreement thereto. Its receipt was duly acknowledged, but no official information has yet been received of the action of the general assembly thereon. It may, however, be very soon expected, as, by the terms of the propositions submitted they were to have been acted upon on or before the first day of the present month.

It was hardly to have been expected that the series of measures passed at your last session with the view of healing the sectional differences which had sprung from the slavery and territorial questions should at once have realized their beneficent purpose. All mutual concession in the nature of a compromise must necessarily be unwelcome to men of extreme opinions. And though without such concessions our Constitution could not have been formed, and can not be permanently sustained, yet we have seen them made the subject of bitter controversy in both sections of the Republic. It required many months of discussion and deliberation to secure the concurrence of a majority of Congress in their favor. It would be strange if they had been received with immediate approbation by people and States prejudiced and heated by the exciting controversies of their representatives. I believe those measures to have been required by the circumstances and condition of the country. I believe they were necessary to allay asperities and animosities that were rapidly alienating one section of the country from another and destroying those fraternal sentiments which are the strongest supports of the Constitution. They were adopted in the spirit of conciliation and for the purpose of conciliation. I believe that a great majority of our fellow-citizens sympathize in that spirit and that purpose, and in the main approve and are prepared in all respects to sustain these enactments. I can not doubt that the American people, bound together by kindred blood and common traditions, still cherish a paramount regard for the Union of their fathers, and that they are ready to rebuke any attempt to violate its integrity, to disturb the compromises on which it is based, or to resist the laws which have been enacted under its authority.

The series of measures to which I have alluded are regarded by me as a settlement in principle and substance—a final settlement of the dangerous and exciting subjects which they embraced. Most of these subjects, indeed, are beyond your reach, as the legislation which disposed of them was in its character final and irrevocable. It may be presumed from the opposition which they all encountered that none of those measures was free from imperfections, but in their mutual dependence and connection they formed a system of compromise the most conciliatory and best for the entire country that could be obtained from conflicting sectional interests and opinions.

For this reason I recommend your adherence to the adjustment established by those measures until time and experience shall demonstrate the necessity of further legislation to guard against evasion or abuse.

By that adjustment we have been rescued from the wide and boundless agitation that surrounded us, and have a firm, distinct, and legal ground to rest upon. And the occasion, I trust, will justify me in exhorting my countrymen to rally upon and maintain that ground as the best, if not the only, means of restoring peace and quiet to the country and maintaining inviolate the integrity of the Union.

And now, fellow-citizens, I can not bring this communication to a close without invoking you to join me in humble and devout thanks to the Great Ruler of Nations for the multiplied blessings which He has graciously bestowed upon us. His hand, so often visible in our preservation, has stayed the pestilence, saved us from foreign wars and domestic disturbances, and scattered plenty throughout the land.

Our liberties, religious and civil, have been maintained, the fountains of knowledge have all been kept open, and means of happiness widely spread and generally enjoyed greater than have fallen to the lot of any other nation. And while deeply penetrated with gratitude for the past, let us hope that His all-wise providence will so guide our counsels as that they shall result in giving satisfaction to our constituents, securing the peace of the country, and adding new strength to the united Government under which we live.

MILLARD FILLMORE.

SPECIAL MESSAGES.

WASHINGTON, *December 9, 1850.*

To the House of Representatives:

I communicate to the House of Representatives a translation of a note of the 5th instant addressed to the Secretary of State by the minister of the Mexican Republic accredited to this Government, relative to a subject* to which the attention of Congress was invited in my message at the opening of the present session.

MILLARD FILLMORE.

[The same message was sent to the Senate.]

WASHINGTON, *December 12, 1850.*

To the Senate of the United States:

I herewith transmit a report of the Secretary of State, with accompanying documents, relating to the African slave trade, in answer to the resolution of the Senate of the 28th of August last.

MILLARD FILLMORE.

WASHINGTON, *December 13, 1850.*

To the Senate and House of Representatives:

I have the pleasure of announcing to Congress the agreement on the part of Texas to the propositions offered to that State by the act of Congress approved on the 9th day of September last, entitled "An act proposing to the State of Texas the establishment of her northern and western boundaries, the relinquishment by the said State of all territory claimed by her exterior to said boundaries and of all her claims upon the United States, and to establish a Territorial government for New Mexico."

By the terms of that act it was required that the agreement of Texas to the propositions contained in it should be given on or before the 1st day of December, 1850. An authenticated transcript of a law passed

*Incursions of Indians of the United States upon the population of the Mexican frontier.

by the legislature of Texas on the 25th day of November, agreeing to and accepting the propositions contained in the act of Congress, has been received. This law, after reciting the provisions of the act of Congress, proceeds to enact and declare as follows, viz:

Therefore, first. *Be it enacted by the legislature of the State of Texas*, That the State of Texas hereby agrees to and accepts said propositions; and it is hereby declared that the said State shall be bound by the terms thereof according to their true import and meaning.

Second. That the governor of this State be, and is hereby, requested to cause a copy of this act, authenticated under the seal of the State, to be furnished to the President of the United States by mail as early as practicable, and also a copy thereof, certified in like manner, to be transmitted to each of the Senators and Representatives of Texas in Congress. And that this act take effect from and after its passage.

C. G. KEENAN,
Speaker of the House of Representatives.

JOHN A. GREER,
President of the Senate.

Approved, November 25, 1850.

P. H. BELL.

From the common sources of public information it would appear that a very remarkable degree of unanimity prevailed, not only in the legislature, but among the people of Texas, in respect to the agreement of the State to that which had been proposed by Congress.

I can not refrain from congratulating Congress and the country on the success of this great and leading measure of conciliation and peace. The difficulties felt and the dangers apprehended from the vast acquisitions of territory under the late treaty with Mexico seem now happily overcome by the wisdom of Congress. Within that territory there already exists one State, respectable for the amount of her population, distinguished for singular activity and enterprise, and remarkable in many respects from her condition and history. This new State has come into the Union with manifestations not to be mistaken of her attachment to that Constitution and that Government which now embrace her and her interests within their protecting and beneficent control.

Over the residue of the acquired territories regular Territorial governments are now established in the manner which has been most usual in the history of this Government. Various other acts of Congress may undoubtedly be requisite for the benefit as well as for the proper government of these so distant parts of the country. But the same legislative wisdom which has triumphed over the principal difficulties and accomplished the main end may safely be relied on for whatever measures may yet be found necessary to perfect its work, so that the acquisition of these vast regions to the United States may rather strengthen than weaken the Constitution, which is over us all, and the Union, which affords such ample daily proofs of its inestimable value.

MILLARD FILLMORE.

WASHINGTON, *December 17, 1850.*

To the Senate of the United States:

I herewith transmit a letter from the Secretary of War, communicating a report of a board of officers to which, in pursuance of a resolution of the Senate passed on the 30th of September last, were submitted the questions proposed therein, relative to the expediency and necessity of creating additional grades of commissioned officers in the Army and of enacting provisions authorizing officers of the Army to exercise civil functions in emergencies to be enumerated and restraining them from usurping the powers of civil functionaries.

MILLARD FILLMORE.

WASHINGTON, *December 30, 1850.*

To the Senate of the United States:

I herewith transmit to the Senate, in reply to their resolution of the 26th instant, a report from the Secretary of State, with accompanying papers.*

MILLARD FILLMORE.

WASHINGTON, *January 3, 1851.*

To the House of Representatives:

By a resolution passed by the House of Representatives on the 24th day of July, 1850, the President was requested to cause to be prepared and communicated to the House certain opinions of the Attorneys-General therein specified. On inquiry I learned that the force employed in the Attorney-General's Office was not sufficient to perform this work; consequently, I employed Benjamin F. Hall, esq., a counselor at law, on the 9th day of September last, to execute it, and requested him to commence it immediately. I informed him that I was not authorized to give any other assurances as to compensation than that it rested with Congress to provide and fix it. I believe Mr. Hall to be in all respects competent and well fitted for the task which he has undertaken, and diligent in the performance of it; and it appears to me that the most just mode of compensation will be to make a per diem allowance of $8 per day for the time actually employed, to be paid on the certificate of the Attorney-General.

I also transmit herewith a portion of the manuscript prepared in pursuance of said resolution, with a letter from Mr. Hall to me indicating the mode in which he thinks the work should be prepared and printed, which appears to me worthy of consideration and adoption by the House.

MILLARD FILLMORE.

*Correspondence with the Austrian chargé d'affaires respecting the appointment or proceedings of the agent sent to examine and report upon the condition and prospects of the Hungarian people during their struggle for independence.

WASHINGTON, *January 10, 1851.*

To the Senate of the United States:

I have the honor herewith to transmit to the Senate a communication from the Secretary of the Navy on the subject of the discipline of the Navy, suggesting such amendments of the law as may be necessary in consequence of the recent act abolishing flogging; to which I respectfully invite the immediate attention of Congress.

MILLARD FILLMORE.

WASHINGTON, *January 14, 1851.*

To the House of Representatives of the United States:

In compliance with the resolution of the House of Representatives adopted July 18, 1850, requesting the President to communicate his views on sundry questions of rank, precedence, and command among officers of the Army and officers of the Navy, respectively, and of relative rank between officers of the Army and Navy when brought into cooperation, I caused to be convened a board of intelligent and experienced officers in each branch of the service to consider the matters involved in said resolutions and to report their opinion for my advice and information.

Their reports have been made, and I have the honor herewith to submit copies of them, together with bills drafted substantially in accordance therewith, on the subject of rank in each branch of the service.

The subject is one of great interest, and it is highly important that it should be settled by legislative authority and with as little delay as possible consistently with its proper examination.

The points on which it will be perceived that the two boards disagree in regard to relative rank between officers of the Army and Navy are not esteemed of very great practical importance, and the adoption of the rule proposed by either would be acceptable to the Executive.

But even if a decision on these shall be suspended, it is hoped that the bills which are designed to regulate rank, precedence, and command in the Army and Navy as separate branches of service may receive the sanction of Congress, with such amendments as may be deemed appropriate, in the course of the present session.

MILLARD FILLMORE.

WASHINGTON, *February 3, 1851.*

To the Senate of the United States:

I transmit to the Senate a report from the Secretary of State, with accompanying papers,* in answer to their resolution of the 30th ultimo.

MILLARD FILLMORE.

*Correspondence relative to the possessory rights of the British Hudsons Bay Company in Oregon.

WASHINGTON, *February 12, 1851.*

To the Senate of the United States:

I transmit herewith a report from the Secretary of State, with accompanying documents,* in answer to the Senate's resolution of the 1st instant.

MILLARD FILLMORE.

WASHINGTON, *February 13, 1851.*

To the Senate of the United States:

I herewith communicate to the Senate, for its consideration, a general convention between the United States and the Swiss Confederation, concluded and signed at Berne on the 25th day of November last by Mr. A. Dudley Mann on the part of the United States and by Messrs. Druey and Frey-Hérosée on the part of the Swiss Confederation. I communicate at the same time a copy of the instructions under which Mr. Mann acted and his dispatch of the 30th November last, explanatory of the articles of the convention.

In submitting this convention to the consideration of the Senate I feel it my duty to invite its special attention to the first and fifth articles. These articles appear to contain provisions quite objectionable, if, indeed, they can be considered as properly embraced in the treaty-making power.

The second clause of the first article is in these words:

> In the United States of America citizens of Switzerland shall be received and treated in each State upon the same footing and upon the same conditions as citizens of the United States born in or belonging to other States of the Union.

It is well known that according to the Constitution of the United States a citizen of one State may hold lands in any other State; and States have, sometimes by general, sometimes by special, laws, removed the disabilities attaching to foreigners not naturalized in regard to the holding of land. But this is not supposed to be a power properly to be exercised by the President and Senate in concluding and ratifying a treaty with a foreign state. The authority naturally belongs to the State within whose limits the land may lie. The naturalization of foreigners is provided for by the laws of the United States, in pursuance of the provision of the Constitution; but when, under the operation of these laws, foreigners become citizens of the United States, all would seem to be done which it is in the power of this Government to do to enable foreigners to hold land. The clause referred to, therefore, appears to me inadmissible.

The fourth clause of the same article provides, among other things, that citizens of Switzerland may, within the United States, acquire, possess, and alienate personal and real estate, and the fifth article grants them the power of disposing of their real estate, which, perhaps, would

*Correspondence with Spain relative to the claim of the owners of the schooner *Amistad* for compensation on account of the liberation of negroes on board said vessel.

CARTOON RIDICULING ABOLITIONISTS—A SLAVE MARKET

ABOLITIONISTS AND SLAVE SELLING

The cartoon reproduced in the upper panel aptly caricatures the individuals associated in the abolition movement; women, aflame with Christian indignation and pity for their black sisters in degradation; ex-slaves, eager to procure the boon of freedom for their less fortunate fellows; and philanthropists who were willing to give their fortunes if the blot on the American escutcheon might be removed. Enduring the jibes of the frivolous, the violence of the mob and the opposition of those whose incomes were affected by agitation, these people persisted until slavery was dead.

They appealed to northern sympathies by portraying the negro father, mother and children sold away from each other for all time on the auction-block. They invested the black parents and children with the tender susceptibilities of white people. This was not generally the case. The slaves in the breeding States of Maryland, Kentucky and Virginia were permitted, even encouraged, to intermingle indiscriminately; the family relation cannot be said to have existed; and they felt no more responsibility for their young than cattle, as the master, to whom each child when it drew breath was worth $100, took charge of its rearing as he would of the rearing of a calf or foal. Kentucky, Virginia and Maryland annually exported more than 25,000 slaves.

The Encyclopedic Index articles, entitled "African Slave Trade," "Abolitionists" and "Slavery," summarize those subjects and then direct the reader to places where the Presidents have discussed the question which dominated all others from 1789 to 1861.

be no otherwise objectionable, if it stood by itself, than as it would seem to imply a power to hold that of which they are permitted to dispose.

These objections, perhaps, may be removed by striking out the second clause of the first article and the words "and real" in the fourth clause. An amendment similar to the last here suggested was made by the Senate in the convention between the United States and the King of Bavaria, the ratification of which, as amended, the Senate advised and consented to on the 15th day of March, 1845.

But there is another and a decisive objection, arising from the last clause in the first article. That clause is in these words:

> On account of the tenor of the federal constitution of Switzerland, Christians alone are entitled to the enjoyment of the privileges guaranteed by the present article in the Swiss Cantons. But said Cantons are not prohibited from extending the same privileges to citizens of the United States of other religious persuasions.

It appears from this that Christians alone are, in some of the Swiss Cantons, entitled to the enjoyment of privileges guaranteed by the first article, although the Cantons themselves are not prohibited from extending the same privileges to citizens of the United States of other religious persuasions.

It is quite certain that neither by law, nor by treaty, nor by any other official proceeding is it competent for the Government of the United States to establish any distinction between its citizens founded on differences in religious beliefs. Any benefit or privilege conferred by law or treaty on one must be common to all, and we are not at liberty, on a question of such vital interest and plain constitutional duty, to consider whether the particular case is one in which substantial inconvenience or injustice might ensue. It is enough that an inequality would be sanctioned hostile to the institutions of the United States and inconsistent with the Constitution and the laws.

Nor can the Government of the United States rely on the individual Cantons of Switzerland for extending the same privileges to other citizens of the United States as this article extends to Christians. It is indispensable not only that every privilege granted to any of the citizens of the United States should be granted to all, but also that the grant of such privilege should stand upon the same stipulation and assurance by the whole Swiss Confederation as those of other articles of the convention.

There have been instances, especially some of recent occurrence, in which the Executive has transmitted treaties to the Senate with suggestions of amendment, and I have therefore thought it not improper to send the present convention to the Senate, inviting its attention to such amendments as appeared to me to be important, although I have entertained considerable doubt whether it would not be better to send back the convention for correction in the objectionable particulars before laying it before the Senate for ratification.

MILLARD FILLMORE.

WASHINGTON, *February 13, 1851.*

To the Senate of the United States:

In answer to the resolution of the Senate of the 10th instant, calling for information relative to a contract alleged to have been made by Mr. I. D. Marks with the Mexican Government, I transmit a report from the Secretary of State and the documents* which accompanied it.

MILLARD FILLMORE.

WASHINGTON, *February 13, 1851.*

To the Senate of the United States:

In compliance with the resolution of the Senate of the 28th of January, 1851, I have the honor to transmit herewith reports from the Secretary of State and Secretary of the Treasury, giving the required correspondence in the case of the British ship *Albion*, seized in Oregon for an alleged violation of the revenue laws.

MILLARD FILLMORE.

WASHINGTON, *February 15, 1851.*

To the Senate of the United States:

In addition to the information heretofore communicated, I now transmit to the Senate a report from the Secretary of State, with accompanying papers,† in answer to their resolution of the 28th ultimo.

MILLARD FILLMORE.

WASHINGTON, *February 15, 1851.*

To the Senate of the United States:

I herewith transmit to the Senate a report‡ from the Secretary of State, in answer to their resolution of the 10th instant.

MILLARD FILLMORE.

WASHINGTON, *February 18, 1851.*

The PRESIDENT OF THE SENATE:

In addition to the papers already transmitted to the Senate in compliance with its resolution of the 28th ultimo, I have the honor herewith to transmit an additional report§ from the Secretary of the Treasury.

MILLARD FILLMORE.

*Relating to drafts upon the Treasury of the United States by Mexico on account of indemnity due that Government in pursuance of the treaty of Guadalupe Hidalgo.

†Additional correspondence relative to the seizure of the British ship *Albion*.

‡Relating to taxation by New Granada on United States citizens when *in transitu* across the Isthmus of Panama, and to the United States mail service at said Isthmus.

§Relating to the seizure of the British ship *Albion*.

EXECUTIVE DEPARTMENT, *February 19, 1851*.

To the Senate of the United States:

I have received the resolution of the Senate of the 18th instant, requesting me to lay before that body, if not incompatible with the public interest, any information I may possess in regard to an alleged recent case of a forcible resistance to the execution of the laws of the United States in the city of Boston, and to communicate to the Senate, under the above conditions, what means I have adopted to meet the occurrence, and whether in my opinion any additional legislation is necessary to meet the exigency of the case and to more vigorously execute existing laws.

The public newspapers contain an affidavit of Patrick Riley, a deputy marshal for the district of Massachusetts, setting forth the circumstances of the case, a copy of which affidavit is herewith communicated. Private and unofficial communications concur in establishing the main facts of this account, but no satisfactory official information has as yet been received; and in some important respects the accuracy of the account has been denied by persons whom it implicates. Nothing could be more unexpected than that such a gross violation of law, such a high-handed contempt of the authority of the United States, should be perpetrated by a band of lawless confederates at noonday in the city of Boston, and in the very temple of justice. I regard this flagitious proceeding as being a surprise not unattended by some degree of negligence; nor do I doubt that if any such act of violence had been apprehended thousands of the good citizens of Boston would have presented themselves voluntarily and promptly to prevent it. But the danger does not seem to have been timely made known or duly appreciated by those who were concerned in the execution of the process. In a community distinguished for its love of order and respect for the laws, among a people whose sentiment is liberty and law, and not liberty without law nor above the law, such an outrage could only be the result of sudden violence, unhappily too much unprepared for to be successfully resisted. It would be melancholy indeed if we were obliged to regard this outbreak against the constitutional and legal authority of the Government as proceeding from the general feeling of the people in a spot which is proverbially called "the Cradle of American Liberty." Such, undoubtedly, is not the fact. It violates without question the general sentiment of the people of Boston and of a vast majority of the whole people of Massachusetts, as much as it violates the law, defies the authority of the Government, and disgraces those concerned in it, their aiders and abettors.

It is, nevertheless, my duty to lay before the Senate, in answer to its resolution, some important facts and considerations connected with the subject.

A resolution of Congress of September 23, 1789, declared:

That it be recommended to the legislatures of the several States to pass laws making it expressly the duty of the keepers of their jails to receive and safe keep therein all prisoners committed under the authority of the United States until they shall be discharged by the course of the laws thereof, under the like penalties as in the case of prisoners committed under the authority of such States respectively; the United States to pay for the use and keeping of such jails at the rate of 50 cents per month for each prisoner that shall, under their authority, be committed thereto during the time such prisoner shall be therein confined, and also to support such of said prisoners as shall be committed for offenses.

A further resolution of Congress, of the 3d of March, 1791, provides that—

Whereas Congress did, by a resolution of the 23d day of September, 1789, recommend to the several States to pass laws making it expressly the duty of the keepers of their jails to receive and safe keep therein all prisoners committed under the authority of the United States: In order, therefore, to insure the administration of justice—

Resolved by the Senate and House of Representatives of the United States of America in Congress assembled, That in case any State shall not have complied with the said recommendation the marshal in such State, under the direction of the judge of the district, be authorized to hire a convenient place to serve as a temporary jail, and to make the necessary provision for the safe-keeping of prisoners committed under the authority of the United States until permanent provision shall be made by law for that purpose; and the said marshal shall be allowed his reasonable expenses incurred for the above purposes, to be paid out of the Treasury of the United States.

And a resolution of Congress of March 3, 1821, provides that—

Where any State or States, having complied with the recommendation of Congress in the resolution of the 23d day of September, 1789, shall have withdrawn, or shall hereafter withdraw, either in whole or in part, the use of their jails for prisoners committed under the authority of the United States, the marshal in such State or States, under the direction of the judge of the district, shall be, and hereby is, authorized and required to hire a convenient place to serve as a temporary jail, and to make the necessary provision for the safe-keeping of prisoners committed under the authority of the United States until permanent provision shall be made by law for that purpose; and the said marshal shall be allowed his reasonable expenses incurred for the above purposes, to be paid out of the Treasury of the United States.

These various provisions of the law remain unrepealed.

By the law of Massachusetts, as that law stood before the act of the legislature of that State of the 24th of March, 1843, the common jails in the respective counties were to be used for the detention of any persons detained or committed by the authority of the courts of the United States, as well as by the courts and magistrates of the State. But these provisions were abrogated and repealed by the act of the legislature of Massachusetts of the 24th of March, 1843.

That act declares that—

No judge of any court of record of this Commonwealth and no justice of the peace shall hereafter take cognizance or grant a certificate in cases that may arise under the third section of an act of Congress passed February 12, 1793, and entitled "An act respecting fugitives from justice and persons escaping from the service of their masters," to any person who claims any other person as a fugitive slave within the jurisdiction of the Commonwealth.

And it further declares that—

> No sheriff, deputy sheriff, coroner, constable, jailer, or other officer of this Commonwealth shall hereafter arrest or detain, or aid in the arrest or detention or imprisonment, in any jail or other building belonging to this Commonwealth, or to any county, city, or town thereof, of any person for the reason that he is claimed as a fugitive slave.

And it further declares that—

> Any justice of the peace, sheriff, deputy sheriff, coroner, constable, or jailer who shall offend against the provisions of this law by in any way acting, directly or indirectly, under the power conferred by the third section of the act of Congress aforementioned shall forfeit a sum not exceeding $1,000 for every such offense to the use of the county where said offense is committed, or shall be subject to imprisonment not exceeding one year in the county jail.

This law, it is obvious, had two objects. The first was to make it a penal offense in all officers and magistrates of the Commonwealth to exercise the powers conferred on them by the act of Congress of the 12th of February, 1793, entitled "An act respecting fugitives from justice and persons escaping from the service of their masters," and which powers they were fully competent to perform up to the time of this inhibition and penal enactment; second, to refuse the use of the jails of the State for the detention of any person claimed as a fugitive slave.

It is deeply to be lamented that the purpose of these enactments is quite apparent. It was to prevent, as far as the legislature of the State could prevent, the laws of Congress passed for the purpose of carrying into effect that article of the Constitution of the United States which declares that "no person held to service or labor in one State, under the laws thereof, escaping into another, shall in consequence of any law or regulation therein be discharged from such service or labor, but shall be delivered up on claim of the party to whom such service or labor may be due" from being carried into effect. But these acts of State legislation, although they may cause embarrassment and create expense, can not derogate either from the duty or the authority of Congress to carry out fully and fairly the plain and imperative constitutional provision for the delivery of persons bound to labor in one State and escaping into another to the party to whom such labor may be due. It is quite clear that by the resolution of Congress of March 3, 1821, the marshal of the United States in any State in which the use of the jails of the State has been withdrawn, in whole or in part, from the purpose of the detention of persons committed under the authority of the United States is not only empowered, but expressly required, under the direction of the judge of the district, to hire a convenient place for the safe-keeping of prisoners committed under authority of the United States. It will be seen from papers accompanying this communication that the attention of the marshal of Massachusetts was distinctly called to this provision of the law by a letter from the Secretary of the Navy of the date of October 28 last.

There is no official information that the marshal has provided any such place for the confinement of his prisoners. If he has not, it is to be regretted that this power was not exercised by the marshal under the direction of the district judge immediately on the passage of the act of the legislature of Massachusetts of the 24th of March, 1843, and especially that it was not exercised on the passage of the fugitive-slave law of the last session, or when the attention of the marshal was afterwards particularly drawn to it.

It is true that the escape from the deputy marshals in this case was not owing to the want of a prison or place of confinement, but still it is not easy to see how the prisoner could have been safely and conveniently detained during an adjournment of the hearing for some days without such place of confinement. If it shall appear that no such place has been obtained, directions to the marshal will be given to lose no time in the discharge of this duty.

I transmit to the Senate the copy of a proclamation issued by me on the 18th instant in relation to these unexpected and deplorable occurrences in Boston, together with copies of instructions from the Departments of War and Navy relative to the general subject. And I communicate also copies of telegraphic dispatches transmitted from the Department of State to the district attorney and marshal of the United States for the district of Massachusetts and their answers thereto.

In regard to the last branch of the inquiry made by the resolution of the Senate, I have to observe that the Constitution declares that "the President shall take care that the laws be faithfully executed," and that "he shall be Commander in Chief of the Army and Navy of the United States, and of the militia of the several States when called into the actual service of the United States," and that "Congress shall have power to provide for calling forth the militia to execute the laws of the Union, suppress insurrections, and repel invasions." From which it appears that the Army and Navy are by the Constitution placed under the control of the Executive; and probably no legislation of Congress could add to or diminish the power thus given but by increasing or diminishing or abolishing altogether the Army and Navy. But not so with the militia. The President can not call the militia into service, even to execute the laws or repel invasions, but by the authority of acts of Congress passed for that purpose. But when the militia are called into service in the manner prescribed by law, then the Constitution itself gives the command to the President. Acting on this principle, Congress, by the act of February 28, 1795, authorized the President to call forth the militia to repel invasion and "suppress insurrections against a State government, and to suppress combinations against the laws of the United States, and cause the laws to be faithfully executed." But the act proceeds to declare that whenever it may be necessary, in the judgment of the President, to use the military force thereby directed to be called forth, the

President shall forthwith, by proclamation, command such insurgents to disperse and retire peaceably to their respective abodes within a limited time. These words are broad enough to require a proclamation in all cases where militia are called out under that act, whether to repel invasion or suppress an insurrection or to aid in executing the laws. This section has consequently created some doubt whether the militia could be called forth to aid in executing the laws without a previous proclamation. But yet the proclamation seems to be in words directed only against insurgents, and to require them to disperse, thereby implying not only an insurrection, but an organized, or at least an embodied, force. Such a proclamation in aid of the civil authority would often defeat the whole object by giving such notice to persons intended to be arrested that they would be enabled to fly or secrete themselves. The force may be wanted sometimes to make the arrest, and also sometimes to protect the officer after it is made, and to prevent a rescue. I would therefore suggest that this section be modified by declaring that nothing therein contained shall be construed to require any previous proclamation when the militia are called forth, either to repel invasion, to execute the laws, or suppress combinations against them, and that the President may make such call and place such militia under the control of any civil officer of the United States to aid him in executing the laws or suppressing such combinations; and while so employed they shall be paid by and subsisted at the expense of the United States.

Congress, not probably adverting to the difference between the militia and the Regular Army, by the act of March 3, 1807, authorized the President to use the land and naval forces of the United States for the same purposes for which he might call forth the militia, and subject to the same proclamation. But the power of the President under the Constitution, as Commander of the Army and Navy, is general, and his duty to see the laws faithfully executed is general and positive; and the act of 1807 ought not to be construed as evincing any disposition in Congress to limit or restrain this constitutional authority. For greater certainty, however, it may be well that Congress should modify or explain this act in regard to its provisions for the employment of the Army and Navy of the United States, as well as that in regard to calling forth the militia. It is supposed not to be doubtful that all citizens, whether enrolled in the militia or not, may be summoned as members of the *posse comitatus*, either by the marshal or a commissioner according to law, and that it is their duty to obey such summons. But perhaps it may be doubted whether the marshal or a commissioner can summon as the *posse comitatus* an organized militia force, acting under its own appropriate officers, without the consent of such officers. This point may deserve the consideration of Congress.

I use this occasion to repeat the assurance that so far as depends on me the laws shall be faithfully executed and all forcible opposition to them suppressed; and to this end I am prepared to exercise, whenever it may become necessary, the power constitutionally vested in me to the fullest extent. I am fully persuaded that the great majority of the people of this country are warmly and strongly attached to the Constitution, the preservation of the Union, the just support of the Government, and the maintenance of the authority of law. I am persuaded that their earnest wishes and the line of my constitutional duty entirely concur, and I doubt not firmness, moderation, and prudence, strengthened and animated by the general opinion of the people, will prevent the repetition of occurrences disturbing the public peace and reprobated by all good men.

MILLARD FILLMORE.

WASHINGTON, *February 25, 1851.*

To the Senate of the United States:

I transmit to the Senate, for its consideration with a view to ratification, a convention between the United States and the Mexican Republic for the protection of a transit way across the Isthmus of Tehuantepec, signed in the City of Mexico on the 25th ultimo.

Accompanying the treaty is a letter from Mr. P. A. Hargous, the present proprietor and holder of the privileges granted by Mexico, signifying his assent to and acceptance of the terms of its provisions. There is also an abstract of title to him from the original grantee and copies of the several powers and conveyances by which that title is derived to him. It may be well that these papers should be returned to be deposited among the archives of the Department of State.

The additional article of the treaty makes an unnecessary reference to the eleventh, twelfth, and thirteenth articles of the treaty of the 22d of June last, because the eleventh, twelfth, and thirteenth articles of the present treaty contain exactly the same provisions as those contained in the same articles of that treaty, as will appear from the copy of the treaty of the 22d of June last, herewith communicated.

MILLARD FILLMORE.

WASHINGTON, *February 26, 1851.*

To the Senate of the United States:

I herewith communicate to the Senate, for its consideration, a convention for the adjustment of certain claims of citizens of the United States against Her Most Faithful Majesty's Government,* concluded and signed this day in the city of Washington by the respective plenipotentiaries.

MILLARD FILLMORE.

*Portugal.

WASHINGTON, *February 27, 1851.*

To the Senate of the United States:

I transmit herewith a report of the Secretary of State, with accompanying documents,* in compliance with the resolution of the Senate of the 17th ultimo.

MILLARD FILLMORE.

WASHINGTON, *February 28, 1851.*

To the Senate of the United States:

In answer to the resolution of the Senate of the 16th ultimo, requesting information touching the difficulties between the British authorities and San Salvador, I transmit a report from the Secretary of State and the documents which accompanied it.

MILLARD FILLMORE.

WASHINGTON, *March 1, 1851.*

Hon. HOWELL COBB,
Speaker of the House of Representatives:

I have the honor herewith to transmit to the House of Representatives manuscript No. 2 of the opinions of the Attorneys-General, prepared in pursuance of its resolution.

MILLARD FILLMORE.

WASHINGTON, *March 3, 1851.*

To the Senate of the United States:

In answer to the resolution of the Senate of the 26th ultimo, calling for information respecting a forcible abduction of any citizen of the United States from the Territory of New Mexico and his conveyance within the limits of the Mexican Republic, I transmit a report from the Secretary of State and the documents which accompanied it.

MILLARD FILLMORE.

PROCLAMATIONS.

BY THE PRESIDENT OF THE UNITED STATES OF AMERICA.

A PROCLAMATION.

Whereas by an act of the Congress of the United States of the 9th of September, 1850, entitled "An act proposing to the State of Texas the establishment of her northern and western boundaries, the relinquishment by the said State of all territory claimed by her exterior to said boundaries and of all her claims upon the United States, and to establish a Territorial government for New Mexico," it was provided that the

*Correspondence relative to prisoners captured by Spanish authorities at or near the island of Contoy, and to projected expeditions to Cuba.

following propositions should be, and the same were thereby, offered to the State of Texas, which, when agreed to by the said State in an act passed by the general assembly, should be binding and obligatory upon the United States and upon the said State of Texas, provided the said agreement by the said general assembly should be given on or before the 1st day of December, 1850, namely:

"First. The State of Texas will agree that her boundary on the north shall commence at the point at which the meridian of 100° west from Greenwich is intersected by the parallel of 36° 30′ north latitude, and shall run from said point due west to the meridian of 103° west from Greenwich; thence her boundary shall run due south to the thirty-second degree of north latitude; thence on the said parallel of 32° of north latitude to the Rio Bravo del Norte, and thence with the channel of said river to the Gulf of Mexico.

"Second. The State of Texas cedes to the United States all her claim to territory exterior to the limits and boundaries which she agrees to establish by the first article of this agreement.

"Third. The State of Texas relinquishes all claim upon the United States for liability of the debts of Texas and for compensation or indemnity for the surrender to the United States of her ships, forts, arsenals, custom-houses, custom-house revenue, arms and munitions of war, and public buildings with their sites, which became the property of the United States at the time of the annexation.

"Fourth. The United States, in consideration of said establishment of boundaries, cession of claim to territory, and relinquishment of claims, will pay to the State of Texas the sum of $10,000,000 in a stock bearing 5 per cent interest, and redeemable at the end of fourteen years, the interest payable half-yearly at the Treasury of the United States.

"Fifth. Immediately after the President of the United States shall have been furnished with an authentic copy of the act of the general assembly of Texas accepting these propositions, he shall cause the stock to be issued in favor of the State of Texas, as provided for in the fourth article of this agreement: *Provided also*, That no more than $5,000,000 of said stock shall be issued until the creditors of the State holding bonds and other certificates of stock of Texas for which duties on imports were specially pledged shall first file at the Treasury of the United States releases of all claim against the United States for or on account of said bonds or certificates in such form as shall be prescribed by the Secretary of the Treasury and approved by the President of the United States: *Provided*, That nothing herein contained shall be construed to impair or qualify anything contained in the third article of the second section of the 'Joint resolution for annexing Texas to the United States,' approved March 1, 1845, either as regards the number of States that may hereafter be formed out of the State of Texas or otherwise;" and

Whereas it was further provided by the eighteenth section of the same act of Congress "that the provisions of this act be, and they are hereby, suspended until the boundary between the United States and the State of Texas shall be adjusted, and when such adjustment shall have been effected the President of the United States shall issue his proclamation declaring this act to be in full force and operation;" and

Whereas the legislature of the State of Texas, by an act approved the 25th of November last, entitled "An act accepting the propositions made by the United States to the State of Texas in an act of the Congress of the United States approved the 9th day of September, A. D. 1850, and entitled 'An act proposing to the State of Texas the establishment of her northern and western boundaries, the relinquishment by the said State of all territory claimed by her exterior to said boundaries and of all her claims upon the United States, and to establish a Territorial government for New Mexico,'" of which act a copy, authenticated under the seal of the State, has been furnished to the President, enacts "that the State of Texas hereby agrees to and accepts said propositions, and it is hereby declared that the said State shall be bound by the terms thereof, according to their true import and meaning:"

Now, therefore, I, Millard Fillmore, President of the United States of America, do hereby declare and proclaim that the said act of the Congress of the United States of the 9th of September last is in full force and operation.

Given under my hand, at the city of Washington, this 13th day of December, A. D. 1850, and the seventy-fifth of the Independence of these United States.

[SEAL.]

MILLARD FILLMORE.

By the President:

DANL. WEBSTER,

Secretary of State.

BY THE PRESIDENT OF THE UNITED STATES.

A PROCLAMATION.

Whereas information has been received that sundry lawless persons, principally persons of color, combined and confederated together for the purpose of opposing by force the execution of the laws of the United States, did, at Boston, in Massachusetts, on the 15th of this month, make a violent assault on the marshal or deputy marshals of the United States for the district of Massachusetts, in the court-house, and did overcome the said officers, and did by force rescue from their custody a person arrested as a fugitive slave, and then and there a prisoner lawfully holden by the said marshal or deputy marshals of the United States, and other scandalous outrages did commit in violation of law:

Now, therefore, to the end that the authority of the laws may be maintained and those concerned in violating them brought to immediate and condign punishment, I have issued this my proclamation, calling on all well-disposed citizens to rally to the support of the laws of their country, and requiring and commanding all officers, civil and military, and all other persons, civil or military, who shall be found within the vicinity of this outrage, to be aiding and assisting by all means in their power in quelling this and other such combinations and assisting the marshal and his deputies in recapturing the above-mentioned prisoner; and I do especially direct that prosecutions be commenced against all persons who shall have made themselves aiders or abettors in or to this flagitious offense; and I do further command that the district attorney of the United States and all other persons concerned in the administration or execution of the laws of the United States cause the foregoing offenders and all such as aided, abetted, or assisted them or shall be found to have harbored or concealed such fugitive contrary to law to be immediately arrested and proceeded with according to law.

Given under my hand and the seal of the United States this 18th day of February, 1851.

[SEAL.] MILLARD FILLMORE.

DANL. WEBSTER,
Secretary of State.

[From Executive Journal of the Senate, Vol. VIII, p. 299.]

WASHINGTON, *March 3, 1851.*

To the Senators of the United States, respectively.

SIR: Whereas divers and weighty causes connected with executive business necessary to be transacted create an extraordinary occasion requiring that the Senate be convened, you are therefore requested, as a member of that body, to attend a meeting thereof to be holden at the Capitol, in the city of Washington, on the 4th day of March instant.

MILLARD FILLMORE.

SPECIAL MESSAGES.

WASHINGTON, *March 4, 1851.*

To the Senate of the United States:

Sundry nominations having been made during the last session of the Senate which were not finally disposed of, I hereby nominate anew each person so nominated at the last session whose nomination was not finally acted on before the termination of that session to the same office for which he was nominated as aforesaid.

MILLARD FILLMORE.

WASHINGTON, *March 10, 1851.*

To the Senate of the United States:

I transmit herewith a report of the Secretary of State, with the accompanying documents,* in compliance with the resolution of the Senate of the 8th instant.

MILLARD FILLMORE.

PROCLAMATIONS.

BY THE PRESIDENT OF THE UNITED STATES.

A PROCLAMATION.

Whereas there is reason to believe that a military expedition is about to be fitted out in the United States with intention to invade the island of Cuba, a colony of Spain, with which this country is at peace; and

Whereas it is believed that this expedition is instigated and set on foot chiefly by foreigners who dare to make our shores the scene of their guilty and hostile preparations against a friendly power and seek by falsehood and misrepresentation to seduce our own citizens, especially the young and inconsiderate, into their wicked schemes—an ungrateful return for the benefits conferred upon them by this people in permitting them to make our country an asylum from oppression and in flagrant abuse of the hospitality thus extended to them; and

Whereas such expeditions can only be regarded as adventures for plunder and robbery, and must meet the condemnation of the civilized world, whilst they are derogatory to the character of our country, in violation of the laws of nations, and expressly prohibited by our own. Our statutes declare "that if any person shall, within the territory or jurisdiction of the United States, begin or set on foot or provide or prepare the means for any military expedition or enterprise to be carried on from thence against the territory or dominions of any foreign prince or state or of any colony, district, or people with whom the United States are at peace, every person so offending shall be deemed guilty of a high misdemeanor and shall be fined not exceeding $3,000 and imprisoned not more than three years:"

Now, therefore, I have issued this my proclamation, warning all persons who shall connect themselves with any such enterprise or expedition in violation of our laws and national obligations that they will thereby subject themselves to the heavy penalties denounced against such offenses and will forfeit their claim to the protection of this Government or any interference on their behalf, no matter to what extremities they may be reduced in consequence of their illegal conduct. And therefore I exhort all good citizens, as they regard our national reputation, as they respect

*Correspondence with the United States minister at Constantinople respecting the liberation of Kossuth and his companions.

their own laws and the laws of nations, as they value the blessings of peace and the welfare of their country, to discountenance and by all lawful means prevent any such enterprise; and I call upon every officer of this Government, civil or military, to use all efforts in his power to arrest for trial and punishment every such offender against the laws of the country.

Given under my hand the 25th day of April, A. D. 1851, and the seventy-fifth of the Independence of the United States.

[SEAL.] MILLARD FILLMORE.

By the President:

W. S. DERRICK,

Acting Secretary of State.

BY THE PRESIDENT OF THE UNITED STATES.

A PROCLAMATION.

Whereas there is reason to believe that a military expedition is about to be fitted out in the United States for the purpose of invading the Mexican Republic, with which this country is at peace; and

Whereas there is reason to apprehend that a portion of the people of this country, regardless of their duties as good citizens, are concerned in or may be seduced to take part in the same; and

Whereas such enterprises tend to degrade the character of the United States in the opinion of the civilized world and are expressly prohibited by law:

Now, therefore, I have issued this my proclamation, warning all persons who shall connect themselves with any such enterprise in violation of the laws and national obligations of the United States that they will thereby subject themselves to the heavy penalties denounced against such offenses; that if they should be captured within the jurisdiction of the Mexican authorities they must expect to be tried and punished according to the laws of Mexico and will have no right to claim the interposition of this Government in their behalf.

I therefore exhort all well-disposed citizens who have at heart the reputation of their country and are animated with a just regard for its laws, its peace, and its welfare to discountenance and by all lawful means prevent any such enterprise; and I call upon every officer of this Government, civil or military, to be vigilant in arresting for trial and punishment every such offender.

Given under my hand the 22d day of October, A. D. 1851, and the seventy-sixth of the Independence of the United States.

MILLARD FILLMORE.

By the President:

J. J. CRITTENDEN,

Acting Secretary of State.

SECOND ANNUAL MESSAGE.

WASHINGTON, *December 2, 1851.*

Fellow-Citizens of the Senate and of the House of Representatives:

I congratulate you and our common constituency upon the favorable auspices under which you meet for your first session. Our country is at peace with all the world. The agitation which for a time threatened to disturb the fraternal relations which make us one people is fast subsiding, and a year of general prosperity and health has crowned the nation with unusual blessings. None can look back to the dangers which are passed or forward to the bright prospect before us without feeling a thrill of gratification, at the same time that he must be impressed with a grateful sense of our profound obligations to a beneficent Providence, whose paternal care is so manifest in the happiness of this highly favored land.

Since the close of the last Congress certain Cubans and other foreigners resident in the United States, who were more or less concerned in the previous invasion of Cuba, instead of being discouraged by its failure have again abused the hospitality of this country by making it the scene of the equipment of another military expedition against that possession of Her Catholic Majesty, in which they were countenanced, aided, and joined by citizens of the United States. On receiving intelligence that such designs were entertained, I lost no time in issuing such instructions to the proper officers of the United States as seemed to be called for by the occasion. By the proclamation a copy of which is herewith submitted I also warned those who might be in danger of being inveigled into this scheme of its unlawful character and of the penalties which they would incur. For some time there was reason to hope that these measures had sufficed to prevent any such attempt. This hope, however, proved to be delusive. Very early in the morning of the 3d of August a steamer called the *Pampero* departed from New Orleans for Cuba, having on board upward of 400 armed men with evident intentions to make war upon the authorities of the island. This expedition was set on foot in palpable violation of the laws of the United States. Its leader was a Spaniard, and several of the chief officers and some others engaged in it were foreigners. The persons composing it, however, were mostly citizens of the United States.

Before the expedition set out, and probably before it was organized, a slight insurrectionary movement, which appears to have been soon suppressed, had taken place in the eastern quarter of Cuba. The importance of this movement was, unfortunately, so much exaggerated in the accounts of it published in this country that these adventurers seem to have been led to believe that the Creole population of the island not only desired to throw off the authority of the mother country, but had resolved upon that step and had begun a well-concerted enterprise for effecting it. The persons engaged in the expedition were generally young and ill informed. The steamer in which they embarked left New Orleans stealthily and without a clearance. After touching at Key West, she proceeded to the coast of Cuba, and on the night between the 11th and 12th of August landed the persons on board at Playtas, within about 20 leagues of Havana.

The main body of them proceeded to and took possession of an inland village 6 leagues distant, leaving others to follow in charge of the baggage as soon as the means of transportation could be obtained. The latter, having taken up their line of march to connect themselves with the main body, and having proceeded about 4 leagues into the country, were attacked on the morning of the 13th by a body of Spanish troops, and a bloody conflict ensued, after which they retreated to the place of disembarkation, where about 50 of them obtained boats and reembarked therein. They were, however, intercepted among the keys near the shore by a Spanish steamer cruising on the coast, captured and carried to Havana, and after being examined before a military court were sentenced to be publicly executed, and the sentence was carried into effect on the 16th of August.

On receiving information of what had occurred Commodore Foxhall A. Parker was instructed to proceed in the steam frigate *Saranac* to Havana and inquire into the charges against the persons executed, the circumstances under which they were taken, and whatsoever referred to their trial and sentence. Copies of the instructions from the Department of State to him and of his letters to that Department are herewith submitted.

According to the record of the examination, the prisoners all admitted the offenses charged against them, of being hostile invaders of the island. At the time of their trial and execution the main body of the invaders was still in the field making war upon the Spanish authorities and Spanish subjects. After the lapse of some days, being overcome by the Spanish troops, they dispersed on the 24th of August. Lopez, their leader, was captured some days after, and executed on the 1st of September. Many of his remaining followers were killed or died of hunger and fatigue, and the rest were made prisoners. Of these none appear to have been tried or executed. Several of them were pardoned upon application of their friends and others, and the rest, about 160 in number, were sent to Spain. Of the final disposition made of these we have no official information.

Such is the melancholy result of this illegal and ill-fated expedition. Thus thoughtless young men have been induced by false and fraudulent representations to violate the law of their country through rash and unfounded expectations of assisting to accomplish political revolutions in other states, and have lost their lives in the undertaking. Too severe a judgment can hardly be passed by the indignant sense of the community upon those who, being better informed themselves, have yet led away the ardor of youth and an ill-directed love of political liberty. The correspondence between this Government and that of Spain relating to this transaction is herewith communicated.

Although these offenders against the laws have forfeited the protection of their country, yet the Government may, so far as consistent with its obligations to other countries and its fixed purpose to maintain and enforce the laws, entertain sympathy for their unoffending families and friends, as well as a feeling of compassion for themselves. Accordingly, no proper effort has been spared and none will be spared to procure the release of such citizens of the United States engaged in this unlawful enterprise as are now in confinement in Spain; but it is to be hoped that such interposition with the Government of that country may not be considered as affording any ground of expectation that the Government of the United States will hereafter feel itself under any obligation of duty to intercede for the liberation or pardon of such persons as are flagrant offenders against the law of nations and the laws of the United States. These laws must be executed. If we desire to maintain our respectability among the nations of the earth, it behooves us to enforce steadily and sternly the neutrality acts passed by Congress and to follow as far as may be the violation of those acts with condign punishment.

But what gives a peculiar criminality to this invasion of Cuba is that, under the lead of Spanish subjects and with the aid of citizens of the United States, it had its origin with many in motives of cupidity. Money was advanced by individuals, probably in considerable amounts, to purchase Cuban bonds, as they have been called, issued by Lopez, sold, doubtless, at a very large discount, and for the payment of which the public lands and public property of Cuba, of whatever kind, and the fiscal resources of the people and government of that island, from whatever source to be derived, were pledged, as well as the good faith of the government expected to be established. All these means of payment, it is evident, were only to be obtained by a process of bloodshed, war, and revolution. None will deny that those who set on foot military expeditions against foreign states by means like these are far more culpable than the ignorant and the necessitous whom they induce to go forth as the ostensible parties in the proceeding. These originators of the invasion of Cuba seem to have determined with coolness and system upon an undertaking which should disgrace their country, violate its laws, and put to hazard the lives of ill-informed and deluded men. You will consider whether further legislation be necessary to prevent the perpetration of such offenses in future.

No individuals have a right to hazard the peace of the country or to violate its laws upon vague notions of altering or reforming governments in other states. This principle is not only reasonable in itself and in accordance with public law, but is ingrafted into the codes of other nations as well as our own. But while such are the sentiments of this Government, it may be added that every independent nation must be presumed to be able to defend its possessions against unauthorized individuals banded together to attack them. The Government of the United States at all times since its establishment has abstained and has sought to restrain the citizens of the country from entering into controversies between other powers, and to observe all the duties of neutrality. At an early period of the Government, in the Administration of Washington, several laws were passed for this purpose. The main provisions of these laws were reenacted by the act of April, 1818, by which, amongst other things, it was declared that—

If any person shall, within the territory or jurisdiction of the United States, begin, or set on foot, or provide or prepare the means for, any military expedition or enterprise to be carried on from thence against the territory or dominions of any foreign prince or state, or of any colony, district, or people, with whom the United States are at peace, every person so offending shall be deemed guilty of a high misdemeanor, and shall be fined not exceeding $3,000 and imprisoned not more than three years.

And this law has been executed and enforced to the full extent of the power of the Government from that day to this.

In proclaiming and adhering to the doctrine of neutrality and nonintervention, the United States have not followed the lead of other civilized nations; they have taken the lead themselves and have been followed by others. This was admitted by one of the most eminent of modern British statesmen, who said in Parliament, while a minister of the Crown, "that if he wished for a guide in a system of neutrality he should take that laid down by America in the days of Washington and the secretaryship of Jefferson;" and we see, in fact, that the act of Congress of 1818 was followed the succeeding year by an act of the Parliament of England substantially the same in its general provisions. Up to that time there had been no similar law in England, except certain highly penal statutes passed in the reign of George II, prohibiting English subjects from enlisting in foreign service, the avowed object of which statutes was that foreign armies, raised for the purpose of restoring the house of Stuart to the throne, should not be strengthened by recruits from England herself.

All must see that difficulties may arise in carrying the laws referred to into execution in a country now having 3,000 or 4,000 miles of seacoast, with an infinite number of ports and harbors and small inlets, from some of which unlawful expeditions may suddenly set forth, without the knowledge of Government, against the possessions of foreign states.

"Friendly relations with all, but entangling alliances with none," has long been a maxim with us. Our true mission is not to propagate our opinions or impose upon other countries our form of government by artifice or force, but to teach by example and show by our success, moderation, and justice the blessings of self-government and the advantages of free institutions. Let every people choose for itself and make and alter its political institutions to suit its own condition and convenience. But while we avow and maintain this neutral policy ourselves, we are anxious to see the same forbearance on the part of other nations whose forms of government are different from our own. The deep interest which we feel in the spread of liberal principles and the establishment of free governments and the sympathy with which we witness every struggle against oppression forbid that we should be indifferent to a case in which the strong arm of a foreign power is invoked to stifle public sentiment and repress the spirit of freedom in any country.

The Governments of Great Britain and France have issued orders to their naval commanders on the West India station to prevent, by force if necessary, the landing of adventurers from any nation on the island of Cuba with hostile intent. The copy of a memorandum of a conversation on this subject between the chargé d'affaires of Her Britannic Majesty and the Acting Secretary of State and of a subsequent note of the former to the Department of State are herewith submitted, together with a copy of a note of the Acting Secretary of State to the minister of the French Republic and of the reply of the latter on the same subject. These papers will acquaint you with the grounds of this interposition of two leading commercial powers of Europe, and with the apprehensions, which this Government could not fail to entertain, that such interposition, if carried into effect, might lead to abuses in derogation of the maritime rights of the United States. The maritime rights of the United States are founded on a firm, secure, and well-defined basis; they stand upon the ground of national independence and public law, and will be maintained in all their full and just extent. The principle which this Government has heretofore solemnly announced it still adheres to, and will maintain under all circumstances and at all hazards. That principle is that in every regularly documented merchant vessel the crew who navigate it and those on board of it will find their protection in the flag which is over them. No American ship can be allowed to be visited or searched for the purpose of ascertaining the character of individuals on board, nor can there be allowed any watch by the vessels of any foreign nation over American vessels on the coast of the United States or the seas adjacent thereto. It will be seen by the last communication from the British chargé d'affaires to the Department of State that he is authorized to assure the Secretary of State that every care will be taken that in executing the preventive measures against the expeditions which the United States Government itself has denounced as not being entitled to the protection of any government no interference shall take place with the lawful commerce of any nation.

In addition to the correspondence on this subject herewith submitted, official information has been received at the Department of State of assurances by the French Government that in the orders given to the French naval forces they were expressly instructed, in any operations they might engage in, to respect the flag of the United States wherever it might appear, and to commit no act of hostility upon any vessel or armament under its protection.

Ministers and consuls of foreign nations are the means and agents of communication between us and those nations, and it is of the utmost importance that while residing in the country they should feel a perfect security so long as they faithfully discharge their respective duties and are guilty of no violation of our laws. This is the admitted law of nations and no country has a deeper interest in maintaining it than the United States. Our commerce spreads over every sea and visits every clime, and our ministers and consuls are appointed to protect the interests of that commerce as well as to guard the peace of the country and maintain the honor of its flag. But how can they discharge these duties unless they be themselves protected? And if protected it must be by the laws of the country in which they reside. And what is due to our own public functionaries residing in foreign nations is exactly the measure of what is due to the functionaries of other governments residing here. As in war the bearers of flags of truce are sacred, or else wars would be interminable, so in peace ambassadors, public ministers, and consuls, charged with friendly national intercourse, are objects of especial respect and protection, each according to the rights belonging to his rank and station. In view of these important principles, it is with deep mortification and regret I announce to you that during the excitement growing out of the executions at Havana the office of Her Catholic Majesty's consul at New Orleans was assailed by a mob, his property destroyed, the Spanish flag found in the office carried off and torn in pieces, and he himself induced to flee for his personal safety, which he supposed to be in danger. On receiving intelligence of these events I forthwith directed the attorney of the United States residing at New Orleans to inquire into the facts and the extent of the pecuniary loss sustained by the consul, with the intention of laying them before you, that you might make provision for such indemnity to him as a just regard for the honor of the nation and the respect which is due to a friendly power might, in your judgment, seem to require. The correspondence upon this subject between the Secretary of State and Her Catholic Majesty's minister plenipotentiary is herewith transmitted.

The occurrence at New Orleans has led me to give my attention to the state of our laws in regard to foreign ambassadors, ministers, and consuls. I think the legislation of the country is deficient in not providing sufficiently either for the protection or the punishment of consuls. I therefore recommend the subject to the consideration of Congress.

Your attention is again invited to the question of reciprocal trade between the United States and Canada and other British possessions near our frontier. Overtures for a convention upon this subject have been received from Her Britannic Majesty's minister plenipotentiary, but it seems to be in many respects preferable that the matter should be regulated by reciprocal legislation. Documents are laid before you showing the terms which the British Government is willing to offer and the measures which it may adopt if some arrangement upon this subject shall not be made.

From the accompanying copy of a note from the British legation at Washington and the reply of the Department of State thereto it will appear that Her Britannic Majesty's Government is desirous that a part of the boundary line between Oregon and the British possessions should be authoritatively marked out, and that an intention was expressed to apply to Congress for an appropriation to defray the expense thereof on the part of the United States. Your attention to this subject is accordingly invited and a proper appropriation recommended.

A convention for the adjustment of claims of citizens of the United States against Portugal has been concluded and the ratifications have been exchanged. The first installment of the amount to be paid by Portugal fell due on the 30th of September last and has been paid.

The President of the French Republic, according to the provisions of the convention, has been selected as arbiter in the case of the *General Armstrong*, and has signified that he accepts the trust and the high satisfaction he feels in acting as the common friend of two nations with which France is united by sentiments of sincere and lasting amity.

The Turkish Government has expressed its thanks for the kind reception given to the Sultan's agent, Amin Bey, on the occasion of his recent visit to the United States. On the 28th of February last a dispatch was addressed by the Secretary of State to Mr. Marsh, the American minister at Constantinople, instructing him to ask of the Turkish Government permission for the Hungarians then imprisoned within the dominions of the Sublime Porte to remove to this country. On the 3d of March last both Houses of Congress passed a resolution requesting the President to authorize the employment of a public vessel to convey to this country Louis Kossuth and his associates in captivity.

The instruction above referred to was complied with, and the Turkish Government having released Governor Kossuth and his companions from prison, on the 10th of September last they embarked on board of the United States steam frigate *Mississippi*, which was selected to carry into effect the resolution of Congress. Governor Kossuth left the *Mississippi* at Gibraltar for the purpose of making a visit to England, and may shortly be expected in New York. By communications to the Department of State he has expressed his grateful acknowledgments for the interposition of this Government in behalf of himself and his associates. This country has been justly regarded as a safe asylum for those whom political events have exiled from their own homes in Europe, and it is recommended to Congress to consider in what manner Governor Kossuth and his companions, brought hither by its authority, shall be received and treated.

It is earnestly to be hoped that the differences which have for some time past been pending between the Government of the French Republic and that of the Sandwich Islands may be peaceably and durably adjusted so as to secure the independence of those islands. Long before the events which have of late imparted so much importance to the possessions of the United States on the Pacific we acknowledged the independence of the Hawaiian Government. This Government was first in taking that step, and several of the leading powers of Europe immediately followed. We were influenced in this measure by the existing and prospective importance of the islands as a place of refuge and refreshment for our vessels engaged in the whale fishery, and by the consideration that they lie in the course of the great trade which must at no distant day be carried on between the western coast of North America and eastern Asia.

We were also influenced by a desire that those islands should not pass under the control of any other great maritime state, but should remain in an independent condition, and so be accessible and useful to the commerce of all nations. I need not say that the importance of these considerations has been greatly enhanced by the sudden and vast development which the interests of the United States have attained in California and Oregon, and the policy heretofore adopted in regard to those islands will be steadily pursued.

It is gratifying, not only to those who consider the commercial interests of nations, but also to all who favor the progress of knowledge and the diffusion of religion, to see a community emerge from a savage state and attain such a degree of civilization in those distant seas.

It is much to be deplored that the internal tranquillity of the Mexican Republic should again be seriously disturbed, for since the peace between that Republic and the United States it had enjoyed such comparative repose that the most favorable anticipations for the future might with a degree of confidence have been indulged. These, however, have been thwarted by the recent outbreak in the State of Tamaulipas, on the right bank of the Rio Bravo. Having received information that persons from the United States had taken part in the insurrection, and apprehending that their example might be followed by others, I caused orders to be issued for the purpose of preventing any hostile expeditions against Mexico from being set on foot in violation of the laws of the United States. I likewise issued a proclamation upon the subject, a copy of which is herewith laid before you. This appeared to be rendered imperative by the obligations of treaties and the general duties of good neighborhood.

In my last annual message I informed Congress that citizens of the

United States had undertaken the connection of the two oceans by means of a railroad across the Isthmus of Tehuantepec, under a grant of the Mexican Government to a citizen of that Republic, and that this enterprise would probably be prosecuted with energy whenever Mexico should consent to such stipulations with the Government of the United States as should impart a feeling of security to those who should invest their property in the enterprise.

A convention between the two Governments for the accomplishment of that end has been ratified by this Government, and only awaits the decision of the Congress and the Executive of that Republic.

Some unexpected difficulties and delays have arisen in the ratification of that convention by Mexico, but it is to be presumed that her decision will be governed by just and enlightened views, as well of the general importance of the object as of her own interests and obligations.

In negotiating upon this important subject this Government has had in view one, and only one, object. That object has been, and is, the construction or attainment of a passage from ocean to ocean, the shortest and the best for travelers and merchandise, and equally open to all the world. It has sought to obtain no territorial acquisition, nor any advantages peculiar to itself; and it would see with the greatest regret that Mexico should oppose any obstacle to the accomplishment of an enterprise which promises so much convenience to the whole commercial world and such eminent advantages to Mexico herself. Impressed with these sentiments and these convictions, the Government will continue to exert all proper efforts to bring about the necessary arrangement with the Republic of Mexico for the speedy completion of the work.

For some months past the Republic of Nicaragua has been the theater of one of those civil convulsions from which the cause of free institutions and the general prosperity and social progress of the States of Central America have so often and so severely suffered. Until quiet shall have been restored and a government apparently stable shall have been organized, no advance can prudently be made in disposing of the questions pending between the two countries.

I am happy to announce that an interoceanic communication from the mouth of the St. John to the Pacific has been so far accomplished as that passengers have actually traversed it and merchandise has been transported over it, and when the canal shall have been completed according to the original plan the means of communication will be further improved. It is understood that a considerable part of the railroad across the Isthmus of Panama has been completed, and that the mail and passengers will in future be conveyed thereon.

Whichever of the several routes between the two oceans may ultimately prove most eligible for travelers to and from the different States on the Atlantic and Gulf of Mexico and our coast on the Pacific, there is little reason to doubt that all of them will be useful to the public, and will liberally reward that individual enterprise by which alone they have been or are expected to be carried into effect.

Peace has been concluded between the contending parties in the island of St. Domingo, and, it is hoped, upon a durable basis. Such is the extent of our commercial relations with that island that the United States can not fail to feel a strong interest in its tranquillity.

The office of commissioner to China remains unfilled. Several persons have been appointed, and the place has been offered to others, all of whom have declined its acceptance on the ground of the inadequacy of the compensation. The annual allowance by law is $6,000, and there is no provision for any outfit. I earnestly recommend the consideration of this subject to Congress. Our commerce with China is highly important, and is becoming more and more so in consequence of the increasing intercourse between our ports on the Pacific Coast and eastern Asia. China is understood to be a country in which living is very expensive, and I know of no reason why the American commissioner sent thither should not be placed, in regard to compensation, on an equal footing with ministers who represent this country at the Courts of Europe.

By reference to the report of the Secretary of the Treasury it will be seen that the aggregate receipts for the last fiscal year amounted to $52,312,979.87, which, with the balance in the Treasury on the 1st July, 1850, gave as the available means for the year the sum of $58,917,-524.36.

The total expenditures for the same period were $48,005,878.68. The total imports for the year ending June 30, 1851, were $215,725,995, of which there were in specie $4,967,901. The exports for the same period were $217,517,130, of which there were of domestic products $178,546,555; foreign goods reexported, $9,738,695; specie, $29,231,880.

Since the 1st of December last the payments in cash on account of the public debt, exclusive of interest, have amounted to $7,501,456.56, which, however, includes the sum of $3,242,400, paid under the twelfth article of the treaty with Mexico, and the further sum of $2,591,213.45, being the amount of awards to American citizens under the late treaty with Mexico, for which the issue of stock was authorized, but which was paid in cash from the Treasury.

The public debt on the 20th ultimo, exclusive of the stock authorized to be issued to Texas by the act of 9th September, 1850, was $62,560,-395.26.

The receipts for the next fiscal year are estimated at $51,800,000, which, with the probable unappropriated balance in the Treasury on the 30th June next, will give as the probable available means for that year the sum of $63,258,743.09.

It has been deemed proper, in view of the large expenditures consequent upon the acquisition of territory from Mexico, that the estimates for the next fiscal year should be laid before Congress in such manner as to distinguish the expenditures so required from the otherwise ordinary demands upon the Treasury.

The total expenditures for the next fiscal year are estimated at $42,-892,299.19, of which there is required for the ordinary purposes of the Government, other than those consequent upon the acquisition of our new territories, and deducting the payments on account of the public debt, the sum of $33,343,198.08, and for the purposes connected, directly or indirectly, with those territories and in the fulfillment of the obligations of the Government contracted in consequence of their acquisition the sum of $9,549,101.11.

If the views of the Secretary of the Treasury in reference to the expenditures required for these territories shall be met by corresponding action on the part of Congress, and appropriations made in accordance therewith, there will be an estimated unappropriated balance in the Treasury on the 30th June, 1853, of $20,366,443.90 wherewith to meet that portion of the public debt due on the 1st of July following, amounting to $6,237,931.35, as well as any appropriations which may be made beyond the estimates.

In thus referring to the estimated expenditures on account of our newly acquired territories, I may express the hope that Congress will concur with me in the desire that a liberal course of policy may be pursued toward them, and that every obligation, express or implied, entered into in consequence of their acquisition shall be fulfilled by the most liberal appropriations for that purpose.

The values of our domestic exports for the last fiscal year, as compared with those of the previous year, exhibit an increase of $43,646,322. At first view this condition of our trade with foreign nations would seem to present the most flattering hopes of its future prosperity. An examination of the details of our exports, however, will show that the increased value of our exports for the last fiscal year is to be found in the high price of cotton which prevailed during the first half of that year, which price has since declined about one-half.

The value of our exports of breadstuffs and provisions, which it was supposed the incentive of a low tariff and large importations from abroad would have greatly augmented, has fallen from $68,701,921 in 1847 to $26,051,373 in 1850 and to $21,948,653 in 1851, with a strong probability, amounting almost to a certainty, of a still further reduction in the current year.

The aggregate values of rice exported during the last fiscal year, as compared with the previous year, also exhibit a decrease, amounting to $460,917, which, with a decline in the values of the exports of tobacco for the same period, make an aggregate decrease in these two articles of $1,156,751.

The policy which dictated a low rate of duties on foreign merchandise, it was thought by those who promoted and established it, would tend to benefit the farming population of this country by increasing the demand and raising the price of agricultural products in foreign markets.

The foregoing facts, however, seem to show incontestably that no such result has followed the adoption of this policy. On the contrary, notwithstanding the repeal of the restrictive corn laws in England, the foreign demand for the products of the American farmer has steadily declined, since the short crops and consequent famine in a portion of Europe have been happily replaced by full crops and comparative abundance of food.

It will be seen by recurring to the commercial statistics for the past year that the value of our domestic exports has been increased in the single item of raw cotton by $40,000,000 over the value of that export for the year preceding. This is not due to any increased general demand for that article, but to the short crop of the preceding year, which created an increased demand and an augmented price for the crop of last year. Should the cotton crop now going forward to market be only equal in quantity to that of the year preceding and be sold at the present prices, then there would be a falling off in the value of our exports for the present fiscal year of at least $40,000,000 compared with the amount exported for the year ending 30th June, 1851.

The production of gold in California for the past year seems to promise a large supply of that metal from that quarter for some time to come. This large annual increase of the currency of the world must be attended with its usual results. These have been already partially disclosed in the enhancement of prices and a rising spirit of speculation and adventure, tending to overtrading, as well at home as abroad. Unless some salutary check shall be given to these tendencies it is to be feared that importations of foreign goods beyond a healthy demand in this country will lead to a sudden drain of the precious metals from us, bringing with it, as it has done in former times, the most disastrous consequences to the business and capital of the American people.

The exports of specie to liquidate our foreign debt during the past fiscal year have been $24,263,979 over the amount of specie imported. The exports of specie during the first quarter of the present fiscal year have been $14,651,827. Should specie continue to be exported at this rate for the remaining three quarters of this year, it will drain from our metallic currency during the year ending 30th June, 1852, the enormous amount of $58,607,308.

In the present prosperous condition of the national finances it will become the duty of Congress to consider the best mode of paying off the public debt. If the present and anticipated surplus in the Treasury should not be absorbed by appropriations of an extraordinary character, this surplus should be employed in such way and under such restrictions as Congress may enact in extinguishing the outstanding debt of the nation.

By reference to the act of Congress approved 9th September, 1850, it will be seen that, in consideration of certain concessions by the State of Texas, it is provided that—

The United States shall pay to the State of Texas the sum of $10,000,000 in a stock bearing 5 per cent interest and redeemable at the end of fourteen years, the interest payable half-yearly at the Treasury of the United States.

In the same section of the law it is further provided—

That no more than five millions of said stock shall be issued until the creditors of the State holding bonds and other certificates of stock of Texas, *for which duties on imports were specially* pledged, shall first file at the Treasury of the United States releases of all claims against the United States for or on account of said bonds or certificates, in such form as shall be prescribed by the Secretary of the Treasury and approved by the President of the United States.

The form of release thus provided for has been prescribed by the Secretary of the Treasury and approved. It has been published in all the leading newspapers in the commercial cities of the United States, and all persons holding claims of the kind specified in the foregoing proviso were required to file their releases (in the form thus prescribed) in the Treasury of the United States on or before the 1st day of October, 1851. Although this publication has been continued from the 25th day of March, 1851, yet up to the 1st of October last comparatively few releases had been filed by the creditors of Texas.

The authorities of the State of Texas, at the request of the Secretary of the Treasury, have furnished a schedule of the public debt of that State created prior to her admission into the Union, with a copy of the laws under which each class was contracted.

I have, from the documents furnished by the State of Texas, determined the classes of claims which in my judgment fall within the provisions of the act of Congress of the 9th of September, 1850.

On being officially informed of the acceptance by Texas of the propositions contained in the act referred to I caused the stock to be prepared, and the five millions which are to be issued unconditionally, bearing an interest of 5 per cent from the 1st day of January, 1851, have been for some time ready to be delivered to the State of Texas. The authorities of Texas up to the present time have not authorized anyone to receive this stock, and it remains in the Treasury Department subject to the order of Texas.

The releases required by law to be deposited in the Treasury not having been filed there, the remaining five millions have not been issued. This last amount of the stock will be withheld from Texas until the conditions upon which it is to be delivered shall be complied with by the creditors of that State, unless Congress shall otherwise direct by a modification of the law.

In my last annual message, to which I respectfully refer, I stated briefly the reasons which induced me to recommend a modification of the present tariff by converting the *ad valorem* into a specific duty wherever the article imported was of such a character as to permit it, and that such a discrimination should be made in favor of the industrial pursuits of our own country as to encourage home production without excluding foreign competition.

The numerous frauds which continue to be practiced upon the revenue by false invoices and undervaluations constitute an unanswerable reason for adopting specific instead of *ad valorem* duties in all cases where the nature of the commodity does not forbid it. A striking illustration of these frauds will be exhibited in the report of the Secretary of the Treasury, showing the custom-house valuation of articles imported under a former law, subject to specific duties, when there was no inducement to undervaluation, and the custom-house valuations of the same articles under the present system of *ad valorem* duties, so greatly reduced as to leave no doubt of the existence of the most flagrant abuses under the existing laws. This practical evasion of the present law, combined with the languishing condition of some of the great interests of the country, caused by overimportations and consequent depressed prices, and with the failure in obtaining a foreign market for our increasing surplus of breadstuffs and provisions, has induced me again to recommend a modification of the existing tariff.

The report of the Secretary of the Interior, which accompanies this communication, will present a condensed statement of the operations of that important Department of the Government.

It will be seen that the cash sales of the public lands exceed those of the preceding year, and that there is reason to anticipate a still further increase, notwithstanding the large donations which have been made to many of the States and the liberal grants to individuals as a reward for military services. This fact furnishes very gratifying evidence of the growing wealth and prosperity of our country.

Suitable measures have been adopted for commencing the survey of the public lands in California and Oregon. Surveying parties have been organized and some progress has been made in establishing the principal base and meridian lines. But further legislation and additional appropriations will be necessary before the proper subdivisions can be made and the general land system extended over those remote parts of our territory.

On the 3d of March last an act was passed providing for the appointment of three commissioners to settle private land claims in California. Three persons were immediately appointed, all of whom, however, declined accepting the office in consequence of the inadequacy of the compensation. Others were promptly selected, who for the same reason also declined, and it was not until late in the season that the services of suitable persons could be secured. A majority of the commissioners convened in this city on the 10th of September last, when detailed instructions were given to them in regard to their duties. Their first meeting for the transaction of business will be held in San Francisco on the 8th day of the present month.

I have thought it proper to refer to these facts, not only to explain the causes of the delay in filling the commission, but to call your attention to the propriety of increasing the compensation of the commissioners. The office is one of great labor and responsibility, and the compensation should be such as to command men of a high order of talents and the most unquestionable integrity.

The proper disposal of the mineral lands of California is a subject surrounded by great difficulties. In my last annual message I recommended the survey and sale of them in small parcels under such restrictions as would effectually guard against monopoly and speculation; but upon further information, and in deference to the opinions of persons familiar with the subject, I am inclined to change that recommendation and to advise that they be permitted to remain as at present, a common field, open to the enterprise and industry of all our citizens, until further experience shall have developed the best policy to be ultimately adopted in regard to them. It is safer to suffer the inconveniences that now exist for a short period than by premature legislation to fasten on the country a system founded in error, which may place the whole subject beyond the future control of Congress.

The agricultural lands should, however, be surveyed and brought into market with as little delay as possible, that the titles may become settled and the inhabitants stimulated to make permanent improvements and enter on the ordinary pursuits of life. To effect these objects it is desirable that the necessary provision be made by law for the establishment of land offices in California and Oregon and for the efficient prosecution of the surveys at an early day.

Some difficulties have occurred in organizing the Territorial governments of New Mexico and Utah, and when more accurate information shall be obtained of the causes a further communication will be made on that subject.

In my last annual communication to Congress I recommended the establishment of an agricultural bureau, and I take this occasion again to invoke your favorable consideration of the subject.

Agriculture may justly be regarded as the great interest of our people. Four-fifths of our active population are employed in the cultivation of the soil, and the rapid expansion of our settlements over new territory is daily adding to the number of those engaged in that vocation. Justice and sound policy, therefore, alike require that the Government should use all the means authorized by the Constitution to promote the interests and welfare of that important class of our fellow-citizens. And yet it is a singular fact that whilst the manufacturing and commercial interests have engaged the attention of Congress during a large portion of every session and our statutes abound in provisions for their protection and encouragement, little has yet been done directly for the advancement of agriculture. It is time that this reproach to our legislation should be removed, and I sincerely hope that the present Congress will not close their labors without adopting efficient means to supply the omissions of those who have preceded them.

An agricultural bureau, charged with the duty of collecting and disseminating correct information as to the best modes of cultivation and of the most effectual means of preserving and restoring the fertility of the soil and of procuring and distributing seeds and plants and other vegetable productions, with instructions in regard to the soil, climate, and treatment best adapted to their growth, could not fail to be, in the language of Washington in his last annual message to Congress, a "very cheap instrument of immense national benefit."

Regarding the act of Congress approved 28th September, 1850, granting bounty lands to persons who had been engaged in the military service of the country, as a great measure of national justice and munificence, an anxious desire has been felt by the officers intrusted with its immediate execution to give prompt effect to its provisions. All the means within their control were therefore brought into requisition to expedite the adjudication of claims, and I am gratified to be able to state that near 100,000 applications have been considered and about 70,000 warrants issued within the short space of nine months. If adequate provision be made by law to carry into effect the recommendations of the Department, it is confidently expected that before the close of the next fiscal year all who are entitled to the benefits of the act will have received their warrants.

The Secretary of the Interior has suggested in his report various amendments of the laws relating to pensions and bounty lands for the purpose of more effectually guarding against abuses and frauds on the Government, to all of which I invite your particular attention.

The large accessions to our Indian population consequent upon the acquisition of New Mexico and California and the extension of our settlements into Utah and Oregon have given increased interest and importance to our relations with the aboriginal race.

No material change has taken place within the last year in the condition and prospects of the Indian tribes who reside in the Northwestern Territory and west of the Mississippi River. We are at peace with all of them, and it will be a source of pleasure to you to learn that they are gradually advancing in civilization and the pursuits of social life.

Along the Mexican frontier and in California and Oregon there have been occasional manifestations of unfriendly feeling and some depredations committed. I am satisfied, however, that they resulted more from the destitute and starving condition of the Indians than from any settled hostility toward the whites. As the settlements of our citizens progress toward them, the game, upon which they mainly rely for subsistence, is driven off or destroyed, and the only alternative left to them is starvation or plunder. It becomes us to consider, in view of this condition of things, whether justice and humanity, as well as an enlightened economy, do not require that instead of seeking to punish them for offenses which are the result of our own policy toward them we should not provide for their immediate wants and encourage them to engage in agriculture and to rely on their labor instead of the chase for the means of support.

Various important treaties have been negotiated with different tribes during the year, by which their title to large and valuable tracts of country has been extinguished, all of which will at the proper time be submitted to the Senate for ratification.

The joint commission under the treaty of Guadalupe Hidalgo has been actively engaged in running and marking the boundary line between the United States and Mexico. It was stated in the last annual report of the Secretary of the Interior that the initial point on the Pacific and the point of junction of the Gila with the Colorado River had been determined and the intervening line, about 150 miles in length, run and marked by temporary monuments. Since that time a monument of marble has been erected at the initial point, and permanent landmarks of iron have been placed at suitable distances along the line.

The initial point on the Rio Grande has also been fixed by the commissioners, at latitude 32° 22′, and at the date of the last communication the survey of the line had been made thence westward about 150 miles to the neighborhood of the copper mines.

The commission on our part was at first organized on a scale which experience proved to be unwieldy and attended with unnecessary expense. Orders have therefore been issued for the reduction of the number of persons employed within the smallest limits consistent with the safety of those engaged in the service and the prompt and efficient execution of their important duties.

Returns have been received from all the officers engaged in taking the census in the States and Territories except California. The superintendent employed to make the enumeration in that State has not yet made his full report, from causes, as he alleges, beyond his control. This failure is much to be regretted, as it has prevented the Secretary of the Interior from making the decennial apportionment of Representatives among the States, as required by the act approved May 23, 1850. It is hoped, however, that the returns will soon be received, and no time will then be lost in making the necessary apportionment and in transmitting the certificates required by law.

The Superintendent of the Seventh Census is diligently employed, under the direction of the Secretary of the Interior, in classifying and arranging in tabular form all the statistical information derived from the returns of the marshals, and it is believed that when the work shall be completed it will exhibit a more perfect view of the population, wealth, occupations, and social condition of a great country than has ever been presented to the world. The value of such a work as the basis of enlightened legislation can hardly be overestimated, and I earnestly hope that Congress will lose no time in making the appropriations necessary to complete the classifications and to publish the results in a style worthy of the subject and of our national character.

The want of a uniform fee bill, prescribing the compensation to be allowed district attorneys, clerks, marshals, and commissioners in civil and criminal cases, is the cause of much vexation, injustice, and complaint. I would recommend a thorough revision of the laws on the whole subject and the adoption of a tariff of fees which, as far as practicable, should be uniform, and prescribe a specific compensation for every service which the officer may be required to perform. This subject will be fully presented in the report of the Secretary of the Interior.

In my last annual message I gave briefly my reasons for believing that you possessed the constitutional power to improve the harbors of our Great Lakes and seacoast and the navigation of our principal rivers, and recommended that appropriations should be made for completing such works as had already been commenced and for commencing such others as might seem to the wisdom of Congress to be of public and general importance. Without repeating the reasons then urged, I deem it my duty again to call your attention to this important subject. The works on many of the harbors were left in an unfinished state, and consequently exposed to the action of the elements, which is fast destroying them. Great numbers of lives and vast amounts of property are annually lost for want of safe and convenient harbors on the Lakes. None but those who have been exposed to that dangerous navigation can fully appreciate the importance of this subject. The whole Northwest appeals to you for relief, and I trust their appeal will receive due consideration at your hands.

The same is in a measure true in regard to some of the harbors and inlets on the seacoast.

The unobstructed navigation of our large rivers is of equal importance. Our settlements are now extending to the sources of the great rivers which empty into and form a part of the Mississippi, and the value of the public lands in those regions would be greatly enhanced by freeing the navigation of those waters from obstructions. In view, therefore, of this great interest, I deem it my duty again to urge upon Congress to make such appropriations for these improvements as they may deem necessary.

The surveys of the Delta of the Mississippi, with a view to the prevention of the overflows that have proved so disastrous to that region of country, have been nearly completed, and the reports thereof are now in course of preparation and will shortly be laid before you.

The protection of our southwestern frontier and of the adjacent Mexican States against the Indian tribes within our border has claimed my earnest and constant attention. Congress having failed at the last session to adopt my recommendation that an additional regiment of mounted men specially adapted to that service should be raised, all that remained to be done was to make the best use of the means at my disposal. Accordingly, all the troops adapted to that service that could properly be spared from other quarters have been concentrated on that frontier and officers of high reputation selected to command them. A new arrangement of the military posts has also been made, whereby the troops are brought nearer to the Mexican frontier and to the tribes they are intended to overawe.

Sufficient time has not yet elapsed to realize all the benefits that are expected to result from these arrangements, but I have every reason to hope that they will effectually check their marauding expeditions. The nature of the country, which furnishes little for the support of an army and abounds in places of refuge and concealment, is remarkably well adapted to this predatory warfare, and we can scarcely hope that any military force, combined with the greatest vigilance, can entirely suppress it.

By the treaty of Guadalupe Hidalgo we are bound to protect the territory of Mexico against the incursions of the savage tribes within our border "with equal diligence and energy" as if the same were made within our territory or against our citizens. I have endeavored to comply as far as possible with this provision of the treaty. Orders have been given to the officers commanding on that frontier to consider the Mexican territory and its inhabitants as equally with our own entitled to their protection, and to make all their plans and arrangements with a view to the attainment of this object. Instructions have also been given to the Indian commissioners and agents among these tribes in all treaties to make the clauses designed for the protection of our own citizens apply also to those of Mexico. I have no reason to doubt that these instructions have been fully carried into effect; nevertheless, it is probable that in spite of all our efforts some of the neighboring States of Mexico may have suffered, as our own have, from depredations by the Indians.

To the difficulties of defending our own territory, as above mentioned, are superadded, in defending that of Mexico, those that arise from its remoteness, from the fact that we have no right to station our troops within her limits and that there is no efficient military force on the Mexican side to cooperate with our own. So long as this shall continue to be the case the number and activity of our troops will rather increase than diminish the evil, as the Indians will naturally turn toward that country where they encounter the least resistance. Yet these troops are necessary to subdue them and to compel them to make and observe treaties. Until this shall have been done neither country will enjoy any security from their attacks.

The Indians in California, who had previously appeared of a peaceable character and disposed to cultivate the friendship of the whites, have recently committed several acts of hostility. As a large portion of the reenforcements sent to the Mexican frontier were drawn from the Pacific, the military force now stationed there is considered entirely inadequate to its defense. It can not be increased, however, without an increase of the Army, and I again recommend that measure as indispensable to the protection of the frontier.

I invite your attention to the suggestions on this subject and on others connected with his Department in the report of the Secretary of War.

The appropriations for the support of the Army during the current fiscal year ending 30th June next were reduced far below the estimate submitted by the Department. The consequence of this reduction is a considerable deficiency, to which I invite your early attention.

The expenditures of that Department for the year ending 30th June last were $9,060,268.58. The estimates for the year commencing 1st July next and ending June 30, 1853, are $7,898,775.83, showing a reduction of $1,161,492.75.

The board of commissioners to whom the management of the affairs of the military asylum created by the act of 3d March last was intrusted have selected a site for the establishment of an asylum in the vicinity of this city, which has been approved by me subject to the production of a satisfactory title.

The report of the Secretary of the Navy will exhibit the condition of the public service under the supervision of that Department. Our naval force afloat during the present year has been actively and usefully employed in giving protection to our widely extended and increasing commerce and interests in the various quarters of the globe, and our flag has everywhere afforded the security and received the respect inspired by the justice and liberality of our intercourse and the dignity and power of the nation.

The expedition commanded by Lieutenant De Haven, dispatched in search of the British commander Sir John Franklin and his companions in the Arctic Seas, returned to New York in the month of October, after having undergone great peril and suffering from an unknown and dangerous navigation and the rigors of a northern climate, without any satisfactory information of the objects of their search, but with new contributions to science and navigation from the unfrequented polar regions. The officers and men of the expedition having been all volunteers for this service and having so conducted it as to meet the entire approbation of the Government, it is suggested, as an act of grace and generosity, that the same allowance of extra pay and emoluments be extended to them that were made to the officers and men of like rating in the late exploring expedition to the South Seas.

I earnestly recommend to your attention the necessity of reorganizing the naval establishment, apportioning and fixing the number of officers in each grade, providing some mode of promotion to the higher grades of the Navy having reference to merit and capacity rather than seniority or date of entry into the service, and for retiring from the effective list upon reduced pay those who may be incompetent to the performance of active duty. As a measure of economy, as well as of efficiency, in this arm of the service, the provision last mentioned is eminently worthy of your consideration.

The determination of the questions of relative rank between the sea officers and civil officers of the Navy, and between officers of the Army and Navy, in the various grades of each, will also merit your attention. The failure to provide any substitute when corporal punishment was abolished for offenses in the Navy has occasioned the convening of numerous courts-martial upon the arrival of vessels in port, and is believed to have had an injurious effect upon the discipline and efficiency of the service. To moderate punishment from one grade to another is among the humane reforms of the age, but to abolish one of severity, which applied so generally to offenses on shipboard, and provide nothing in its stead is to suppose a progress of improvement in every individual among seamen which is not assumed by the Legislature in respect to any other class of men. It is hoped that Congress, in the ample opportunity afforded by the present session, will thoroughly investigate this important subject, and establish such modes of determining guilt and such gradations of punishment as are consistent with humanity and the personal rights of individuals, and at the same time shall insure the most energetic and efficient performance of duty and the suppression of crime in our ships of war.

The stone dock in the navy-yard at New York, which was ten years in process of construction, has been so far finished as to be surrendered up to the authorities of the yard. The dry dock at Philadelphia is reported as completed, and is expected soon to be tested and delivered over to the agents of the Government. That at Portsmouth, N. H., is also nearly ready for delivery; and a contract has been concluded, agreeably to the act of Congress at its last session, for a floating sectional dock on the Bay of San Francisco. I invite your attention to the recommendation of the Department touching the establishment of a navy-yard in conjunction with this dock on the Pacific. Such a station is highly necessary to the convenience and effectiveness of our fleet in that ocean, which must be expected to increase with the growth of commerce and the rapid extension of our whale fisheries over its waters.

The Naval Academy at Annapolis, under a revised and improved system of regulations, now affords opportunities of education and instruction to the pupils quite equal, it is believed, for professional improvement, to those enjoyed by the cadets in the Military Academy. A large class of acting midshipmen was received at the commencement of the last academic term, and a practice ship has been attached to the institution to afford the amplest means for regular instruction in seamanship, as well as for cruises during the vacations of three or four months in each year.

The advantages of science in nautical affairs have rarely been more strikingly illustrated than in the fact, stated in the report of the Navy Department, that by means of the wind and current charts projected and prepared by Lieutenant Maury, the Superintendent of the Naval Observatory, the passage from the Atlantic to the Pacific ports of our country has been shortened by about forty days.

The estimates for the support of the Navy and Marine Corps the ensuing fiscal year will be found to be $5,856,472.19, the estimates for the current year being $5,900,621.

The estimates for special objects under the control of this Department amount to $2,684,220.89, against $2,210,980 for the present year, the increase being occasioned by the additional mail service on the Pacific Coast and the construction of the dock in California, authorized at the last session of Congress, and some slight additions under the head of improvements and repairs in navy-yards, buildings, and machinery.

I deem it of much importance to a just economy and a correct understanding of naval expenditures that there should be an entire separation of the appropriations for the support of the naval service proper from those for permanent improvements at navy-yards and stations and from ocean steam mail service and other special objects assigned to the supervision of this Department.

The report of the Postmaster-General, herewith communicated, presents an interesting view of the progress, operations, and condition of his Department.

At the close of the last fiscal year the length of mail routes within the United States was 196,290 miles, the annual transportation thereon 53,272,252 miles, and the annual cost of such transportation $3,421,754.

The length of the foreign mail routes is estimated at 18,349 miles and the annual transportation thereon at 615,206 miles. The annual cost of this service is $1,472,187, of which $448,937 are paid by the Post-Office Department and $1,023,250 are paid through the Navy Department.

The annual transportation within the United States, excluding the service in California and Oregon, which is now for the first time reported and embraced in the tabular statements of the Department, exceeds that of the preceding year 6,162,855 miles, at an increased cost of $547,110.

The whole number of post-offices in the United States on the 30th day of June last was 19,796. There were 1,698 post-offices established and 256 discontinued during the year.

The gross revenues of the Department for the fiscal year, including the appropriations for the franked matter of Congress, of the Departments, and officers of Government, and excluding the foreign postages collected for and payable to the British post-office, amounted to $6,727,-866.78.

The expenditures for the same period, excluding $20,599.49, paid under an award of the Auditor, in pursuance of a resolution of the last Congress, for mail service on the Ohio and Mississippi rivers in 1832 and 1833, and the amount paid to the British post-office for foreign postages collected for and payable to that office, amounted to $6,024,566.79, leaving a balance of revenue over the proper expenditures of the year of $703,299.99.

The receipts for postages during the year, excluding the foreign postages collected for and payable to the British post-office, amounted to $6,345,747.21, being an increase of $997,610.79, or 18.65 per cent, over the like receipts for the preceding year.

The reduction of postage under the act of March last did not take effect until the commencement of the present fiscal year. The accounts for the first quarter under the operation of the reduced rates will not be settled before January next, and no reliable estimate of the receipts for the present year can yet be made. It is believed, however, that they will fall far short of those of the last year. The surplus of the revenues now on hand is, however, so large that no further appropriation from the Treasury in aid of the revenues of the Department is required for the current fiscal year, but an additional appropriation for the year ending June 30, 1853, will probably be found necessary when the receipts of the first two quarters of the fiscal year are fully ascertained.

In his last annual report the Postmaster-General recommended a reduction of postage to rates which he deemed as low as could be prudently adopted unless Congress was prepared to appropriate from the Treasury for the support of the Department a sum more than equivalent to the mail services performed by it for the Government. The recommendations of the Postmaster-General in respect to letter postage, except on letters from and to California and Oregon, were substantially adopted by the last Congress. He now recommends adherence to the present letter rates and advises against a further reduction until justified by the revenue of the Department.

He also recommends that the rates of postage on printed matter be so revised as to render them more simple and more uniform in their operation upon all classes of printed matter. I submit the recommendations of the report to your favorable consideration.

The public statutes of the United States have now been accumulating for more than sixty years, and, interspersed with private acts, are scattered through numerous volumes, and, from the cost of the whole, have become almost inaccessible to the great mass of the community. They also exhibit much of the incongruity and imperfection of hasty legislation. As it seems to be generally conceded that there is no "common law" of the United States to supply the defects of their legislation, it is most important that that legislation should be as perfect as possible, defining every power intended to be conferred, every crime intended to be made punishable, and prescribing the punishment to be inflicted. In addition to some particular cases spoken of more at length, the whole criminal code is now lamentably defective. Some offenses are imperfectly described and others are entirely omitted, so that flagrant crimes may be committed with impunity. The scale of punishment is not in all cases graduated according to the degree and nature of the offense, and is often rendered more unequal by the different modes of imprisonment or penitentiary confinement in the different States.

Many laws of a permanent character have been introduced into appropriation bills, and it is often difficult to determine whether the particular clause expires with the temporary act of which it is a part or continues in force. It has also frequently happened that enactments and provisions of law have been introduced into bills with the title or general subject of which they have little or no connection or relation. In this mode of legislation so many enactments have been heaped upon each other, and often with but little consideration, that in many instances it is difficult to search out and determine what is the law.

The Government of the United States is emphatically a government of written laws. The statutes should therefore, as far as practicable, not only be made accessible to all, but be expressed in language so plain and simple as to be understood by all and arranged in such method as to give perspicuity to every subject. Many of the States have revised their public acts with great and manifest benefit, and I recommend that provision be made by law for the appointment of a commission to revise the public statutes of the United States, arranging them in order, supplying deficiencies, correcting incongruities, simplifying their language, and reporting them to Congress for its action.

An act of Congress approved 30th September, 1850, contained a provision for the extension of the Capitol according to such plan as might be approved by the President, and appropriated $100,000 to be expended under his direction by such architect as he should appoint to execute the same. On examining the various plans which had been submitted by different architects in pursuance of an advertisement by a committee of the Senate no one was found to be entirely satisfactory, and it was therefore deemed advisable to combine and adopt the advantages of several.

The great object to be accomplished was to make such an addition as would afford ample and convenient halls for the deliberations of the two Houses of Congress, with sufficient accommodations for spectators and suitable apartments for the committees and officers of the two branches of the Legislature. It was also desirable not to mar the harmony and beauty of the present structure, which, as a specimen of architecture, is so universally admired. Keeping these objects in view, I concluded to make the addition by wings, detached from the present building, yet connected with it by corridors. This mode of enlargement will leave the present Capitol uninjured and afford great advantages for ventilation and the admission of light, and will enable the work to progress without interrupting the deliberations of Congress. To carry this plan into effect I have appointed an experienced and competent architect. The corner stone was laid on the 4th day of July last with suitable ceremonies, since which time the work has advanced with commendable rapidity, and the foundations of both wings are now nearly complete.

I again commend to your favorable regard the interests of the District of Columbia, and deem it only necessary to remind you that although its inhabitants have no voice in the choice of Representatives in Congress, they are not the less entitled to a just and liberal consideration in your legislation. My opinions on this subject were more fully expressed in my last annual communication.

Other subjects were brought to the attention of Congress in my last annual message, to which I would respectfully refer. But there was one of more than ordinary interest, to which I again invite your special attention. I allude to the recommendation for the appointment of a commission to settle private claims against the United States. Justice to individuals, as well as to the Government, imperatively demands that some more convenient and expeditious mode than an appeal to Congress should be adopted.

It is deeply to be regretted that in several instances officers of the Government, in attempting to execute the law for the return of fugitives from labor, have been openly resisted and their efforts frustrated and defeated by lawless and violent mobs; that in one case such resistance resulted in the death of an estimable citizen, and in others serious injury ensued to those officers and to individuals who were using their endeavors to sustain the laws. Prosecutions have been instituted against the alleged offenders so far as they could be identified, and are still pending. I have regarded it as my duty in these cases to give all aid legally in my power to the enforcement of the laws, and I shall continue to do so wherever and whenever their execution may be resisted.

The act of Congress for the return of fugitives from labor is one required and demanded by the express words of the Constitution.

The Constitution declares that—

> No person held to service or labor in one State, under the laws thereof, escaping into another, shall, in consequence of any law or regulation therein, be discharged from such service or labor, but shall be delivered up on claim of the party to whom such service or labor may be due.

This constitutional provision is equally obligatory upon the legislative, the executive, and judicial departments of the Government, and upon every citizen of the United States.

Congress, however, must from necessity first act upon the subject by prescribing the proceedings necessary to ascertain that the person is a fugitive and the means to be used for his restoration to the claimant. This was done by an act passed during the first term of President Washington, which was amended by that enacted by the last Congress, and it now remains for the executive and judicial departments to take care that these laws be faithfully executed. This injunction of the Constitution is as peremptory and as binding as any other; it stands exactly on the same foundation as that clause which provides for the return of fugitives from justice, or that which declares that no bill of attainder or *ex post facto* law shall be passed, or that which provides for an equality of taxation according to the census, or the clause declaring that all duties shall be uniform throughout the United States, or the important provision that the trial of all crimes shall be by jury. These several articles and clauses of the Constitution, all resting on the same authority, must stand or fall together. Some objections have been urged against the details of the act for the return of fugitives from labor, but it is worthy of remark that the main opposition is aimed against the Constitution itself, and proceeds from persons and classes of persons many of whom declare their wish to see that Constitution overturned. They avow their hostility to any law which shall give full and practical effect to this requirement of the Constitution. Fortunately, the number of these persons is comparatively small, and is believed to be daily diminishing; but the issue which they present is one which involves the supremacy and even the existence of the Constitution.

Cases have heretofore arisen in which individuals have denied the binding authority of acts of Congress, and even States have proposed to nullify such acts upon the ground that the Constitution was the supreme law of the land, and that those acts of Congress were repugnant to that instrument; but nullification is now aimed not so much against particular laws as being inconsistent with the Constitution as against the Constitution itself, and it is not to be disguised that a spirit exists, and has been actively at work, to rend asunder this Union, which is our cherished inheritance from our Revolutionary fathers.

In my last annual message I stated that I considered the series of measures which had been adopted at the previous session in reference to the agitation growing out of the Territorial and slavery questions as a final settlement in principle and substance of the dangerous and exciting subjects which they embraced, and I recommended adherence to the adjustment established by those measures until time and experience should demonstrate the necessity of further legislation to guard against evasion or abuse. I was not induced to make this recommendation because I thought those measures perfect, for no human legislation can be perfect. Wide differences and jarring opinions can only be reconciled by yielding something on all sides, and this result had been reached after an angry conflict of many months, in which one part of the country was arrayed against another, and violent convulsion seemed to be imminent. Looking at the interests of the whole country, I felt it to be my duty to seize upon this compromise as the best that could be obtained amid conflicting interests and to insist upon it as a final settlement, to be adhered to by all who value the peace and welfare of the country. A year has now elapsed since that recommendation was made. To that recommendation I still adhere, and I congratulate you and the country upon the general acquiescence in these measures of peace which has been exhibited in all parts of the Republic. And not only is there this general acquiescence in these measures, but the spirit of conciliation which has been manifested in regard to them in all parts of the country has removed doubts and uncertainties in the minds of thousands of good men concerning the durability of our popular institutions and given renewed assurance that our liberty and our Union may subsist together for the benefit of this and all succeeding generations.

MILLARD FILLMORE.

SPECIAL MESSAGES.

WASHINGTON, *December 12, 1851.*

To the Senate of the United States:

I transmit to the Senate, for its consideration with a view to ratification, a treaty of friendship, commerce, and navigation between the United States and the Republic of Costa Rica, signed in this city on the 10th day of July last.

MILLARD FILLMORE.

WASHINGTON, *December 15, 1851.*

To the Senate of the United States:

I transmit to the Senate a report* of the Secretary of State, in answer to their resolution of the 8th of March last.

MILLARD FILLMORE.

WASHINGTON, *December 15, 1851.*

To the Senate of the United States:

I have received a resolution of the Senate, adopted on the 12th instant, in the following terms:

Resolved, That the President of the United States be requested to communicate to the Senate, if not inconsistent with the public interest, any information the Executive may have received respecting the firing into and seizure of the American steamship *Prometheus* by a British vessel of war in November last near Greytown, on the Mosquito Coast, and also what measures have been taken by the Executive to ascertain the state of the facts and to vindicate the honor of the country.

*Relating to the free navigation of the St. Lawrence, St. John, and other large rivers, and to the free enjoyment of the British North American fisheries by United States citizens.

In answer to this request I submit to the Senate the accompanying extracts from a communication addressed to the Department of State by Mr. Joseph L. White, as counsel of the American, Atlantic and Pacific Ship Canal Company, dated 2d instant.

This communication is the principal source of the information received by the Executive in relation to the subject alluded to, and is presumed to be essentially correct in its statement of the facts. Upon receiving this communication instructions such as the occasion seemed to demand were immediately dispatched to the minister of the United States in London. Sufficient time has not elapsed for the return of any answer to this dispatch from him, and in my judgment it would at the present moment be inconsistent with the public interest to communicate those instructions. A communication, however, of all the correspondence will be made to the Senate at the earliest moment at which a proper regard to the public interest will permit.

At the same time instructions were given to Commodore Parker, commanding the Home Squadron, a copy of which, so far as they relate to the case of the *Prometheus*, is herewith transmitted to the Senate.

MILLARD FILLMORE.

WASHINGTON, *December 16, 1851.*

To the Senate of the United States:

In answer to the resolution of the Senate of the 9th instant, requesting information in regard to the imprisonment of John S. Thrasher at Havana, I transmit a report from the Secretary of State and the documents which accompanied it.

MILLARD FILLMORE.

WASHINGTON, *December 16, 1851.*

To the Senate of the United States:

In answer to the resolution of the Senate of the 8th instant, requesting the communication of a dispatch* addressed to the Department of State by Mr. Niles, late chargé d'affaires of the United States at Turin, I transmit a report from the Secretary of State, which is accompanied by a copy of the dispatch.

MILLARD FILLMORE.

WASHINGTON, *December 23, 1851.*

To the House of Representatives:

I transmit to the House of Representatives a report from the Secretary of State, in answer to the first part† of a resolution of the 15th Decem-

* On the subject of a ship canal between the Atlantic and Pacific oceans.

† Relating to the conclusion of a treaty between Spain, France, and Great Britain in respect to the island of Cuba.

ber, 1851, and also a report from the Secretary of the Navy, in answer to the remaining part* of the same resolution.

MILLARD FILLMORE.

WASHINGTON, *December 23, 1851.*

To the House of Representatives:

In answer to a resolution of the House of Representatives of the 15th instant, requesting information in regard to the imprisonment, trial, and sentence of John S. Thrasher in the island of Cuba, I transmit a report from the Secretary of State and the documents which accompanied it.

MILLARD FILLMORE.

WASHINGTON, *December 29, 1851.*

To the Senate and House of Representatives:

I transmit herewith a copy of a letter of the 26th instant, addressed to the Secretary of State by the contractors for paying the next installment due to Mexico pursuant to the treaty of Guadalupe Hidalgo, representing the necessity of an immediate appropriation by Congress of the money necessary for that purpose.

MILLARD FILLMORE.

WASHINGTON, *January 2, 1852.*

To the House of Representatives:

As a further answer to the resolution of the House of Representatives of the 15th ultimo, calling for information respecting the imprisonment, trial, and sentence of John S. Thrasher in the island of Cuba, I transmit another report from the Secretary of State.

MILLARD FILLMORE.

WASHINGTON, *January 2, 1852.*

To the House of Representatives of the United States:

I transmit to the House of Representatives a copy of the resolution adopted by the Legislative Council of Canada, together with the copy of the note by which the resolution was communicated to this Government, expressing the satisfaction of that Council at receiving intelligence of certain donations in aid of the reconstruction of the library of the Canadian Parliament.

MILLARD FILLMORE.

[The same message, dated January 6, 1852, was sent to the Senate.]

*Pertaining to the relative strength of the British, French, and United States squadrons in the West India seas, and whether additional appropriations are necessary to increase the United States force on that station.

WASHINGTON, *January 3, 1852.*

To the Senate of the United States:

I nominate Elisha Whittlesey and Elias S. Terry to be commissioners under the seventeenth article of the treaty concluded with the Cherokee tribe of Indians at New Echota on the 29th day of December, 1835, to adjudicate the claim of David Taylor for 640 acres of land, which has been duly appraised in accordance with the terms of the ninth article of said treaty, but not paid for. The facts of the case will more fully appear in the accompanying papers from the Department of the Interior.

MILLARD FILLMORE.

WASHINGTON, *January 5, 1852.*

To the House of Representatives:

I transmit to the House of Representatives a report of the Secretary of State, relative to the persons belonging to the expedition of Lopez who were taken prisoners in Cuba and afterwards sent to Spain, and who have now been pardoned and released by Her Catholic Majesty. The appropriation the expediency of which is suggested in the report I cordially commend to the consideration of Congress, with the single additional suggestion that to be available it should be promptly made.

MILLARD FILLMORE.

[The same message was sent to the Senate.]

WASHINGTON, *January 9, 1852.*

To the House of Representatives:

In answer to a resolution of the House of Representatives of the 15th ultimo, requesting information in regard to the Territory of Utah, I transmit a report from the Secretary of State, to whom the resolution was referred.

MILLARD FILLMORE.

WASHINGTON, *January 12, 1852.*

To the House of Representatives:

In answer to the resolution of the House of Representatives of the 5th instant, I herewith transmit to it a report and accompanying papers* from the Secretary of State.

MILLARD FILLMORE.

WASHINGTON, *January 16, 1852.*

To the House of Representatives:

I transmit a copy of a letter which has been addressed to me by the secretary of the Territory of Utah since my recent message to the House

*Relating to a circular issued by the secretary of state for the British colonial department relative to the employment in the British West India colonies of free blacks and liberated slaves from the United States.

of Representatives in answer to its resolution requesting information in regard to the affairs of that Territory.

MILLARD FILLMORE.

WASHINGTON, *January 19, 1852.*

To the Senate and House of Representatives of the United States:

I transmit to Congress a report from the Secretary of State, accompanied by a letter to him from the contractors for paying the installment of Mexican indemnity due on the 31st May next, and respectfully invite attention to the subject.

MILLARD FILLMORE.

WASHINGTON, *January 20, 1852.*

To the Senate and House of Representatives of the United States:

I communicate to both Houses of Congress a report from the Department of State, containing copies of the correspondence which has taken place between that Department and the minister of the United States in Paris respecting the political occurrences which have recently taken place in France.

MILLARD FILLMORE.

WASHINGTON, *January 22, 1852.*

To the Senate of the United States:

In compliance with a resolution of the Senate passed March 13, 1851, I herewith transmit a report of the Secretary of War, containing information in regard to the claims of citizens of California for services rendered and for money and for property furnished in 1846 and 1847 in the conquest of that country.

MILLARD FILLMORE.

WASHINGTON, *January 23, 1852.*

To the House of Representatives:

I transmit a report from the Secretary of State and the documents which accompanied it, upon the subject of a resolution of the House of Representatives of yesterday, relative to the Mexican indemnity.

MILLARD FILLMORE.

WASHINGTON, *January 28, 1852.*

To the House of Representatives:

In answer to the resolution of the House of Representatives of the 15th ultimo, requesting information respecting the seizure and confiscation of the bark *Georgiana*, of Maine, and brig *Susan Loud*, of Massachusetts,* I transmit a report from the Secretary of State and the documents which accompanied it.

MILLARD FILLMORE.

* By the Spanish or Cuban authorities.

WASHINGTON, *January 28, 1852.*

To the House of Representatives:

In answer to the resolution of the House of Representatives of the 7th August, 1850, and the 17th December, 1851, requesting information touching the claims of citizens of the United States on the Government of Portugal, I transmit a report from the Secretary of State and the documents which accompanied the same.

MILLARD FILLMORE.

WASHINGTON, *February 9, 1852.*

To the Senate of the United States:

I transmit to the Senate, for its consideration with a view to ratification, a treaty of friendship, commerce, and navigation between the United States and the Republic of Peru, concluded and signed at Lima on the 26th day of July last.

A copy of a dispatch of Mr. J. R. Clay, the chargé d'affaires of the United States at Lima, to the Secretary of State, bearing date the 6th December last, is also transmitted for the information of the Senate.

MILLARD FILLMORE.

WASHINGTON, *February 10, 1852.*

To the Senate and House of Representatives:

I transmit to Congress a copy of the instruction dispatched from the Department of State to the minister of the United States at London respecting the attack on the United States steamer *Prometheus* in the harbor of San Juan de Nicaragua by the British brig of war *Express*, and also a copy of the dispatches of Mr. Lawrence to that Department and of his correspondence with Her Britannic Majesty's principal secretary of state for foreign affairs on the same subject.

MILLARD FILLMORE.

EXECUTIVE CHAMBER,
Washington City, February 10, 1852.

To the Senate and House of Representatives of the United States:

I transmit herewith a report from the Secretary of the Interior, containing a report from Thomas U. Walter, architect for the extension of the Capitol.

MILLARD FILLMORE.

WASHINGTON, *February 12, 1852.*

To the House of Representatives:

In answer to the resolution of the House of Representatives of the 26th of December last, requesting information in regard to the seizure of the brig *Arve** at Jeremie, in the island of St. Domingo, I transmit a report from the Secretary of State and the documents by which it was accompanied.

MILLARD FILLMORE.

WASHINGTON, *February 12, 1852.*

To the Senate of the United States:

In compliance with the resolution of the Senate of the 26th ultimo, requesting information upon the subject of the mission of Mr. Balistier, late consul at Singapore, to eastern Asia, I transmit a report from the Secretary of State and the documents which accompanied it.

MILLARD FILLMORE.

WASHINGTON, *February 13, 1852.*

To the Senate of the United States:

I transmit herewith, for the constitutional action of the Senate, treaties recently concluded with certain Indian tribes at Traverse des Sioux, Mendota, Pembina, and Fort Laramie, together with communications from the Department of the Interior and other documents connected therewith.

MILLARD FILLMORE.

WASHINGTON, *February 14, 1852.*

To the House of Representatives:

I communicate to the House of Representatives herewith a report to me, dated the 13th instant, from the Secretary of the Interior, respecting the delay and difficulty in making the apportionment among the several States of the Representatives in the Thirty-third Congress, as required by the act of 23d May, 1850, in consequence of the want of full returns of the population of the State of California, and suggesting the necessity for remedial legislation.

The subject is one of much importance, and I earnestly commend it to the early consideration of Congress.

MILLARD FILLMORE.

[The same message was sent to the Senate.]

WASHINGTON, *February 16, 1852.*

To the Senate and House of Representatives of the United States:

I transmit to Congress a letter addressed to the Secretary of State by the commissioner of the United States under the convention with Brazil, setting forth the obstacles which have impeded the conclusion of the business of that commission.

MILLARD FILLMORE.

*By Haytien authorities.

WASHINGTON, *February 16, 1852.*

To the Senate of the United States:

I herewith communicate to the Senate, for its consideration with a view to ratification, a treaty of commerce and navigation concluded by the minister resident of the United States at Constantinople with the chargé d'affaires of the Shah of Persia at the same place. The treaty is in the Persian and French languages, but is accompanied by an English translation. A copy of the correspondence between the Department of State and the legation of the United States at Constantinople on the subject is also herewith communicated.

MILLARD FILLMORE.

WASHINGTON, *February 18, 1852.*

To the House of Representatives:

In answer to the resolution of the House of Representatives requesting the official correspondence respecting an alleged misunderstanding between Captain Long, of the Navy of the United States, and Louis Kossuth, I transmit reports from the Secretaries of State and of the Navy and the papers which accompanied them.

MILLARD FILLMORE.

WASHINGTON, *March 1, 1852.*

To the Senate and House of Representatives of the United States:

In compliance with the provisions of the act of Congress of the 11th August, 1848, I transmit to that body the copy of a dispatch from the commissioner *ad interim* of the United States at Canton, together with the copy of certain rules and regulations for masters, officers, and seamen of vessels of the United States of America at the free ports of China, which accompanied said dispatch, and which are submitted for the revision of Congress.

MILLARD FILLMORE.

WASHINGTON, *March 4, 1852.*

To the House of Representatives of the United States:

In compliance with the resolution of the House of Representatives of the 17th ultimo, I transmit herewith a report from the Secretary of the Navy and a report from the Solicitor of the Treasury Department in relation to the accounts of Prosper M. Wetmore, late navy agent in the city of New York.

MILLARD FILLMORE.

WASHINGTON, *March 4, 1852.*

To the Senate and House of Representatives of the United States:

I transmit to Congress a letter addressed to me by the governor of the Territory of Minnesota, with the statements to which it refers, of the disbursements up to the 1st of January last of the money appropriated by the act approved June 11, 1850, for the erection of public buildings in that Territory.

MILLARD FILLMORE.

WASHINGTON, *March 4, 1852.*

To the Senate and House of Representatives of the United States:

I transmit to Congress a dispatch addressed to the Secretary of State by the minister of the United States at Mexico, and the papers therein referred to, relative to the cemetery which has been constructed in the neighborhood of that city as a place of sepulture for the remains of the officers and soldiers of the United States who died or were killed in that vicinity during the late war, and for such citizens of the United States as may hereafter die there. A copy of the report of the agent who was sent for the purpose of superintending the work is also herewith transmitted. It will be seen that a sum of $2,500 or $3,000, in addition to the amount appropriated by the act of Congress approved September 28, 1850, is represented to be necessary to carry the objects of that appropriation into full effect. I accordingly recommend that provision therefor may be made.

MILLARD FILLMORE.

WASHINGTON, *March 25, 1852.*

To the House of Representatives:

As a further answer to the resolution of the House of Representatives of the 5th of January last, requesting information in regard to a circular of Her Britannic Majesty's secretary of state for colonial affairs in respect to the encouragement of the emigration of colored laborers from the United States to the British West India islands, I transmit another dispatch addressed to the Department of State by the minister of the United States at London.

MILLARD FILLMORE.

WASHINGTON, *March 26, 1852.*

To the Senate and House of Representatives of the United States:

At the close of the commission to adjudicate upon the claims of citizens of the United States under the treaty of Guadalupe Hidalgo I directed a list to be made of papers which had been presented to that commission, and, pursuant to the act of Congress approved 3d March, 1849, the papers themselves to be carefully arranged and deposited for safe-keeping in the Department of State. I deemed all this necessary as well for the interest of the claimants as to secure the Government against fraudulent claims which might be preferred hereafter. A few days since I was surprised to learn that some of these papers had been fraudulently abstracted by one of the claimants, and upon the case being made known to me by the Secretary of State I referred it to the Attorney-General for the purpose of ascertaining what punishment could be inflicted upon the person who had been guilty of this offense.

I now communicate to you his opinion and that of the attorney of the United States for this District, by which you will perceive that it is doubtful whether there be any law for punishing the very grave offense of fraudulently abstracting or mutilating the papers and public documents in the several Departments of this Government. It appears to me that the protection of the public records and papers requires that such acts should be made penal and a suitable punishment inflicted upon the offender, and I therefore bring the subject to your consideration, to enable you to act upon it should you concur with me in this opinion.

MILLARD FILLMORE.

WASHINGTON, *March 26, 1852.*

To the House of Representatives:

In compliance with the resolution of the House of Representatives of the 18th instant, I transmit a copy of the correspondence with John P. Gaines, governor of the Territory of Oregon, relative to the seat of government of said Territory.

MILLARD FILLMORE.

WASHINGTON, *March 29, 1852.*

To the Senate of the United States:

In compliance with the resolution of the Senate of the 24th instant, relating to the extension of the Capitol, I have the honor to submit herewith a report from the Secretary of the Interior, which furnishes, it is believed, the required information.

MILLARD FILLMORE.

WASHINGTON CITY, *March 29, 1852.*

To the Senate of the United States:

I have the resolution of your honorable body adopted in executive session March 24, 1852, by which I am requested to return to the Senate the resolution advising and consenting to the appointment of George C. Laurason as collector of the customs for the district of New Orleans, provided a commission had not been issued to him, and in reply thereto I would respectfully state that prior to the receipt of said resolution I had signed the commission to Mr. Laurason and transmitted it to the Secretary of the Treasury, to whom your resolution was immediately referred; and I have the honor now to transmit his reply, by which it will be seen that the commission, after having been duly executed, was sent to the First Comptroller, where it still remains. I suppose, according to the doctrine laid down in the case of Marbury *v.* Madison (1 Cranch R., 137), the appointment must be deemed complete, and nothing short of the removal of Mr. Laurason can enable me again to submit his nomination to the consideration of the Senate; but as the commission has not been technically issued to Mr. Laurason, I deem it most respectful to comply with your request by returning the copy of the resolution which notified me that the Senate advised and consented to his appointment.

MILLARD FILLMORE.

WASHINGTON CITY, *April 6, 1852.*

To the House of Representatives:

In compliance with the resolution of the House of the 31st ultimo, I have the honor herewith to transmit a report from the Secretary of War, accompanied by the original manuscript report of Captain Thomas J. Crane, dated February 3, 1844, on the best mode of improving the navigation of the Ohio River at the Falls of Louisville, together with the original maps accompanying the same.

MILLARD FILLMORE.

WASHINGTON, *April 8, 1852.*

To the Senate of the United States:

I herewith transmit to the Senate, in reply to their resolution of the 4th ultimo, a report from the Secretary of State, with accompanying papers.*

MILLARD FILLMORE.

WASHINGTON, *April 19, 1852.*

To the Senate and House of Representatives of the United States:

I invite the attention of Congress to the state of affairs in the Territory of Oregon, growing out of a conflict of opinion among the authorities of that Territory in regard to a proper construction of the acts of Congress approved the 14th August, 1848, and 11th June, 1850, the former entitled "An act to establish a Territorial government of Oregon," and the latter entitled "An act to make further appropriations for public buildings in the Territories of Minnesota and Oregon." In order to enable Congress to understand the controversy and apply such remedy with a view to adjust it as may be deemed expedient, I transmit—

1. An act of the legislative assembly of that Territory, passed February 1, 1851, entitled "An act to provide for the selection of places for the location and erection of public buildings of the Territory of Oregon."

2. Governor Gaines's message to the legislative assembly of the 3d February, 1851.

3. The opinion of the Attorney-General of the United States of 23d

*Relating to the relations between the United States and Japan.

April, in regard to the act of the legislative assembly of the 1st February, 1851.

4. The opinion of the supreme court of Oregon, pronounced on the 9th December, 1851.

5. A letter of Judge Pratt of the 15th December, 1851, dissenting from that opinion.

6. Governor Gaines's letter to the President of the 1st January, 1852.

7. Report of the Attorney-General of the United States on that letter, dated 22d March, 1852.

If it should be the sense of Congress that the seat of government of Oregon has not already been established by the local authorities pursuant to the law of the United States for the organization of that Territory, or, if so established, should be deemed objectionable, in order to appease the strife upon the subject which seems to have arisen in that Territory I recommend that the seat of government be either permanently or temporarily ordained by act of Congress, and that that body should in the same manner express its approval or disapproval of such laws as may have been enacted in the Territory at the place alleged to be its seat of government, and which may be so enacted until intelligence of the decision of Congress shall reach there.

MILLARD FILLMORE.

WASHINGTON, *May 1, 1852.*

To the Senate of the United States:

I transmit to the Senate, for their consideration and advice with regard to its ratification, a convention between the United States and the Free and Hanseatic Republics of Hamburg, Bremen, and Lubeck, signed in this city by their respective plenipotentiaries on the 30th day of April, A. D. 1852, for the mutual extension of the jurisdiction of consuls. A copy of a note from the special plenipotentiary of Hamburg, Bremen, and Lubeck accompanies the convention.

MILLARD FILLMORE.

WASHINGTON, *May 5, 1852.*

To the Senate of the United States:

On the 3d of March, 1849, a general convention of peace, amity, commerce, and navigation between the United States and the Republic of Guatemala, by Elijah Hise, the chargé d'affaires of the United States to that Republic, on the part of this Government, and by Señor Don Jose Mariano Rodriguez, minister for foreign affairs, on the part of the Government of Guatemala. This convention was approved by the Senate on the 24th of September, 1850, and by a resolution of the 27th of that month that body authorized the ratification of this Government to be exchanged for the ratification of the Government of Guatemala at any time prior to the 1st of April, 1851. I accordingly ratified the convention on the 14th of November, 1850, but there was then no person in this country authorized to effect the exchange of ratifications on the part of the Guatemalan Government, and the United States had no diplomatic representative there. When, however, in the summer of 1851, Mr. J. Bozman Kerr proceeded to Nicaragua as the chargé d'affaires of the United States, he was empowered and instructed, when he should have concluded the business, which it was presumed would not have detained him long, in Nicaragua, to repair to Guatemala and effect the exchange on the part of this Government. Circumstances, however, have hitherto prevented him from accomplishing this object. Meanwhile Señor Don Felipe Molina has been received as chargé d'affaires of Guatemala here, and has been empowered to effect the exchange on the part of that Government.

I accordingly recommend that the Senate authorize a further extension of the period for exchanging the ratifications, in order that the convention may go into operation. It is presumed that if this recommendation should be adopted a few weeks from the date of the decision of the Senate upon the subject would be necessary to complete the preparations for carrying it into effect.

MILLARD FILLMORE.

WASHINGTON, *May 29, 1852.*

To the Senate of the United States:

The resolution of the Senate of the 6th instant, requesting the "papers and proofs on file in any of the Executive Departments touching the claim of Samuel A. Belden & Co., of Brownsville, Tex., against the Mexican Government for injuries inflicted upon said Belden & Co., as alleged by them in violation of the treaty of Guadalupe Hidalgo," was referred to the heads of those Departments, and the documents herewith transmitted have been reported to me from the Department of State as comprising all on the files of that Department called for by the resolution, with the exception of those of a diplomatic character. As the claim referred to is a subject of negotiation with the Mexican Government, it is not deemed expedient at this juncture to make public the documents which have been reserved. According to the reports of the Secretary of the Treasury, of the Secretary of the Interior, of the Secretary of War, of the Secretary of the Navy, and of the Postmaster-General, there are no papers in their respective Departments relative to the claim of Messrs. Belden & Co.

MILLARD FILLMORE.

WASHINGTON, *June 1, 1852.*

To the Senate of the United States:

I communicate to the Senate herewith, for its constitutional action thereon, eighteen treaties negotiated with Indian tribes in California, as described in the accompanying letter of the Secretary of the Interior, dated the 22d ultimo, with a copy of the report of the superintendent of Indian affairs for the State of California and other correspondence in relation thereto.

MILLARD FILLMORE.

WASHINGTON, *June 11, 1852.*

To the Senate of the United States:

I transmit to the Senate, for its consideration with a view to ratification, a convention between the United States and the Sultan of Borneo, signed at Bruni on the 23d of June, 1850. A copy of two dispatches to this department from Mr. Balestier, who concluded the convention on the part of this Government, one dated the 22d of April and the other the 24th June, 1851, is also transmitted for the information of the Senate. As the period limited for the exchange of the ratifications, which is to be effected at Bruni, will expire on the 23d instant, I recommend that if the Senate should approve the convention authority may be given to perform that ceremony within a year from that date. The instrument would have been submitted to the Senate in season for the ratification to be exchanged within the stipulated time had not Mr. Balestier's arrival with it in the United States been unavoidably delayed.

MILLARD FILLMORE.

WASHINGTON, *June 11, 1852.*

To the Senate and House of Representatives:

I transmit to Congress a report from the Secretary of State, on the subject of the disorders on the Rio Grande frontier, and recommend the legislation which it suggests, in order that the duties and obligations of this Government occasioned thereby may be more effectually discharged and the peace and security of the inhabitants of the United States in that quarter more efficiently maintained.

MILLARD FILLMORE.

WASHINGTON, *June 14, 1852.*

To the Senate and House of Representatives:

I transmit herewith, for your consideration, a report from the Secretary of State, accompanied by a communication from His Excellency Señor Don A. Calderon de la Barca, envoy extraordinary and minister plenipotentiary of Her Catholic Majesty, claiming indemnity for those Spanish subjects in New Orleans who sustained injury from the unlawful violence of the mob in that city consequent upon hearing the news of the execution of those persons who unlawfully invaded Cuba in August, 1851. My own views of the national liability upon this subject were expressed in the note of the Secretary of State to Mr. Calderon of the 13th November, 1851, and I do not understand that Her Catholic Majesty's minister controverts the correctness of the position there taken. He, however, insists that the thirteenth article of the treaty of 1795 promises indemnity for such injuries sustained within one year after the commencement of war between the two nations, and although he admits this is not within the letter of the treaty, yet he conceives that, as between two friendly nations, it is within the spirit of it.

This view of the case is at his request submitted for your consideration, but whether you may deem it correct or not, there is, perhaps, one ground upon which this indemnity, which can not be large in amount, may be granted without establishing a dangerous precedent, and the granting of which would commend itself to the generous feelings of the entire country, and that is this: The Queen of Spain, with a magnanimity worthy of all commendation, in a case where we had no legal right to solicit the favor, granted a free pardon to all the persons who had so unjustifiably invaded her dominions and murdered her subjects in Cuba, in violation of her own laws as well as those of the United States and the public law of nations. Such an act of mercy, which restored many misguided and unfortunate youth of this country to their parents and friends, seems to me to merit some corresponding act of magnanimity and generosity on the part of the Government of this country, and I think that there can be none more appropriate than to grant an indemnity to those Spanish subjects who were resident among us and who suffered by the violence of the mob, not on account of any fault which they themselves had committed, but because they were the subjects of the Queen of Spain. Such an act would tend to confirm that friendship which has so long existed between the two nations and to perpetuate it as a blessing to both, and I therefore recommend it to your favorable consideration.

MILLARD FILLMORE.

WASHINGTON, *June 22, 1852.*

To the Senate of the United States:

I transmit herewith a report from the Secretary of State, with the accompanying documents,* in compliance with the Senate's resolution of the 29th of April last.

MILLARD FILLMORE.

WASHINGTON, *June 22, 1852.*

To the Senate of the United States:

I transmit to the Senate, for its consideration with a view to ratification, a convention for the mutual delivery of criminals fugitives from justice in certain cases between the United States on the one part and Prussia and other States of the Germanic Confederation on the other part, signed in this city on the 16th instant.

MILLARD FILLMORE.

*Correspondence of the American chargé at Vienna on the subject of the apprehension and imprisonment by the Austrian authorities of Rev. Charles L. Brace, an American citizen.

WASHINGTON, *June 23, 1852.*

To the Senate of the United States:

I transmit herewith a report from the Secretary of State, with the accompanying documents,* in compliance with the Senate's resolution of the 3d instant.

MILLARD FILLMORE.

WASHINGTON, *June 26, 1852.*

To the Senate of the United States:

I transmit and commend to the consideration of the Senate a report from the Secretary of State, touching the convention between the United States and the Mexican Republic for the mutual extradition of fugitives from justice in certain cases, which convention I submitted to the Senate soon after I entered upon the office of President of the United States.

MILLARD FILLMORE.

DEPARTMENT OF STATE,
Washington, June 26, 1852.

The PRESIDENT OF THE UNITED STATES:

It was understood that at the close of the Administration of your predecessor an extradition treaty was concluded in this city between the United States and the Mexican Republic, which, however, was submitted to the Senate by yourself, but before I entered upon my present office.

It is presumed that as the treaty has not been returned to this Department the Senate has made no decision in regard to it.

The necessity for a compact upon that subject between the two Governments, whose territories, being conterminous, afford great facilities for wrongdoers in the one to screen themselves from punishment by seeking refuge in the other, would at all times be obvious, but at the present juncture may be considered as urgent.

I would consequently suggest that the attention of the Senate be respectfully invited to the matter, in order that if the treaty before them should be deemed objectionable another, embodying such amendments as may be supposed to be necessary, may be proposed to the Mexican Government.

Respectfully submitted.

DANL. WEBSTER.

WASHINGTON, *June 26, 1852.*

To the Senate of the United States:

I have received and taken into respectful consideration the resolution of the Senate of yesterday, adopted in executive session, requesting information in regard to supposed negotiations between the United States and Great Britain and between the United States and the Republics of Nicaragua and Costa Rica, respectively. Any information which may be in the possession of the Executive on these subjects shall in due time be laid before the Senate, but it is apprehended that it would not comport with the public interests to communicate it under existing circumstances.

MILLARD FILLMORE.

*Correspondence relative to the withdrawal of Mr. Hülsemann, chargé d'affaires from Austria to the United States.

WASHINGTON, *June 26, 1852.*

To the Senate of the United States:

I have received the resolution of the Senate of the 11th instant, passed in executive session, making inquiry respecting supposed propositions of the King of the Sandwich Islands to convey the sovereignty of those islands to the United States and requesting all official information in my possession touching the subject.

This request has been taken into the most respectful consideration, but the conclusion at which I have arrived is that the public interest would not be promoted, but, on the contrary, might under circumstances of possible occurrence, be seriously endangered if it were now to be complied with.

MILLARD FILLMORE.

WASHINGTON CITY, *July 1, 1852.*

To the Senate of the United States:

On the 26th ultimo I received a resolution of the Senate, passed in executive session, in the following words:

Resolved, That the President of the United States be requested to inform the Senate, if not in his opinion incompatible with the public interest, whether any convention or compact has been entered into on the part of the United States and the Government of Great Britain whereby the two Governments jointly recommend or advise the Republics of Costa Rica and Nicaragua, or either of those Republics, and the Mosquito Indians, inhabiting the Mosquito Coast, in Central America, on matters affecting their several and respective boundaries, or whereby any recommendation or advice is given to either of said Republics or said Indians respecting the territorial rights thereafter to be enjoyed or observed by them respectively, or in any other manner affecting or regulating the relations hereafter to be maintained between said Republics themselves, or either of them, and the said Indians concerning their territorial boundaries or other matters thereto appertaining. And if there be any such convention or compact, then that the President be requested to communicate the same, or a copy thereof, to the Senate, and to inform the Senate whether the same was made at the request or invitation of either of said Republics or of said Indians, or with their privity, approbation, or consent. And that the President be further requested to communicate to the Senate copies of all correspondence between the Executive and Great Britain, or with either of said Republics of Central America, touching said convention, and of all documents connected therewith. And if such convention or compact has been made, that the President be further requested to inform the Senate whether the same has been formally communicated to the respective Governments of Nicaragua and Costa Rica and the Mosquito Indians on the part of the Governments of Great Britain and the United States, and in what form such communications have been made to them, and that he lay before the Senate copies of any instructions that have been given to the representatives or agents of the United States at Nicaragua and Costa Rica touching such convention and the matters therein contained, with copies of like instructions to any naval officer of the United States relating to or in any manner concerning the said convention or its communication to said Republics or said Indians.

On the same day I returned the following answer to that resolution:

I have received and taken into respectful consideration the resolution of the Senate of yesterday, adopted in executive session, requesting information in regard to supposed negotiations between the United States and Great Britain and between the United States and the Republics of Nicaragua and Costa Rica, respectively. Any information which may be in the possession of the Executive on these subjects shall in due time be laid before the Senate, but it is apprehended that it would not comport with the public interests to communicate it under existing circumstances.

Great was my surprise to observe this morning in one of the public journals a statement of what purports to be a proposition, jointly signed by Her Britannic Majesty's minister here and the Secretary of State, for the adjustment of certain claims to territory between Nicaragua, Costa Rica, and the Mosquito Indians. I have caused immediate inquiry to be made into the origin of this highly improper publication, and shall omit no proper or legal means for bringing it to light. Whether it shall turn out to have been caused by unfaithfulness or breach of duty in any officer of this Government, high or low, or by a violation of diplomatic confidence, the appropriate remedy will be immediately applied, as being due not only to this Government, but to other governments. And I hold this communication to be especially proper to be made immediately by me to the Senate, after what has transpired on this subject, that the Senate may be perfectly assured that no information asked by it has been withheld and at the same time permitted to be published to the world.

This publication can not be considered otherwise than as a breach of official duty by some officer of the Government or a gross violation of the confidence necessary always to be reposed in the representatives of other nations. An occurrence of this kind can not but weaken the faith so desirable to be preserved between different governments and to injure the negotiations now pending, and it merits the severest reprobation.

MILLARD FILLMORE.

WASHINGTON CITY, *July 2, 1852.*

To the Senate of the United States:

I herewith transmit, for the advice and consent of the Senate, a treaty recently negotiated with the Chickasaw Nation of Indians.

The nature and objects of the treaty are fully explained by the report of Mr. Harper, who negotiated it in behalf of the United States.

MILLARD FILLMORE.

WASHINGTON, *July 2, 1852.*

To the Senate and House of Representatives:

By an act of Congress approved on the 10th day of February, 1852, an appropriation of $6,000 was made for the relief of *American citizens* then lately imprisoned and pardoned by the Queen of Spain, intended to provide for the return of such of the Cuban prisoners as were citizens of the United States who had been transported to Spain and there pardoned by the Spanish Government. It will be observed that no provision was

A Proclamation:
by the
President of the United States.

Whereas information has been received, that sundry lawless persons, principally persons of color, combined and confederated together, for the purpose of opposing by force, the execution of the Laws of the United States, did, at Boston, in Massachusetts, on the 15th, of this month, make a violent assault on the Marshal or Deputy Marshals of the United States, for the District of Massachusetts, in the Court House, and did overcome the said Officers, and did, by force, rescue from their custody, a person, arrested as a fugitive Slave, and, then and there, a prisoner lawfully holden by the said Marshal, or Deputy Marshals of the United States, and other scandalous outrages did commit in violation of law.
Now Therefore, to the end, that the

PRESIDENT FILLMORE'S FUGITIVE SLAVE PROCLAMATION.

found to have harbored or concealed such fugitive, contrary to law, to be immediately arrested and proceeded with according to law.

Given under my hand and the Seal of the United States, this 18 day of February, 1851.

Millard Fillmore

[illegible]ter,

[illegible] retary of State

LAST PAGE OF FILLMORE'S FUGITIVE SLAVE PROCLAMATION.

made for such foreigners or aliens as were engaged in the Cuban expedition, and who had shared the fate of American citizens, for whose relief the said act was intended to provide. I now transmit a report from the First Comptroller, with accompanying papers, from which it will be perceived that fifteen foreigners were connected with that expedition, who were also pardoned by the Queen of Spain, and have been transported to the United States under a contract made with our consul, at an expense of $1,013.34, for the payment of which no provision has been made by law. The consul having evidently acted with good intentions, the claim is submitted for the consideration of Congress.

MILLARD FILLMORE.

WASHINGTON, *July 13, 1852.*

To the House of Representatives:

In answer to the resolution of the House of Representatives requesting information relative to the policy of the Government in regard to the island of Cuba, I transmit a report from the Department of State and the documents by which it was accompanied.

MILLARD FILLMORE.

EXECUTIVE MANSION,
Washington City, July 26, 1852.

To the Senate of the United States:

In obedience to your resolution adopted in executive session June 11, 1852, I have the honor herewith to communicate a report* from the Secretary of the Interior, containing the information called for by that resolution.

MILLARD FILLMORE.

WASHINGTON, *July 27, 1852.*

To the Senate of the United States:

In answer to the resolution of the Senate of the 19th instant, requesting the correspondence between the Government of the United States and that of the Mexican Republic respecting a right of way across the Isthmus of Tehuantepec, I transmit a report from the Department of State and the documents by which it was accompanied.

MILLARD FILLMORE.

WASHINGTON, *July 29, 1852.*

To the Senate of the United States:

In compliance with the resolution of the Senate of the 27th instant, I transmit the copy of the notes† of Mr. Luis de la Rosa and Mr. J. M. Gonzales de la Vega, which it requests.

MILLARD FILLMORE.

*Relating to the boundary line between the United States and Mexico.

†Upon the subject of the American and Mexican boundary commission.

WASHINGTON, *July 31, 1852.*

To the Senate of the United States:

I communicate to the Senate herewith, for its constitutional action thereon, nineteen treaties negotiated by commissioners on the part of the United States with various tribes of Indians in the Territory of Oregon, accompanied by a letter to me from the Secretary of the Interior and certain documents having reference thereto.

MILLARD FILLMORE.

WASHINGTON, *August 2, 1852.*

To the Senate of the United States:

In answer to the resolution of the Senate of the 23d ultimo, requesting information in regard to the fisheries on the coasts of the British possessions in North America, I transmit a report from the Acting Secretary of State and the documents by which it was accompanied. Commodore M. C. Perry, with the United States steam frigate *Mississippi* under his command, has been dispatched to that quarter for the purpose of protecting the rights of American fishermen under the convention of 1818.

MILLARD FILLMORE.

WASHINGTON, *August 9, 1852.*

To the House of Representatives of the United States:

I transmit a report from the Acting Secretary of State and the documents by which it was accompanied, in answer to a resolution of the House of Representatives of the 22d ultimo, on the subject of the fisheries, and state for the information of that House that the United States steam frigate *Mississippi* has been dispatched to the fishing grounds on the coasts of the British possessions in North America for the purpose of protecting the rights of American fishermen under the convention between the United States and Great Britain of the 20th of October, 1818.

MILLARD FILLMORE.

WASHINGTON, *August 10, 1852.*

To the Senate of the United States:

I transmit a copy of the certificate of the exchange of the ratifications of the general convention of peace, amity, commerce, and navigation between the United States and the Republic of San Salvador, signed at Leon, in Nicaragua, on the 2d of January, 1850. It will be seen that the exchange was not effected until the 2d of June last, but that it was stipulated that the convention was not to be binding upon either of the parties thereto until the Senate of the United States should have duly sanctioned the exchange.

The Senate by its resolution of the 27th of September, 1850, authorized the exchange to take place at any time prior to the 1st of April, 1851.

Mr. Kerr, the chargé d'affaires of the United States to Nicaragua, however, who was authorized to make the exchange on the part of this Government, was unavoidably detained in that Republic, in consequence of which the exchange could not be effected within the period referred to.

The expediency of sanctioning the exchange which has been made by Mr. Kerr, and of authorizing the convention to go into effect, is accordingly submitted to the consideration of the Senate.

MILLARD FILLMORE.

WASHINGTON, *August 12, 1852.*

To the Senate of the United States:

In answer to the resolution of the Senate dated the 20th ultimo, requesting information in regard to controversies between the consul of the United States at Acapulco and the Mexican authorities, I transmit a report from the Secretary of State and the documents by which it was accompanied.

MILLARD FILLMORE.

WASHINGTON, *August 13, 1852.*

To the Senate of the United States:

I transmit a report from the Secretary of State upon the subject of the relations between the United States and the Republics of Nicaragua and Costa Rica, in Central America, which has been delayed longer than I desired in consequence of the ill health of the Secretary of State.

MILLARD FILLMORE.

WASHINGTON, *August 14, 1852.*

To the Senate of the United States:

I have received a resolution from your honorable body of the 6th instant, appearing to have been adopted in open legislative session, requesting me "to inform the Senate, if not incompatible with the public interests, whether any propositions have been made by the King of the Sandwich Islands to transfer the sovereignty of these islands to the United States, and to communicate to the Senate all the official information on that subject in my possession;" in reply to which I have to state that on or about the 12th day of June last I received a similar resolution from the Senate adopted in executive or secret session, to which I returned an answer stating that in my opinion a communication of the information requested at that juncture would not comport with the public interest. Nothing has since transpired to change my views on that subject, and I therefore feel constrained again to decline giving the information asked.

MILLARD FILLMORE.

WASHINGTON, *August 21, 1852.*

To the Senate of the United States:

In answer to the resolution of the Senate of the 9th instant, requesting information touching the Lobos Islands, I transmit a report from the Secretary of State and the documents by which it was accompanied. The instructions to the squadron of the United States called for by the resolution will be communicated on an early future occasion.

MILLARD FILLMORE.

WASHINGTON, *August 27, 1852.*

To the Senate of the United States:

In answer to the resolution of the Senate of the 14th ultimo, requesting a copy of the correspondence of Mr. R. M. Walsh while he was employed as a special agent of this Government in the island of St. Domingo, I transmit a report from the Secretary of State and the documents by which it was accompanied.

MILLARD FILLMORE.

WASHINGTON, *August 27, 1852.*

To the Senate of the United States:

I transmit a further report from the Secretary of State relative to the Lobos Islands. This report is accompanied by a copy of the orders of the Navy Department to Commodore McCauley, requested by the resolution of the Senate of the 9th instant.

MILLARD FILLMORE.

WASHINGTON, *August 27, 1852.*

To the Senate of the United States:

As it is not deemed advisable that the instruction to Mr. R. M. Walsh,* a copy of which is herewith transmitted, should be published at this time, I communicate it confidentially to the Senate in executive session.

MILLARD FILLMORE.

WASHINGTON, *August 27, 1852.*

To the Senate of the United States:

I transmit to the Senate, for its consideration with a view to ratification, a supplementary convention relative to commerce and navigation between the United States and the Netherlands, signed in this city on the 26th instant.

MILLARD FILLMORE.

*Special agent of the United States in the island of St. Domingo.

WASHINGTON, *August 27, 1852*.

To the Senate of the United States:

I transmit to the Senate, for its consideration with a view to ratification, a convention between the United States and Belgium for regulating the right of inheriting and acquiring property, signed in this city on the 25th instant.

MILLARD FILLMORE.

WASHINGTON, *August 31, 1852*.

To the Senate of the United States:

In answer to the resolution of the Senate of the 21st instant, requesting information in respect to foreign postal arrangements, and especially cheap ocean postage, I transmit a report of the Secretary of State and the documents by which it was accompanied.

MILLARD FILLMORE.

EXECUTIVE ORDERS.

WASHINGTON CITY,
May 17, 1852.

The SECRETARY OF WAR.

MY DEAR SIR: I have just issued an authority to Hugh Maxwell, collector at New York, under the eighth section of the act of April 20, 1818, to arrest any unlawful expedition that may be attempted to be fitted out within his district, and I have given him power to call upon any military and naval officers that may be there to aid him in the execution of this duty; and I will thank you to issue the necessary instructions to the proper military officer in that district.

I am, your obedient servant,

MILLARD FILLMORE.

WASHINGTON CITY,
Tuesday, June 29, 1852—12.30 o'clock p. m.

SIR:* The tolling bells announce the death of the Hon. Henry Clay. Though this event has been long anticipated, yet the painful bereavement could never be fully realized. I am sure all hearts are too sad at this moment to attend to business, and I therefore respectfully suggest that your Department be closed for the remainder of the day.

I have the honor to be, your obedient servant,

MILLARD FILLMORE.

*Addressed to the heads of the several Executive Departments.

WASHINGTON, *September 13, 1852*.

General JOS. G. TOTTEN.

SIR: I have to acknowledge the receipt of your favor of the 11th instant and to say that I shall be pleased if you will cause the necessary surveys, projects, and estimates for determining the best means of affording the cities of Washington and Georgetown an unfailing and abundant supply of good and wholesome water to be made as soon as possible.

I am, very respectfully, your obedient servant,

MILLARD FILLMORE.

[From the Daily National Intelligencer, October 26, 1852.]

EXECUTIVE MANSION,
Washington, Monday Morning, October 25, 1852.

The ACTING SECRETARY OF STATE and the SECRETARIES OF THE TREASURY, INTERIOR, WAR, NAVY, the ATTORNEY-GENERAL and POSTMASTER-GENERAL.

GENTLEMEN: The painful intelligence received yesterday enforces upon me the sad duty of announcing to the Executive Departments the death of the Secretary of State. Daniel Webster died at Marshfield, in Massachusetts, on Sunday, the 24th of October, between 2 and 3 o'clock in the morning.

Whilst this irreparable loss brings its natural sorrow to every American heart and will be heard far beyond our borders with mournful respect wherever civilization has nurtured men who find in transcendent intellect and faithful, patriotic service a theme for praise, it will visit with still more poignant emotion his colleagues in the Administration, with whom his relations have been so intimate and so cordial.

The fame of our illustrious statesman belongs to his country, the admiration of it to the world. The record of his wisdom will inform future generations not less than its utterance has enlightened the present. He has bequeathed to posterity the richest fruits of the experience and judgment of a great mind conversant with the greatest national concerns. In these his memory will endure as long as our country shall continue to be the home and guardian of freemen.

The people will share with the Executive Departments in the common grief which bewails his departure from amongst us.

In the expression of individual regret at this afflicting event the Executive Departments of the Government will be careful to manifest every observance of honor which custom has established as appropriate to the memory of one so eminent as a public functionary and so distinguished as a citizen.

The Acting Secretary of State will communicate this sad intelligence to the diplomatic corps near this Government and, through our ministers abroad, to foreign governments.

The members of the Cabinet are requested, as a further testimony of respect for the deceased, to wear the usual badges of mourning for thirty days.

I am, gentlemen, your obedient servant,

MILLARD FILLMORE.

THIRD ANNUAL MESSAGE.

WASHINGTON, *December 6, 1852.*

Fellow-Citizens of the Senate and of the House of Representatives:

The brief space which has elapsed since the close of your last session has been marked by no extraordinary political event. The quadrennial election of Chief Magistrate has passed off with less than the usual excitement. However individuals and parties may have been disappointed in the result, it is, nevertheless, a subject of national congratulation that the choice has been effected by the independent suffrages of a free people, undisturbed by those influences which in other countries have too often affected the purity of popular elections.

Our grateful thanks are due to an all-merciful Providence, not only for staying the pestilence which in different forms has desolated some of our cities, but for crowning the labors of the husbandman with an abundant harvest and the nation generally with the blessings of peace and prosperity.

Within a few weeks the public mind has been deeply affected by the death of Daniel Webster, filling at his decease the office of Secretary of State. His associates in the executive government have sincerely sympathized with his family and the public generally on this mournful occasion. His commanding talents, his great political and professional eminence, his well-tried patriotism, and his long and faithful services in the most important public trusts have caused his death to be lamented throughout the country and have earned for him a lasting place in our history.

In the course of the last summer considerable anxiety was caused for a short time by an official intimation from the Government of Great Britain that orders had been given for the protection of the fisheries upon the coasts of the British Provinces in North America against the alleged encroachments of the fishing vessels of the United States and France. The shortness of this notice and the season of the year seemed to make it a matter of urgent importance. It was at first apprehended that an increased naval force had been ordered to the fishing grounds to carry into effect the British interpretation of those provisions in the convention of 1818 in reference to the true intent of which the two Governments differ. It was soon discovered that such was not the design of Great Britain, and satisfactory explanations of the real objects of the measure have been given both here and in London.

The unadjusted difference, however, between the two Governments as to the interpretation of the first article of the convention of 1818 is still a matter of importance. American fishing vessels, within nine or ten years, have been excluded from waters to which they had free access for twenty-five years after the negotiation of the treaty. In 1845 this exclusion was relaxed so far as concerns the Bay of Fundy, but the just and liberal intention of the home Government, in compliance with what we think the true construction of the convention, to open all the other outer bays to our fishermen was abandoned in consequence of the opposition of the colonies. Notwithstanding this, the United States have, since the Bay of Fundy was reopened to our fishermen in 1845, pursued the most liberal course toward the colonial fishing interests. By the revenue law of 1846 the duties on colonial fish entering our ports were very greatly reduced, and by the warehousing act it is allowed to be entered in bond without payment of duty. In this way colonial fish has acquired the monopoly of the export trade in our market and is entering to some extent into the home consumption. These facts were among those which increased the sensibility of our fishing interest at the movement in question.

These circumstances and the incidents above alluded to have led me to think the moment favorable for a reconsideration of the entire subject of the fisheries on the coasts of the British Provinces, with a view to place them upon a more liberal footing of reciprocal privilege. A willingness to meet us in some arrangement of this kind is understood to exist on the part of Great Britain, with a desire on her part to include in one comprehensive settlement as well this subject as the commercial intercourse between the United States and the British Provinces. I have thought that, whatever arrangements may be made on these two subjects, it is expedient that they should be embraced in separate conventions. The illness and death of the late Secretary of State prevented the commencement of the contemplated negotiation. Pains have been taken to collect the information required for the details of such an arrangement. The subject is attended with considerable difficulty. If it is found practicable to come to an agreement mutually acceptable to the two parties, conventions may be concluded in the course of the present winter. The control of Congress over all the provisions of such an arrangement affecting the revenue will of course be reserved.

The affairs of Cuba formed a prominent topic in my last annual message. They remain in an uneasy condition, and a feeling of alarm and irritation on the part of the Cuban authorities appears to exist. This feeling has interfered with the regular commercial intercourse between the United States and the island and led to some acts of which we have a right to complain. But the Captain-General of Cuba is clothed with no power to treat with foreign governments, nor is he in any degree under the control of the Spanish minister at Washington. Any communication which he may hold with an agent of a foreign power is informal and matter of courtesy. Anxious to put an end to the existing inconveniences (which seemed to rest on a misconception), I directed the newly appointed minister to Mexico to visit Havana on his way to Vera Cruz. He was respectfully received by the Captain-General, who conferred with him freely on the recent occurrences, but no permanent arrangement was effected.

In the meantime the refusal of the Captain-General to allow passengers and the mail to be landed in certain cases, for a reason which does not furnish, in the opinion of this Government, even a good presumptive ground for such prohibition, has been made the subject of a serious remonstrance at Madrid, and I have no reason to doubt that due respect will be paid by the Government of Her Catholic Majesty to the representations which our minister has been instructed to make on the subject.

It is but justice to the Captain-General to add that his conduct toward the steamers employed to carry the mails of the United States to Havana has, with the exceptions above alluded to, been marked with kindness and liberality, and indicates no general purpose of interfering with the commercial correspondence and intercourse between the island and this country.

Early in the present year official notes were received from the ministers of France and England inviting the Government of the United States to become a party with Great Britain and France to a tripartite convention, in virtue of which the three powers should severally and collectively disclaim now and for the future all intention to obtain possession of the island of Cuba, and should bind themselves to discountenance all attempts to that effect on the part of any power or individual whatever. This invitation has been respectfully declined, for reasons which it would occupy too much space in this communication to state in detail, but which led me to think that the proposed measure would be of doubtful constitutionality, impolitic, and unavailing. I have, however, in common with several of my predecessors, directed the ministers of France and England to be assured that the United States entertain no designs against Cuba, but that, on the contrary, I should regard its incorporation into the Union at the present time as fraught with serious peril.

Were this island comparatively destitute of inhabitants or occupied by a kindred race, I should regard it, if voluntarily ceded by Spain, as a most desirable acquisition. But under existing circumstances I should look upon its incorporation into our Union as a very hazardous measure. It would bring into the Confederacy a population of a different national stock, speaking a different language, and not likely to harmonize with the other members. It would probably affect in a prejudicial manner the industrial interests of the South, and it might revive those conflicts of opinion between the different sections of the country which lately shook the Union to its center, and which have been so happily compromised.

The rejection by the Mexican Congress of the convention which had been concluded between that Republic and the United States for the protection of a transit way across the Isthmus of Tehuantepec and of the interests of those citizens of the United States who had become proprietors of the rights which Mexico had conferred on one of her own citizens in regard to that transit has thrown a serious obstacle in the way of the attainment of a very desirable national object. I am still willing to hope that the differences on the subject which exist, or may hereafter arise, between the Governments will be amicably adjusted. This subject, however, has already engaged the attention of the Senate of the United States, and requires no further comment in this communication.

The settlement of the question respecting the port of San Juan de Nicaragua and of the controversy between the Republics of Costa Rica and Nicaragua in regard to their boundaries was considered indispensable to the commencement of the ship canal between the two oceans, which was the subject of the convention between the United States and Great Britain of the 19th of April, 1850. Accordingly, a proposition for the same purposes, addressed to the two Governments in that quarter and to the Mosquito Indians, was agreed to in April last by the Secretary of State and the minister of Her Britannic Majesty. Besides the wish to aid in reconciling the differences of the two Republics, I engaged in the negotiation from a desire to place the great work of a ship canal between the two oceans under one jurisdiction and to establish the important port of San Juan de Nicaragua under the government of a civilized power. The proposition in question was assented to by Costa Rica and the Mosquito Indians. It has not proved equally acceptable to Nicaragua, but it is to be hoped that the further negotiations on the subject which are in train will be carried on in that spirit of conciliation and compromise which ought always to prevail on such occasions, and that they will lead to a satisfactory result.

I have the satisfaction to inform you that the executive government of Venezuela has acknowledged some claims of citizens of the United States which have for many years past been urged by our chargé d'affaires at Caracas. It is hoped that the same sense of justice will actuate the Congress of that Republic in providing the means for their payment.

The recent revolution in Buenos Ayres and the Confederated States having opened the prospect of an improved state of things in that quarter, the Governments of Great Britain and France determined to negotiate with the chief of the new confederacy for the free access of their commerce to the extensive countries watered by the tributaries of the La Plata; and they gave a friendly notice of this purpose to the United States, that we might, if we thought proper, pursue the same course. In compliance with this invitation, our minister at Rio Janeiro and our

THE FIRST JAPANESE-AMERICAN TREATY

THE FIRST JAPANESE TREATY

Japan's ports were closed to foreigners. Mariners wrecked on her shores got short shrift. The natives refused to enter into commercial relations with any save their fellows. In 1832, 1845, and 1849, vessels were sent to establish commercial relations with Japan, but without avail. Finally Commodore M. C. Perry, bearing instructions prepared by Webster, set sail in November, 1852, with a respectable naval force, prepared to secure a treaty by persuasion, if possible, and by force if necessary. He succeeded; two Japanese ports were opened to our trade.

The upper left-hand panel shows Perry, attended by his marines and sailors, forcing an audience upon the authorities. The upper right-hand panel contains the portraits (from daguerreotypes) of the Japanese Commissioners. The main picture shows their reception in the White House, the treaty being carried in the box held by one of the envoys' suite.

See the articles entitled "Japan" and "Japan, Treaties with," in the Encyclopedic Index, for a full statement of the history of that nation and of our relations with her.

chargé d'affaires at Buenos Ayres have been fully authorized to conclude treaties with the newly organized confederation or the States composing it. The delays which have taken place in the formation of the new government have as yet prevented the execution of those instructions, but there is every reason to hope that these vast countries will be eventually opened to our commerce.

A treaty of commerce has been concluded between the United States and the Oriental Republic of Uruguay, which will be laid before the Senate. Should this convention go into operation, it will open to the commercial enterprise of our citizens a country of great extent and unsurpassed in natural resources, but from which foreign nations have hitherto been almost wholly excluded.

The correspondence of the late Secretary of State with the Peruvian chargé d'affaires relative to the Lobos Islands was communicated to Congress toward the close of the last session. Since that time, on further investigation of the subject, the doubts which had been entertained of the title of Peru to those islands have been removed, and I have deemed it just that the temporary wrong which had been unintentionally done her from want of information should be repaired by an unreserved acknowledgment of her sovereignty.

I have the satisfaction to inform you that the course pursued by Peru has been creditable to the liberality of her Government. Before it was known by her that her title would be acknowledged at Washington, her minister of foreign affairs had authorized our chargé d'affaires at Lima to announce to the American vessels which had gone to the Lobos for guano that the Peruvian Government was willing to freight them on its own account. This intention has been carried into effect by the Peruvian minister here by an arrangement which is believed to be advantageous to the parties in interest.

Our settlements on the shores of the Pacific have already given a great extension, and in some respects a new direction, to our commerce in that ocean. A direct and rapidly increasing intercourse has sprung up with eastern Asia. The waters of the Northern Pacific, even into the Arctic Sea, have of late years been frequented by our whalemen. The application of steam to the general purposes of navigation is becoming daily more common, and makes it desirable to obtain fuel and other necessary supplies at convenient points on the route between Asia and our Pacific shores. Our unfortunate countrymen who from time to time suffer shipwreck on the coasts of the eastern seas are entitled to protection. Besides these specific objects, the general prosperity of our States on the Pacific requires that an attempt should be made to open the opposite regions of Asia to a mutually beneficial intercourse. It is obvious that this attempt could be made by no power to so great advantage as by the United States, whose constitutional system excludes every idea of distant colonial dependencies. I have accordingly been led to order an appropriate naval force to Japan, under the command of a discreet and intelligent officer of the highest rank known to our service. He is instructed to endeavor to obtain from the Government of that country some relaxation of the inhospitable and antisocial system which it has pursued for about two centuries. He has been directed particularly to remonstrate in the strongest language against the cruel treatment to which our shipwrecked mariners have often been subjected and to insist that they shall be treated with humanity. He is instructed, however, at the same time, to give that Government the amplest assurances that the objects of the United States are such, and such only, as I have indicated, and that the expedition is friendly and peaceful. Notwithstanding the jealousy with which the Governments of eastern Asia regard all overtures from foreigners, I am not without hopes of a beneficial result of the expedition. Should it be crowned with success, the advantages will not be confined to the United States, but, as in the case of China, will be equally enjoyed by all the other maritime powers. I have much satisfaction in stating that in all the steps preparatory to this expedition the Government of the United States has been materially aided by the good offices of the King of the Netherlands, the only European power having any commercial relations with Japan.

In passing from this survey of our foreign relations, I invite the attention of Congress to the condition of that Department of the Government to which this branch of the public business is intrusted. Our intercourse with foreign powers has of late years greatly increased, both in consequence of our own growth and the introduction of many new states into the family of nations. In this way the Department of State has become overburdened. It has by the recent establishment of the Department of the Interior been relieved of some portion of the domestic business. If the residue of the business of that kind—such as the distribution of Congressional documents, the keeping, publishing, and distribution of the laws of the United States, the execution of the copyright law, the subject of reprieves and pardons, and some other subjects relating to interior administration—should be transferred from the Department of State, it would unquestionably be for the benefit of the public service. I would also suggest that the building appropriated to the State Department is not fireproof; that there is reason to think there are defects in its construction, and that the archives of the Government in charge of the Department, with the precious collections of the manuscript papers of Washington, Jefferson, Hamilton, Madison, and Monroe, are exposed to destruction by fire. A similar remark may be made of the buildings appropriated to the War and Navy Departments.

The condition of the Treasury is exhibited in the annual report from that Department.

The cash receipts into the Treasury for the fiscal year ending the 30th June last, exclusive of trust funds, were $49,728,386.89, and the expenditures for the same period, likewise exclusive of trust funds, were $46,-007,896.20, of which $9,455,815.83 was on account of the principal and interest of the public debt, including the last installment of the indemnity to Mexico under the treaty of Guadalupe Hidalgo, leaving a balance of $14,632,136.37 in the Treasury on the 1st day of July last. Since this latter period further purchases of the principal of the public debt have been made to the extent of $2,456,547.49, and the surplus in the Treasury will continue to be applied to that object whenever the stock can be procured within the limits as to price authorized by law.

The value of foreign merchandise imported during the last fiscal year was $207,240,101, and the value of domestic productions exported was $149,861,911, besides $17,204,026 of foreign merchandise exported, making the aggregate of the entire exports $167,065,937. Exclusive of the above, there was exported $42,507,285 in specie, and imported from foreign ports $5,262,643.

In my first annual message to Congress I called your attention to what seemed to me some defects in the present tariff, and recommended such modifications as in my judgment were best adapted to remedy its evils and promote the prosperity of the country. Nothing has since occurred to change my views on this important question.

Without repeating the arguments contained in my former message in favor of discriminating protective duties, I deem it my duty to call your attention to one or two other considerations affecting this subject. The first is the effect of large importations of foreign goods upon our currency. Most of the gold of California, as fast as it is coined, finds its way directly to Europe in payment for goods purchased. In the second place, as our manufacturing establishments are broken down by competition with foreigners, the capital invested in them is lost, thousands of honest and industrious citizens are thrown out of employment, and the farmer, to that extent, is deprived of a home market for the sale of his surplus produce. In the third place, the destruction of our manufactures leaves the foreigner without competition in our market, and he consequently raises the price of the article sent here for sale, as is now seen in the increased cost of iron imported from England. The prosperity and wealth of every nation must depend upon its productive industry. The farmer is stimulated to exertion by finding a ready market for his surplus products, and benefited by being able to exchange them without loss of time or expense of transportation for the manufactures which his comfort or convenience requires. This is always done to the best advantage where a portion of the community in which he lives is engaged in other pursuits. But most manufactures require an amount of capital and a practical skill which can not be commanded unless they be protected for a time from ruinous competition from abroad. Hence the necessity of laying those duties upon imported goods which the Constitution authorizes for revenue in such a manner as to protect and encourage the labor of our own citizens. Duties, however, should not be fixed at a rate so high as to exclude the foreign article, but should be so graduated as to enable the domestic manufacturer fairly to compete with the foreigner in our own markets, and by this competition to reduce the price of the manufactured article to the consumer to the lowest rate at which it can be produced. This policy would place the mechanic by the side of the farmer, create a mutual interchange of their respective commodities, and thus stimulate the industry of the whole country and render us independent of foreign nations for the supplies required by the habits or necessities of the people.

Another question, wholly independent of protection, presents itself, and that is, whether the duties levied should be upon the value of the article at the place of shipment, or, where it is practicable, a specific duty, graduated according to quantity, as ascertained by weight or measure. All our duties are at present *ad valorem*. A certain percentage is levied on the price of the goods at the port of shipment in a foreign country. Most commercial nations have found it indispensable, for the purpose of preventing fraud and perjury, to make the duties specific whenever the article is of such a uniform value in weight or measure as to justify such a duty. Legislation should never encourage dishonesty or crime. It is impossible that the revenue officers at the port where the goods are entered and the duties paid should know with certainty what they cost in the foreign country. Yet the law requires that they should levy the duty according to such cost. They are therefore compelled to resort to very unsatisfactory evidence to ascertain what that cost was. They take the invoice of the importer, attested by his oath, as the best evidence of which the nature of the case admits. But everyone must see that the invoice may be fabricated and the oath by which it is supported false, by reason of which the dishonest importer pays a part only of the duties which are paid by the honest one, and thus indirectly receives from the Treasury of the United States a reward for his fraud and perjury. The reports of the Secretary of the Treasury heretofore made on this subject show conclusively that these frauds have been practiced to a great extent. The tendency is to destroy that high moral character for which our merchants have long been distinguished, to defraud the Government of its revenue, to break down the honest importer by a dishonest competition, and, finally, to transfer the business of importation to foreign and irresponsible agents, to the great detriment of our own citizens. I therefore again most earnestly recommend the adoption of specific duties wherever it is practicable, or a home valuation, to prevent these frauds.

I would also again call your attention to the fact that the present tariff in some cases imposes a higher duty upon the raw material imported than upon the article manufactured from it, the consequence of which is that the duty operates to the encouragement of the foreigner and the discouragement of our own citizens.

For full and detailed information in regard to the general condition of our Indian affairs, I respectfully refer you to the report of the Secretary of the Interior and the accompanying documents.

The Senate not having thought proper to ratify the treaties which have been negotiated with the tribes of Indians in California and Oregon, our relations with them have been left in a very unsatisfactory condition.

In other parts of our territory particular districts of country have been set apart for the exclusive occupation of the Indians, and their right to the lands within those limits has been acknowledged and respected. But in California and Oregon there has been no recognition by the Government of the exclusive right of the Indians to any part of the country. They are therefore mere tenants at sufferance, and liable to be driven from place to place at the pleasure of the whites.

The treaties which have been rejected proposed to remedy this evil by allotting to the different tribes districts of country suitable to their habits of life and sufficient for their support. This provision, more than any other, it is believed, led to their rejection; and as no substitute for it has been adopted by Congress, it has not been deemed advisable to attempt to enter into new treaties of a permanent character, although no effort has been spared by temporary arrangements to preserve friendly relations with them.

If it be the desire of Congress to remove them from the country altogether, or to assign to them particular districts more remote from the settlements of the whites, it will be proper to set apart by law the territory which they are to occupy and to provide the means necessary for removing them to it. Justice alike to our own citizens and to the Indians requires the prompt action of Congress on this subject.

The amendments proposed by the Senate to the treaties which were negotiated with the Sioux Indians of Minnesota have been submitted to the tribes who were parties to them, and have received their assent. A large tract of valuable territory has thus been opened for settlement and cultivation, and all danger of collision with these powerful and warlike bands has been happily removed.

The removal of the remnant of the tribe of Seminole Indians from Florida has long been a cherished object of the Government, and it is one to which my attention has been steadily directed. Admonished by past experience of the difficulty and cost of the attempt to remove them by military force, resort has been had to conciliatory measures. By the invitation of the Commissioner of Indian Affairs, several of the principal chiefs recently visited Washington, and whilst here acknowledged in writing the obligation of their tribe to remove with the least possible delay. Late advices from the special agent of the Government represent that they adhere to their promise, and that a council of their people has been called to make their preliminary arrangements. A general emigration may therefore be confidently expected at an early day.

The report from the General Land Office shows increased activity in its operations. The survey of the northern boundary of Iowa has been completed with unexampled dispatch. Within the last year 9,522,953 acres of public land have been surveyed and 8,032,463 acres brought into market.

	Acres.
In the last fiscal year there were sold	1,553,071
Located with bounty-land warrants	3,201,314
Located with other certificates	115,682
Making a total of	4,870,067
In addition there were—	
Reported under swamp-land grants	5,219,188
For internal improvements, railroads, etc	3,025,920
Making an aggregate of	13,115,175

Being an increase of the amount sold and located under land warrants of 569,220 acres over the previous year.

The whole amount thus sold, located under land warrants, reported under swamp-land grants, and selected for internal improvements exceeds that of the previous year by 3,342,372 acres; and the sales would without doubt have been much larger but for the extensive reservations for railroads in Missouri, Mississippi, and Alabama.

	Acres.
For the quarter ending 30th September, 1852, there were sold	243,255
Located with bounty-land warrants	1,387,116
Located with other certificates	15,649
Reported under swamp-land grants	2,485,233
Making an aggregate for the quarter of	4,131,253

Much the larger portion of the labor of arranging and classifying the returns of the last census has been finished, and it will now devolve upon Congress to make the necessary provision for the publication of the results in such form as shall be deemed best. The apportionment of representation on the basis of the new census has been made by the Secretary of the Interior in conformity with the provisions of law relating to that subject, and the recent elections have been made in accordance with it.

I commend to your favorable regard the suggestion contained in the report of the Secretary of the Interior that provision be made by law for the publication and distribution, periodically, of an analytical digest of all the patents which have been or may hereafter be granted for useful inventions and discoveries, with such descriptions and illustrations as may be necessary to present an intelligible view of their nature and operation. The cost of such publication could easily be defrayed out of the patent fund, and I am persuaded that it could be applied to no object more acceptable to inventors and beneficial to the public at large.

An appropriation of $100,000 having been made at the last session for the purchase of a suitable site and for the erection, furnishing, and fitting up of an asylum for the insane of the District of Columbia and of the Army and Navy of the United States, the proper measures have been adopted to carry this beneficent purpose into effect.

By the latest advices from the Mexican boundary commission it appears that the survey of the river Gila from its confluence with the Colorado to its supposed intersection with the western line of New Mexico has been completed. The survey of the Rio Grande has also been finished from the point agreed on by the commissioners as "the point where it strikes the southern boundary of New Mexico" to a point 135 miles below Eagle Pass, which is about two-thirds of the distance along the course of the river to its mouth.

The appropriation which was made at the last session of Congress for the continuation of the survey is subject to the following proviso:

Provided, That no part of this appropriation shall be used or expended until it shall be made satisfactorily to appear to the President of the United States that the southern boundary of New Mexico is not established by the commissioner and surveyor of the United States farther north of the town called "Paso" than the same is laid down in Disturnell's map, which is added to the treaty.

My attention was drawn to this subject by a report from the Department of the Interior, which reviewed all the facts of the case and submitted for my decision the question whether under existing circumstances any part of the appropriation could be lawfully used or expended for the further prosecution of the work. After a careful consideration of the subject I came to the conclusion that it could not, and so informed the head of that Department. Orders were immediately issued by him to the commissioner and surveyor to make no further requisitions on the Department, as they could not be paid, and to discontinue all operations on the southern line of New Mexico. But as the Department had no exact information as to the amount of provisions and money which remained unexpended in the hands of the commissioner and surveyor, it was left discretionary with them to continue the survey down the Rio Grande as far as the means at their disposal would enable them or at once to disband the commission. A special messenger has since arrived from the officer in charge of the survey on the river with information that the funds subject to his control were exhausted and that the officers and others employed in the service were destitute alike of the means of prosecuting the work and of returning to their homes.

The object of the proviso was doubtless to arrest the survey of the southern and western lines of New Mexico, in regard to which different opinions have been expressed; for it is hardly to be supposed that there could be any objection to that part of the line which extends along the channel of the Rio Grande. But the terms of the law are so broad as to forbid the use of any part of the money for the prosecution of the work, or even for the payment to the officers and agents of the arrearages of pay which are justly due to them.

I earnestly invite your prompt attention to this subject, and recommend a modification of the terms of the proviso, so as to enable the Department to use as much of the appropriation as will be necessary to discharge the existing obligations of the Government and to complete the survey of the Rio Grande to its mouth.

It will also be proper to make further provision by law for the fulfillment of our treaty with Mexico for running and marking the residue of the boundary line between the two countries.

Permit me to invite your particular attention to the interests of the District of Columbia, which are confided by the Constitution to your peculiar care.

Among the measures which seem to me of the greatest importance to its prosperity are the introduction of a copious supply of water into the city of Washington and the construction of suitable bridges across the Potomac to replace those which were destroyed by high water in the early part of the present year.

At the last session of Congress an appropriation was made to defray the cost of the surveys necessary for determining the best means of affording an unfailing supply of good and wholesome water. Some progress has been made in the survey, and as soon as it is completed the result will be laid before you.

Further appropriations will also be necessary for grading and paving the streets and avenues and inclosing and embellishing the public grounds within the city of Washington.

I commend all these objects, together with the charitable institutions of the District, to your favorable regard.

Every effort has been made to protect our frontier and that of the adjoining Mexican States from the incursions of the Indian tribes. Of about 11,000 men of which the Army is composed, nearly 8,000 are employed in the defense of the newly acquired territory (including Texas) and of emigrants proceeding thereto. I am gratified to say that these efforts have been unusually successful. With the exception of some partial outbreaks in California and Oregon and occasional depredations on a portion of the Rio Grande, owing, it is believed, to the disturbed state of that border region, the inroads of the Indians have been effectually restrained.

Experience has shown, however, that whenever the two races are brought into contact collisions will inevitably occur. To prevent these collisions the United States have generally set apart portions of their territory for the exclusive occupation of the Indian tribes. A difficulty occurs, however, in the application of this policy to Texas. By the terms of the compact by which that State was admitted into the Union she retained the ownership of all the vacant lands within her limits. The government of that State, it is understood, has assigned no portion of her territory to the Indians, but as fast as her settlements advance lays it off into counties and proceeds to survey and sell it. This policy manifestly tends not only to alarm and irritate the Indians, but to compel them to resort to plunder for subsistence. It also deprives this

Government of that influence and control over them without which no durable peace can ever exist between them and the whites. I trust, therefore, that a due regard for her own interests, apart from considerations of humanity and justice, will induce that State to assign a small portion of her vast domain for the provisional occupancy of the small remnants of tribes within her borders, subject, of course, to her ownership and eventual jurisdiction. If she should fail to do this, the fulfillment of our treaty stipulations with Mexico and our duty to the Indians themselves will, it is feared, become a subject of serious embarrassment to the Government. It is hoped, however, that a timely and just provision by Texas may avert this evil.

No appropriations for fortifications were made at the two last sessions of Congress. The cause of this omission is probably to be found in a growing belief that the system of fortifications adopted in 1816, and heretofore acted on, requires revision.

The subject certainly deserves full and careful investigation, but it should not be delayed longer than can be avoided. In the meantime there are certain works which have been commenced, some of them nearly completed, designed to protect our principal seaports from Boston to New Orleans and a few other important points. In regard to the necessity for these works, it is believed that little difference of opinion exists among military men. I therefore recommend that the appropriations necessary to prosecute them be made.

I invite your attention to the remarks on this subject and on others connected with his Department contained in the accompanying report of the Secretary of War.

Measures have been taken to carry into effect the law of the last session making provision for the improvement of certain rivers and harbors, and it is believed that the arrangements made for that purpose will combine efficiency with economy. Owing chiefly to the advanced season when the act was passed, little has yet been done in regard to many of the works beyond making the necessary preparations. With respect to a few of the improvements, the sums already appropriated will suffice to complete them; but most of them will require additional appropriations. I trust that these appropriations will be made, and that this wise and beneficent policy, so auspiciously resumed, will be continued. Great care should be taken, however, to commence no work which is not of sufficient importance to the commerce of the country to be viewed as national in its character. But works which have been commenced should not be discontinued until completed, as otherwise the sums expended will in most cases be lost.

The report from the Navy Department will inform you of the prosperous condition of the branch of the public service committed to its charge. It presents to your consideration many topics and suggestions of which I ask your approval. It exhibits an unusual degree of activity in the operations of the Department during the past year. The preparations for the Japan expedition, to which I have already alluded; the arrangements made for the exploration and survey of the China Seas, the Northern Pacific, and Behrings Straits; the incipient measures taken toward a reconnoissance of the continent of Africa eastward of Liberia; the preparation for an early examination of the tributaries of the river La Plata, which a recent decree of the provisional chief of the Argentine Confederation has opened to navigation—all these enterprises and the means by which they are proposed to be accomplished have commanded my full approbation, and I have no doubt will be productive of most useful results.

Two officers of the Navy were heretofore instructed to explore the whole extent of the Amazon River from the confines of Peru to its mouth. The return of one of them has placed in the possession of the Government an interesting and valuable account of the character and resources of a country abounding in the materials of commerce, and which if opened to the industry of the world will prove an inexhaustible fund of wealth. The report of this exploration will be communicated to you as soon as it is completed.

Among other subjects offered to your notice by the Secretary of the Navy, I select for special commendation, in view of its connection with the interests of the Navy, the plan submitted by him for the establishment of a permanent corps of seamen and the suggestions he has presented for the reorganization of the Naval Academy.

In reference to the first of these, I take occasion to say that I think it will greatly improve the efficiency of the service, and that I regard it as still more entitled to favor for the salutary influence it must exert upon the naval discipline, now greatly disturbed by the increasing spirit of insubordination resulting from our present system. The plan proposed for the organization of the seamen furnishes a judicious substitute for the law of September, 1850, abolishing corporal punishment, and satisfactorily sustains the policy of that act under conditions well adapted to maintain the authority of command and the order and security of our ships. It is believed that any change which proposes permanently to dispense with this mode of punishment should be preceded by a system of enlistment which shall supply the Navy with seamen of the most meritorious class, whose good deportment and pride of character may preclude all occasion for a resort to penalties of a harsh or degrading nature. The safety of a ship and her crew is often dependent upon immediate obedience to a command, and the authority to enforce it must be equally ready. The arrest of a refractory seaman in such moments not only deprives the ship of indispensable aid, but imposes a necessity for double service on others, whose fidelity to their duties may be relied upon in such an emergency. The exposure to this increased and arduous labor since the passage of the act of 1850 has already had, to a most observable and injurious extent, the effect of preventing the enlistment of the best seamen in the Navy. The plan now suggested is designed to promote a condition of service in which this objection will no longer exist. The details of this plan may be established in great part, if not altogether, by the Executive under the authority of existing laws, but I have thought it proper, in accordance with the suggestion of the Secretary of the Navy, to submit it to your approval.

The establishment of a corps of apprentices for the Navy, or boys to be enlisted until they become of age, and to be employed under such regulations as the Navy Department may devise, as proposed in the report, I cordially approve and commend to your consideration; and I also concur in the suggestion that this system for the early training of seamen may be most usefully ingrafted upon the service of our merchant marine.

The other proposition of the report to which I have referred—the reorganization of the Naval Academy—I recommend to your attention as a project worthy of your encouragement and support. The valuable services already rendered by this institution entitle it to the continuance of your fostering care.

Your attention is respectfully called to the report of the Postmaster-General for the detailed operation of his Department during the last fiscal year, from which it will be seen that the receipts from postages for that time were less by $1,431,696 than for the preceding fiscal year, being a decrease of about 23 per cent.

This diminution is attributable to the reduction in the rates of postage made by the act of March 3, 1851, which reduction took effect at the commencement of the last fiscal year.

Although in its operation during the last year the act referred to has not fulfilled the predictions of its friends by increasing the correspondence of the country in proportion to the reduction of postage, I should, nevertheless, question the policy of returning to higher rates. Experience warrants the expectation that as the community becomes accustomed to cheap postage correspondence will increase. It is believed that from this cause and from the rapid growth of the country in population and business the receipts of the Department must ultimately exceed its expenses, and that the country may safely rely upon the continuance of the present cheap rate of postage.

In former messages I have, among other things, respectfully recommended to the consideration of Congress the propriety and necessity of further legislation for the protection and punishment of foreign consuls residing in the United States; to revive, with certain modifications, the act of 10th March, 1838, to restrain unlawful military expeditions against the inhabitants of conterminous states or territories; for the preservation and protection from mutilation or theft of the papers, records, and archives of the nation; for authorizing the surplus revenue to be applied to the payment of the public debt in advance of the time when it will become due; for the establishment of land offices for the sale of the public lands in California and the Territory of Oregon; for the construction of a road from the Mississippi Valley to the Pacific Ocean; for the establishment of a bureau of agriculture for the promotion of that interest, perhaps the most important in the country; for the prevention of frauds upon the Government in applications for pensions and bounty lands; for the establishment of a uniform fee bill, prescribing a specific compensation for every service required of clerks, district attorneys, and marshals; for authorizing an additional regiment of mounted men for the defense of our frontiers against the Indians and for fulfilling our treaty stipulations with Mexico to defend her citizens against the Indians "with equal diligence and energy as our own;" for determining the relative rank between the naval and civil officers in our public ships and between the officers of the Army and Navy in the various grades of each; for reorganizing the naval establishment by fixing the number of officers in each grade, and providing for a retired list upon reduced pay of those unfit for active duty; for prescribing and regulating punishments in the Navy; for the appointment of a commission to revise the public statutes of the United States by arranging them in order, supplying deficiencies, correcting incongruities, simplifying their language, and reporting them to Congress for its final action; and for the establishment of a commission to adjudicate and settle private claims against the United States. I am not aware, however, that any of these subjects have been finally acted upon by Congress. Without repeating the reasons for legislation on these subjects which have been assigned in former messages, I respectfully recommend them again to your favorable consideration.

I think it due to the several Executive Departments of this Government to bear testimony to the efficiency and integrity with which they are conducted. With all the careful superintendence which it is possible for the heads of those Departments to exercise, still the due administration and guardianship of the public money must very much depend on the vigilance, intelligence, and fidelity of the subordinate officers and clerks, and especially on those intrusted with the settlement and adjustment of claims and accounts. I am gratified to believe that they have generally performed their duties faithfully and well. They are appointed to guard the approaches to the public Treasury, and they occupy positions that expose them to all the temptations and seductions which the cupidity of peculators and fraudulent claimants can prompt them to employ. It will be but a wise precaution to protect the Government against that source of mischief and corruption, as far as it can be done, by the enactment of all proper legal penalties. The laws in this respect are supposed to be defective, and I therefore deem it my duty to call your attention to the subject and to recommend that provision be made by law for the punishment not only of those who shall accept bribes, but also of those who shall either promise, give, or offer to give to any of those officers or clerks a bribe or reward touching or relating to any matter of their official action or duty.

It has been the uniform policy of this Government, from its foundation to the present day, to abstain from all interference in the domestic affairs of other nations. The consequence has been that while the nations of Europe have been engaged in desolating wars our country has pursued its peaceful course to unexampled prosperity and happiness. The wars in which we have been compelled to engage in defense of the rights and honor of the country have been, fortunately, of short duration. During the terrific contest of nation against nation which succeeded the French Revolution we were enabled by the wisdom and firmness of President Washington to maintain our neutrality. While other nations were drawn into this wide-sweeping whirlpool, we sat quiet and unmoved upon our own shores. While the flower of their numerous armies was wasted by disease or perished by hundreds of thousands upon the battlefield, the youth of this favored land were permitted to enjoy the blessings of peace beneath the paternal roof. While the States of Europe incurred enormous debts, under the burden of which their subjects still groan, and which must absorb no small part of the product of the honest industry of those countries for generations to come, the United States have once been enabled to exhibit the proud spectacle of a nation free from public debt, and if permitted to pursue our prosperous way for a few years longer in peace we may do the same again.

But it is now said by some that this policy must be changed. Europe is no longer separated from us by a voyage of months, but steam navigation has brought her within a few days' sail of our shores. We see more of her movements and take a deeper interest in her controversies. Although no one proposes that we should join the fraternity of potentates who have for ages lavished the blood and treasure of their subjects in maintaining "the balance of power," yet it is said that we ought to interfere between contending sovereigns and their subjects for the purpose of overthrowing the monarchies of Europe and establishing in their place republican institutions. It is alleged that we have heretofore pursued a different course from a sense of our weakness, but that now our conscious strength dictates a change of policy, and that it is consequently our duty to mingle in these contests and aid those who are struggling for liberty.

This is a most seductive but dangerous appeal to the generous sympathies of freemen. Enjoying, as we do, the blessings of a free Government, there is no man who has an American heart that would not rejoice to see these blessings extended to all other nations. We can not witness the struggle between the oppressed and his oppressor anywhere without the deepest sympathy for the former and the most anxious desire for his triumph. Nevertheless, is it prudent or is it wise to involve ourselves in these foreign wars? Is it indeed true that we have heretofore refrained from doing so merely from the degrading motive of a conscious weakness? For the honor of the patriots who have gone before us, I can not admit it. Men of the Revolution, who drew the sword against the oppressions of the mother country and pledged to Heaven "their lives, their fortunes, and their sacred honor" to maintain their freedom, could never have been actuated by so unworthy a motive. They knew no weakness or fear where right or duty pointed the way, and it is a libel upon their fair fame for us, while we enjoy the blessings for which they so nobly fought and bled, to insinuate it. The truth is that the course which they pursued was dictated by a stern sense of international justice, by a statesmanlike prudence and a far-seeing wisdom, looking not merely to the present necessities but to the permanent safety and interest of the country. They knew that the world is governed less by sympathy than by reason and force; that it was not possible for this nation to become a "propagandist" of free principles without arraying against it the combined powers of Europe, and that the result was more likely to be the overthrow of republican liberty here than its establishment there. History has been written in vain for those who can doubt this. France had no sooner established a republican form of government than she manifested a desire to force its blessings on all the world. Her own historian informs us that, hearing of some petty acts of tyranny in a neighboring principality, "the National Convention declared that she would afford succor and fraternity to all nations who wished to recover their liberty, and she gave it in charge to the executive power to give orders to the generals of the French armies to aid all citizens who might have been or should be oppressed in the cause of liberty." Here was the false step which led to her subsequent misfortunes. She soon found herself involved in war with all the rest of Europe. In less than ten years her Government was changed from a republic to an empire, and finally, after shedding rivers of blood, foreign powers restored her exiled dynasty and exhausted Europe sought peace and repose in the unquestioned ascendency of monarchical principles. Let us learn wisdom from her example. Let us remember that revolutions do not always establish freedom. Our own free institutions were not the offspring of our Revolution. They existed before. They were planted in the free charters of self-government under which the English colonies grew up, and our Revolution only freed us from the dominion of a foreign power whose government was at variance with those institutions. But European nations have had no such training for self-government, and every effort to establish it by bloody revolutions has been, and must without that preparation continue to be, a failure. Liberty unregulated by law degenerates into anarchy, which soon becomes the most horrid of all despotisms. Our policy is wisely to govern ourselves, and thereby to set such an example of national justice, prosperity, and true glory as shall teach to all nations the blessings of self-government and the unparalleled enterprise and success of a free people.

We live in an age of progress, and ours is emphatically a country of progress. Within the last half century the number of States in this Union has nearly doubled, the population has almost quadrupled, and our boundaries have been extended from the Mississippi to the Pacific. Our territory is checkered over with railroads and furrowed with canals. The inventive talent of our country is excited to the highest pitch, and the numerous applications for patents for valuable improvements distinguish this age and this people from all others. The genius of one American has enabled our commerce to move against wind and tide and that of another has annihilated distance in the transmission of intelligence. The whole country is full of enterprise. Our common schools are diffusing intelligence among the people and our industry is fast accumulating the comforts and luxuries of life. This is in part owing to our peculiar position, to our fertile soil and comparatively sparse population; but much of it is also owing to the popular institutions under which we live, to the freedom which every man feels to engage in any useful pursuit according to his taste or inclination, and to the entire confidence that his person and property will be protected by the laws. But whatever may be the cause of this unparalleled growth in population, intelligence, and wealth, one thing is clear—that the Government must keep pace with the progress of the people. It must participate in their spirit of enterprise, and while it exacts obedience to the laws and restrains all unauthorized invasions of the rights of neighboring states, it should foster and protect home industry and lend its powerful strength to the improvement of such means of intercommunication as are necessary to promote our internal commerce and strengthen the ties which bind us together as a people.

It is not strange, however much it may be regretted, that such an exuberance of enterprise should cause some individuals to mistake change for progress and the invasion of the rights of others for national prowess and glory. The former are constantly agitating for some change in the organic law, or urging new and untried theories of human rights. The latter are ever ready to engage in any wild crusade against a neighboring people, regardless of the justice of the enterprise and without looking at the fatal consequences to ourselves and to the cause of popular government. Such expeditions, however, are often stimulated by mercenary individuals, who expect to share the plunder or profit of the enterprise without exposing themselves to danger, and are led on by some irresponsible foreigner, who abuses the hospitality of our own Government by seducing the young and ignorant to join in his scheme of personal ambition or revenge under the false and delusive pretense of extending the area of freedom. These reprehensible aggressions but retard the true progress of our nation and tarnish its fair fame. They should therefore receive the indignant frowns of every good citizen who sincerely loves his country and takes a pride in its prosperity and honor.

Our Constitution, though not perfect, is doubtless the best that ever was formed. Therefore let every proposition to change it be well weighed and, if found beneficial, cautiously adopted. Every patriot will rejoice to see its authority so exerted as to advance the prosperity and honor of the nation, whilst he will watch with jealousy any attempt to mutilate this charter of our liberties or pervert its powers to acts of aggression or injustice. Thus shall conservatism and progress blend their harmonious action in preserving the form and spirit of the Constitution and at the same time carry forward the great improvements of the country with a rapidity and energy which freemen only can display.

In closing this my last annual communication, permit me, fellow-citizens, to congratulate you on the prosperous condition of our beloved country. Abroad its relations with all foreign powers are friendly, its rights are respected, and its high place in the family of nations cheerfully recognized. At home we enjoy an amount of happiness, public and private, which has probably never fallen to the lot of any other people. Besides affording to our own citizens a degree of prosperity of which on so large a scale I know of no other instance, our country is annually affording a refuge and a home to multitudes, altogether without example, from the Old World.

We owe these blessings, under Heaven, to the happy Constitution and Government which were bequeathed to us by our fathers, and which it is our sacred duty to transmit in all their integrity to our children. We must all consider it a great distinction and privilege to have been chosen by the people to bear a part in the administration of such a Government. Called by an unexpected dispensation to its highest trust at a season of embarrassment and alarm, I entered upon its arduous duties with extreme diffidence. I claim only to have discharged them to the best of an humble ability, with a single eye to the public good, and it is with devout gratitude in retiring from office that I leave the country in a state of peace and prosperity.

MILLARD FILLMORE.

SPECIAL MESSAGES.

WASHINGTON, *December 7, 1852.*

To the Senate of the United States:

I transmit to the Senate, for its consideration with a view to ratification, a treaty of friendship, commerce, and navigation, between the United States and the Oriental Republic of Uruguay, signed at Montevideo on the 28th of August last.

MILLARD FILLMORE.

WASHINGTON, *December 8, 1852.*

To the Senate of the United States:

I transmit to the Senate, for its consideration with a view to ratification, an additional article, signed in this city on the 16th ultimo, to the convention for the mutual delivery of criminals fugitives from justice in certain cases between the United States on the one part and Prussia and other States of the Germanic Confederation on the other part, concluded on the 15th of June, 1852.

MILLARD FILLMORE.

WASHINGTON, *January 4, 1853.*

To the Senate of the United States:

In answer to the resolution of the Senate of the 30th ultimo, requesting information in regard to the establishment of a new British colony in Central America, I transmit a report from the Secretary of State and the documents by which it was accompanied.

MILLARD FILLMORE.

WASHINGTON, *January 4, 1853.*

To the Senate of the United States:

In answer to the Senate's resolution of the 3d instant, calling for information relative to a proposed tripartite convention on the subject of the island of Cuba, I transmit to the Senate a report from the Secretary of State and the papers which accompanied it.

MILLARD FILLMORE.

WASHINGTON, *January 12, 1853.*

To the Senate of the United States:

In pursuance of the eleventh article of the treaty with the Chickasaw Indians signed on the 20th day of October, 1832, I herewith transmit a recommendation from the Secretary of the Treasury for the investment of a portion of the funds belonging to said nation, for the purpose of obtaining the advice and consent of the Senate to make the investment as therein recommended.

MILLARD FILLMORE.

WASHINGTON, *January 12, 1853.*

To the Senate of the United States:

In reply to the resolution of your honorable body of the 5th instant, I herewith communicate a report of the Secretary of the Interior giving the information* required.

MILLARD FILLMORE.

*Relating to the Mexican boundary commission.

To the Senate of the United States:

In answer to the resolution of the Senate dated the 13th ultimo, requesting further information in regard to the imprisonment of the United States consul and of other American citizens in the castle at Acapulco, I transmit a report from the Secretary of State and the documents by which it is accompanied.

MILLARD FILLMORE.

JANUARY 17, 1853.

WASHINGTON, *January 17, 1853.*

To the Senate and House of Representatives:

I transmit herewith a communication lately received at the Department of State from the minister of Her Most Catholic Majesty, accompanied by a letter of instructions from the Spanish Government relative to the case of the *Amistad*. In Mr. Calderon's communication reference is had to former letters addressed by him to the Department of State on the same subject, copies of which are herewith transmitted, and an earnest wish is expressed that a final settlement of this long-pending claim should be made. The tone of the letter of instructions from Mr. Manuel Bertran de Lis is somewhat more peremptory than could be wished, but this circumstance will not, probably, prevent Congress from giving his suggestions the attention to which they may be entitled.

The claim of the Spanish Government on behalf of its subjects interested in the *Amistad* was the subject of discussion during the Administration of President Tyler between the Spanish minister and Mr. Webster, then Secretary of State. In an elaborate letter of the latter, addressed to the Chevalier d'Argais on the 1st of September, 1841, the opinion is confidently maintained that the claim is unfounded. The Administration of President Polk took a different view of the matter. The justice of the claim was recognized in a letter from the Department of State to the Spanish minister of the 19th of March, 1847, and in his annual message of the same year the President recommended its payment.

Under these circumstances the attention of Congress is again invited to the subject. Respect to the Spanish Government demands that its urgent representation should be candidly and impartially weighed. If Congress should be of opinion that the claim is just, every consideration points to the propriety of its prompt recognition and payment, and if the two Houses should come to the opposite conclusion it is equally desirable that the result should be announced without unnecessary delay.

MILLARD FILLMORE.

WASHINGTON, *January 18, 1853.*

To the Senate and House of Representatives of the United States:

I have the honor herewith to transmit a report from the Secretary of the Interior, from which it appears that the efforts of that Department to induce the Indians remaining in Florida to migrate to the country assigned to their tribe west of the Mississippi have been entirely unsuccessful. The only alternative that now remains is either to compel them by force to comply with the treaty made with the tribe in May, 1832, by which they agreed to migrate within three years from that date, or allow the arrangement made with them in 1842, referred to in the Secretary's report, by which they were permitted to remain in the temporary occupancy of a portion of the peninsula until the Government should see fit to remove them, to continue.

It can not be denied that the withholding so large a portion of her territory from settlement is a source of injury to the State of Florida; and although, ever since the arrangement above referred to, the Indians have manifested a desire to remain at peace with the whites, the presence of a people who may at any time and upon any real or fancied provocation be driven to acts of hostility is a source of constant anxiety and alarm to the inhabitants on that border.

There can be no doubt, also, that the welfare of the Indians would be promoted by their removal from a territory where frequent collisions between them and their more powerful neighbors are daily becoming more inevitable.

On the other hand, there is every reason to believe that any manifestation of a design to remove them by force or to take possession of the territory allotted to them would be immediately retaliated by acts of cruelty on the defenseless inhabitants.

The number of Indians now remaining in the State is, it is true, very inconsiderable (not exceeding, it is believed, 500), but owing to the extent of the country occupied by them and its adaptation to their peculiar mode of warfare, a force very disproportioned to their numbers would be necessary to capture them, or even to protect the white settlements from their incursions. The military force now stationed in that State would be inadequate to these objects, and if it should be determined to enforce their removal or to survey the territory allotted to them some addition to it would be necessary, as the Government has but a small force available for that service. Additional appropriations for the support of the Army would also, in that event, be necessary.

For these reasons I have deemed it proper to submit the whole matter to Congress, for such action as they may deem best.

MILLARD FILLMORE.

WASHINGTON, *January 19, 1853.*

To the House of Representatives:

In answer to the resolution of the House of Representatives of the 27th ultimo, requesting information relative to the claims on Spain in the cases of the bark *Georgiana* and the brig *Susan Loud*, I transmit a report from the Secretary of State, to whom the resolution was referred.

MILLARD FILLMORE.

WASHINGTON, *January 21, 1853.*

To the Senate of the United States:

In compliance with the resolution of the Senate of the 10th instant, requesting certain correspondence relative to Central America, I transmit a report from the Secretary of State and the documents by which it was accompanied.

MILLARD FILLMORE.

WASHINGTON, *January 24, 1853.*

To the House of Representatives of the United States:

In obedience to a resolution of your honorable body of December 27, 1852, in reference to claims of custom-house officers for additional pay, I have the honor herewith to transmit a report from the Secretary of the Treasury giving the desired information; and in answer to the seventh interrogatory, asking "whether in my opinion further legislation is necessary or advisable either to protect the Treasury from unjust claims or to secure to the claimants their just rights," I would state that in my opinion no further legislation is necessary to effect either object. My views on this subject will be more fully seen on reference to an opinion given by me to the Secretary of the Treasury, a copy of which is annexed to his report.

MILLARD FILLMORE.

WASHINGTON, *January 24, 1853.*

To the Senate of the United States:

In answer to the resolution of the Senate of the 14th instant, relative to the award of the Emperor Louis Napoleon, of France, in the case of the brig *General Armstrong*, I transmit a report from the Secretary of State and the documents by which it was accompanied.

MILLARD FILLMORE.

WASHINGTON, *January 27, 1853.*

To the Senate of the United States:

In answer to the resolution of the Senate of the 13th instant, requesting a copy of correspondence and other documents relative to Nicaragua, Costa Rica, and the territory claimed by the Mosquito Indians, I transmit a report of the Secretary of State, to whom the resolution was referred.

MILLARD FILLMORE.

WASHINGTON, *January 27, 1853.*

To the House of Representatives:

Since my last message to your honorable body, communicating a report from the Treasury Department, in answer to your resolution of the 3d instant [27th ultimo?], in reference to the compensation of weighers and gaugers, further communications on that subject have been received from New Orleans, which have just been reported to me by the Secretary of the Treasury and which I deem it my duty to communicate to the House.

MILLARD FILLMORE.

WASHINGTON, *February 3, 1853.*

To the Senate of the United States:

I transmit herewith to the Senate in a new draft the convention with the Swiss Confederation, originally negotiated at Berne and concluded in that city on the 25th of November, 1850. On the 7th of March, 1851, it was considered by the Senate of the United States, whose assent was given to it with certain amendments, as will appear from the Journal of the Senate of that day. The convention was sent back to Switzerland with these alterations, which were taken into consideration by the Government of that Confederation, whose action in the premises will be learned by a letter from its President of the 5th of July, 1852.

The modifications which the Government of the Swiss Confederation are desirous of introducing into the amendments made by the Senate of the United States and the articles affected by them are not inconsistent with the object and spirit of those amendments, and appear to me to proceed upon a reasonable principle of compromise.

I have thought it expedient, in submitting them to the Senate with a view to their advice and consent to the ratification of the treaty in its present form, to have the entire instrument taken into a continuous draft, as well the portions—by far the greater part—already assented to by the Senate as the modifications proposed by the Government of the Swiss Confederation in reference to these amendments. In preparing the new draft a few slight alterations have been made in the modifications proposed by the Swiss Government.

Should the convention receive the approbation of the Senate in its present form, it will be immediately transmitted to Switzerland for ratification by the Swiss Confederation.

The delays which have taken place in the negotiation of this treaty have been principally caused by the want of a resident diplomatic agent of the United States at Berne, and are among the reasons for which an appropriation for a chargé d'affaires to that Government has recently, by my direction, been recommended in a letter from the Department of State to the chairman of the Committee on Foreign Relations of the Senate.

MILLARD FILLMORE.

WASHINGTON, *February 3, 1853.*

To the Senate of the United States:

In compliance with the resolution of the Senate of the 11th ultimo, asking for information with regard to the execution of the postal convention between the United States and Great Britain, I transmit a report from the Secretary of State and the documents which accompanied it.

MILLARD FILLMORE.

WASHINGTON, *February 7, 1853.*

To the Senate and House of Representatives:

Having in my message to Congress at the opening of the session adverted to the pending negotiations between this Government and that of Great Britain relative to the fisheries and commercial reciprocity with the British American Provinces, I transmit for the information of Congress the accompanying report from the Department of State on the present state of the negotiations, and I respectfully invite the attention of the two Houses to the suggestion in the latter part of the report.

MILLARD FILLMORE.

WASHINGTON, *February 9, 1853.*

To the Senate and House of Representatives:

I herewith transmit a communication from the Secretary of the Navy, accompanied by the first part of Lieutenant Herndon's report of the exploration of the valley of the Amazon and its tributaries, made by him in connection with Lieutenant Lardner Gibbon, under instructions from the Navy Department.

MILLARD FILLMORE.

WASHINGTON, *February 14, 1853.*

To the Senate of the United States:

I herewith communicate to the Senate, for its consideration with a view to ratification, a convention on the subject of the extradition of fugitives from justice between the United States and Belgium, concluded and signed in this city on the 11th instant by the respective plenipotentiaries.

MILLARD FILLMORE.

WASHINGTON, *February 18, 1853.*

To the Senate and House of Representatives:

I transmit a report from the Secretary of State, embodying the substance of recent communications made by the minister of Her Britannic Majesty to the Department of State on the subject of the interoceanic canal by the Nicaragua route, which formed the chief object of the treaty between the United States and Great Britain of the 19th April, 1850, and the relations of Great Britain to the protectorate of Mosquito, which she expresses herself desirous of relinquishing on terms consistent with her honorable engagements to the Indians of that name.

In consequence of these communications and other considerations stated in the report, it is deemed advisable by the Department that our diplomatic relations with the States of Central America should be placed on a higher and more efficient footing, and this measure meets my approbation. The whole subject is one of so much delicacy and importance that I should have preferred, so near the close of my Administration, not to make it the subject of an Executive communication. But inasmuch as the measure proposed can not, even if deemed expedient by my successor, take effect for near a twelvemonth unless an appropriation is made by this Congress, I have thought it my duty to submit the report of the Department to the two Houses. The importance of the measure seemed to require an exposition somewhat in detail of the grounds on which it is recommended.

MILLARD FILLMORE.

WASHINGTON, *February 18, 1853.*

To the Senate of the United States:

I transmit to the Senate, with the view to its ratification, a convention which was yesterday concluded between the United States and Great Britain for the establishment of international copyright.

MILLARD FILLMORE.

WASHINGTON, *February 19, 1853.*

To the Senate of the United States:

In answer to the resolution of the Senate of the 14th instant, relative to the fisheries on the coasts of Florida, I transmit herewith a report from the Secretary of State and the documents which accompanied it.

MILLARD FILLMORE.

WASHINGTON, *February 21, 1853.*

To the Senate of the United States:

In compliance with your resolution of the 19th of February instant, I herewith communicate a report from the Secretary of War, containing the report of Lieutenant Meigs, of the Engineer Corps, on the surveys, projects, and estimates for supplying the cities of Washington and Georgetown with an unfailing and abundant supply of water.

MILLARD FILLMORE.

WASHINGTON, *February 21, 1853.*

To the Senate of the United States:

I have the honor to transmit herewith a report from the Secretary of the Treasury of the 21st instant, in reference to the reinvestment of certain moneys belonging to the Chickasaw Nation of Indians which will come into the Treasury during the succeeding vacation of the Senate, and I respectfully concur in the recommendation made by the Secretary.

MILLARD FILLMORE.

WASHINGTON, *February 23, 1853.*

To the Senate of the United States:

I transmit to the Senate, for advice and consent with a view to ratification, a convention between the United States and Her Britannic Majesty for the adjustment of certain claims of citizens of the United States on the British Government and of British subjects on the Government of the United States, signed in London on the 8th instant. Although it is stipulated by the terms of the first article of the convention that the commissioner on the part of this Government shall be appointed by the President of the United States, it is not understood that this stipulation was intended to dispense with the concurrence of the Senate in such appointment.

MILLARD FILLMORE.

WASHINGTON, *February 25, 1853.*

To the Senate of the United States:

I transmit to the Senate, for its consideration with a view to ratification, a consular convention concluded in this city on the 23d instant between the United States and His Majesty the Emperor of the French.

MILLARD FILLMORE.

WASHINGTON, *February 26, 1853.*

To the Senate of the United States:

I transmit a copy of a proclamation of yesterday, which I deemed it advisable to issue, relative to an extraordinary session of the Senate on the 4th of March next.

MILLARD FILLMORE.

WASHINGTON, *February 28, 1853.*

To the Senate of the United States:

In answer to the resolution of the Senate of the 17th January last, requesting information in regard to the fisheries on the coasts of the British North American Provinces, I transmit a report from the Secretary of State and the documents which accompanied it.

MILLARD FILLMORE.

WASHINGTON, *February 28, 1853.*

To the Senate of the United States:

I herewith transmit, for the consideration and advice of the Senate, a treaty recently entered into with the Apache Indians in New Mexico by Colonel Sumner and Mr. Greiner, acting on behalf of the United States, together with the letter of Colonel Sumner on the subject of the treaty and reports thereon from the Commissioner of Indian Affairs and the Secretary of the Interior.

MILLARD FILLMORE.

PROCLAMATION.

BY THE PRESIDENT OF THE UNITED STATES OF AMERICA.

A PROCLAMATION.

The attention of the President having been called to the proceedings of Congress at the close of its session on the 4th of March, 1851, from which it appears that the constitutional term of that body was held not to have expired until 12 o'clock at noon of that day, and a notice having been issued, agreeably to former usage, to convene the Senate at 11 o'clock a. m. on the 4th of March next, it is apparent that such call is in conflict with the decision aforesaid:

Now, therefore, as well for the purpose of removing all doubt as to the legality of such call as of establishing a precedent of what is deemed a proper mode of convening the Senate, I, Millard Fillmore, President of the United States, have considered it to be my duty to issue this my proclamation, revoking said call and hereby declaring that an extraordinary occasion requires the Senate of the United States to convene for the transaction of business at the Capitol, in the city of Washington, on Friday, the 4th day of March next, at 12 o'clock at noon of that day, of which all who shall at that time be entitled to act as members of that body are hereby required to take notice.

Given under my hand and the seal of the United States, at Washington, this 25th day of February, A. D. 1853, and of the Independence of the United States the seventy-seventh.

[SEAL.]

MILLARD FILLMORE.

By the President:

EDWARD EVERETT,

Secretary of State.

Franklin Pierce

March 4, 1853, to March 4, 1857

SEE ENCYCLOPEDIC INDEX.

HOME AT CONCORD, NEW HAMPSHIRE, OF

FRANKLIN PIERCE

With official portrait engraved from copy of original in steel

Franklin Pierce

Franklin Pierce

FRANKLIN PIERCE was born in Hillsboro, N. H., November 23, 1804. Was the fourth son of Benjamin and Anna Pierce. His father was a citizen of Massachusetts; was a soldier in the War of the Revolution, attaining the rank of captain and brevet major. After peace was declared he removed from Massachusetts to New Hampshire and located near what is now Hillsboro. His first wife was Elizabeth Andrews, who died at an early age. His second wife, the mother of Franklin Pierce, was Anna Kendrick, of Amherst, N. H. He was sheriff of his county, a member of the State legislature and of the governor's council, and was twice chosen governor of his State (as a Democrat), first in 1827 and again in 1829. For many years he was declared to be "the most influential man in New Hampshire." He died in 1839. Franklin was given an academic education in well-known institutions at Hancock, Francestown, and Exeter, and in 1820 was sent to Bowdoin College. His college mates there were John P. Hale, his future political rival; Professor Calvin E. Stowe; Sergeant S. Prentiss, the distinguished orator; Henry W. Longfellow, and Nathaniel Hawthorne, his future biographer and lifelong friend. He graduated in 1824, being third in his class. After taking his degree he began the study of law at Portsmouth in the office of Levi Woodbury, where he remained about a year. Afterwards spent two years in the law school at Northampton, Mass., and in the office of Judge Edmund Parker, at Amherst, N. H. In 1827 was admitted to the bar and began practice in his native town. Espoused the cause of Andrew Jackson with ardor, and in 1829 was elected to represent his native town in the legislature, where by three subsequent elections he served four years, the last two as speaker. In 1833 was elected to represent his native district in the lower House of Congress, where he remained four years; served on the Judiciary and other important committees. His first important speech in the House was delivered in 1834 upon the necessity of economy and of watchfulness against frauds in the payment of Revolutionary claims. In 1834 married Miss Jane Means Appleton, daughter of Rev. Jesse Appleton, president of Bowdoin College. In 1837 was elected to the United States Senate. On account of ill health of his wife, deeming it best for her to return to New Hampshire, on June 28, 1842, resigned his seat, and returning to his home resumed the practice of the law. In 1838 he changed his residence from Hillsboro to Concord. In 1845 declined an appointment to the United States Senate to fill a vacancy. Also declined the nomination for governor, tendered by the Democratic State convention, and in 1845 an appointment to the office of Attorney-General of the United States, tendered by President Polk. In 1846, when the war with Mexico began, he enlisted as a private in a volunteer company organized at Concord; was soon afterwards commissioned colonel of the Ninth Regiment of Infantry; March 3, 1847, was commissioned brigadier-general in the Volunteer Army, and on March 27 embarked for Mexico, arriving at Vera Cruz June 28. August 6, 1847, joined General Scott with his brigade at Puebla, and soon set out for the capture of the City of Mexico. Took part in the battle of Contreras September 19, 1847, in which engagement he was severely injured by being thrown from his horse. The next day, not having recovered, he undertook to accompany his brigade in action against the enemy, when he fainted. He persisted in remaining on duty in the subsequent operations of the Army. His conduct and services were spoken of in high terms by his superior officers, Generals Scott, Worth, and Pillow. Before the battle of Molino del Rey was appointed one of the American commissioners in the effort for peace, a truce being declared for that purpose. The effort failed and the fighting was renewed. Participated in the battle of Molino del Rey and continued on duty till peace was declared. Resigned his commission in March, 1848, and returned to his home. The same month the legislature of his State voted him a sword of honor in appreciation of his services in the war. Resumed his law practice and was highly successful. In 1850 was a member of the constitutional convention which met at Concord to amend the constitution of New Hampshire, and was chosen to preside over its deliberations; he favored the removal of the religious-test clause in the old constitution, by which Roman Catholics were disqualified from holding office in the State, and also the abolition of any "property qualification;" he carried these amendments through the convention, but the people defeated them at the election. In January, 1852, the Democratic State convention of New Hampshire declared for him for President, but in a letter January 12 he positively refused to permit the delegation to present his name. The national convention of the party met at Baltimore June 1, 1852. On the fourth day he was nominated for President, and was elected in November, receiving 254 electoral votes, while his opponent, General Scott, received only 42. Was inaugurated March 4, 1853. In 1856 was voted for by his friends in the national Democratic convention for renomination, but was unsuccessful. Upon the expiration of his term as President he retired to his home at Concord, where he resided the remainder of his life. Died October 8, 1869, and was buried at Concord.

INAUGURAL ADDRESS.

MY COUNTRYMEN: It is a relief to feel that no heart but my own can know the personal regret and bitter sorrow over which I have been borne to a position so suitable for others rather than desirable for myself.

The circumstances under which I have been called for a limited period to preside over the destinies of the Republic fill me with a profound sense of responsibility, but with nothing like shrinking apprehension. I repair to the post assigned me not as to one sought, but in obedience to the unsolicited expression of your will, answerable only for a fearless, faithful, and diligent exercise of my best powers. I ought to be, and am, truly grateful for the rare manifestation of the nation's confidence; but this, so far from lightening my obligations, only adds to their weight. You have summoned me in my weakness; you must sustain me by your strength. When looking for the fulfillment of reasonable requirements, you will not be unmindful of the great changes which have occurred, even within the last quarter of a century, and the consequent augmentation and complexity of duties imposed in the administration both of your home and foreign affairs.

Whether the elements of inherent force in the Republic have kept pace with its unparalleled progression in territory, population, and wealth has been the subject of earnest thought and discussion on both sides of the ocean. Less than sixty-four years ago the Father of his Country made "the" then "recent accession of the important State of North Carolina to the Constitution of the United States" one of the subjects of his special congratulation. At that moment, however, when the agitation consequent upon the Revolutionary struggle had hardly subsided, when we were just emerging from the weakness and embarrassments of the Confederation, there was an evident consciousness of vigor equal to the great mission so wisely and bravely fulfilled by our fathers. It was not a presumptuous assurance, but a calm faith, springing from a clear view of the sources of power in a government constituted like ours. It is no paradox to say that although comparatively weak the new-born nation was intrinsically strong. Inconsiderable in population and apparent resources, it was upheld by a broad and intelligent comprehension of rights and an all-pervading purpose to maintain them, stronger than armaments. It came from the furnace of the Revolution, tempered to the necessities of the times. The thoughts of the men of that day were as practical as their sentiments were patriotic. They wasted no portion of their energies upon idle and delusive speculations, but with a firm and fearless step advanced beyond the governmental landmarks which had hitherto circumscribed the limits of human freedom and planted their standard, where it has stood against dangers which have threatened from abroad, and internal agitation, which has at times fearfully menaced at home. They proved themselves equal to the solution of the great problem, to understand which their minds had been illuminated by the dawning lights of the Revolution. The object sought was not a thing dreamed of; it was a thing realized. They had exhibited not only the power to achieve, but, what all history affirms to be so much more unusual, the capacity to maintain. The oppressed throughout the world from that day to the present have turned their eyes hitherward, not to find those lights extinguished or to fear lest they should wane, but to be constantly cheered by their steady and increasing radiance.

In this our country has, in my judgment, thus far fulfilled its highest duty to suffering humanity. It has spoken and will continue to speak, not only by its words, but by its acts, the language of sympathy, encouragement, and hope to those who earnestly listen to tones which pronounce for the largest rational liberty. But after all, the most animating encouragement and potent appeal for freedom will be its own history—its trials and its triumphs. Preeminently, the power of our advocacy reposes in our example; but no example, be it remembered, can be powerful for lasting good, whatever apparent advantages may be gained, which is not based upon eternal principles of right and justice. Our fathers decided for themselves, both upon the hour to declare and the hour to strike. They were their own judges of the circumstances under which it became them to pledge to each other "their lives, their fortunes, and their sacred honor" for the acquisition of the priceless inheritance transmitted to us. The energy with which that great conflict was opened and, under the guidance of a manifest and beneficent Providence, the uncomplaining endurance with which it was prosecuted to its consummation were only surpassed by the wisdom and patriotic spirit of concession which characterized all the counsels of the early fathers.

One of the most impressive evidences of that wisdom is to be found in the fact that the actual working of our system has dispelled a degree of solicitude which at the outset disturbed bold hearts and far-reaching intellects. The apprehension of dangers from extended territory, multiplied States, accumulated wealth, and augmented population has proved to be unfounded. The stars upon your banner have become nearly threefold their original number; your densely populated possessions skirt the shores of the two great oceans; and yet this vast increase of people and territory has not only shown itself compatible with the harmonious action of the States and Federal Government in their respective constitutional spheres, but has afforded an additional guaranty of the strength and integrity of both.

With an experience thus suggestive and cheering, the policy of my Administration will not be controlled by any timid forebodings of evil from expansion. Indeed, it is not to be disguised that our attitude as a nation and our position on the globe render the acquisition of certain possessions not within our jurisdiction eminently important for our protection, if not in the future essential for the preservation of the rights of commerce and the peace of the world. Should they be obtained, it will be through no grasping spirit, but with a view to obvious national interest and security, and in a manner entirely consistent with the strictest observance of national faith. We have nothing in our history or position to invite aggression; we have everything to beckon us to the cultivation of relations of peace and amity with all nations. Purposes, therefore, at once just and pacific will be significantly marked in the conduct of our foreign affairs. I intend that my Administration shall leave no blot upon our fair record, and trust I may safely give the assurance that no act within the legitimate scope of my constitutional control will be tolerated on the part of any portion of our citizens which can not challenge a ready justification before the tribunal of the civilized world. An Administration would be unworthy of confidence at home or respect abroad should it cease to be influenced by the conviction that no apparent advantage can be purchased at a price so dear as that of national wrong or dishonor. It is not your privilege as a nation to speak of a distant past. The striking incidents of your history, replete with instruction and furnishing abundant grounds for hopeful confidence, are comprised in a period comparatively brief. But if your past is limited, your future is boundless. Its obligations throng the unexplored pathway of advancement, and will be limitless as duration. Hence a sound and comprehensive policy should embrace not less the distant future than the urgent present.

The great objects of our pursuit as a people are best to be attained by peace, and are entirely consistent with the tranquillity and interests of the rest of mankind. With the neighboring nations upon our continent we should cultivate kindly and fraternal relations. We can desire nothing in regard to them so much as to see them consolidate their strength and pursue the paths of prosperity and happiness. If in the course of their growth we should open new channels of trade and create additional facilities for friendly intercourse, the benefits realized will be equal and mutual. Of the complicated European systems of national polity we have heretofore been independent. From their wars, their tumults, and anxieties we have been, happily, almost entirely exempt. Whilst these are confined to the nations which gave them existence, and within their legitimate jurisdiction, they can not affect us except as they appeal to our sympathies in the cause of human freedom and universal advancement. But the vast interests of commerce are common to all mankind, and the advantages of trade and international intercourse must always present a noble field for the moral influence of a great people.

With these views firmly and honestly carried out, we have a right to expect, and shall under all circumstances require, prompt reciprocity. The rights which belong to us as a nation are not alone to be regarded, but those which pertain to every citizen in his individual capacity, at home and abroad, must be sacredly maintained. So long as he can discern every star in its place upon that ensign, without wealth to purchase for him preferment or title to secure for him place, it will be his privilege, and must be his acknowledged right, to stand unabashed even in the presence of princes, with a proud consciousness that he is himself one of a nation of sovereigns and that he can not in legitimate pursuit wander so far from home that the agent whom he shall leave behind in the place which I now occupy will not see that no rude hand of power or tyrannical passion is laid upon him with impunity. He must realize that upon every sea and on every soil where our enterprise may rightfully seek the protection of our flag American citizenship is an inviolable panoply for the security of American rights. And in this connection it can hardly be necessary to reaffirm a principle which should now be regarded as fundamental. The rights, security, and repose of this Confederacy reject the idea of interference or colonization on this side of the ocean by any foreign power beyond present jurisdiction as utterly inadmissible.

The opportunities of observation furnished by my brief experience as a soldier confirmed in my own mind the opinion, entertained and acted upon by others from the formation of the Government, that the maintenance of large standing armies in our country would be not only dangerous, but unnecessary. They also illustrated the importance—I might well say the absolute necessity—of the military science and practical skill furnished in such an eminent degree by the institution which has made your Army what it is, under the discipline and instruction of officers not more distinguished for their solid attainments, gallantry, and devotion to the public service than for unobtrusive bearing and high moral tone. The Army as organized must be the nucleus around which in every time of need the strength of your military power, the sure bulwark of your defense—a national militia—may be readily formed into a well-disciplined and efficient organization. And the skill and self-devotion of the Navy assure you that you may take the performance of the past as a pledge for the future, and may confidently expect that the flag which has waved its untarnished folds over every sea will still float in undiminished honor. But these, like many other subjects, will be appropriately brought at a future time to the attention of the coordinate branches of the Government, to which I shall always look with profound respect and with trustful confidence that they will accord to me the aid and support which I shall so much need and which their experience and wisdom will readily suggest.

In the administration of domestic affairs you expect a devoted integrity in the public service and an observance of rigid economy in all departments, so marked as never justly to be questioned. If this reasonable expectation be not realized, I frankly confess that one of your leading hopes is doomed to disappointment, and that my efforts in a very important particular must result in a humiliating failure. Offices can be properly regarded only in the light of aids for the accomplishment of these objects, and as occupancy can confer no prerogative nor importunate desire for preferment any claim, the public interest imperatively demands that they be considered with sole reference to the duties to be performed. Good citizens may well claim the protection of good laws and the benign influence of good government, but a claim for office is what the people of a republic should never recognize. No reasonable man of any party will expect the Administration to be so regardless of its responsibility and of the obvious elements of success as to retain persons known to be under the influence of political hostility and partisan prejudice in positions which will require not only severe labor, but cordial cooperation. Having no implied engagements to ratify, no rewards to bestow, no resentments to remember, and no personal wishes to consult in selections for official station, I shall fulfill this difficult and delicate trust, admitting no motive as worthy either of my character or position which does not contemplate an efficient discharge of duty and the best interests of my country. I acknowledge my obligations to the masses of my countrymen, and to them alone. Higher objects than personal aggrandizement gave direction and energy to their exertions in the late canvass, and they shall not be disappointed. They require at my hands diligence, integrity, and capacity wherever there are duties to be performed. Without these qualities in their public servants, more stringent laws for the prevention or punishment of fraud, negligence, and peculation will be vain. With them they will be unnecessary.

But these are not the only points to which you look for vigilant watchfulness. The dangers of a concentration of all power in the general government of a confederacy so vast as ours are too obvious to be disregarded. You have a right, therefore, to expect your agents in every department to regard strictly the limits imposed upon them by the Constitution of the United States. The great scheme of our constitutional liberty rests upon a proper distribution of power between the State and Federal authorities, and experience has shown that the harmony and happiness of our people must depend upon a just discrimination between the separate rights and responsibilities of the States and your common rights and obligations under the General Government; and here, in my opinion, are the considerations which should form the true basis of future concord in regard to the questions which have most seriously disturbed public tranquillity. If the Federal Government will confine itself to the exercise of powers clearly granted by the Constitution, it can hardly happen that its action upon any question should endanger the institutions of the States or interfere with their right to manage matters strictly domestic according to the will of their own people.

In expressing briefly my views upon an important subject which has recently agitated the nation to almost a fearful degree, I am moved by no other impulse than a most earnest desire for the perpetuation of that Union which has made us what we are, showering upon us blessings and conferring a power and influence which our fathers could hardly have anticipated, even with their most sanguine hopes directed to a far-off future. The sentiments I now announce were not unknown before the expression of the voice which called me here. My own position upon this subject was clear and unequivocal, upon the record of my words and my acts, and it is only recurred to at this time because silence might perhaps be misconstrued. With the Union my best and dearest earthly hopes are entwined. Without it what are we individually or collectively? What becomes of the noblest field ever opened for the advancement of our race in religion, in government, in the arts, and in all that dignifies and adorns mankind? From that radiant constellation which both illumines our own way and points out to struggling nations their course, let but a single star be lost, and, if there be not utter darkness, the luster of the whole is dimmed. Do my countrymen need any assurance that such a catastrophe is not to overtake them while I possess the power to stay it? It is with me an earnest and vital belief that as the Union has been the source, under Providence, of our prosperity to this time, so it is the surest pledge of a continuance of the blessings we have enjoyed, and which we are sacredly bound to transmit undiminished to our children. The field of calm and free discussion in our country is open, and will always be so, but never has been and never can be traversed for good in a spirit of sectionalism and uncharitableness. The founders of the Republic dealt with things as they were presented to them, in a spirit of self-sacrificing patriotism, and, as time has proved, with a comprehensive wisdom which it will always be safe for us to consult. Every measure tending to strengthen the fraternal feelings of all the members of our Union has had my heartfelt approbation. To every theory of society or government, whether the offspring of feverish ambition or of morbid enthusiasm, calculated to dissolve the bonds of law and affection which unite us, I shall interpose a ready and stern resistance. I believe that involuntary servitude, as it exists in different States of this Confederacy, is recognized by the Constitution. I believe that it stands like any other admitted right, and that the States where it exists are entitled to efficient remedies to enforce the constitutional provisions. I hold that the laws of 1850, commonly called the "compromise measures," are strictly constitutional and to be unhesitatingly carried into effect. I believe that the constituted authorities of this Republic are bound to regard the rights of the South in this respect as they would view any other legal and constitutional right, and that the laws to enforce them should be respected and obeyed, not with a reluctance encouraged by abstract opinions as to their propriety in a different state of society, but cheerfully and according to the decisions of the tribunal to which their exposition belongs. Such have been, and are, my convictions, and upon them I shall act. I fervently hope that the question is at rest, and that no sectional or ambitious or fanatical excitement may again threaten the durability of our institutions or obscure the light of our prosperity.

But let not the foundation of our hope rest upon man's wisdom. It will not be sufficient that sectional prejudices find no place in the public deliberations. It will not be sufficient that the rash counsels of human passion are rejected. It must be felt that there is no national security but in the nation's humble, acknowledged dependence upon God and His overruling providence.

We have been carried in safety through a perilous crisis. Wise counsels, like those which gave us the Constitution, prevailed to uphold it. Let the period be remembered as an admonition, and not as an encouragement, in any section of the Union, to make experiments where experiments are fraught with such fearful hazard. Let it be impressed upon all hearts that, beautiful as our fabric is, no earthly power or wisdom could ever reunite its broken fragments. Standing, as I do, almost within view of the green slopes of Monticello, and, as it were, within reach of the tomb of Washington, with all the cherished memories of the past gathering around me like so many eloquent voices of exhortation from heaven, I can express no better hope for my country than that the kind Providence which smiled upon our fathers may enable their children to preserve the blessings they have inherited.

MARCH 4, 1853.

SPECIAL MESSAGES.

WASHINGTON, *March 21, 1853*.

To the Senate of the United States:

In answer to the resolution of the Senate of the 17th instant, respecting certain propositions to Nicaragua and Costa Rica relative to the settlement of the territorial controversies between the States and Governments bordering on the river San Juan, I transmit a report from the Secretary of State and the documents by which it was accompanied.

FRANKLIN PIERCE.

WASHINGTON, *March 21, 1853*.

To the Senate:

The eleventh article of the treaty with the Chickasaw Indians of the 20th October, 1832, provides that certain moneys arising from the sales of the lands ceded by that treaty shall be laid out under the direction of the President of the United States, by and with the advice and consent of the Senate, in such safe and valuable stock as he may approve of, for the benefit of the Chickasaw Nation.

The report of the Secretary of the Treasury of the 15th instant, herewith transmitted, shows that the sum of $58,100 5 per cent stock, created under the act of 3d March, 1843, now stands on the books of the

Treasury in the name of the Secretary of the Treasury, as trustee for the Chickasaw national fund. This stock, by the terms of its issue, is redeemable on the 1st July next, when interest thereon will cease. It therefore becomes my duty to lay before the Senate the subject of reinvesting this amount under the same trust.

The second section of the act of 11th September, 1841 (the first section of which repeals the provisions of the act of 7th July, 1838, directing the investment of the Smithsonian fund in the stocks of the States), enacts that "all other funds held in trust by the United States, and the annual interest accruing thereon, when not otherwise required by treaty, shall in like manner be invested in stocks of the United States bearing a like rate of interest."

I submit to the Senate whether it will advise and consent that the Secretary of the Treasury be authorized, under my direction, to reinvest the above-mentioned sum of $58,100 in stocks of the United States under the same trust.

FRANKLIN PIERCE.

WASHINGTON, *March 21, 1853.*

To the Senate of the United States:

In answer to the resolution of the Senate of the 18th of January last, calling for further correspondence touching the revolution in France of December, 1851, I transmit a report from the Secretary of State and the documents by which it was accompanied.

FRANKLIN PIERCE.

EXECUTIVE CHAMBER, *March 25, 1853.*

To the Senate of the United States:

I nominate Mrs. Mary Berard to be deputy postmaster at "West Point," N. Y., the commissions for said office having exceeded $1,000 for the year ending the 30th June, 1852. Mrs. B. has held said office since the 12th of May, 1848, under an appointment of the Post-Office Department.

FRANKLIN PIERCE.

EXECUTIVE ORDERS.

EXECUTIVE OFFICE, *March 23, 1853.*

Believing that the public interests involved in the erection of the wings of the United States Capitol will be promoted by the exercise of a general supervision and control of the whole work by a skillful and competent officer of the Corps of Engineers or of the Topographical Corps, and as the officers of those corps are more immediately amenable to the Secretary of War, I hereby direct that the jurisdiction heretofore exercised over the said work by the Department of the Interior be transferred to the War Department, and request that the Secretary of War will designate to the President a suitable officer to take charge of the same.

FRANKLIN PIERCE.

BY THE PRESIDENT OF THE UNITED STATES.

WASHINGTON, *April 20, 1853*.

The President has, with deep sorrow, received information that the Vice-President of the United States, William R. King, died on the 18th instant at his residence in Alabama.

In testimony of respect for eminent station, exalted character, and, higher and above all station, for a career of public service and devotion to this Union which for duration and usefulness is almost without a parallel in the history of the Republic, the labors of the various Departments will be suspended.

The Secretaries of War and Navy will issue orders that appropriate military and naval honors be rendered to the memory of one to whom such a tribute will not be formal, but heartfelt from a people the deceased has so faithfully served.

The public offices will be closed to-morrow and badges of mourning be placed on the Executive Mansion and all the Executive Departments at Washington.

FRANKLIN PIERCE.

GENERAL ORDERS, NO. 11.

WAR DEPARTMENT,
ADJUTANT-GENERAL'S OFFICE,
Washington, April 20, 1853.

I. The following order announces to the Army the death of William Rufus King, late Vice-President of the United States:

WAR DEPARTMENT,
Washington, April 20, 1853.

With deep sorrow the President announces to the Army the death of William Rufus King, Vice-President of the United States, who died on the evening of Monday, the 18th instant, at his residence in Dallas County, Ala.

Called into the service of his country at a period in life when but few are prepared to enter upon its realities, his long career of public usefulness at home and abroad has always been honored by the public confidence, and was closed in the second office within the gift of the people.

From sympathy with his relatives and the American people for their loss and from respect for his distinguished public services, the President directs that appropriate honors to his memory be paid by the Army.

JEFFERSON DAVIS,
Secretary of War.

II. On the day next succeeding the receipt of this order at each military post the troops will be paraded at 10 o'clock a. m. and this order read to them.

The national flag will be displayed at half-staff.

At dawn of day thirteen guns will be fired. Commencing at 12 o'clock m. seventeen minute guns will be fired and at the close of the day the national salute of thirty-one guns.

The usual badge of mourning will be worn by officers of the Army and the colors of the several regiments will be put in mourning for the period of three months.

By order:

S. COOPER,
Adjutant-General.

[From the Daily National Intelligencer, April 21, 1853.]

GENERAL ORDER.

NAVY DEPARTMENT,
April 20, 1853.

With deep sorrow the President announces to the officers of the Navy and Marine Corps the death of William Rufus King, Vice-President of the United States, who died on the evening of Monday, the 18th instant, at his residence in Alabama.

Called into the service of his country at a period of life when but few are prepared to enter upon its realities, his long career of public usefulness at home and abroad has always been honored by the public confidence, and was closed in the second office within the gift of the people.

From sympathy with his relatives and the American people for their loss and from respect for his distinguished public services, the President directs that appropriate honors be paid to his memory at each of the navy-yards and naval stations and on board all the public vessels in commission on the day after this order is received by firing at dawn of day thirteen guns, at 12 o'clock m. seventeen minute guns, and at the close of the day the national salute, by carrying their flags at half-mast one day, and by the officers wearing crape on the left arm for three months.

J. C. DOBBIN,
Secretary of the Navy.

FIRST ANNUAL MESSAGE.

WASHINGTON, D. C., *December 5, 1853.*

Fellow-Citizens of the Senate and of the House of Representatives:

The interest with which the people of the Republic anticipate the assembling of Congress and the fulfillment on that occasion of the duty imposed upon a new President is one of the best evidences of their capacity to realize the hopes of the founders of a political system at once complex and symmetrical. While the different branches of the Government are to a certain extent independent of each other, the duties of all alike have direct reference to the source of power. Fortunately, under this system no man is so high and none so humble in the scale of public station as to escape from the scrutiny or to be exempt from the responsibility which all official functions imply.

Upon the justice and intelligence of the masses, in a government thus organized, is the sole reliance of the confederacy and the only security for honest and earnest devotion to its interests against the usurpations and encroachments of power on the one hand and the assaults of personal ambition on the other.

The interest of which I have spoken is inseparable from an inquiring, self-governing community, but stimulated, doubtless, at the present time by the unsettled condition of our relations with several foreign powers, by the new obligations resulting from a sudden extension of the field of enterprise, by the spirit with which that field has been entered and the amazing energy with which its resources for meeting the demands of humanity have been developed.

Although disease, assuming at one time the characteristics of a widespread and devastating pestilence, has left its sad traces upon some portions of our country, we have still the most abundant cause for reverent thankfulness to God for an accumulation of signal mercies showered upon us as a nation. It is well that a consciousness of rapid advancement and increasing strength be habitually associated with an abiding sense of dependence upon Him who holds in His hands the destiny of men and of nations.

Recognizing the wisdom of the broad principle of absolute religious toleration proclaimed in our fundamental law, and rejoicing in the benign influence which it has exerted upon our social and political condition, I should shrink from a clear duty did I fail to express my deepest conviction that we can place no secure reliance upon any apparent progress if it be not sustained by national integrity, resting upon the great truths affirmed and illustrated by divine revelation. In the midst of our sorrow for the afflicted and suffering, it has been consoling to see how promptly disaster made true neighbors of districts and cities separated widely from each other, and cheering to watch the strength of that common bond of brotherhood which unites all hearts, in all parts of this Union, when danger threatens from abroad or calamity impends over us at home.

Our diplomatic relations with foreign powers have undergone no essential change since the adjournment of the last Congress. With some of them questions of a disturbing character are still pending, but there are good reasons to believe that these may all be amicably adjusted.

For some years past Great Britain has so construed the first article of the convention of the 20th of April, 1818, in regard to the fisheries on the northeastern coast, as to exclude our citizens from some of the fishing grounds to which they freely resorted for nearly a quarter of a century subsequent to the date of that treaty. The United States have never acquiesced in this construction, but have always claimed for their fishermen all the rights which they had so long enjoyed without molestation. With a view to remove all difficulties on the subject, to extend the rights of our fishermen beyond the limits fixed by the convention of 1818, and to regulate trade between the United States and the British North American Provinces, a negotiation has been opened with a fair prospect of a favorable result. To protect our fishermen in the enjoyment of their rights and prevent collision between them and British fishermen, I deemed it expedient to station a naval force in that quarter during the fishing season.

Embarrassing questions have also arisen between the two Governments in regard to Central America. Great Britain has proposed to settle them by an amicable arrangement, and our minister at London is instructed to enter into negotiations on that subject.

A commission for adjusting the claims of our citizens against Great Britain and those of British subjects against the United States, organized under the convention of the 8th of February last, is now sitting in London for the transaction of business.

It is in many respects desirable that the boundary line between the United States and the British Provinces in the northwest, as designated in the convention of the 15th of June, 1846, and especially that part which separates the Territory of Washington from the British possessions on the north, should be traced and marked. I therefore present the subject to your notice.

With France our relations continue on the most friendly footing. The extensive commerce between the United States and that country might, it is conceived, be released from some unnecessary restrictions to the mutual advantage of both parties. With a view to this object, some progress has been made in negotiating a treaty of commerce and navigation.

Independently of our valuable trade with Spain, we have important political relations with her growing out of our neighborhood to the islands of Cuba and Porto Rico. I am happy to announce that since the last Congress no attempts have been made by unauthorized expeditions within the United States against either of those colonies. Should any movement be manifested within our limits, all the means at my command will be vigorously exerted to repress it. Several annoying occurrences have taken place at Havana, or in the vicinity of the island of Cuba, between our citizens and the Spanish authorities. Considering the proximity of that island to our shores, lying, as it does, in the track of trade between some of our principal cities, and the suspicious vigilance with which foreign intercourse, particularly that with the United States, is there guarded, a repetition of such occurrences may well be apprehended.

As no diplomatic intercourse is allowed between our consul at Havana and the Captain-General of Cuba, ready explanations can not be made or prompt redress afforded where injury has resulted. All complaint on the part of our citizens under the present arrangement must be, in the first place, presented to this Government and then referred to Spain. Spain again refers it to her local authorities in Cuba for investigation, and postpones an answer till she has heard from those authorities. To avoid these irritating and vexatious delays, a proposition has been made to provide for a direct appeal for redress to the Captain-General by our consul in behalf of our injured fellow-citizens. Hitherto the Government of Spain has declined to enter into any such arrangement. This course on her part is deeply regretted, for without some arrangement of this kind the good understanding between the two countries may be exposed to occasional interruption. Our minister at Madrid is instructed to renew the proposition and to press it again upon the consideration of Her Catholic Majesty's Government.

For several years Spain has been calling the attention of this Government to a claim for losses by some of her subjects in the case of the schooner *Amistad*. This claim is believed to rest on the obligations imposed by our existing treaty with that country. Its justice was admitted in our diplomatic correspondence with the Spanish Government as early as March, 1847, and one of my predecessors, in his annual message of that year, recommended that provision should be made for its payment. In January last it was again submitted to Congress by the Executive. It has received a favorable consideration by committees of both branches, but as yet there has been no final action upon it. I conceive that good faith requires its prompt adjustment, and I present it to your early and favorable consideration.

Martin Koszta, a Hungarian by birth, came to this country in 1850, and declared his intention in due form of law to become a citizen of the United States. After remaining here nearly two years he visited Turkey. While at Smyrna he was forcibly seized, taken on board an Austrian brig of war then lying in the harbor of that place, and there confined in irons, with the avowed design to take him into the dominions of Austria. Our consul at Smyrna and legation at Constantinople interposed for his release, but their efforts were ineffectual. While thus in prison Commander Ingraham, with the United States ship of war *St. Louis*, arrived at Smyrna, and after inquiring into the circumstances of the case came to the conclusion that Koszta was entitled to the protection of this Government, and took energetic and prompt measures for his release. Under an arrangement between the agents of the United States and of Austria, he was transferred to the custody of the French consul-general at Smyrna, there to remain until he should be disposed of by the mutual agreement of the consuls of the respective Governments at that place. Pursuant to that agreement, he has been released, and is now in the United States. The Emperor of Austria has made the conduct of our officers who took part in this transaction a subject of grave complaint. Regarding Koszta as still his subject, and claiming a right to seize him within the limits of the Turkish Empire, he has demanded of this Government its consent to the surrender of the prisoner, a disavowal of the acts of its agents, and satisfaction for the alleged outrage. After a careful consideration of the case I came to the conclusion that Koszta was seized without legal authority at Smyrna; that he was wrongfully detained on board of the Austrian brig of war; that at the time of his seizure he was clothed with the nationality of the United States, and that the acts of our officers, under the circumstances of the case, were justifiable, and their conduct has been fully approved by me, and a compliance with the several demands of the Emperor of Austria has been declined.

For a more full account of this transaction and my views in regard to it I refer to the correspondence between the chargé d'affaires of Austria and the Secretary of State, which is herewith transmitted. The principles and policy therein maintained on the part of the United States will, whenever a proper occasion occurs, be applied and enforced.

The condition of China at this time renders it probable that some important changes will occur in that vast Empire which will lead to a more unrestricted intercourse with it. The commissioner to that country who has been recently appointed is instructed to avail himself of all occasions to open and extend our commercial relations, not only with the Empire of China, but with other Asiatic nations.

In 1852 an expedition was sent to Japan, under the command of Commodore Perry, for the purpose of opening commercial intercourse with that Empire. Intelligence has been received of his arrival there and of his having made known to the Emperor of Japan the object of his visit. But it is not yet ascertained how far the Emperor will be disposed to abandon his restrictive policy and open that populous country to a commercial intercourse with the United States.

It has been my earnest desire to maintain friendly intercourse with the Governments upon this continent and to aid them in preserving good understanding among themselves. With Mexico a dispute has arisen as to the true boundary line between our Territory of New Mexico and the

Mexican State of Chihuahua. A former commissioner of the United States, employed in running that line pursuant to the treaty of Guadalupe Hidalgo, made a serious mistake in determining the initial point on the Rio Grande; but inasmuch as his decision was clearly a departure from the directions for tracing the boundary contained in that treaty, and was not concurred in by the surveyor appointed on the part of the United States, whose concurrence was necessary to give validity to that decision, this Government is not concluded thereby; but that of Mexico takes a different view of the subject.

There are also other questions of considerable magnitude pending between the two Republics. Our minister in Mexico has ample instructions to adjust them. Negotiations have been opened, but sufficient progress has not been made therein to enable me to speak of the probable result. Impressed with the importance of maintaining amicable relations with that Republic and of yielding with liberality to all her just claims, it is reasonable to expect that an arrangement mutually satisfactory to both countries may be concluded and a lasting friendship between them confirmed and perpetuated.

Congress having provided for a full mission to the States of Central America, a minister was sent thither in July last. As yet he has had time to visit only one of these States (Nicaragua), where he was received in the most friendly manner. It is hoped that his presence and good offices will have a benign effect in composing the dissensions which prevail among them, and in establishing still more intimate and friendly relations between them respectively and between each of them and the United States.

Considering the vast regions of this continent and the number of states which would be made accessible by the free navigation of the river Amazon, particular attention has been given to this subject. Brazil, through whose territories it passes into the ocean, has hitherto persisted in a policy so restricted in regard to the use of this river as to obstruct and nearly exclude foreign commercial intercourse with the States which lie upon its tributaries and upper branches. Our minister to that country is instructed to obtain a relaxation of that policy and to use his efforts to induce the Brazilian Government to open to common use, under proper safeguards, this great natural highway for international trade. Several of the South American States are deeply interested in this attempt to secure the free navigation of the Amazon, and it is reasonable to expect their cooperation in the measure. As the advantages of free commercial intercourse among nations are better understood, more liberal views are generally entertained as to the common rights of all to the free use of those means which nature has provided for international communication. To these more liberal and enlightened views it is hoped that Brazil will conform her policy and remove all unnecessary restrictions upon the free use of a river which traverses so many states and so large a part of the continent. I am happy to inform you that the Republic of

Paraguay and the Argentine Confederation have yielded to the liberal policy still resisted by Brazil in regard to the navigable rivers within their respective territories. Treaties embracing this subject, among others, have been negotiated with these Governments, which will be submitted to the Senate at the present session.

A new branch of commerce, important to the agricultural interests of the United States, has within a few years past been opened with Peru. Notwithstanding the inexhaustible deposits of guano upon the islands of that country, considerable difficulties are experienced in obtaining the requisite supply. Measures have been taken to remove these difficulties and to secure a more abundant importation of the article. Unfortunately, there has been a serious collision between our citizens who have resorted to the Chincha Islands for it and the Peruvian authorities stationed there. Redress for the outrages committed by the latter was promptly demanded by our minister at Lima. This subject is now under consideration, and there is reason to believe that Peru is disposed to offer adequate indemnity to the aggrieved parties.

We are thus not only at peace with all foreign countries, but, in regard to political affairs, are exempt from any cause of serious disquietude in our domestic relations.

The controversies which have agitated the country heretofore are passing away with the causes which produced them and the passions which they had awakened; or, if any trace of them remains, it may be reasonably hoped that it will only be perceived in the zealous rivalry of all good citizens to testify their respect for the rights of the States, their devotion to the Union, and their common determination that each one of the States, its institutions, its welfare, and its domestic peace, shall be held alike secure under the sacred ægis of the Constitution.

This new league of amity and of mutual confidence and support into which the people of the Republic have entered happily affords inducement and opportunity for the adoption of a more comprehensive and unembarrassed line of policy and action as to the great material interests of the country, whether regarded in themselves or in connection with the powers of the civilized world.

The United States have continued gradually and steadily to expand through acquisitions of territory, which, how much soever some of them may have been questioned, are now universally seen and admitted to have been wise in policy, just in character, and a great element in the advancement of our country, and with it of the human race, in freedom, in prosperity, and in happiness. The thirteen States have grown to be thirty-one, with relations reaching to Europe on the one side and on the other to the distant realms of Asia.

I am deeply sensible of the immense responsibility which the present magnitude of the Republic and the diversity and multiplicity of its interests devolves upon me, the alleviation of which so far as relates to the immediate conduct of the public business, is, first, in my reliance on the wisdom and patriotism of the two Houses of Congress, and, secondly, in the directions afforded me by the principles of public polity affirmed by our fathers of the epoch of 1798, sanctioned by long experience, and consecrated anew by the overwhelming voice of the people of the United States.

Recurring to these principles, which constitute the organic basis of union, we perceive that vast as are the functions and the duties of the Federal Government, vested in or intrusted to its three great departments—the legislative, executive, and judicial—yet the substantive power, the popular force, and the large capacities for social and material development exist in the respective States, which, all being of themselves well-constituted republics, as they preceded so they alone are capable of maintaining and perpetuating the American Union. The Federal Government has its appropriate line of action in the specific and limited powers conferred on it by the Constitution, chiefly as to those things in which the States have a common interest in their relations to one another and to foreign governments, while the great mass of interests which belong to cultivated men—the ordinary business of life, the springs of industry, all the diversified personal and domestic affairs of society—rest securely upon the general reserved powers of the people of the several States. There is the effective democracy of the nation, and there the vital essence of its being and its greatness.

Of the practical consequences which flow from the nature of the Federal Government, the primary one is the duty of administering with integrity and fidelity the high trust reposed in it by the Constitution, especially in the application of the public funds as drawn by taxation from the people and appropriated to specific objects by Congress.

Happily, I have no occasion to suggest any radical changes in the financial policy of the Government. Ours is almost, if not absolutely, the solitary power of Christendom having a surplus revenue drawn immediately from imposts on commerce, and therefore measured by the spontaneous enterprise and national prosperity of the country, with such indirect relation to agriculture, manufactures, and the products of the earth and sea as to violate no constitutional doctrine and yet vigorously promote the general welfare. Neither as to the sources of the public treasure nor as to the manner of keeping and managing it does any grave controversy now prevail, there being a general acquiescence in the wisdom of the present system.

The report of the Secretary of the Treasury will exhibit in detail the state of the public finances and the condition of the various branches of the public service administered by that Department of the Government.

The revenue of the country, levied almost insensibly to the taxpayer, goes on from year to year, increasing beyond either the interests or the prospective wants of the Government.

At the close of the fiscal year ending June 30, 1852, there remained in the Treasury a balance of $14,632,136. The public revenue for the fiscal year ending June 30, 1853, amounted to $58,931,865 from customs and to $2,405,708 from public lands and other miscellaneous sources, amounting together to $61,337,574, while the public expenditures for the same period, exclusive of payments on account of the public debt, amounted to $43,554,262, leaving a balance of $32,425,447 of receipts above expenditures.

This fact of increasing surplus in the Treasury became the subject of anxious consideration at a very early period of my Administration, and the path of duty in regard to it seemed to me obvious and clear, namely: First, to apply the surplus revenue to the discharge of the public debt so far as it could judiciously be done, and, secondly, to devise means for the gradual reduction of the revenue to the standard of the public exigencies.

Of these objects the first has been in the course of accomplishment in a manner and to a degree highly satisfactory. The amount of the public debt of all classes was on the 4th of March, 1853, $69,190,037, payments on account of which have been made since that period to the amount of $12,703,329, leaving unpaid and in continuous course of liquidation the sum of $56,486,708. These payments, although made at the market price of the respective classes of stocks, have been effected readily and to the general advantage of the Treasury, and have at the same time proved of signal utility in the relief they have incidentally afforded to the money market and to the industrial and commercial pursuits of the country.

The second of the above-mentioned objects, that of the reduction of the tariff, is of great importance, and the plan suggested by the Secretary of the Treasury, which is to reduce the duties on certain articles and to add to the free list many articles now taxed, and especially such as enter into manufactures and are not largely, or at all, produced in the country, is commended to your candid and careful consideration.

You will find in the report of the Secretary of the Treasury, also, abundant proof of the entire adequacy of the present fiscal system to meet all the requirements of the public service, and that, while properly administered, it operates to the advantage of the community in ordinary business relations.

I respectfully ask your attention to sundry suggestions of improvements in the settlement of accounts, especially as regards the large sums of outstanding arrears due to the Government, and of other reforms in the administrative action of his Department which are indicated by the Secretary; as also to the progress made in the construction of marine hospitals, custom-houses, and of a new mint in California and assay office in the city of New York, heretofore provided for by Congress, and also to the eminently successful progress of the Coast Survey and of the Light-House Board.

Among the objects meriting your attention will be important recommendations from the Secretaries of War and Navy. I am fully satisfied that the Navy of the United States is not in a condition of strength and efficiency commensurate with the magnitude of our commercial and other interests, and commend to your especial attention the suggestions on this subject made by the Secretary of the Navy. I respectfully submit that the Army, which under our system must always be regarded with the highest interest as a nucleus around which the volunteer forces of the nation gather in the hour of danger, requires augmentation, or modification, to adapt it to the present extended limits and frontier relations of the country and the condition of the Indian tribes in the interior of the continent, the necessity of which will appear in the communications of the Secretaries of War and the Interior.

In the administration of the Post-Office Department for the fiscal year ending June 30, 1853, the gross expenditure was $7,982,756, and the gross receipts during the same period $5,942,734, showing that the current revenue failed to meet the current expenses of the Department by the sum of $2,042,032. The causes which, under the present postal system and laws, led inevitably to this result are fully explained by the report of the Postmaster-General, one great cause being the enormous rates the Department has been compelled to pay for mail service rendered by railroad companies.

The exhibit in the report of the Postmaster-General of the income and expenditures by mail steamers will be found peculiarly interesting and of a character to demand the immediate action of Congress.

Numerous and flagrant frauds upon the Pension Bureau have been brought to light within the last year, and in some instances merited punishments inflicted; but, unfortunately, in others guilty parties have escaped, not through the want of sufficient evidence to warrant a conviction, but in consequence of the provisions of limitation in the existing laws.

From the nature of these claims, the remoteness of the tribunals to pass upon them, and the mode in which the proof is of necessity furnished, temptations to crime have been greatly stimulated by the obvious difficulties of detection. The defects in the law upon this subject are so apparent and so fatal to the ends of justice that your early action relating to it is most desirable.

During the last fiscal year 9,819,411 acres of the public lands have been surveyed and 10,363,891 acres brought into market. Within the same period the sales by public purchase and private entry amounted to 1,083,495 acres; located under military bounty-land warrants, 6,142,360 acres; located under other certificates, 9,427 acres; ceded to the States as swamp lands, 16,684,253 acres; selected for railroad and other objects under acts of Congress, 1,427,457 acres; total amount of lands disposed of within the fiscal year, 25,346,992 acres, which is an increase in quantity sold and located under land warrants and grants of 12,231,818 acres over the fiscal year immediately preceding. The quantity of land sold during the second and third quarters of 1852 was 334,451 acres; the amount received therefor was $623,687. The quantity sold the second and third quarters of the year 1853 was 1,609,919 acres, and the amount received therefor $2,226,876.

The whole number of land warrants issued under existing laws prior to the 30th of September last was 266,042, of which there were outstanding at that date 66,947. The quantity of land required to satisfy these outstanding warrants is 4,778,120 acres.

Warrants have been issued to 30th of September last under the act of 11th February, 1847, calling for 12,879,280 acres, under acts of September 28, 1850, and March 22, 1852, calling for 12,505,360 acres, making a total of 25,384,640 acres.

It is believed that experience has verified the wisdom and justice of the present system with regard to the public domain in most essential particulars.

You will perceive from the report of the Secretary of the Interior that opinions which have often been expressed in relation to the operation of the land system as not being a source of revenue to the Federal Treasury were erroneous. The net profits from the sale of the public lands to June 30, 1853, amounted to the sum of $53,289,465.

I recommend the extension of the land system over the Territories of Utah and New Mexico, with such modifications as their peculiarities may require.

Regarding our public domain as chiefly valuable to provide homes for the industrious and enterprising, I am not prepared to recommend any essential change in the land system, except by modifications in favor of the actual settler and an extension of the preemption principle in certain cases, for reasons and on grounds which will be fully developed in the reports to be laid before you.

Congress, representing the proprietors of the territorial domain and charged especially with power to dispose of territory belonging to the United States, has for a long course of years, beginning with the Administration of Mr. Jefferson, exercised the power to construct roads within the Territories, and there are so many and obvious distinctions between this exercise of power and that of making roads within the States that the former has never been considered subject to such objections as apply to the latter; and such may now be considered the settled construction of the power of the Federal Government upon the subject.

Numerous applications have been and no doubt will continue to be made for grants of land in aid of the construction of railways. It is not believed to be within the intent and meaning of the Constitution that the power to dispose of the public domain should be used otherwise than might be expected from a prudent proprietor, and therefore that grants of land to aid in the construction of roads should be restricted to cases where it would be for the interest of a proprietor under like circumstances thus to contribute to the construction of these works. For the practical operation of such grants thus far in advancing the interests of the States in which the works are located, and at the same time the substantial interests of all the other States, by enhancing the value and promoting the rapid sale of the public domain, I refer you to the report of the Secretary of the Interior. A careful examination, however, will show that this experience is the result of a just discrimination and will be far from affording encouragement to a reckless or indiscriminate extension of the principle.

I commend to your favorable consideration the men of genius of our country who by their inventions and discoveries in science and arts have contributed largely to the improvements of the age without, in many instances, securing for themselves anything like an adequate reward. For many interesting details upon this subject I refer you to the appropriate reports, and especially urge upon your early attention the apparently slight, but really important, modifications of existing laws therein suggested.

The liberal spirit which has so long marked the action of Congress in relation to the District of Columbia will, I have no doubt, continue to be manifested.

The erection of an asylum for the insane of the District of Columbia and of the Army and Navy of the United States has been somewhat retarded by the great demand for materials and labor during the past summer, but full preparation for the reception of patients before the return of another winter is anticipated; and there is the best reason to believe, from the plan and contemplated arrangements which have been devised, with the large experience furnished within the last few years in relation to the nature and treatment of the disease, that it will prove an asylum indeed to this most helpless and afflicted class of sufferers and stand as a noble monument of wisdom and mercy.

Under the acts of Congress of August 31, 1852, and of March 3, 1853, designed to secure for the cities of Washington and Georgetown an abundant supply of good and wholesome water, it became my duty to examine the report and plans of the engineer who had charge of the surveys under the act first named. The best, if not the only, plan calculated to secure permanently the object sought was that which contemplates taking the water from the Great Falls of the Potomac, and consequently I gave to it my approval.

For the progress and present condition of this important work and for its demands so far as appropriations are concerned I refer you to the report of the Secretary of War.

The present judicial system of the United States has now been in operation for so long a period of time and has in its general theory and much of its details become so familiar to the country and acquired so entirely the public confidence that if modified in any respect it should only be in those particulars which may adapt it to the increased extent, population, and legal business of the United States. In this relation the organization of the courts is now confessedly inadequate to the duties to be performed by them, in consequence of which the States of Florida, Wisconsin, Iowa, Texas, and California, and districts of other States, are in effect excluded from the full benefits of the general system by the functions of the circuit court being devolved on the district judges in all those States or parts of States.

The spirit of the Constitution and a due regard to justice require that all the States of the Union should be placed on the same footing in regard to the judicial tribunals. I therefore commend to your consideration this important subject, which in my judgment demands the speedy action of Congress. I will present to you, if deemed desirable, a plan which I am prepared to recommend for the enlargement and modification of the present judicial system.

The act of Congress establishing the Smithsonian Institution provided that the President of the United States and other persons therein designated should constitute an "establishment" by that name, and that the members should hold stated and special meetings for the supervision of the affairs of the Institution. The organization not having taken place, it seemed to me proper that it should be effected without delay. This has been done; and an occasion was thereby presented for inspecting the condition of the Institution and appreciating its successful progress thus far and its high promise of great and general usefulness.

I have omitted to ask your favorable consideration for the estimates of works of a local character in twenty-seven of the thirty-one States, amounting to $1,754,500, because, independently of the grounds which have so often been urged against the application of the Federal revenue for works of this character, inequality, with consequent injustice, is inherent in the nature of the proposition, and because the plan has proved entirely inadequate to the accomplishment of the objects sought.

The subject of internal improvements, claiming alike the interest and good will of all, has, nevertheless, been the basis of much political discussion and has stood as a deep-graven line of division between statesmen of eminent ability and patriotism. The rule of strict construction of all powers delegated by the States to the General Government has arrayed itself from time to time against the rapid progress of expenditures from the National Treasury on works of a local character within the States. Memorable as an epoch in the history of this subject is the message of President Jackson of the 27th of May, 1830, which met the system of internal improvements in its comparative infancy; but so rapid had been its growth that the projected appropriations in that year for works of this character had risen to the alarming amount of more than $100,000,000.

In that message the President admitted the difficulty of bringing back the operations of the Government to the construction of the Constitution set up in 1798, and marked it as an admonitory proof of the necessity of guarding that instrument with sleepless vigilance against the authority of precedents which had not the sanction of its most plainly defined powers.

Our Government exists under a written compact between sovereign States, uniting for specific objects and with specific grants to their general agent. If, then, in the progress of its administration there have been departures from the terms and intent of the compact, it is and will ever be proper to refer back to the fixed standard which our fathers left us and to make a stern effort to conform our action to it. It would seem that the fact of a principle having been resisted from the first by many of the wisest and most patriotic men of the Republic, and a policy having provoked constant strife without arriving at a conclusion which can be regarded as satisfactory to its most earnest advocates, should suggest the inquiry whether there may not be a plan likely to be crowned by happier results. Without perceiving any sound distinction or intending to assert any principle as opposed to improvements needed for the protection of internal commerce which does not equally apply to improvements upon the seaboard for the protection of foreign commerce, I submit to you whether it may not be safely anticipated that if the policy were once settled against appropriations by the General Government for local improvements for the benefit of commerce, localities requiring expenditures would not, by modes and means clearly legitimate and proper, raise the fund necessary for such constructions as the safety or other interests of their commerce might require.

If that can be regarded as a system which in the experience of more than thirty years has at no time so commanded the public judgment as to give it the character of a settled policy; which, though it has produced some works of conceded importance, has been attended with an expenditure quite disproportionate to their value and has resulted in squandering large sums upon objects which have answered no valuable purpose, the interests of all the States require it to be abandoned unless hopes may be indulged for the future which find no warrant in the past.

With an anxious desire for the completion of the works which are regarded by all good citizens with sincere interest, I have deemed it my duty to ask at your hands a deliberate reconsideration of the question, with a hope that, animated by a desire to promote the permanent and substantial interests of the country, your wisdom may prove equal to the task of devising and maturing a plan which, applied to this subject, may promise something better than constant strife, the suspension of the powers of local enterprise, the exciting of vain hopes, and the disappointment of cherished expectations.

In expending the appropriations made by the last Congress several cases have arisen in relation to works for the improvement of harbors which involve questions as to the right of soil and jurisdiction, and have threatened conflict between the authority of the State and General Governments. The right to construct a breakwater, jetty, or dam would seem necessarily to carry with it the power to protect and preserve such constructions. This can only be effectually done by having jurisdiction over the soil. But no clause of the Constitution is found on which to rest the claim of the United States to exercise jurisdiction over the soil of a State except that conferred by the eighth section of the first article of the Constitution. It is, then, submitted whether, in all cases where constructions are to be erected by the General Government, the right of soil should not first be obtained and legislative provision be made to cover all such cases.

For the progress made in the construction of roads within the Territories, as provided for in the appropriations of the last Congress, I refer you to the report of the Secretary of War.

There is one subject of a domestic nature which, from its intrinsic importance and the many interesting questions of future policy which it involves, can not fail to receive your early attention. I allude to the means of communication by which different parts of the wide expanse of our country are to be placed in closer connection for purposes both of defense and commercial intercourse, and more especially such as appertain to the communication of those great divisions of the Union which lie on the opposite sides of the Rocky Mountains.

That the Government has not been unmindful of this heretofore is apparent from the aid it has afforded through appropriations for mail facilities and other purposes. But the general subject will now present itself under aspects more imposing and more purely national by reason of the surveys ordered by Congress, and now in the process of completion, for communication by railway across the continent, and wholly within the limits of the United States.

The power to declare war, to raise and support armies, to provide and maintain a navy, and to call forth the militia to execute the laws, suppress insurrections, and repel invasions was conferred upon Congress as means to provide for the common defense and to protect a territory and a population now widespread and vastly multiplied. As incidental to and indispensable for the exercise of this power, it must sometimes be necessary to construct military roads and protect harbors of refuge. To appropriations by Congress for such objects no sound objection can be raised. Happily for our country, its peaceful policy and rapidly increasing population impose upon us no urgent necessity for preparation, and leave but few trackless deserts between assailable points and a patriotic people ever ready and generally able to protect them. These necessary links the enterprise and energy of our people are steadily and boldly struggling to supply. All experience affirms that wherever private enterprise

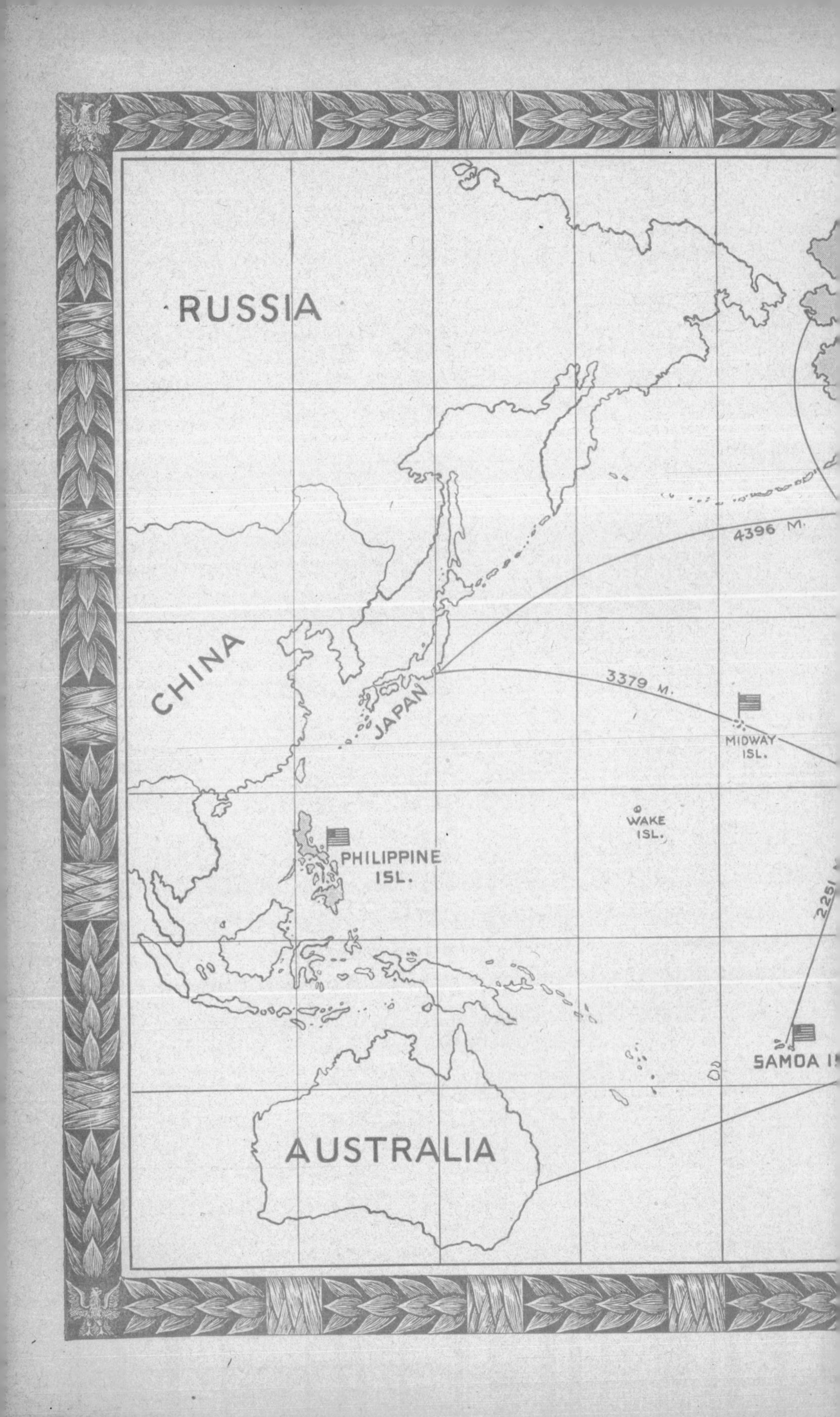
RUSSIA
CHINA
JAPAN
4396 M.
3379 M.
MIDWAY
ISL.
WAKE
ISL.
PHILIPPINE
ISL.
SAMOA I
AUSTRALIA